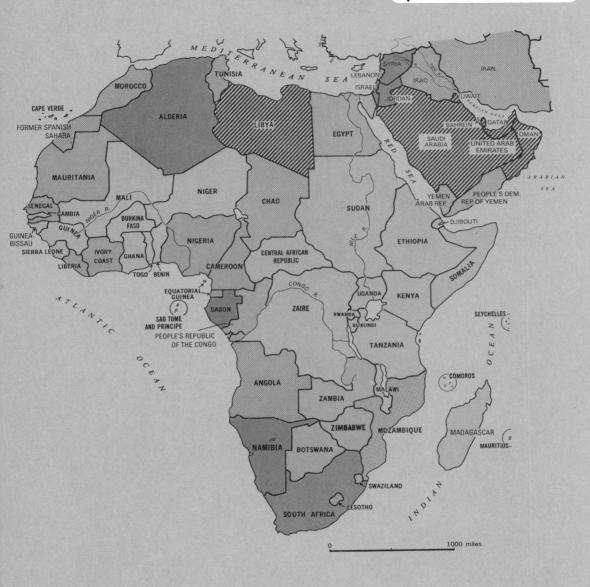

Gross national product per capita, 1983

$400 and less $401 to $1,635 $1,636 to $5,500   More than $5,500   No data

Source: The World Bank Atlas, 1986

AFRICA AND THE MIDDLE EAST

ECONOMICS
OF
DEVELOPMENT

ECONOMICS OF DEVELOPMENT

Second Edition

Malcolm Gillis
DUKE UNIVERSITY

Dwight H. Perkins
HARVARD UNIVERSITY

Michael Roemer
HARVARD UNIVERSITY

Donald R. Snodgrass
HARVARD UNIVERSITY

W. W. NORTON & COMPANY
New York London

Library of Congress Cataloging in Publication Data
Economics of development
  Bibliography: p.
  Includes index.
  1. Developing countries—Economic policy.
2. Economic development. I. Gillis, Malcolm.
HC59.7.E314   1987   338.9   87–5701

ISBN 0-393-95548-6

W. W. Norton & Company, Inc.,
500 Fifth Avenue, New York, N. Y. 10110

W. W. Norton & Company, Ltd.,
37 Great Russell Street, London WC1B 3NU

2 3 4 5 6 7 8 9 0

For Elizabeth, Julie, Linda, and Anne

CONTENTS

Preface

The consequences of economic development regularly make headlines. Japan, in ruins after World War II, becomes an economic superpower thirty years later and challenges the primacy of American industry. South Korea, widely regarded as a hopeless case after the devastation of the Korean War, bids in turn to challenge Japan for export markets. Malaysia, with less than half the average income of Chile as recently as 1963, takes only twenty years to equal Chile. Oil exporting countries, attempting to short-cut the normally slow accumulation of wealth by nations, manage to extract unprecedented revenues from consumers around the world, until the OPEC system weakens in the mid-1980s. Mexico, Brazil, Argentina, and other countries go deeply into debt to finance their development, then present world capital markets with a financial crisis when they are unable to repay. Public health makes such great strides after World War II that populations start growing dramatically. World population surpasses five billion, and three out of four live in developing countries. But during the 1980s overpopulation and drought conspire to create famine in Africa's Sahel; governments and rock stars respond with grain, money, and much fanfare.

Newspapers, and especially television, have bombarded our senses with these and other stories about development. The developing world no longer seems exotic or remote, and few doubt that the struggle for development will profoundly affect the way people live in the industrial countries. Enhanced awareness about development creates an opportunity for those of us who write textbooks, but also presents two challenges.

The first challenge is to keep up with the news. Development texts deal with contemporary history as well as tools of analysis and must be revised to reflect current events and thinking. The Second Edition of *Economics of Development* utilizes data published as recently as 1985 by the World Bank, United Nations, and other sources. It also pays more attention to matters of greatest current interest. Sections have been expanded or added on third-world debt, economic stabilization, the new protectionism, capital mobility, population trends, and the destruction of tropical forests. The country examples have been updated where appropriate and new ones incorporated to illustrate important issues.

The second challenge is more difficult. News stories about third-world countries make development seem an exciting but ephemeral subject: it would appear necessary only to keep up with the latest events to capture the essence of the topic. But the reality is deeper. The challenge of a textbook is to distinguish between the merely evanescent and the truly enduring aspects of development. The forces underlying economic change are sometimes barely perceptible. But they can be powerful, radically altering a country's standard of living in two or three generations.

To meet this challenge, the second edition incorporates the distinguishing features of the first: (1) The text makes extensive use of the theoretical tools of classical and neoclassical economics, in the belief that these tools contribute substantially to our understanding of development. (2) The book draws heavily upon decades of empirical studies by economists and economic historians, studies that have uncovered and explained the structure of development, or at least narrowed our zones of ignorance. (3) *Economics of Development* deals explicitly with both the political and institutional framework in which economic development take place. (4) This edition presents many real-country examples to illustrate major points, drawing upon the authors' collective experience of more than ninety years of work on development issues. (5) The book recognizes the diversity of development experience reflected in these country examples, acknowledging that the lessons of theory and history can only be applied within certain institutional and national contexts. The ingredients causing economic failure in one set of circumstances might, in different circumstances or with a different recipe, lead to economic success.

ORGANIZATION

The second edition retains the organization of the first. Part I introduces the concept and measurement of development, some theories developed to explain it, and the body of data that has been amassed to recognize and define development when it takes place. Because planning has been closely associated with development, two chapters discuss the process and techniques of national planning.

People make development happen and people benefit from it. Part II deals with the contribution of human resources to development and with the transformation of human lives as a consequence of development. Chapters are included on population, labor, education, and health.

Capital, the other major physical input in the growth process, is the subject of Part III. It deals with saving and investment, fiscal policy, financial policy, and foreign aid and investment.

International trade binds developing countries to industrial countries and offers potentially effective strategies for accelerating the development process. Part IV explores these strategies.

In Part V, the lessons of earlier chapters are applied and extended to help understand development of the major sectors: agriculture, natural resources, and industry, with a final chapter on a pervasive institution of developing countries, the public enterprise.

SUPPLEMENTS

To help serve the needs of students and instructors, two supplements now accompany the text. A *Study Guide and Workbook* by Bruce Bolnick of Northeastern University provides review material, self-tests, and problem sets that will help students to grasp the major points more firmly. An *Instructor's Manual,* also by Bruce Bolnick, provides lecture and discussion topics along with answers to the problem sets in the workbook.

ACKNOWLEDGMENTS

In the course of writing two editions, we have accumulated many debts to generous colleagues who have read chapters, reviewed the entire book, tested the manuscript in their classes, or otherwise encouraged us: Paul Albanese (Middlebury College), Ralph Beals (Amherst College), Richard Bird (University of Toronto), Bruce Bolnick (Northeastern University), Paul Clark (Williams College), David Dapice (Tufts University), James Duesenberry (Harvard University), Sebastian Edwards (University of Southern California), Alfred J. Field (University of North Carolina), Lester Gordon (Harvard University), Arnold Harberger (University of Chicago), Sue Horton (University of Toronto), Alan Kelley (Duke University), Anne Krueger (Duke University), Charles McLure (Stanford University), Malcolm McPherson (Harvard University), Caroline Schwartz (Emory University), David Singer (University of Connecticut), Joseph Stern (Harvard University), and Louis Wells (Harvard University). Though we cannot list their names, we would also like to thank the nearly fifty teachers who responded to a detailed questionnaire about the First Edition.

Ricardo Godoy's dedicated work on the data for the First Edition was carried forward by Kit Crowe, who updated the tables and coordinated textual revisions with admirable energy and efficiency. Marty Ferry produced and revised the entire manuscript. JoAnne Giovino, Gretchen O'Connor, and Andrea Yelle gave support at various stages of revision. At W. W. Norton, Donald Lamm continued to encourage us, while Drake McFeely and Patty Peltekos transformed the manuscript into the book you are reading now.

We have worked toward a book that meets the expectations of all these people, and we thank them for helping us.

Durham	M.G.
Cambridge	D.H.P.
Cambridge	M.R.
Cambridge	D.R.S.

January 1987

PART 1

THEORY AND PATTERNS

Introduction: Worlds Apart

The people around the village of Jalab, in Senegal, West Africa, and many rural towns of Georgia in the United States depend upon the same essential crop: peanuts.[1] West Africa and the United States are two of the biggest commercial producers of peanuts. The story of their cultivation and marketing is the story of two very different worlds.

Slave ships carried peanuts to the American South because colonists needed a high-protein, high-caloric staple to feed their captives. Growing conditions proved ideal, especially in Georgia, where cultivation thrived and where today nearly half the American crop is harvested. Peanuts are the eleventh most valuable crop grown in the United States, worth half a billion dollars a year.

John Johnston, a thirty-four-year-old Georgia peanut farmer, cultivates 540 acres of peanuts and another 650 acres of corn. His ground is prepared for planting by tractor. Government-sponsored research has discovered improved combinations of seed and fertilizer, and the extension service ensures that farmers know how to use them. Pesticides are sprayed on Johnston's crop from airplanes. Combine harvesters pick the ripe plant and separate the peanuts for drying. Johnston sells his crop to a broker in nearby Blakely, where the peanuts are stored in modern warehouses. The broker sells them to processors through larger brokers in Atlanta, New York, or Chi-

---

1. This narrative is adapted from a television film by Otto C. Honegger, *The Nguba Connection,* jointly produced by WGBH Boston, Swiss TV Zurich and Swedish TV (SK2). We are grateful for permission to use this material. Names have been fictionalized.

cago. The price received by Johnston is maintained above the world-market price by a U.S. government support program that restricts imports, limits domestic acreage, and protects the farmer from price fluctuations. Research, mechanization, efficient marketing, government price supports, and hard work enable Johnston to net as much as $100,000 from his peanuts in a good year. At this income, the Johnston family lives in comfort, enjoying the wide variety of goods—basics and luxuries—available to affluent Americans.

In Senegal, Cherno Sar grows peanuts on his small farm near Jalab. Like Johnston, Sar inherited his land, which is the sole support for his family of five, plus three relatives. Like Johnston, Sar cultivates relatively good land for peanuts and he has begun to mechanize what was until recently a hand-picked harvest. But his plows are not as productive as Johnston's combines, while fertilizers and insecticides are either unavailable or too expensive. Sar's yields are about a fifth of Johnston's. And his output must be sold to a government corporation that pays the farmer well below the world-market price in order to extract tax revenue for the government. Storage facilities are rudimentary and much of the harvested crop may be lost to blight, insects, or bad weather. The small size of their farm, poor yields, low prices, and storage losses keep the Sar family very poor. Eight people must live on only $400 of cash income in a good year, much less than John Johnston's field workers, who earn $100 a week when they work and are extremely poor by American standards. Even though the Sars grow much of their own food, their diet is inadequate, consisting mostly of millet made into a gruel. Jalab has no electricity, no school, no clinic, no shops. Cherno's wife draws water from a village well a few hundred yards from their hut, much closer than for most farm families in Senegal. For every hundred children born in his village, twenty will probably never see their first birthday.

Not all Senegalese are as poor as Cherno Sar. In Dakar, the modern capital, officials of the government peanut marketing corporation work in air-conditioned offices, own cars, and live in substantial houses, enjoying some of the same comforts as the Johnstons in Georgia. Their children attend the best schools in the country and, if necessary, can be treated in a nearby modern hospital. Of course these officials are part of a minority group in Senegal, a group favored by birth, education, urban benefits, and income over the vast majority of poor, small farmers. The peanuts the government buys are mostly exported. The resulting government revenues help pay the salaries of government workers, who are much better off than Cherno Sar; the foreign exchange helps to pay for imports that are consumed largely by people in the cities.

In each country the political process reinforces disparities. John Johnston is represented in Washington by a congressman who is responsive to his needs. Congressmen representing farm states remain powerful enough, even in a predominantly urban country, to perpetuate the government's price supports, agricultural research, and extension system that have been so beneficial to farmers like John Johnston. Cherno Sar has little or no political influence. Although farm families like his make up most of Senegal's population, it is the minority urban dwellers who command most of the government's attention and resources. Sar is virtually helpless to influence the price the groundnut marketing corporation pays for his crop or what services the government provides him and his family.

Nor is there any international mechanism to reduce the vast disparities between people like the Johnstons who live in North America, Europe, and Japan, and the much greater numbers of people like the Sars who live in Africa, Asia, and Latin America. Although national fiscal policy can transfer income from rich to poor within a country, no international fiscal mechanism exists. Foreign aid has been conceived as a method of transfer from rich to poor nations, but it is voluntary and grossly inadequate for the task. Discussions have taken place about international price supports, such as those that exist within many countries, that would raise the incomes poor countries earn from their commodity exports. But differing national interests make agreement on such schemes unlikely. U.S. restriction of peanut imports, which discriminate against the Sars and help the Johnstons, are only one of hundreds of trade restrictions that slow international development.

Why do disparities like these exist? Why are Sengalese farmers—and three billion like them in other countries—so poor while Americans and Europeans are rich? What could be done about it, by Sengalese or Americans? And what is *likely* to happen? These questions, and many others suggested by them, are the subject of this book.

THE THIRD WORLD

The two worlds of the peanut farmer are sharply defined and widely separated by geography, income, standard of living, and economic, social, and political structure. They make it easy to see the differences between "development" and "underdevelopment." But the world is complex, and such simplified, dichotomous examples cannot do justice to the many-dimensional continuum that explains economic development. The bulk of this text is devoted to exploring that continuum, and no single chapter can do the work of an entire book. This chapter will orient you within the variegated world of developed and underdeveloped countries. Before attempting that, however, we need to sort out some terms.

Terminology: Rich and Poor Countries

The countries with which this book is concerned have been referred to by many different terms. All these terms are intended to contrast their state or rate of change with those of the more modern, advanced, developed countries, so that terms tend to be found in pairs. The starkest distinction is between **backward** and **advanced** economies, or between **traditional** and **modern** ones. The "backward" economy is traditional in its economic relationships, in ways that will be described in the next chapter. However precisely and neutrally the term can be defined, it retains perjorative connotations, a touch of condescension, and is therefore not much used today. In any case, the implication of stagnation is inappropriate for in most countries economic and social relationships are changing in important ways.

The more popular classification terms implicitly put all countries on a continuum based on their **degree of development.** Thus we speak of the distinctions between **developed and underdeveloped** countries, **more and less developed** ones, or, to recognize continuing change, **developed and developing** countries. The degree of optimism implicit in "developing countries" and the handy acronym, LDCs, for "less developed countries," make these the two most widely used terms.[2] Developed countries are also frequently called the **industrial countries,** in recognition of the close association between development and industrialization.

A dichotomy based simply on income levels, the **poor** versus the **rich countries,** has been refined by the World Bank[3] and combined with a second distinction, based on type of economic organization, to yield a five-part classification that is useful for some analytical purposes. The developing countries are divided by income into **low income** (less than $400 per capita in 1983) and **middle income** (between $400 and about $6,900 in 1983). The third category of developing countries consists of five petroleum exporters (Oman, Libya, Saudi Arabia, Kuwait, and the United Arab Emirates), whose incomes ranged from $6,300 to $23,000 per capita in 1983, but whose economies are more traditional than industrialized; the World Bank calls this anomalous group the "capital-surplus oil exporters." The **industrial economies** are divided into **market** (Western capitalist) and **nonmarket** (Eastern Communist) economies.

The term now in greatest vogue, especially in international forums, is the **third world.** Perhaps the best way to define it is by elimination. Take the industrialized market economies of Western Europe, North America, and the Pacific (the "first" world), and the industrialized but centrally planned economies of Eastern Europe (the "second" world); the rest of the countries constitute the third world. All third-world countries are developing countries and these include all of Latin America and the Caribbean, Africa, the Middle East, and all Asia except Japan. The geographic configuration of this group has led to a parallel distinction—**north** (first and second worlds) versus **south** —that is also in current vogue. But the south or third world encompasses a wide variety of nations. The obvious differences between the wealthy (if structurally underdeveloped) oil exporters and the very low-income, poorly endowed countries have led some to add fourth and fifth worlds to the classification. Political motivations create further exceptions: South Africa and Israel are usually not considered part of the third world; nor are Spain and Portugal, former colonial powers, although in many respects they are less developed countries.

2. Recently, the initials "LDC" have been used, especially by the United Nations, to designate the "least developed" countries, those with incomes below $100 per capita (among other characteristics). In this book "LDC" is used to mean "less developed country (or countries)."

3. The World Bank, formally titled the International Bank for Reconstruction and Development (IBRD), is owned by the governments of its 148 member countries. The Bank borrows funds on private capital markets in the developed countries and lends to the developing countries. Its affiliate, the International Development Association (IDA), receives contributions from the governments of developed countries and lends to the low-income countries at concessional terms (very low interest rates and long repayment periods). The World Bank and IDA are important and influential development agencies. See Chapter 14 for a more complete discussion.

It is necessary to be aware of these various terminologies and classifica-
tions, and to recognize their exceptions and inconsistencies. But it is not wise
to dwell too long over them. No system can capture all important dimensions of development and provide a perfectly consistent, manageable framework. Because there is no compelling selection of terms, we make none in
this book. The less developed countries will be called that, as well as developing or third-world countries. When one country or several do not fit a general observation, we will name the exceptions and desist from adding new
terms to a field that is already awash in classification schemes.

Terminology: Growth and Development

While the labels used to distinguish one set of countries from another can
vary, one must be more careful with the terms used to describe the development process itself. The terms **economic growth** and **economic development**
are sometimes used interchangeably, but there is a fundamental distinction
between them. *Economic growth* refers to a rise in national or per-capita
income and product.[4] If the production of goods and services in a nation
rises, by whatever means, one can speak of that rise as economic growth.
Economic development implies more. What has been happening in South
Korea since 1960, for example, is fundamentally different from what has
been happening in Libya as a result of the discovery of petroleum. Both
countries experienced a large rise in per-capita income, but in Libya this rise
was achieved by foreign corporations staffed largely by foreign technicians
who produced a single product consumed mainly in the United States and
Western Europe. Although the government and people of Libya have
received large amounts of income from their oil, they have had little to do
with producing that income. The effect of petroleum development has been
much as if a rich nation had decided to give Libya large amounts of grant
aid.

Libya's experience is not usually described as economic development.
Economic development, in addition to a rise in per-capita income, implies
fundamental changes in the structure of the economy, of the kind observed
in South Korea since 1960. Two of the most important of these structural
changes are the rising share of industry—along with the falling share of agriculture—in national product and an increasing percentage of people who
live in cities rather than the countryside. In addition, countries that enter
into economic development usually pass through periods of accelerating,
then decelerating, population growth during which the nation's age structure
changes dramatically. Consumption patterns also change as people no longer
have to spend all of their income on necessities, but instead move on to consumer durables and eventually to leisure time products and services.

A key element in economic development is that the people of the country
must be major participants in the process that brought about these changes
in structure. Foreigners can be and inevitably are involved as well, but they
cannot be the whole story. Participation in the process of development

4. Income per capita is measured as the gross national product (the value of all goods and
services produced by a country's economy in a year) divided by the population.

implies participation in the enjoyment of the benefits of development as well as the production of those benefits. If growth only benefits a tiny, wealthy minority, whether domestic or foreign, it is not development.

Modern economic growth, the term used by Nobel laureate Simon Kuznets, refers to the current economic epoch as contrasted to, say, the epoch of merchant capitalism or the epoch of feudalism. The epoch of modern economic growth is still going on so all of its features are not yet clear, but the key element has been the application of science to problems of economic production, which in turn has led to industrialization, urbanization, and even an explosive growth in population.

The widely used term, **modernization,** refers to much more than the economy. One can speak of the modernization of a society or of a political system, for example. But it is difficult to give the term a precise meaning. Too often there is a tendency to equate modernization with becoming more like the United States or Western Europe. Is it reasonable to say that the Soviet Union is not modern because it is not democratic or that Japan is not modern because it still maintains certain ways of organizing business based more on its own traditions than on practices in the West? Because of the vague and misleading nature of the term, we will not use it further here.

Finally, it should always be kept in mind that while *economic development* and *modern economic growth* involve much more than a rise in per-capita income or product, there can be no development without economic growth.

A DEVELOPMENT CONTINUUM

Much can be learned about the nature of structural change during development and about the many differences within the developing world from a ten-minute perusal of Table 1–1. These data are from the World Bank and use its five-part classification. The wide disparity of per-capita income among the groups of countries is not surprising because they are classified that way. In Chapter 3 we will discuss the shortcomings of using national income per capita to compare the well-being of country populations, but it remains the most useful single indicator.[5] The industrialized market countries as a group have an average per-capita GNP over eight times that of the middle-income countries, of which Mexico and the Philippines are typical examples, and *forty* times that of the poorest thirty-five countries, of which India and Tanzania are examples.

A predominant structural characteristic of development is the growing share of both income produced and labor employed in industry. An average 73 percent of the labor force is engaged in agriculture in the low-income countries, contrasted with 44 percent in the middle group and only 6 percent for the industrial market economies. Moreover this characteristic structural shift is taking place more rapidly in the middle-income countries, whose

5. One of the major problems with income comparisons, differences in national price structures, can be overcome by using a physical measure of economic welfare, of which per capita energy consumption has as much validity as any. The relative levels shown in Column 2 of Table 1–1 conform very closely to those of per-capita income.

TABLE 1-1   Development Characteristics of Groups[a] and Selected Countries

	GNP per capita, 1983 ($)	Energy consumption per capita, 1983 (kg. of oil equivalent)	Labor force: share in agriculture, 1981 (%)	Life expectancy at birth, 1983 (years)	Adult literacy rate, 1980 (%)[b]
Low-income countries[c]	*260 (200)*	*276 (80)*	*73 (72)*	*59 (51)*	*52 (40)*
Ethiopia	120	19	80	43	15
Bangladesh	130	36	74	50	26
Mali	160	22	73	45	10
Tanzania	240	38	83	51	79
India	260	182	71	55	36
China	300	455	74	67	66
Ghana	310	111	53	59	na
Sri Lanka	330	143	54	69	85
Kenya	340	109	78	57	47
Pakistan	390	197	57	50	24
Middle-income countries[d]	*1,310*	*745*	*44*	*61*	*65*
Senegal	440	151	77	46	10
Bolivia	510	292	50	51	63
Indonesia	560	204	58	54	62
Egypt	700	532	50	58	44
Philippines	760	252	46	64	75
Nigeria	770	150	54	49	34
Guatemala	1,120	178	55	60	na
Colombia	1,430	786	26	64	81
Cuba	na	1,042	23	75	95
Malaysia	1,860	702	50	67	60
Brazil	1,880	745	30	64	76
South Korea	2,010	1,168	34	67	93
Mexico	2,240	1,332	36	66	83
High-income oil exporters[e]	*12,370*	*3,858*	*46*	*59*	*32*
Saudi Arabia	12,230	3,536	61	56	25
Industrial market economies[f]	*11,060*	*4,733*	*6*	*76*	*99*
United Kingdom	9,200	3,461	2	74	99
Japan	10,120	2,929	12	77	99
Germany (West)	11,430	4,156	4	75	99
United States	14,110	7,030	2	75	99
East European non-market economies[g]	*na*	*4,279*	*17*	*70*	*99*
Germany (East)	na	5,370	10	71	na
Soviet Union	na	4,505	14	69	100

Source: World Bank, *World Development Report 1985* (Washington, D.C., 1985), pp. 174–75, 188–89, 214–15; World Bank, *World Development Report 1983* (Washington, D.C., 1983), pp. 148–149.

[a] Includes countries with population of one million or more only; all group averages are weighted by population; na = not available. Figures in parentheses for low-income countries exclude China and India.

[b] Estimates are generally for years not more than two years distant from 1980.

[c] Thirty-five countries with per-capita incomes of less than $400. China and India, with 75 percent of the population, dominate the statistics for this group. Figures in parentheses exclude China and India.

[d] Fifty-nine countries with per capita incomes of $400 to $6,900.

[e] Oman, Libya, Saudi Arabia, Kuwait, and United Arab Emirates.

[f] Nineteen countries with per-capita incomes of $4,780 or more. Includes all Western Europe except Greece, plus Canada, United States, Japan, Australia, and New Zealand.

[g] Eight countries in East Europe: Hungary, Albania, Bulgaria, Czechoslovakia, East Germany, Poland, Romania, and the Soviet Union.

manufacturing growth rates are generally higher than those for the low-income group (or for the industrial countries, except Japan). Thus in India and Tanzania, with over 70 percent of the labor force in agriculture, manufacturing output is growing at 4 percent a year or less, while in Mexico and the Philippines with 36 and 46 percent, respectively, of their workers in agriculture, manufacturing has been growing at 6 to 7 percent a year as shown in Table 1–2.

Rising income is not the only end of development. People aspire to stay healthier and become better educated. Indicators for each of these aspects of well-being are included in Table 1–1, and they are closely correlated with per-capita income. Life expectancy, only fifty-one years in poor countries excluding China, is seventy-six years in the rich countries. But the most dramatic contrast is in adult literacy: only 40 percent of the adult population can read in low-income countries excluding China, compared with 65 per-

TABLE 1–2 Growth of Output and Population of Groups[a] and Selected Countries, 1965–1983 (percent per year)

	GNP per capita, 1965–1983	Population 1983[b]	Manufacturing 1965–1983
Low-income countries	*2.7(0.7)*	*1.9 (2.7)*	*4.3 (4.6)*
Ethiopia	0.5	2.1	5.8
Bangladesh	0.5	2.6	8.7[c]
Mali	1.2	2.7	na
Tanzania	0.9	3.4	0.5[d]
India	1.5	2.1	4.1
China	4.4	1.2	na
Ghana	−2.1	3.9	−0.7
Sri Lanka	2.9	2.1	4.3
Kenya	2.3	4.3	4.0
Pakistan	2.5	2.7	6.6
Middle-income countries	*3.4*	*2.4*	*6.8*
Senegal	−0.5	2.7	0.8[d]
Bolivia	0.6	2.8	2.8
Indonesia	5.0	2.1	11.0
Egypt	4.2	2.3	9.3[d]
Philippines	2.9	2.4	6.5
Nigeria	3.2	3.3	11.3
Guatemala	2.1	2.9	5.5
Colombia	3.2	2.1	4.9
Cuba	na	1.1	na
Malaysia	4.5	2.3	10.6[d]
Brazil	5.0	2.2	7.2
South Korea	6.7	1.7	15.8
Mexico	3.2	2.7	7.4
High-income oil exporters	*3.8*	*3.1*	*9.5[d]*
Saudi Arabia	6.7	3.1	9.1
Industrial market economies	*2.5*	*0.5*	*2.3*

Source: World Bank, *World Development Report 1985* (Washington, D.C., 1985), pp. 174–77, 212–13. World Bank, *World Development Report 1984* (Washington, D.C., 1984), pp. 220–21.

[a] Groups defined as in Table 1–1 (notes a–f); group averages are weighted, except for manufacturing growth, which is a median. Figures in parentheses for low-income countries exclude China and India.

[b] Crude birth rate minus crude death rate.

[c] 1960–1982.

[d] 1970–1982.

cent in the middle group; in industrial countries virtually all adults are literate.

In each category there is considerable variance and hence there are some interesting exceptions. China is a low-income country that consumes more energy per capita than many middle-income countries; while Nigeria, which is both a middle-income nation and an oil exporter, has one of the lowest levels of energy consumption in the world. The agricultural labor-force share in Malaysia is about twice that of Colombia and Cuba, though Malaysia enjoys a higher income. Cubans live as long as British and Americans. And two-thirds or more of Sri Lankan, Tanzanian, and Chinese adults have learned to read, more than in middle-income countries like Senegal, Egypt, and Nigeria. In Cuba and Korea, however, over 90 percent can read, almost as many as in the industrial countries. Behind these and other variations in development lie many factors: different resource endowments, governments' varying ideologies and policies, cultural differences, colonial experience, war, and historical accident. In many cases variations suggest new theories of development and we will explore some of these in later chapters.

However, development is inherently a dynamic process, not always a predictable one, that cannot be completely captured by Table 1–1. Most less developed countries have experienced growth in incomes since 1965 and many have enjoyed substantial growth, as Table 1–2 shows. Even in the low-income countries, which account for over half the world's population, per-capita GNP grew by 2.7 percent a year (though without India and China the rate was below 1 percent a year). For some, such as Sri Lanka, Kenya, and Pakistan, growth was fast enough to double incomes in thirty years. Middle-income countries did much better, with per-capita GNP growing by 3.4 percent a year, which is why some of those countries rose from low- to middle-income status during the period. Indonesia, Brazil, and South Korea are the standouts in the table, growing at 5 percent to almost 7 percent a year. Nevertheless, over the eighteen years from 1965 to 1983, even the middle-income countries increased their per-capita incomes by only 17 percent relative to the industrial world.

The middle-income countries in particular experienced relatively rapid growth in manufacturing (Table 1–2), thus moving through the inevitable structural change that reduces the share of income produced and labor employed in agriculture. From 1965 to 1981, a short period in the history of economic development, the share of the labor force in agriculture fell from 77 to 73 percent in low-income countries and, more dramatically, from 57 to 44 percent in middle-income countries.

Perhaps the most remarkable changes in the third world since 1965 have been the virtually universal improvement in health conditions and the wide spread of education, as documented in Table 1–3. The death rate in low-income countries fell from 17 per thousand in 1965 to 11 per thousand in 1983. For middle-income countries the decline was from 15 to 10 per thousand, putting this group almost on a par with the industrial countries. Thus although the life expectancies shown in Table 1–1 are low relative to those in industrial countries, they represent average increases of about eight years over the eighteen-year period. Moreover, these improvements have been

TABLE 1–3   Progress in Social Well-Being for Groups[a] and Selected Countries, 1965–1983

| | Crude death rate, per 1000 | | Medical pro- fessionals[b] per 100 thousand | | Percentage of age group enrolled in primary school | |
	about 1965	about 1983	about 1965	about 1980	about 1965	about 1982
Low-income countries	*17(21)*	*11(16)*	*23(18)*	*40(17)*	*62(45)*	*85(70)*
Ethiopia	19	20	18	18	11	46
Bangladesh	22	16	na	17	49	60
Mali	27	21	33	47	24	27
Tanzania	22	16	52	39	32	98
India	21	13	36	45	74	79
China	13	7	na	116	na	100[c]
Ghana	16	10	35	144	69	76
Sri Lanka	8	6	49	89	93	100[c]
Kenya	17	12	64	194	54	100[c]
Pakistan	21	15	42	46	40	44
Middle-income countries	*15*	*10*	*36*	*68*	*84*	*100[c]*
Senegal	23	19	43	79	40	48
Bolivia	21	16	55	na	73	86
Indonesia	20	13	14	52	72	100[c]
Egypt	19	11	94	170	75	78
Philippines	12	7	165	29	100[c]	100[c]
Nigeria	23	17	20	41	32	98
Guatemala	16	9	38	73	50	73
Colombia	12	7	152	183	84	100[c]
Cuba	8	6	209	409	100[c]	100[c]
Malaysia	12	6	92	na	90	92
Brazil	12	8	110	na	100[c]	96
South Korea	12	6	70	355	100[c]	100
Mexico	11	7	154	na	92	100[c]
High-income oil exporters	*19*	*11*	*33*	*193*	*43*	*76*
Saudi Arabia	20	12	27	145	24	67
Industrial market economies	*10*	*9*	*467*	*737*	*100[c]*	*100[c]*
United Kingdom	12	12	616	868	92	100[c]
Japan	7	6	524	545	100	100
Germany (West)	12	12	444	810	na	100
United States	9	9	983	907	100[c]	100
East European non-market economies	*8*	*11*	*512*	*1055*	*100[c]*	*100[c]*
Germany (East)	14	13	na	na	100[c]	94
Soviet Union	7	10	565	1370	100[c]	100[c]

Source: World Bank, *World Development Report 1985* (Washington, D.C., 1985), pp. 212–13, 220–23.
   [a] Groups defined as in Table 1–1; figures in parentheses for low-income countries exclude China and India; all group averages are weighted by population.
   [b] Medical professional is defined as physicians and nurses.
   [c] Actual percentage is over 100, because repeaters who are beyond primary-school age are counted as enrollees.

enjoyed by every country in our list, regardless of their economic performance. The numbers of physicians and nurses have also increased relative to
the population in most countries, although the concentration of these health
professionals in urban areas in many countries reduces the impact they
might have on health status, especially in the poorest countries. That healthier populations have also meant higher population growth (Table 1–2) is an
important consideration, as discussed in Chapter 7.

   The spread of primary education, which now covers over 90 percent of the
population in developing countries, is also shown in Table 1–3. Remarkable
strides have been made by countries like Tanzania, which now has virtually

all of its eligible students in primary school and has raised its adult literacy rate from 10 percent of the adult population at independence to over 75 percent today; and also by countries such as Ethiopia, Kenya, Ghana, and Nigeria.

It is sometimes easy to become pessimistic about further progress in developing nations, especially when confronted by gloomy predictions about their future economic growth and by the myriad problems afflicting LDCs, many of which will be catalogued in this book. As an antidote to discouragement, one needs to keep in mind the considerable economic development that has already taken place and the gratifying improvements in health and education status that mark even the poorest countries. There remains the question of how these benefits have been distributed among the populace, a topic taken up in Chapter 4 and in Part II.

FOCUS OF THE BOOK

Approaches to Development

This book is not for readers who are looking for a simple explanation of why some nations are still poor or of how poverty can be overcome. Library shelves are full of studies explaining how development will occur if only a nation will increase the amount it saves and invests or intensify its efforts to export. For several decades in the mid-twentieth century, industrialization through import substitution—the replacement of imports with home-produced goods—was considered by many as the shortest path to development. More recently, labor-intensive techniques, income redistribution, and provision of basic human needs to the poor have gained popularity as keys to development. Many economists now counsel governments to depend substantially on unfettered markets to set prices and allocate resources. Another school of thought suggests that development is only possible if preceded by a revolution that eliminates existing elites and replaces the market with central planning. A different theme is that development will only be possible if there is a massive shift of resources, in the form of foreign aid and investment, from the richest nations to the poorest.

No single factor is responsible for underdevelopment and no single policy or strategy can set in motion the complex process of economic development. A wide variety of explanations and solutions to the development problem make sense if placed in the proper context and make no sense at all outside that set of circumstances. Mobilization of saving is essential for accelerated growth in most cases, but sometimes may come second to a redistribution of income if extreme poverty threatens political stability or forestalls the mobilization of human resources. Import substitution has carried some countries quite far towards economic development, but export promotion has helped others when import substitution bogged down. Prices that are badly distorted from their free-market values can stifle initiative and hence growth, but removing those distortions leads to development only where other conditions are met as well. Moreover, some, but certainly not all, centrally planned economies have achieved sustained periods of development with prices that bear little relation to those determined by market forces. Finally, where nations are ruled by leaders backed by interests hostile to development, those leaders and their constituents must be removed from power before growth can occur; but not all developing nations are ruled by such people.

This book is not neutral toward all issues of development. Where controversy exists we shall point it out. Indeed, the authors of this book differ among ourselves over some questions of development policy. But we do share a common point of view on certain basic points.

First of all, this text makes extensive use of the theoretical tools of classical and neoclassical economics in the belief that these tools contribute substantially to our understanding of development problems and their solution. The text does not rely solely or even primarily on theory, however. For three decades and more, development economists and economic historians have been building up an empirical record against which these theories can be tested and this book draws heavily on many of these empirical studies. We try to give real-country examples for virtually all of the major points made in this book. In part these examples come from the individual country and cross-country comparative studies of others, but they also draw extensively from our own personal experiences working on development issues around the world. Among the four of us, we have been fortunate enough to study and work over long periods of time in Bolivia, Chile, China, Colombia, Ghana, Indonesia, Kenya, Korea, Malaysia, Peru, Sri Lanka, and Tanzania. At one time or another, at least one from this group of nations has exemplified virtually all approaches to development now extant.

While this book draws extensively on the tools of classical and neoclassical economic theory, development involves major issues for which these economic theories do not provide answers, or at best provide only partial answers. Economic theory tends to take the **institutional context** (the existence of markets, of a banking system, of international trade, etc.) as given. But development is concerned with how one creates institutions that facilitate development in the first place. How, for example, does a nation acquire a government interested in and capable of promoting economic growth? Can efficiently functioning markets be created in countries that currently lack them, or should the state take over the functions normally left to the market elsewhere? Is a fully developed financial system a precondition for growth, or can a nation do without at least some parts of such a system? Is land reform necessary for development, and, if so, what kind of land reform? These institutional issues and many others like them are at the heart of the development process and will reappear in different guises in the following chapters.

Organization

This book is divided into five parts. Part I examines the main factors that prevent development from taking place and the kinds of structural change that occur once growth is underway. Structural change, of course, does not just happen as a result of impersonal and uncontrolled forces. It is often the result of deliberate planning and the first part of the book, therefore, also provides an introduction to the theory and practice of development planning.

Economic development is first and foremost a process involving people. People are the prime movers of development and its beneficiaries. Part II, therefore, deals with how human resources are transformed in the process of economic development and how that transformation contributes to the development process itself. There are chapters on population, labor, education, and health.

The other major physical input in the growth process is capital, and Part III is concerned with how capital is mobilized and allocated for development purposes. Where, for example, do the savings come from and how are they transformed into investment? What kind of financial system is consistent with rapid capital accumulation? Will inflation enhance or hinder the process and what role is played by foreign aid and investment?

One of the most fundamental issues facing a developing nation is the degree to which that nation should integrate its economy with the economies of the rest of the world. These international trade and interdependence strategies are the subject of Part IV.

Finally, issues such as technological change and various kinds of institutional reform often differ significantly between sectors of the economy. The problems of agriculture are different from those of industry and natural resource development is different from either of the other two. In Part V, therefore, problems of economic development are approached from this sectoral point of view.

Starting Modern Economic Growth

The era of modern economic growth is only two centuries old. Before the late eighteenth century there were individuals and families who became rich, but nations as a whole and most of the people in them were poor. An economy was seen as a pie of fixed size. One could cut oneself a bigger piece of the pie, but only by taking away a portion that originally belonged to someone else. Few saw the possibility of increasing the size of the pie so that all could have larger slices.

But the essence of modern economic growth is that, on average, the per-capita income of all people in a nation rises, not just the income of a select few. And as per-capita income rises, other fundamental changes occur that affect the way people live. The household as a production unit declines and is replaced by larger enterprises that find it economic to locate near each other. The result is that more people live in cities and work in factories rather than on farms. As incomes rise and urbanization takes place, behavior within the household also changes. Families no longer want large numbers of children and so the birth rate begins to fall. Modern economic growth, therefore, involves fundamental structural changes in the way both production and society are organized.

In the late eighteenth century England began to transform its economy, a process that would later be called the Industrial Revolution. By the middle of the nineteenth century other nations in Europe and North America had begun similar transformations, and toward the end of the century the first non-European population, the Japanese, had begun to industrialize. Two world wars and the Great Depression interrupted industrialization in the already advanced nations and slowed the spread of economic advance to other parts of the globe. The Second World War, however, also undermined the strength of European colonialism and set the stage for a widespread effort to industrialize the large numbers of newly independent nations.

One of the key characteristics of modern economic growth, therefore, is that it did not begin everywhere in the world at the same time. Instead it spread slowly across Europe and North America, but did not break out of areas dominated by European culture (except for Japan) until the 1950s and 1960s. In parts of the world the process has yet to begin.

Between those parts of the world that have achieved sustained growth and those that have not, a gap in the standard of living has inevitably opened up. The average European, American, or Japanese enjoys a material way of life that is many times richer than that experienced by even large parts of the elites of India or Africa. But there is nothing inevitable or permanent about this gap. In the nineteenth century England was far ahead of the rest of the world, whereas today England is not even in the top ten of the richest nations in terms of per-capita income. In the early 1950s Japan was poorer than such centers of European poverty as Spain or Greece, but by the mid 1980s Japanese income per capita was comparable to that of richer Western European nations such as France.

This chapter focuses on why these gaps in income between nations open up. Why is it that some nations began developing earlier than others? What has prevented some nations from entering into modern economic growth even today? Are the barriers that have inhibited development the result of conditions internal to the country affected or is the lack of development in some nations today the result of externally imposed forces? A related question is whether the barriers to growth in nations are the same everywhere or whether particular conditions in one country act to inhibit growth while similar conditions elsewhere do little harm because the context is different. In much the same spirit, are there "prerequisites" that must be in place, such as a modern banking system, before growth can occur, or are there often substitutes available for particular prerequisites?

Throughout most of this book, the emphasis is on the kinds of changes that occur once modern economic growth is underway and how government policy can accelerate or slow that change. This chapter, by contrast, will emphasize what is required to initiate growth. A central theme of this chapter is that the failure to achieve sustained development is as much a political and social phenomenon as it is economic. Politics and social structure, of course, also shape development once it is underway, but a failure to get growth started at all is foremost a political and social problem. This point will be illustrated first with a brief glance at the great diversity in the historical experience of today's developing nations.

The Developing Nations: A Glance at History

The two features common to all traditional societies are a low per-capita income and an absence of modern economic growth. Beyond these simple common features is a great diversity of national experience about which valid generalizations are difficult to make. The use of terms such as third world, less developed countries, or developing nations tends to obscure this diversity by implying that all nations, except those already rich, have a common experience that transcends any differences in their background and current conditions. In fact the differences between developing nations are so great that one cannot really understand their development problems without taking these differences into account.

Even within Europe on the eve of industrialization there were great differences between societies, and these differences have much to do with why development began first in the West and spread only gradually to the East. In England, for example, laborers were free to change jobs and migrate to distant places, and commerce and banking had reached a high level of sophistication in the centuries preceding the Industrial Revolution. But Russia in the mid-nineteenth century was still feudal: Most peasants were tied to their lord's estate for life, and commerce, industry, and transport were still in a primitive state.

In Asia, Latin America, and Africa the range of political and cultural experience is more diverse than that which existed within Europe. Great empires, such as those of China and Japan, had over one thousand years' of self-governing experience and they thought of themselves as a single unified people, rather than as a collection of ethnically distinct tribes or regions. By premodern standards China and Japan also had high levels of urbanization and commerce, and they shared Confucian values that emphasized the importance of education. Long years of comparative stability contributed to a population increase that resulted in the great shortage of arable land relative to population that still exists in the region today. Because of the comparative sophistication of premodern commerce in East Asia, European and American merchants were never able to play a significant role in the management of domestic commerce in the region. And as Chinese and Japanese merchants gradually acquired an understanding of foreign markets, they were able to compete successfully with representatives of the industrialized world in that sphere as well.

COLONIALISM AND INDEPENDENCE

At the other end of this spectrum with respect to self-government and commercial sophistications are several Southeast Asian and African nations. Indonesia, Nigeria, and Pakistan, for example, were really the arbitrary creations of Dutch and British colonialism, which brought together diverse groups of people who shared little in common and had no desire to maintain these externally imposed boundaries. Both Indonesia in 1958 and Nigeria in the late 1960s had to fight wars to keep their new nations together. In 1971 Pakistan also fought a civil war to hold the eastern and western portions of the nation together, but the effort failed and the independent state of Bangladesh was formed out of what had been East Pakistan.

Experience with commerce in many parts of Southeast Asia and Africa was also quite limited and illiteracy was often nearly universal. Throughout the colonial era in Indonesia and many parts of sub-Saharan Africa, foreign trade and large-scale domestic commerce were almost entirely in the hands of Europeans. Small-scale commerce, particularly in the countryside, was sometimes controlled by local people, but usually it was in the hands of minorities who had immigrated from other poor but commercially more advanced nations. Thus local commerce in much of Southeast Asia was in the hands of Chinese, that in East Africa was mainly managed by Indians, while in West Africa Lebanese often played a central role. Because of inexperience the local people could not effectively compete with either these immigrant groups or the Europeans and because they could not compete, they did not gain much experience with trade or finance. This was one of the many vicious circles so common to the plight of poor nations.

Not all experiences with colonialism were the same. In India a tiny number of British ruled a vastly populated subcontinent. By necessity the British had to train large numbers of Indians to handle all but the very top jobs in the bureaucracy and army. At the time of independence in 1948, Indians were already running most of their own affairs because there were enough trained and experienced personnel to do so. But in Indonesia there were fewer than one thousand university or other postsecondary school graduates at the time of independence, and in Zaire there were hardly any. Prior to independence even the lower levels of the central bureaucracy in Indonesia had been manned by the Dutch and those in Zaire by Belgians. In comparison, India and China in the 1940s had hundreds of thousands of university graduates.

Latin America's historical heritage is different from that of either Asia or Africa. Independence in most of the region was achieved in the early nineteenth century, not after World War II as in Asia and Africa. Although there were local populations in the region when the Europeans first arrived, the indigenous populations were suppressed or enslaved. So to meet growing labor requirements, the elites turned to voluntary and forced immigration of Europeans and Africans. Spanish and Portuguese immigrants ruled; the Africans were enslaved until late in the nineteenth century. Ignored or pushed aside, the original population continued to exist, but in varying numbers: Peru and Bolivia maintained large indigenous populations, whereas in Argentina native peoples nearly disappeared.

North America above the Rio Grande was also peopled by immigrants who suppressed the local population. In both North and South America slavery existed in some regions and not in others, but there were important differences between the types of colonial rule. In the north the Indian population was more thoroughly suppressed; hence, it was small and isolated and not a factor when economic development began. European immigrants were from the economically most advanced parts of Europe where feudal values and structures had already been partially dismantled. But Spanish and Portuguese immigrants came from an area that by the nineteenth century was one of the more backward parts of Europe. The feudal values and structures that still dominated this region accompanied these colonists to the New World. Likewise, there were also great differences within Latin America. Argentina, for example, is largely a nation of European immigrants;

Mexico, Peru, and Bolivia have large Indian populations but few of African descent; and the population of Haiti is mainly descended from former African slaves.

THE DEVELOPING NATIONS: A BRIEF TAXONOMY

It is impossible to summarize all the important differences between nations in the developing world, but those with the greatest bearing on the potential for modern economic growth in the region would include:

Differences between nations with a long tradition of emphasis on education and an elite that was highly educated, as contrasted to nations where illiteracy was nearly universal.

Countries with fairly highly developed systems of commerce, finance, and transport mainly run by local people versus countries where these activities were almost entirely in the hands of European or Asian immigrant minorities.

Nations peopled by those who shared a common language, culture, and sense of national identity versus nations where there was a great diversity of language, culture, and no common sense of national identity or shared common goals.

Nations with long traditions of self-government versus those with no experience with even limited self-government until the 1950s or 1960s.

This list could be extended but the point is made. Economic development as we shall see requires both a government capable of directing or supporting a major growth effort and a people who can work effectively in and manage the enterprises and other organizations that arise in the course of development. Nations with people who have at least some relevant education and experience in economic affairs and which have governments able to support those people are better positioned for development than nations where the people have little relevant experience and where diverse groups within the nation are still arguing over their shares in what they believe, wrongly for the most part, to be a pie of fixed size.

THE CONCEPT OF SUBSTITUTES

Given the great diversity in developing-country experience, it would be a counsel of despair to suggest that the way to begin development is first to recreate the kinds of political, social, and economic conditions that existed in Western Europe or North America when those regions entered into modern economic growth. England prior to the Industrial Revolution had centuries of experience with merchant capitalism, but does it follow that Ghana or Indonesia must also acquire long experience with merchant capitalism before economic development would be feasible? If the answer were yes, these nations would be doomed to another century or more of poverty.

Fortunately there is no standard list of barriers that must be overcome or prerequisites that must be in place before development is possible. Instead, as the economic historian Alexander Gerschenkron pointed out, for most presumed prerequisites there are usually **substitutes**. The main point of this concept is best illustrated with an example from Gerschenkron's own work.[1]

Capital, like labor, is of course necessary for development, and much more will be said about both in later chapters. But Marx and others went a step further and argued that there must be an original or prior accumulation of capital before growth can take place. The basic idea came from looking at the experience of England where, Marx argued, trade, exploitation of colonies, piracy, and other related measures led to the accumulation of great wealth that in the late eighteenth century could be converted into investment in industry. Is such an accumulation a *prerequisite* for development everywhere or at least for a large number of countries? In the absence of a prior accumulation of capital, does economic development thereby become impossible?

In Europe the answer was clearly no. One did have to find funds that could be invested in industry but they did not have to come out of the accumulated wealth of the past. Germany, for example, had little in the way of an original accumulation of capital when modern economic growth began there. But Germany did have a banking system that could create funds which were then lent to industrialists. How banks create funds is not our concern here—the point is that banks can create accounts that investors can draw upon, and the creation of those accounts depends in no significant way on long years of prior savings and accumulation by merchants or other wealthy individuals.

Russia in the nineteenth century had neither an original accumulation of wealth nor a banking system capable of creating large enough levels of credit. Instead Russia turned to the taxing power of the state. The government could and did tax funds away from people and use this tax revenue for investment in industry. Russia also imported capital from abroad. Thus the government's use of taxation was a *substitute* for an underdeveloped banking system, and elsewhere a modern banking system was a *substitute* for an original accumulation of capital.

Similar examples of substitutes in today's world abound. Latin American countries, for example, rely heavily on financial institutions to mobilize and allocate savings. Sub-Saharan African countries, in contrast, rely more on fiscal institutions (the government budget). Factories in advanced nations with well-developed commercial networks rely on central distributors to supply them with spare parts. Rural industries in China, where commerce is less developed, make spare parts in their own foundries. As already pointed out, a number of nations in the developing world today have substantial numbers of people with training and experience in areas relevant to economic development, while the number of such people in other nations is miniscule. The most common substitute for this lack of relevant experience is to import foreigners who have the required experience. For reasons that will become apparent in later chapters, foreigners are frequently not very good substitutes for experienced local talent, but where the latter is missing they can fill the gap until local talent is trained.

1. Alexander Gerschenkron, *Economic Backwardness in Historical Perspective* (Cambridge, Mass.: Harvard University Press, 1962), Chapter 2.

Therefore, in the following discussion of political and social barriers to development and of what is required to initiate development, we shall not be looking for three or four universal causes of poverty or a similar number of prerequisites that must always be in place before growth is possible. Instead we shall attempt to identify some of the more common political and social barriers to development, recognizing that the presence of these barriers or the absence of prerequisites does not guarantee the continuation of poverty. There are usually ways around, or substitutes for, any single barrier or prerequisite, but the existence of many of these barriers or the absence of a wide variety of desirable preconditions will at least make economic development more difficult and in some cases impossible.

The closest one can come to a single prerequisite without which economic development would be impossible lies not in the realm of politics or social structure but in whether or not a nation has access to the discoveries of modern science and innovators to adapt these discoveries for the marketplace. The industrial economy of the twentieth century would be inconceivable in the absence of the knowledge arising from such fields as chemistry, physics, and biology. A high percentage of the products in common use today, ranging from electric power to antibiotics, did not even exist prior to the advent of modern science.

While science is crucial to economic development, it is also clear that no nation today is really cut off from the main fruits of that science. Some of the great civilizations of the past probably were unable to expand beyond a certain level primarily from a lack of scientific discovery and technological advancement. It is also the case today that nations with educational and research capabilities of their own, such as South Korea and Mexico, can often make more and better use of many scientific discoveries. But even the most poorly endowed nations have access to much of what modern science has contributed since the fruits of scientific discovery are often embodied in products domestically manufactured using comparatively simple processes or imported as finished goods from more advanced nations. Developing countries do not have to rediscover the basic laws of thermodynamics. For many purposes they only need to understand those laws and how they can be usefully applied, or imitate others' applications of those laws, a much easier task than making the discovery in the first place. The issue of why some nations gained access to modern science earlier than others, therefore, is mainly of historical interest and won't be pursued further here.

In the eyes of some economists a failure to enter into modern economic growth is mainly the result of economic forces within the developing nation. Since the remainder of this book is concerned with these economic forces, we shall put them aside in this chapter. As the following chapters will make clear, however, there is no single economic barrier to development that accounts for why so few countries were able to initiate growth prior to the middle of the twentieth century. Savings rates in many of these countries were too low to pay for the investment needed to achieve development, but the crucial question is why were savings rates low. Poverty alone is not a cause of low savings rates. Even very poor nations, such as Japan in the late nineteenth century, were able to mobilize large amounts of savings. Japan

could mobilize large amounts of savings in part because it had a strong governmental structure with a tradition of extracting large tax payments from
the population.

Therefore, while there are economic causes for the prevalence of poverty
in large parts of the world, economic explanations alone cannot account for
why particular economic barriers exist. Economists are uncomfortable when
they leave the realm of economic explanations, in part because the tools of
economic analysis are of only limited help outside the sphere for which they
were designed. But if one is seriously interested in understanding why some
nations have had so much trouble initiating growth, there is little choice but
to explore the relationship between economic development on the one hand,
and political systems and social values on the other.

POLITICAL OBSTACLES TO DEVELOPMENT

Economic development in England in the eighteenth century began with little direct assistance from the government, but since that time government's
role in development has risen steadily to a point where successful growth is
not really possible without the active support of a government. In subsequent chapters the role of many kinds of specific governmental policies in
promoting economic development will be explained in detail. For our purposes here one mainly needs to know that an active, positive role for government is essential. It follows that if a government is unwilling or unable to
play such a role, then the government itself can be considered a barrier to
development or a fundamental cause of poverty.

Political Stability

To begin with, governments must be able to create and maintain a **stable
environment** for modern enterprises, whether public or private. At a minimum, civil war, sustained insurrection, or invasion by hostile forces must be
avoided. It is an obvious point but one frequently forgotten in discussions of
the nature of development. Prolonged instability connected with civil war
and foreign invasion go a long way toward explaining why China failed to
enter into modern economic growth prior to 1949. By extension, the creation of a stable environment after 1949 helps to explain why growth began
after 1949. More recently Vietnam was obviously not in a position to
develop its economy on a sustained basis in the 1950s and 1960s. China and
Vietnam are extreme cases, but a much longer list of nations, including Bolivia, Pakistan, Ghana, and many others, have experienced prolonged domestic political instability of a kind that has inhibited growth. Bolivia, for
example, has had one hundred and fifty governments since independence in
1825. Investors will not put their money into projects that pay off only over
the long run if, in the short run, a change of government could lead to the
project's being confiscated or rendered unprofitable by new laws and other
restrictions. Where instability is particularly rife, a common solution among
the wealthy has been to stop investing in the local economy and to ship off a

large part of their wealth to banks in Switzerland or to indulge in conspicuous consumption.

Political Independence

But a stable environment alone is not enough. Colonial governments were usually quite stable, often for very long periods of time. There were rebellions against British rule in India, French rule in North Africa, and Japanese rule in Korea, but these rebellions were generally short-lived or on the periphery of the colony. Furthermore, most colonial governments had a very specific interest in creating a stable environment for private business. Yet few, if any, European or Japanese colonies experienced anything that could be described as sustained economic development. Part of the explanation is that the stable environment created was often only for the benefit of a small number of traders and investors from the colonizing nation, whereas the citizens of the colonies themselves received little such support. Probably a more important part of the explanation, however, is that most colonial governments made only limited investments in training local people, in developing electric power resources, or in promoting industry. Thus, in most cases political independence was necessary before modern economic growth was possible. Conceivably, colonial governments could have promoted genuine development, but for the most part they did not. Later in this chapter we shall return to the question of whether or not relations between rich and poor countries today continue to possess some of the features that characterized the colonial era.

Government Support of Development

The immediate concern here is whether there are many governments of developing countries today that, for domestic reasons of their own, are unwilling to do what is necessary to achieve growth. Since virtually all leaders of developing nations regularly make speeches about the need for growth and appoint commissions to draw up development plans, the answer seems obvious, but nothing could be further from the truth.

The decision to pursue economic development, like most other economic decisions, involves hard choices or **trade-offs.** While there are many people whose position is improved by economic development, in the early stages at least, there are usually people whose position becomes worse off. If those who become worse off in the short run are in a position to topple the government, that government will be unwilling or unable to take the steps necessary to promote growth. The nature of the problem is best illustrated by the experience of a number of developing nations that have attempted to devalue their currencies, to eliminate excessive staffing of public enterprises, or to remove subsidies on basic consumer goods.

Devaluation of a nation's currency as a policy option for promoting development will be discussed at length in Chapter 17. Here all we need to know is that for some countries, economic growth requires a more rapid development of those countries' exports and a restriction of imports. Devaluing the currency relative to foreign currencies accomplishes both ends by lowering the prices of the nations' exports (in terms of foreign prices) and raising the

prices of imports to the domestic consumer (in terms of local currency). But
when governments as diverse as those of Ghana and Peru carried out a devaluation (in 1971 and 1968, respectively), those governments immediately
fell. The reason was very simple. The people most dependent on imported
consumer products whose prices had risen were the urban well-to-do,
including the military and the civil service elite, who also held most of the
political power in these countries. While devaluation made good sense in
terms of the economic interests of the nation as a whole, it did not make economic sense to the narrower interests of the groups (the bureaucrats and the
military) best able to prevent it.

Analagous situations can be found in a number of less developed countries
and are endemic to large parts of the developing world. In Sri Lanka and
Bangladesh, for example, political supporters of the government, or others
who could cause trouble if unemployed, have been forced on the managing
boards of public enterprises. The result is a large number of overstaffed and
hopelessly inefficient enterprises that are unable to contribute to national
savings mobilization efforts or to deliver goods and services effectively. To
fire these unnecessary employees is not usually politically feasible, but to
continue employing them is to settle for little or no growth. In Egypt the
problem is both an overvalued currency and large subsidies on food and
other basic necessities, subsidies that are a major drain on the government
budget, making it difficult for that government to find funds for development purposes. When the Egyptian government started to remove these subsidies in 1977, however, the immediate result was widespread urban rioting
contained only by the government's decision to reverse its policy and keep
the subsidies.

While problems such as those described in the previous two paragraphs
are the most common reasons for governments' being unwilling to take the
steps necessary to promote growth, there are other reasons that need to be
mentioned. Some nations, for example, feel that certain international goals
should take precedence over domestic developmental goals. President
Sukarno in Indonesia, during the period he held real power (1948–1965),
was more interested in international affairs, such as leadership of the third
world or military confrontation with Singapore and Malaysia, than in economic development. A number of Arab states have devoted a sizeable share
of their surplus resources to three decades of confrontation and war with
Israel. No doubt both President Sukarno and the leaders of these Arab states
would have preferred to have economic development as well as confrontation, but their resources were limited and they had to choose between goals.
They did not opt for economic development.

Other nations have concentrated their energies on achieving what could
be termed **social goals** rather than economic development. In the definition
used in this book, economic development includes both growth and wide
distribution of the benefits of growth. While some nations have pursued
growth but not development, there are also several nations that have sacrificed growth at least for a time in order to achieve wider distribution and
other social goals. Cuba in the 1960s, for example, experienced little eco-

nomic growth in large part because energies were concentrated on achieving a major redistribution of income, education, and other benefits in favor of the poorest elements of the society. China's Cultural Revolution (1966–76) was even more ambitious. There the ultimate goal of at least some of the nation's leaders was to eliminate all class distinctions and to minimize the role of material incentives, and the leaders were willing to sacrifice growth at least temporarily to achieve those objectives. Growth and distributive goals, as will become clear in Chapter 4, need not be in conflict. To the contrary, certain kinds of income redistribution can make an important contribution to more rapid growth, but as China's and Cuba's experiences of the 1960s indicate, they can also be in conflict, and when they are in conflict, governments do not always choose growth.

From these various examples it should be clear that one of the reasons many nations are still underdeveloped is that their governments have been unable or unwilling to pursue policies that would achieve development. After all, governments represent various interests in the society, and in some cases it has proved impossible to pursue developmental goals and maintain sufficient support from those interests to stay in office, while in other cases government leaders themselves have preferred to pursue objectives that were in conflict with development. An important question is why governments have found themselves in these situations, but the answers would take us deep into the nature of politics and society in developing nations, and would divert us from this book's main task of explaining economic development.

SOCIAL VALUES AS OBSTACLES TO DEVELOPMENT

Whether a society's values and structure lead to political systems that impede or foster modern economic growth, clearly such values have a direct bearing on whether or not development occurs. Much of the analysis of the relationship between values and development has arisen out of concern with how societies create a sufficient number of entrepreneurs to lead the development effort. Societies that lacked a sufficient number of entrepreneurs, it was argued, failed to initiate a sustained period of growth. And the origins of this insufficiency lay in the way different societies were structured.

Entrepreneurship

The concept of the **entrepreneur** or **entrepreneurship** was developed by the economist Joseph Schumpeter, who put the entrepreneur at the center of his *The Theory of Economic Development,* originally published (in German) in 1911. The entrepreneur was someone who could take a new technical discovery or a new method of management and make practical use of it in his factory or business. It was one thing to develop a new technique or invention, but unless someone actually put that technique to practical use, to turn it into an **innovation,** it would have little or no impact on economic development. The entrepreneur who played this crucial role was someone who had the imagination to see the potential for profit from the innovation, the initiative to carry out the task of introducing the innovation, and a willingness to take a calculated risk that the effort might fail and lead to a loss rather than a profit. An entrepreneur was not necessarily either a manager of the enterprise using the innovation or a supplier of capital (investment funds) to that enterprise. An entrepreneur was an innovator, and while he might manage his own enterprise or supply his own capital, he might also hire a manager or borrow his capital from a bank.

Schumpeter raised basic questions about whether entrepreneurship was really necessary once industrial development had reached an advanced level. In advanced industrial economies innovation tends to become routinized. Corporations have their own large research laboratories, and managers more or less automatically turn the results of that research into new products or new methods of producing old products. Innovations no longer require the bold imagination of a few unique entrepreneurs. How to introduce innovations can be taught to thousands of future managers at any good business school.

Schumpeter's insight concerning advanced industrial economies is directly relevant to developing countries. If innovation can be routinized in advanced economies, why not in developing economies as well? After all, it does not take much imagination or daring to see that a railroad or a chemical fertilizer plant may make a major contribution to a developing country's economy. The value of such innovations is clear to all, and the task for the developing nation is to find the capital and managerial talent to pay for and run the new enterprise. Actually technological transfer is never this simple, as will be amply demonstrated in later chapters.

Thus, there is still some role for entrepreneurship in today's developing world, and the question then becomes, what is it in a society that creates an adequate number of entrepreneurs, or, alternatively, what has blocked the development of entrepreneurship in other societies? One of the best known explanations, from Everett Hagen of MIT, is that entrepreneurs come disproportionately from **blocked minorities.** The basic idea is that certain individuals in a traditional society are prevented from rising to the more conventional sources of prestige, power, and wealth, such as high government office. The reason they are prevented from rising up through the conventional hierarchy may be that they are members of a religious minority subjected to discrimination or because they are immigrants from abroad and not "natives" of the country. If these blocked minorities had previously enjoyed a high status, they have a particularly keen desire to restore themselves to a position of wealth and prestige. Since they cannot join the army or the civil service, the one route open to them is to become wealthy through entrepreneurship.

The examples of blocked minorities that have supplied large numbers of entrepreneurs is a long one. The list includes Parsees in India, Jews in Europe, Chinese in Southeast Asia, Indians and Lebanese in Africa, and so on. In looking at the oldest developed nations of northern and western Europe and North America, the connection between minority status and entrepreneurs becomes more remote except in a fairly trivial sense. Everyone in the United States is a member of a minority group of some kind, for example, but only a few of those minorities have been blocked from rising up any of the ladders of power and prestige, and those blocked minorities have not yet been the major suppliers of entrepreneurship.

The real question, however, is not whether there is some correlation between minority status and entrepreneurial qualities in certain individuals. In Latin America, for example, most industrialists have been of Lebanese, Arab, Jewish, Basque, German, or Italian origin rather than from the dominant populations of Spanish or Portuguese origin. The logical explanation for this phenomenon, however, has little to do with these people's minority status. Their immigrant background gave these people a greater knowledge of and often access to foreign sources of supply, and hence they often became importers.[2] When the nations of Latin America began to restrict imports in order to promote local industry, it was natural for these former importers who already knew the markets to move into manufacturing to preserve their position in those markets.

Similar although slightly different arguments can be made about the Chinese in Southeast Asia or the Indians and Lebanese traders in Africa. The Chinese, Indians, and Lebanese who emigrated to these regions came from societies (described briefly above) where commerce was already highly developed by premodern standards. Commerce in much of Southeast Asia and Africa, in contrast, was much less developed and hence the local populations had little experience as merchants or moneylenders. Is it really surprising that under such circumstances it was the more experienced immigrant populations that, together with the European colonialists, ended up in charge of the commerce that arose during the colonial period?

Motivation for Development

Even if it is difficult to establish a clear causal connection between certain types of minority-group status and entrepreneurship, there remains the question of what factors beside minority status cause people to become entrepreneurs. One idea first put forward by the Harvard psychologist, David McClelland, is that of **need achievement.** McClelland proposes achievement as a psychological need and observes that certain societies produce a large number of people with a high level of desire to improve themselves in order to get ahead financially or to be recognized as the best at some endeavor. Such societies will produce large numbers of entrepreneurs and hence will develop.

There seems to be little reason to dispute the notion that success in business, as in many other activities, is somehow connected with a need to achieve. The controversy surrounding the term instead centers around two other issues. There is first of all the question of whether one can come up with plausible and independent methods of measuring need achievement that can then be compared with economic performance. Proponents of the concept argue that they have developed such measurable concepts and that the correlation clearly exists, whereas a considerable body of skeptics

2. Albert O. Hirschman, *A Bias for Hope* (New Haven: Yale University Press, 1971) pp. 96–97.

remains to be convinced. A second question is whether need achievement is

something that must exist in adequate amounts before development can occur or whether appropriate motivation is something that arises more or less automatically as economic development creates opportunities for people to exploit.

The nature of this latter issue can be illustrated with an historical example. Malaya had long been known to have rich resources of tin. When European industrialization created a rapidly rising demand for tin, the question arose as to who would develop the Malayan mines. The two main groups in Malaya were the Malays and the Chinese, both possessing rich but very different cultures. The Malays lived in villages on the coast, grew rice, fished in surrounding bountiful seas, and showed little inclination to go deep into the jungle where most of the tin was located. Chinese migrants from extremely poor regions of South China possessed little land in Malaya and wanted most of all to accumulate money to send back to their families in China, where they one day hoped to return themselves. The Chinese were willing to go into the jungle to mine tin even though the risk of death from malaria was extremely high. A majority of the first miners to settle in what is now the capital city of Kuala Lumpur, for example, died of malaria. But at least some of the Chinese who survived these and similar mining camps accumulated funds and started other businesses; they soon came to dominate those parts of the colonial commercial economy not in the hands of the British. The Malays remained as fishermen and farmers right into the middle of the twentieth century.

One interpretation of this experience is to say that the Chinese possessed a strong desire to achieve and the Malays did not, and hence the Chinese got ahead economically and the Malays did not. A somewhat different interpretation is to point out that in the nineteenth century the Malays had few rational reasons for wanting to mine tin, since their wants were met under more favorable conditions on the coast and the disadvantages of going into the jungle were high. By the time the risks had fallen, the Chinese and British were in command of virtually the entire mining and commercial network in the country and evinced little interest in making way for Malay participation. Only when a Malay-dominated government came to power after independence were the firms forced to open opportunities for Malays. The question then became whether the Malays would respond to the opportunities being created. So far the response has been slow, but it is occurring. Values suitable to the new environment of opportunity do not arise overnight, nor do the skills that come only with experience. In short, motivation in this case is not just determined by the opportunities of the moment but is rooted in the experience of the past as well.

Clearly the problem of appropriate motivation for economic development exists in some developing societies, and for various reasons certain cultures seem more resistant to change than others. It is also clear that the problem of motivation is not confined to the issue of what creates entrepreneurs. Development requires effective managers and a hard working and disciplined labor force, and motivation presumably has something to do with these people as well. But once these obvious points have been made, it is difficult to say much more with any conviction. We have only a general idea of what the appropriate kinds of motivation are for economic development to be successful, and an even hazier notion of how that motivation is created. We suspect, however, that an environment full of economic opportunity eventually brings forth the desired response. At one time it was held by many that only those who believed in the Protestant version of the Christian ethic made successful entrepreneurs. Today as development spreads across the globe, the ranks of entrepreneurs include people of all religious persuasions—Catholics, Hindus, Buddhists, Zoroastrians, and numerous others.

INTERNATIONAL OBSTACLES TO DEVELOPMENT

Up to this point our analysis of the obstacles to development has concentrated on political systems and social values that are internal to the less developed world. To the extent that these internal conditions are the main causes of a lack of economic growth in the past, successful development will depend on internal solutions. But many economists and others argue that the main barriers to development today lie with conditions external to the developing world. Specifically, the existence of already rich and industrialized nations, it is argued, creates international political and economic pressures that hamper the growth efforts of today's poor nations.

Before reviewing the various arguments that stress the negative political and economic aspects of the relations between rich and poor countries, it is useful to present a brief synopsis of some of the beneficial economic aspects for poor nations in a world where some nations are already rich. These positive economic elements are less controversial, and with them in mind, one can ask whether they are outweighed by the negative side of the ledger.

One important part of any argument about the positive side of rich-poor relations is based on the concept of the gains from trade. Since these gains are considered in some detail in Chapter 15, only a brief listing of these gains will be attempted here.

Gains from Trade: A Preliminary View

To begin with, the **theory of comparative advantage** states that nations with different endowments of capital, labor, and natural resources will gain by specializing in those areas where their relative costs are low and importing where their relative costs of production are high. Further, the greater the difference in endowments between countries—and the differences between rich and poor countries are great indeed—the greater these gains from trade are likely to be. In certain extreme cases, but ones that occur in the real world, a nation possesses one resource or factor such as land or oil in such abundance that it is impossible to make effective internal use of all of that resource. Trade makes it possible to use this surplus resource because the country can export what is not needed at home to purchase things that are needed. Saudi Arabia could not possibly use all the petroleum it is capable of producing, or Canada all of the wheat from its great plains. Trade thus becomes what is sometimes referred to as a **vent for surplus.**

Other gains from trade include the fact that real capital goods can only be transferred from rich to poor nations (and vice versa) through trade. In addition, there is the fact that some countries' export-producing enterprises are among the nation's most progressive businesses because they have to be to survive international competition. The example set by these progressive firms then influences the operation of domestic enterprises.

Drawing on Experience

The gains from trade, however, encompass only a part of the economic advantages of poor nations that exist in a world where some countries have already achieved sustained development. The term used by Gerschenkron to describe this broader phenomenon is the **advantages of backwardness.** Developing countries are in a position to learn from the experience of already advanced nations. The most obvious area in which these advantages exist is the realm of science and technology. But the advantages are not confined to science and technology.

By the middle of the twentieth century, advanced nations had acquired a great deal of experience with management of enterprises, with national economic policymaking, and even with widely different kinds of economic systems. In the late eighteenth century, laissez-faire capitalism was probably the only system capable of achieving modern economic growth in England. During World War I, however, wartime conditions led Germany and others to experiment with close state management of the economy. In the 1930s the Soviet Union, building on the World War I experience of others, developed what we know today as the Soviet-type or socialist system of planned economy. When China opted for a fully socialized economy in the 1950s, Chinese planners were able to draw on Soviet experience, often to the extent of simply translating Soviet planning rules and regulations into Chinese and then putting them into effect. The Chinese later modified the Soviet planning system to make it more suitable to Chinese conditions, but the point is that without prior Soviet experience, China would have had to move much more cautiously in setting up a centrally planned economy. In a similar fashion, South Korea learned much from the experience of Japan about how to operate a privately owned but state-managed economy.

There are situations, of course, where having a wide range of choices makes it possible for a country to make the wrong choice. Some nations would be better off if they had no range of options and instead had to follow a single optimal or at least feasible development path. But other nations have benefited from being able to make choices that took into account their own local economic, political, and social conditions.

Imperialism

While almost everyone acknowledges the potential advantages of learning from the experience of others, many have argued that this potential is seldom realized in practice because advanced nations create barriers to the progress of poor nations. Many economists and other scholars have attempted to explain the nature and sources of these barriers imposed on the less-developed world, but the largest group of theorists in one way or another owe an intellectual debt to Marx, the British economist Hobson, and Lenin, the architect of the Russian revolution.

Marxian Approaches to Development One of the centerpieces of Karl Marx's theory of capitalist development was the view that the rate of profits on capital inevitably declines as growth takes place.[3] These profits were produced by labor from the **surplus,** or the excess, of what was needed to meet the subsistence needs of that labor. Competition in the face of this declining rate of profit leads to stronger capitalists swallowing up the weaker, who then join the ranks of the proletariat or workers. Economic crises or depressions become more severe as development proceeds, and the wages of workers may actually decline as capitalists squeeze them harder in a desperate attempt to keep profits up. The end result is a revolution that overthrows the rule of the capitalist class.

By the late nineteenth and early twentieth century, there was little evidence to support the view that the rate of profit was declining, and it was clear that real wages were rising. At the same time, however, the capitalist powers of Europe were vigorously expanding their colonial empires. The question then became whether there was a connection between the two phenomena. Workers in the colony also produced a surplus. If the imperial power could drain off enough of that colonial surplus, it could maintain profits at home and perhaps have enough left over to raise the wages of workers so that they would not become restless.

Conversely, from the colonial country's point of view, its development was severely inhibited because its surplus was being drained off abroad. In the absence of this surplus, the colonial nation had few resources of its own to invest while at the same time it was receiving only small amounts of investment from abroad.

In this form the basic propositions of the theory can be tested empirically. The issue is mainly whether the flow of surplus, or profits and tax revenues, from the colonial to the imperialist nation was large enough to keep the profit rate in the capitalist nation high or to keep the rate of investment in the colonial nation low. The issue is not whether this drain of surplus made a few Englishmen and others very rich, but whether it accounted for a large share of the total profits of the capitalist world. More important from the point of view of development, was the drain of surplus large enough relative to the national product of the colonial country to have a significant impact on the investment, and hence development, prospects of that country?

The end of colonialism in much of the world did not by itself necessarily change this situation. Capitalist nations could continue to accomplish much of what was achieved by colonialism through private investment activities abroad. Even many early proponents of this Marxian viewpoint, however, recognized that it was difficult to find quantitative data with which to support the argument in this form.

A different tack taken by other scholars is that what was lost was a poten-

---

3. Karl Marx, *Das Kapital,* the first volume of which was published in 1867.

tial, rather than actual, surplus. The drain of profits from the developing world might not be large, but measures taken by the capitalist nations prevented the developing nations from producing the surplus that would have existed in the absence of capitalist pressures from abroad. Some argued, for example, that free-trade policies imposed on the developing world made it impossible to protect infant industries, and hence those industries did not develop. The resources that would have gone to produce industrial output and funds for further investment instead lay idle. It is argued that free trade, leading to imports of manufactured cloth and the like, also destroyed local handicrafts, thereby further contributing to the unemployment of domestic resources. Still other scholars have argued that the drain of profits was real enough, but hidden by the way prices are set for goods transferred from the industrial to the developing nation. Multinationals, it is argued, charge much higher prices when they sell to developing countries than when they sell the same product at home.

Modern Theories of Imperialism Modern theories of imperialism or of the nature of relations between rich and poor nations continue to use many of these older themes, but there has been a definite shift of emphasis. There are also many differences in analysis and emphasis among scholars writing about imperialism. Broadly, however, these scholars share the view that slow growth, extreme inequality, and high levels of unemployment in developing nations arise out of unequal relations of power both between rich and poor nations, and between classes within the poorer developing nations. Furthermore, a solution to these problems of poverty requires a fundamental change in these power relations usually involving the elimination of capitalist class structures and values.[4]

As to why capitalist nations are inherently imperialistic, the important point is not so much a declining rate of profit shored up by returns from abroad as it is the need of capitalist firms to secure a reliable supply of natural resources. Capitalist firms, therefore, are interested in protecting their investments abroad, and to that end they want a large military force at home and abroad capable of providing that protection. But workers in capitalist societies also benefit from this large military force even though they gain nothing, or less than nothing, from foreign investments. In the absence of such military expenditures, scholars like Stanford economist Paul Baran have argued, there would be a great depression and large-scale unemployment in capitalist countries.[5] This belief is based on a Keynesian-like analysis of the sources of unemployment. In addition to avoiding unemployment, workers in the large defense industries benefit directly from military expenditures. Thus the presence of democracy in the capitalist world does not prevent imperialism because large numbers of voters in that world see imperialism, at least indirectly, as being in their interests.

For poor nations attempting to develop, the emphasis has shifted away

---

4. Keith Griffin and John Gurley, "Radical Analyses of Imperialism, the Third World, and the Transition to Socialism," *Journal of Economic Literature* 23, no. 3 (September 1985): 1090–91.

5. Paul Baran, *The Political Economy of Growth* (New York: Monthly Review Press, 1957).

from the role of a direct drain of surplus to collusion between advanced-nation capitalists and antigrowth forces within the developing nation. The issue is not as much the drain of surplus abroad as it is the misuse of that surplus at home.

There are many variations on this basic theme. Some scholars argue that it is in the interest of advanced-nation capitalists to keep raw materials from developing nations flowing. Industrial growth within the developing nation would be harmful to both goals since local industrial products would compete with imports and would also bid for local raw materials. The old ruling classes made up of landlords and other feudal elements also have no interest in promoting the rise of industrial capitalists who would compete with them for power, and who might find it in the interest of industry to advocate such measures as land reform. Although some commercial capitalists exist in such societies, it is argued that they too tend to side with foreign investors and the feudal ruling class because they make their living from the existing pattern of trade and do not want competition from newer patterns. Even the workers in modern establishments share this viewpoint, because their wages are so much higher than the average. The end result is an alliance of foreign investors backed by their governments, feudal landlords, and merchant capitalists and their workers, who together keep a government in power that does little to promote development.

Income Inequality and the Demand for Luxury Products Another variation on this theme is that put forward by the prominent Brazilian economist Celso Furtado.[6] Furtado starts from the proposition, for which there is much evidence, that poor nations in the early stages of development tend to have a very unequal distribution of income. As a result demand for industrial products in these societies tends to be concentrated on luxury products such as automobiles, since the poor have little money left over after purchasing food and housing. It is precisely luxury goods such as automobiles that are usually either imported from abroad or produced domestically by foreign firms. Local enterprises and investors lack the capital or know-how to produce such sophisticated products in the early stages of development. Foreign investors have an interest in keeping the distribution of income unequal because that is what keeps up demand for products only they can produce. The local ruling class has the same interest because they are the beneficiaries of this unequal distribution. Growth is slow because foreign investors only invest the minimum necessary to maintain control of the local market.

A key link in this argument is the connection between income inequality and the demand for luxury products. It is a link that can be tested empirically by observing what happens to demand in a given country when income is redistributed in a way to achieve greater equality. Although the tests are not conclusive because of the limitations of the data used, the results so far indicate that a major redistribution of income does not lead to large shifts in the structure of demand. The demand for a luxury good such as automobiles

6. Celso Furtado, "The Brazilian 'Model' of Development," in *The Political Economy of Development and Underdevelopment,* Charles K. Wilber, ed. (New York: Random House, 1979), pp. 324–33.

might fall, but there is little change in the demand for steel, cement, and machine tools, to mention only a few important items.

The common theme of these theories of imperialism, therefore, is that local elites combine with foreign capitalist powers to keep a government in power that pursues policies that put obstacles in the way of economic development. The differences among the theories are mainly over the reason why this collusion of antigrowth forces exists, not whether it exists.

There is also variation in emphasis about which policies, when forced on the poor of the developing world, most prohibit their prospects for a rise from poverty. Some continue to stress how in the developing world, the imposition of free-trade policies leads to an overemphasis on investment in natural resources and an underinvestment in industry. Others argue that foreign investment in developing nations, far from enriching those nations, is later returned to the industrialized world through repatriated profits, artificially low prices for developing country exports, and high interest payments on developing country debt. More will be said about these specific policies in later chapters.

While there are variations on how the imperialism of the industrialized world and the dependency of the developing world stifle growth and promote inequality, scholars who make these arguments tend to share a common view that progress for a developing nation is possible only if its ties to the international capitalist system are severed. It is this claim for universality, however, that is the weakest point in these analyses of the relationship between rich and poor nations. It is simply too easy to demonstrate that some countries with close ties to the capitalist world-economic system have achieved rapid economic growth and, in a few cases, even a reduction in inequality. Taiwan is the clearest case in point where both rapid growth and falling inequality have been achieved by increasing the island's integration into the international economic system, not by decreasing that involvement. A much longer list of nations has achieved rapid growth by exporting more to the capitalist world, growth in which most have shared in the benefits but not on an equal basis.

If the claim to universality is dropped and the argument is simply that some nations are hurt by becoming entangled in the capitalist economic system, few would object. The issue then becomes one of how, and under what circumstances, to become involved in world trade and capital movements, not whether to become involved at all. Few economists today, for example, would argue with the proposition that Mexico and Brazil would be better off if they had avoided becoming so dependent on loans from Western banks in the 1970s.

In a similar vein, Ethiopia under the rule of Emperor Haile Selassie was afraid of many key development-oriented reforms precisely because they would undermine the government's domestic sources of support. Certainly the Selassie government's ability to stay in power was also reinforced by continuing support from such countries as the United States. Similar situations involving external political support from France, Britain, and others can be found elsewhere. On the other hand, when Ethiopia overthrew Haile Selassie and switched its main international ties from the United States to the Soviet

Union and Cuba, the nation's economy continued to stagnate and suffer from famine. Even in the case of Ethiopia, poverty was only in part the result of the nation's ties to the capitalist economic and political system.

Clearly international influences operating through politics as well as economics can have a profound impact on the course of a nation's development. Warfare is an extreme form of the negative influences that are possible, but there are many subtler effects on both the positive and negative side of the ledger. Which effects are likely to predominate in any given country depends on the particular historical circumstances in which that country finds itself.

The one clear conclusion is that there is no single cause for why some nations took longer to initiate growth than others or for why some have yet to enter into sustained modern economic growth even today. Nor is there any single set of explanations that applies to all countries. Instead there are a wide variety of reasons for the continued poverty of nations, some of which apply in certain cases but not in others. The list of elements, both internal and external, that may have some negative influence on the prospects for development is almost infinite. And yet a large number of countries have managed to enter into sustained periods of economic development, and the number of such nations is growing. The political and social barriers to development are being overcome among an ever-widening proportion of the world's people.

3

Growth and Structural Change

There is a popularly held view that the main problem of economic development is to initiate the process. Once started, the rise to becoming a modern industrial state proceeds more or less automatically. The analogy is to an airplane that requires great energy and a skilled pilot to get off the ground, but once it has taken off soars easily through the air to its destination.

The concept of a **takeoff** is seen frequently in the development literature and is at the center of economic historian Walt Rostow's analysis of the stages of economic growth.[1] When the term means simply that a country has entered into a period of modern economic growth, it causes few problems. Frequently, however, the term has been used in ways that imply much more. Specifically, there has often been the implication that development once started proceeds automatically along well-traveled routes until the country becomes a modern industrialized nation.

The first problem with the concept is that, once started, economic development does not necessarily proceed without interruption. Economic development itself, particularly in its early stages, can create enormous social and political tensions that can undermine the stability so necessary for growth. The classic example from the early part of the twentieth century is in the case of Argentina. To many observers in the 1910s and 1920s, Argentina seemed well on its way to becoming a modern industrial state. At the time it was considered more advanced than Canada. But as urbanization and industrialization progressed, the expanding Argentinian working class became increas-

---

1. Walt W. Rostow, *Stages of Economic Growth* 2d ed. (New York: Cambridge University Press, 1960; 2d ed. 1971).

ingly alienated from the nation's leadership. Juan Peron was able to use this alienation to build a political organization that brought him to power in 1946. To keep his support, however, Peron carried out measures that were popular with his constituents, such as price control of food grains and enlarged military expenditures, but that stifled growth and divided society into sharply contending classes. More importantly, long after Peron left office, the forces he unleashed prevented the nation from establishing a consensus behind any government that would maintain stability and promote growth.

More recent examples of similar connections between the early stages of economic development and political instability can be found in Pakistan and Iran. In the 1960s Pakistan experienced a decade of fairly rapid industrialization, but most of this industrialization was concentrated in the western half of the country. East Pakistan made few gains and the people there felt that the west was developing at their expense. It matters little now whether West Pakistan exploited East Pakistan: the people in the east perceived that they were the losers. The result was a civil war, the splitting of an already geographically divided country into two nations with the formation of Bangladesh, and subsequent instability and economic stagnation in Bangladesh.

Iran presents a variation on the same theme. Oil revenues in the 1950s and 1960s fueled rapid industrial development, which accelerated even more dramatically after the quadrupling of the price of oil in 1973. Oil revenues, however, were also used extravagantly in the purchase of weapons, in large capital-intensive projects such as the Teheran subway, and in fueling corruption among Iran's elite. Iran's new wealth, far from buying stability, increased the alienation of the great majority of the people who felt that the nation's wealth was being monopolized by a corrupt few. When combined with other deeply felt grievances, such as those of the religious fundamentalists led by Ayatollah Khomeini, the result was a year of rioting and demonstrations culminating in the fall of the Shah and his army.

Once started, therefore, economic development can come to an abrupt halt. Even when a nation's development continues, it does not necessarily proceed along a predetermined path. Alternate paths to growth exist. While a nation's choice among those paths is limited, a nation can shift paths at least to some extent.

There are, however, some features of the development process that are common to all nations. The next sections of this chapter introduce a framework of analyzing why some growth rates are higher than others and for explaining what we know about the patterns of development that have occurred in the past and are likely to occur in the future. Attempts to determine the basic sources and patterns of growth have followed two very different approaches—one empirical and the other theoretical. One group of economists, best represented by Simon Kuznets of Harvard and the World Bank's Hollis Chenery, has attempted to discern patterns of development through an analysis of data on the gross national product and the structure of that product for dozens of nations around the world and through time. The search has been for patterns that are common to all nations, or more realistically, to a large subgroup of nations.

The second approach has been to construct theories of how the structure
of a nation's economy could be expected to change given various assumptions about the conditions facing that nation. This theoretical approach has a long tradition stretching back to Adam Smith and David Ricardo of the eighteenth and nineteen centuries, and in more recent decades includes the growth models of Roy Harrod, Evsey Domar, Robert Solow, W. Arthur Lewis, John Fei, Gustav Ranis, and many others.

In economics the ultimate objective is to develop theories whose validity can then be tested with the data available. Therefore, the empirical or data-based approach and the theoretical approach are not two different ways of looking at a given problem, but are two parts of what is really a single approach. In the field of economic development, however, the process being studied is so complex and theorizing is at such an early stage in its own evolution that one can still speak of two quite different approaches to an analysis of the patterns of development.

ESTIMATING GROSS NATIONAL PRODUCT

Before we can talk about the empirical approach to an analysis of the sources of growth and of the patterns of development, however, it is important to understand both the strengths and particularly the weaknesses of the data used to measure those patterns. In essence the analysis of patterns of development involves relating trends in gross national product per capita to trends in the various components of gross national product. **Gross national product** (GNP) is the sum of the value of finished goods and services produced by a society during a given year and excludes **intermediate goods** (goods used up in the production of other goods, such as the steel used in an automobile or the chips that go into a computer). **Gross domestic product** (GDP) is similar to GNP except that it excludes income earned by citizens of a country who are resident abroad but includes all production within the country including that that involves payments of income to people outside the country.

The share of a sector or component of GNP such as manufacturing or agriculture is measured by the **value-added** contributed by that sector. Value-added refers to the addition to the value of the product at a particular stage of production. Thus the value-added of the cotton textile industry is the value of the textiles when they leave the factory minus the value of raw cotton used in their manufacture. This, in turn, is equal to the payments to the factors of production: wages paid to labor plus profits, interest, depreciation of capital, and rents for buildings and land.

The great advantage of the GNP concept is that it encompasses all of a nation's economic activity in a few summary statistics that are mutually consistent. The alternative of describing growth in terms of tons of steel and kilowatt-hours of electricity either leaves out much economic activity or, in an effort to be inclusive, involves the hopelessly complex discussion of thousands of individual products. The analysis of individual products in physical terms can be misleading, particularly in the measurement of broad economic change over time. Cotton textile output, for example, may fall over time but textiles made from artificial fibers may be increasing by more than enough to offset that fall. Gross national product provides a consistent technique for adding these two different trends together.

If the concept of gross national product has certain advantages, it also has certain important limitations, particularly when comparing patterns of development in a wide variety of developing countries. One difficulty is that poor countries usually have poor statistical services; data from certain sectors of poor countries, such as agriculture and handicrafts, are the worst of all. Estimates of the gross national product of many developing nations are based on fairly reliable statistics on modern industrial and mining enterprises combined with estimates of rural-sector performance based on small samples or outright guesses.

In addition to data limitations, there are basic methodological issues that get in the way of reliable estimates.

What Is Included in GNP?

To begin with, there is a problem with the definition of gross national product. The proper way to calculate GNP is to add up all the goods and services produced by a country and which are then sold on the market. In adding up steel and mangos, one can use either the prices at which steel and mangos were sold on the market **(market prices),** or one can use the cost of all factor inputs (labor, capital, land) used to produce a ton of steel or a bushel of mangos. The latter method is referred to as pricing at **factor cost.** Many valuable contributions to society are therefore excluded from gross national product. When housework and child care are performed by paid servants or day-care employees, for example, they are included in GNP, but when they are performed by unpaid members of the household they do not enter GNP. In developing countries a very large number of activities do not enter the market. Much of what is produced by the agricultural sector, to take the most important example, is consumed by the farm household and never reaches the market. Strictly speaking one cannot meaningfully discuss the changing share of agriculture in GNP but only the changing share of the marketed agricultural product in GNP. Because this strict definition of GNP would severely limit the usefulness of comparing structural change among nations where agriculture is the dominant sector, the usual practice is to include farm output consumed by the producer, valuing that produce at the prices of marketed farm produce. While making GNP a more meaningful indicator of the productive capacity of a developing economy, this procedure turns GNP into a somewhat arbitrary concept. If nonmarketed agricultural produce is included, for example, why not include household-provided child-care services?

Exchange-Rate Conversion Problems

A second methodological problem arises when attempting to convert the GNP of several different countries into a single currency. To compare the changing economic structure of several countries as per-capita income rises, one must measure the per-capita income figures in a common currency. The shortcut to accomplishing this goal is to use the official exchange rate between dollars and each national currency. For example, to convert Bangladesh GNP from taka into dollars, the official exchange rate between taka and dollars (nearly 28 taka per dollar in 1986) is used. One problem with this procedure is that exchange rates, particularly those of developing countries, are frequently highly distorted. Trade restrictions make it possible for an official exchange rate to be substantially different from a rate determined by free trade.

But even an accurate estimate of the exchange rate that would prevail under a free-trade regime would not eliminate the problem. A significant part of GNP is made up of what are called **non-traded goods** and **services,** that is, goods that do not and often cannot enter into international trade. Electric power, for example, can be imported only in rare cases from an immediate neighbor with a surplus to sell (the U.S. imports some electricity from Canada, for example). For the most part electric power must be generated within a country, and it makes little sense to talk about the international market or the international market price for electric power. By definition, internal transportation cannot be traded, although many transport inputs, such as trucks, can be imported. Wholesale and retail trade or elementary school teachers are nontraded services. The wages of workers in these nontraded services are less influenced by any international market.

Gross national product converted to dollars by exchange rates that are determined by the flow of traded goods will give misleading comparisons if the ratio of prices of nontraded goods to prices of traded goods is different in the countries being compared. The way around this problem is to pick a set of prices prevailing in one of the countries and use that set of prices to value the goods of all countries being compared. The essence of the procedure can be illustrated with the simple numerical exercise presented in Table 3–1. The two economies in the table are called the United States and India, and each economy produces one traded commodity (steel) and one nontraded service (measured by the number of retail sales people). The price of steel is given in dollars in the United States and rupees in India, and the exchange rate is based on the ratio of the prices of the traded good (in this case, steel). The value of the services of retail sales personnel is estimated in the most commonly used way, which is to assume the value of the service is equal to the wages of the service personnel. The two methods of converting Indian GNP into U.S. dollars are presented in the table. Clearly, one gets very different results depending on which method is used.

The example in Table 3–1 exaggerates the differences in results obtained from the two methods mainly because the nontraded-services sector is larger relative to total GNP than would normally be the case. Systematic estimates using the two different methods on a select group of countries are presented in Table 3–2. While the differences in results between the two methods are not as great as in our numerical illustration, they are still substantial. Furthermore there is a reasonably systematic relation between the degree to which the exchange-rate conversion method understates GNP and the level of development of the country. For Germany and the United States, whose per-capita GNPs were not far apart in 1970, the exchange-rate con-

TABLE 3-1   Exchange Rate versus Individual Price Methods of Converting GNP into a Single Currency

	United States			India		
	quantity	price (in U.S. dollars)	Value of output (in billion U.S. dollars)	quantity	price (rupees)	Value of output in billion rupees
steel (million tons)	100	200 per ton	20	8	1,600 per ton	13
retail sales personnel (millions)	2	5,000 per person per year	10	4	4,000 per person per year	16
Total GNP (in local currency)			30			29

Official exchange rate, based on steel prices, = 1,600/200 or Rs8 = U.S. $1.

1. Indian GNP in U.S. dollars calculated by using the official exchange rate:

$$\frac{29}{8} = \text{U.S. \$3.6 billion.}$$

2. Indian GNP in U.S. dollars calculated by using U.S. prices for each individual product or service and applying that price to Indian quantities:

steel 8 million $\times$ \$ 200 = \$ 1.6 billion
retail sales personnel 4 million $\times$ \$5,000 = $\underline{\$20 \quad \text{billion}}$
GNP = \$21.6 billion.

3. Ratio of B to A:

$$\frac{21.6}{3.6} = 6.0.$$

TABLE 3-2   Gross Domestic Product[a] Per Capita in 1975 in U.S. Dollars

	Using official exchange rate conversion (1)	Using dollar prices for each individual product (2)	Ratio (2) ÷ (1) (3)
United States	7,176	7,176	1.00
Germany (West)	6,797	5,953	0.88
France	6,428	5,977	0.93
Japan	4,474	4,907	1.10
United Kingdom	4,134	4,588	1.11
Italy	3,440	3,861	1.12
Hungary	2,125	3,559	1.68
Colombia	568	1,609	2.83
Korea	583	1,484	2.54
Kenya	241	470	1.95
India	146	470	3.22

Source: World Bank, *World Tables,* Vol. 1, 3d ed., Economic Data, (Johns Hopkins University Press, 1983) p. 568.
[a] Gross domestic product (GDP) is similar to gross national product (GNP). GDP can be derived from GNP by subtracting payments to a country's own factors (labor and capital) from abroad and adding payments to foreign factors remitted abroad. In brief GDP includes everything produced within a country whoever receives the income, but excludes income received by residents of the country from abroad.

version is a reasonable approximation of what is obtained when converting German GNP into dollars using the better method. For India, however, the ratio between the two results is 3.23 to 1. With differences of that magnitude, exchange-rate conversions are misleading.

Other Index-Number Problems

The issue being discussed here is part of a larger group of issues generally referred to as **index-number problems.** Index-number problems arise not only in the comparison of two countries using two different currencies, but also in the study of the growth of a single country over a long period of time. As growth occurs it usually happens that relative prices change—that is, the prices of some commodities fall while the prices of others rise. If the country is experiencing **inflation,** which is a sustained increase in the general price level, all prices are rising, but some rise faster than others so that relative prices still change. To eliminate the impact of inflation on the statistics, economists measure *real* increases (actual growth) rather than *nominal* increases (where the prices also grow) in GNP. The proper procedure is to recalculate GNP in each year using the prices of only one year. But which year does one pick? Estimates of the growth rate will differ as one uses the prices of different years, just as the ratio of Indian to United States GNP will vary if one uses Indian prices to value both countries' GNP in one case and United States prices in another.

A hypothetical illustration of the impact of base year versus current year prices is presented in Table 3–3. In this example a higher growth rate is achieved using base-year rather than current-year prices. This happens because the relative price of the industrial product (television sets) is higher in the base year than in the current year, and thus the faster growing industrial product accounts for a larger share of total product when base-year prices are used. In most countries the industrial sector is growing faster than the agricultural sector, and hence a set of prices that gives the industrial sector a larger weight in national product will result in a higher GNP growth rate.

TABLE 3–3 Base-Year versus Current-Year Price Calculations of GNP

Product per year	Base Year (1960)		Current Year (1982)	
	quantity	price (in U.S. dollars)	quantity	price (in U.S. dollars)
television sets (millions)	1	300	50	100
wheat (million tons)	100	200	200	300

1. GNP index using *base-year* prices:

$$100 \times \frac{(50 \times 300) + (200 \times 200)}{(1 \times 300) + (100 \times 200)} = 271.$$

2. GNP index using *current-year* prices:

$$100 \times \frac{(50 \times 100) + (300 \times 200)}{(1 \times 100) + (300 \times 100)} = 216.$$

Data problems, therefore, are pervasive whenever one studies the aggregate performance of an economy as it evolves over time or compares the aggregate performance of two different economies. When comparing the steel ingot output of two nations it is possible to say precisely how many more tons of steel one of the nations produces when compared to the other. There is no comparable precision when one compares large aggregates such as GNP. A certain ambiguity is always present when these figures are used to measure the sources of growth or to search for similarities in the development patterns across countries or over time.

ONE-SECTOR GROWTH MODELS

In Chapters 7 through 14 we shall analyze how the quality and quantity of labor and of savings and investment are mobilized and used to promote economic development. The theory explaining the relationship between these inputs and the growth in national product is based on the **production function.** At the individual firm or microeconomic level, the production function tells how much the output of a firm or factory, such as a textile mill, will increase if the number of workers or the number of spindles and looms rises by a given amount. These are mathematical expressions, often derived from engineering specifications, that relate given amounts of physical inputs to the amount of physical output that can be produced with those inputs. Often, for convenience, microeconomic production functions are expressed in money values rather than in physical quantities.

At the national or economy-wide level, production functions describe the relationship of the size of a nation's labor force and its stock of capital with the level of that nation's gross national product. These economy-wide relationships are called **aggregate production functions.** They measure increases in the value of output or national product, given the value of increases in such inputs as the stock of capital and the labor force. Because both inputs and outputs are measured in aggregate terms (national capital stock, GNP), index-number and other measurement problems of the kind just described do introduce some ambiguity into the interpretation of economy-wide production functions. Still, it is the one tool we have for relating inputs and output at the national level within a consistent framework. For that reason, it is useful to see what this aggregate production function can tell us about how inputs contribute to growth before turning in later chapters to how those inputs can be mobilized.

The Harrod-Domar Model

The simplest and best known production function used in the analysis of economic development was developed independently during the 1940s by economists Roy Harrod of England and Evsey Domar of MIT, primarily to explain the relationship between growth and unemployment in advanced capitalist societies.[2] But the Harrod-Domar model has been used extensively

2. Roy F. Harrod, "An Essay in Dynamic Theory," *Economic Journal* (1939): 14–33; and Evsey Domar, "Capital Expansion, Rate of Growth, and Employment," *Econometrica* (1946): 137–47 and "Expansion and Employment," *American Economic Review* 37 (1947): 34–55.

in developing countries as a simple way of looking at the relationship between growth and capital requirements.

The underlying assumption of the model is that the output of any economic unit, whether a firm, an industry, or the whole economy, depends upon the amount of capital invested in that unit. Thus if we call output Y and the stock of capital K, then output can be related to capital stock by

$$Y = K/k, \qquad\qquad [3\text{--}1]$$

where k is a constant, called the capital-output ratio. To convert this into a statement about the growth of output, we use the notation Δ to represent increases in output and capital, and write

$$\Delta Y = \Delta K/k. \qquad\qquad [3\text{--}2]$$

The growth rate of output, g, is simply the increment in output divided by the total amount of output, $\Delta Y/Y$. If we divide both sides of Equation 3–2 by Y, then

$$g = \Delta Y/Y = \Delta K/Y \cdot 1/k. \qquad\qquad [3\text{--}3]$$

For the whole economy, ΔK is the same as investment, I, which must equal savings, S. Hence, $\Delta K/Y$ becomes I/Y, and this is equal to S/Y, which can be designated by the savings rate, s, a percentage of national product. Equation 3–3 can then be converted to

$$g = s/k, \qquad\qquad [3\text{--}4]$$

which is the basic Harrod-Domar relationship for an economy.

Underlying this equation is the view that capital created by investment in plant and equipment is the main determinant of growth and that it is savings by people and corporations that make the investment possible. The **capital-output ratio** is simply a measure of the productivity of capital or investment. If an investment of $3,000 in a new plant and new equipment makes it possible for an enterprise to raise its output by $1,000 a year for many years into the future, then the capital-output ratio for that particular investment is 3:1. Economists often use the term **incremental capital-output ratio,** abbreviated ICOR, because in studying growth one is mainly interested in the impact on output of additional or incremental capital. The incremental capital-output ratio measures the productivity of additional capital while the (average) capital-output ratio refers to the relationship between a nation's total stock of capital and its total national product.

For economic planners, given this simple equation, the task is straightforward. (A more detailed description of the role of economic planning is given in Chapter 6.) The first step is to try to come up with an estimate of the incremental capital-output ratio (k in Equation 3–3) for the nation whose plan is being drawn up. There are two alternatives for the next step. Either planners can decide on the rate of economic growth (g) they wish to achieve, in which case the equation will tell them the level of savings and investment necessary to achieve that growth. Or planners can decide on the rate of savings and investment that is feasible or desirable, in which case the equation will tell planners the rate of growth in national product that can be achieved.

This procedure can be applied to the economy as a whole, or it can be applied to each sector or each industry. Incremental capital-output ratios, for example, can be calculated separately for agriculture and industry. Once planners decide how much investment will be allocated to each sector, the Harrod-Domar equations determine the growth rates to be expected in each of the two sectors.

Production Functions

At the heart of this kind of analysis is the explicit or implicit assumption that the incremental capital-output ratio is a single fixed number. This assumption is consistent with a production function that employs fixed proportions of capital and labor and constant returns to scale, like that depicted in Figure 3–1. Output in this figure is represented by **isoquants,** which are combinations of inputs (labor and capital in this case), that produce equal amounts of output. Only two isoquants are shown in this diagram. The L-shape of the isoquants indicates production processes that use fixed proportions of capital and labor. For example, it takes capital (plant and equipment) of $10 million and 100 workers to produce 100,000 tons of cement. If more workers are added without investing in more capital, output will not rise above 10,000 tons per year. Because the diagram is also drawn with **constant returns to scale,** if capital in the cement industry is doubled to $20 million and labor is doubled to 200 workers, output also doubles to 200,000 tons per year.

Most economists, however, believe that the production function for many industries, and for the economy as a whole, looks more like that depicted in Figure 3–2. In this figure, if one starts with output of 100,000 tons at point *a,*

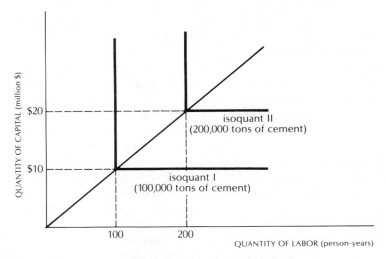

FIGURE 3–1   Production Function with Fixed Coefficients. With constant returns to scale, the isoquants will be L-shaped and the production function will be the straight line through their minimum-combination points.

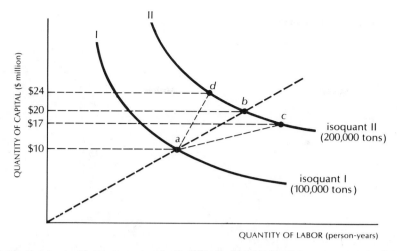

FIGURE 3–2 Neoclassical (Variable Proportions) Production Function. Instead of requiring fixed factor proportions, as in Figure 3–1, output can be achieved with varying combinations of labor and capital. This is called a **neoclassical** production function. The isoquants are curved, rather than L-shaped.

using $10 million of capital and 100 workers (not shown in the figure), the industry could be expanded in any of three ways. If industry planners decide to expand at constant factor proportions and move to point *b* on isoquant II, the situation would be identical to the fixed proportions case of Figure 3–1. But production of 200,000 tons could be achieved by using more labor and less capital, a more *labor intensive* method, at a point like *c* on isoquant II. In that case the incremental capital-output ratio falls to 1.4:1, if the price of cement is $50 a ton. Or if a more *capital-intensive* method is desired, such as the production technique given by *d* on isoquant II, the ICOR would rise to 2.8:1.

If the production function facing a nation is neoclassical, then the capital-output ratio becomes a variable that is to some extent under the control of policymakers in the government. Considering production functions like those in Figure 3–2 from the industry level, policymakers in developing countries in which capital is scarce can try to induce manufacturers and farmers to employ more labor-intensive technologies. Then, for a given amount of savings and investment, both growth and employment can be higher. At the level of the whole economy, policy will encourage labor-intensive technologies as well as encourage investment in the more labor-intensive industries, reducing the demand for investment and saving on both counts. The kinds of tools that policymakers may use to accomplish this reduction in the capital-output ratio are discussed in depth in several chapters of this text, especially Chapters 8, 13, and 17.

The appropriate incremental capital-output ratio will vary among countries and, for a single country, over time. Poor countries, with low savings rates and surplus (unemployed and underemployed) labor, can achieve higher growth rates by economizing on capital and utilizing as much labor as possible. As economies grow and per-capita income rises, savings rates tend to increase and the labor surplus diminishes. Thus the ICOR shifts upwards.

TABLE 3–4   Selected Incremental Capital-Output Ratios

Country	Incremental capital-output ratio (1970–1981)[a]
United States	6.6
Norway	6.7
Japan	7.4
South Korea	3.3
Indonesia	2.6
India	6.0
Argentina	13.3
Brazil	2.8
Venezuela	6.8
Ivory Coast	4.2
Kenya	4.0
Tanzania	5.2

Source: World Bank, *World Tables, Vol. 1, 3d ed., Economic Data* (Baltimore: Johns Hopkins University Press, 1983) pp. 9, 23, 39, 85, 87, 95, 101,103, 123, 175, 239, 247, and 257.
[a]These ratios were derived by dividing the average share of gross domestic investment in gross domestic product by the rate of growth in gross domestic product, both figures being for the years 1970–1981.

In the more advanced countries it can be higher than in the developing countries without sacrificing growth. And resource-rich developing countries, such as those exporting petroleum, can afford more capital-intensive development than other LDCs. These shifts in the ICORs can come about through market mechanisms as prices of labor and capital change in response to changes in supplies. As growth takes place, savings become relatively more abundant and hence the price of capital falls while employment and wages rise. Thus all producers increasingly economize on labor and use more capital. Alternatively, in Soviet-type and other planned economies, the planners can allocate investment in ways that move the economy towards an appropriate ICOR. Finally, technological change and "learning by doing" can play important roles. Both can contribute to increased productivity of all factors of production, which reduces the ICOR. In Figures 3–1 and 3–2, increased factor productivity can be represented by a shifting inward of each isoquant toward the origin.

Data on incremental capital-output ratios for a few selected countries are presented in Table 3–4. These ratios vary from under 3:1 to 7:1 and even higher. Some of these differences can be explained by the point made earlier that richer nations such as the United States, Norway, and Japan tend to have higher ratios because capital is less expensive relative to labor than in poorer countries in the early stages of development. Other differences, however, such as those between Korea and India, have little to do with differences in the relative scarcity of capital. These differences are more likely to be the result of the differences between nations in the efficiency with which capital and other inputs are managed.

Sources of Growth

The simple Harrod-Domar production function, therefore, obscures some of the basic differences in growth performance between nations. One wants to know much more about why the capital-output ratio varies so much. To that end, economists such as Robert Solow and Edward Denison have

attempted to explain the sources of growth with a different form of the production function, one that allows the analyst to separate out the various causes of growth rather than subsume all of these other causes in the capital-output ratio.

The production function used in this analysis is neoclassical like that depicted in Figure 3–2. However, more factors of production are included. The function relates increases in output to increases in inputs of capital, skilled and unskilled labor, and other variables. This method also attempts to separate out the contribution made by rises in the efficiency with which inputs are used. The production function takes the following form:

$$Y = f(K, L, T, A), \tag{3–5}$$

where

$Y =$ output or national product
$K =$ the stock of capital
$L =$ the size of the labor force
$T =$ the stock of arable land and natural resources
and $\quad A =$ increases in the productivity or efficiency with which inputs are used.

The next step is to convert this production function into a form that makes measuring the contribution of each input possible. The deriviation of this new form of the equation involves calculus and so is presented in the appendix to this chapter. The resulting equation is

$$g_N = a + W_K \cdot g_K + W_L \cdot g_L + W_T \cdot g_T, \tag{3–6}$$

where

$g =$ the growth rate of any variable
$W =$ the share in income of any input, (e.g., the share of wages)
$N =$ national product
$K =$ the capital stock
$L =$ labor
$T =$ arable land and natural resources
and $\quad a =$ the variable measuring the shift in the production function resulting from greater efficiency in the use of inputs.

Data for each of these variables can be found in the statistical handbooks of many nations and the contribution of each of these variables to growth can thus be measured and identified.

A simple numerical example illustrates the way in which this equation is used. Assume the following values for the variables in the equation:

$g_N = .06$ (a GNP growth rate of 6 percent a year)
$g_K = .07$ (capital stock rises at 7 percent a year)
$g_L = .02$ (the labor force increases at 2 percent a year)
$g_T = .01$ (arable land is rising by one percent a year).

The share of labor in national income is 60 percent ($W_L = 0.6$), the share of capital is 30 percent ($W_K = 0.3$), and the share of land is ten percent

($W_T = 0.1$). By substituting these figures into Equation 3–6 we get:

$$0.06 = a + 0.3 \cdot 0.07 + 0.6 \cdot 0.02 + 0.1 \cdot 0.01$$

Solving for a, we get $a = 0.026$.

What these figures tell us is that productivity growth is 2.6 percent a year and thus accounts for just under half of the total growth of GNP of 6 percent a year.

Growth accounting or **sources of growth analysis,** as this method has been called, has been carried out for many nations. Because of variations in the way different economists carry out growth accounting, it is not possible to summarize the results of these calculations in a simple table. Two conclusions that have arisen from this empirical work, however, provide an important basis for much of the analysis in subsequent chapters.

First, most efforts to measure the sources of growth have indicated that increases in productivity or efficiency (a in Equation 3–6) account for a much higher proportion of growth than was believed to be the case before these calculations were made. Increases in the capital stock frequently account for much less than half of the increase in output, particularly in rapidly growing countries. Second, while capital does not contribute as much to growth as assumed in early growth models, capital does tend to play a larger role in growth in today's developing countries than it did in those nations that had already achieved high levels of per-capita national product by the 1980s. Furthermore, some of the increases in efficiency or productivity involve advances in technology that are embodied in capital equipment. Thus mobilization of capital remains a major concern of policymakers in developing countries and is the subject of four chapters in this text (Chapters 11–14), but mobilization of labor and improvements in the quality of that labor are also important (Chapters 9–10). And of equal or even greater importance is the productivity of these inputs or the efficiency with which they are used. The sources of differences in productivity and efficiency are not the subject of a single chapter but are a recurring theme throughout this book.

THE CHANGING STRUCTURE OF OUTPUT

Structural change in the course of economic development thus involves rises in productivity while it also involves increases in the capital stock relative to other inputs such as labor. In the numerical example above, the incremental capital-labor ratio was 3.5:1 ($.07 \div .02$). Structural change also involves major shifts between the sectors that make up the output side of the production function equation. These shifts in the structure of output or national product are the subject of the remainder of this chapter. In this chapter we are mainly concerned with the relationship between these sectors as growth takes place. In later chapters (notably Chapters 18–20) we shall look at development within each of these sectors individually.

One clear pattern of changing economic structure in the course of economic development is that, as per-capita income rises, the share of industry in gross national product rises also. While it is possible to conceive of a situation in which a nation moves from a condition of poverty to one of wealth while concentrating on agriculture, this kind of growth has yet to occur. Every country that has achieved a high per-capita income has also experienced a population shift—where the majority moves from rural areas and farming to cities and industrial jobs. All have also experienced an increase in industrial value-added in gross national product.

There are two principal reasons for this. The first is **Engel's law.** In the nineteenth century Ernst Engel discovered that as incomes of families rose, the proportion of their budget spent on food declined. Since the main function of the agricultural sector is to produce food, it follows that demand for agricultural output would not grow as rapidly as demand for industrial products and services, and hence the share of agriculture in national product would decline. This relationship holds for all countries that have experienced sustained development.

A second reason has reinforced the impact of the first: productivity in the agricultural sector has risen as growth has progressed. People require food to survive, and if a household had to devote all of its energies to producing enough of its own food, it would have no surplus time to make industrial products or to grow surplus food that could be traded for industrial products. In the course of development, however, increased use of machinery and other new methods of raising crops have made it possible for an individual farmer in the United States, for example, to produce enough food to feed, and feed very well, another seventy to eighty people. As a result only 3 percent of the work force of the United States is in farming, while the others have been freed to produce elsewhere.

The rising share of industry also helps to explain why, as incomes rise, an increasing percentage of every country's population lives in cities rather than in the countryside. There are **economies of scale** in the manufacture of many industrial products. The existence of economies of scale implies that output per unit of input rises as the firm size increases; that is, a large industrial enterprise in an industry such as steel will produce more steel per dollar cost (made up from the cost of coal, iron ore, limestone, labor, plant machinery and electricity) than will a smaller enterprise. Furthermore it makes sense for many different kinds of industrial enterprises to locate in the same place so that common support facilities, such as electric power stations, transport, and wholesalers, can also operate at an efficient level. The result is that industry leads to the growth of cities, and the growth of cities itself tends to increase the share of manufacturing and some services in gross national product. In the rural economies of most poor countries, for example, food processing is done in the home and is not usually included in gross national product calculations at all. In urbanized nations, in contrast, food processing is often done in large factories, and the value-added produced by these factories is included in the share of the manufacturing sector.

Even though the rising share of manufacturing in gross national product and the declining share of agriculture is a pattern common to all nations, it does not follow that the rates of change are the same in each country. In fact planners around the world have been plagued by the question of how much to emphasize agriculture versus industry during the course of development. The Chinese in the 1950s, for instance, tried to follow the Soviet example of putting most of their investment into industry, hoping that agriculture would somehow take care of itself. Disastrous harvests in 1959 through 1961 forced the government to put more resources, notably chemical fertilizer, into agriculture, but machinery, steel, and related industries continued to receive the lion's share of investment. Food production grew, but only just fast enough to hold per-capita consumption constant since population grew at 2 percent a year. When wages and farm incomes began to rise in the late 1970s, however, constant per-capita output was perceived as being insufficient, and the government once again greatly increased the share of investment going to agriculture. In the 1980s they took the even more radical step of abandoning collectivized agriculture in what proved to be a successful move to raise agricultural production at an accelerated rate.

For a decade and more after independence some African nations also felt that agriculture required little help. Increased food requirements could be met by the simple expedient of expanding the amount of land under cultivation. But population continued to grow, at rates over 3 percent a year in many countries, and the supply of readily available arable land became exhausted. On the edge of the Sahel desert the overuse of fragile land has contributed to severe ecological damage that, together with a change in weather patterns, has brought about widespread famine in the region.

In fact, virtually every government in the developing world has struggled with the question of the proper relationship between agricultural and industrial development. Would a greater awareness of the historical relationship between agriculture and industry in countries undergoing development improve performance in these countries? If planners knew that the share of agriculture in national product always remained above 40 percent until per-capita income rose above $500, those planners would have a target to aim at. Investment in agriculture could be kept at a level to ensure that the share did not fall below 40 percent. But what if there were no consistent patterns among countries at comparable levels of development?

Hollis Chenery and his coauthors, for example, found that there was no single pattern for the changes in shares and that to talk meaningfully about consistent patterns at all, the nations of the world had to be divided into three subgroups: large countries, meaning countries with a population over 15 million in 1960; small countries that emphasize primary (agriculture plus mining) exports; and small countries that emphasize industrial exports.[3] Even within these subgroups there was enormous variation. Figure 3–3, for example, compares Chenery's large-country pattern, estimated in this case from a sample of nineteen countries, with the actual historical performance of several European countries plus Japan. As is apparent from this figure, the average performance of these nine industrialized nations is similar to the trend estimated by Chenery and Taylor, but no single country was on the trend line.

3. H. B. Chenery and M. Syrquin, *Patterns of Development, 1950–1970* (London: Oxford University Press, 1975); and H. B. Chenery and L. J. Taylor, "Development Patterns: Among Countries and over Time," *Review of Economics and Statistics* (November 1968): 391–416.

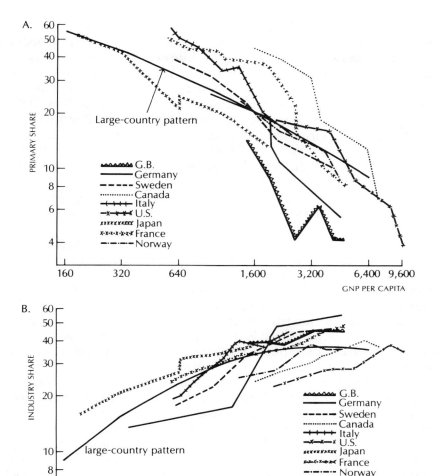

FIGURE 3–3 Development Patterns. Chenery's large-country patterns are compared here to the actual, historical performance of nine countries. Panel A depicts the primary share, and Panel B the industry share. *Source:* H. Chenery and L. J. Taylor, "Development Patterns" *Review of Economics and Statistics* (November 1968), p. 401. Per-capita GNP has been converted from 1964 to 1983 prices using a conversion ratio of 3.2:1.

Chenery and his coauthors often speak of the trends they have estimated as being the **normal pattern** of development for large (or small) countries. The term has contributed to a good deal of misunderstanding and misuse of the results. Planners have compared these estimated trends with the actual performance of their country, and if their own industrial share has grown more rapidly than the trend, they have congratulated themselves for a good performance. Or if the share has grown at a rate below the general trend line they have concluded that something had to be done to correct a poor performance. In either case a deviation from the trend was seen as a cause for concern. But these patterns are nothing more than the average results obtained from comparing many diverse patterns. They are not a guide to what a country ought to do. Perhaps someday we shall be in a position to say that one trend makes more efficient use of a nation's resources than another trend or leads to a faster overall growth rate. Today all we have are data and estimates that give us a general idea of the trends to expect as economic development occurs. Under the circumstances it is better to drop the term *normal pattern* from the vocabulary and speak of **average pattern.** On the average the primary share (agriculture plus mining) of GNP in large countries falls from 32 percent at $600 per capita (in 1983 prices) to 19 percent at $1,600 per capita, but the variation around that trend is so great that these patterns provide only the crudest of guides to planners.

Two-Sector Models

Long before the concept of GNP was invented or economists had many statistics of any kind to work with, they recognized the fundamental importance of the relationship between industry and agriculture. To better understand the nature of that relationship, they began to design simple models to explain the key connections between the two sectors. The best known of the earlier models appeared in David Ricardo's *The Principles of Political Economy and Taxation,* published in 1817. In his model Ricardo included two basic assumptions that have played an important role in two-sector models ever since. First, he assumed that the agricultural sector was subject to **diminishing returns:** given increases in inputs lead to continually smaller increases in output. The reason is that crops require land and land is limited. To increase production, Ricardo felt, farmers would have to move onto poorer and poorer land, thus making it more and more costly to produce a ton of grain. Second, Ricardo put forward the concept that today is called **labor surplus.** Britain in the early nineteenth century still had a large agricultural work force, and Ricardo felt that the industrial sector could draw away the surplus labor in the rural sector without causing a rise in wages in either the urban or rural areas.

The concept of labor surplus is closely related to concepts such as rural unemployment and underemployment or disguised unemployment. **Rural unemployment** is formally much the same as urban unemployment. When there are people who desire work, are actively looking for work, and cannot find work, they are said to be **unemployed.** Very few people in rural areas of developing countries are unemployed in this sense. While most rural people have jobs, those jobs are not very productive. In many cases there is not enough work to employ the entire rural work force full time. Instead members of farm families all work part time, sharing what work there is. Economists call this **underemployment** or **disguised unemployment,** because some members of the rural work force could be removed entirely without a fall in production. Some remaining workers would simply change from part-time to full-time effort.

Underemployment and other features of developing-country labor markets will be discussed at greater length in Chapter 8. Here we are mainly interested in how an agricultural sector with diminishing returns and surplus or underemployed labor affects the development of the industrial sector. Put differently, if the industrial sector grows at a certain rate, how fast must the agricultural sector grow in order to avoid a drag on industry and on overall economic development? And will accelerated population growth help or make matters worse? To answer these and related questions we shall develop a **simple two-sector model.**

The modern version of the two-sector labor-surplus model was first developed by W. Arthur Lewis.[4] Lewis, like Ricardo before him, pays particular attention to the implications of surplus labor for the distribution of income, and hence it is the Lewis version of that labor-surplus model that is most relevant to the discussion in Chapter 4. The concern in this chapter, however, is with the relationship between industry and agriculture, and that relationship is more completely worked out in a version of the labor-surplus model developed by John Fei and Gustav Ranis.[5] Therefore it is the Fei-Ranis version of the model that is used in the discussion in this chapter.

The Production Function

Our starting point is the agricultural sector and the **agricultural production function.** A production function, as indicated earlier, tells us how much output we can get for a given amount of input. In our simple agricultural production function we assume two inputs, labor and land, produce an output, such as grain. The production function of Figure 3–4 differs from that of Figure 3–2, because instead of showing two inputs, labor and capital, on the axes, it shows output and one input, labor. Because increases in labor must

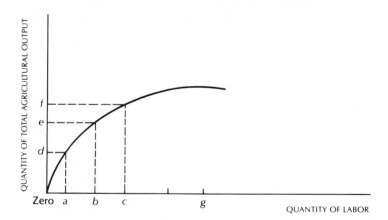

FIGURE 3–4 The Production Function. In this figure, a rise in the labor force from *a* to *b* leads to an increase in output of *de*, while an equal increase in labor from *b* to *c* leads to a smaller rise in output. At point *g* further increases in the amount of labor used do not lead to any rise in output at all. Beyond point *g* the marginal product of labor is zero or negative, so additional labor causes no increase or a reduction in output.

4. W. Arthur Lewis, *The Theory of Economic Growth* (Homewood, Ill.: Richard Irwin, 1955).

5. Gustav Ranis and John C. H. Fei, *Development of the Labor Surplus Economy* (Homewood, Ill.: Richard Irwin, 1964).

be combined with either a fixed amount of land or with land of decreasing quality, the production function indicates diminishing returns. Put differently, the **marginal product of labor** is falling, which means that each additional unit of labor produces less and less output.

The next step in constructing our model is to show how rural wages are determined. The standard assumption in all labor surplus models from Ricardo to the present time is that rural wages will not fall below a minimum level. Thus in its more general form the concept of labor surplus includes not only situations where the marginal product of labor is zero, but also situations where the marginal product of labor is above zero but less than the minimum below which rural wages will not fall. In the Fei-Ranis model and in other labor-surplus theories the usual assumption is that rural wages do not fall below the **average product** of farm labor in households with a labor surplus. The logic behind this view is that a laborer in a farm household will not look for work outside the household unless he or she can earn at least as much as he would receive by staying at home. These concepts in diagrammatic form are presented in Figure 3–5.

Figure 3–5 can be derived directly from Figure 3–4. The *total* product per unit of labor in Figure 3–4 is converted into the *marginal product* per unit of labor of Figure 3–5. The concept of a minimum wage (represented by the dotted line *hi*) was then added to the diagram. This minimum wage is also sometimes called an **institutionally fixed wage** to contrast it with wages determined by market forces. In a perfectly competitive market, wages will equal the marginal product of labor for reasons that will be discussed at greater length in Chapter 8. Thus once labor is withdrawn from agriculture to a point where the marginal product rises above the minimum wage (point *h* in Figure 3–5), wages in agriculture will follow the marginal product curve.

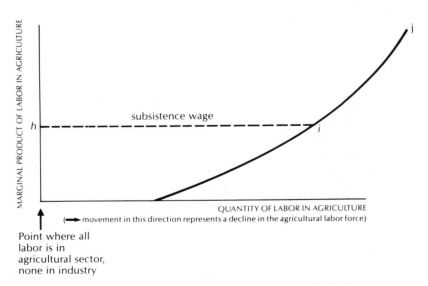

FIGURE 3–5 Marginal Product of Labor in Agriculture. As the quantity of agricultural labor decreases, the marginal product increases.

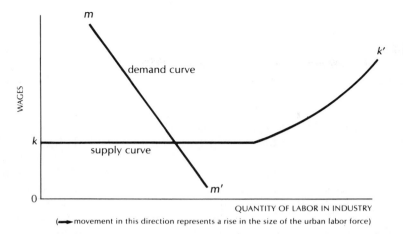

FIGURE 3-6 **The Supply and Demand for Industrial Labor.** The supply curve, *kk'*, is drawn directly from Figure 3–5. Demand, *mm'*, is derived from the industrial production function.

To hire away from the farm, factories in the city will have to pay at least as much as the workers are earning on the farm. Thus the line *hij* in Figure 3–5 can be thought of as the **supply curve of labor** facing the industrial sector. Actually the usual assumption is that the supply curve of labor in industry is a bit above the line *hij* because factories must pay farmers a bit more than they are receiving in agriculture to get them to move.

The key feature of this supply curve of labor is that unlike more common supply curves, it does not rise steadily as one moves from left to right but has a substantial horizontal portion. Formally this means that the supply curve of labor up to point *i* is **perfectly elastic. Elasticity**[6] is a concept used to refer to the percentage change occurring in one variable (in this case, the supply of labor) arising from a given percentage change in another variable (in this case, wages). Perfect elasticity occurs when the ratio of these two percentages equals infinity. From the point of view of the industrial sector this means that that sector can hire as many workers as it wants without having to raise wages until the amount of labor is increased beyond point *i*.

The final steps are to add a demand curve for labor in the industrial sector (Figure 3–6) and then to combine the three figures into a single model. As we see in Figure 3–6, it can be derived from the industrial production function. To simplify our model, this step is ignored and we have simply drawn in the demand curve *mm'*. The supply curve in Figure 3–6 is derived from Figure 3–5. 0*k* in Figure 3–6 is assumed to be slightly higher than the subsistence wage in Figure 3–5. The supply curve of labor to industry turns up when withdrawal of labor from agriculture can no longer be accomplished without

6. The term **elasticity** refers to the percentage change in one variable that results from a percentage change in another variable and is presented as a ratio. In the case discussed here, the elasticity is the ratio of the percentage change in the supply of labor ($\Delta L/L$) to the percentage change in the wage rate ($\Delta W/W$). Algebraically,

$$\text{elasticity} = \frac{\Delta L/L}{\Delta W/W} = \frac{\Delta L}{\Delta W} \cdot \frac{W}{L}.$$

In the case of perfect elasticity, this ratio approaches infinity.

a decline in agricultural output (when the marginal product of labor rises above zero) because at that point the relative price of agricultural produce will rise, necessitating a commensurate rise in urban wages. The demand curve for labor in industry is determined by the marginal product of labor in industry, and hence the demand curve can be derived from the industrial production function.[7]

To combine Figures 3–4, 3–5, and 3–6, one additional piece of information is needed, the size of the nation's labor force. Many models use total population rather than the labor force, and this switch has little effect if the labor force is closely correlated with total population. The size of the labor force in Figure 3–7 is represented by the line zero to p, as labeled in Panel A. In order to combine the three figures, Figure 3–4's relation to the others is made clearer if it is flipped so that an increase in labor is represented by moving from right to left rather than the reverse. Handled this way, a movement from left to right represents both a decline in the agricultural labor force and a rise in the industrial labor force, that is, a transfer of labor from agriculture to industry.

If an economy starts with its entire population in agriculture, it can remove a large part of that population *(pg)* to industry or other employment without any reduction in farm output. Industry will have to pay that labor a wage a bit above subsistence (the difference between $p''k$ and $p'h$) to get it to move, but as long as there is some way of moving the food consumed by this labor from the rural to the urban areas, industrialization can proceed without putting any demands on agriculture. Even if agriculture is completely stagnant, industry can grow. As industry continues to grow, however, it will eventually exhaust the supply of surplus labor. Further removals of labor from agriculture will lead to a reduction in farm output. A shift in industrial demand to *mm* will force industry to pay more for the food of its workers; that is, the *terms of trade* between industry and agriculture will turn against industry and in favor of agriculture. It is this shift in terms of trade that accounts for the rise in the supply curve of labor between g'' and i''. Industry must pay more to get the same amount of food to feed its workers.

The Fei-Ranis model can be used to explore the implications of population growth and a rise in agricultural productivity, among other things. To simplify, if one assumes that there is a close relationship between population and the labor force, then an increase in population from, say, p to t will not increase output at all. The elastic portion of both the urban and rural labor supply curves will be extended by $p't'$ and $p''t''$ respectively, thus postponing the day when industrialization will cause wages to rise.[8] This point where wages begin to rise is sometimes referred to as the **turning point.** Most important, if population rises without any increase in food output, the average

7. A factory owner under competitive conditions is willing to pay up to but no more than what a laborer contributes to increase the volume of output of the factory. The increase in output value contributed by the last laborer hired is by definition the marginal revenue product of that laborer.

8. In the industrial labor supply and demand part of Figure 3–7, panel C, it is also necessary to move the labor demand curves to the left since the zero point on the horizontal axis has been moved to the left. These new demand curves, $s's'$, $m'm'$, and $n'n'$, therefore, are really the same as *ss*, *mm*, and *nn*. That is, the quantity of labor demanded at any given price is the same for $s's'$ as *ss* and so on.

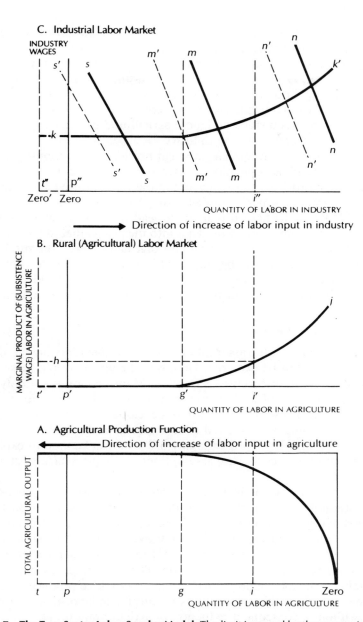

FIGURE 3-7 **The Two-Sector Labor Surplus Model.** The limit imposed by the country's population (zero to *p* in Panel A), coupled with the agricultural production function, allows us to analyze the effects of industry wages on the mix between agricultural and industrial labor.

amount of food available per capita will fall. From the standpoint of everyone but a few employers who want to keep wages low and profits high, population growth is an unqualified disaster. Wages may actually fall in the urban areas, and the welfare of the great mass of farmers will certainly fall. It is a model such as this, even if only imperfectly understood, that people often have in mind when they speak of population growth in wholly negative terms.

How fast agricultural production must grow depends on what happens to a number of different variables. If industry's demand for labor is growing very rapidly, for example, agricultural productivity must grow rapidly enough to keep the terms of trade from turning sharply against industry, thereby cutting into industrial profits and slowing or halting industrial growth.[9] On the other hand, as long as there is a surplus of labor and no population growth, it is possible to ignore agricultural productivity growth and concentrate one's resources on industry.

David Ricardo, using similar although not identical reasoning, was concerned with keeping population growth down to avoid using poorer and poorer land in order to get a sufficient food supply. He also feared the impact of increasing wages, which he saw as leading to a two-fold disaster. Following Thomas Malthus, he argued that would lead to workers having more children. Further, higher wages would cut into the profits that initially provided the funds for investment in capital and that had allowed the rural surplus labor to move to cities and be employed in industry. Modern labor-surplus theorists would not agree with Ricardo's harsh policy prescriptions, but they would see the problems facing today's developing countries in a similar light.

The Neoclassical Model

By changing many of the assumptions in the labor-surplus model, many of its implications can be explored. Here we take up the implications of one assumption, the labor-surplus assumption. Many economists simply do not agree that a surplus of labor exists in today's developing nations, even in India or China. These economists have developed an alternative two-sector model that is sometimes referred to as a **neoclassical model.**

The framework developed in Figure 3–7 can also be used to explore the implications of the neoclassical assumptions. A simple neoclassical model is presented in Figure 3–8.

The implications of population or labor force growth in the neoclassical model are quite different from what they were in the labor surplus model. An increase in population and labor in agriculture will raise farm output (see dotted line *t* in Figure 3–8A), and any removal of labor from agriculture will cause farm output to fall. Thus in a neoclassical model population growth is not such a wholly negative phenomenon. The increase in labor is much less of a drain on the food supply since that labor is able to produce much or all of its own requirements, and there is no surplus of labor that can be transferred without a consequent reduction in agricultural output.

If industry is to develop successfully, simultaneous efforts must be made to ensure that agriculture grows fast enough to feed workers in both the rural and urban sectors at ever-higher levels of consumption and to prevent the terms of trade from turning against industry. A stagnant agricultural sector, that is one with little new investment or technological progress, will cause

---

9. Agricultural productivity in the model presented here refers to a shift in the agricultural production function causing a given amount of labor input in agriculture to produce a larger amount of agricultural output.

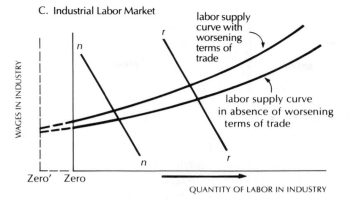

C. Industrial Labor Market

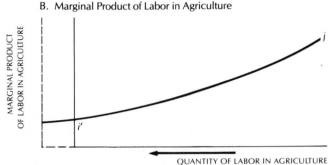

B. Marginal Product of Labor in Agriculture

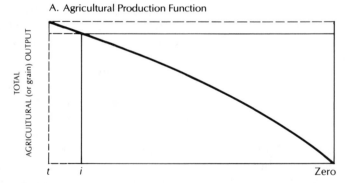

A. Agricultural Production Function

FIGURE 3–8 A "Neoclassical" Two-Sector Model. The key difference between Figures 3–7 and 3–8 is the agricultural production function (Figure 3–8A). Limited land resources do lead to slightly diminishing returns in the agricultural sector, but the curve never flattens out; that is, the marginal product of labor never falls to a minimum subsistence level so there is no minimum subsistence or **institutionally fixed** wage in Figure 3–8B. Wages instead are always determined by the marginal product of labor in agriculture. Finally, the supply curve of labor to industry no longer has a horizontal section. Since removal of labor from agriculture increases the marginal product of labor remaining in agriculture, industry must pay an amount equal to that marginal product plus a premium to get labor to migrate to the cities. The supply curve of labor to industry rises for another reason as well. As labor is removed from agriculture, farm output falls; and in order to extract enough food from the agricultural sector to pay its workers, industry must pay higher and higher prices for food. Only if industry is in a position to import food from abroad will it be able to avoid these worsening terms of trade. If imports are not available, rising agricultural prices will lead to a higher marginal revenue product, and hence higher wages, for workers in agriculture. As in the labor surplus case, industry will have to pay correspondingly higher wages to attract a labor force.

wages of urban workers to rise rapidly, thereby cutting into profits and the funds available for industrial development. Where in the labor-surplus model planners can ignore agriculture until the surplus of labor is exhausted, in the neoclassical model there must be a balance between industry and agriculture from the beginning.

Two-sector models of both the labor-surplus and neoclassical type can become very elaborate, with dozens or even hundreds of equations used to describe different features of the economy. These additional equations and assumptions will also have an influence on the kinds of policy recommendations an economist will derive from the model. But at the core of these more elaborate models are the labor-surplus and neoclassical assumptions about the nature of the agricultural production function.

These same points can be made in a less abstract way by turning to Chinese and African examples of the relationship between industry and agriculture during economic development.

Labor Surplus in China

In China by the 1950s most arable land was already under cultivation, and further increases in population and the labor force contributed little to increases in agricultural output. Urban wages rose in the early 1950s, but then leveled off and remained unchanged for twenty years between 1957 and 1977. If allowed to do so, tens of millions of farm laborers would have happily migrated to the cities despite urban wage stagnation. Only legal restrictions on rural-urban migration, backed up by more than a little force, held this migration to levels well below what would have been required to absorb the surplus. Population growth that averaged 2 percent a year up until the mid-1970s continued to swell the ranks of those interested in leaving the countryside. In short, China over the past three decades was a labor-surplus country.

As pointed out earlier, China did invest in agriculture, but only enough to maintain, not to raise, per-capita food production. The rural-urban migration that did occur was not fast enough to eliminate the rural labor surplus, but it was enough to require farmers to sell more of their production to the cities. Thus the prices paid to farmers for their produce were gradually raised, while the prices paid by farmers for urban products remained constant or fell—that is, the rural-urban *terms of trade* shifted slowly but markedly in favor of agriculture.

To get out of this labor-surplus situation, Chinese planners in the late 1970s had both to accelerate the transfer of workers from rural to urban employment and to take steps to keep the rural pool of surplus labor from constantly replenishing itself. Accelerating the growth of urban employment was accomplished by encouraging labor-intensive consumer goods (textiles, electronics, etc.) and service industries (restaurants, taxis, etc.). To feed this increase in urban population, the government both increased food imports, shifted more investment funds to agriculture, and allowed a further improvement in the rural-urban terms of trade.

To keep the rural pool of surplus labor from replenishing itself, plan-

ners slowed those kinds of farm mechanization that had the effect of reducing the rural demand for labor. Most important, planners attacked the surplus at its source by a massive effort to bring down the birth rate. By 1980 the population growth rate in China had slowed from 2 to 1.2 percent a year. By the early 1980s China was still a labor-surplus country, but the pursuit of similar policies under similar conditions had removed South Korea's labor surplus by the mid-1960s, and much the same thing occurred in Japan at an even earlier date.

Labor Surplus in Africa

Africa, as already pointed out, had low population densities relative to the availability of arable land. In nations such as Kenya, increases in population could be readily accommodated in the 1950s and 1960s by opening up new land or by converting land to more intensive uses (for example, from pasture to crops). Therefore, increased population was more or less matched by rises in agricultural production. Food output, at least in the richer nations such as Kenya, kept up with the needs of both the expanding rural population and with the even more rapidly growing urban sector. Planners felt little pressure either to improve the rural-urban terms of trade or to increase state investment in agriculture. In short, until recently Kenya fit reasonably well the assumptions of the neoclassical model.

Because Kenya's land resources were not unlimited and because population growth continued at the extraordinarily high rate of close to 4 percent per annum, by the late 1970s Kenya was beginning to acquire some of the characteristics of a labor-surplus economy; and planners were having to adjust to the policy implications (more investment and better prices for agriculture, a greater effort to reduce population growth) of these new conditions.

This discussion of the relations between the agricultural and industrial sectors during the process of economic development has gone as far as we can productively go at this stage. Analysis of the patterns of development using data on shares of the two sectors in GNP provided an insight into the patterns that have occurred in the past and might be expected to recur in the future. Two-sector models have made it possible to go a step further and to acquire an understanding of some of the reasons why different patterns of industrial and agricultural development might occur. In later chapters the validity of the labor-surplus versus neoclassical assumptions for today's developing world will be explored at greater length. There will also be extended discussions of the nature and problems of industrial and agricultural development that will include further consideration of the nature of relations between the two sectors.

To know precisely which industries would develop at each stage in a nation's growth would be a very valuable piece of information for economists. Plans could be drawn up that could concentrate a nation's energies on particular industries at particular stages. If all industrial development began with textiles, for example, then planners could focus their attention on getting a textile industry started and worry about other sectors later. Similarly, if only nations with high per-capita incomes could support the efficient production of automobiles, planners in countries beginning development would know that they should avoid investing resources in the automobile industry until a later stage.

Empirical Approaches

Chenery and Taylor[10] have used the terms **early industries, middle industries,** and **late industries. Early industries** are those that supply goods essential to the populations of poor countries and are produced with simple technologies so that their manufacture can take place within the poor country. In statistical terms the share of these industries in GNP rises at low levels of per-capita income, but that share stops rising when income is still fairly low and stagnates or falls thereafter. Typically included in this group are food processing and textiles. **Late industries** are those whose share in GNP continues to rise even at high levels of per-capita income. This group includes many consumer durables (refrigerators, cars) as well as other metal products. **Middle industries** are those that fall in between the other two categories.

Unfortunately, it is frequently difficult to decide in which category a particular industry belongs. For many industries the nineteenth-century experience of European nations or of the United States is a poor guide because many industries that are important today did not even exist then. The nuclear power industry, for example, did not exist prior to World War II, and even the chemical-fertilizer sector as we think of it today did not really begin until well into the twentieth century.

Cross-section data get rid of this particular problem but introduce many others. In several Arab states petroleum accounts for a large share of GNP because these nations have unusually rich underground resources. In Malaysia soil and climate have been favorable to the rise of rubber, palm oil, and timber. Singapore and Hong Kong, which have no natural resources to speak of, have taken advantage of their vast experience in foreign trade to develop textiles, electronics, and other manufactures for export. In short, the share of particular industries in the GNP of individual countries is determined by endowments of natural resources, historical heritages of experience with commerce and trade, and many other factors. There is no single pattern of industrial development, or even two or three patterns, that all nations must follow as they progress out of poverty. Some industries where the techniques used are easier to master, such as textiles, are more likely to

10. Chenery and Taylor, "Development Patterns."

get started in the early stages of development than others, such as the manufacture of commercial aircraft. And there is some regularity in the patterns of what people consume as they move from lower to higher incomes. Engel's law has already been mentioned as a part of the explanation for the declining share of agriculture in GNP. The same law has much to do with why the share of food processing within industry falls as per-capita income rises. But before planners can decide which industries to push in one country, they must know the particular conditions facing that country as well as these more general patterns.

Theoretical Approaches

Economists' debates on balanced and unbalanced growth predate much of the quantitative work on patterns of development. **Balanced growth** advocates such as Ragnar Nurkse or Paul Rosenstein-Rodan[11] argued that countries have to develop a wide range of industries simultaneously if they are ever to succeed in achieving sustained growth. What would happen in the absence of balanced growth has often been illustrated with a story of a hypothetical country that attempted to begin development by building a shoe factory. The factory is built, workers are hired and trained, and the factory begins to turn out shoes. Everything goes well until the factory tries to sell the shoes it is producing. The factory workers themselves use their increased income to buy new factory-made shoes; but of course they are able to produce far more shoes than they need for themselves or their families. The rest of the population is mainly poor farmers whose income has not risen, and hence they cannot afford to buy factory-made shoes. They continue to wear cheap homemade sandals. The factory in turn, unable to sell its product, goes bankrupt and the effort to start development comes to an end.

The proposed solution to this problem is to build a number of factories simultaneously. If a textile mill, a flour mill, a bicycle plant, and many other enterprises could be started at the same time, the shoe factory could sell its shoes to the workers in these factories as well. In turn, shoe-factory workers would use their new income to buy bicycles, clothing, and flour, thus keeping the other new plants solvent. This kind of development is sometimes referred to as **balanced growth on the demand side** because the industries developed are determined by the demand or expenditure patterns of consumers (and investors). **Balanced growth on the supply side** refers to the need to build a number of industries simultaneously to prevent supply bottlenecks from occurring. Thus, in building a steel mill, planners need to make sure that iron and coal mines and coking facilities are also developed, unless imports of these inputs are readily available. At a more aggregated level, it is also necessary to maintain a balance between the development of industry

11. Ragnar Nurkse, *Problems of Capital Formation in Underdeveloped Countries* (New York: Oxford University Press, 1953); and Paul N. Rosenstein-Rodan, "Problems of Industrialization of Eastern and Southeastern Europe," *Economic Journal* (June–September 1943), reprinted in *The Economics of Underdevelopment*, A. N. Agarwala and S. P. Singh, eds. (New York: Oxford University Press, 1963).

and agriculture. Otherwise, as pointed out earlier, the terms of trade might turn sharply against industry, thereby bringing growth to a stop.

One problem with the balanced-growth argument is that in its pure form it is a counsel of despair. A poor country with little or no industry is told that it must either start up a wide range of industries simultaneously or resign itself to continued stagnation. This across-the-board program has sometimes been referred to as a **big push** or a **critical minimum effort**. By whatever name, it is discouraging advice for a poor nation that is taxing its managerial and financial resources to the limit just to get a few factories started.

In the discussion of patterns of industrial development, however, we pointed out that there is little evidence that all nations have to follow a set pattern. Some nations have emphasized one set of industries while other nations concentrated on different ones. Proponents of **unbalanced growth**, especially Albert Hirschman, recognize these differences and use them to suggest a very different pattern of industrial development.[12] Nations, they say, could and did concentrate their energies on a few sectors during the early stages of development. In most cases there was little danger of producing more shoes than could be sold.

Certain industrial products have ready markets, even among the rural poor and even in the absence of a big push towards development. A worker in a nineteenth-century factory, for example, could produce forty times as much cotton yarn per day as a peasant with a spinning wheel in a dark rural cottage. From the peasants' point of view, therefore, it made sense to buy factory yarn and to concentrate his effort on a more productive activity, such as weaving that yarn into cloth. Initially much of this yarn was imported into places like India and China from factories in Britain, but it was not long before entrepreneurs in China and India discovered that cotton yarn could be produced more cheaply at home than purchased as an import. Thus they substituted domestic production for imports. **Import substitution**, as this process is called, is one way a nation can find a ready market for one of its own industries. The market is already there, and all a country's planners have to do is ensure that the domestic industry can compete effectively with the imported product. How this can be done is a subject to which we shall return in Chapter 16. Here the main point is that import substitution is one way of beginning industrialization on a limited and selective basis rather than with a balanced "big push." Another way is to rely on exports, as England did during the Industrial Revolution. If it is impossible to sell all of a factory's product at home, it is often possible to sell the product abroad, assuming that product could be produced at a cost that is competitive.

Backward and Forward Linkages

Unbalanced growth advocates such as Hirschman, however, did not content themselves with simply pointing out an escape from the dilemma posed by balanced growth proponents. Hirschman developed the unbalanced growth

---

12. Albert O. Hirschman, *The Strategy of Economic Development* (New Haven: Yale University Press, 1958).

idea into a general interpretation of how development ought to proceed. The central concept in Hirschman's theory is that of **linkages**. Industries are linked to other industries in ways that can be taken into account in deciding on a development strategy. Industries with **backward linkages** make use of inputs from other industries. Automobile manufacturing, for example, uses the products of machinery and metal-processing plants, which in turn make use of large amounts of steel. The building of an automobile manufacturing plant, therefore, will create a demand for machinery and steel. Initially this demand may be supplied by imports, but eventually local entrepreneurs will see that they have a ready market for domestically made machinery and steel, and this demand stimulates them to set up such plants. Planners interested in accelerating growth, therefore, will emphasize industries with strong backward linkages because it is these industries that will stimulate production in the greatest number of additional sectors.

Forward linkages occur in industries that produce goods that then become inputs into other industries. Rather than start with automobiles, planners might prefer to start at the other end by setting up a steel mill. Seeing that they had a ready domestic supply of steel, entrepreneurs might then be stimulated to set up factories that would make use of this steel. In a similar way successful drilling for oil will encourage a nation to set up its own refineries and petrochemical complexes rather than ship its crude oil to other nations for processing.

Both forward and backward linkages set up pressures that lead to the creation of new industries, which in turn create additional pressures, and so on. These pressures can take the form of new profit opportunities for private entrepreneurs, or pressures can build through the political process and force governments to act. Private investors, for example, might decide to build factories in a given location without at the same time providing adequate housing facilities for the inflow of new workers or roads with which to supply the factories and transport their output. In such cases government planners might be forced to construct public housing and roads.

While on the surface the balanced and unbalanced growth arguments appear to be fundamentally inconsistent with each other, when stated in less extreme forms they can be seen as opposite sides of the same coin. Almost everyone would agree that there is no single pattern of industrialization that all nations must follow. On the other hand, quantitative analysis suggests that there are patterns that are broadly similar among large groups of nations. While nations with large amounts of foreign trade can follow an unbalanced strategy for some time, a nation cannot pick any industry or group of industries it desires and then concentrate exclusively on those industries throughout the nation's development, following in effect an extreme form of an unbalanced growth strategy. The very concept of linkages suggests that extreme imbalances of this sort will set up pressures that will force a nation back toward a more balanced path. Thus the ultimate objective is a degree of balance in the development program. But planners have a choice between attempting to maintain balance throughout the development process or first creating imbalances with the knowledge that linkage pressures will eventually force them back toward the balance. In terms of

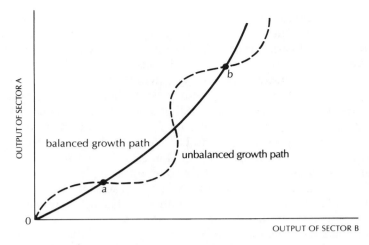

FIGURE 3–9 Balanced and Unbalanced Growth Paths. The solid line between points *a* and *b* is shorter than the dotted line, but because of the impact of linkages, a country travelling along the dotted line may get from point *a* to *b* in less time than a country travelling along the solid line or balanced growth path.

Figure 3–9, the issue is whether to follow the steady balanced path represented by a solid line or the unbalanced path represented by a dashed line. The solid line is shorter, but under certain conditions a nation might get to any given point faster by following the dashed line.

APPENDIX: DERIVING THE SOURCES OF GROWTH EQUATION

There are six steps to deriving the sources of growth equation from the standard aggregate production function. To simplify the presentation, we shall assume that there are only two factors of production, capital and labor.

1. Assume an aggregate production function:

$$Y = F(K, L, t), \qquad [3\text{–}7]$$

which is continuous and homogeneous to degree one, where

Y = national income or product
K = capital stock
t = time (shift in basic production function)
L = labor force.

2. Differentiate this production function with respect to time.

$$\frac{dY}{dt} = \left(\frac{\delta F}{\delta K} \cdot \frac{dK}{dt}\right) + \left(\frac{\delta F}{\delta L} \cdot \frac{dL}{dt}\right) + \left(\frac{\delta F}{\delta t} \cdot \frac{dt}{dt}\right) \qquad [3\text{–}8]$$

3. Divide through by Y, and insert L and K in equation.

$$\frac{1}{Y} \cdot \frac{dY}{dt} = \frac{1}{Y}\left(\frac{\delta F}{\delta K} \cdot \frac{dK}{dt} \cdot K \cdot \frac{1}{K} + \frac{\delta F}{\delta L} \cdot \frac{dL}{dt} \cdot L \cdot \frac{1}{L} + \frac{\delta F}{\delta t}\right) \qquad [3\text{–}9]$$

4. Rearrange terms.

$$\frac{dY/dt}{Y} = \frac{(\delta F/\delta K)\,K}{Y} \cdot \frac{(dK/dt}{K} + \frac{(\delta F/\delta L)\,L}{Y} \cdot \frac{dL/dt}{L} + \frac{\delta F/dt}{Y}, \qquad [3\text{--}10]$$

where

$$G_Y = \frac{dY/dt}{Y} = \text{growth rate of income,}$$

$$G_K = \frac{dK/dt}{K} = \text{growth rate of capital,}$$

$$G_L = \frac{dL/dt}{L} = \text{growth rate of labor force,}$$

$$W_K = \frac{(\delta F/\delta K)\,K}{Y} = \text{share of product of capital in national income.}$$

5. Assume perfect competition so that wages and the interest rate equal the marginal product of labor and capital respectively, if

$$\frac{\delta F}{\delta L} = \text{ wage rate,}$$

then

$$W_L = \frac{(\delta F/\delta L)\,L}{Y} = \text{share of product of labor in national income,}$$

and if

$$\frac{\delta F}{\delta K} = i \text{ (rate of interest),}$$

then

$$W_K = \frac{(\delta F/\delta K) \cdot K}{Y}$$

and

$$a = \frac{\delta F/\delta t}{Y} = \text{increase in output as share of income not} \atop \text{explained by increase in factors.}$$

6. Substitute G_Y, G_L, G_K, W_L, W_K, and a into Equation 3–10, which then gives one the sources of growth equation:

$$G_Y = (W_K \cdot G_K) + (W_L \cdot G_L) + a. \qquad [3\text{--}11]$$

This equation can also be rewritten in the form,

$$a = (\text{the ``residual''}) = G_Y - (W_K \cdot G_K) - (W_L \cdot G_L). \qquad [3\text{--}12]$$

Countries with reasonably good statistical systems regularly publish data on the growth rate of national product (G_Y) and the labor force (G_L). Data on the growth rate of the capital stock (G_K) are more difficult to find because estimates of the capital stock are readily available only for industrialized nations. Economists who work with developing country data, therefore, sometimes rewrite the $W_K \cdot G_K$ component of Equation 3–11. By not inserting K into Equation 3–10, that part of Equation 3–10 becomes

$$\frac{dF}{dK} \cdot \frac{dK/dt}{Y},$$

where

$$\frac{dF}{dK} = \text{the interest rate as previously assumed}$$

and

$$\frac{dK/dt}{Y} = I = \text{the share of gross domestic investment} \atop \text{in gross domestic product.}$$

The share of gross domestic investment (I), or capital formation in gross domestic product, is regularly calculated for most countries.

Data on the shares of labor income in national income (W_L) are the total wages and salaries paid to workers plus the inputed wages of farmers. The share of capital income in national income (W_K) is made up of interest income and profits. In a two factor model, W_K would encompass all property income, including the rent on land.

When economists such as Edward Denison calculate the sources of growth, they generally use more than two factors of production. Labor, for example, is usually divided into unskilled and skilled labor of various types. Foreign exchange earnings are sometimes treated as a separate factor of production from capital, and so on. There often is an attempt to break down the residual measure of productivity increases (a) into its various components. Some of these refinements can be used in estimating the sources of growth in developing countries, but others are not possible because of the limited availability of relevant developing-country data.

4

Development and Human Welfare

In Chapter 1 economic growth was defined simply as a rise in national or per-capita income and product. Economic development, it was said, implies more than this: growth plus fundamental changes in the structure of the economy, a rise in the share of national product originating in the industrial sector, urbanization, participation by the nationals of the country itself in the process by which these changes are brought about. Despite the many caveats raised in Chapter 3 which must be applied to efforts to measure growth and development, it is evident that most developing countries really are growing and developing in the senses implied by these definitions.

The question to be taken up in this chapter is the meaning of that growth and development for the three billion citizens of the third world. Are growth and development improving their living conditions as time goes by? If so, to what extent and in what ways? If their welfare is not improving, or not improving very fast, what kinds of changes in development patterns and process could improve this outcome? And how can they be brought about?

Logically speaking, economic growth and development are necessary, but not sufficient, conditions for improving the physical well-being of large numbers of people. If there is no growth, then some people can be made better off only by taking income and assets from others. In poor countries, even if a few people are very rich, the potential of this kind of redistribution is severely limited. Even if the metaphorical pie were cut into precisely equal pieces for all, the slices would be very thin indeed.[1]

Economic growth, by contrast, opens up the possibility of making at least some people better off without making anyone worse off. In metaphorical

---

1. There is, however, a view which argues that if assets are redistributed first, faster growth will result. This is taken up in the last section of this chapter.

terms the pie becomes larger; but how is it sliced? Does every piece increase in size or only those received by the fortunate few? Might some people receive even smaller slices of the pie despite the larger total to be distributed?

There are at least three reasons why we cannot assume that a higher per-capita GNP necessarily means higher incomes for all, or even most, families. First, governments promote economic development not just to improve the welfare of their citizens but also, and sometimes primarily, to augment the power and glory of the state and its rulers. Much of the wealth of ancient Egypt was invested in the pyramids. Some modern LDCs buy ballistic missile systems, develop their own atomic bombs, or construct elaborate capital city complexes in deserts and jungles. The gains from growth can be channeled largely to such expensive projects and thus provide little immediate benefit to the nation's citizens.

Second, resources may be heavily invested in further growth, so that significant consumption gains are put off to a later date. If the process continues indefinitely, that later date never arrives. In extreme cases, such as the Soviet collectivization drive of the 1930s, consumption levels may actually be depressed, even to the point of starvation, so that still faster growth can be achieved. Normally, such extreme measures are within the power only of totalitarian governments.

Third, income and consumption may increase but those who are already relatively well off may get all or most of the benefits. The rich get richer, the old saw says, and the poor get poorer. (In another version, the poor get children.) This is what poor people often think is happening. Sometimes they are right.

The question of who benefits from economic growth and development is not a new one. In Victorian England, for example, rising inequalities in income and wealth, and persistent, even worsening, poverty among the lower classes were issues widely perceived and frequently debated. Social philosophers such as Karl Marx and novelists like Charles Dickens made these phenomena their major themes. Defenders of the status quo responded either by denying that things were as bad as the critics charged or by arguing that the conditions they deplored were a necessary part of a process of change that would ultimately benefit all strata of society.

Despite the efforts of a few nineteenth-century pioneers in "economic arithmetic" and of subsequent economic historians, we do not know precisely what the dimensions of nineteenth-century inequality and poverty were. It is known, however, that things improved in the developed capitalist countries in the early part of the twentieth century. During this period most governments of industrializing Western states enacted reforms (antitrust legislation, progressive taxation, unemployment insurance, social security, and after 1930, stabilizing monetary and fiscal policies) that helped to mitigate the worst inequalities and assure some minimal living standard for all members of society. Contrary to Marx, who had predicted ever-worsening inequality and instability leading to the collapse of the "bourgeois system" itself, workers in the rich capitalist countries ultimately did reach an era of mass consumption that allowed them to share in the gains from economic development.

But what about the masses of people in Asia, Africa, and Latin America
who remain desperately poor by the standards of the ordinary citizen of a
rich Western country, or even by those of a worker in an East European
socialist state? As industrialization proceeds and their nations' GNPs rise,
what happens to their individual economic welfare? When can they hope to
reach an era of mass consumption?

The last twenty years have seen an enormous rise of interest in the problems of inequality and poverty in the less developed countries. This discussion has replayed, with variations, some of the themes heard in the industrial
countries a century or more ago. There is no country in which everyone is
equally poor, although some exceedingly low-income countries may
approach this state of affairs through "shared poverty."[2] As economic growth
occurs, inequality is generated because people's incomes rise at varying rates.
During the early years of the current period of interest in economic development, roughly 1950–65, it was possible to forget this fact because there were
hardly any available statistics on the distribution of income in developing
countries. Sometimes people did assume that because per-capita GNP was
rising everyone was getting better off. If certain sections of the population
were not benefiting, it was only a matter of time, some argued, until the benefits of development would "trickle down" to them.

Doubts about whether development was really reaching the poor began in
India as early as 1960. By the late 1960s enough income distribution statistics had been compiled for India and other LDCs to rock the complacent.
These newly gathered data revealed what was for many a shocking reality.
Not only was income inequality generally much higher in poor countries
than in rich countries, something generally appreciated, but: (1) inequality
was apparently rising in many developing countries; (2) in fact the mass of
people in some countries were not benefiting at all from development; (3)
finally, and more controversially, some writers claimed that the poor were
actually becoming worse off, at least in certain large and very poor countries
such as India and Bangladesh.

Much scholarly work and policymaking concern have resulted from these
disclosures. In the following pages we will consider what has been learned,
dealing first with concepts of economic welfare, then with the facts of what
has been happening, next with theories about the causes and effects of
inequality and poverty, and finally with possible policies to help ameliorate
inequality.

CONCEPTS AND MEASURES

Income Distribution

The most common way to evaluate the effect of development on **welfare**
(economic well-being) is through the study of income distribution. The two
types of income distribution generally cited are the functional distribution

2. In some poor societies, anthropologists have argued, inequalities are small because few
people control significant amounts of land or capital and the community bands together to
ensure a minimal consumption standard for all.

and size distribution. The **functional distribution** refers to the division among the factors of production, traditionally identified as land, labor, and capital. The **size distribution** refers to the distribution of income of all kinds among individuals or families, which are divided into categories based on levels of family income. The latter is most commonly used as a direct measure of welfare.[3] Since income distribution, according to most theories, is determined largely by ownership patterns of the productive factors and the role each factor plays in the production process, the functional distribution of income is important as a cause of welfare levels. For example, if ownership of land and capital is narrowly distributed, then anything that enhances the returns to these factors will tend to worsen the size distribution of income. Conversely, a higher return to unskilled labor, the most widely distributed resource, will make for a more equal size distribution.

There are many practical problems involved in measuring the size distribution of income. Ideally, average income over several years should be used since earners in LDCs often experience wide income fluctuations as a result of the vagaries of nature, markets, and their own governments. Cumulated lifetime income would be an even better measure, because earnings also vary systematically with age. But such refinements are usually not practical and most studies take income over a particular recent period (a month or year) as their basis. Other practical decisions involve precisely how to define income and how to collect data. Usually a sample survey of households is undertaken. Even when considerable care and ingenuity are exercised the resulting statistics are likely to be of questionable accuracy. Respondents may not know what their income is, or they may be afraid to disclose it, perhaps out of fear that their taxes will go up. Generally, reported incomes are understated. If a household income survey is projected over all households, the total ought to be equal the household share of national income implied in the national estimates.[4] In practice a shortfall of "only" 15 or 20 percent is regarded as a good result for a household income survey. In general, the uncertainties of these statistics require the analyst to tread cautiously when trying to interpret them.

Once the data have been collected, the next step is to analyze them. Respondents (either individuals or households) are first ranked by income size. The best ranking criterion is actually household income per capita, since family members in LDCs usually pool their incomes and welfare is affected by both the total income received and the number of family members to be supported.

---

3. One could argue that the distribution of consumption or wealth should be measured instead. Consumption measures the volume of goods and services actually consumed, so it could be equated with material welfare. But income represents *potential consumption,* including a part of the potential which is not realized in the current period because it is saved to yield higher consumption later on. Wealth, finally, defines the potential to earn *and* to consume, especially when human capital is included in the definition of wealth (see Chapters 9 and 10). But the distribution of wealth is notoriously hard to measure and statistics on wealth distribution are rare.

4. **National income** equals gross national product less depreciation and indirect taxes; the household share of national income would also exclude profits retained (not distributed as dividends) by corporations.

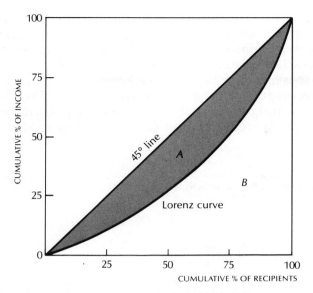

FIGURE 4–1 Lorenz Curve. The further the Lorenz curve bends away from the 45° line, the greater is the inequality of income distribution. Dividing the shaded area (A) by the total area under the 45° line (A + B) gives one measure of inequality, the Gini concentration ratio.

The data can be arranged in various ways. The most common method is the **Lorenz curve,** which is illustrated in Figure 4–1. To draw a Lorenz curve, income recipients are ranked from lowest income to highest along the horizontal axis. The Lorenz curve itself shows the percentage of total income accounted for by any cumulative percentage of recipients. The shape of this curve indicates the degree of inequality in the income distribution. The curve must by definition touch the 45° line at the lower left corner (zero percent of recipients must receive zero percent of income) and at the upper right corner (100 percent of recipients must receive 100 percent of income). If all recipients had the same income, the Lorenz curve would lie along the 45° line (perfect equality). If only one individual or household received income, it would trace the lower and right-hand borders of the diagram (perfect inequality). In the general case, it lies somewhere in between. The inequality of the distribution curve is greater the further it bends away from the 45° line of perfect equality (the shaded area *A* is greater).

Inequality Measures

Statisticians have long been interested in finding a single numerical measure that adequately expresses the degree of overall inequality present in an income distribution. All common statistical measures, such as the range and standard deviation, have serious faults. The most frequently used measure, the **Gini concentration ratio,** is derived from the Lorenz curve. This ratio is most easily understood as the value of area *A* divided by area *A* plus *B* in Figure 4–1. That is, the larger the share of the area between the 45° line and the Lorenz curve, the higher the value of the Gini concentration ratio. One can see from Figure 4–1 that the theoretical range of the Gini ratio is from zero (perfect equality) to one (perfect inequality). In practice, values measured in national income distributions have a much narrower range—normally from about .20 to .60. Some examples are shown in Table 4–1.

Like all other indicators that have been proposed to measure inequality, the Gini concentration ratio has its problems. For one thing Lorenz curves can intersect, so that curves of different shapes could generate the same Gini ratio. This happens because one distribution is very unequal in one part of

TABLE 4–1 Income Distribution in Selected Countries[a]

Country	% of income received by: Lowest 40%	% of income received by: Highest 20%	Gini concentration ratio[b]
Low-income countries			
Bangladesh	17.1	46.9	.389
Tanzania	16.0	50.4	.420
India	16.2	49.4	.407
Sri Lanka	19.2	43.4	.345
Kenya	8.9	60.4	.550
Indonesia	14.4	49.4	.430
Middle-income countries			
Egypt	16.5	48.0	.403
Philippines	14.2	54.0	.459
Zambia	10.8	61.1	.534
Ivory Coast	10.1	57.2	.554
Costa Rica	12.0	54.8	.486
Tunisia	11.4	55.0	.494
Colombia	9.4	59.4	.530
Peru	7.0	61.0	.569
Korea (South)	16.9	45.3	.378
Brazil	7.0	66.6	.605
Malaysia	11.2	56.1	.500
Taiwan	20.0	41.4	.331
Mexico	9.9	57.7	.520
Argentina	14.1	50.3	.440
Uruguay	14.3	47.4	.421
Venezuela	10.3	54.0	.495
Industrial market economies			
Japan	21.9	37.5	.285
United Kingdom	18.5	39.7	.328
France	16.4	45.8	.395
West Germany	20.4	39.5	.308
Australia	15.4	47.1	.404
Canada	17.1	40.0	.344
Sweden	20.5	41.7	.324
United States	17.2	39.9	.344
Socialist countries			
Yugoslavia	18.7	38.7	.317
Hungary	20.5	35.8	.284

Source: Montek S. Ahluwalia, "Inequality, Poverty and Development," *Journal of Development Economics* 3 (1976): 340–41; World Bank, *World Development Report 1985* (New York: Oxford University Press, 1985): 228–29.

[a] Dates of the surveys underlying these estimates vary by country, ranging between 1965 and 1982. Countries are categorized and ranked by their GNP per capita in 1975.

[b] Approximate Gini concentration ratios calculated from grouped data (that is, from data that have been aggregated by income size groups).

its range, say, from the bottom to around the middle, while another is
unequal in a different part, say, in terms of the income shares of the very richest families. For another, the extreme nature of the reference standard, perfect equality, makes the measure generally insensitive to changes in distribution. This insensitivity is greatest for changes in the incomes of low-income groups, which may be small in absolute terms but still important in percentage terms to the poor households themselves, and also perhaps an important form of redistribution in policy terms.[5]

Any measure that tries to encompass the entire Lorenz curve in a single statistic must contain an element of arbitrariness. One way around this is to look only at a particular part of the curve. Thus if we are interested in how the poor are faring, we might examine the absolute and relative incomes of the poorest 30 or 40 percent of the distribution. Conversely if we are interested in the concentration of wealth at the top of the distribution, the top 5, 10, or 20 percent could be studied. This tells us what we want to know for particular purposes, but at the cost of generality; it ignores what is going on in the rest of the distribution.

TABLE 4–2   Comparisons of Income Distribution in Tanzania, Egypt, and Indonesia

Country	Income shares						Gini concentration ratio
	Bottom 20%	Second 20%	Third 20%	Fourth 20%	Top 20%	Top 10%	
Tanzania (1969)	5.8	10.2	13.9	19.7	50.4	35.6	.420
Egypt (1974)	5.8	10.7	14.7	20.8	48.0	33.2	.403
Indonesia (1976)	6.6	7.8	12.6	23.6	49.4	34.0	.430

Source: World Bank, *World Development Report 1985* (New York: Oxford University Press, 1985), pp. 228–29.

Some of these points are illustrated in Table 4–2, which compares the income distributions of Tanzania, Egypt, and Indonesia during the years 1970–75. All three countries had fairly unequal income distributions, but which was the most unequal? The Gini concentration ratio says Indonesia, yet the bottom 20 percent of the distribution did better in Indonesia than in either of the other two countries. And Tanzania gave a large share of total income to households in the highest quintile of income recipients. So which distribution is really more unequal? In a borderline case like this, there is no clear answer. Indonesia's distribution was more unequal in some senses, Tanzania's in others. Egypt's distribution was less unequal than the other two in most, but not quite all, respects. The crossing Lorenz curves produced by these distributions are shown in Figure 4–2.

5. In the Philippines in 1970–71, the lowest 20 percent of the income distribution received only 5.2 percent of total income while the top 10 percent of households got 38.5 percent of total income. Taking 1 percent of total income from the richest group and giving it to the lowest 20 percent would raise the income of the poor by 19 percent, a meaningful increase. Yet it would lower the Gini concentration ratio only from .461 to .445, assuming that the redistributive gain is shared equally by the lowest two deciles.

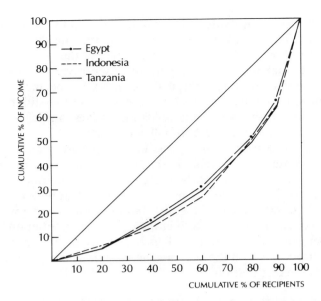

FIGURE 4-2 Lorenz Curves for Income Distribution in Tanzania, Egypt, and Indonesia, c. 1970–1975. When Lorenz curves intersect, as do the curves for Tanzania, Egypt, and Indonesia, there is no clear measure of relative inequality.

Poverty Measures

While inequality is clearly a matter of relative incomes, the concept of **poverty** implies that households are poor in some absolute sense. But what absolute standard is there that can be used to distinguish between poor and nonpoor households? One could perhaps identify poverty through its specific manifestations: starvation, severe malnutrition, illiteracy, substandard clothing and housing. But there is more to poverty than that. Fundamentally, poverty is usually defined in social terms. The "poor" are those who must live below whatever has been defined as the minimum acceptable standard in a given time and place. It is in this sense that the poor are always with us. Thus while practically everyone in the United States receives a higher income than almost everyone in, say, Chad, there are still poor people in the United States and nonpoor people in Chad. Different standards apply in the two places. So poverty is not entirely a matter of absolute levels of living. Its real basis is psychological. The poor are those who feel deprived of what is enjoyed by other people in the society of which they consider themselves to be a part (their "reference group," in psychological terms). Reference groups are probably expanding as education and communication improve. Formerly, peasants might compare their own status to that of the village elites at most. Now they are becoming increasingly aware of the living standards of urban elites in their own countries, and even of standards that prevail in the rich countries. So the sense of deprivation may well be growing.

Measurement of the amount of poverty existing in a country usually begins with the drawing of a **poverty line.** Ideally, this line should be defined in terms of household income per capita. Households with per-capita incomes below the poverty line are defined as poor while those with incomes above the line are not poor. The simplest measure of the extent of poverty is the percentage of poor households in the total. A better measure would take account of the extent to which the incomes of the poor fall below the poverty line. Reduction of poverty would therefore be measured through a fall in the percentage of poor households in the total and also through increases in the absolute incomes of the poor.

Table 4–3 illustrates these points using as an example one of the most successful cases of poverty and inequality alleviation. Sri Lanka in 1953 had a low per-capita income, relatively great inequality (as measured by the Gini ratio), and a large population of poor people (defined here as receiving a monthly per-capita income below 100 rupees in 1963 prices). Over the succeeding two decades inequality declined and outstanding progress was made in reducing poverty, as can be seen from the rise in the mean income of the bottom 40 percent of the income distribution and from the sharp decline in the percentage of households below the poverty line. Note that this was achieved with only modest growth in average income; according to the statistics, monthly income per capita rose only 28 percent in 20 years, while the average income of households in the lowest four deciles of the distribution rose by 71 percent. Few developing countries have been able to duplicate this achievement.

The poverty analyst can apply similar or different standards across differing times and places. World Bank publications sometimes refer to the quantity and distribution of "absolute poverty" in the world; these calculations are made using a single global poverty line.[6]

TABLE 4–3   Changes in Income Distribution and Poverty in Sri Lanka, 1953–1973

Measure	1953	1963	1973
Income shares of quintiles			
Bottom 20%	5.2	4.5	7.2
Second quintile	9.3	9.2	12.1
Third quintile	13.3	13.8	16.3
Fourth quintile	18.4	20.2	21.6
Top 20%	53.8	52.3	42.9
Gini concentration ratio	.46	.45	.35
Mean monthly income per capita, (rupees)[a]	117	134	150
Mean monthly income of bottom 40% (rupees)[a]	42	46	72
Percent of households below 100 rupees/month[a]	63	59	41

Source: Gary S. Fields, *Poverty, Inequality and Development* (Cambridge: Cambridge University Press, 1980), p. 197.
[a] In 1963 prices.

---

6. For a probing discussion of these measurement problems, see Amartya K. Sen, *On Economic Inequality* (New York: W. W. Norton, 1973). A good short discussion is provided by Richard Szal and Sherman Robinson, "Measuring Income Inequality," in *Income Distribution and Growth in the Less-Developed Countries,* Charles R. Frank and Richard C. Webb, eds. (Washington, D.C.: Brookings Institution, 1977), pp. 491–533.

Before leaving the topic of income distribution measures, we should note that equality is not the same thing as equity. *Equality* is an objective statistical measure used mainly to determine how far any actual distribution diverges from the standard. *Equity* is a normative (ethical) concept: what is equitable depends on one's values. Many Americans, for example, believe in "equality of opportunity," but think that considerable inequality of results may be justified by interpersonal differences in ability, effort, training, willingness to take risks, and stage in the life cycle. Thus, quite apart from the fact that there is a trade-off between equity and economic growth (policymakers may have to permit more inequality than they would like because of the need to provide incentives for people to produce more), most concepts of equity allow for some degree of inequality in the distribution of income.

Basic Human Needs and Social Indicators

The poverty approach measures purchasing power in the hands of the poor. But some students of development, including many from disciplines other than economics, object to using income as the measure of welfare. Of course, they maintain, higher incomes help make it possible for people to live better and longer, but why don't we look to see whether these changes actually occur? Efforts to measure a wide variety of social indicators have been going on for several years. More recently interest has centered on seeing whether **basic human needs** are being satisfied. Lists of basic human needs can differ, but most versions include minimal levels of nutrition, health, clothing, shelter, and opportunities for individual freedom and advancement. Some of these, at least, can be measured.

For some years now the United Nations Research Institute for Social Development (UNRISD), located in Geneva, has been compiling a data bank of social indicators. A selection of its data is shown in Table 4–4. Some of the indicators listed—infant deaths, life expectancy, protein consumption, and adult literacy—reflect the degree to which basic human needs are satisfied in countries at different levels of GNP per capita. Others (newsprint consumption, radios, and motor vehicles) indicate consumption of items that might be regarded as less basic. Remaining indicators are less directly related to welfare. Some, such as fertilizer use and electricity consumption, measure the sophistication of the economy. Finally, a fourth group of indicators, represented in Table 4–4 by densities of physician and hospital services, indicate levels of services which may contribute to basic needs satisfaction, which is itself measured more directly by other indicators.[7]

Two interesting points come out of an examination of Table 4–4. One is that as a general rule improvement in social indicators goes hand-in-hand with a rise in per-capita GNP. In Table 4–4 it is striking that every time we move to a higher income group the average value of each social indicator for the countries represented in UNRISD's data bank increases. But the second point is that variation among countries within each income class is large.

---

7. Besides being an approach to measuring welfare, basic human needs is also a strategy for welfare-oriented development. This aspect is discussed in the last section of the chapter.

TABLE 4–4 Illustrative Social Indicators for 1970

Indicator	GNP per capita (1971)									
	< $150		$150–$500		$500–$1,000		$1,000–$2,000		> $2,000	
Infant deaths/ 1,000 live births	136	(41)	109	(33)	50	(18)	32	(13)	18	(4)
Life expectancy at birth (years)	46	(9)	52	(6)	66	(6)	70	(2)	72	(2)
Thousand inhabitants/ physician	33.4	(24.5)	8.6	(8.5)	2.1	(2.5)	0.9	(0.6)	0.7	(0.2)
Thousand inhabitants/ hospital bed	1.3	(1.1)	0.6	(0.5)	0.4	(0.5)	0.2	(0.1)	0.1	(0)
Protein consumption/ head/day (gms)	55	(11)	61	(13)	75	(16)	90	(16)	92	(8)
Adult literacy (%)	37	(22)	49	(21)	84	(6)	89	(11)	99	(0)
Newsprint consumption (kg/head)	0.3	(0.4)	1.3	(1.2)	5	(2.9)	9.8	(12.6)	23.6	(11.3)
Radios/1,000 inhabitants	55	(91)	87	(68)	184	(105)	206	(104)	401	(282)
Motor vehicles/ 1,000 inhabitants	5	(3)	16	(11)	45	(25)	106	(67)	250	(117)
Fertilizer use (kg/ha of arable land)	9	(13)	46	(76)	57	(45)	131	(118)	346	(224)
Electricity consumption (kwh/head)	41	(44)	271	(238)	1,031	(655)	1,675	(834)	5,065	(3,020)

Source: UNRISD Research Data Bank. Figures in parentheses are standard deviations.

This is demonstrated by the high values for standard deviations shown in the table.[8]

One problem with social indicators is that it is hard to combine them to obtain an overall view of a nation's material well-being. An imaginative move in this direction has been made by the Washington-based Overseas Development Council (ODC). The ODC's "physical quality of life index" (PQLI) is an aggregation of three widely available indicators of the basic human needs variety: life expectancy at age one, the infant mortality rate, and the literacy rate.[9] Any such index is necessarily arbitrary. Nevertheless, the PQLI does produce some interesting and intuitively appealing results, which are interpreted by its compilers to suggest that the richest countries do not always enjoy the highest quality of life, and that at least a few countries, such as Sri Lanka, Cuba, Guyana, and South Korea, have been able to

8. The standard deviation is a measure of the average variation among observations. It can be defined as

$$(d^2/n)^{1/2},$$

where d is the deviation of each observation from the mean and n is the number of observations. A large standard deviation indicates a wide spread among the observations, while a small one suggests that most observations have values close to the mean.

9. Each indicator is assigned a scaled value from 0 to 100, with the best and worst known cases serving as the limits of the scale. An unweighted average of the three is then taken. See Morris David Morris, *Measuring the Condition of the World's Poor. The Physical Quality of Life Index* (New York: Pergamon Press for the Overseas Development Council, 1979).

TABLE 4-5   Physical Quality of Life Index (PQLI) for Selected Countries, 1970–75 Average

Country	GNP per capita (dollars), 1970–75 Average	Life expectancy at age one (years)	Infant mortality (per 1,000 live births)	Percent literate (age 15 and over)	PQLI
India	133	56	122	34	43
Tanzania	154	52	162	28	31
Pakistan	155	57	121	16	38
Sri Lanka	179	70	45	81	82
Indonesia	203	55	137	60	48
Kenya	213	56	119	23	39
China	300	65	78	60	69
Bolivia	332	52	108	40	43
South Korea	464	67	47	88	82
Colombia	526	67	97	81	71
Ghana	595	56	156	25	35
Malaysia	692	67	75	53	66
Brazil	912	65	82	66	68
Chile	1,137	67	77	88	77

Source: Morris David Morris, *Measuring the Condition of the World's Poor. The Physical Quality of Life Index* (New York: Pergamon Press for the Overseas Development Council, 1979), pp. 128–135.

achieve a comparatively high quality of life at levels of per-capita income well below those of the industrialized nations. The correlation between the PQLI and per-capita GNP, however, is quite high, and the largest deviations are caused by obvious cases such as the oil-exporting countries, which have high GNP and low PQLI. Values of the PQLI for selected countries are shown in Table 4–5.

Distribution Weights

A few years ago a study group convened by the World Bank proposed a novel and ingenious way to integrate the study of economic growth and welfare, involving the use of **distribution weights**.[10] These are illustrated in Table 4–6, which compares six countries for which income distribution estimates separated by several years are available. During the periods concerned these countries had average annual GNP growth rates ranging from 4.5 percent for India to 9.3 percent for South Korea. Their initial income distributions varied from quite egalitarian (Korea), through moderately egalitarian (India and Sri Lanka), to very unequal (Brazil, Colombia, and Peru). The distribution of amounts added to total income during the periods studied also differed among the six countries. In Colombia and Sri Lanka inequality declined; in the other countries it rose.

These varying development experiences can be evaluated using three different weighting schemes:

First, conventional national accounting implicitly uses **base-year income share** as its weighting system. In measuring GNP, statisticians do not disaggregate income into different income groups; they simply measure total income for the entire population. But under this aggregate measure, if the top 20 percent of households received half the income in the basic year, their

10. Hollis Chenery et al., *Redistribution with Growth* (London: Oxford University Press, 1974).

TABLE 4-6   Illustration of Distribution Weights

| Country | Period | Income growth | | | Growth rate using: | | | Initial Gini coefficient |
		Upper 20%	Middle 40%	Lowest 40%	Income weights	Population weights	Poverty weights	
South Korea	1964–70	10.6	7.8	9.3	9.3	9.0	9.0	.34
Brazil	1960–70	8.4	4.8	5.2	6.9	5.7	5.4	.56
Colombia	1964–70	5.6	7.3	7.0	6.2	6.8	7.0	.57
Peru	1961–71	4.7	7.5	3.2	5.4	5.2	4.6	.59
Sri Lanka	1963–70	3.1	6.2	8.3	5.0	6.4	7.2	.45
India	1954–64	5.1	3.9	3.9	4.5	4.1	4.0	.40

Source: Hollis Chenery et al., *Redistribution with Growth* (London: Oxford University Press, 1974), p. 42.

income growth gets a 50 percent weighting in figuring out the growth rate of society's income (GNP). By this criterion Korea grew more than twice as fast as India and the other countries fell in between.

Second, **population weights** give each income group a weight equal to its share in total population. This is an egalitarian approach that weights everyone's income growth equally. Under population weighting Korea remains the country with the best performance, but Colombia and Sri Lanka, in which the income distribution improved during the period, begin to look better relative to the others, in which the distribution worsened.

Third, **poverty weights** would go a step further and assign a greater weight to income growth for the poor. Various weights could be used; the ones employed in Table 4–6 imply a moderately pro-poor bias: whereas population weights are 0.2, 0.4, and 0.4 respectively for the three income groups, the poverty weights selected were 0.1, 0.3, and 0.6. In other words income gains for the poorest group are valued at one and one-half times as much as under the population weights scheme, gains for the middle group at three-quarters as much, and gains for the richest group at half as much. Under this weighting scheme, as the table shows, Colombia's and Sri Lanka's performances look even better, while Brazil slips from its original position of second to fourth place.

These weighting schemes evaluate the *change in welfare* during the period. They should be read in conjunction with the initial degree of inequality, which is shown in the right-hand column of Table 4–6. Thus while India and Korea showed increases in inequality during the period, evaluation of their performance should be tempered by the fact that they started from relatively equal initial distributions. Brazil and Peru, by contrast, experienced worsening of distributions that were already highly unequal to begin with.

The flexibility of the distribution-weights approach is appealing, but there are difficulties with it, both in principle and in practice. Who makes the value judgments implicit in the choice of weights? Those economists who have proposed the reweighting schemes are egalitarian-minded, but do their values coincide with those of poor societies and their governments? University of Chicago economist Arnold Harberger has demonstrated that seemingly modest reweighting schemes imply that society is willing to accept a large loss in efficiency in return for some redistribution, and he has gone on to argue that most governments reveal by their actions that they are not in fact so interested in redistribution as such.[11] Harberger believes that governments instead show commitment to the satisfaction of basic human needs for food, education, health services, and so on. Yet not to reweight also implies a value judgment—namely, in favor of the existing distribution of income.

A practical impediment to widespread use of reweighting schemes is the weakness of statistics on the distribution of income. For most developing countries the analyst is fortunate to have one reasonably reliable estimate of the distribution of income. In very few instances are there the two or more comparable estimates required to say how the benefits of economic growth have been distributed. Even in a country like Sri Lanka, a pioneer both in the collection of income-distribution statistics and in the redistribution of income, questions have been raised about whether the improvement of income distribution thought to have occurred between the early 1960s and the early 1970s actually took place.

Universally acceptable measures have not been found and never will be. Development brings about many changes, and any evaluation of its effect on welfare will inevitably depend on how one weights each type of change. Varying degrees of emphasis on growth, inequality, and poverty will lead to varying assessments. A system of distributive weights can express one evaluator's values, but the values of other observers may well diverge. Agreement is possible only in the loose sense that most people would regard successful development (in welfare terms) as encompassing rising per-capita output, reduced poverty, improved health and longevity, and a least no dramatic worsening of inequality.

PATTERNS OF INEQUALITY AND POVERTY

In his 1955 presidential address to the American Economic Association, Simon Kuznets put forward the proposition that the relationship between the level of per-capita GNP and inequality in the distribution of income may take the form of an inverted U. That is, as per-capita income rises, inequality may initially rise, reach a maximum at an intermediate level of income, and then decline as income levels characteristic of an industrial country are reached. Kuznets based this proposition on mere fragments of data available at the time for estimating income distributions in a few rich and poor countries, and on trends in distribution over time in a very few European countries.

Evidence for Kuznets' Inverted U

Kuznets' insight has held up well in later years as much larger bodies of data have been amassed. We now have estimates of income distribution in more than seventy countries, although some of these estimates are of dubious quality. Data published by the World Bank, covering fifty-eight countries for

11. Arnold Harberger, "Basic Needs versus Distributional Weights in Social Cost-Benefit Analysis," *Economic Development and Cultural Change* 32, no. 4 (April 1984), pp. 455–77.

which estimates were made between 1965 and 1982, are summarized in
Table 4–7. Inequality can be measured in this table using any of three measures: the share of total income received by the poorest 40 percent, the share of the top 20 percent, or the Gini concentration ratio. By any of these measures, inequality first rises, then falls, just as Kuznets predicted in 1955. Other studies have obtained similar results.

Most of our evidence on the relationship of inequality to per-capita income comes from this kind of **cross-section data;** that is, from estimates made at approximately the same time for countries at low, middle, and high levels of per-capita income. **Time-series data**—comparable estimates at different times for particular countries—are much rarer. For many countries there is only one good estimate of income distribution (at most!), while even where two or more surveys have been made differences in their design and execution may make it hard to compare results. Accordingly the questions of whether low-income countries will necessarily see a rise in inequality as they move to semideveloped status, and whether they can then expect inequality to decline once more as they achieve a high level of development, remain open.

But if, as seems likely, there is a tendency toward the inverted-U relationship, two important questions arise. What causes this pattern of changing inequality through the development process? And how predetermined is it? That is, how much latitude is there for differences either in the circumstances of particular countries or in the policies they follow to make a different pattern of inequality consistent with economic growth?

A starting point in answering these questions is the observation that per-capita GDP, using Kuznets' hypothesized curvilinear relationship, explains —in statistical terms—only about one-quarter of the intercountry variations in Gini coefficients reflected in the data summarized in Table 4–7. Thus, while "Kuznets' Law" clearly holds in terms of averages, at least in cross-section data, its application to any particular country is rather limited.

TABLE 4–7   **Estimates of Inequality and Poverty in Relation to GNP Per Capita (unweighted averages within groups)**

Country groups	Number of countries included	Percent of income received by: Lowest 40%	Highest 20%	Gini concentration ratio	Mean income of lowest 40% (dollars)	GNP per capita[a] (dollars)
Low-income countries	11	14.2	50.9	.427	97	256
Lower-middle-income countries	16	11.3	53.5	.505	240	867
Upper-middle-income countries	12	14.0	49.1	.428	937	2,623
Industrial market economies	18	18.8	40.2	.331	4,065	8,664
East European nonmarket economies	1	20.5	35.8	.284	671	1,309

Source: Ahluwalia, "Inequality, Poverty and Development," 340–41; World Bank, *Development Report 1985,* 228–29.
[a] In 1975, measured in 1983 dollars.

Exceptional Cases

There are many cases in which individual countries depart substantially from the norms. Sri Lanka, South Korea, and Taiwan all have relatively equal income distributions among developing countries. In Latin America, Argentina and Uruguay have inequality measures far below the normally high levels for the region. Several developed capitalist countries have no more inequality than Yugoslavia, a socialist state. Notable deviations on the other side include a number of African and Latin American countries with unusually high inequality (for example, Kenya, Ivory Coast, Zambia, Peru, Brazil, Mexico, and Venezuela), as well as Malaysia and the Philippines in Asia. Among developed countries, France stands out for its high level of inequality. Statistics for all these countries can be examined by referring back to Table 4–1.

Analysts have tried to increase the percentage of statistically explained variation in the degree of inequality among countries by adding more independent variables to the equation. One result that emerges clearly from this effort is that socialist countries have much less inequality than nonsocialist countries with comparable GNP per capita.[12] Since socialist countries must, for incentive purposes, maintain wage differentials comparable to those existing in nonsocialist countries, their lower inequality must be attributable mainly to the drastic restrictions they maintain on private ownership of land and capital facilities, assets whose ownership is very unequally distributed in nonsocialist countries.

Among the nonsocialist countries, three factors help to explain inequality in both low-income and high-income countries. Relatively high enrollment rates in primary and secondary schools and a higher GNP growth rate appear to be associated with reduced inequality, given the level of GNP per capita, while a higher growth rate of population goes with greater inequality. Together these factors can raise the total explained variation in a statistical cross-section analysis to about 50 percent.[13] This still leaves a lot of room for country-to-country variation, which has not yet been fit into a general explanatory framework.

Other Explanatory Factors

There have been attempts to identify the types of societies (in social and political as well as economic terms) in which inequality is likely to be high or low. One such study, which measured inequality in terms of the share of income received by the lowest 60 percent of the income distribution, found that relatively equal income distributions are typically found in two kinds of countries: very poor nations dominated by small-scale or communal (jointly farmed) agriculture and well-developed nations in which major efforts have

12. It should be stressed that while inequality is low for the socialist countries, absolute income is also relatively low. East Germany, the richest country in this group, had a per-capita income only two-thirds that of its nonsocialist counterpart, West Germany.

13. See Montek S. Ahluwalia, "Income Inequality: Some Dimensions of the Problem," in Hollis Chenery et al., *Redistribution with Growth,* pp. 3–37; and "Inequality, Poverty and Development," *Journal of Development Economics* 3 (1976): 307–42.

been made to improve human resources.[14] This conclusion is consistent with
the Kuznets hypothesis but more suggestive of the factors that may be associated with the inverted-U pattern. The very poor countries may be quite egalitarian, it says, but only if their economies are dominated by small peasant farms and not by large farms or mines. Rich countries can also be egalitarian, but only if their people have been permitted to share in development by upgrading the productivity of the labor resources that they supply to the economy.

By implication, countries with intermediate income levels are likely to have considerable inequality. This same study found the income share of the poorest 60 percent to be smallest of all where well-entrenched foreign or military elites control the most productive economic sectors and receive most of the benefits of development.

There is a school of thought that is pessimistic about prospects that development will better either the absolute or the relative position of the poor.[15] Much of this pessimism stems from study of the South Asian experience. The pessimism does not have strong empirical backing, however, since most studies show that the poor generally do benefit from a rise in GNP, both in terms of absolute income gains and in terms of their share in total income.

Logically speaking, if the income share of the poor rises with growth, their absolute income must rise by definition, since they are getting an increasing share of an increasing total. But what of the situation, apparently common in the early stages of development, in which their share declines?

How Growth Reduces Poverty

The conclusion one reaches will depend on the definition of poverty adopted, but if we define a single worldwide poverty line, it is clear that economic growth is strongly associated with a reduction in poverty. Using the data that lie behind Table 4–7, for example, we can ask ourselves how much of the intercountry variation in the absolute mean income of the poor (defined here as the lowest 40 percent of the distribution) can be explained statistically using per-capita GNP as the sole explanatory variable. The answer turns out to be a high 94 percent. In other words, while there are many reasons why people may be poor in an absolute sense, the most important one is that they live in poor countries. Other studies have reached similar conclusions.[16]

Another indication of the close association between poverty and low national income per capita is the locational pattern of world poverty. Calculations made by the World Bank in 1975 show that over half the world's poor (defined as per-capita income below $75) lived in the low-income countries of South Asia. Overall, 79 percent of the poor lived in countries with per-

14. See Irma Adelman and Cynthia Taft Morris, *Economic Growth and Social Equity in Developing Countries* (Stanford, Calif.: Stanford University Press, 1973).

15. See Adelman and Morris, *Economic Growth,* as well as *Poverty and Landlessness in Rural Asia* (Geneva: International Labour Office, 1977).

16. See, for example, Ahluwalia, "Income Equality," and his "Inequality, Poverty, and Development."

capita GNP of less than $265 in 1975 prices.[17] There are of course absolutely poor people in other regions, such as Latin America and the Middle East, but their numbers are much smaller. Most of these poor people live in rural areas.

Is there any need to qualify the strongly indicated conclusions that poverty is associated with low national per-capita income and tends to be eradicated as per-capita income rises? Only, perhaps, in two respects. First, we have been analyzing absolute poverty using a global poverty line. Relative poverty is far more persistent. There are not many people living on $75 a year in the United States, but there are many who must live on incomes far below a reasonable U.S. standard. Second, some time-series studies for particular countries have shown stagnation or even decline in the incomes of the poor and increases in the number of poor people or both. Many of these findings have been challenged, but they do at least serve to warn us not to assume complacently that economic growth will necessarily eliminate poverty either automatically or rapidly.

The Determinants of Income Distribution

The most ambitious efforts made to study the determinants of income distribution and the effects of various policies consist of comprehensive models of income distribution as it emerges from the overall workings of an economy. In one of the best-known studies, quantitative economists Irma Adelman and Sherman Robinson modeled the South Korean economy.[18] Their computable general equilibrium (CGE) model (see further discussion in Chapter 6) included specifications of price and quantity adjustments in both factor and product markets, and it allowed for substitution possibilities in production and consumption in response to changes in relative prices. A dynamic version of the model projected investment by sector on the basis of profitability, expectations, and government financial policies. The model forecasted that economic growth would continue in Korea, but that most of the gains would go to the urban population and the income distribution would steadily worsen. Experimental runs of the model to simulate the effects of various policy packages showed that most policies would have little effect on income distribution. Some supposedly anti-poverty policies actually proved to yield disproportionate benefits to the rich and the middle-income group. The most promising policies for bettering income distribution were those that improved the internal terms of trade for agricultural producers and those that encouraged rural-urban migration. Foreign trade policies had significant impacts on inequality and poverty, working largely through these two factors.

The global statistics and research that we have been discussing cannot fully reveal the extent or causes of poverty in particular countries. The following four case histories help to round out the picture. If they achieve nothing else, they show that one should be cautious in generalizing about

17. World Bank, *Prospects for Developing Countries, 1978–85* (Washington, D.C.: November 1977), p. 8.

18. Irma Adelman and Sherman Robinson, *Income Distribution Policy in Developing Countries. A Case Study of Korea* (Stanford, Calif.: Stanford University Press, 1978).

development, inequality, and poverty. Much depends on the circumstances of the individual country and the type of development pursued.

South Korea

South Korea has enjoyed a high rate of economic growth, with the evident benefits of poverty alleviation and basic needs satisfaction. The Korean development pattern has been highly equitable, relative to virtually all other developing countries, both because assets, especially land, were distributed relatively equally before rapid growth began, and because Korea pursued a pattern of development that did not greatly concentrate income or wealth. When Korea emerged from Japanese colonial rule at the end of World War II, the many large production units which had been Japanese-owned were either nationalized or broken up and redistributed. Two land reforms subdivided the larger agricultural holdings and virtually eliminated tenancy (in which land is owned by one person but farmed by another, who pays rent for its use). The rapid economic growth which began in the early 1960s emphasized the modernization of small and medium-sized firms. Foreign ownership was held to a minimum. Manufacturing for export boomed, absorbing a larger share of labor-force growth than in almost any other country. The Korean educational system, which accommodated all children at its lower levels and then rigorously selected the few best performers for continuation to its higher levels, supported both equity and growth. All these factors contributed to a rapid decline in poverty. Inequality probably rose slightly as development proceeded, especially in the 1970s, when shortages of skilled labor emerged, but it remained low relative to other third-world countries and comparable to inequality in the most developed western countries. Korea, then, is a clear-cut case of rapid growth with equity.

Brazil

Like Korea, Brazil has grown rapidly, but with consequences for human welfare that are more equivocal. Brazil is a large, naturally rich country that has made impressive strides toward creation of a modern, diversified economy. Some of its industries and modern cities bear comparison with those in the rich countries. Besides this urban boom, Brazil has also had important areas of agricultural progress, such as the development of soybeans as a major export crop alongside coffee and other traditional items. But Brazilian economic growth has been uneven both in time (it has gone through several stop-and-go phases) and space. Whole sections of the country, most notoriously the northeast, have been largely excluded from development. Even the big, modern cities in the south (Rio de Janeiro, São Paulo, Belo-Horizonte) have appalling urban slums, sometimes located side-by-side to luxurious, architecturally impressive, new constructions. Many of the factors that have led to equitable growth in Korea are reversed in Brazil: asset ownership is highly concentrated; there has been no land reform; access to education is uneven and heavily influenced by economic factors; development, in both manufacturing and agriculture, has emphasized large production units; technologies adopted have tended to be capital-intensive. The results are very high inequality and very little progress toward poverty alleviation, despite rapid growth of the economy and some increases in the real incomes of the poor.

Sri Lanka

Sri Lanka, in contrast to Korea and Brazil, grew at average or low rates until a change of government in 1977 led to a radical shift in economic policies. As a result of the country's open democratic system of government and the articulateness of its well-educated electorate, all Sri Lankan governments since independence in 1948 have had to be populist to survive. A system of social benefits that included cheap staple foods, and free schooling and medical services, helped to produce a healthy, literate populace. Inequality was kept relatively low, and despite low income levels, the worst manifestations of poverty (premature deaths, malnutrition, illiteracy) have been remarkably absent from Sri Lankan society. The trouble is that economic growth did not occur fast enough either to provide adequate financing for the welfare system or to give employment to the growing labor force, especially of educated youths seeking white-collar jobs. A foreign-exchange crisis in the early 1960s led to many shortages, slower growth, and cutbacks in social services. Chronic popular dissatisfaction led to repeated changes in government at the polls and an unsuccessful youth revolt in 1971. In 1977 a new right-wing government inaugurated an effort to accelerate growth by emphasizing labor-intensive manufacturing, irrigation, and tourism. Sri Lanka is something of an aberration, which tends to be viewed either favorably or unfavorably by development specialists, depending on their biases. Perhaps what it really demonstrates is the interactions between development and a strongly democratic system of government, the latter hardly a common feature in third-world countries.

India

India, like Brazil, is a big country with areas of dynamism and areas of stagnation. Also like Brazil, it has emphasized inward-looking development to build a self-sufficient, sub-continental economy. Like Sri Lanka, India is a poor country and has not grown very rapidly. Some parts of India, such as Bombay and the Punjab, have in fact grown rapidly, through either industrialization or successful adoption of the Green Revolution in food-grain production. Others, like Bihar state, remain desperately poor. One southern state, Kerala, has a Sri Lanka-like pattern of high basic-needs satisfaction together with low income and growth. Overall inequality measures for India come out rather low because there are so many poor people and only relatively small classes of the comfortable or rich. About 50 percent of the population lives below the officially defined poverty line. Whether the poor have gained or lost from development in India has been hotly debated. The most recent analyses suggest that the proportion of people who are poor has changed little since the 1950s.

THEORIES OF INEQUALITY AND POVERTY

Questions of poverty and inequality and their relationship to economic growth have been emphasized in some periods in the history of economic thought and relegated to the background during other periods. One stage at which they figured prominently was the classical period of economic theorizing, particularly in the work of David Ricardo, who wrote in the early 1800s, when England was a developing country.

Ricardo's Two-Sector Model

We saw in Chapter 3 that Ricardo pioneered the two-sector model of development. His analysis suggested that if England did not abolish the corn laws, which protected grain farmers from foreign competition, and allow imports of food to fuel its industrial revolution, income would be redistributed from capitalists to landlords. (Wages, he assumed, would remain at the subsistence level.) Since Ricardo regarded landlords as spendthrifts and thought that economic growth was financed by the savings of the thrifty capitalist class, he concluded that this redistribution would harm economic growth.

Although his theory was innovative and internally consistent, all Ricardo's predictions about income distribution and economic growth turned out to be wrong. Rent has not taken a growing share of national income in industrializing countries, but in fact has remained a rather small share. The profit share has not been squeezed out. And wages have not been held to the subsistence level but have risen, at least in the later stages of industrial development; the share of wages in national income, if anything, has tended to rise. There are several reasons why actual trends have not matched those predicted in Ricardo's model. One is that England did adopt free trade, as Ricardo wanted. But even if it had not, diminishing returns would probably have been largely offset by technological change, which would have made it possible to grow increasing amounts of food on land of given quantity and quality. Ricardo also overestimated the strength of the Malthusian population mechanism, which he thought would hold wages at the subsistence level.

Marx's View

Karl Marx also believed that capitalist development would create an increasingly unequal distribution of income. Capitalists, he thought, had an incentive to create a "reserve army of the unemployed" whose brooding presence would ensure that the wages of employed laborers stayed at the subsistence level. (Marx hotly rebutted the Malthusian theory that demographic forces created the labor surplus, calling this line of thinking an insult to the working class.) In Marxian thought, the owners of capital dominate both the economy and the "bourgeois state." But as capitalism develops, the rate of profit falls and crises occur, causing firms to fail and industrial concentration to rise. Eventually, in a final apocalyptic crisis, capitalism itself collapses, to be replaced by socialism. Only then, according to Karl Marx, can the lot of the workers improve.

Marx's theory provided no better guide to the future evolution of income distribution than Ricardo's. Like Ricardo, Marx has been influential not because his theory proved to be prophetic but because of the analytical approach that he used.

The Neoclassical Theory

The dominant theory used today to explain income distribution in developing countries was worked out in the late nineteenth and early twentieth centuries. This is the **neoclassical (marginal productivity) theory,** which postulates that all factors of production (now more numerous than three, to take account of quality differences) are in scarce supply, and that their rates of return are set equal to their marginal products in competitive factor markets. This theory, although heavily criticized, has yet to be supplanted in analyses of developed countries.

The Labor-Surplus Model

It was W. Arthur Lewis who first observed that conditions in less developed countries are in some ways more similar to those which prevailed in the industrialized countries before the Industrial Revolution than they are to conditions in those same countries today. The most useful theory to analyze the workings of the early-stage developing economy, therefore, might be one built on classical rather than neoclassical assumptions. It was this insight that led Lewis to his celebrated model of "economic development with unlimited supplies of labor," which utilized the Ricardo-Marx assumption that labor is available in unlimited quantity at a fixed real wage, rather than being a scarce factor of production which has to be bid away from other uses, as in the neoclassical theory. Lewis's surplus-labor model, as pointed out in Chapter 3, was further developed by John Fei, Gustav Ranis, and others. The implications of the surplus-labor model for the importance of agricultural development and the role played by population growth were discussed in the previous chapter. What remains is to bring out the implications of the model for the distribution of income.

The labor-surplus model suggests that inequality will first increase and later diminish as development takes place. In other words its implications are consistent with Kuznets' generalization about what has actually occurred. There are two reasons for expecting the initial rise in inequality to take place. One is that the share of the capitalists (who in the Lewis version of the model could be either private capitalists or governments running state-owned enterprises) rises as the size of the modern, or capitalist, sector increases. The second reason is that inequality in the distribution of labor income also rises during the early period, when increasing but still relatively small numbers of laborers are moving from the subsistence wage level to the capitalist-sector wage level, which Lewis says tends to run about 30 percent higher in real terms.

This tendency toward increasing inequality is finally reversed, as explicitly depicted in the Fei-Ranis extension of the Lewis model (see Chapter 3). When all the surplus labor is finally absorbed into modern-sector employment, labor becomes a scarce factor of production, and further increases in demand require increases in real wages to bid labor away from marginal uses. It is the resulting rise in the general wage level, the model suggests, that brings about the eventual downturn in inequality, as well as the long-awaited abolition of poverty, at least by former standards.

In the Lewis version of the labor-surplus model, inequality is not only a necessary effect of economic growth—it is simultaneously a cause of growth. Inequality—that is, a distribution of income that favors high-income groups —contributes to growth because the high-income groups are the elements of society that save, and saving is essential for increasing productive capacity and thus bringing about output growth. In a famous quotation, Lewis says that "the central problem in the theory of economic development is to understand the process by which a community which was previously saving and investing 4 or 5 percent of its national income converts itself into an economy where voluntary saving is running about 12 to 15 percent of the national income or more."[19] The answer, he argues, lies with the 10 percent of the population which receives 40 percent or more of national income in labor-surplus countries. Growth occurs when they save more, not because their marginal propensity to save increases, but because their aggregate income and share in total income go up. This happens because the profit share in income increases with the growth of the modern sector while the wage share remains constant.

Not only does inequality contribute to growth, but attempts to redistribute income "prematurely" run the risk of stifling economic growth. As in Ricardo's theory, anything that raises urban wages cuts into profits, and hence into savings and economic growth. Some of the factors that could have this effect include a rise in the price of food relative to the price of manufactured goods, and actions, by trade unions or government, to bargain for or legislate increased modern-sector wages. This would gain little anyway because, as noted earlier, in poor countries there is little to redistribute; everyone will benefit in time, the Lewis model suggests, if they wait for the development process to run its course. A temporary increase in inequality is the price that must be paid for these gains.

The implications of the labor-surplus model have been presented at some length because this has been the dominant model for the past twenty years. It is far from universally accepted, however, and is subject to increasing challenge today. Some of the questions that have been raised about the model include the following. Will the capitalists actually save or will they indulge in luxury consumption? If they do save, will they necessarily invest at home or will they seek higher rates of return abroad? How fast will the capitalist

19. W. Arthur Lewis, "Economic Development with Unlimited Supplies of Labor," *The Manchester School* 22 (May 1954): 155.

(modern) sector absorb labor, particularly since it may be using capital-intensive technology imported from the developed countries and inappropriate to the factor endowment of a poor labor-surplus economy? (See Chapter 8 for discussion of this issue.) Finally, can governments in today's developing countries afford to wait for the accumulation process to work and for the benefits of growth eventually to be distributed throughout the society, or do poverty, population growth, and political instability require interventions to redistribute income sooner?

There are probably no firm, categorical answers to these questions. Some capitalists will save and invest their savings locally, while others will consume their high income or invest abroad. What they do probably depends on a complex set of factors relating to the characteristics of the upper-income group in a particular country and to the local investment climate. Nor does making the government the capitalist necessarily solve the problem. Although a few governments have been able to follow the Soviet model of rapid accumulation under a system of state capitalism, many others have proved unable to evolve the combination of discipline and incentives needed for publicly owned enterprises to generate surpluses (see Chapter 21).

STRATEGIES FOR GROWTH WITH EQUITY

Countries in Asia, Africa, and Latin America have demonstrated the difficulties of trying to redistribute before growing. "Socialism" has been a popular watchword in many of these countries, connoting immediate redistribution through direct controls on economic activity, elaborate social service networks, consumer subsidies, reliance on cooperatives, and other populist devices. Especially when undertaken by "soft states," which find it difficult to enforce their own mandates on the populace, these measures have generally failed to achieve their redistributive objectives and have often stifled economic growth. Burma, Ghana and Jamaica are three examples among many. Moreover, even when carried out relatively successfully, they achieve income redistribution only in a rather limited sense. This appears to have been the case, for example, in the Peruvian "national revolution," which redistributed income to the urban working class but left the poorest elements of society (poor peasants, mainly of Indian origin) comparatively untouched. Many similar cases could be cited.

Is there then no alternative to the stern growth-versus-equality trade-off postulated by W. Arthur Lewis? Contemporary development thinking and experience have in fact suggested three alternative models. If Lewis's classical model may be characterized as "grow first, then redistribute," the alternatives could be described as a radical "redistribute first, then grow" model and two reformist models: "redistribution with growth" and "basic human needs."

Redistribute First, then Grow

The **radical model** is epitomized by the experience of the Asian socialist economies, especially the People's Republic of China. Socialist development in these countries has begun with the expropriation of capitalists and land-lords. Their property has then either been subdivided among small-scale pro-ducers, or more often, placed under some system of collective ownership. Confiscation has two kinds of effects on income distribution. The immediate impact is to eliminate the property income of the previous owner and assign this income either to the state or to the new owners of the subdivided prop-erty. This immediate effect can have a substantial impact on income distri-bution if the amount of profit or rent involved is large. In the longer run, however, the second effect of confiscation can be even more important. This effect works through the productivity of the confiscated asset (factory, farm, etc.) under its new ownership and management. If the asset is managed as efficiently, or more efficiently, than under the prior ownership, then the redistributive effect holds up over the long run. If, however, the asset is less productive under the new arrangement, then some of the redistributive effect is dissipated. The old owner has lost his property income but the new owners have not benefited proportionately. The management of a confis-cated asset is thus an important determinant of its redistributive effect.

Countries which pursue a radical pattern of development are not exempted from the need to amass a surplus and reinvest it productively if they wish to grow. Development in the Soviet Union, which followed a basic-industry strategy, involved a continuous effort to hold down consump-tion and squeeze a surplus out of the general population, particularly the peasants. Inequality was limited because most property income accrued to the state, but many of the material benefits of economic growth were denied to the population until the Khrushchev reforms of the 1960s provided the first hint of a possible emerging era of mass consumption.

By contrast, the People's Republic of China has tried to follow a more bal-anced development pattern. By offsetting the emphasis on heavy industry with attention to smaller scale, decentralized, and more labor-intensive pro-duction units—by "walking on two legs," as the Chinese say—and by not stinting on basic human services, China has apparently been able to achieve a more equitable pattern of development, and in a much poorer country, then was achieved by the USSR.

The Chinese Communists contend that their development experience has little to teach other countries that operate under different social systems. It is true that some features of the Chinese approach are probably available only to a strong regime that gained power through a revolution. Yet a modified version of the "redistribute then develop" approach has been used in Taiwan and South Korea, where rural landholdings were redistributed shortly after World War II and development has proceeded rapidly and comparatively equitably.

Redistribution with Growth

The desire to avoid both the extremes of concentrated industrial develop-ment as depicted by the Lewis model and radical restructuring of asset ownership has naturally led to a determined search for a middle way—*redistribution with growth,* as a study sponsored by the World Bank called it. Is there, in other words, a way in which the gains from economic growth can be redistributed so that over time the income distribution gradually improves—or at least does not worsen—as growth proceeds?

The basic idea of redistribution with growth (RWG) is that government policies should influence the pattern of development in such a way that low-income producers (in most countries, located primarily in agriculture and small-scale urban enterprises) will see improved earning opportunities and simultaneously receive the resources necessary to take advantage of them. According to the World Bank study group, seven types of policy instruments could be employed to this end: (1) measures to alter the prices of labor and capital, to encourage the employment of unskilled labor; (2) "dynamic redistribution" of assets by directing investment to areas in which the poor may be owners of assets, such as land or small shops; (3) greater education to improve literacy, skills, and access to the modern economy; (4) more progressive taxation; (5) public provision of consumption goods, such as basic foods, to the poor; (6) intervention in commodity markets to aid poor producers and consumers; and (7) development of new technologies that will help make low-income workers more productive. All these policy possibilities are discussed in other chapters of this book.

The way in which these elements could be combined into an effective national policy package will naturally vary with a country's circumstances. A rural-based, equity-oriented, development strategy is often proposed for large, predominantly rural countries such as India.[20] For these countries, it is argued, the time required for the modern sector to soak up all the surplus labor existing in the traditional sector would be far too long for any reasonable standard of equity to be achieved, or political stability to be maintained. A strategy emphasizing rural development, it is hoped, will bring about a much more equitable pattern of development than could ever be attained through emphasis on urban and industrial growth. (Rural development is discussed in Chapter 18.)

On the other hand, countries in which the modern sector is large relative to the traditional sector face a less severe trade-off. These countries can hope to have an integrated, modern economy in a much shorter period and in the meantime have a much larger surplus available to redistribute to the traditional sector through social services and rural development projects.

The RWG approach has attracted a lot of interest among those who want to see the welfare of the third-world poor improve but wish to avoid violent social revolution. Indeed the reader may note that many of the ideas included in the RWG package are treated sympathetically in this book. Yet one must accept that the changes brought about by such a strategy will occur slowly in most countries. Development is usually a gradual business, and even the changes in equality and poverty that were projected by the World Bank's study group, which was intellectually and emotionally committed to the approach, struck many readers as disappointingly small and gradual.

---

20. For example, see John Mellor, *The New Economics of Growth: A Strategy for India and the Developing World* (Ithaca, N.Y.: Cornell University Press, 1976).

Pessimism about how fast economic development, even if it is poverty-focused, can improve the well-being of the poor in most LDCs is one factor contributing to interest in the **basic human needs** (BHN) approach. Although advocates of RWG and BHN share the same objectives, they differ on the best means of achieving them. Whereas RWG stresses increases in the productivity and purchasing power of the poor, BHN emphasizes the provision of public services, along with entitlements to the poor to make sure they receive the services provided.

The BHN strategy is designed to provide several basic commodities and services to the poor: staple foods, water and sanitation, health care, primary and nonformal education, and housing. The strategy includes two important elements. First, it requires finance to ensure that these basic needs can be provided at costs that the poor can afford. Second, the strategy includes service networks to distribute these services in forms appropriate for consumption by the poor, especially in areas where the poor live.

The possibility of using fiscal policy to ameliorate poverty is discussed in Chapter 12. Redistribution of income through a combination of progressive taxation and public expenditures on social service programs has been an important part of twentieth-century reform movements in western industrial countries. The potential of this form of redistribution for less developed countries has traditionally been downplayed because the public sector is smaller in these countries and thus has less revenue-raising power; because the government pursues multiple objectives in its tax and expenditure policies and thus cannot devote itself wholeheartedly to redistribution; and because of the many difficulties of identifying, designing, and implementing public consumption and investment projects that can affect the incomes of the poor. However, there is a more positive side to the picture. Many LDCs now collect 20 percent or more of the GNP in the form of government revenues. Taxes can be made more progressive in developing countries, even when direct (income) taxes are paid by only a small fraction of the population. Indirect taxes, such as customs duties, excises, turnover taxes, and sales taxes with exemptions, can lend an element of progressivity. Finally, much can be done through the expenditure side of the budget to improve the distribution of benefits from public services. Some of these possibilities will be discussed in Chapters 9 and 10, which deal with education and health.

For BHN programs to redistribute income, services must be offered on a subsidized basis. Otherwise redistribution will not work, either because the poor will spend too much of their meager income on the services offered or because they will be deterred by high user charges and not take advantage of them at all. If the poor do not consume the services offered, the income transfer can be perverse, as is the case with government-run universities in many countries, which admit selectively and charge low fees, thus subsidizing the well-to-do. For the poor to be reached, appropriate forms of service must be emphasized: primary schools instead of universities, village clinics instead of intensive-care units in urban hospitals. Second, the system must be extended to the poor in their villages and urban slums. There must actually be schools and clinics, teachers and primary health workers, and they must work where the poor live. So far most LDC social service networks have not met this challenge, although there are some honorable exceptions.

Much of the appeal of BHN derives from its link to the notion of investment in human capital. Many kinds of education, health, and other social expenditures can improve the quality of human resources. When such expenditures are directed particularly toward the poor, as for instance in primary education or rural community health programs, they become ways to reduce poverty by increasing the productivity of the poor.

KEY POLICY ISSUES

Probably the single most promising way of achieving greater equity during growth under the reformist approach is to give greater emphasis to *employment creation.* By appropriate price incentives and other measures to absorb more labor in relatively productive forms of employment, the inequality generated by the Lewis-type employment shift can be mitigated and the labor surplus can be eliminated in a shorter time. (This subject is discussed in detail in Chapter 8.)

The other touchstone of equitable growth is the relationship between the *prices of rural and urban outputs.* If farm prices are held down to depress urban wages and increase the investible surplus, then the majority of the poor who live in the rural areas and depend mainly on agriculture for a living will suffer. (There are also likely to be food supply problems; see Chapter 18.) Of course, if agricultural prices rise too high, growth will be choked off. But an equity-focused strategy rules out the squeeze-the-farmer approach that has often been attempted in the past and remains in effect in some LDCs today.

Finally, one can ask whether governments of less developed countries will in fact act to take advantage of these opportunities to reduce inequality arising during the course of economic growth. This is an important question of political economy. Marxists argue that governments are controlled by particular social classes and act in the best interests of those classes. Certainly, many third world governments are heavily influenced by civilian or military elites and for this reason are much less prone to egalitarian reform in their actions than in their verbal pronouncements. But political motivations are perhaps more mixed than the Marxists believe. Some governments may be inclined to make limited reforms for essentially conservative reasons: to forestall upheavals or demands for more radical changes. Others may be motivated toward reform by a different kind of political incentive: in countries where ethnic, tribal, or religious distinctions form an important basis for political activity, it may not be the rich but rather a large, less wealthy social group whose interests are primarily reflected in government policy. In such cases—for example, the Malays of Malaysia—ambitious redistributive programs may be launched even by relatively conservative governments.

5

Planning, Markets, and Politics

Virtually all developing countries undertake national planning. This widespread practice was encouraged by a confluence of historical factors. At the end of World War II the Soviet Union emerged as the second world power, using central planning and controls to transform its economy from near-backwardness to near-modernity in just thirty years. India's leaders, whose intellectual roots in British socialism encouraged a commitment to national planning, saw lessons for India in the Russian experience. During the early 1960s India became a model for other newly independent states that also took up national planning. The United States, then the principal aid donor, and the World Bank, which it dominated, encouraged this trend. Both donors had been impressed by the success of the Marshall Plan in reconstructing Europe, which was attributed to the ample provision of capital and cooperative planning by the European countries. The widespread influence of Keynesian economics, which encouraged macroeconomic forecasting and fiscal planning, also stimulated development planning.

PLANS AND MARKETS

To understand the rationale for national planning in a developing country, it is necessary to sort out several concepts that tend to blur in debates about planning: **mixed economy,** in which government interventions are superimposed on a market-based system; **socialist economy,** in which direct controls typically predominate over market forms; and **national planning,** which can be helpful in making either system function well, especially in developing countries.

Mixed Economies

Most countries depend largely upon the market to allocate goods, services, and factors of production. Three arguments favor market allocation over the alternative, direct controls by government of the quantities produced and sold. First, reliance on markets encourages private economic activity, providing scope for pluralistic societies, democratic government, and individual liberties. Second, the market can allocate thousands of different products among consumers, reflecting their preferences, and thousands of productive inputs among producers, tasks that if handled by the state would require enormous governmental responsibility with attendant high costs for decision-making and control. Third, markets are more flexible than governments and better able to adapt to changing conditions, automatically providing incentives for growth, innovation, and structural change that governments either cannot manage or are slow to achieve.

Despite these substantial advantages, there are some circumstances in which markets do not perform well on their own. Economists have identified a number of cases, called **market failures,** where the market system, left to itself, may not operate efficiently. Those in the following list and the corresponding interventions are not the only ones possible, but include the market failures that seem particularly important for developing countries.

1. Growing concentration and **monopoly power,** where one seller gains control of a market, seem to be features of modern economies. In developing countries, economies of scale may be so large relative to market size that monopoly is inevitable in some industries, while **oligopoly** (a market with few firms) is probably the rule in most others outside of agriculture, fishing, handicraft industries, transportation, retail trade, and personal services. Monopolistic firms are able to raise their prices, and consequently their profits, by restricting their output, so that consumers pay more and obtain less than they would in a purely competitive market. In large economies, governments can try to limit the exercise of monopoly pricing by regulating the size of firms and breaking up the largest ones. In all economies, the threat of competing imports could be effective but is seldom used. Price controls are employed more frequently in developing countries. If government cannot prevent monopoly pricing, it can capture some of the benefits from monopolists by taxing the resulting profits at high rates.

2. **External economies** are benefits of a project, such as a hydroelectric dam, that are enjoyed by people not connected with the project, such as the downstream farmer whose production rises because the dam prevents floods. External economies are important benefits in many economic "overhead" investments, such as dams, roads, railroads, and irrigation schemes. Although in principle the beneficiaries could be charged for all external benefits, in practice they cannot be: it may be difficult and costly to control

access to the facilities and difficult even to identify the beneficiaries or the extent to which they benefit. Hence a private investor would not be able to realize revenue from this aspect of the project's output. Because private investors cannot easily charge for externalities and because such projects take large investments with long repayment periods, private investors are unlikely to undertake them. Governments do so instead. Another kind of external economy is central to the balanced growth strategy discussed in Chapter 3. If several industries are started at the same time, the resulting labor force may be large enough to create an internal market for the output of all industries and backward linkages may create adequate markets for producer goods industries. But a single private investor who depended on these newly created markets would not invest without strong assurances that the other investments would take place simultaneously. Government must play a role to ensure that these external benefits can be realized.

3. **External diseconomies** are costs not borne by the firm. The pollution of air and water is a widely recognized problem in the industrial world and increasingly so in the developing countries. Since polluters would bear all the costs of reduced emissions and effluents, but benefit only as average members of the population of the affected area, they have little incentive to control pollution on their own. The same situation arises with **common resources,** such as forests, fisheries, or open grazing land, which can be used by many people who do not own them. Once a certain number of entrants, such as loggers, fishermen, or herders, are exploiting the new resource, new entrants cause the cost of logging, fishing, or grazing to rise per unit output for *all* entrants. Thus the new entrant faces unit costs only slightly greater than the average for all prior entrants. But at some point an extra fisherman means so many fish are caught that few will be spawned for next season. In this case, society as a whole faces a much higher marginal cost, which includes the increased difficulty of catching fish—felt by all fishermen, old and new. In the case of both pollution and common resources, some kind of intervention by government—preferably a tax but frequently control over access—is ordinarily required to force private producers to bear costs closer to the social cost and consequently to reduce pollution or common resource exploitation to levels closer to the social optimum.

4. Market prices may not reflect the changes in economic structure required for development. The most frequently cited example is the **infant industry,** one brand-new to a society, whose productivity increases and whose costs fall over time because managers and workers are "learning by doing." This effect can justify a **protective tariff** (a tax on imports of the industry's good) or **initial subsidy** (where the government bears some start-up costs) to protect an infant industry, but only if the tariff or subsidy is reduced as productivity rises. The infant industry argument has even greater force for the economy as a whole because experience in all industries creates a more skilled and productive labor force, making all activities more attractive for investors. This "infant economy" phenomenon is closely akin to the balanced growth strategy because it also depends on external economies: as trained, experienced workers leave one employer to work for another, the second firm benefits from the training provided by the first. Sector-wide (or even economy-wide) protective tariffs could be justified by this effect,

although a devalued exchange rate combined with offsetting taxes on traditional exports would be a superior intervention, for reasons that will be explored in Part IV.

5. In developed economies consumers "vote" with their dollars for the goods the economy should produce. But in developing economies, remoteness, poverty, and illiteracy exclude large numbers of subsistence farmers and their families from large segments of goods and money markets. With an insignificant share of the dollar votes, these groups have little influence on the types of goods and services offered. Special efforts are required to bring them into the monetary economy. Even for those in the monetary economy there is inadequate information about markets and products, so many consumers remain ignorant about the goods and services being offered, and workers know little about job opportunities.[1] **Institutional underdevelopment** is characteristic and, as explained in Chapter 2, rigidities abound. Perhaps the best example is in banking, which generally remains urban-based and employs standards of service, modeled on Western banking methods, that exclude most of the rural and much of the poor urban population. In some countries retail and wholesale trade is dominated by racial minorities, such as the Indians and Pakistanis in East Africa, the Lebanese in parts of West Africa, and the Chinese in Southeast Asia. Although these entrepreneurially inclined people often do reach out to remote and poor populations, their commercial success engenders suspicion of their prices, practices, and intentions, and governments typically discourage their activities.

With this last point, the discussion shades into questions of national goals and policies. To a considerable extent market economies require intervention not only because of market failures but also because societies impose on them national goals that even well-functioning markets cannot satisfy. Establishing policies that favor poorer majorities over entrepreneurially accomplished minorities is one example. If Malaysian and Indonesian Chinese or Kenyan Indians already dominate the distribution system of those countries, then unguided economic growth is likely to improve their relative position over time. To expand the role of the indigenous majority and allow it to "catch up" requires governmental intervention. More generally, in market economies growth is often led by—and hence favors—people and firms that are already successful, thus concentrating income at least initially, as we saw in the discussion of Kuznets' proposition in Chapter 4. It is only after growth has been rapid for some time that all groups begin to benefit substantially and the income distribution begins to equalize. But the alleviation of poverty, relative and absolute, is often considered too urgent to await the operation of market forces, and intervention is considered necessary. This may be true for other goals as well, such as greater employment creation or reduced dependence on foreign goods, capital, technology, and skills. Even accelerated growth, typically served well by market economies, may require intervention if savings levels are initially low.

1. One group, future generations, is necessarily excluded from current decision-making. Parents and governments act for this group by such means as saving, investing, and educating. Public investment may be influenced by use of a social discount rate, explained in the next chapter, which reflects a desire to improve the welfare of future generations.

These are some of the reasons that governments intervene in market economies. This combination of market allocation and government intervention yields the **mixed economy,** which characterizes all the non-socialist countries. The particular interventions chosen are not always ideal. Worse, they often work against the goals they are supposed to achieve. The most egregious examples—minimum wages that concentrate incomes and reduce employment, interest rate ceilings that reduce and bias investment, tariffs and import controls that intensify dependence on imports, food price controls that discourage farm production—will be explored in later chapters. Nevertheless, because markets are imperfect and governments have political goals that markets must serve, intervention is the rule. Usually interventions work best and avoid undesired side effects if they work through market mechanisms, operating indirectly through prices to alter supply and demand, rather than operating directly through controls. A central role of planning in a mixed economy is to structure these interventions to achieve their aims with minimal incidental costs.

Socialist Economies

Socialism can be defined as government ownership and control of the means of production. Whether a country is socialist or not is a matter of degree. The clear examples are the Communist countries—the Soviet Union, the Eastern European countries, China, North Korea, Vietnam, and Cuba—in which government ownership and control dominate industry and services and strongly influence agriculture. Some Western European countries, such as Sweden and Great Britain, have had socialist governments that nationalized key industries, and many other countries have large state-owned enterprise sectors, but these economies retain the market character of mixed economies. Socialism and the market are not inimical. In fact, Oskar Lange, an influential socialist economist, proposed a system of market socialism under which publicly owned firms would compete in markets at prices set by a central planning authority to represent real costs to society.[2] The ill-fated economic liberalization of Czechoslovakia during the late 1960s and the more successful reforms of Hungary and Yugoslavia all centered on attempts to employ some of Lange's proposals. China's recent economic reforms have introduced private initiative into agriculture and even private ownership into some trade and service activities, with good results, especially in agriculture. (See box, p. 119.)

Nevertheless the dominant characteristic of the Soviet and other communist economies is government control over production. Whereas *in mixed economies the market sets prices* as signals for production and consumption, *in Soviet-type economies central planners control the quantities* produced and consumed. Prices become irrelevant to production and investment decisions. But prices, along with quantity rationing, still regulate demand, because no government is able to give directives to each household about its complete consumption basket. Prices also serve an accounting function,

2. Oskar Lange, "On the Economic Theory of Socialism," in *On the Economic Theory of Socialism,* ed. B. Lippincott, (Minneapolis: University of Minnesota Press, 1938).

determining how much income is transferred from households to government-owned producers (and vice versa, through wage payments), among producers, and from producers to the government.

The leaders who designed the Soviet economic system began from the premise that market forces, whatever their theoretical merits, were in practice hopelessly chaotic, and thus prices determined by the market could not be relied on to guide production. This basic view of the market was reinforced by the pronounced emphasis in the Soviet Union, and later in China, on machinery and steel as leading sectors in their industrialization programs. Since neither economy had much of a steel or machinery industry to begin with, planners were faced with an extreme form of the infant industry problem and with very large external economies, because the main demand for steel was from a machinery sector that did not yet exist. Neither Soviet nor Chinese planners were willing to build a machinery sector first and then wait for the growing demand for steel to accommodate an efficient steel industry. In general the price system is less effective when the change in economic structure being contemplated is rapid and massive. What the Soviet Union desired in the 1930s when it introduced this system, and what China also wanted in the 1950s, was precisely such a rapid and massive restructuring of economies that were fundamentally agricultural into ones that were based on machinery and steel.

The ways in which the Soviet Union and, until the 1980s, China drew up plans are not radically different from the procedures followed in mixed economies described in these chapters. The problems of deciding on goals, the role of bureaucratic politics (described later in this chapter), and even formal planning techniques such as input-output analysis (which will be examined closely in Chapter 6) are as much present in the Soviet Union and China as in mixed economies. What separates a centrally planned economy of the Soviet type from the others is the way in which plans are carried out. Once broad goals and quantitative targets for individual industries have been decided, planners give direct orders to firms on how much to produce. Firms cannot buy the necessary inputs in a market but must apply to government organizations for the delivery of needed items. The firm must pay money for these items, but willingness to pay does not determine whether it gets them. Only if the plan says it should receive a certain amount of steel will that amount actually be delivered.

In reality, the Soviet-type system does not follow the plan quite so rigidly. A variety of devices, both legal and illegal, provide some flexibility. Nevertheless many allocations which in mixed economies are handled by impersonal market forces are decided by government bureaucrats in centrally planned economies. The centrally planned system therefore puts a premium on having large numbers of people trained to manage the complex tasks of deciding which firms ought to get particular inputs. Hundreds and even thousands of different kinds of inputs must be parceled out to tens of thousands of individual enterprises. If the inputs go to the wrong enterprises, those enterprises will have surpluses piling up in their warehouses while other enterprises operate below capacity.

The advantage of this system is that it gives central planners a high degree of control over the economy and with that control, the power to quickly restructure key sectors. The system, however, does not put a high premium on the efficiency with which inputs are used. The problems of inefficiency increase if people with skills adequate to manage such a system are in short supply, as is often the case in developing countries. China had sufficient numbers of such people or was able to train them with Soviet help in the 1950s, but by the late 1970s China began to experiment with greater use of market forces in order to reduce inefficiency.

Few other developing countries have had the administrative and decision-making capacity to control production through central planning. Among the developing nations only North Korea, Vietnam, Cuba, and China have tried. Tanzania, avowedly socialist, has placed the majority of modern industries under public ownership, nationalized much wholesale and retail trade, and attempted to socialize its agriculture. Nevertheless the government has not tried to set output targets and most units, public or private, respond to market-determined prices. Interventions in setting these prices, though substantial, are no greater in Tanzania than in many non-socialist developing countries such as Bolivia, Kenya, and Indonesia. India based its first development plans on Soviet models that emphasized investment in capital goods and other heavy industries and espoused public ownership of these sectors. Yet India's ostensibly socialist economy remains predominately market-based, while South Korea, avowedly capitalist, produces more of its output in public enterprises than does India.

National Planning

It should be evident by now that planning is a tool useful in both mixed and socialist economies. In Soviet-type economies planning is essential because production and investment are controlled centrally and the controllers have to balance supplies and demands themselves. Planning must determine all the basic quantities of an economy for each sector and type of good: consumer demand, government consumption, investment, trade balances, production by commodity and industry, requirements for intermediate goods and raw materials, allocations of labor and finance.

Planning in mixed economies carries less of a burden but still covers a wide range of potential activities. Our discussion of mixed economies suggested that a set of market interventions may be needed either to correct for market failures or to induce markets to achieve social and political ends that government imposes on them. Such interventions can be numerous, conflicting, and counterproductive unless they are carefully planned with specific goals and priorities in mind. When government invests directly, as in infrastructure and public enterprises, it needs to select only the most productive projects, because budgetary constraints will limit these investments. Government is also responsible for the macroeconomic guidance of the mixed economy. To reach their targets for economic growth, redistribution of income, and stabilization of the economy, governments attempt to manipulate the tools at their disposal: taxation and public spending, control of the money supply and interest rates, management of the foreign exchange regime. To make these tools work, governments require macroeconomic perspectives of the economy, projections of its future course, and predictions of how alternative policy packages might influence that course.

THE PLANNING PROCESS

Development planning is embedded in the politics and bureaucracy of a country. This section describes how political leaders and government officials affect development plans, then analyzes the process of creating plans. After discussing the impact of decentralization and participation, the section concludes with a description of a national plan.

The Politics of Planning

A rudimentary description of the planning process would include political leaders who set the goals and agree to a final plan of action for achieving them; planners—economists and other technicians—who translate the goals into proposed actions; and technicians, such as engineers and agricultural extension officers, who carry out these actions and thus implement the plan.

But this simple description masks many important qualifications. Who, for instance, are the political leaders, how are they chosen, and for whom do they speak? In democracies like the United States, India, Kenya, and Colombia, the voters select their leaders, presumably choosing among candidates whose views on national goals are known. But election campaigns seldom elicit consistent sets of priorities in the detail needed for national planning, and so provide only the roughest of guidelines for elected leaders. More crucially, in pluralistic societies political leaders are influenced by various special interest groups, such as large farmers, unions, manufacturers, doctors, teachers, and the military. Political leaders' views on national goals must bend to accommodate such constituencies, whether before or after an election, so that development priorities will be influenced at least as much by entrenched interest groups as by electoral majorities.

Authoritarian governments such as the Soviet Union, China, South Korea, Chile, and Zaire, may appear better able to establish goals based on ideology, national aspirations, or the interests of constituencies that propel them to power. But even governments willing to use repression face limits to their freedom of action. Few dictators can defy public opinion indefinitely: in the past twenty-five years popular unrest has either overthrown authoritarian leaders or caused the military to give up power in countries as diverse as Poland, the Philippines, Peru, Argentina, South Korea, Nigeria, and Ghana. Special interest groups, especially those with economic or military power, can also influence the actions of authoritarian regimes, either indirectly by swaying public opinion or directly by threatening hostile actions such as strikes or coups.

The planners, who interpret the goals and design plans to achieve them, are not simply technicians. They also participate in the political system. Indeed high-level planners owe their success as much to their political acumen as to their technical skills, and they have economic concerns as intense as any interest group. Planners, though removed from the political arena, may still be influenced by their reading of the needs and entreaties of particular constituencies, such as small farmers, factory owners, or civil servants, whether out of conviction or self-interest. And the same is true of the technicians who implement plans; their power over the realization of national goals is at least as great as that of the political leaders or planners.

The picture becomes more complex once the several layers of government are introduced: central, regional, and local administration; different departments or ministries within each layer; and semi-autonomous agencies with a variety of missions. Each of these separate bureaucracies may have its own point of view on development issues, yet national plans have somehow to reconcile diverse views if they are to guide the many organs of government. Harvard-based political scientist Graham Allison uses the term *bureaucratic politics* to describe the complexity of reaching binding decisions in this environment.[3]

The problem of bureaucratic politics is immediately apparent if we look beyond the central planning unit that provides the macroeconomic framework and has the final word on projects to be included in the plan. In a good planning system the central planners will engage the planning units of sectoral ministries in preparing plans. But the viewpoints of a central planner do not generally coincide with those of sectoral planners in agriculture, industry, education, and other fields. Each has a different technical perspective; each works for a different political boss and within a different bureaucracy; each faces the judgment of a different public or interest group; and each tends to identify its own view with the national interest. Conflict between these units on the shape of the plan is likely. Then consider their respective ministers, politicians who are particularly sensitive to their own constituencies. Different segments of the public, pressure groups, other politicians, their own bureaucrats, local constituencies, or even family groups may exert varying influences on ministers. Short-term considerations tend to dominate long-term ones and economic rationality and efficiency are not paramount.[4]

The plan that emerges from this mélange of public opinion, special interest groups, political leaders, planners, implementers, and competing bureaucracies is often one of compromise, and even then some key party may not support it. The complexities of the planning process need to be borne in mind in the balance of this and the next chapter. The exposition may at times seem to imply the idealized existence of a philosopher-king who expresses national aspirations and of skillful technicians who can manipulate policy instruments to implement such aspirations if they understand the economy well enough. But this is only a device necessary to explain certain points and the reader should not forget that the planning process is deeply embedded in an intricate political, economic, social, and bureau-

3. Graham T. Allison, *The Essence of Decision: Explaining the Cuban Missile Crisis* (Boston: Little, Brown, 1971).
4. David K. Leonard, "The Political Realities of African Management," (Binghampton, N.Y.: Institute for Development Anthropology, September 1985), explores these pressures and the nature of decisionmaking in an African context.

cratic system that makes it function very differently from the ideal. Later chapters will elaborate on the interactions of economic policy and pressure-group politics in specific contexts, such as trade, taxation, and investment. The same forces that thwart reforms in these areas are also likely to influence planning and implementation.

Planning as Process

The planning process can be divided into four steps. In the first step, political leaders identify *goals,* which are translated into quantitative targets for growth, employment creation, income distribution, poverty alleviation, and so forth. Political leaders must also establish goal *priorities* to guide planners in the likely case that some goals conflict. The identification and prioritizing of goals results in a **welfare function,** which provides planners with a measure of the extent to which their plans will satisfy national goals. The measure can be expressed mathematically as an arbitrarily weighted sum of specific goal targets as described in Chapter 6. This formulation would suggest more precision than is possible in measuring goal achievement; in any case, it is rarely employed. It is more common to specify a target increase in one or more of the goals, such as a 6 percent annual increase in GNP and a 4 percent increase in employment, and then to instruct planners to develop programs that achieve these targets. A third alternative would be a welfare function that simply ranks goals, telling planners to consider, for example, both growth and employment, but to give higher priority to employment.

At this point in the idealized process the planner takes over. The second step is to measure the availabilities of scarce resources during the plan period: savings, foreign capital, government revenues, export earnings, skilled workers, and so forth. These, together with administrative and organizational limitations, are the **constraints** that will limit the economy's ability to achieve its targets. Third, most of the planning effort goes into identifying the various **means** *(activities* or *instruments)* that might be employed to achieve national goals. These include investment projects, such as building roads, irrigation networks, factories, and health centers, to be included in the national plan; policies or price incentives, such as changes in the exchange rate or interest rates, wage targets, tax reforms, or subsidies, that may induce private firms and individuals to promote national development goals; and institutional changes, such as the establishment of development banks or the reorganization of agricultural services, which may remove obstacles to change and support other development activities.

Finally, the planner undertakes the mechanical process of selecting from among the possible activities those that will do most to achieve national goals (the welfare function) without violating any of the resource or organizational constraints. The result of this process is a **development plan** that lays out the activities to be undertaken over the next several years (usually five). The process of selecting activities can be done by formal models, as described in the next chapter, but it is usually done informally, by trial and error.

This traditional planning sequence works only if political leaders specify national goals and priorities fairly clearly for the planners. Unfortunately, political leaders are not always willing to do so. Most leaders prefer grand but ambiguous statements of goals, leaving room for inevitable maneuver. Whereas planners think in terms of several years, political considerations dictate much shorter horizons. In any case leaders cannot rationally specify priorities in the abstract without first having at least an approximate notion of the *trade-offs* among goals: for example, how much national growth (if any) would be sacrificed in order to increase employment in a remote region?

A change in sequence can help circumvent this impasse. Planners can start by assuming alternative sets of goals and priorities, then preparing alternative plans (sets of activities), each designed to perform best under a different set of priorities. This provides the political decision-maker with a measure of the trade-offs among different goals. It also reduces the choice among competing goals to a set of particular investments and policies, which is easier to grasp than the more abstract concept of goal fulfillment.[5]

Perhaps, after all, it is the *process* of planning that is important, rather than the resulting plan. Recognizing that politicians inevitably have compelling concerns outside economics, the planners can be most constructive by trying to insert economic considerations more firmly into political decision-making, quantifying the elements that can be measured by economists, and identifying those elements that are not quantifiable. This is partly a matter of educating political leaders about economics in general and their own economies in particular. By presenting and explaining the trade-offs involved in choices between alternative projects or strategies, the planner can help the politician trace through the economic implications of planning decisions and highlight both the constraints and opportunities provided by the economic system. Over time, the process of educating politicians through planning may lead to more informed political decisions and consequently to improved economic performance, which is in any case the ultimate goal of development planning.[6]

Decentralization and Participation

In the 1950s and early 1960s planning for the mixed economies of developing countries was focused on the macroeconomics of growth and on broad strategic issues: feasible growth rates, savings targets, strategies for industrialization, and so forth. Consequently efforts were concentrated on establishing national planning agencies that could take a broad view of economic activity and command the respect of sectoral ministries and provincial governments. The precise design has varied, depending on each government's traditions and its seriousness about national planning. Today these agencies include planning commissions reporting to a prime minister or president, separate ministries, and divisions of the finance ministry. To help planning agencies

---

5. Michael Roemer, "Planning by Revealed Preference," *World Development* 4, no. 9 (1976): 775–83, explains why this planning sequence may be both necessary and desirable.
6. Tony Killick offers a perceptive view of the economic planner's role in politically motivated decision-making in "The Possibilities of Development Planning," *Oxford Economic Papers* 28, no. 2 (1976): 161–84.

become effective policy coordinators, governments have assigned them some form of fiscal control. All planning agencies write a development plan that includes a long-term, usually five-year, budget for government investment. However, the power of the purse lies in annual development budgets, which allocate government savings and foreign aid to investment projects. A planning agency that shares this power with the finance ministry is usually better able to enforce its views on other ministries and local governments. Central planning agencies have professional staffs, most often trained in economics, that are concerned with macroeconomic analysis, project planning, and annual budgeting.

As the planning systems evolved, it became apparent that planning could not be confined to one central agency. Sectoral ministries, such as agriculture, industry, transportation, and health, became responsible for proposing and implementing investment projects in their areas. Regional and local governments have acquired varying degrees of responsibility for smaller, local projects and some services because they have the depth of knowledge necessary for sound planning and usually a greater awareness of local needs. They are also responsible for implementing development programs, for which their commitment is essential. In order to tap their knowledge and gain their commitment, many governments have assigned relevant planning tasks to ministries and local governments.

These reasons to *decentralize* planning have been reinforced by development strategies that emphasize rural projects, poverty alleviation, and small-scale industry. Programs with these aims require extensive administrative coverage, such as widespread extension services or marketing arrangements, and consequently involve many national agencies and local govenments. Central coordination becomes more difficult as the number of agencies increases, and some planning must be done at intermediate levels before the national planning agency can incorporate all relevant information into a comprehensive form and thus coordinate the national plan.

A further argument for decentralization has come from a growing acceptance of the principle that *participation* is an essential ingredient to development. One kind of participation is the sharing of the economic benefits of development by a broad spectrum of people at all levels of society. Rapid growth of employment in all sectors and increased productivity on small farms are two essential ingredients of a participative strategy. But proponents usually go beyond economics and suggest that people ought to have a hand in guiding their own destinies by participating in the planning and design of projects that affect them. For example, the route of a new farm-to-market road ought to be decided in consultation with the villagers and farmers who are affected by the road. Participation is valued for the intrinsic satisfaction it gives to all participants and also because it may promote democratic government at the local level, loosen the grip of local and national elites, and infuse project planning with the practical realities of local attitudes and conditions. Participation can also be viewed as an attempt to enfranchise the economically and politically weak, to give them a chance to influence planning in ways that under centralized planning are possible only for entrenched interest groups.

What emerges from this mélange of national, sectoral, regional, local, and popular planning? Do all the requirements of national coordination, ministry responsibility, local government involvement, and popular participation leave any room for a feasible, let alone an ideal, planning system? In practice there have been a variety of accommodations, with periodic shifts in emphasis and in bureaucratic power. Nevertheless, some general principles can be advanced to cope with the competing demands on planning.

Central planning agencies in mixed economies ought, at a minimum, to provide four functions. First, decisions on national goals need to be drawn from the political process and translated into quantified targets where possible. Next, central planners are responsible for all macroeconomic, long-term balancing of the resource constraints on development. Whatever the details of the plan, they must fit within a consistent macroeconomic framework in which domestic and foreign saving will finance investment, export receipts and foreign capital will cover imports, demands for skilled labor can be met, and so on. Third, and really a part of the resource constraints problem, central planners need to indicate the budget constraints within which each decentralized planning agency must work. To ensure that decentralized planners come to grips with matters of priority, rather than leave this to the central unit, they must be forced to fit their proposals within a realistic investment budget. Fourth, the central planners need to provide standards for project design and selection, so that decentralized planners can identify the activities to be included in the plan. These start with a translation of national strategies and priorities into guidelines for selecting projects, and include a set of rules and national prices for conducting cost-benefit analysis to aid project selection, as described in the next chapter.

Within this framework set by central planning, the sectoral ministries, regional governments, and local authorities would, ideally, carry out a similar set of functions at their respective levels. Using project design and appraisal guidelines provided by national authorities, the sectoral and regional planners identify potential projects, design them, evaluate them as contributors to national goals, and, if they pass the test, propose them to central planning. The investment budget constraint set by central planning is then used as a test of priorities. There is ample scope for decentralized planners to exercise judgment about their areas of expertise within the constraints set by central planning and even to develop a case for increased allocations if enough good projects can be prepared.

In a model system, participative planning would follow the same pattern at the local level. Local planners suggest priority areas for development projects and place budgetary constraints on the projects that could be considered for each locality. In addition, to a greater degree than is true at higher levels of planning, local and ministerial technicians should be available to consult with popular representatives or the people themselves, offering guidance on technical and economic matters, answering questions, and posing alternatives. The essence of planning at this level is the same as elsewhere: those involved should be able to make their own choices, but they must choose within a realistic set of constraints and with knowledge of the costs and benefits of alternative choices.

The end result of the planning process discussed here is a national (or regional) development plan, a document containing a blueprint for the economy over the next several years. Although development planners are guided by economic analysis and may employ models of the types described in the next chapter, plans are not solely economic documents. They are political statements, buttressed by economic descriptions and projections. What is found in a typical development plan?

The best way to find out, of course, is to read one. Development plans are now written, generally every five years, by most of the hundred-plus developing countries, and they have found their way into libraries all over the world that specialize in economics, politics, and area studies. A reader sampling these will find a common, though not rigid, pattern. Opening statements by political leaders are followed by an introduction that establishes the national goals which the plan is to serve. Later in the first chapters, some—probably ambitious—targets will be announced for national income, investment, exports, poverty alleviation, education, health, and employment.

National Goals as Presented in Two Development Plans

Kenya

Improvements of the well-being of the people remain our dominant aim. The plan focuses sharper attention on measures to deal with the alleviation of poverty through emphasis on continued growth, raising household incomes by creating more income-earning opportunities, increasing the output and quality of services provided by Government, and improving income distribution throughout the nation. . . .

The target set for overall annual growth of the economy is 6.3 percent [per year]. . . . Considering the constraints that we face, it is an ambitious goal. The most severe constraints will be our balance of payments. . . . Two other constraints . . . are the gaps between Government revenue and expenditure, and the gap between the savings that are available within the country and the amount of investment required to meet the goals we have set. . . .

[I]n agriculture, development of arid and semi-arid areas is accorded a high priority . . . There will also be an emphasis on the promotion of agriculture exports. . . . In manufacturing, our emphasis will shift from producing goods for our domestic use to the more difficult challenge of increasing our exports in highly competitive world markets. . . . The dispersal of industrial activity throughout the country is another important objective. . . .

For the private sector [increased efficiency] entails the promotion of competition and reduction of restrictions . . . For the public sector, emphasis has been placed on making marketing institutions, local authorities and operating ministries more efficient.

—Republic of Kenya, *Development Plan, 1979–1983*

[T]he Repelita II [Second Plan] goals are: first, to raise the nation's living standard and prosperity, and, second, to lay a firm foundation for the next development stage. . . . Enhancing development means a faster increase in production of goods and services. Production increases must run parallel to and be balanced with equal production dispersion and expansion of employment opportunities, as well as equitable redistribution of the benefits.

In order to achieve [these goals], production in agriculture must increase by around 4.6 percent per year, in industry by around 13.0 percent, in mining by around 10.1 percent . . . With a population growth rate around 2.3 percent per year, income per capita will increase by around 5.0 percent. . .

Constant efforts will be directed toward mobilizing forces in the interest of national development by supporting self-reliance in stimulating the initiative and active participation of the entire nation. . . . It is estimated that local savings will increase from 11.6 to 17.8 percent [of national income] . . . [and] that only around 16 percent of development expenditure will be derived from foreign aid [by the end of the plan]. Gross exports will increase by 23.9 percent per year.

—Republic of Indonesia, *The Second Five-Year Development Plan, 1974–75 to 1978–79* (translated from Indonesian)

The early chapters of a plan will review the economy and the progress in achieving the targets of the previous plan, although this may be put in a separate document. Most plans have been based upon some macroeconomic analysis of the constraints on achieving economic goals and often the rough outlines will be presented: target growth requires so much investment and so much saving, and implies import levels that suggest so much export growth and foreign aid; manpower planning shows shortages in the following kinds of skills, which will be imported; and so forth. In many cases it may appear that constraints can be satisfied when in fact they cannot be. The resource needs have been dictated by infeasible targets, but it requires further calculations or a close knowledge of the economy to discover that the resources are not there. This is not necessarily bad. Plans reach a domestic political audience and leaders want to appear to be offering measurable progress. Ambitious goals may even spur some participants to greater effort, although this incentive can evaporate if the gap between targets and achievement remains large. Plans have also been negotiating documents, particularly during the 1960s, used to support requests for aid from foreign governments, the World Bank, and other aid donors.

Incentives to private investors generally take the forms of tax relief and subsidy schemes. The relative price structure of the economy and its implied incentives are taken as given. To induce private investors to act in ways consistent with national priorities, government may offer tax holidays, accelerated depreciation, export subsidies, and other incentives. Frequently these are catalogued in the plan. Sometimes the scope for private investment is specified for each industry, but not often.

Sectoral chapters provide the bulk of most plans. These cover agriculture, fishing, forestry, mining, manufacturing, power, water supplies, financial institutions, health, education, and other areas. Each may begin with general descriptions of the sector and changes in the past five years, perhaps followed by some statements of priorities and policies. Then comes the meat of the plan: public-sector investment projects are described, sometimes at length. These are the "shopping lists" of projects the government would like to undertake. Priorities may be implied (though seldom stated), but it is certain that far more is listed than will be implemented. Some of these projects are probably quite far along in their design and financing by the time the plan is published. Some projects have probably been appraised and may have been submitted to an aid donor for consideration. Most others—at various stages of appraisal, design, or imagination—will only be sketched in the plan. A large fraction of these will remain paper projects.

One other section receives considerable attention: the government's long-run **development budget.** This surfaces in various places depending on the plan, but is essentially an amalgam of those development projects, probably introduced in the sectoral chapters, that are included in the budget for the next five years. Some indication of financing prospects may be included here or in the chapter(s) on macroeconomic constraints. The development budget is the battleground for financial allocations and implementation. Regardless of what the sectoral project lists show, the crucial task for ministry, regional, or public enterprise planners is to get their projects inserted into the development budget.

The **annual government budget,** though related to the development plan, is a separate document that involves a different process from development planning. The annual budget is under the control of a ministry of finance (often called the treasury). It is typically separated into two parts: the **current** or **operating budget** and the annual **capital** or **development budget.** The latter includes government investments and derives from the development plan's long-run budget. In the early years of a development plan, the annual capital and long-run development budgets may look quite similar. But as time passes the economic situation most often deviates from the projections in the development plan and the annual capital budget becomes increasingly divorced from the long-range development plan. The current budget contains expenses, such as the salaries of civil servants, teachers, and the military, and interest paid on the national debt, that recur each year. These items are counted as government consumption in the national accounts. The operating budget also includes transfers, such as subsidies and social security payments, that are not included in the national accounts. Development expenditures frequently have implications for future operating budgets. For example, a program to invest in rural health centers or additional primary schools implies increased wages to health workers and teachers in the future.

IMPLEMENTATION

As blueprints for development, long-range plans have not worked very well. Although a few countries have had considerable success in carrying out their

plans and others have done well over the course of a plan period or two, by
and large the record is poor. Few countries fulfill their macroeconomic goals or implement many of their projects over most plan periods. This should not be surprising, nor should it deter countries from continuing to plan. Planning is not a blueprint for detailed development. It has other functions, as we have seen: it stimulates a dialogue between politicians and planners; serves as a domestic political statement and in a few countries as a vehicle for public discussion; and can be an international aid-negotiating tool.

Still, the shortcomings of plans cannot be written off that easily. Even admitting the need for political statements and allowing for the inherent benefits of a plan dialogue, it probably remains true that plans do not fulfill the expectations of politicians, planners, the populace, or aid donors. What has gone wrong and what can be done to make planning more meaningful?

Economic Forecasting

Imperfections in economic forecasting and in planning models—both discussed in Chapter 6—create one set of problems. Regardless of the perfection of the model, no country's future can be forecast with great accuracy for as long as five years ahead. This point need not be elaborated for anyone who has been reading a newspaper during the 1970s and 1980s, when commodity price swings, OPEC oil pricing, abrupt shifts in government policies, and persistent inflation have wrecked most economists' forecasts. Add to these worldwide phenomena political crises and natural disasters—floods, drought, earthquakes, extreme temperatures—and the limitations of forecasting are clear. This is equally true for developed and developing countries, except that the latter generally are not so well insulated from such shocks and suffer more intensely from them. Changing conditions require that multiyear plans be supplemented by annual budgets, periodic reviews, and in extreme cases, early revision. In Soviet-type economies where enterprises must follow plan directives because of the absence of market influences, the key plan is not the widely advertised five-year plan but the annual plan, and even the annual plan must frequently be revised during the course of the year.

Nor are the forecasting models very good. One characteristic of underdevelopment is poor data. Although efforts over the past three decades have improved available data enormously, much remains to be done and important indicators are simply not measured in many of the poorer countries. The models that are in general use have severe limitations, as discussed in Chapter 6. As predictors of future outcomes based on past data, these models depend critically on continuity and some kind of equilibrium. Yet discontinuity and disequilibrium are the essence of developing economies. It is risky, for example, to depend on econometric estimates of a savings supply function in countries where interest rates have been controlled and kept at low levels; or an import function in countries where the level of imports is determined each year by administrative controls over import licenses. Improvements are being made in these models, but it takes time to adopt newer models for general use in planning and forecasting.

With very few exceptions (e.g., Singapore, South Korea, and China) developing countries must count administrative and organizational capacity among the constraints on development. Their administrative systems lack **absorptive capacity:** they cannot utilize all the resources that could be made available. For the dozens of countries that became independent after World War II, local capacity to govern was typically limited by the policies of the departing colonial powers and the new government was barely able to maintain the services already offered. Independence brought enhanced expectations that growth could be accelerated, implying expansion of all sectors, especially government. If investment was to be expanded, government had to increase its project formulation and implementation, activities that use managers and administrators intensively, putting an added burden on perhaps the scarcest resource for many of the developing countries.

As all governments expanded their traditional activities to spur development, many governments moved into areas previously left to the private sector. The spread of public enterprise into all phases of the economy is documented in Chapter 21. This expansion further drained government's managerial capacity, because the civil service had to provide enterprise managers and technicians as well as informed administrators to supervise the new public corporations. In the fully socialized economy based on the Soviet model, the need for informed administrators for supervisory and managerial roles is even greater because so few decisions are governed by market forces.

The suspicions about private enterprise that led many governments to nationalize some industries also led them to intervene in the market, through import controls, investment licensing, and regulation of wages, interest rates, and commodity prices. These and other interventions require large bureaucracies to administer the myriad of regulations that inevitably mushroom under such regimes. Government regulations prevent otherwise competitive markets from squeezing profits to the minimum level necessary for continued participation by firms and individuals. The higher-than-necessary profits created by regulations are called **rents.** Import restrictions, for example, reduce the supply of imported commodities and raise their prices on domestic markets. But importers pay no more to foreign suppliers because of the restrictions. The importer who can obtain a license from the authorities can earn large profits, so the license itself has value. To obtain licenses and earn these rents, potential importers go to great lengths, including bribery of officials. Similarly, price controls over food grains and other commodities cause producers to limit the supplies available in official markets. Instead, they divert their sales to illegal **parallel** or **black markets** in which deprived consumers are willing to pay higher prices. Competition for import licenses diverts importers' time from productive activities and raises the share of rents spent on bribes. In parallel markets, higher operating costs, including the costs of avoiding detection and prosecution, will also squeeze profits. Such *rent-seeking* behavior wastes scarce resources and reduces potential growth.[7] This waste can be reduced by phasing out controls and

---

7. Anne O. Krueger, "The Political Economy of Rent-Seeking," *American Economic Review* 64, no. 3 (1974): 291–303. Robert H. Bates argues that in some African countries price-

permitting the market to regulate through prices, something it does well.

Recent trends in development have intensified the need for trained administrators and technicians. Strategies that emphasize labor-intensive development through small farms and industries, poverty relief through basic needs provided by government, and participative planning, require an administrative structure that reaches more widely and deeply into the villages and countryside than in the past. These strategies are appealing because they try to reach the most deprived members of society. But because such programs draw heavily upon one of society's scarcest resources, it may be difficult to implement them effectively or efficiently.

It is not surprising then that even with a will to implement all of the well-designed projects in a development plan, the civil service often has been unable to complete the task. In the long run the solution lies in recruiting, and training civil servants with appropriate skills, providing them with material and psychic incentives, and adopting strategies that depend less on direct governmental involvement. However, education, even in the long run, is no panacea, as Chapter 9 makes clear. It is not always obvious just what the appropriate skills are, how to instill them in students, how to ensure that those students end up in suitable government jobs, and how to motivate them to serve the interests of the people government is trying to help.

Bureaucratic Politics—Once More

Even if governments had the capacity to implement, would they have the collective will? The concept of bureaucratic politics was introduced earlier in this chapter when we described the way competing bureaucracies force compromises in national plans. Even if plans reflect a strong consensus of interested parties, and especially if they do not, the path toward implementation is hazardous. Implementers are different people from planners. In a ministry of agriculture, for example, the planning unit that works with the central planners on agricultural projects then hands these over to operating divisions—crops or livestock, for example—for implementation. If these programs are innovative, if they shift allocations from one crop or region to another, if they require any kind of change, they are likely to encounter some resistance, both from office heads and field personnel. Officials may resent change because it is threatening to their established way of operating; they may (and likely do) feel pressure from a different constituency, such as local farmers (probably large ones) and traders; and they may have a more realistic view of what can be accomplished. The latter emphasizes the importance of incorporating the views of operating personnel in planning, but this is not easy to arrange for a large ministry and seldom is done effectively. Whatever the locus or causes of resistance, it can obviously endanger any project in the hands of the implementers.

Complexity increases and implementation prospects become dimmer when a project cuts across several agencies. A multipurpose dam, requiring the cooperation of ministries of public works, water, power, and agriculture,

---

distorting interventions are used as a means of exerting government control, especially over small farmers; see *Markets and States in Tropical Africa* (Berkeley: University of California Press, 1981).

involves many politicians, planners, and implementers with potentially con-flicting interests. The motives may be petty—a resentment of change that reduces one's control; or large—a genuine belief that, for example, hydro-electric power operations are reducing the potential for needed irrigation. Whatever the case, so long as there are implementers in the long chain of operations who resist the project, it can fail. Obviously, this is not inevitable, because some very complex projects have been completed successfully. But the danger is there and much of the inability to implement can be traced to these conflicts.[8]

Examples can be multiplied at length, but the addition of two more inter-est groups should illustrate sufficiently. Each of the governmental actors is sensitive to some outside group, such as large farmers, a particular local gov-ernment, labor unions, manufacturing trade associations, or influential friends. When the interests of these groups are threatened, they can try to act openly by opposing features of the plan they do not like, or they can work against implementation by convincing those in the chain of operation to work against the project. The methods are sometimes obvious and some-times subtle, as numerous and various as all the ways that well-placed people have for influencing the actions governments take. Even the potential bene-ficiaries themselves may resist change, either because they do not fully understand the new program or because they have other concerns that would be better served by different policies.

Finally, aid donors enter the picture. They will try to ensure that needed resources are made available for any project that they are financing. In a world of scarcity, especially scarce administrative capacity, this often means that some other project goes without the needed resources and may be delayed or may fail. Donors' priorities thus can have considerable influence over which projects are implemented.

There is no easy solution to these problems; they are inherent in govern-ment. Participative, consultative planning can help to alleviate some of the dangers. Plans should be responsive to the views of those who must imple-ment them. However, since change is the nature of development and some projects are necessarily radical, it is inevitable that implementation will meet resistance on many fronts. Drastic measures may be necessary to make these programs succeed, and continuing effective political commitment is essen-tial. Because it is, and because such commitment can be costly to a govern-ment, planners cannot lightly suggest large-scale, radical projects nor try to impose many of them at once.

THE RESURGENCE OF THE MARKET

This chapter began by describing the historical influences that promoted national planning and government intervention, especially in developing

---

8. A systematic view of these implementational difficulties is presented by Donald Warwick, "Integrating Planning and Implementation: A Transactional Approach," in *Planning Educa-tion for Development,* ed. R. Davis, vol. 1 (Cambridge, Mass.: Center for Studies in Education and Development, Harvard University, 1980).

economies. That tide has ebbed in the past decade. Most developing coun-

tries still plan, and Japan's state-guided capitalism has given planning new respectability even in western industrial countries. But governments are increasingly turning back to the market as a mechanism to regulate the economy and propel development.

What accounts for the resurgence of market-oriented approaches to development? One factor is the difficulty of making and implementing comprehensive national plans, for the many reasons cited in this chapter. These failures became especially evident during the 1970s, when the international economic environment changed so drastically and rapid adjustment became imperative in every country. The structural changes needed to reduce consumption of petroleum products, for example, were accomplished best where oil prices were allowed to rise and market forces induced users to conserve energy. Moreover, the cumulative demands of planning and the resulting interventions on governments' limited managerial capacity began to affect economic performance in many developing countries, some of which started to see the private sector as an increasingly attractive partner in development. And the examples of South Korea, Taiwan, Singapore, and Brazil, all of which sustained rapid growth for close to two decades with market-oriented economies, convinced many that the market was worth another look.

Both the International Monetary Fund (IMF) and the World Bank encouraged this trend by putting large sums of money behind programs to liberalize developing economies. The IMF's *stabilization packages* tried to help governments to restore balance to their budgets and foreign payments, while the World Bank's *structural adjustment* loans supported measures to remove controls and "get prices right," which means getting them closer to market-determined levels. The Reagan administration's "supply-side" economics also encouraged a return to market-regulated economies, even though the administration was a late arrival to the supply-side business: the whole field of development has always been a supply-side phenomenon, because the overriding problem is to increase an economy's capacity to produce goods and services. From the opposite end of the ideological spectrum, China's economic reforms of the 1980s have made the market a respectable proposition even for socialist-oriented third world countries, as described in the case study.

Reforming Central Planning in China

Following the death of Mao Zedong in 1976, the new Chinese leadership under Deng Xiaoping was dissatisfied with the rate of progress under Soviet-style central planning. China's gross national product continued to grow at between 4 and 5 percent a year in the two decades prior to 1976, but the economy was by some measures becoming much less efficient. A growing share of GNP was going into capital formation and more energy per unit of GNP was required just to maintain this GNP growth rate. For these reasons, among others, the leadership began experimenting with reforms in the planning and management of the economy in the late

1970s. In October 1985, they announced a major decision to continue moving the economy away from reliance on central planning toward greater use of market forces.

As the Chinese have experimented with these reforms, they have faced a complex task. One of their early steps was to make a higher share of key commodities, such as steel and cement, available for purchase on the open market rather than through administrative allocation by the central planners. But the prices of steel, cement, and other key inputs had often remained unchanged for one or two decades and no longer reflected the relative scarcities of these items in the economy. Under centrally planned allocation, distorted relative prices made little difference, but as goods became available on the market, these distorted prices gave the wrong signals to producers, leading them to demand too much of those products that were priced too low and too little of those that were priced too high.

To bring prices more into line with relative scarcities, the Chinese government freed the prices of many goods sold on the open market while retaining tight control of that portion of those same goods that were allocated by central planners. The problem then became one of preventing people from obtaining goods on the controlled market and reselling them at higher prices on the uncontrolled market. In some cases, notably for certain agricultural commodities, central allocation was eliminated altogether and prices were allowed to find their equilibrium level. Pent-up excess demand from the past, however, caused inflationary price increases when this latter step was taken.

None of these problems are insurmountable, but it is likely to be a decade or more before China has completed the process of changing its economic system and has learned how to manage the resulting mix of market and planned allocation of commodities efficiently.

Will the ebbing tide of planning and controls begin to flow again? It probably will, because every major shift in economic fashion tends to be carried too far and because over time the faults of any system become more apparent. In planning versus the market, as in most such issues, the question is one of balance and the proportions may differ for different countries. The general view of this book is that a balance closer to market determination is probably more effective for most mixed as well as socialist economies in the 1980s, but that a role will always exist for planning, especially for planning to guide the market itself. The precise definition of that role is a major theme of this book.

6

Planning Models

The national development plan described in Chapter 5 is a product of engineering feasibility studies, economic analysis, and politics. In this chapter we assume that the engineers have done their work and we leave aside the intricacies of bureaucratic and national politics in order to concentrate on economic models that aid national planning. We are now in the unrealistic but instructive world of the philosopher-king who establishes national goals and the economic technicians who determine how to manage the economy to achieve these goals.

Planning models can be valuable tools for planners. First, models impose the discipline of consistency on both the data used and the plans derived; the next section explains the role in planning of consistency and a related concept, optimality. Second, alternative economic projections and alternative development strategies can be tested through planning models, giving policymakers a systematic view of the range of possible outcomes and of the trade-offs among different strategies. Third, setting up a model is one of the best ways to marshal all extant data on an economy and to reveal crucial relationships about which data are inadequate. Models thus establish a research agenda designed to improve economic policymaking.

Six planning models are covered: a simple Keynesian macroeconomic growth model, interindustry (input-output) analysis and its extension, the social accounting matrix, linear programming, computable general equilibrium models, and cost-benefit analysis.

CONSISTENCY AND OPTIMALITY

The distinction between **consistency** and **optimality planning** can be illustrated with a simple example. If a traveler has a two-week vacation and a budget of $3,000 to spend, she may ask whether she has enough time and money to travel to Kenya to see its game parks. Are her plans (to visit Kenya's game parks) *consistent* with her resources (two weeks and $3,000)? This consistency problem becomes an optimality problem if asked another way: How far can the traveler go, and how much can she see, in two weeks with only $3,000 to spend? How can the traveler make *optimal* use of her resources?

A consistent plan can be illustrated in terms of the **production possibility frontier** of Figure 6–1. The production possibility frontier shows the maximum feasible output of two goods, *X* (say, necessities) and *Y* (say, luxuries), in an economy with a given endowment of productive resources over a given period such as one, five, or twenty years. The more of good *Y* the economy wants to produce, the less of good *X* it can produce, because resources (land, labor, capital) must be taken from the production of necessities *(X)* to be used in production of more luxuries *(Y)*. Consistency models ensure that any plan resulting from them would place the economy *within* its frontier, at a point like *A,* or at best *on* the frontier, at a point like *B*. Any point, like *C,* beyond the frontier is unobtainable.

To illustrate an optimal plan it is necessary to review the concept of **indifference curves,** illustrated in Figure 6–2. The individual's indifference curve assumes that a single consumer may purchase two goods, *X* (necessities) and *Y* (luxuries) in various combinations. If the consumer were to purchase quantities X_a and Y_a, he or she would achieve a certain level of satisfaction. Other combinations of purchases, such as X_b and Y_b, may yield the same level of satisfaction to the consumer. If so, then points *a* and *b* lie on the

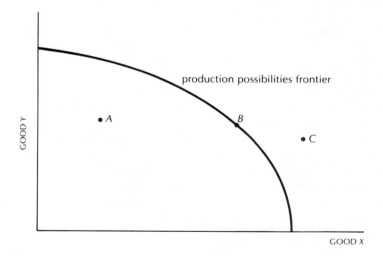

FIGURE 6–1 Consistency. Consistency as shown by the Production Possibility Frontier. Points such as *A* or *B*, below or on the frontier, are consistent with this economy's endowment. Point *C*, beyond the frontier, is not.

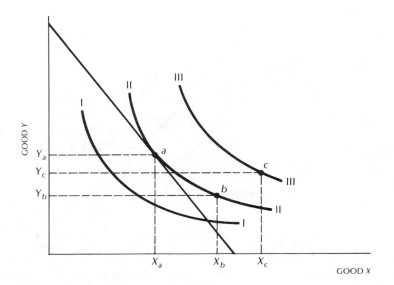

FIGURE 6–2   Indifference Curves and the Budget Constraint. Each indifference curve traces out a series of points that yield an individual the same level of satisfaction. The budget line shows the possible purchases of both goods for a given income and relative price. A consumer's highest possible level of satisfaction occurs at the tangency of the budget line and an indifference curve.

same indifference curve, labelled II in the diagram. Indifference curve II is the locus of all combinations of the two goods that give the same satisfaction to the consumer as does the combination X_a and Y_a. Any indifference curve to the northeast of II, such as curve III, contains combinations of the two goods that yield greater satisfaction to the consumer than does any point on curve II. That is, the combination X_c and Y_c is preferred by the consumer to X_a and Y_a (or to X_b and Y_b). Similarly, combinations along curve I, to the southwest of curve II, are inferior to those along curve II.

Introduction of the **budget line** (or **constraint**) completes the picture. The budget line gives the combinations of goods X and Y that can be purchased by the consumer within the limits of the person's income. (The slope of the budget line gives the relative price of one good, Y, in terms of the other, X.) The consumer can maximize his or her level of satisfaction by consuming at point a, where the budget line is tangent to indifference curve II. The consumer cannot reach any other point on curve II, such as b, and still satisfy the budget constraint. (Nor would he want to, since he is indifferent between combinations a and b.) Any combination of purchases on higher indifference curves, such as point c on curve III, would require more income than the consumer has. And there is no need to accept less satisfaction on a curve such as I, even though it lies partly within the budget constraint, since greater satisfaction is achievable at point a.

It takes very restrictive assumptions to use indifference curves, which are valid for individuals, to represent the consumption choices for an entire community or country. However, the concept of **community indifference curves** is useful—and often used—to demonstrate many theories in economics. Figure 6–3 shows a set of community indifference curves super-

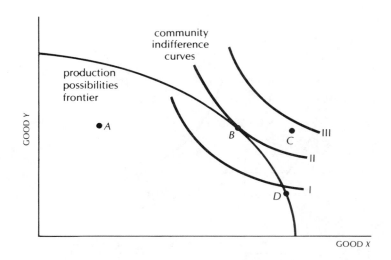

FIGURE 6-3   Optimality as Shown by the Production Possibilities Frontier. Indifference curves I, II, and III represent the consumption preferences for an entire community, analogous to those for an individual. The production frontier is analogous to the individual's budget constraint. The optimal combination of the two goods, X and Y, is given by point B, where indifference curve II is tangent to the production frontier. The country cannot achieve a higher level of satisfaction, such as indifference curve III, given its resource and production constraints.

imposed on the production frontier of Figure 6–1. In planning models, society's welfare is represented by an **objective** or **welfare function** that measures the nation's development goals in a way that will be explained later in this chapter. The community indifference curves of Figure 6–3 can also represent increasing values of this objective function. An optimal planning model seeks solutions like point B in Figure 6–3 for which the value of the objective function is at its maximum given the resource (and hence the production) constraints on an economy.

KEYNESIAN GROWTH MODELS

The simplest and best known consistency model for planning is the Harrod-Domar model, introduced in Chapter 3:

$$g = s/k, \qquad\qquad [6-1]$$

in which g is the annual growth rate of gross domestic (or national) product, s is the saving rate, and k is the incremental capital-output ratio. If k is known, then planners can decide on a target rate of growth (g) and calculate the consistent rate of saving (s) needed to obtain that growth. Alternatively, they can determine a feasible rate of saving and calculate the growth rate consistent with it.

The Harrod-Domar equation is the basis of many macroeconomic growth models, some of which can be quite elaborate. To illustrate these models, a still quite simple version would begin by turning the Harrod-Domar investment relationship, Equation 6–1, into a more realistic form, such as

$$\Delta Y_t = Y_t - Y_{t-1} = (1/k)\Delta K_{t-1} = (1/k)(I_{t-1} - \delta K_{t-1}), \qquad [6\text{–}2]$$

which can be written as

$$Y_t = Y_{t-1} + (1/k)(I_{t-1} - \delta K_{t-1}). \qquad [6\text{–}3]$$

In Equation 6–2, Y is gross domestic (or national) product, K is the capital stock, I is gross investment (i.e., it includes an allowance to replace depreciated capital), k is the ICOR of Equation 6–1, and δ is the rate of depreciation of existing capital stock. The subscripts refer to the current year, t, and the previous year, t-1. Note that here we simplify by assuming it takes investment just a year before it can produce output. This is the entire supply side of our elementary model, indicating how much the economy can produce.

The demand side of the model, showing how output is used, can be contained in five equations, all in the spirit of Keynesian macroeconomic (multiplier) analysis:

$$S_t = sY_t \qquad [6\text{–}4]$$
$$I_t = S_t + F_t \qquad [6\text{–}5]$$
$$M_t = mY_t \qquad [6\text{–}6]$$
$$M_t = E_t + F_t \qquad [6\text{–}7]$$
$$C_t = Y_t - I_t + F_t. \qquad [6\text{–}8]$$

The new variables are S = gross domestic saving, F = foreign saving (the same as foreign aid plus foreign investment), M = imports of goods and services, E = exports of goods and services, and C = consumption. The parameters are s, the domestic saving rate, and m, the import rate, known as the propensity to import. They, like k, are assumed to be known values. Equation 6–4 is a Keynesian saving function, in which saving is a constant proportion, s, of income. Equation 6–5 says that gross investment must be financed by domestic saving and foreign saving. Equation 6–6 determines imports as a constant fraction, m, of income, while equation 6–7 says that imports must be financed by export earnings and foreign capital (saving). Equation 6–8 determines consumption as a residual between income and saving, but puts it in terms of domestic investment and foreign saving, using Equation 6–5.

Any system of independent, linear equations, such as the six of our model (Equations 6–3 through 6–8), can be solved if the number of equations equals the number of unknowns. In this model, however, there are ten variables (Y_t, Y_{t-1}, K_{t-1}, I_t, I_{t-1}, S_t, F_t, M_t, E_t, and C_t), four too many. Three of them, the so-called "lagged" variables, Y_{t-1}, K_{t-1}, and I_{t-1}, are considered to be known, because they represent values from an earlier year for which we presumably have data. A fourth, E_t, is usually estimated separately, because exports depend on factors outside the model, mainly domestic supply capacity for export goods and the state of world markets. That leaves just six unknowns to be found from the six equations, and the model can be solved for all variables.

Suppose, however, that another variable, F_t, the flow of foreign saving (aid plus foreign investment), were also estimated independently of the model.

This is quite realistic since foreign aid is a matter for negotiation and private foreign investment in LDCs is not always closely related to domestic economic variables. Then we have a model with only five unknowns (Y_t, I_t, S_t, M_t, and C_t), but six equations, so the model is **overdetermined**: one of the six equations cannot be satisfied, except by chance. Put another way, one of the equations—and we are not sure yet which one—is not necessary for the model; it is **redundant**. This kind of redundancy is characteristic of planning models.

To see which equations might be redundant, let us trace through the working of the model. Potential national income (measured, let us say, as GNP) is already known from the first equation, since it depends only upon lagged variables, those determined in the previous year. Thus both saving (Equation 6–4) and imports (Equation 6–6) can be found directly. However, each of these variables also appears in another equation. Saving helps determine investment from Equation 6–5. But what if government has a target income growth rate? Then to make income grow at the target rate in the following year, t+1, investment must be

$$I_t = k(Y_{t+1} - Y_t) + K_t. \qquad [6\text{–}9]$$

This is merely a rearrangement of Equation 6–3, with a change of subscripts to the next period, which says that gross investment must be adequate to increase income from Y_t to Y_{t+1} and to cover depreciation of the existing capital stock, K_t. With foreign capital fixed, the target level of investment from Equation 6–9 might require national saving more or less than that forthcoming from Equation 6–4. If more, then the economy will not grow at the target rate, because Equation 6–4 sets a limit to the level of saving, a level inconsistent with the growth target. Saving becomes a **binding constraint** on investment growth. If Equation 6–9 requires less saving than available, the growth target is consistent with saving behavior and the saving Equation (6–4) is redundant.

Imports might present another problem. Imports include both consumer and producer goods, the requirements of which are determined by national income (Equation 6–6). But what if the separately estimated level of exports and foreign capital give a different level of financeable imports from Equation 6–7? If more can be financed, then Equation 6–7 is redundant and the model is consistent. If, however, the sum of exports plus foreign capital is less than necessary imports, then income cannot reach the target level of Y_t; it would have to be lower to get along with fewer imports. In this case the foreign exchange equation (Equation 6–7) becomes a binding constraint on production. Moreover, since most capital goods are imported (an important feature left out of this simple model), the shortage of imports would prevent investment from being high enough to attain the growth target.

This fairly primitive macroeconomic planning model is one version of the **two-gap model** developed by Stanford University economist Ronald McKinnon, Chenery, and others.[1] The two gaps refer to Equation 6–5, which bal-

1. Ronald McKinnon, "Foreign Exchange Constraints in Economic Development," *Economic Journal* 74 (1964): 388–409; and Hollis Chenery and Alan Strout, "Foreign Assistance and Economic Development," *American Economic Review* 56 (1966): 679–733.

ances investment against domestic and foreign saving, and Equation 6–7,
which balances imports against export earnings and foreign saving. Under the model's rigid assumptions, only one of these equations will be in balance on the basis of previously determined values of the variables. This becomes the binding constraint, the other being redundant. After the fact, both equations will be in balance, but the redundant one will balance because of subsequent adjustments in the variables, as, for example, a drop in exports or in investments. Targets are consistent with resource constraints (the two balance equations, Equations 6–5 and 6–7) only if one is just balanced and the other redundant, in which case no greater growth can be achieved without some structural change in the economy or a greater influx of foreign resources; or if both are redundant, in which case higher targets can be achieved.

Models like this one can be made much more complicated by **disaggregating** some of the relationships, breaking them into component variables and relationships; by separating the economy and model into sectors, such as agriculture, industry, and services; and by adding factors of production, such as various categories of labor, natural resources, kinds of imports, and so forth. Each new factor of production adds a resource balance or constraint equation, so that these become multi-gap models. But the basic principles of solution and of planning remain the same.

INTERINDUSTRY MODELS

Input-Output Analysis

Macroeconomic models, such as the Keynesian growth models, lack detailed information on the many agricultural, industrial, and service industries that make up an economy. The interactions—or **linkages**—between these sectors is of crucial significance for planners, who simultaneously need to keep overall macroeconomic balances in view to ensure consistency. The tool designed to accomplish these tasks is the **input-output** or **interindustry table.** Its two inventors suggest its flexibility and usefulness. The Russian-born economist Wassily Leontief developed input-output tables at Harvard during the 1930s to help understand the workings of a modern economy and later to help with postwar planning in the United States. About the same time, though working independently, the Russian economist Leonid Kantorovich developed the same tool to help planners in his country set quantity targets for Soviet production, allowing both for final demands and for the use of intermediate products within industry. The two economists eventually won Nobel prizes for their efforts.

The essence of an input-output table is to display the flow of output from one industry to another and to final users (consumers, investors, and exporters). A highly simplified example is shown in Table 6–1, which contains only four sectors: primary products, manufactured consumer goods, manufactured producer goods, and services. Sectors shown in rows are producing industries, while those shown in columns are users. For example, row 1, "Primary industry," indicates that agriculture, forestry, and mining pro-

TABLE 6–1 Simplified Input-Output Table (Flow Matrix), Value in Dollars

	1. Primary industry	2. Manufactured consumer goods	3. Manufactured producer goods	4. Services	5. Total inter-mediate use	6. Final use	7. Total use
		As Users					
1. Primary industry	20	75	50	0	145	255	400
2. Manufactured consumer goods	0	30	0	0	30	270	300
3. Manufactured producer goods	60	60	75	0	195	55	250
4. Services	40	15	50	70	175	175	350
5. Total purchases	120	180	175	70	545		
6. Value added	280	120	75	280		755	
7. Total output	400	300	250	350			1,300

(Row label along left margin: "As Producers")

duced $20 (million, billion, or whatever unit is convenient) worth of products used within the sector (e.g., feed for livestock); it produced $75 worth sold to consumer goods manufacturers (e.g., wheat for bakeries or cotton for textiles); $50 worth sold to producer goods industries (e.g., wood for pulp or iron ore for steel); and nothing to services. These intermediate uses totaled $145 (column 5). Final products, such as corn for consumption or cocoa for export, were valued at $255, so that total output was $400. Similarly, producer goods manufacturers sold $60 worth of output, such as chemicals, to consumer goods manufacturers (row 3, column 2), and so on.

Each producer is also a user of intermediate goods and its purchases are shown in the columns of the input-output table. For example, consumer goods manufacturers bought $75 worth of primary products, which we know from inspecting row 1, and also $30 from within the sector (e.g., textiles used in clothing), $60 from producer goods industries (e.g., chemicals or paper used in printing), and $15 from services (e.g., banking services, transportation of goods). Total purchases for this sector, given in row 5, were $180. These industries added value of $120, including wages, rents, depreciation, interest, and profits, so that total output was valued at $300. This must be equal to the total output shown in row 2 for manufactured consumer goods. The difference is that each row shows output allocated according to uses (including final demand), while each column shows the costs and profit of producing that output. Rules of accounting tell us that these must give the same total. This applies to the total columns (5, 6, and 7) and rows as well. Column 6, "Final use," gives the sum of consumption plus investment plus exports less imports by sector. Add these and the result must be gross national product, $755. Row 6 gives value added by sector, the sum of which must also yield GNP.

National input-output tables are much larger than the example shown here. Small ones may have fifteen to twenty sectors, while those developed for the United States economy have close to five hundred sectors. Moreover, the columns giving final uses and the rows giving value-added may be broken down into their components and considerably refined. Quantities of capital, labor, and essential imports (goods not produced in the country) can be added as rows to the bottom of the table, showing the investment, labor, and foreign exchange requirements of expanded output.

To turn the input-output flow matrix into a usable tool for planning or analysis, a crucial assumption is required. Interindustry tables are based on observations of a single year's activity for each sector, merely a snapshot of the economy. If it is assumed that the ratio of purchases and value added to total production is fixed for every industry and will prevail in the future, then this accountant's snapshot of costs becomes an economist's production function with fixed coefficients. It says that for any industry, inputs and costs must expand proportionally with output. The flow matrix of Table 6–1 can be converted into a matrix of ratios, called **input-output coefficients,** which is done in Table 6–2. Each column in Table 6–1 has been divided through by its total, so that the second column, for example, now gives the ratios of inputs to output for consumer goods industries: each unit requires 0.25 of primary goods, 0.10 of consumer goods, 0.20 of producer goods, 0.05 of services, and 0.40 of value-added.

The resulting matrix of coefficients, known as the A-matrix, can be seen as a set of production functions for each sector shown in columns. These fixed-coefficient production functions are often called **Leontief production functions.** The **elements** (coefficients) of input-output matrices are usually designated a_{ij}, the subscripts referring to the row (i, for input) and column (j), in that order. Thus, a_{12} is the output of primary products needed per unit of consumer goods, a value of 0.25, while a_{43} is the 0.20 units of services needed to produce one unit of manufactured producer goods.

The Leontief matrix is particularly suited to solving the following kind of problem: starting with a target growth rate for an economy over five years, planners can estimate a bill of "final" goods—those commodities and services purchased by private consumers, investors, government, and foreign importers—that will be demanded at the higher income level. Approximately how much output will be required from each branch of industry to produce that set of final goods? If we can estimate the required output, then it should be possible to determine roughly the amount and kinds of investment needed to produce it. The latter is of course the heart of a development plan. Input-output analysis answers these questions at a highly aggregated level and does not give precise, detailed guidance to planners, but the results

---

TABLE 6–2   Coefficients Matrix[a]

	1. X_1	2. X_2	3. X_3	4. X_4
1. Primary goods (X_1)	.05	.25	.20	.00
2. Consumer goods (X_2)	.00	.10	.00	.00
3. Producer goods (X_3)	.15	.20	.30	.00
4. Services (X_4)	.10	.05	.20	.20
5. Total purchases	.30	.60	.70	.20
6. Value added	.70	.40	.30	.80
7. Total output	1.00	1.00	1.00	1.00

[a] For flow matrix of Table 6–1.

are useful indicators or guidelines to more specific planning of investment projects.

The answer to the central question, how much of each good, is not immediately obvious. Let us say that 100 units of manufactured consumer goods will be required. We know from Table 6-2 that this will require, for example, 20 units of producer goods (coefficient $a_{32} \times 100$). But the story does not end there, because to manufacture those inputs, producer goods industries will in turn purchase, for example, 4 units of primary goods (20 units needed for consumer goods times a_{13}, or 20×0.20). To produce this 4 units, primary industries require 0.6 units (4×0.15) of producer goods, and so on, through an endless chain of outputs and inputs. How can we solve the problem?

Start by asking a simpler question: for any level of output of the four products, which we now label X_1 through X_4, how much of one product, primary goods (X_1) will be required? The answer is

$$X_1 = a_{11} X_1 + a_{12} X_2 + a_{13} X_3 + a_{14} X_4 + F_1. \qquad [6\text{--}10]$$

This says that enough X_1 must be produced to cover the input needs of each of the producing sectors, given by the input-output coefficient times the level of output, or $a_{ij}X_j$, plus the amount of X_1 needed for final demand, F_1. The same is true for each of the other products, giving

$$X_1 = a_{11} X_1 + a_{12}X_2 + a_{13}X_3 + a_{14}X_4 + F_1 \qquad [6\text{--}10]$$
$$X_2 = a_{21}X_1 + a_{22}X_2 + a_{23}X_3 + a_{24}X_4 + F_2 \qquad [6\text{--}11]$$
$$X_3 = a_{31}X_1 + a_{32}X_2 + a_{33}X_3 + a_{34}X_4 + F_3 \qquad [6\text{--}12]$$
$$X_4 = a_{41}X_1 + a_{42}X_2 + a_{43}X_3 + a_{44}X_4 + F_4. \qquad [6\text{--}13]$$

We already know the values for F_1 through F_4, because these are the final goods required by our growth targets. Since we have four equations (Equations 6–10 through 6–13) and four unknowns (the values of total output, X_1 through X_4), we can solve this set of linear simultaneous equations for each of the outputs and get our answer that way. This is a mechanical process that any student of intermediate algebra (or a computer) can easily complete.[2]

This basic calculation, yielding the total production needed for any bill of final goods, is at the heart of planning in the Soviet Union, where it is called the method of **materials balances,** and in China. When the requirements of total production are checked against the capacity in each sector, it becomes a test of consistency: Is present capacity adequate for projected final uses, industry by industry? If not, as is likely in any growing economy, plans must provide enough investment in additional capacity so that each sector can produce the required output. The resulting requirement for investment can then be checked against available savings and foreign investment, one of the constraints of the macroeconomic model. Similarly, requirements for labor of varying skills, for imports (foreign exchange), and for other scarce factors of production can be measured against anticipated supplies. One of these constraints, **manpower requirements,** has received considerable attention

---

2. For those who know matrix algebra, this set of equations can be solved by inverting I-A, where I is the identity matrix and A is the Leontief matrix of Table 6-2. The result is a matrix of **direct plus indirect** input coefficients, usually labeled r_{ij}. The matrix is called the **Leontief inverse.**

from education planners who utilize input-output techniques to project the
demands for education implied by growth targets.

Thus the input-output table can provide a comprehensive but detailed model of the economy, one capable of tracing through the implications for all resources of any output or growth target. This is the most complete form of consistency planning that is now done, although only a minority of developing countries—including South Korea, Malaysia, India, and Mexico—have used it in this way. Despite its power, the input-output model has some serious drawbacks. First, the assumption of fixed coefficients rules out the real possibility that targets may be met not by proportional growth of all factors of production but through the substitution of abundant factors, like unskilled labor, for scarce ones, like capital. This possibility was suggested in Chapter 3 when the Harrod-Domar model was contrasted with a neoclassical production function. The concept of substitution is central not only to neoclassical economic theory, but also to much real-world economics. To take only one recent problem, the fuel crisis of the 1970s was solved partly by substitution of more abundant fuels, like coal, for oil.

The fuel crisis also suggests the need for **technological innovations,** or improvements, another possibility not handled easily by interindustry methods. Any time new technologies appear, new coefficients are required in the Leontief table. If planners anticipate such changes they can make approximate allowances by adjusting the initial coefficients, for example, by reducing petroleum inputs relative to outputs as oil prices rise. Nor can tables of fixed coefficients handle economies of scale and learning by doing, both of which increase factor productivity with growth. Although some nonlinear methods are available to incorporate these shifts in productivity, they are quite complex and have not been widely used for macroeconomic planning.[3]

Social Accounting Matrix

As complex as an input-output matrix can become, it describes only a portion of an economy and leaves many essential policy concerns untouched. An innovation of the 1970s, the **social accounting matrix** or SAM, amplifies the Leontief model to accommodate far more economic data. The social accounting matrix can be extended in several directions beyond the input-output matrix, which is embedded within the SAM. A row and a column can be added for each of the domestic production factors—land, labor of different skills, and capital of different types—and for the outside world. These factors, which can also be included in Leontief tables, permit a disaggregated look at value added and at imports, exports and foreign capital flows.

The major innovation of the social accounting matrix is the addition of a row and a column representing each of the institutions that make up the economy: households, firms, and government. By dividing households into different income categories and firms into different types and sizes (publicly owned versus private firms, large versus small firms, corporations versus

---

3. For an introductory text on input-output analysis, see Hollis Chenery and Paul Clark, *Interindustry Economics* (New York: Wiley, 1959).

partnerships or family-owned businesses), the planner can obtain a detailed picture of who owns and supplies the different factors of production, who receives various kinds of income and how much, in what kinds of industries and organizations workers of various skills are employed, and so forth. This detail gives a comprehensive picture of how production in an economy results in the observed income distribution among households (or, in the jargon of mathematically minded economists, how production relationships *map* into income distribution). Thus the SAM can be used to assess how specific policy interventions, such as measures to increase exports or saving, might change the distribution of income. Further, the addition of a row and column for the capital account enables the SAM to map the flow of savings from various institutions into investments by these and other institutions, which is called the **flow of funds matrix.**

Social accounting matrices serve four purposes in economic planning. At the most basic level, SAMs provide a comprehensive and consistent framework to organize masses of economic data, including the national accounts, household budget surveys, income tax information, financial market accounts, and other sources. Once organized into a SAM and added up in the relevant rows and columns, this data can be checked to ensure internal consistency. Second, when this has been done, the SAM provides a detailed and comprehensive picture of the economy. Third, the SAM highlights areas where data are missing and thus defines an agenda for research. Fourth, when this economic picture has been completed, the SAM can be converted into a dynamic model of the economy and used by planners to determine how various interventions might affect the economy in detail.

Though much more comprehensive and powerful than a Leontief matrix, the social accounting matrix still suffers from the same major drawback: it represents a linear, fixed-coefficients world, and models based solely on it fail to convey the potential for substitution, productivity growth, and changes in institutional behavior. Its data requirements are enormous, perhaps beyond the capability of most developing countries. But social accounting matrices are a potentially valuable organizing framework for data collection and research in all countries.[4]

Linear Programming

Input-output analysis is useful for answering the question: Do we have adequate resources to achieve our targets? Planners often ask a different question: Given our resources, how can we use them to achieve our goals to the greatest extent possible? That is, instead of planning a merely consistent use of resources, we would like to plan an optimal allocation of resources. Linear programming is a technique used to answer the second question. At the core of a linear programming model is the same input-output table used in consistency planning. It also includes a set of resource constraints, as in consistency models. The major difference is in the treatment of goals. Consistency models start with specific values for one or more goals, which we called targets. Linear programming uses a **welfare** or **objective function** instead.

4. Social accounting matrices are introduced by Graham Pyatt and Erik Thorbecke in *Planning Techniques for a Better Future* (Geneva: International Labour Office, 1976).

An objective function is simply an algebraic expression that contains one

variable for each of the goals that must be taken into account. To combine
these into one formula, each goal must have a **priority** or **welfare weight,**
which expresses its importance relative to other goals. Such weights are arbitrary because economics provides no scientific guidance to selecting values
for priority weights. Thus, for example, a government may hold three quantifiable economic goals important: (1) increase in national income (G_1); (2)
employment creation (G_2); and (3) additional income for the poorest 40 percent of society (G_3). Say the first goal is arbitrarily given a weight of 1. If
employment creation—which would have to be measured in terms of wages
paid to new jobholders—is considered half as important, then its weight, w_2,
would be 0.5; and if redistribution, expressed as increases in income to the
poorest 40 percent, is considered 75 percent more valuable than income
increases on average, then its weight, w_3, would be 0.75. (Weight w_3 is not
1.75, because increases in income to an average recipient are already
counted with a weight of one in G_1. Here we only want to count the added
weight if the recipient is poor.) Thus the objective function would be

$$W = w_1G_1 + w_2G_2 + w_3G_3 = G_1 + 0.5G_2 + 0.75G_3. \qquad [6\text{-}14]$$

A linear program would choose the activities or quantities of output that
would maximize the value of the objective function, subject to two sets of
constraints. First, production of each good must satisfy the input-output
relationships of the Leontief inverse matrix. In order to obtain high values
for Equation 6–14, the model will emphasize production in those activities
that give rapid growth, high employment, and income for the poor. But
whatever activities it selects, it must provide for enough output of each commodity and service to ensure that the required intermediate inputs are produced. Second, the production of these goods and services must satisfy the
resource constraints and not use more factors of production than the economy has available. In practice, and because this is a model of linear equations, only one of the resources will be used fully, exhausting its supply.
Other resources will generally not be fully employed; these are redundant.

The model works, in effect, by trying out a first solution, consisting of outputs and resource inputs that are consistent. This set of values results in a
trial value for the objective function. The model (or more correctly, the computer program that simulates the model) then searches for a set of variables
which, while still consistent, will improve the value of the objective function.
Eventually the program will find a value of the objective function upon
which it cannot improve. This is the solution, the set of outputs and resource
inputs that maximizes the welfare function. The process can be viewed in
terms of Figure 6–3 as a search from within the production frontier (a point
such as A) to find the point of tangency of the objective function with the
production frontier (point B).

Linear programming is a step forward in sophistication from input-output
analysis. It depends upon the same assumptions, however, and is therefore
limited in the same ways. Programming has been widely and effectively used
in certain microeconomic applications in agriculture and industry, such as
combining nutrients to feed livestock for maximum biological growth or

planning industrial processes to minimize costs. Its use as a sectoral or national planning tool has been limited to experiments, principally by academic economists, to apply the technique and draw general lessons about economies such as Brazil, Chile, India, Israel, Mexico, and South Korea. These experiments have shown that linear programming is useful not so much for its detailed portrayal of optimal resource allocations, but, perhaps paradoxically, for the macroeconomic picture it provides, based on detailed analysis. Its particular strength is in measuring the trade-offs among different development strategies. The financial and manpower costs of building, calibrating, and operating a realistic linear program are large, however, and so far few governments have tried to apply the technique. Nevertheless, as human and computer capacities increase over time, linear programming may find increasing uses in macroeconomic and sectoral planning.[5]

Computable General Equilibrium Models

Linear programming models are suited to situations in which planners have substantial direct control over an economy's production decisions or prices. They are less useful in mixed economies where markets determine outcomes and planners can only influence economic decisions at a remove, in ways explained in later chapters. To represent the complex market-based interactions of mixed economies and the kinds of policy interventions that are feasible, economists have developed the **computable general equilibrium model** or CGE. CGEs come in many forms, from relatively simple models of a few equations to models as comprehensive as the social accounting matrix, on which they can be based.

The key technical innovation of CGEs is that they escape the constraints of linearity. Neoclassical production functions are used to represent production relationships, so that not only can the interindustry format be represented, but the possibilities of factor substitution, productivity increases, and economies of scale can be included. Similarly, consumption functions that permit substitutability among consumer goods can be introduced. Indeed, the complexities of these models are limited only by the imaginations of their builders and the costs of economists' time and computer solutions, both of which can be high.

A technical explanation and assessment of these complex models is far beyond the scope of this text. They have emerged as a policy analysis tool only in the past decade and are still in a formative stage. Their major technical weakness is that they can be very sensitive to the kinds of relationships and the values of parameters that are built into them. Too often such relationships and parameters are based more on the assumptions or biases of the model-builders than on solid empirical foundations. Despite this, CGEs have great potential for sophisticated analyses of development strategies and policies.[6]

---

5. The standard text on the economic theory of linear programming is Robert Dorfman, Paul Samuelson, and Robert Solow, *Linear Programming and Economic Analysis* (New York: McGraw-Hill, 1958).

6. Advanced students should consult Kemal Dervis, Jaime de Melo, and Sherman Robinson, *General Equilibrium Models for Developing Countries* (Cambridge, England: Cambridge University Press, 1982).

Although much attention is, quite correctly, paid to the macroeconomic setting of development plans, the bulk of most published plans consists of descriptions of projects and their costs. Correspondingly, one of the most used tools of development planning is **project appraisal,** also called **cost-benefit analysis.** This technique has its genesis in the kind of analysis done by private firms on their alternative investment prospects. When a firm lays out its investment plans (called capital budgets), it tries to select investments that will yield the highest profit for a given amount of finance. Three basic elements are involved in this calculation.

Present Value

The first is the **net cash flow** of an investment, which measures the difference between the cash revenues from the sale of the product and the cash outlays on investment, material inputs, salaries and wages, purchased services, and so forth. Costs that do not deplete the cash resources of the firm, of which depreciation is the most prominent example, are not counted.

The second element involves the observation that cash received in the future is less valuable than cash received immediately, because in the interim the firm could earn interest (or profits) on these funds by investing them in bonds or savings accounts (or in additional, revenue-earning production facilities). For example, a firm or individual, asked to choose between $1,000 today or $1,000 next year, would take the money now and place it in a savings account earning, say, 8 percent a year. Then after one year the interest payment would boost the savings account balance to $1,080. So the prospect of $1,000 a year from now should be evaluated as equivalent to only $1,000 \div 1.08 = $926. This process, reducing the value of future flows because funds earn interest over time, is called **discounting.** Because interest is also earned on previous interest, discounting must allow for **compound interest.** In the second year another 8 percent would be earned on the balance of $1,080, increasing it to $1,166. The payment of $1,000 two years from now would then be discounted to yield a **present value** of only $1,000 \div 1.166 = $858. A general expression for the present value, P, is

$$P = F/(1 + i)^n \qquad [6\text{--}15]$$

where F is the value to be realized in the future ($1,000 in our example), i is the interest rate (8 percent) and n is the number of years. As the interest rate or the delay in payment increases, the present value decreases.

An investment project will result in a series of net cash flows over time: large outflows in the early years, as investments are made, then becoming positive, perhaps gradually, as the new facilities begin to generate revenue in excess of recurrent costs. Such a **time profile** of net cash flow is depicted in Figure 6–4; it is the most common of several possible profiles. To summarize the value of this net cash flow in a single number, each year's net cash flow is multiplied by the respective discount factor and the resulting present values are added to give the **net present value** (NPV). Thus,

$$\text{NPV} = \sum_{t=0}^{n} (B_t - C_t)/(1 + i)^t \qquad [6\text{--}16]$$

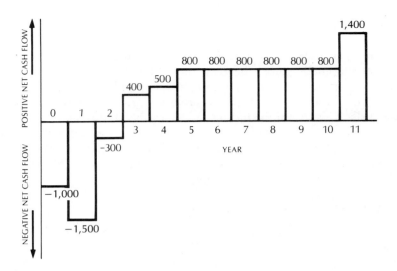

FIGURE 6–4   Time Profile for Investment: Net Cash Flow. The cash flow of a project can be represented by a bar diagram. Cash outflows are shown by bars below the horizontal axis; inflows by bars above the axis. Years 0 and 1 show investment in construction and equipment, hence negative cash flows; Year 2 is the start-up period; Years 3 and 4 show gradually increasing output and cash inflows; Years 5 through 10 show steady output and cash inflows; and the project is assumed to end in Year 11, when the salvage value of equipment swells the cash inflow.

where B_t and C_t are the benefits (revenues) and costs, including investment, in each year, t; i is the discount rate; and n is the life of the project. For a firm, the correct discount rate is the average cost at which additional funds may be obtained from all sources, the firm's cost of capital.

If the net present value of a project, discounted at the firm's average cost of capital, happens to equal zero, this implies that the project will yield a net cash flow just large enough both to repay the principal of all funds invested in the project and to pay the interest and dividends required by lenders and shareholders. In that case, when NPV = 0, the discount rate has a special name, the **internal rate of return** (IRR). If the net present value is positive, then the project can cover all its financial costs with some profit left over for the firm. If negative, the project cannot cover its financial costs and should not be undertaken. Clearly the higher the net present value, the better the project.

Another measure of project desirability is the **benefit-cost ratio,**

$$\text{BCR} = \sum_{t=0}^{n} B_t (1 + i)^{-t} / \sum_{t=0}^{n} C_t (1 + i)^{-t}. \qquad [6\text{--}17]$$

When NPV = 0, BCR = 1, so that desirable projects have NPV greater than zero or BCR greater than one. Although the BCR can be useful, it has the disadvantage that its precise value depends on sometimes arbitrary decisions about which cash flows to include in the numerator and which in the denominator. Neither the NPV nor the IRR calculation suffers from this ambiguity. However, the IRR has a different problem: there will be more

than one IRR for a cash flow if at any time after the initial investment the
cash flow again turns negative.

The cash flow of Figure 6–4 is discounted at a rate of 12 percent in Table 6–3, using Equation 6–16. The net present value is a positive $518, indicating that the investment project will earn enough to repay the total investment ($2,500 over years 0 and 1) with a surplus of $518.

This brings us to the third element in project appraisal, comparison among projects. We already know that a project should be considered for investment only if its net present value is positive. But how to choose among many projects, all with positive NPVs? The answer is to select that set of projects which will yield the highest total net present value for the entire investment budget. This assumes that the firm has a set of alternative projects to consider at any one time and an investment budget that can accommodate several but not all of these.

TABLE 6–3   Net Present Value

Year	Cash flow[a] from Figure 6–4 ($)	Discount factor[b] at 12%	Present Value[c] ($)
0	− 1,000	1.000	− 1,000
1	− 1,500	0.893	− 1,340
2	− 300	0.797	− 239
3	400	0.712	285
4	500	0.636	318
5	800	0.567	454
6	800	0.507	406
7	800	0.452	362
8	800	0.404	323
9	800	0.361	289
10	800	0.322	258
11	1,400	0.287	402
Net Present Value[d]			+518

[a] Cash flow $= (B_t − C_t)$ from Equation 6–16.
[b] Discount factor $= 1/(1+i)^t$ from Equation 6–16. In this example, $i = 12\%$; t takes the value of each year, 0 to 11. Discount factors for a range of discount rates are readily available in discount tables. (See, for example, the appendix table in Michael Roemer and Joseph J. Stern, *The Appraisal of Development Projects* [New York: Praeger, 1975]).
[c] Present value $=$ cash flow x discount factor.
[d] Net present value $=$ algebraic sum of the present values.

Opportunity Costs

A country wishing to derive the greatest possible future income (or consumption) from the resources available for investment faces the same problem as the investing firm. The only difference is that the country is interested in resource flows and their **opportunity costs,** rather than cash flows. When any project in the public or private sector uses goods and services, it denies these to other possible projects. For example, investment in a dam requires utilization of savings that could otherwise be invested in a rural road or a textile factory; cotton used in that factory could otherwise have been exported to earn foreign exchange; or the labor used to build the road might have otherwise been used to build the dam or to grow cotton. To society the cost of undertaking a project is the value of the resources—goods and services—used to invest in and operate the new facilities. The value of these resources is measured in terms of the net benefits they would have provided if used in some alternative project, the opportunity cost.

A simple illustration should capture this point. A textile factory is built and hires labor away from the rural areas. To the textile firm, the cost of labor is the wages paid. To society, however, the cost is the reduction in the value of production, net of costs, in the rural areas. If ten laborers migrate to take jobs in the new factory, their opportunity cost would be the reduction in agricultural output due to their leaving the farm, net of the non-labor recurrent costs of producing that output. This reduction in net output is the value of the marginal product of price theory and is the opportunity cost of labor in this situation.[7] Similarly, if the investment in the textile mill means that savings will be drawn away from other projects that would on average have earned a return of 12 percent, then the opportunity cost of capital is 12 percent and this should be used as the discount rate in evaluating the textile mill. Because project appraisals are most conveniently done at **constant prices,** netting out inflation, the discount rate is a *real* rate of interest, also net of inflation. If, in this example, inflation were 10 percent a year, the corresponding nominal interest rate, the rate observed in the market, would be 23 percent.[8]

Foreign exchange plays a special role in cost-benefit analysis. Most developing countries face a shortage of foreign exchange, in the sense that export revenues and foreign investment are not adequate to finance the imports needed to achieve growth and other development targets. When a project requires imports, such as capital equipment or raw materials, it reduces the foreign exchange available to other projects. If it yields additional foreign exchange, by exporting its output or by substituting domestic production for imports, it benefits other projects by providing more foreign purchasing power. Thus, the opportunity cost or benefit of any good that could be imported or exported should be measured as the net amount of foreign exchange the good represents. For example, the cotton used in the textile mill might have been exported otherwise; if so, its opportunity cost would be the foreign currency it would have earned as an export. If the cloth produced by the mill would have been imported in the absence of the project, its opportunity cost (a benefit in this case) would be the foreign exchange that would otherwise have been spent on cloth imports.

Shadow Prices

The opportunity costs of goods and services are estimated for the economy as a whole and are called **shadow prices** or **social opportunity costs.** The first

---

7. The value of the marginal product of a factor of production can be defined as the price of a commodity multiplied by the additional physical output which results when one unit of the factor is added to the production process with all other factors held constant.

8. The formula relating these is: $1 + i_n = (1 + i_r)(1 + p)$, where i_n is the nominal rate of interest, i_r is the real rate, and p is the rate of inflation. Normally we know the nominal rate and need to calculate the real rate:

$$i_r = \frac{1 + i_n}{1 + p} - 1 = \frac{i_n - p}{1 + p}.$$

For small values of i_n and p, i_r can be approximated by $i_r = i_n - p$.

approximation of a shadow price—for land, labor, capital, foreign exchange —is the price paid by private participants in the market. Many interferences in the market distort market prices from their social opportunity cost: taxes and subsidies of all kinds, monopoly power, minimum wages, interest rate controls, tariffs and import quotas, price controls, and so forth. Prices that are observed in the market need to be adjusted for these effects before a good approximation of shadow prices can be found. A simple example is the wage of textile workers. If the government imposes minimum-wage regulations, the factory will probably have to pay a wage above the opportunity costs of rural migrants and urban workers who are outside the formal, protected urban wage sector.

Estimation of shadow prices is a research task that requires intimate knowledge of the workings of an economy, both its macroeconomic relationships and the microeconomic behavior of its factor markets. It is a task to be undertaken by a central planning agency, which then instructs other planning units—ministries, public enterprises, regional and local governments—in the application of these economy-wide shadow prices to the appraisal of development projects. The use of a single set of shadow prices by all planning agencies and public enterprises is one key to decentralized participative planning, coordinated to achieve national goals. Not only does shadow price estimation help improve the selection of development projects, but the estimation of these opportunity costs teaches the researchers a great deal about the working of the economy, itself an important by-product for a central planning agency.

Although there remains much controversy among economists on the precise estimation of shadow prices, some general results have emerged for a wide range of developing countries. First, and most significant, the shadow foreign exchange rate tends to be higher than the official rate in terms of local currency per dollar, perhaps 10 to 50 percent higher. This reflects the widespread use of import duties and quotas, as well as the reluctance of many countries to devalue their exchange rate despite the inflation of domestic prices. Part IV explores these problems. As a consequence, any export project that earns more foreign exchange than it uses, or any import-substituting project that saves more than it uses, gets a boost from the shadow exchange rate. In terms of the net cash flow profile of Figure 6–4, application of the shadow rate to such projects will raise the positive net cash flows of years 3 through 11 proportionately more than it raises the negative flows of years 0 through 2, giving the project a higher net present value at the same discount rate.

Although salaries and wages of skilled employees probably require no adjustment from market to shadow prices, it is frequently true that the opportunity cost of unskilled workers is lower than the wage in formal, urban labor markets. Thus any project using unskilled labor, especially if it is located in a rural area, gets a boost because the shadow wage reduces costs without changing benefits.

The social discount rate can represent either the opportunity cost of investment and saving in the private sector, or the rate at which policymakers wish to discount future benefits. The first method yields discount rates of 10 to 15 percent for the LDCs. The second approach usually employs a lower discount rate, but entails a shadow price of investment that raises the effective cost of capital. In either case discounting at social rates treats capital as a very scarce factor, discouraging any project with high initial investment costs, long gestation periods, and low net cash flows in the productive years. This system favors projects that generate their net benefits early, because these can be reinvested in other productive projects for continued growth, and projects that use abundant resources, especially labor, instead of scarce ones like capital.

Project Appraisal and National Goals

Project appraisal using social opportunity costs is a simple and powerful device to further certain national goals. Its underlying tenet is that saving should be allocated to investments yielding the greatest future income or consumption, automatically accommodating the goal of efficient resource use to promote maximum growth. This further implies that scarce resources, like foreign exchange, are more highly valued than the market would indicate. The subsidiary goals of improving foreign exchange earnings or reducing dependence on imports are also built in, because any project that efficiently increases exports or reduces imports is given a correspondingly higher net present value by the shadow exchange rate. Once the central planners establish a system of appraisal with shadow prices, then every agency that designs, evaluates, and proposes investment projects is automatically incorporating these national goals in their work.

An illustration of the power of shadow pricing is contained in Table 6–4. It depicts two projects with identical cash flows. However, one project (the textile mill) earns more foreign exchange than the other (a telecommunications system), net of foreign exchange expenditures, and also uses more labor. Because the shadow wage rate is below the market rate, the economic net present value of both projects is raised, but the more labor-intensive textile project benefits more (panel 2). When the shadow exchange rate is applied, the net present value of the exchange-earning textile mill is raised considerably, but that of the telecommunications system, which is a net user of foreign exchange, falls and becomes negative (panel 3).

Not all national goals can be conveniently incorporated into project appraisal, however. Two are of particular concern. The use of low shadow wages for unskilled workers will encourage employment creation but only insofar as this is efficient, in the sense that workers' opportunity cost is below the net benefit they would produce in the project. Government may, however, want to encourage employment beyond this point, because a job is the most significant way that people can participate in development and employed workers may be deemed politically more stable than the unemployed. If projects such as rural public works employ people inefficiently for the sake of employment, then the role of cost-benefit analysis is to estimate the cost of the employment in terms of the greater net benefits that might be earned if investment and labor were allocated to other projects that employ fewer people.

A second class of goals, income redistrubution or poverty alleviation, can also be served by project appraisal, because low shadow wages encourage the

1. Take two projects with identical cash flows, but project A earns more net foreign
exchange and uses more labor than project B:

Project	Investment (first year)	Net annual cash flow (next 5 years)	Net present value at 10%
A. Textile mill of which:	−1,000	+300	+137
Net foreign exchange earned	− 500	+400	
Wages paid	− 350	−100	
B. Telecommunications system of which:	−1,000	+300	+137
Net foreign exchange earned	− 800	0	
Wages paid	− 100	− 50	

2. *Shadow wage* is 75% of market wage, so all wage costs reduced by 25%. This results in
the following net cash flows:

	Investment	Net Annual Flow	NPV (10%)
A. Textile mill	− 913	+325	+319
B. Telecommunications system	− 975	+313	+212

3. *Shadow exchange rate* is 20% above official rate, so net foreign exchange flow is raised
by 20%. This results in the following net cash flows:

	Investment	Net Annual Flow	NPV (10%)
A. Textile mill	−1,100	+380	+340
B. Telecommunications system	−1,160	+300	− 23

employment of low-income labor. The impact may be weak, however,
because distributional goals are still subordinate to efficient growth in the
cost-benefit framework. Situations requiring structural change and large
investments to alleviate poverty may not measure up to the high efficiency
standard of project analysis in the short run. For this reason some economists have suggested, and some governments have considered, using **welfare
weights** in project analysis. These would place a higher value on net additional income to certain target groups, such as families in the lower 40 percent of the income distribution. (We have already seen such a welfare weight:
w_3 of the linear programming objective function, Equation 6–14, gave an
additional value of 75 percent to any income going to the poorest 40 percent
of society.) Then projects generating such incomes would have higher NPVs
than otherwise and would tend to be selected more frequently.

The method is potentially powerful, but has its dangers as well. The welfare premiums are arbitrary weights, subject to planners' or politicians' judgments. This in itself is not bad, but these weights can so overwhelm the
other, economically based shadow prices that project selection comes down
to a choice based almost entirely on arbitrary weights. This gives a false sense
of precision.

Shadow prices based on existing economic conditions are not value free,
either. They imply a welfare weighting scheme that accepts the existing
income distribution and the resulting pattern of demand. A compromise is
to keep the two goals separate, making measurements of net present values
using only the economic variables, then identifying separately the redistribu-

tional benefits of projects. The two can be compared, giving the decision-makers a trade-off to consider and the opportunity to make clear choices of goal priorities.

We have skirted an issue of terminology. When a firm undertakes investment analysis, it can be called **commercial project appraisal,** which uses *market* prices. Traditionally, once *shadow prices* are introduced to reflect the goal of efficient growth and the real scarcities of productive factors, it has been called **social project appraisal.** The implication may be too large, however, because only economic, and not other social, goals are incorporated. The World Bank, which undertakes a large fraction of the project analysis done in the world, has shifted to a more accurate terminology. It calls the second form **economic project appraisal.** The term *social appraisal* is reserved for a third stage, in which welfare weights are applied to reflect distributional goals. But readers should be wary, because this distinction has not been universally accepted.

Transforming Market Prices into Shadow Prices

If governments undertake projects on the basis of economic appraisals, using shadow prices, an implementation problem arises. A firm, whether a public or private enterprise, can only be financially sound if it covers costs and earns a profit at market prices. The shadow prices of planners exist only on paper; no one pays them or receives them in the marketplace. For example, consider a public enterprise producing paper; its investment is encouraged by the planning ministry because it employs many workers whose opportunity cost is low. However, the enterprise must pay its workers not the low shadow wage, but the higher minimum wage set by the government. If this causes the firm to lose money it could go bankrupt, in which case the economic benefits to the country would be lost. (A private firm, of course, would never undertake such an investment.) Hence if the government wants the project implemented, it would have to compensate the enterprise. The most effective compensation would be a direct subsidy to wages, up to the difference between the shadow and minimum wages. Not only would this improve the firm's cash flow, but it would also give the firm an incentive to use more labor because its wage costs would be lower. This is precisely what government wants: to employ more workers, an abundant resource with low opportunity costs, and less of other, relatively scarce factors of production, like capital and foreign exchange.

The same holds for any production factor that is shadow-priced: labor, capital, foreign exchange, and specific commodities. Whenever shadow prices push projects that are commercially unprofitable into the realm of the economically profitable, a subsidy may have to be paid to induce a firm to undertake the project. And, conversely, if economically undesirable projects are nevertheless profitable at market prices, government should consider imposing taxes to discourage firms from undertaking such projects.

This leads to a more general point about shadow prices. They represent the opportunity costs that ideally functioning markets should be generating to give the right price signals to private producers and consumers. If any of the market imperfections, discussed in Chapter 5, intervene to distort mar-

ket prices from this ideal, then one object of government policy might be to
move all market prices towards shadow prices, either by removing imperfections or by imposing compensatory taxes and subsidies. If government can
accomplish this, then resources would be used efficiently—that is, according
to their relative scarcities. Generally, this would promote economic growth,
although some interventions might still be necessary to accommodate externalities, infant industries, and institutional deficiencies.

Policies that move market prices towards shadow prices are at the core of
"getting prices right." This implies both a reduction in controls and the
movement of prices toward opportunity costs, which may require changes in
indirect taxation and other changes in market prices. Government ownership can be consistent with "getting prices right"; indeed, this is the essence
of Lange's system of market socialism, mentioned in Chapter 5. Later
chapters will suggest some of the elements of a price structure that approxi-
mates opportunity costs: market-determined wages (Chapter 8), interest
rates (Chapter 13), and exchange rates (Part IV). The kinds of market failures
covered in Chapter 5 may warrant deviations from market-determined
prices, but these need to be carefully designed, moderate, and temporary.
Finally, as discussed in Chapter 5, not all national goals are served by enforcing shadow prices on the market, since these accept and tend to perpetuate
existing structural conditions, especially the distribution of income. If certain social goals and shadow prices are in conflict, the government must
either choose between competing goals or seek compromise solutions. The
nature of this choice is explored at many junctures in the rest of this book.[9]

9. For an introductory text on project analysis see Michael Roemer and Joseph J. Stern, *The
Appraisal of Development Projects* (New York: Praeger, 1975). A range of alternative treatments
at a more advanced level is given in the bibliography at the end of this book.

PART 2

HUMAN RESOURCES

7

Population

The chapters in this part deal with the human factor in economic development. People play a dual role in the development process: on the one hand they are its ultimate beneficiaries; on the other they provide the most important input into the process of production growth and transformation that is called economic development.

In view of this dual role, what attitude should one take toward the growth of population at the family, national, and global level? Should population growth be limited on the ground that it creates more mouths to feed and bodies to clothe, frequently in households and societies that are having trouble feeding the mouths and clothing the bodies that they already have? World population projections and estimates of natural resource availability can make frightening reading. Yet each new individual can also bring additional labor power, and even more important, additional human spark and creativity to help solve the many problems that society faces. The argument for some form of population limitation is strong, but agreement is not universal, and there are important social, political, and moral issues to be weighed.

The decision of how many children to have is an intimately personal one. Traditionally, it has been left to the choice of the couple involved, although all societies condition these individual decisions in many ways. Arguments for conscious policy intervention must depend either on the rationale that couples do not know how to achieve their desired family size or find it too expensive to do so, and thus must be helped to achieve it, or on the belief that individual reproductive choices impose excessive social costs at the national or international levels or both. Arguments against intervention may appeal either to the value of freedom for the individual or to the alleged advantages of a larger population for a nation or other social group.

The view of humans as an economic resource has quantitative and qualitative dimensions. Often in economic theory the quantitative aspect is emphasized while the qualitative aspect is downplayed or ignored. Many economic models assume that labor is **homogeneous** (undifferentiated) and thus can be measured satisfactorily by counting bodies, or hours or days of work. Other models make only a broad distinction between skilled and unskilled labor. Few take any account of the importance of gender. Such models, although useful for revealing particular truths, are extreme simplifications, since the study of economic development clearly demonstrates that the qualitative aspects of the human contribution to production are at least as important as the quantitative aspects.

Development specialists often talk about "developing human resources" or "investing in human capital." The analogy to natural resources and physical capital is appropriate in many ways. But it can be misleading if it is taken to imply that the nature of "human resources" and their contribution to production are understood as fully as the contributions of a lathe, a road, or a ton of bauxite. The role of human resources is far more complex and mysterious than any of these. To what extent, and in what ways, human resources can be created through an investment-like process are questions to be addressed in Chapters 8–10. This chapter lays a foundation for the later discussion by reviewing some of what is known about population and development.

DEMOGRAPHIC MEASURES

Demography, the study of population, has its own specialized vocabulary. The **birth rate,** also called the **crude birth rate,** is births per thousand of population. Likewise, the (crude) **death rate** is deaths per thousand of population. The **rate of natural increase** is the difference between the birth rate and the death rate, but it is conventionally measured in percentage terms or per hundred rather than per thousand. Say an LDC has a population of 10 million at the start of a given year. During that year it experiences 400,000 births and 150,000 deaths. If net international migration is zero (that is, if the number of immigrants equals the number of emigrants), its population at the end of the year will be 10,250,000. The midyear or average population is used in calculating the birth rate, death rate, and rate of natural increase, which in this case turn out to be 39.5, 14.8, and 2.47 respectively.

One way of expressing the growth potential of a population is through its **doubling time.** For a population that is growing at a constant rate, doubling time is approximately 70 divided by the growth rate. Thus a population growing at 1 percent a year doubles in about 70 years, while one growing at a steady 2 percent per annum will be twice as large in just 35 years, and a population growing at 3 percent a year will double in 23 years and a few months.

Crude birth and death rates reflect the interaction of two factors: the age structure of a population, and its age-specific fertility and death rates. Comparisons of crude birth and death rates across populations with very different **age structures** (different shares of various age groups in the total population) can be misleading. For example, some LDCs have crude death rates as low as those in the developed countries, but the **age-specific death rates** in these LDCs are much higher. (In other words, a higher percentage of people in each age group die annually.) The explanation is that the populations of the LDCs are much younger; the main reason why few people die in these countries is that the population is concentrated in age ranges (older children and youth) where death rates are low.

Thus for some purposes it is important to use age-specific demographic rates. The **infant death rate** is a measure which differs sharply between rich and poor countries. It is defined as deaths in the first year of life per thousand live births. Thus if 40,000 of the 400,000 babies born in our hypothetical country die before reaching their first birthdays, the infant death rate is 100. Similar age-specific death rates can be calculated for any particular age group.

Life expectancy is defined as the average number of additional years that people of a given age can expect to live, assuming that age-specific death rates remain constant. **Life expectancy at birth** is the most frequently used version of this measure.

The **fertility** of a population refers to its propensity to have children. An **age-specific fertility rate** is the average number of children born each year to women in a particular age group. The **total fertility rate** is the sum of the age-specific fertility rates applying to a particular group (cohort) of women as they move through their reproductive years. In other words, it is the number of children the average woman will have in her lifetime if age-specific fertility rates remain constant.

A Brief History of Human Population

We hear many expressions of concern about high rates of population growth and rising population densities in places such as Egypt, Mexico, and Bangladesh. But rising population densities are a very old story. For years people have been saying, "This cannot continue," yet it does. How do current demographic trends fit into the history of human experience?

World population has been growing more or less continuously since the appearance of life on earth, but the rate of growth has accelerated tremendously in the past two hundred years. Four demographic eras in the history of humanity can be distinguished.[1]

The Preagricultural Era For perhaps half a million years, humankind *(Homo sapiens)* lived a precarious existence as hunters, gatherers, and at

1. Based on Lester R. Brown, *In the Human Interest* (New York: W. W. Norton, 1974), pp. 20–21; for an informative and enjoyable longer presentation, see Carlo Cipolla. *The Economic History of World Population* (Harmondsworth, England: Penguin Books, 1962).

least occasionally, cannibals. Population density, the number of people per square kilometer, was very low. It had to be, since a given population required a vast extent of land to sustain itself. The birth rate was probably high, but the death rate was nearly as high and the rate of natural increase was very low. When this unimaginably long era ended with the introduction of settled agriculture about twelve thousand years ago, the world's population was perhaps no more than 100 million.

From Settled Agriculture to the Industrial Revolution The development of settled agriculture revolutionized the capacity of the earth to sustain human life. During the years leading up to the Industrial Revolution of the late eighteenth and early nineteenth centuries, the food supply grew and became more reliable. The death rate fell, life expectancy increased, and population growth gradually accelerated to around 0.5 percent a year. This growth, however, was set back at intervals by plagues, famines, and wars—a self-perpetuating cycle that could wipe out as much as half the population in a given area. For example, the Black Death, or bubonic plague, killed one-third of the population of Europe in the fourteenth century. Nevertheless, by 1800 the population of the world was about 1.7 billion.

From the Industrial Revolution to World War II The Industrial Revolution, which marked the start of modern economic growth, further expanded the population-carrying capacity of the earth. Innovations in industry were matched by innovations in agriculture, permitting the transfer of labor to industry while raising the productivity of the remaining agricultural laborers high enough to feed the growing urban population. Improved transportation, especially transcontinental railroads and fast, reliable ocean shipping, further boosted world food output, making it possible to grow more basic foodstuffs in the areas best suited for this activity and to get supplies to food-deficit areas quickly in emergencies. Famines declined in frequency and severity. Food prices fell in many parts of the world. Meanwhile, modern medicine, sanitation, and pharmaceutical production began to develop. All these factors helped to reduce the death rate. Population growth accelerated, reaching about 1 percent per annum by World War II. This third demographic era lasted until 1945, when the population of the world was slightly less than 2.5 billion.

A feature of the third demographic era was major change in the location of world population. Between 1846 and 1930, more than fifty million people left Europe to settle in other parts of the world. The United States received the bulk of them, while smaller numbers went to Canada, Brazil, Argentina, Chile, South Africa, Australia, and New Zealand. It is estimated that the proportion of world population that was of "European stock" grew from 22 percent in 1846 to 35 percent in 1930, when the Great Depression put an end to mass international migration.[2] During this same period millions of laborers and merchants from overpopulated India and China moved to less densely settled areas in Southeast Asia, Africa, the South Pacific, and elsewhere. The existence of colonial empires facilitated this movement.

2. For discussion, see Cipolla, *Economic History,* pp. 101–4.

The Post-World War II Period The latest demographic era has seen further dramatic improvements in food supply and disease control. Techniques introduced in the developed countries during the preceding era spread throughout the globe. People became more aware of famines and epidemics in "remote" parts of the world and less willing to tolerate them. The result was a veritable revolution in death rates and life expectancy. Plummeting death rates in many areas caused rates of natural increase to rise to 2 or even 3 percent. The doubling time of world population shortened drastically. This fourth demographic era is only four decades old, yet population has doubled to 5 billion in 1987.

Despite the dramatic acceleration of change and foreshortening of the demographic eras, population growth has slowed in some parts of the world. The industrial countries have experienced a **demographic transition.** Initially, these countries had both high birth and high death rates, a pattern followed by a decrease in the death rate. This, in turn, raised the rate of natural increase. Some years later, this was followed by a drop in the death rate, which lowered natural increase to around 1 percent. The demographic transition as it occurred in England and Wales is depicted in Figure 7–1.

During the present demographic era, the developing countries have apparently begun to experience a demographic transition of their own. Shortly after World War II death rates began to fall almost everywhere. The causes of this drop in mortality are discussed in Chapter 10. Death rates in the LDCs began to decline at much lower levels of per-capita income and fell much

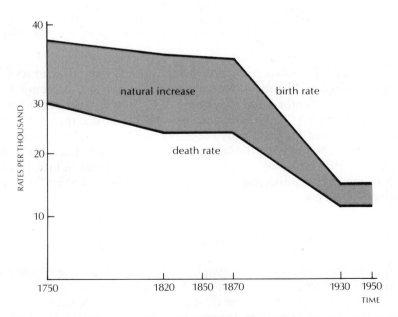

FIGURE 7–1 The Demographic Transition in England and Wales, 1750–1950. The decline in the death rate preceded the decline in the birth rate, creating a period of fairly rapid (about 1 percent per annum) natural increase in the late eighteenth and early nineteenth centuries. After 1870 the birth rate fell more rapidly, sharply reducing the rate of natural increase. *Source:* Carlo Cipolla, *The Economic History of World Population* (Harmondsworth, England: Penguin Books, 1962), p. 85.

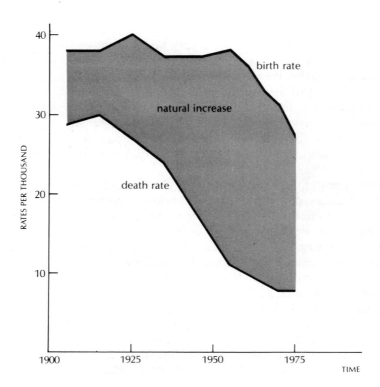

FIGURE 7–2 The Demographic Transition of Ceylon (Sri Lanka), 1900–1975. The death rate fell very sharply after 1920. There was no decline in the birth rate until about 1960. Very high rates of natural increase (over 2 percent per annum) were experienced in the 1950s and 1960s.

faster than these rates had previously fallen in the developed countries. An example is given in Figure 7–2—drawn to the same scale as Figure 7–1—which depicts the demographic experience of Ceylon (now Sri Lanka) during the twentieth century. These early and sharp death rate declines, which have now been achieved for practically the entire population of the world, have not always been followed by the lagged decline in the birth rate evident in Sri Lanka since 1955. In some countries the birth rate has fallen little, if at all. Just how the "new demographic transition" will work in the third world is a question to which we will return.

THE PRESENT DEMOGRAPHIC SITUATION

The world today exhibits a demographic dualism. The developed countries of Europe and North America have passed through the demographic transition, with crude birth rates of less than twenty and rates of natural increase below 1 percent. Their populations are aging and their growth rates are likely to remain low.[3] In some developed countries current fertility is only suffi-

3. But demographic behavior does sometimes surprise the experts. They are confounded, for example, by the post-World War II "baby boom" in the United States.

cient to replace the existing population. Zero population growth (ZPG), promoted by some as a desirable target in view of limitations on natural resources, may not be far away in industrialized countries

By contrast, the less developed countries are at a much earlier stage in the demographic transition—if indeed they are entering a comparable transition process at all. Many low-income countries have crude birth rates of forty or more. Yet their crude death rates are below twenty, and sometimes less than ten. This combination produces rates of natural increase of 2 to 3 percent, or even more. Since three-fourths of the world's population lives in developing countries, the average growth rate of world population is nearly 2 percent as shown in Table 7–1.

TABLE 7–1 World Population by Region and Development Category, 1983

	Total Population		Population density (per square kilometer)	Annual growth rate 1973–83 (%)
	number (in millions)	(% of total)		
Region				
Africa	531	11	18	2.8
Asia and the Pacific[a]	2,671	57	76	2.0
Europe	810	17	29	0.7
North and Central America	389	8	17	1.5
South America	255	5	15	2.2
Development category[b]				
Developing countries	3,500	76	49	2.1
Low-income	2,335	50	74	2.0
Middle-income	1,165	25	29	2.4
High-income oil exporters	18	<1	4	5.1
Developed countries	1,115	24	21	0.7
Market economics	729	16	24	0.7
Nonmarket economies	386	8	16	0.8
World Total	4,656	100	35	1.8

Source: World Bank, *World Development Report 1985* (New York: Oxford University Press, 1985); *World Bank Atlas 1985* (Washington, D.C. 1985).
[a] Kampuchea, for which population in mid-1983 was not available, is not included.
[b] Includes countries with population of 1 million or more only.

Table 7–2 shows some demographic and population-structure characteristics of countries at different levels of GNP per capita. Part A of this table reflects the demographic transition pattern. With only minor aberrations, such as those caused by the atypically low birth rates of India and China, birth rates decline steadily as one moves up the income scale from countries with per-capita incomes below $300 to countries with annual incomes of $5,000 or more. Death rates also tend to decline as income rises. Middle-income countries have high rates of natural increase. Table 7–3 gives the same information as Table 7–2 for selected countries, providing some idea of the range of intercountry variation.

The infant death rate is a particularly sensitive measure of death rate decline, falling by 88 percent from the poorest group of countries in Table 7–2 to 12 percent in the richest group. This fall in infant deaths causes more

TABLE 7–2   Demographic and Population Characteristics of Countries by Level of GNP Per
Capita, 1983

A. *Demographic Characteristics*

Income group	Crude birth rate (per 1,000)	Crude death rate (per 1,000)	Rate of natural increase (%)	Infant death rate (per 1,000 live births)
Below $300[a]	37 (43)	14 (16)	2.3 (2.7)	99 (110)
$300–$500[b]	23 (44)	8 (15)	1.5 (2.9)	50 (109)
$500–$1,000	38	13	2.5	93
$1,000–$2,000	31	8	2.3	64
$2,000–$5,000	25	9	1.5	47
Above $5,000	15	9	0.5	12

B. *Population Characteristics*

Income group	Population below 15 years, 1980 (% of total)	Growth rate of urban population 1973–1983 (%)	Urban population (% of total)
Below $300[a]	41 (45)	4.8 (5.9)	22 (19)
$300–$500[b]	38 (45)	na (5.0)	22 (27)
$500–$1,000	43	4.7	29
$1,000–$2,000	39	4.0	58
$2,000–$5,000	32	0.9	63
Above $5,000	22	1.2	76

Source: World Bank, *World Development Report 1985* (New York: Oxford University Press, 1985); Dorothy L. Nortman, *Population and Family Planning Programs: A Compendium of Data through 1983* (New York: Population Council, 1985).
[a] Figures in parentheses exclude India.
[b] Figures in parentheses exclude China.

children to survive, creating population structures in which children make up very large fractions of the population (see Tables 7–2B and 7–3B). Countries with this age structure are said to have a high **dependency ratio,** or ratio of nonworking-age population (conventionally defined as zero to fourteen, and sixty-five and over) to working-age population. A high dependency ratio depresses per-capita income by requiring that the output of a given number of producers be shared among a larger number of consumers.

The spatial distribution of the population is another concern in many low-income countries. *Urbanization* is an inevitable concomitant of development (Table 7–2B). Many people have argued that the growth of urban areas through migration from the countryside is proceeding too fast and causing serious social problems. Yet third-world governments that have tried to staunch the flow have found the task all but impossible. The reason is that people have found they can better themselves in several ways by moving to the cities. Not only do they earn higher incomes than they could have obtained in the rural areas, but they gain better access to schooling for their children and social services of other kinds. This is what people seek in rural-urban migration, and studies have shown that by and large they find it. This raises an important question: if rural-urban migration is good for the people who move, is it really bad for society? It is true that there are external social costs associated with the migration process: congestion may make it harder to provide adequate urban infrastructure (housing, roads, sewers, etc.) and social services. (To some extent these costs arise because governments feel

TABLE 7-3   Demographic and Population Characteristics of Selected Countries, 1983

A. *Demographic Characteristics*

Country	Crude birth rate (per 1,000)	Crude death rate (per 1,000)	Rate of natural increase (%)	Infant death rate (per 1,000 live births)
Latin America				
Bolivia	44	16	2.8	123
Brazil	30	8	2.2	70
Chile	24	6	1.8	40
Colombia	28	7	2.1	53
Peru	34	11	2.3	98
Africa				
Ghana	49	10	3.9	97
Kenya	55	12	4.3	81
Tanzania	50	16	3.4	97
Asia				
China	19	7	1.2	38
India	34	13	2.1	93
Indonesia	34	13	2.1	101
South Korea	23	6	1.7	29
Malaysia	29	6	2.3	29
Pakistan	42	15	2.7	119
Sri Lanka	27	6	2.1	
				37

B. *Population Characteristics*

Country	Population below 15 years (% of total)	Average growth rate of urban population, 1973–1983 (%)	Population density (per square kilometer)	Urban population (% of total)
Latin America				
Bolivia	43	3.3	5	43
Brazil	38	4.1	15	71
Chile	32	2.4	15	82
Colombia	39	2.9	24	66
Peru	41	3.6	14	67
Africa				
Ghana	46	5.3	54	38
Kenya	52	8.0	32	17
Tanzania	48	8.6	22	14
Asia				
China	37	na	107	21
India	39	4.2	223	24
Indonesia	41	4.8	81	24
South Korea	33	4.8	408	62
Malaysia	39	3.5	45	31
Pakistan	45	4.3	112	29
Sri Lanka	37	2.9	233	26

Source: World Bank, *World Development Report 1985* (New York: Oxford University Press, 1985); Dorothy L. Nortman, *Population and Family Planning Programs: A Compendium of Data through 1983* (New York: Population Council, 1985).

obliged to provide facilities to urban populations that they do not provide to rural populations.) But the common perception of urbanization as a problem also contains an element of class bias. Ruling elites sometimes feel threatened by rapid growth in the number of poor people who live, so to speak, within marching distance of the palace.

Some third-world governments have tried to accelerate the development of secondary towns or backward regions of the country. To the extent that these policies attempt to counteract the existing pattern of incentives affecting the location of population and economic activity, they frequently fail. To make them succeed, governments have to commit large amounts of their own resources to the backward areas in the form of infrastructure and public facilities. It may be that nothing less than a radical shift in development strategy to a genuine emphasis on the intensification and diversification of the rural economy will do the job.

THE DEMOGRAPHIC FUTURE

When extrapolated into the future, even modest-seeming population growth rates quickly generate projected total populations that may seem unthinkable. For example, continued growth at 1.8 percent (the average growth rate in 1978–83) would bring world population to 6.3 billion by the year 2000 and 15.3 billion by 2050. Even if population growth were cut to 1 percent, the world would still be headed toward 5.5 billion inhabitants in 2000 and 9 billion by 2050.

This type of projection, beloved by popular writers, makes frightening reading for many. It is hard to imagine life in a world with two or three times as many people as there are today. How will this expanded population live? How will the globe's finite supplies of space and natural resources be affected? Shouldn't population growth be slowed down? *Can* it be slowed down? These are obviously vital questions that concern everyone.

Linear extrapolations of current trends are not valid because there are grounds for expecting that the developing countries, like the industrial countries before them, will undergo a demographic transition. But it is already evident that there will be some differences in the experiences of the two groups of countries. The decline in death rates in the developing countries has been occurring at much lower levels of per-capita income than previously. But it is not yet known how fast birth rates will fall. In the last two decades or so the beginnings of birth rate decline have become visible in many, although not yet all, developing countries. As Table 7–4 shows, the crude birth rate in the third world fell by one-third between 1960 and 1983. China, which cut its birth rate by half, made a major contribution to this reduction. A few smaller countries (such as Singapore, Hong Kong, Malaysia, and Cuba) experienced comparable birth rate declines. But many countries, including most of those in Africa, have yet to take much part in birth rate decline. No one can say with any precision how far and fast this trend toward lower birth rates will move. Demographic projections are adjusted up or down as each new census or survey result comes in.

It is certain, however, that world population will become much bigger in the future than it is now. This is assured by the phenomenon of **demographic momentum.** Fertility reduction takes time to bring population growth to a halt because populations that have been growing rapidly have large numbers

TABLE 7–4   Crude Birth Rate Decline in Eighty-nine Developing Countries[a], 1960–83

Region	Crude birth rate		% Decline 1960–1983	1983 Population of included countries (in millions)
	1960	1983		
Africa	48	46	4	518.7
Asia				
China	40	19	53	1,019.1
Others[b]	44	35	20	1,496.1
Latin America	42	31	26	378.2
Total	43	31	28	3,412.1

Source: World Bank, *World Development Report 1985* (New York: Oxford University Press, 1985), pp. 174–75, 212–13.
[a] Includes countries with population of 1 million or more; all group averages are weighted by population.
[b] Excludes Kampuchea, for which population in mid-1983 was not available. Includes Indonesia and Papua New Guinea.

of people in, or about to enter, the most fertile age brackets. Even if all couples were to start today to have only enough children to replace themselves in the population—that is called the **replacement level of fertility**—growth would continue into the early part of the twenty-first century. It has been estimated that if the whole world were to achieve the replacement level of fertility by the year 2000, world population would still grow to 8.1 billion by 2050.[4]

THE CAUSES OF POPULATION GROWTH

So there will be continuing growth of world population well into the next century. Most of this growth will occur in the third world. Viewpoints on this prospect vary widely, and discussions of world population frequently turn acrimonious, especially when they are conducted on a global or ideological level. Questions of whose population is to be limited, and by what means, become very sensitive. Before we can confront such issues intelligently, we must consider what is known about both the causes and the effects of rapid population growth. In particular, a course on economic development must concern itself with the two-way relationship between the growth of population and the rise in average income levels and structural change that we term economic development. We deal first with economic development as a cause of population growth.

Malthus and His World

The most famous and influential demographic theorist of all time was Thomas R. Malthus (1766–1834). His pessimistic view of the principles underlying human reproduction and the prospects of economic development is well known. Malthus believed that "the passion between the sexes" would cause population to expand as long as food supplies permitted. People

4. See Thomas Frejka, *The Future of Population Growth* (New York: Population Council, 1973).

would generally not limit procreation below the biological maximum. Should wages somehow rise above the subsistence level, they would marry younger and bear more children. But this situation could only be temporary. In time, the rise in population growth would create an increase in labor supply, which would press against fixed land resources and eventually, through diminishing returns, cause wages to fall back to the subsistence level. If this process went too far, famines and rising deaths would result. Malthus did not think that the growth of food supply could stay ahead of population growth in the long run. In a famous example he argued that food supplies grow according to an arithmetic (additive) progression while population follows an explosive geometric (multiplicative) progression.

We can see that in the grim Malthusian world population growth is limited primarily by factors working through the death rate, which he called "positive checks." In this deceptively mild phrase Malthus included all the disasters that exterminate people in large numbers: famines, wars, and epidemics. It was these phenomena, he believed, which generally constitute the operative limitation on population. Only in later editions of his famous *Essay on the Principle of Population* did he concede the possibility of a second, less drastic, category of limiting factors: "preventive checks" working through the birth rate. What Malthus had in mind here were primarily measures of "restraint," such as a later age of marriage. Unlike latter-day "Malthusians" he was not an advocate of birth control, which as a minister he considered immoral. Even while grudgingly recognizing that humankind might voluntarily control its own numerical growth, however, Malthus invested little hope in the possibility.

The gloominess of the Malthusian theory is not surprising considering that its author lived during the early years of the Industrial Revolution. In all prior history (that is, through the first two demographic eras outlined above) population had tended to expand in response to economic gains. Now with unprecedented economic growth underway in the world he knew, what could Malthus expect except an acceleration of natural increase as death rates fell? That indeed was happening during his lifetime.

Malthus did not live to witness the rest of the European demographic transition. As we have seen in Figure 7–1, the early decline in death rates was followed, with a lag, by a fall in fertility; beginning in the middle of the nineteen century, dramatic increases in wages were recorded. Why did all this happen? Wages rose, despite accelerating population growth, because capital accumulation and technical change offset any tendency for the marginal product of labor to decline. It appears that the death rate fell through a combination of the indirect effects of higher incomes (better nutrition and living conditions) and the direct effects of better preventive and curative health measures. The fall in the birth rate is harder to understand. Theoretically there is good reason to expect, as Malthus did, that fertility would rise, not fall, as income went up. There are both biological and economic reasons for this expectation. Healthier, better fed women have a greater biological capacity to conceive, carry a child full term, and give birth to a healthy infant. In addition, people marry earlier when times are good and better-off families have the financial capacity to support more children. Why then do increases in income seem to lead to declines in fertility? An answer to this question must be sought in post-Malthusian demographic theory.

Mechanisms for Reducing Birth Rates

The first stage of the demographic transition is marked by a decline in the death rate, particularly a fall in the number of deaths among infants and young children. This in itself is a very good thing and no humane person or government would want to reverse the trend. The question of how to reduce the rate of population growth therefore narrows down to a matter of cutting the birth rate.

By definition, three kinds of demographic change can affect the crude birth rate. The first is change in the structure of the population in terms of age groups and sexes. An increase in the share of people of reproductive age (roughly fifteen to forty-five) will increase the birth rate, as was seen earlier in the discussion of demographic momentum. Conversely, if the population begins to have a high proportion of older people, as is happening in many industrial countries now, the birth rate is depressed. Similarly, unbalancing the sex ratio (for example, through migration of males) will reduce the birth rate, while correcting a previously unbalanced ratio will increase it. However, these structural effects are quantitatively important only in rather special circumstances.

The second kind of demographic mechanism that influences the birth rate is change in the proportion of the adult population that is married. This can be affected both by the number of adults who get married, and stay married, at some time in their lives, and by the initial age at which people marry.

The third factor is the marital fertility rate, the number of children born to the average married couple. Most historical birth rate changes are primarily attributable to a fall in marital fertility. However, later age of marriage has also been important in some cases, for example in the fall of the Irish birth rate after the potato famine of the 1840s. It has been suggested that there are three basic preconditions for a significant decline in marital fertility.

(1) Fertility must be subject to conscious choice; it must be socially acceptable for a couple to decide how many children they want to have. (2) Reduced fertility must be seen as advantageous; there must be perceived social and economic benefits to having fewer children. (3) Effective techniques of fertility reduction must be available; couples must know about them and agree to employ them.[5]

Some theorists believe the first and third preconditions are only facilitating influences. The active force working for lower birth rates, they argue, is perceived incentives for individuals to have fewer children.

Modern Theories of Fertility

To understand how people use the available mechanisms for reducing births, economists and demographers have tried to explain fertility in terms of sup-

5. Michael S. Teitelbaum, "Relevance of Demographic Transition Theory for Developing Countries," *Science* 188 (May 2, 1977): 420–25.

ply and demand. Looked at this way, a family planning program works mainly on the supply side. It can reduce the birth rate by making it easier and cheaper for people to regulate the number of births and come closer to their desired family size. It may also affect the demand side of this equation —the number of children people want to have—but probably not by much. The social motivations that led the government to undertake a family planning program—perceived crowding and strain on national resources, perhaps some pressure from foreign aid organizations—are likely to be very different from the private considerations that influence individuals. Couples are unlikely to be moved by general, remote-sounding arguments.

Why, then, do people have children? Is it because they are moved by Malthus's "passion between the sexes" and do not know how to prevent the resulting births? Or do they have many children because they are tradition-bound, custom-ridden? Or is it perhaps rational in some social settings? All three positions help to explain birth rates. The case for the first one was stated by a Latin American doctor at an international conference a few years ago. "People don't really want children," he said. "They want sex, and they don't know who to avoid the births that result." This viewpoint captures the element of spontaneity which is inevitably present in the reproductive process. Yet the evidence suggests that all societies consciously control human fertility. In no known case does the number of children that the average woman has over the course of her childbearing years even approach her biological capacity to bear children. All societies practice methods of inhibiting conception, aborting pregnancies, and disposing of unwanted infants, even those which have had no contact with modern birth control methods.

It is sometimes said that many children are the social norm in traditional societies, that society looks askance at couples who have no or few children, that a man who lacks wealth can at least have children, that a woman's principal socially recognized function in a traditional society is to bear and rear children. Such norms and attitudes are important, but they are probably not the dominant factors in human fertility. The determinants of fertility are evidently a complex combination of forces, but social scientists in recent years have given increasing credence to the elements of individual rationality in the process. Simply stated, their thesis asserts that most families in traditional societies have many children because it is rational for them to do so. By the same token people in modern societies have fewer children because that is rational behavior in the circumstances in which they live. It follows that to reduce fertility in developing countries it is necessary to alter the incentives.

Although some would regard it as a cold, inhumane way of looking at the matter, it is nevertheless true that children impose certain costs upon their parents and confer certain benefits in return. To the extent that couples are influenced by these benefits and costs, are able to calculate them, and are capable of carrying out their reproductive plans, it follows that to reduce the birth rate it will be necessary to increase the ratio of costs to benefits.

The benefits of having children can be classified as economic and psychic. Within a few years of their birth, children may supplement family earnings by working. On family farms and in other household enterprises there is usually something that even a very young child can do to increase production. And in many poor societies large numbers of children work for wages outside the home. In the longer run children provide a form of social security in societies lacking institutional programs to assist the elderly. In some cultures it is considered especially important to have a son who survives to adulthood; in view of high infant and child mortality, this can motivate couples to keep having children until two or three sons have been born. Besides these economic benefits, which are probably more important in a low-income society than in a more affluent one, children can also yield psychic benefits, as all parents know.

The costs of children can also be categorized as economic and psychic. Economic costs can be further divided into explicit (monetary) and implicit (opportunity) costs. Children entail cash outlays for food, clothing, shelter, and sometimes for hired childcare services and education. Implicit costs arise when childcare by a member of the family (usually, but not always, the mother) involves a loss of earning time. Psychic costs include anxiety and loss of leisure-time activities. Some of the costs felt by parents parallel costs of population growth experienced at the national level. For example, more children in a family may mean smaller inheritances of agricultural land, an example of a natural resources constraint operating at the family level. Similarly, it may be harder to send all the children in a larger family to school; this reflects the pressures on social investment which are felt when population growth is rapid.

Viewing childbearing as an economic decision has several important implications. (1) Fertility should be higher when children can earn incomes or contribute to household enterprises at a young age than when they cannot. (2) Reducing infant deaths should lower fertility because fewer births are needed to produce a given desired number of surviving children. (3) The introduction of an institutionalized social security system should lower fertility. (4) Fertility should fall when there is an increase in opportunities for women to work in jobs that are relatively incompatible with childbearing, essentially work outside the home. (5) Fertility should be higher when income is higher because the explicit costs are more easily borne.

The first four theoretical predictions have been pretty well verified in empirical studies. The fifth, however, is in glaring conflict with observed reality. In the real world fertility is usually negatively related to income—not positively, as the theory predicts. The negative relationship shows up both in time-series data: that is, fertility usually declines through time as income rises; and in cross-section data: fertility is generally higher in poor countries than in rich countries; also, in most societies middle- and upper-income families have fewer children than poor families.

Several theorists have attempted to explain this anomaly. University of Chicago theorist Gary Becker, a principal formulator of "the new household economics," views children as a kind of consumer durable that yields benefits over time. Couples maximize a joint (expected) utility function in which the "goods" they can "buy" are (1) number of living children, (2) "child quality" (a vector of characteristics including education and health), and (3) conventional goods and services. The constraints faced by parents in Becker's model are (1) their time and (2) the cost of purchased goods and services. Becker explains the fact that fertility falls as income rises over time by saying that the cost of children tends to rise, especially because the opportunity cost of the parents' time goes up. He believes that the spread of contraceptive knowledge also plays a part. Given the rising cost of child *quantity,* Becker argues that many parents opt to invest in child *quality,* perhaps spending more money on a decreasing number of children.[6]

Whereas Malthus erred in basing his theory of population on an assertion that human nature is immutable, Becker has been criticized for going too far in the opposite direction and exaggerating both the extent to which couples can select their family sizes and the extent to which they apply a benefit-cost calculation in doing so. Although others argue that socially conditioned changes in tastes and values are an important part of the demographic transition, Becker regards tastes as given.

Rivaling Becker's purely economic model of fertility is the more eclectic framework of University of Pennsylvania demographer Richard Easterlin, who directly addresses people's motivation to use available means of fertility control. He says this is determined by two factors. One of them is the demand for children, defined as the number of surviving children a couple would have if fertility regulation were costless; this is essentially a matter of tastes, which Easterlin (in contrast to Becker) believes do change over time. The second factor influencing people's interest in fertility control is natural fertility, which Easterlin defines as their potential output of children if fertility were not deliberately limited; this is determined partly by biology and partly by culture. Besides motivation to limit fertility, Easterlin believes the cost of controlling fertility is another important influence on the actual use of means to limit births. To Easterlin, cost includes not only market costs, such as the cost of contraceptives, but also psychic costs deriving, for example, from social disapproval of particular fertility limitation practices. Easterlin thus explains declining fertility in the real world as the combined effect of changing tastes and the declining cost of fertility control.[7]

For the population policymaker, Becker's theory emphasizes the importance of changing incentives to have children if one wishes to reduce fertility, while Easterlin's approach points to the need to change tastes and reduce market and psychic costs of practicing birth control.

ANALYZING THE EFFECTS OF RAPID POPULATION GROWTH

Two questions are important for population policy. What are the effects of population growth on development of human welfare? And if population

6. See Gary Becker, *A Treatise on the Family* (Cambridge, Mass.: Harvard University Press, 1981).

7. See Richard Easterlin, "Modernization and Fertility: A Critical Essay," in *Determinants of Fertility in Developing Countries,* vol. 2, ed. R. Bulatao and R. Lee (New York: Academic Press, 1983), pp. 562–86.

growth is thought to have harmful effects, how can these harmful effects best be reduced or eliminated?

163
ANALYZING THE
EFFECTS OF
RAPID POPULA-
TION GROWTH

Optimum Population

The theory reviewed in the preceding section implies that at the family level, population tends toward an optimum, in the sense that people have the number of children they consider beneficial to their overall welfare. Yet when asked, many parents in LDCs say that they would rather have fewer children than they have. Also, several studies show that rates of sickness and death are higher among children in large families, especially those with a later birth order. So perhaps parents' judgments about an optimal family size change after they have become parents and have formed a more realistic appraisal of the costs and benefits of children.

When the issue of the relationship between population and welfare is transferred from the family level to the national level, the question that arises is whether individual preferences should be allowed to determine how large a population a country has. What are the effects of population growth on development and human welfare? Is there a case for the state to intervene to curb, or in some instances perhaps to encourage, human reproduction?

We can begin to attack this issue by considering the relationship between per-capita income and the size of the population in a given country. Would per-capita income be higher or lower if the population were larger than it is? In dynamic terms, which are more relevant for policy, the question is whether the future growth of per-capita income would be faster or slower if the rate of population growth were increased or reduced.

An answer to this question can be reached through successive approximations. The oldest and simplest answer is that with every mouth comes a pair of hands. This implies that economic activity is scale-neutral, that per-capita income is unaffected by the size or growth rate of the population. But this ancient piece of folk wisdom is all too obviously an oversimplification. It ignores the role of nonlabor resources and the possibility (which so concerned Ricardo and Malthus) that diminishing returns will be encountered as population expands.

A somewhat more sophisticated approach that meets this objection is the optimum population theory: for any given country at any particular time with a fixed supply of nonlabor resources, there is a unique population size at which per-capita income is maximized. The idea is that at suboptimal levels of population, per-capita income is lower than it could be because there is not enough labor to utilize the available nonlabor resources efficiently, while at population levels above the optimum, per-capita income is also lower because there is too much labor and diminishing returns set in. This relationship is graphed in Figure 7–3.

The optimum population theory is consistent with the intuition that there can be underpopulated countries and overpopulated countries. It is not hard to believe that immigration into the United States, Canada, and Australia during the nineteenth century raised per-capita income in those countries. (It is harder to think of underpopulated countries in today's world.) Nor is it implausible to think that Bangladesh's per-capita income would rise if some

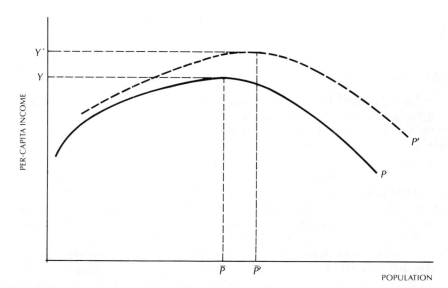

FIGURE 7–3 The Theory of Optimum Population. Curve P shows that, at levels of population below P̄, an increase in population leads to an increase in income per capita, but beyond P̄, more population reduces average income. P̄ is the optimum level of population. Discoveries of new resources, capital accumulation, or technological change can shift the curve upwards to P′, with a new, higher optimum population, P̄′.

millions of its population could somehow be made to disappear. The trouble with the approach is that it is a static framework and can take only limited account of dynamic factors. Capital accumulation, technical change, and natural-resource discoveries make it possible simultaneously to raise per-capita income and to increase the optimum population over time.

Dynamic Effects of Population Growth

Figure 7–3 depicts what economists call comparative statics. The optimum population theory is a static model showing how income per capita is determined, given population, stocks of other resources, and technology. It enables us to see how income per capita is affected, say, by a one-time improvement in technology, but it does not attempt to show what would happen through time as population and capital stocks grow, as supplies of resources stabilize or decline, and as technology changes. A dynamic model would try to do that.

The pioneering work in developing a dynamic model of population's effect on material welfare was published in 1958 by Princeton University demographer Ansley Coale and Duke University economist Edgar Hoover, who created a macroeconomic model of population growth and development in India.[8] Coale and Hoover concluded that a reduction in the birth

8. Ansley J. Coale and Edgar M. Hoover, *Population Growth and Economic Development in Low-Income Countries: A Case Study of India's Prospects* (Princeton: Princeton University Press, 1958).

rate in India would accelerate growth in per-capita income for two important reasons. First, at the household level, slower population growth would reduce the dependency ratio, and this in turn would lower the consumption and raise savings at any given level of income. Second, at the societal level, slower population growth would reduce the share of public sector resources that must be used to provide social services to the growing population and increase the share that can be invested to raise average income.

Most subsequent research has supported the findings of Coale and Hoover. In a recent comprehensive review of population change and development, the World Bank found that rapid population growth depresses private savings and necessitates capital widening (the spreading of available capital over increasing numbers of workers) instead of capital deepening (more capital per worker), which would raise productivity and per-capita income.[9] In addition, many writers have called attention to the deleterious effects of population growth on the environment. Rising population densities have caused deforestation in many parts of the third world as rural people move up the hillsides in search of more agricultural land and firewood. Depletion of all nonrenewable resources is accelerated by rapid population growth. Maintaining a stable or rising per-capita food supply has not been so great a problem as Malthus anticipated, but it has proven difficult in wide areas of sub-Saharan Africa. The World Bank, among many others, has also pointed to the impact of growing total population on urbanization, which brings with it extra costs that society must bear.

Despite the heavy weight of opinion behind the view that rapid population growth is harmful in the contemporary third-world environment, there has always been a dissenting minority who doubt that faster population growth retards growth in per-capita income, or who even argue that it is beneficial. It is true that no clear-cut negative correlation between the growth rate of population and the growth rate of per-capita income has even been established empirically. Writers such as the Australian economist Colin Clark, the Danish economist Ester Boserup, and most recently Julian Simon of the University of Illinois have all maintained that population growth can enhance growth in per-capita income by inducing technological change and greater investment demand, thus making it possible to realize economies of scale and stimulating change.[10] As Rati Ram (University of Illinois) and Theodore W. Schultz (University of Chicago) have pointed out, the longer life spans that accompany falling death rates and faster population growth in the LDCs do increase the incentives for investment in human capital and make labor more productive.[11]

9. See *World Development Report 1984* (New York: Oxford University Press, 1984), pp. 51–206.

10. See Colin Clark, "The 'Population Explosion' Myth," *Bulletin of the Institute of Development Studies,* Sussex, England (May 1969); id. "The Economics of Population Growth and Control: A Comment," *Review of Social Economy* 28, no. 1 (March 1970): 449–66; Ester Boserup, *The Conditions of Agricultural Growth* (Chicago: Aldine, 1965); and Julian Simon, *The Ultimate Resource* (Princeton: Princeton University Press, 1981).

11. Rati Ram and Theodore W. Schultz, "Life Span, Savings, and Productivity," *Economic Development and Cultural Change* 27, no. 3 (April 1979): 394–421.

Despite these opposing arguments, most analysts would agree that in the circumstances of nearly all LDCs slower population growth would probably permit per-capita income to rise more rapidly. There are two distinct reasons for this belief. First, in many LDCs population density in relation to land and other natural resources is already so high that it is reasonable to believe that it depresses per-capita income. This applies to many Asian countries, to Egypt, and to several Caribbean islands. It does not apply, however, to certain land-rich areas in sub-Saharan Africa and South America. In addition, however, rapid population growth (whether or not population density is already high) presses on scarce capital resources, inhibiting capital deepening and making it hard to improve levels of public services. This second point applies to nearly all LDCs, including those with low population densities.

Recall from the earlier discussion of fertility determinants that while some of the pressures created by high population growth and density are felt by individuals, others are not. For example, excessive growth in the number of school-age children will make it difficult for society to provide schooling of adequate quality for everyone. Although a reduction in the average number of children per family would contribute to a solution of this problem, particular couples would not find publicly financed educational facilities any better if they had fewer children (although they *would* be better able to meet the private costs of schooling). One argument for policy intervention to bring about a more moderate rate of population growth is that such social diseconomies can be avoided.

It is also argued that rapid population control in particular countries can produce external diseconomies at the international level. There are nationalistic reasons, related to prestige and sometimes also to military power, why particular nation-states may want to have larger populations. But these motivations can be disruptive to international relations and the welfare of other countries. They may contribute to the likelihood of war by making larger armies possible and by heightening competition for land and other resources. They may create pressures for migration from densely populated countries to other countries whose population growth is under control. For all these reasons there is a case for an international effort to limit world population. The main problem is to decide whose population is to be limited. Possibilities of doing much about population at the global level are limited by the linkage of the population problem to other issues of international politics, and by the locus of population policy, which is at the national level.

POPULATION POLICY

Most LDC governments today are on record as favoring slower population growth and have formulated policies, usually family planning programs, for attempting to achieve it. Some of the strongest commitments have come from Asian governments. Latin American governments, when they provide family planning services officially or permit private organizations to do so, usually justify their actions mainly or entirely as efforts to promote the welfare of mothers and children. Some African governments are committed to population growth limitation, while others are indifferent or openly prona- talist (see boxed example on Kenya). The population policies of Communist regimes have varied among countries and from time to time. China has achieved what is probably the most effective control over population ever attained by any government through its "planned births" campaign (see boxed example).

Population and Family Planning in Kenya

Kenya is an example of an African country with a current low population density, but a high growth rate and explosive demographic potential. With a crude birth rate of fifty-five per thousand and a crude death rate of twelve (see Table 7–3), Kenya has one of the highest rates of natural increase observed anywhere. And this growth shows no signs of slowing down anytime soon. A survey taken in the late 1970s found that Kenyans regarded eight children as an ideal family size, up from six in the 1960s. The current doubling time of Kenya's population is just over sixteen years.

Why Kenyans are so very fertile is not clear. Although Nairobi, the cap- ital, is a prosperous, modern city, the country is still nearly 90 percent rural. The per-capita GNP of $340 (1983) is very unequally distributed. Water shortages severely restrict the cultivatability of much of Kenya's land, while in some of the most fertile areas there are large farms. Many Kenyans, therefore, must make a living from holdings that are either too small or too poorly watered to ensure an adequate income.

Surprisingly, the Kenyan government adopted a policy of population limitation as early as 1966. Despite substantial international aid, however, the national family planning program has been unable to make much headway. It is said that the late President Jomo Kenyatta, who issued the 1966 statement, subsequently refused to lend public support to family planning. A part of the problem was Kenya's keen tribal rivalries, which made each group fear that if it adopted birth limitation it would only be boosting the power of its competitors. In recent years, however, as the dangers of continued rapid population growth have become both evi- dent and imminent, President Moi's government has actively supported a revived family planning effort.

Population and Family Planning in China

China has made unique progress toward gaining control over the growth of its massive population, particularly since 1971. By doing so, it has not only made a large numerical impact on the total population of the globe but it has also provided some lessons to other low-income countries interested in fertility reduction. Some of the techniques used to reduce the number of births in China, however, many not be transferable to other political and cultural settings or would not be widely acceptable because of the loss of personal freedom they involve.

Population policy in China has been anything but constant. After the Communist takeover in 1949 Chairman Mao Zedong repeatedly expressed the view that "revolution plus production" would solve all problems, with no need to limit population growth. China's first census, conducted in 1953, revealed a population (nearly 600 million) which shook this complacency. But birth control campaigns in 1956–1958 and 1962–1966 had only limited results and were interrupted by Mao's famous policy reversals, the "Great Leap Forward" of 1960 and the "Cultural Revolution" of the late 1960s. Only in 1971 was a serious and sustained effort launched. At that time the crude birth rate, already reduced by the disruptions of the Cultural Revolution, stood at thirty. By 1983 it had been cut to nineteen.

The "Planned Births" campaign of 1971 was reportedly launched at the personal initiative of Premier Zhou Enlai. It established three reproductive norms (*wan xi shao*): later marriage, long spacing between births, and fewer children. To implement these norms, the highly committed post-Mao leadership set birth targets for administrative units at all levels throughout China. Responsibility for achieving these targets was placed in the hands of officials heading units ranging from the province of 2–90 million people down to the production team of 250–800. The national government conducted information and motivation campaigns to persuade people to have fewer children, but it was left to local officials to fill out many details of the program and finance much of its cost. A wide range of contraceptives was offered and family planning was closely linked to efforts to improve child and maternal health care.

While national officials maintained that participation in the program was voluntary, local officials with targets to fulfill often applied pressure. At the production-team level, "birth planning" became intensely personal, as couples were required to seek approval to have a child in a particular year. (The application could be accepted, or they might be asked to wait a year or two.) Such extreme methods seem to have worked and been reasonably well accepted in China, presumably because of its cohesive social structure, and strong government authority from the national down to the neighborhood level.

The most popular form of birth limitation in China has been the intrauterine device (IUD). The other two major forms have been abortion and sterilization of both women and men. China is researching contraceptive technologies such as low-cost "paper pills," "morning-after pills," and male contraceptive pills.

The *wan xi shao* campaign lowered fertility, but population projections continued to be a matter for concern and in 1979 the "One Child" campaign was promulgated. Couples were now told that "only children are better children" and were urged to take a pledge to stop at one. Those who do so often receive special incentives, such as an income supplement, extra maternity leave, and preferential treatment when applying for public housing. The "One Child" campaign flies in the face of traditional son-preference by asking half of China's couples to stop reproducing before they have had a male child, but it nevertheless seems to be succeeding in bringing about further reductions in fertility. The target now is to stabilize the population at about 1.2 billion early in the twenty-first century.

Although some aspects of China's population program will doubtless remain unique, countries interested in strengthening their own programs could learn from China's strong information activities, its use of a wide range of contraceptive methods, and its decentralization of many aspects of planning and implementation to local authorities.

Political, moral, and religious problems have arisen in connection with population policy in a number of countries. Some countries are pronatalist for nationalistic reasons. This may be caused by a desire to have enough people to hold areas of low population density against external challenges. Other countries (Guyana, Lebanon, Nigeria, and Malaysia, to name a few) have internal racial, tribal, religious, or ethnic divisions that make population policy a sensitive matter, since it involves the balance of power among the various groups. Still other countries have provoked adverse political reactions by adopting means of population control that were regarded as excessively zealous, offensive to local belief, or callous in their disregard of individual rights. Indira Gandhi's surprising defeat in India's 1977 general election was attributed in part to the population policy of her emergency government. Despairing of controlling population growth by conventional means, the government added male sterilization to its list of promoted family planning methods. Incentives were offered to those who agreed to be sterilized, and quotas were assigned to officials charged with carrying out the program in different parts of the country. Problems arose when force was allegedly used against low-status individuals by officials anxious to fill their quotas. The result was a setback not only for Indira Gandhi's government but also for Indian family planning.

The thinking about population and development reviewed here casts light on both the rationale for population policy in the LDCs and the proper design of programs to reduce fertility. The rationale for population policy must be grounded in consideration of the effects of rapid population growth in a low-income country. Its design should pay attention to the modern theories of fertility determination.

There are two main arguments for the promotion of family planning in an LDC. One is that, through information dissemination and access to contraceptives, couples can be assisted to realize their reproductive plans. As discussed earlier, the second argument is that high fertility has social costs that are not taken into account by individuals but should be offset by government on behalf of society by subsidizing family planning, penalizing couples who have many children, or both. The first argument enjoys wide support, while the second is more controversial. The World Bank's 1984 *World Devel-*

opment Report supported both arguments, while a recent review of population and development sponsored by the National Academy of Sciences accepts the first one, saying that family planning programs, like public health and farm extension activities, help diffuse useful knowledge. But this review found evidence on social diseconomies arising from population growth in the LDCs to be inconclusive.[12]

Policy Alternatives

The alternatives facing a policymaker who wishes to reduce population growth can be grouped into three categories: family planning, population redistribution, and more drastic measures like abortion or sterilization.

In essence, **family planning programs** do two things: they make one or more forms of contraception more widely or cheaply available, or both; and they undertake information and propaganda activities to urge people to use them. These programs have achieved good results in some cases but have had little or no discernible effect in others. They appear to work best where there is a pre-existing desire for smaller families, at least in some parts of the population. Most of the family planning programs which have been relatively successful in reaching a large number of "acceptors" and retaining a large stock of "current users" over time are to be found in countries which are developing rapidly at attaining higher literacy, reduced infant death rates, and more widespread female employment outside the home.[13] In countries where these factors are absent, family planning tends to catch on among the relatively well-off, the urbanized, and the educated, but it spreads very slowly among the rest of the population.

The record, however, is not clear-cut. In some parts of rural Indonesia, family planning has had a measurable effect on the birth rate, despite comparatively low levels of income, education, and health services (see the following boxed example). Integrating contraceptive services with other services, especially maternal and child health services, seems to help. Even if population growth is not reduced, enabling women to improve the spacing of births has health and welfare benefits that women recognize and that contribute to acceptance of the program.

Population and Family Planning in Indonesia

Indonesia is the fifth most populous country in the world. Its 160 million people inhabit a chain of islands stretching some three thousand miles along the equator. Two-thirds of all Indonesians live on Java and Bali, small islands that make up only 7 percent of the land area. In the rural areas of Java and Bali, population densities are among the highest in the world, land holdings are small and shrinking, and decent jobs are hard to find.

---

12. See World Bank, *World Development Report 1984* (New York: Oxford University Press, 1984), pp. 51–206, and National Academy of Sciences, *Population Growth and Economic Development: Policy Questions* (Washington, D.C.: National Academy Press, 1986).

13. This list of factors is based on empirical research. Some of the reasons why these factors should be influential were suggested earlier.

For many years transmigration to the less fertile, but relatively uncrowded "outer islands" of Sumatra, Kalimantan, and Sulawesi has been promoted as a way of easing population pressure in Java and Bali. But this has never made a dent in population growth in these core islands, nor has it lowered existing densities. Indeed, while some migrants move toward available agricultural land in the outer islands, many others flock to Java's cities, where the best income-earning opportunities are concentrated.

Indonesia's population policy reversed gears in the late 1960s. Sukarno, the ardent nationalist who was president from 1945 to 1966, often proclaimed his belief that Indonesia had too few people, not too many. "We have rich natural resources," he said. "We need more people to exploit them." Yet Sukarno's government failed to develop the country's resources, and by the mid-1960s Indonesia's masses were desperately short of food, clothing, and medical care.

Suharto, the second president, tried to rebuild the economy. He also declared approval of population limitation, and in 1970 an official family planning program was launched. Although most people in Indonesia are still poor and ill-educated, this program has succeeded beyond anyone's expectation. Greatest attention was paid to, and greatest success achieved in, the rural parts of Java and Bali. The program was imaginatively conceived, well managed, and implemented largely through existing village institutions. Pills were used as the main method of contraception. By 1980 fertility in key areas had fallen by 15–20 percent. In other areas fertility remained high, while in still others it was low, but only because of low female fecundity resulting from ill-health and malnutrition.

During the 1980s fertility reduction in Indonesia has been further spurred by rapid expansion of educational opportunities. Parents now see greater possibilities for sending their children to high school and college, and are limiting the number of children they have as a way to save more, so as to realize these dreams. Indonesia's official goal is to cut fertility in half by the year 2000, or even by 1990 if possible. Although these ambitious targets may not be realized, a determined government will still have succeeded in improving a critical demographic situation under circumstances that experts considered quite unfavorable for family planning.

A second broad approach to population policy would be to try to move people from one part of the country to another to improve the fit between population and the availability of land and other resources. This **population redistribution** may help to accommodate a growing total population in limited circumstances, but the magnitude of the effect is not likely to be great. First, there must be empty but habitable space into which people can be moved. Then, particularly if the government is going to organize the movement, a considerable investment of capital and formidable organizational capacity will be required. It is hard to move enough people to make a real difference, as experience in Brazil, Indonesia, and elsewhere shows. We have already noted that the kind of mass international population redistribution which was a major factor in the nineteenth century is not likely to be significant in today's world, although smaller movements of people (motivated by political as well as economic considerations) are still taking place.

Methods of population control more drastic than contraception, such as abortion and sterilization, have played an important part in the slowdown of population growth in several European, South American, and East Asian countries. These methods are often regarded as objectionable on moral grounds. When forced on resisting populations, as they were in India during the emergency of the mid-1970s, they can backfire. Yet when acceptable to local mores, they may help to bring about a rapid decline in fertility.

The "Developmentalist" Approach

Some people, with diverse perspectives, argue that governments should worry less about population policy and should concentrate more on *economic development,* leaving it to the demographic transition to bring about a decline in fertility. At the United Nations World Population Conference, held in Bucharest in 1974, a popular slogan was, "Take care of the people and the population will take care of itself." There and elsewhere, verbal wars have been waged between "family planners" and "developmentalists." Ideology often becomes entwined in the debate. Marxist spokesmen routinely contend that population pressure in capitalist countries is merely one more manifestation of class conflict. In a socialist society the problem will disappear because it will be possible to organize society "scientifically," thus providing full employment and satisfaction of everyone's basic needs. In the meantime, capitalist efforts to promote family planning are seen as just one more futile attempt to stave off the coming revolution. Interestingly, the Reagan administration in the United States has provided a mirror image of this argument by contending that population would be less of a problem if LDC governments gave freer rein to private enterprise.

The earlier review of facts and theories suggests that family planning versus development is a false dichotomy. The real issue is not whether to have family planning or development, but what mix of the two is best in a particular set of circumstances. Family planning alone is unlikely to reduce the birth rate; we have seen that it seldom works well in settings where there has been little development. Moreover its effects on marital fertility need support from a trend toward a higher age of marriage, and this is also more likely to come about in a more rapidly developing society.

Yet family planning has made its own independent contribution to LDC fertility decline in recent years, as studies have shown.[14] In Latin America and the Caribbean about 40 percent of couples now practice family planning; in Asia about 30 percent use it, and in the Middle East and North

---

14. W. Parker Mauldin and Bernard Berelson, "Conditions of Fertility Decline in Developing Countries, 1965–75," *Studies in Family Planning* 9, no. 5 (1978). See also "Fertility and Family Planning Surveys: An Update," *Population Reports* Series M, no. 8 (September—October 1985), Johns Hopkins University.

Africa about 20 percent. The use of contraceptive methods has clearly reduced fertility in these areas. In sub-Saharan Africa, the area with the highest levels of fertility and rates of natural increase, only 10 percent of couples practice family planning.[15] In reality family planning and development are more complements than substitutes.

Selective Interventions

In the past decade there has been much interest in ways of modifying the development process to increase its impact on fertility. This has been called "population policy beyond family planning" or "the search for selective interventions."[16] Quite a number of selective interventions—that is, specific policies, that may reduce fertility—have been proposed: increased education for girls, especially the attainment of basic literacy for all women in countries which have not yet reached this target; increased job opportunities for women outside the home; formal social security systems—a realistic option only for middle-income countries; a ban on child labor; compulsory schooling up to a certain age; a rise in the status of women, which will give them greater control over their own lives. The use of monetary incentives and disincentives geared to the number of children per family has also been advocated. The trouble with these is that while they may discourage parents from having an additional child, they frequently penalize those children already born.

The reduction of infant mortality can be considered another form of "selective intervention." According to the "child replacement thesis," the number of children that a couple has is geared to the number it expects to survive; accordingly, if survival prospects improve, then the birth rate—if not necessarily the rate of natural increase—will fall.

Finally, a rise in the legal minimum age of marriage has been proposed in some countries. It is doubtful that this will have any effect if there are deeply engrained norms favoring early-marriage. More impact is likely from the kinds of selective interventions discussed above, since these may affect both marital fertility and the age of marriage.

One country that has emphasized selective interventions, albeit in rather special circumstances, is Singapore. There 60 percent of the population lives in public housing, and nearly everyone is heavily dependent on the government for a variety of social services. In its campaign to limit population growth, the government of Singapore has discriminated among users of public services on the basis of how many children they have. People with large families pay higher maternity fees, get lower priority in school selection, and receive no extra income tax deductions on housing or space. Abortion and sterilization (male and female) are available on demand at nominal fees. All this is backed up by a determined information campaign. Singapore's tough policy has contributed to a dramatic fall in population growth, although

15. See "Fertility and Family Planning Surveys: An Update," September–October 1985.

16. For a thoughtful discussion, see Ronald G. Ridker, ed., *Population and Development: The Search for Selective Interventions* (Baltimore and London: Johns Hopkins University Press for Resources for the Future, 1976).

rapid economic and social change in the southeast Asian city-state has probably had an even greater impact.

A somewhat broader proposition is that *improvement in the distribution of
income* will lower the birth rate. (The complementary proposition, that
unequal income distribution leads to higher fertility, has also been put forward.) This makes sense, since poor households have perhaps three-quarters
of the babies born in a developing society and it is their income which must
therefore rise if an increase in income is to bring about a decline in fertility. A
related idea is that a generally equitable pattern of development, including
improving social services for the poor, will convince people that their lives
are improving and that they are gaining increasing control over their own
destinies, leading to an especially rapid decline in fertility. These are attractive hypotheses and there is some evidence to support them, but it is not
conclusive.

8

Labor's Role

The dual role of people in economic development—as both the beneficiaries of development and a major productive resource—is particularly evident in discussing labor and employment. Labor employed in economic activity can be interpreted as both a cost and a benefit. It is a cost—if it has an alternative use and thus a positive marginal product, as discussed below—in the same sense that use of other productive resources represents a cost. But it is also a potential benefit, in two senses. First, in some situations, because of market imperfections, it may be possible to increase production with policies that better organize the available labor and by adopting technologies more appropriate to the factor endowments of less developed countries. Second, regardless of the impact on aggregate output, increased employment of poor people may be an effective and relatively low-cost way to increase their share of total income.

A perplexing problem is how best to measure the quality of labor used in production. Given the supplies of capital and natural resources available, and given a range of applicable technologies, the level of GNP attainable will depend on the amount of labor available. But what is "the amount of labor available"? We could simply count the number of people potentially available for work—that is, the number of people who are not underage, overage, or infirm—but this could be misleading. Labor productivity, or quality, varies widely in the real world, depending on several factors.

One important set of influences is people's attitudes and values. How much value is attached to the goods and services that can be earned by working? Are people willing to abandon traditional social settings and take up jobs in unfamiliar environments, such as factories, mines, and plantations? Do they come to work on time? Do they exert themselves on the job? Can they tolerate routinized operations? Is saving for future purposes important to them or do they live for the moment? Although economic theories usually abstract from the effects of values and attitudes on productivity, in the real world they are significant. These values and attitudes are acquired, not inborn. The work of sociologists and psychologists indicates that they are created primarily by experiences in the home, in school, and on the job. In a sense they are thus a consequence of economic development, but they are also one of its causes. The subject is not yet well-enough understood for values and attitudes to be readily manipulated as a means of promoting development, although many governments make efforts in this direction.

A second set of factors affecting labor productivity is the skills possessed by the population. If values and attitudes refer to the way people look at the world, skills are what they know how to do. Only some skills are relevant to economic development in a particular environment. One needs to know different things to work effectively in an Asian rice field, a Detroit auto factory, or an Arctic fishing community; skills that are vital in one of these settings may well be useless in another. Compared to attitudes and values, skills are acquired in a more straightforward and easily understood manner. The process can be called education, although the term is used here in a broader sense than is usual.

Finally, labor productivity is influenced by the health and nutrition of the working population. People must possess the physical and mental stamina necessary, first to learn economically useful skills and then to apply them in the workplace. Education and health each merit their own chapters, and are taken up in Chapters 9 and 10. Here we concentrate on quantitative aspects of the human factor in development.

ANALYZING EMPLOYMENT ISSUES

Economists look at a number of factors in order to analyze labor's role: growth in the number of laborers, patterns of employment, the structure of the markets in which labor is provided, and methods of measuring labor supply and its utilization. Here, we take up each one in turn.

Growth of Labor Supply

A major difference between the development challenge faced by today's LDCs and that overcome by the industrial countries in the early phase of their own development is the unprecedented growth rate of labor supply that exists in the third world. In most countries the number of people who want to work is currently increasing at 2 percent or more a year. Since nearly all adult males and many adult females seek work outside the home, the rise in the number of potential workers is linked closely to the increase in total population. In Chapter 7 we saw that a major component in the post World War II "population explosion" has been the survival of many more children from

TABLE 8–1 Growth of Labor Force, 1960–2000[a]

| | Annual Percent Growth Rate | | |
| | Actual | | Projected |
	1960–70	1970–82	1980–2000
Low- and middle-income Asia	1.8	2.1	2.0
Latin America and Caribbean	2.4	2.6	2.7
Middle East and North Africa	2.0	2.6	3.2
Sub-Saharan Africa	2.0	2.2	3.3
All developing economies	1.8	2.1	2.2
Industrial market economies	1.2	1.2	0.5
East European nonmarket economies	0.9	1.0	0.5

Source: World Bank, *World Development Report, 1984* (New York: Oxford University Press, 1984); pp. 258–59.
[a] Weighted averages based on 1983 population.

infancy to adulthood. This means that accelerated population growth tends to be followed, with a lag of about 15 years, by a similar acceleration of labor-force growth. It also means that a slowdown in population growth will not result immediately in reduced labor force growth. Growth in the LDC labor force speeded up in the 1960s and 1970s, and is expected to remain rapid through the remainder of this century, as Table 8–1 demonstrates.

Patterns of Employment

One of the best known characteristics of labor in third-world countries is that most people work in agriculture. The pattern is most pronounced in the poorest countries and varies systematically with the level of development. As per-capita income rises, the share of agricultural workers tends to fall, while the shares of both industrial and service workers rise as we see in Table 8–2. Individual countries follow this pattern, with some case-to-case variations as depicted in Table 8–3.

Another well-known feature of LDC labor is that most workers are paid low wages by the standards of the industrial countries. Labor in developing countries is generally plentiful, relative to the supplies of complementary resources that could raise labor productivity and permit higher wages to be paid. Nearly all complementary resources are scarce: capital equipment, arable land, foreign exchange, and also those less tangible but important resources, entrepreneurship and managerial capacity. Thus, low wages are

TABLE 8–2 Employment Shares in a Typical Developing Country

| | Level of per-capita GNP in 1983 dollars | | | | |
% of employment in:	$320	$960	$1,600	$2,560	$3,200
Primary production	66	49	39	30	25
Industry	9	21	26	30	33
Services	25	30	35	40	42

Source: Based on Hollis Chenery and Moises Syrquin, with the assistance of Hazel Elkington, *Patterns of Development 1950–1970* (London: Oxford University Press for the World Bank, 1975), pp. 20–21.

TABLE 8–3 Employment Shares in some Representative Countries,[a] 1981

	Agriculture	Industry	Services
Low-income countries	*73*	*13*	*15*
Tanzania	83	6	11
India	71	13	16
China	74	13	13
Ghana	53	20	27
Sri Lanka	54	14	32
Kenya	78	10	12
Pakistan	57	20	23
Middle-income countries	*44*	*22*	*35*
Bolivia	50	24	26
Indonesia	58	12	30
Peru	40	19	41
Colombia	26	21	53
Malaysia	50	16	34
Brazil	30	24	46
South Korea	34	29	37
Chile	19	19	62
Industrial market economies	*6*	*38*	*56*
United Kingdom	2	42	56
Japan	12	39	49
Germany (West)	4	46	50
Australia	6	33	61
United States	2	32	66
East European non-market economies	*17*	*44*	*39*
Czechoslovakia	11	48	41
Poland	31	39	30
USSR	14	45	41

Source: World Bank, *World Development Report 1985* (New York: Oxford University Press, 1985), pp. 214–15.
[a] Groups defined as in Table 1–1 (notes a–g).

easily understood from the perspective of an elementary supply-demand analysis.

It is not demeaning to third-world workers, however, to note that another cause of low productivity and pay is the characteristics of the workers themselves. Through no fault of their own, few of them have the education and experience required for high-productivity labor. In Indonesia in 1980 only 32 percent of adults had completed primary school, a mere 10 percent had gone on to secondary education, and a microscopic 0.5 percent had been to a university. Few indeed had worked in a factory or had other good opportunities for on-the-job training. In many LDCs these proportions are even lower. Often LDC workers lack even the capacity to do sustained physical labor because their health and nutritional status is low.

Yet LDCs also have in their work forces persons of consummate learning and outstanding abilities. Another characteristic of LDC labor is that differentials among the wages received by different skills and education levels are wider than in developed countries. Skilled manual workers in developed countries may earn 20–40 percent more than their unskilled counterparts. In Asia, the equivalent skill differential is likely to be 40–80 percent, in Latin America 70–100 percent, and in Africa even more. The extra earnings for educated workers are also much larger in developing countries. In part these large earnings differentials exist because the rarity of skills and schooling attracts a larger market premium. Another factor may be segmented LDC labor markets, discussed in the following section.

A final characteristic of LDC labor is that often large amounts of it are underutilized. For reasons to be discussed below, not all of this underutilization takes the form of visible unemployment, as it is known in the industrial countries. Much of it is what has been called **disguised unemployment.** That is, people have some kind of a job, and may even work long hours, but their contribution to output is low. With some reallocation of resources and improvement of institutions, their labor could be made much more productive. This is a major challenge for development policy.

To recapitulate, low wages and productivity, large wage differentials, rapid growth of labor supply, and underutilization of the existing supply of labor are all characteristic of third-world countries. Since hardly any generalizations apply to *all* LDCs, however, there are naturally many intercountry variations. For example, most Asian countries are now entering a period of declining labor-force growth, while others, such as those in sub-Saharan Africa, are still in a period of accelerating growth (see Table 8–1). Similarly, the degree of labor underutilization varies greatly, depending mainly on the supply of arable land and other complementary resources in relation to working-age population.

The Structure of Labor Markets

It is useful to think of labor services as being bought and sold in markets like other goods and services. The economists' conception of a **perfect** market describes one in which, given certain assumptions, the market allocates goods efficiently, through prices. However, labor markets everywhere are notoriously imperfect, and none are more so than those of the LDCs. Thus, wages (the "price" of labor) are not entirely determined by competitive forces. This section will describe a pattern of segmented labor markets, which may help to explain wage and employment determination in the LDCs.

A "typical" LDC could be represented by a three-tiered employment structure, consisting of an urban formal sector, an urban informal sector, and rural employment. Figure 8–1 is a schematic representation of these three markets.

The **urban formal sector** is where almost everyone would like to work if they could. It consists of the government and large-scale enterprises, such as banks, insurance companies, factories, and trading houses. People welcome the opportunity to work in a modern facility and be associated with a prestigious name, but the main attractions of formal-sector employers are that they pay the highest wages and offer the steadiest employment. One reason they pay more is that they hire virtually all the university- and secondary-school educated labor in the country. But they also tend to pay more for given types of labor, for several reasons: because the government presses them to do so, to "cream" the best (and presumably most productive) workers available, because they want to be known as "model employers," and partly no doubt because they can simply afford to do so. With wages

A. FORMAL MARKET

FIGURE 8–1 **The Three-Tiered Employment Structure.** A. Wage (W_F) is above market-clearing level; there is a queue ($L_F - E_F$) of job applicants. B. Wage (W_I) clears the market but is lower than the formal sector wage (W_F) in Figure 8–1A. C. Wage (W_R) clears the market but is lower than the urban informal sector wage (W_I in Figure 8–1B); supply of labor is highly elastic.

held above market-clearing levels by legislation, custom, and other factors (W_F in Figure 8–1A), there is nearly always a queue of workers ($E_F - L_F$ in Figure 8–1A) waiting for jobs with urban formal-sector employers. A routine job-opening announcement may attract hundreds, or even thousands, of applicants.

Side by side with the large urban formal-sector establishments—or more likely, in the alleys behind them—are the smaller enterprises of the **urban informal sector.** These shops and curbside establishments produce and trade a wide range of goods and services, sometimes competing with the larger enterprises and at other times filling in the gaps that the formal-sector firms do not find it profitable to enter. Sometimes this sector provides jobs for migrants who have come to town from the rural areas seeking work in the urban formal sector but have been unable to find it. However, studies in several third-world cities indicate that many of the people who earn their income in this way are long-time urban residents and veterans at their particular lines of work.

The urban informal sector is easily entered; one can set oneself up as a street hawker or in dozens of other lines of work with only a tiny amount of capital. For those who lack even the ten to one-hundred dollars of capital needed to be self-employed, there is always the opportunity to work for others, albeit at wages far below those offered by the urban formal sector. Domestic servants form one such group, a large and important one in every

B. INFORMAL URBAN MARKET

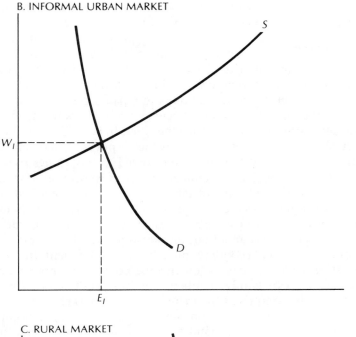

C. RURAL MARKET

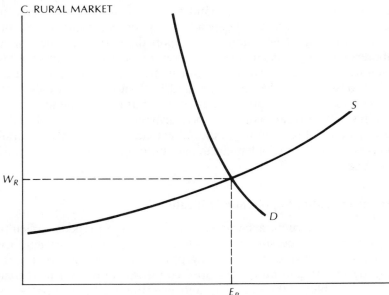

developing country. The urban informal sector can provide incredible amounts of low-wage employment. A few years ago in Jakarta, the capital of Indonesia, it was estimated that drivers of a tricycle-like form of public transportation called the *becak* numbered between 200,000 and 400,000.

Because of the ease in which it is entered, the urban informal-sector labor market tends to be in equilibrium (Figure 8–1B). New entrants can generally find something to do, even if their presence tends to drive down wages slightly for all participants.

Although in visualizing the urban informal sector one tends to think first of massive urban agglomerations such as Mexico City, Lagos, and Calcutta, smaller cities and towns also provide significant amounts of urban informal sector employment. Market centers and small towns often draw rural workers to participate in activities linked to the farm economy: marketing and processing of local agricultural produce, distribution of basic consumer goods and farm inputs, transportation, and repair services.

Even the urban informal sector is likely to pay higher wages than the **rural labor market,** those who work outside the cities. In part this wage differential is illusory because urbanities have to pay higher prices for food and housing than rural residents, and they are often forced to buy things (water, fuel, building materials) which are obtainable free (that is, without monetary cost —although large expenditures of labor time are often required) in rural areas. But even after allowance has been made for differences in living costs, surveys indicate that most urban residents, even recent rural-urban migrants, are better off than all but the wealthiest rural residents.

As assumed by dual-economy models of development (presented in Chapter 3), in rural districts of low-income countries, employment commonly means work by family members, not for wages but for a share in the output of a family enterprise. Still, there is always a market for hired labor, at least on a seasonal basis. Depending on the amount of population pressure and the prevailing pattern of land tenure, there will be a large or small number of people who must depend on wage employment because they have no land to farm, or not enough to support their families. These agricultural laborers typically make up the very lowest income stratum in a poor country. Even when the number of such unfortunates is small, however, rural households commonly trade labor back and forth at different times of the year, sometimes on a cooperative or barter basis but more often for wages in cash or kind. While rural people are primarily engaged in agricultural work, a variety of small-scale nonagricultural activities (trade, services, crafts) provides an important supplement to agricultural employment in many developing countries.

Measuring Labor Supply and Utilization

Because of the structural complexity of LDC labor markets, difficulties arise in defining and measuring concepts that are relatively straightforward in developed countries. The two key problems concerning policymakers in both developed and underdeveloped countries are measuring the supply of labor available to the economy and determining how fully the available labor supply is being utilized.

In developed countries labor supply is measured through the **labor force** concept. The labor force consists of everyone who has a job or is actively looking for one. Labor force in developed countries is determined largely by the size of the total population, its composition in terms of age groups and sex, and those social factors, such as educational patterns and the willingness of women to work outside the home, that determine the participation rates of the different segments of the population. There is some short-term responsiveness (elasticity) to the supply of labor. It can be large under unusual circumstances, as when women in many countries went to work in factories for the first time during World War II. But normally the short-term elasticity is low. Developed countries experiencing full employment, as many European nations did during the 1950s, can easily have their economic growth constrained by the available supply of labor.

In LDC conditions, available labor force is generally not a constraint on development, although skilled labor and management can be very scarce. Typically, more people would like to work than are working, and many of those who are working are underutilized. Moreover, the meaning of "having a job" or "actively looking for work" is often hard to pin down in the LDC context, where multiple job-holding, part-time work, and work for one's own family all tend to be more common than in a developed country. The number of "discouraged workers" (those who have stopped looking for work because they believe none is available) is also likely to be greater in underdeveloped than in developed countries. Using the conventional definitions, women participate increasingly in the labor force as development proceeds and the number of jobs outside the home rises. This suggests that at low levels of development there is a large reserve of female labor not apparent in the statistics, but ready to come forth when reasonably attractive work opportunities open up. In fact, of course, these women are already working hard in the home, where by convention they are not counted as part of the labor force.

Labor underutilization in developed countries is measured primarily through the concept of **unemployment.** The unemployed are defined as those who do not have a job but are actively looking for one. The familiar **rate of unemployment** is total unemployment as a percentage of the labor force. In industrial countries the rate of unemployment is a closely watched indicator of economic performance.

In developing countries the rate of unemployment understates labor underutilization, often by a large factor. Surveys have indicated that India has a lower rate of unemployment than the United States. Yet most observers would agree that underutilization of labor supply is much greater in India than in the United States. Semideveloped countries with per-capita income levels much higher than India's (for example, Malaysia, the Philippines or almost any Latin American country) have also been measured in surveys as having far higher rates of unemployment. One reason for these anomalies is suggested by analyzing the types of people who are reported as unemployed when labor force surveys are carried out in developing countries. Many of them are young and live in urban areas; they are far better educated than the population in general, have never worked before, or both. The inference is clear. The unemployed, as measured in these surveys, tend to be those who can afford to remain unemployed while they search for the type of job, undoubtedly in the urban formal sector, that they want and for which they believe their educational attainment qualifies them. They are in fact likely to come from the better-off families in the society and to be supported by their parents through an extended period of search for the "right" job.

The very poor may appear less often in the unemployment statistics of the developing countries, and when they do appear they do not remain unemployed for so long. Because they lack resources, they cannot be without work for more than a brief period or they and their families will starve. They must therefore accept almost any job that becomes available. It has been ironically observed that in a poor country unemployment is a luxury. Unemployment is usually part of a job search that can be long and costly. Those best situated to make this search are the relatively privileged. Because LDCs lack unemployment insurance and other forms of social support common in the developed countries, job seekers must be supported either by their families (which sometimes make large sacrifices for the purpose) or by such casual work as they can find.

If the standard concept of unemployment is an inadequate measure of labor underutilization in developing countries, what better measure might be devised? This is a complex matter because there are, in fact, several different kinds of underutilization common in LDCs, and it is hard to encompass them all in any single measure. These are defined in Table 8–4.

TABLE 8–4 Types of Labor Underutilization in Developing Countries

Type	Unemployment	Underemployment
Visible	Mostly urban new entrants	Rural labor; seasonal
Invisible	Mostly women ("discouraged workers")	Rural labor + urban informal sector ("disguised unemployment")

It has been argued that disguised unemployment (the lower right-hand quadrant of Table 8–4) is the major form of labor underutilization in poor countries. Workers in this category are fully, but unproductively, employed in the rural sector or urban informal sector. Standard examples include the street vendor who sits for hours just to make one or two low-value sales, the shoeshine boy, and the goatherd. These people, it is argued, contribute little or nothing to production. Like those who are conventionally classified as unemployed, they could be put to work somewhere else in the economy at low or zero opportunity cost. We will discuss the merits of this argument as a guide to development policy later on. The important point here is that while this category of labor underutilization may be large and important, it is exceedingly difficult to define and measure precisely.

One country profile of labor underutilization, based on a framework similar to Table 8–4, was provided by the 1970 International Labor Office (ILO) employment mission to Colombia.[1] Visible unemployment in urban areas was running at 14 percent of the labor force, but the mission estimated that when discouraged workers and the underemployed (those working involuntarily shortened hours) were taken into account, urban labor underutilization rose to at least 25 percent. If disguised unemployment, as indicated by extremely low income, was added in, then it rose to one-third of the labor

---

1. International Labor Office, *Towards Full Employment* (Geneva: ILO, 1970), pp. 13–28.

force. In rural areas everyone was apparently employed at the peak season, but at least one-sixth of the labor force earned incomes low enough to be characterized as disguised unemployment.

Other Ways to Measure Labor Underutilization

Other possible approaches to the problem of measuring labor underutilization are the estimation of surplus labor, the replacement of a labor-use criterion with an income criterion, and attempts to measure the quality of labor utilization.

In the surplus-labor approach two magnitudes are estimated: the amount of labor available and the amount needed to produce the current level of output, using some specified technology. The difference between these two is labor surplus. The technique has been applied most frequently to the agricultural sectors of Asian and African countries. Some of the best known estimates are for Indian agriculture. For example, in a well-known 1966 article, S. Mehra reported a surplus equal to 17 percent of available labor.[2] The problem with this approach is that it is difficult to specify either available supply or needs precisely and unambiguously. In particular, "needs" can be defined only in relation to a specific technology. With a different technology a very different quantity of labor may be "needed." Thus the econometric approach can be only a notional indicator of disguised unemployment.

The difficulty of measuring labor underutilization in developing countries has led some analysts to propose abandoning the attempt entirely and substituting an effort to answer a different, if related, question. David Turnham, a British economist, has proposed that unemployment in developing countries should be redefined in terms of earnings.[3] He argues that low productivity is a more common situation than unemployment and represents a greater waste of resources. Employed workers earning low incomes are a bigger social problem than the unemployed sons of the middle class.[4] A useful definition of unemployment would therefore focus on low productivity regardless of cause. Income differentials provide an objective basis for defining marginal occupations. Under Turnham's alternative scheme, therefore, attention would focus on the measurement of income rather than unemployment or hours of work.

Turnham's emphasis on poverty is welcome in its own right. But in analyzing degrees and forms of labor utilization we cannot focus exclusively on the result—low income. We must also look at the causes. What would be most useful for the formulation of employment policy is a scheme for measuring the quality of "hardness" of employment. Although several such schemas have been proposed, none has yet gained widespread acceptance.[5]

2. S. Mehra, "Surplus Labor in Indian Agriculture," *Indian Economic Review* (April 1966).

3. David Turnham, assisted by Ingelies Jaeger, *The Employment Problem in Less Developed Countries: A Review of Evidence* (Paris: Organization for Economic Cooperation and Development, 1971).

4. The latter, however, may be a bigger political problem because the unemployed and their families may be well placed to put pressure on the government.

5. See, for example, Philip M. Hauser, "The Measurement of Labour Utilization," *Malayan Economic Review* 19, no. 1 (April 1974): 16–34, and his "The Measurement of Labour Utilization—More Empirical Results," *Malayan Economic Review* 22, no. 1 (April 1977): 10–25.

Because of the many difficulties of defining and measuring labor utilization, it is not certain just how the overall degree of labor utilization varies with the level of economic development. The highest rates of visible unemployment, often reaching 10 to 20 percent of the labor force, have been measured in the urban areas of low- and middle-income countries. According to broader definitions of underutilization, still larger shares of the labor force are underutilized and overall underutilization is probably greatest in the poorest countries. Disguised forms of underutilization are relatively more important in the poorest countries than in the somewhat richer ones. In the semideveloped countries covered by labor utilization surveys, disguised unemployment was significant but quantitatively somewhat less than open unemployment.

Nor is it easy for trends to be established with certainty. Many observers suspect that the degree of labor underutilization in most LDCs increased during the 1970s, but a recent careful review of the data showed that this cannot be proven with existing statistics.[6]

LABOR REALLOCATION

We cannot talk about employment policy in developing countries without broaching an issue that has been debated extensively by development theorists: how can underutilized labor be used in a development strategy? In theoretical writings of the 1950s it was frequently asserted that large numbers of people engage in work which adds nothing to national output. Two well-known writers who emphasized this idea and made it a cornerstone of their analyses of how development proceeds were the late Finnish economist Ragnar Nurkse and Nobel Laureate W. Arthur Lewis.[7] Nurkse saw the reallocation of surplus labor to more productive uses, especially labor-intensive construction projects, as a major source of capital formation and economic growth. Lewis envisaged a similar reallocation process except that he pictured the "capitalist sector," essentially industry, as the principal employer of the surplus labor. (Chapters 3 and 4 discuss Lewis's theory in detail.) Both theorists regarded the labor reallocation process as practically costless, although they did discuss the problem of how to capture from the agricultural sector the food necessary to feed the reallocated laborers.

This approach to development theory instituted a long-running debate on two issues: what extra laborers actually contribute to LDC agricultural production, and how readily any excess labor can be mobilized in industry or construction projects. The consensus emerging from this debate can be summarized as follows. First, extra laborers do increase agricultural production, contrary to Nurkse's and Lewis's assumption. In technical economic terms, the marginal product of labor is almost always positive, not zero, although it

6. Peter Gregory, "An Assessment of Changes in Employment Conditions in Less Developed Countries," *Economic Development and Cultural Change* 28, no. 4 (July 1980): 673–700.

7. Ragnar Nurkse, *Problems of Capital Formation in Underdeveloped Countries* (Oxford: Basil Blackwell, 1957; first published in 1953); W. Arthur Lewis, "Economic Development with Unlimited Supplies of Labour," *The Manchester School* (May 1954).

may be very low, such as in densely populated Asian countries. At least this is true on a year-round basis. If there is really such a thing as zero-marginal product labor, the condition is likely to be seasonal. Second, even if forgone output were zero or negligible, there are other costs associated with the physical movement of labor from agricultural pursuits to industry or construction. This point will be discussed shortly. Third, although long-term growth consists of reallocating labor to higher-productivity uses, there are no free, or even very easy, gains to be had in the short run.

In more positive terms, it can be said that in almost all countries and times there are opportunities to work at some positive wage and marginal product, even though these may be very low. Some may remain unemployed despite such opportunities; they probably reject the wage offered because it is too low to compensate for their loss of "leisure" and the chance to search for a better paid job.

Costs and Benefits of Reallocating Labor

If this is so, how should an LDC government look at an employment-creating development project? In Chapter 6 we saw that any development project can be evaluated through social cost-benefit analysis. An important part of the social cost of any input is its "opportunity cost"—its value in its next best alternative use. Labor hired for an urban formal-sector project might well be drawn from the urban informal sector. The worker who moves out of the urban informal sector may in turn be replaced by someone from the rural sector. In this example, the output lost is that of the worker who was formerly in the rural sector—the worker at the end of the employment chain. For this reason, some analysts believe that the wage paid to casual agricultural laborers provides a good measure of the social cost of unskilled labor.

However, this measure, while a good indicator of output forgone through labor reallocation, probably understates the true social cost of employing labor, which has other components that are likely to be significant.

One such significant component is **induced migration.** An influential model of rural-urban migration, developed by John R. Harris and Michael P. Todaro and described more fully in the following section, implies that migrating workers are essentially participants in a lottery of relatively high-paid jobs in the towns.[8] When new urban jobs are created, the lottery becomes more attractive to potential migrants. Depending on their responsiveness to this improved opportunity, it is possible that more than one worker will migrate for each job created. If this happens, then the output forgone may be that of two or more agricultural workers, not just one. Familial ties may multiply this effect. If a male worker migrates and brings his family with him, additional output may be forgone because the wife and children find fewer employment opportunities in the town that in the rural areas; for example, they do not have land on which to grow food.

In addition to forgone output, certain **costs of urbanization** should be taken into account in computing the social cost of urban job creation. Some

---

8. John R. Harris and Michael P. Todaro, "Migration, Unemployment and Development: A Two-Sector Analysis," *American Economic Review* 60 (March 1970), pp. 126–42.

of these costs are internalized by the worker, and presumably taken into account in the migration decision: the higher cost of food, housing, and other items in the town. Other costs are external and must be borne by society as a whole: social services that are provided only to the urban population or that are more expensive in the town, pollution, congestion, additional security requirements. It is these costs that make many third-world governments frown on urbanization, however much they may desire industrialization.

Finally, there is the possibility of a reduction in national savings, which has worried development theorists and Soviet-style economic planners alike. If labor which has been adding little to agricultural output but has been consuming a larger share of that product is withdrawn from the sector, who controls the food thus freed up? The government's aim is to find a way to transfer the food that the rural worker was consuming in order to feed the same worker in the city. What it fears is that the remaining rural population will simply increase its per-capita consumption. Since the urban labor force must be fed—from imports, if not from domestic production—the planners' concern is that aggregate national consumption will rise and national savings will fall, reducing the growth rate of GNP.[9] During the 1930s this concern moved Soviet planners to drastic measures to extract a surplus from a resistant rural population. Governments of less developed countries generally have neither the means nor the desire to suppress food consumption, so they may indeed experience some decline in savings. This is far from pure loss, however, because the added consumption is a gain to some members of society. In any case there are other means to increase saving than coercive controls over food consumption.

The primary benefit of urban employment is added output. A highly productive project may easily repay all the costs discussed above. By contrast, low-productivity, make-work projects in urban areas may incur costs with few offsetting benefits. Labor-intensive projects in rural areas, especially those employing seasonally underutilized labor, may also waste resources but are likely to be more beneficial because they do not require workers to migrate. These projects are discussed toward the end of this chapter.

A secondary benefit of urban job creation is the training it may provide. In LDCs opportunities to learn skills useful in the modern economy are concentrated in urban areas. For example, the ability to operate and repair machinery of all kinds is typically rare. A worker who comes to town can acquire these skills. In doing so he may benefit himself if he can find employment as a skilled worker and obtain higher wages. But he also confers an "external benefit" on society because everyone benefits when bus drivers, auto mechanics, appliance repairmen, and others who work with machinery learn to do their jobs better. This applies to both employers, who can hire labor from a more skilled pool, and consumers, who get better at service at lower prices.

9. The problem is exacerbated by the fact that the new urban workers get higher wages and thus want to consume more food than they were consuming in the rural areas.

It is evident that developing through the reallocation of low-productivity labor is a more complex business than Nurkse and Lewis imagined in the 1950s. Nevertheless, employment expansion remains an important means of both expanding output and redistributing income. A government that can create projects in which the marginal product of labor exceeds its social cost, taking into account all the elements discussed here, can achieve both of these objectives simultaneously. Output goes up and additional income is put in the hands of poor, unskilled workers. Less productive forms of employment creation, in which the social cost of labor exceeds its marginal product, would be acceptable as redistributive measures if a degree of income redistribution is desired and other ways of achieving it are unavailable. But this would achieve more equity only at the cost of less growth.

Internal Migration

As GNP rises and the structure of employment changes, there is bound to be movement of workers and their families from place to place. Most of this internal migration is from rural to urban areas. A long succession of theorists has argued that economic factors dominate the decision to migrate. Some early writers distinguished between "pull" and "push" factors. They said that rural-urban migration can result either from favorable economic developments in the town or from adverse developments in the countryside. The Harris-Todaro model of rural-urban migration, introduced in the previous section, integrates these two sets of factors by focusing on the wage differential which pulls rural workers to the city. Yet there is something to the older notion. Just as eighteenth-century English cottagers were pushed into the town by the Enclosure Movement, so peasants in eastern India move to Calcutta primarily because of wretched conditions in the surrounding countryside, rather than outstanding income or employment opportunities in Calcutta itself. By contrast, the growth of dynamic third-world cities such as São Paulo and Nairobi could be attributed at least partly to "pull" factors.

The Harris-Todaro model of rural-urban migration is an important formulation of the role of economic incentives in the migration decision. The model assumes that migration depends primarily on a comparison of wages in the rural and urban labor markets. That is,

$$M_t = f(W_u - W_r), \qquad [8-1]$$

where M_t is the number of rural to urban migrants in time period t, f is a response function, W_u is the urban wage, and W_r is the rural wage. Since there is unemployment if the town (assume that there is none in the countryside) and every migrant cannot expect to find a job there, the model postulates that the *expected* urban wage is compared to the rural wage. The expected urban wage is the actual wage times the probability of finding a job, or

$$W_u^* = pW_u, \qquad [8-2]$$

where W_u^* = expected urban wage and p = probability of finding a job.

A simple way of defining p is

$$p = E_u/(E_u + U_u), \qquad [8\text{--}3]$$

where E_u = urban employment, and U_u = urban unemployment. In this formulation all members of the urban labor force are assumed to have equal chances of obtaining the jobs available, so that W_u^* becomes simply the urban wage times the urban unemployment rate. Migration in any given time period then depends on three factors: the rural-urban wage gap, the urban unemployment rate, and the responsiveness of potential migrants to the resulting opportunities.

$$M_t = h(pW_u - W_r), \qquad [8\text{--}4]$$

where M_t = migration in period t, and h = response rate of potential migrants.

As long as W_u^* exceeds W_r, the model predicts that rural-urban migration will continue. It will only stop when migration has forced down the urban wage or forced up urban unemployment sufficiently that $W_u^* = W_r$. It is also possible that W_r is greater than W_u^*, in which case there will be a flow of disappointed urban job-seekers back to the countryside.

Critics of the Harris-Todaro model point out that the equilibrium condition specified by the model is seldom attained. It is common for urban wages to be, say, 50 or 100 percent higher than rural wages and for urban unemployment to run at 10 to 20 percent of the labor force. If the figures stay in this range, the expected urban wage (W_u^*) remains above the rural wage (W_r). Migration in practice does not seem to close the gap between W_u^* and W_r as the model predicts. Nor can the theory account fully for "reverse migration" from town to country, which is significant in many countries. Some "reverse migrants" may indeed be disappointed urban job-seekers returning home in despair, but even more of this two-way or "circular" migration may be intentional. Workers, especially young, unattached males, often migrate temporarily to towns, mines, or plantations, work for a while and amass savings, which they then take back to the rural areas to invest in land, farm improvements, or marriage. This pattern of migration has been especially evident in parts of Africa, perhaps because in many African cultures women normally tend the crops after the men have planted them. The opportunity cost of absent males outside the planting season is thus low.

Economic factors are not the only important influences on migration decisions. Studies have shown that distance and social ties are also significant. Migrants to expanding urban areas tend to come from nearby rural regions, while peasants who have been pushed out of their native districts by a calamity are likely to go to the nearest large town. People also tend to migrate to areas where members of their family, village, or ethnic group have settled. Finally, some migrants, especially young males, are attracted by the "bright lights" and excitement of the city. But the view common in the 1950s and earlier—that people come for the "bright lights" regardless of the personal economic benefit—has been discredited by Harris and Todaro and others.

Although most internal migration in developing countries undoubtedly involves rural-to-urban movement, interregional differences in economic opportunity can bring about substantial rural-to-rural movement as well. Countries fortunate enough to possess lightly settled but cultivable regions often try to bring about such movement as a matter of public policy, as we saw in Chapter 7. Unless there are massive physical or legal barriers to settlement of these relatively empty areas, however, these interregional movements tend to occur spontaneously. This has happened in Nepal, for instance, where farmers have moved from the densely packed Kathmandu Valley into the southern *terai* region, and in many parts of Africa and South America. Unforced movements of population from one region of a country to another are likely to be socially beneficial. People make these moves to benefit themselves and their families. Even in the most congested slums of such major LDC cities as São Paulo, Lagos, and Jakarta, migrants report that they are better off than they were in the rural areas and generally they do not want to go back.

Society is likely to benefit as well from an improved spatial allocation of labor relative to other resources. However, two factors could make social costs greater than benefits. First, distorted incentives, such as artificially high wages and subsidized urban services, can inflate private benefits. Second, external costs such as congestion, pollution, and crime are borne equally by migrants, who benefit from migration, and by their predecessors, who do not. If these distortions and externalities are large, social costs may exceed benefits.

International Migration

International migration is frequently regarded as a different matter altogether. To bring a degree of cool rationality to this often heated subject, it is helpful to distinguish between unskilled labor and skilled or educated labor. This distinction may not matter when we look at the problem from the global point of view: it has been argued that world GNP is maximized when everyone works where his salary, and therefore presumably his productivity, is greatest. But it is important when we examine the problem from the viewpoint of the LDCs because skilled and unskilled labor have different opportunity costs.

There are two reasons why the migration of educated, highly skilled labor is abhorrent to most third-world countries and has been stigmatized as the "brain drain." One is that such people represent one of the LDCs' scarcest resources. The other is that in most cases their education has been time-consuming, expensive, and heavily subsidized by the state. Their departure for foreign lands can thus be costly. Not only are their services lost, but the cost of training a replacement is likely to be high. Yet if they are so productive at home, why are they not paid enough to keep them there? The answer may be nonmarket influences on the salary structure. For example, if most doctors and engineers work for the government and their salaries are held down to avoid politically embarrassing salary differentials, it is not surprising that many of them seek an opportunity to emigrate. Often international agencies, which recruit in a worldwide labor market, pay far more for the same skills than national governments. This is the reason why one can find Pakistani experts working in Egypt, for example, even as Egyptian experts are employed in Pakistan, despite the likelihood that both groups could work more effectively in their own countries.

While it probably raises world GNP, international migration of the educated worsens the distribution of income between rich and poor countries. For this reason the Indian economist Jagdish Bhagwati has proposed a "tax on the brain drain," to be collected by the governments of developed countries to which professional and technical personnel from underdeveloped countries have migrated.[10] The proceeds of the tax would be transferred to the poor countries as partial compensation for the loss of talent that they have suffered.

In contrast, international migration of unskilled labor can be beneficial to the country of emigration. Unskilled workers are a more plentiful resource, and their loss is therefore likely to be felt less keenly by the sending economy. There are even significant offsetting benefits. One is remittances: unskilled migrants are less likely to take their families along, and are thus more likely to send money back. This makes labor a kind of national export. For countries such as Turkey, Algeria, and Egypt, worker remittances are a traditional source of foreign-exchange earnings. A second potential benefit is training. Unskilled workers who go abroad generally return to their native lands after a few years, bringing back usable skills acquired abroad.

Recently some LDC governments have begun to look more favorably on worker emigration. Despairing of generating enough employment at home, they have begun to encourage their people to go abroad, at least for a while. The South Asian countries for example took advantage of lucrative employment opportunities in the Middle East during the oil boom of the 1970s. When education is particularly cheap, even the emigration of trained personnel may be encouraged. The Philippines has been exporting doctors and nurses in quantity for years.

EMPLOYMENT POLICY

It is clear that the origin of the employment problem in the developing countries is the rapid growth of population and labor force. The supply of labor has increased sharply relative to the natural resource base. Although capital stock has usually risen even faster, it has generally not been deployed in ways that absorb as much labor as might have been possible. It was once thought that the solution to the employment problem in most LDCs would be industrialization. Certainly this was the premise, for example, of India's first two five-year plans. But the actual situation in that while industrial sector employment has grown rapidly in many cases, it has been unable to absorb the expanding labor force. A simple example will help to explain why this is so.

10. Jagdish Bhagwati and Martin Partington, *Taxing the Brain Drain: A Proposal* (Amsterdam: North-Holland, 1976).

Labor Absorption through Industrialization

Industrial sectors in developing countries typically grow rapidly from a low base. In low-income countries between 1965 and 1983, value-added in industry (defined to include manufacturing, utilities, and construction) grew at an average rate of 7.1 percent a year. Yet employment growth in the sector was only 60 percent as fast, or 4.3 percent a year. The amount of industrial employment growth expected from a given rate of output growth can be expressed by the following formula:

$$\Delta E_i = \eta g(V_i)S_i, \qquad\qquad [8\text{--}5]$$

where ΔE_i = annual employment growth in industry, expressed in percentage points of labor force growth; η = an elasticity relating the growth of employment to the growth of value-added; $g(V_i)$ = growth in industrial value-added, expressed in percentage points; S_i = industrial employment as a fraction of total employment. Industry absorbed 9 percent of the labor force in low-income countries in 1965, so:

$$\Delta E_i = 0.6 \times 7.1 \times 0.09 = 0.4. \qquad\qquad [8\text{--}6]$$

This means that only four-tenths of 1 percent of the labor force was absorbed by industrial expansion each year. Yet the labor force grew at 2.1 percent a year from 1965 to 1983. The implication is that less than one-fifth of the workers entering the labor force could find jobs in industry. The rest had to do the best they could in primary production in the service sector.

Is this too pessimistic a depiction of the problem? On the brighter side it can be noted that only direct employment creation in industry has been taken into account. Some additional **indirect job creation** can be expected in sectors with either forward or backward linkages to the industrial sector, such as service activities that distribute its products, and agricultural and mining activities that supply its inputs (linkages within the industrial sector are already accounted for in the model). Indirect job creation can be significant in some circumstances, such as when the capacity to process domestically produced primary commodities is expanded, but it is frequently less important for the type of import-substituting industrialization (which has few forward or backward linkages) experienced by many LDCs. Chapter 16 will discuss this in detail.

Secondary job creation also occurs as workers employed in high-paying industrial jobs spend their incomes. Businesses supplying them with consumer goods of various kinds prosper, thus creating additional employment.

Since industrial jobs are often some of the most productive and desirable ones in the economy, it is important to ask what can be done to improve industrial employment creation. In terms of the formula given above, raising ΔE_i requires increasing η, $g(V_i)$, S_i, or some combination of them. Industry's share in employment (S_i) will rise only gradually through time. In the medium term, industrial labor absorption can be increased by raising either the growth rate of sectoral value-added, $g(V_i)$, or the employment elasticity, which is η.

There are a few countries that have been able to expand industrial employment much more rapidly than average. These are also the countries that have achieved greatest success in exporting labor-intensive manufactured products. Outstanding among them are South Korea, Taiwan, Hong Kong, and Singapore, sometimes known collectively as the "Gang of Four." There are two separate aspects to their achievement. First, by breaking into the export market, they have been able to reach higher growth rates of industrial output, $g(V_i)$, because they have not had to depend on growth of the domestic market for manufactured goods. Second, they have experienced high values of η because the goods they have chosen to export are those which use large amounts of their most plentiful resource, labor. These countries have experienced values of η of around 0.8 instead of the more typical 0.4 to 0.6. Thus Korea after 1963 was able to absorb as much as half of its total labor force growth in manufactured exports alone, at a time when most LDCs were absorbing less than 5 percent of labor force growth in this activity.[11] Can other LDCs take lessons in employment policy from South Korea and the other members of the "Gang of Four"? We will take up this question in the next section.

The generally poor employment performance of industry is particularly distressing when we remember that the sector should not only be soaking up a good share of labor force growth, but also gradually drawing labor away from less productive forms of employment in peasant agriculture, petty services, and cottage industry. When industry fails to achieve either of these ends, employment in these less productive sectors will have to rise rather than fall. This can lead to stagnant, or even declining, levels of productivity and income. There is evidence that this is in fact happening, especially in some of the poorest and least rapidly growing countries.

Although the above discussion has been couched in terms of industry, it can easily be extended to cover the entire urban formal sector. Large trading companies, financial organizations, transport and communication facilities, public utilities, and the like may collectively be even more important for intersectoral labor transfer than industry. And they, too, often fail to increase their employment fast enough to satisfy development planners.

Elements of a Solution

In principle the problem of labor underutilization could be attacked on either the supply or the demand side. In practice, however, little can be done to bring about a supply-side adjustment. Labor supply grows steadily from year to year. It is hard to discourage people from seeking work. Nor would most policymakers wish to do so, given the advantages of employment creation as a means of income redistribution, and the psychological and political advantages of enabling everyone to participate in the economy. The only real supply-side potential is to reduce the growth of labor supply in the long run by reducing population growth.

Some years ago it was widely believed that increasing the supply of certain types of skilled labor would produce a strong expansionary effect on

11. Susumu Watanabe, "Exports and Employment: The Case of the Republic of Korea," *International Labour Review* 106, no. 6 (December 1972): 495–526.

employment generally through increased absorption of complementary unskilled labor. Thus India in its early postindependence years moved fast to eliminate a suspected manpower bottleneck by expanding the supply of engineers, thinking that employment in construction and other activities would be increased in this way. The number of Indian engineers increased rapidly. The effect on general employment is hard to determine, but the effect on the engineers was clear-cut: there were soon far too many of them, and many of them were unemployed. The moral is that while skill shortages can constrain employment and output growth, they can sometimes be eliminated relatively quickly and easily through expansion of education and training programs, or through migration. In other countries, where education is less developed, skill formation may be much more difficult and time-consuming.

Since the potential for correcting the labor-market disequilibrium by working on the supply side is quite limited, policy must concentrate on the demand side of the equation. Many different kinds of policy affect the economy's ability to create jobs for a growing labor force. Wage, industrial promotion, fiscal, foreign trade, education, and population policies—all have important implications for employment. For this reason other chapters of this book make frequent references to employment, supplementing the discussion in the present chapter.

We have already noted the importance of two different approaches to employment creation. One is to stimulate output, especially in relatively high-productivity and high-wage sectors of the economy. The other is to try to increase the amount of labor used to produce a given amount of output. The first approach is discussed in Chapters 18 and 20, which deal with the growth of the agricultural and industrial sectors. The second will be examined here.

Production can be made more labor-intensive in two general ways. One is to alter relative prices and thus create incentives for businesses to substitute labor for capital. The other is to develop technologies more appropriate to the factor proportions prevailing in developing countries.

Factor Pricing Distortions

The prices of labor and capital faced by modern-sector firms in less developed countries are frequently distorted in ways that make capital artificially cheap relative to labor. This distortion can inhibit labor absorption at several levels. At the sectoral level it can promote the growth of sectors that are technologically better suited to capital-intensive production (for example, basic metals) and hinder the growth of sectors that tend to be more labor intensive (for example, textiles). At the level of interfirm competition, it can promote the appearance and growth of plants using relatively capital-intensive technologies (these may be large, foreign-owned, or both) and accelerate the decline and disappearance of more labor-intensive units. At the plant level it can promote the use of machines in place of men and women.

Where do these factor price distortions originate ? In most cases some sort of government action is involved. Artificially high wages may be imposed on modern-sector firms by minimum-wage laws that are intended to protect workers' incomes, by government support of trade union demands, or by pressure on firms (especially foreign and state-owned enterprises) to be "model employers." Some governments levy payroll or social security taxes on modern-sector payrolls, thus raising the cost of labor to the employer. When jobs once done by foreigners are taken over by citizens, nationalist pressures cause salaries to be kept at their previously high, internationally competitive levels.

All these policies promote the welfare of one relatively small group at the expense of a much larger group. Minimum-wage laws and similar measures, if effectively enforced (and often they are not), make wages and working conditions better for those workers fortunate enough to get jobs in modern-sector firms. But by raising the cost of labor, minimum-wage laws limit the ability of existing firms to absorb more workers and inhibit the creation of more enterprises like them. In other words, minimum wages improve the well-being of the relatively small group of modern-sector employees at the cost of the much larger group that is either unemployed or working in the informal and rural sectors.

Why do governments of countries with serious employment problems enact such measures as minimum-wage laws? The answer lies in points of political economy that have been discussed in earlier chapters. Relatively small but well-organized, vocal, and visible groups of modern-sector workers, nearly always located in urban areas, use their political power to press for enactment of these laws, or for increases in the statutory minimum once a system of minimum wages is established. Under this kind of system the government is typically held directly responsible for the earnings of workers in the protected sectors. If it resists a strongly backed demand for a rise in the minimum wage, it is inviting political trouble. Of course the government is also responsible for the welfare of those who lose from the wage increase because their chances of ever getting a job in the protected high-wage sector are reduced. But their loss is less easily perceived than the wage gain of the protected workers, and the government is less likely to be held accountable for it.

Artificially cheap capital can reinforce the effect of artificially expensive labor. Many LDCs maintain legal ceilings on interest rates. These make capital equipment cheaper for those preferred customers who can obtain the credit necessary to buy it. (For the rest, of course, capital may become more expensive, or even unobtainable, as banks and other financial institutions direct the available funds to their preferred customers.) Overvaluation of the domestic currency in terms of foreign exchange can have a similar effect. It forces the imposition of a licensing system for foreign exchange, imports or both, and this in turn makes artificially cheapened capital goods available to those who can obtain the necessary licenses.

Like minimum wages, interest ceilings, foreign exchange control, and import licensing are enacted to serve the interests of influential minorities. In the case of Pakistan, for example, New York University economist Lawrence White has shown how preferred access to imports and credit led to the increasing concentration of industry and commerce in the hands of an elite group known as "The Twenty Families."[12] Licensing systems also receive strong support from officials of the license-granting authorities, who can earn substantial illicit income from the bestowal of their favors.

Another way governments help to make capital artificially cheap is by gearing investment incentives to the amount of capital invested. Often a firm that invests $50 million is given a longer tax holiday or a shorter write-off period than one that invests only $5 million. This creates incentives for capital-intensive industries to set up in the country and for firms facing a range of possible technologies to select more capital-intensive modes of production.

Correcting Factor Price Distortion

What can be done to correct these factor price distortions? Certainly the most straightforward approach is for governments to avoid the kinds of price-distorting policies mentioned above, or if they have already instituted them, to deregulate as soon as possible. Often, however, they are reluctant to do so, either because of concern for the welfare of workers already holding modern-sector jobs, or because of the political power of those who benefit from artificially high wages or artificially cheap capital and foreign exchange.

When price distortions cannot be changed by direct means, it may be possible to offset them by taxes or subsidies. Some economists argue that artificially high labor costs faced by modern-sector employers should be countered by a wage subsidy. This advice has been followed rarely, if at all, although a few countries have adopted investment incentives that depend in part on the number of jobs an investor creates.

An important question about all proposals for correcting factor price distortions is how great their employment-creating effect is likely to be. Technically speaking, this depends on the **elasticity of substitution,** which can be defined as

$$\sigma = \frac{\Delta\,(K/L)}{\Delta\,(w/r)} \cdot \frac{w/r}{K/L},$$

where K is the amount of capital, L the amount of labor, w the wage rate, r the cost of capital, and Δ signifies a change. The elasticity of substitution is thus the percentage change in the capital/labor ratio, $\Delta(K/L)/(K/L)$, that results from a given percentage change in the ratio of the price of labor to that of capital, $\Delta(w/r)/(w/r)$. (The expression w/r is also called the *wage-rental ratio.*) Thus, if a 10 percent decline in the wage-rental ratio leads to a 5 percent fall in the capital-labor ratio, then the elasticity of substitution is 0.5. In these circumstances a 10 percent decline in the wage-rental ratio would mean that in the future it would take 5 percent less investment (capital) to employ a given amount of labor; alternatively, a given amount of investment would employ 5 percent more workers.

Debates over the efficiency of employment creation through correction of factor price distortions have ranged the "elasticity optimists" against the

12. Lawrence White, *Industrial Concentration and Economic Power in Pakistan* (Princeton: Princeton University Press, 1974).

"elasticity pessimists." The optimists have argued that the employment effects are likely to be large because investors tend to be rational profit maximizers who have a range of possible outputs and technologies open to them. When faced with cheaper labor relative to capital, they will therefore make two kinds of adjustment: they will concentrate on goods that can be produced relatively efficiently using a lot of labor relative to capital; and they will tend to use more labor-intensive technologies in all their operations. (The optimists assume that these investors actually have a "shelf" of "appropriate technologies" available to them, an issue that will be explored in the following section.)

The pessimists, on the other hand, argue that the response to a change in the wage-rental ratio may be small or nonexistent. There certainly are modern industries whose technologies permit little substitution of labor for capital. Examples include the "process industries" such as petrochemicals and wood pulp. In such industries, highly capital-intensive technologies may be absolutely more efficient than any less capital-intensive alternatives. That is, they may use less capital per unit of output as well as less labor. In many cases these technical characteristics are linked to economies of scale: a plant must be very large, as well as highly capital-intensive, to be efficient. An LDC government might well think twice before establishing such an industry, but it would be ill-advised to try to make it labor-intensive.

The elasticity pessimists also point out that many firms sell in oligopolistic markets and therefore do not necessarily have to maximize profits; that they may prefer the most "modern" (and therefore capital-intensive) technologies for their own sake; and that they may produce goods mainly for middle-class consumption, to which capital-intensive technologies are better suited than labor-intensive technologies. For all these reasons the pessimists argue against the policies advocated by the optimists. They would expect, for example, that a wage subsidy would do more to increase business profits than to expand employment.

Figures 8-2 and 8-3 show the differences between what the pessimists and the optimists have in mind. Which is the better depiction of the real world? It might seem a simple matter to calculate the elasticity of substitution in developing countries and settle the argument once and for all. And indeed many econometric estimates have been made. Quite a number of these studies have found the value of σ to range from 0.5, not a dramatically high value but high enough to encourage the elasticity optimists, up towards 1.0. But other writers have criticized these estimates on various grounds: they assume labor and capital to be homogeneous—that is, of uniform quality—when in fact they are not; they ignore the roles of other factors of production, such as management; they often deal with industries that are defined so broadly as to encompass a variety of outputs; and so on. Modest changes in assumptions, the critics note, can lead to large differences in conclusions.

Thus the debate between the optimists and the pessimists is not so easily settled, at least not by econometric means. However, there remain good reasons for believing that the relative prices of labor and capital can make a significant difference for employment creation. First, whatever the range of technologies available for producing a particular item, factor prices can have

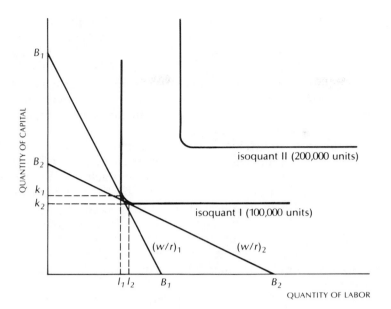

FIGURE 8–2 Factor Substitution with Relatively Fixed Factor Proportions (Low Elasticity of Substitution). Possibilities for producing given levels of output with different factor combinations are severely limited. When the wage-rental ratio falls from $(w/r)_1$ to $(w/r)_2$, there is little effect on the amounts of labor and capital used to produce 100,000 units of output.

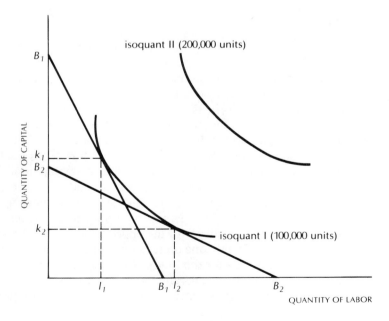

FIGURE 8–3 Factor Substitution with Relatively Variable Factor Proportions (High Elasticity of Substitution). Possibilities for producing given levels of output with different factor combinations are much greater than in Figure 8–2. When the wage-rental ratio falls, the amount of capital used is sharply reduced while employment expands significantly.

an important influence on employment by affecting the choice of goods to be produced. Recall the example of the successful exporters of labor-intensive manufacturers mentioned earlier. Second, even if the technology of a core production process is fixed and capital-intensive, opportunities exist for using large amounts of labor in subsidiary operations such as materials handling. Similarly, in construction some operations are best done by machines at almost any wage-rental ratio, but others lend themselves to labor-intensive methods if labor costs are low enough.

Third, employers are much more responsive to relative factor prices if they are forced to sell their products in competitive markets than if they can sell in oligopolistic markets. An important study conducted in Indonesia by Harvard Business School professor Louis Wells showed that while the non-maximizing behaviors cited by the elasticity pessimists are real enough, businessmen indulge them much more freely under oligopolistic market conditions.[13] When the competition forces then to seek the most profitable technologies and factor proportions, both domestic and foreign businessmen find ways to economize on capital and substitute more labor in labor-rich, capital-scarce countries.

A broad statement of the conclusion which emerges from these three points is that open competition promotes appropriate factor choices. Increasing the degree of competition, both within a given economy and among economies (as we will see in Chapters 16 and 17), can go a long way toward validating the assumptions of the elasticity optimists and making it possible to promote employment by reducing factor price distortions.

The Role of Technology

For the employment problem to be solved, or even significantly ameliorated, technology appropriate to the factor endowments of the low- and middle-income countries is clearly needed. Does such technology already exist? If not, how can it be brought into existence?

Everyone agrees that much of the technology used in high-income countries is inappropriate to the needs of low- and middle-income countries. Since the beginning of their industrialization processes the United States and Europe have had a scarcity of labor relative to other factors of production. Nearly all their innovations have accordingly aimed at saving labor. The result in almost all sectors of production has been a sequence of increasingly mechanized and automatically controlled technologies, each more appropriate than the last for a country with scarce labor and plentiful capital—but less and less appropriate for a country with the opposite factor endowments.

Excessive capital intensity is only one dimension of the inappropriateness of developed-country technology for the LDCs. Since the economies of even the smaller industrial countries are generally much larger than those of even the most populous developing countries, the technology is frequently

13. Louis T. Wells, "Economic Man and Engineering Man: Choice of Technology in a Low-Wage Country," in *The Choice of Technology in Developing Countries: Some Cautionary Tales,* C. Peter Timmer et al., eds. (Cambridge, Mass.: Harvard University Center for International Affairs, 1975), pp. 69–93.

designed to be efficient at a much larger scale of operation than the developing countries can hope to attain in the foreseeable future. In addition the
borrowed technology may necessitate the use of skills that are unavailable in
poor countries, and thus may require the importation of foreign technicians.
Finally, it may be designed to produce the wrong type or grade of product:
for example, no-iron synthetic fabrics in countries where cotton is cheaper
and where there is plenty of labor to wash and press cotton garments.

Despite the dimensions of inappropriateness, technology developed in
rich countries is often transferred intact for use in poor countries. This is not,
after all, surprising. Well over 90 percent of the world's expenditure on technology research and development is made in rich countries. Third-world
countries invite multinational corporations to invest in their leading sectors.
They obtain equipment through official aid programs. The investors and aid
givers, East or West, can only provide what they know and have available.
Hence the transfer of inappropriate technology.

Technology Policies

When technology available from the developed countries is inappropriate,
where is more appropriate technology to be obtained? Four possible sources
can be distinguished.[14] First, LDCs can use developed-country technologies
but make peripheral modifications, for example, in materials handling. Second, they can borrow old technologies from the industrial countries. American technology of twenty, thirty, or even fifty years ago may be more
appropriate to the setting of, say, India, than the methods and machines used
in the United States today. A third possible source of appropriate technology
is selective borrowing from the industrial countries. Former British, French,
American, and Dutch colonies in Southeast Asia gradually learned after
independence that Japanese equipment was often better suited to their needs
than the equipment they had formerly imported from the metropolitan
country. Now equipment from Korea, Taiwan, and mainland China is
replacing Japanese equipment. Fourth, developing countries can do their
own research and development to evolve technologies specifically designed
to fit local conditions. It is sometimes said that traditional indigenous technologies developed over the years by local farmers, craftsmen, and fishermen
provide a promising basis for this work.

But if these alternative channels of technological development are really
open, why does so much of the technology used in the third world remain so
obviously inappropriate? One important reason has already been suggested:
when competitive pressures are absent, incentives to adapt to local conditions are weak. Another barrier is communication difficulties. It is hard for
someone sitting in Surabaya or São Paulo to know just what technologies—
new and modern, or older vintages—are available in New York or Nagasaki.
Finally, it must be said that most third-world governments have not yet fully
awakened to the need to promote local research and development. Their

14. This paragraph and the two which follow are based on Frances Stewart, "Technology
and Employment in LDCs," *Employment in Developing Nations,* Edgar O. Edwards, ed. (New
York and London: Columbia University Press, 1974), pp. 83–132.

universities are usually preoccupied with teaching, and official research institutes in various field are often either slow to be set up or experience severe staffing difficulties once they open their doors. Sometimes in these circumstances the most useful research and development work is done by foreign firms with a long history of operations in the country.

The British economist Frances Stewart has distinguished three schools of thought on technology policies for third-world countries. The first group, which she calls "the price incentive school," stresses "getting the prices right," in the belief that factor prices that reflect social costs will not only lead to the selection of the most efficient techniques out of the currently available range, but will also create incentives for more appropriate technologies to be developed. The opposing "technologist school" believes that this mechanism of induced innovation cannot be relied upon to do the job, and that a conscious decision to invest more in technological development is needed. Finally, there is "the radical reform school," which takes a broader view of the matter. This school argues that both the array of goods produced and the methods used to produce them are inherent features of social systems. One cannot expect anything but capital-intensive methods and products targeted for middle-class consumption from the multinational corporations. Creation of appropriate technologies and use of appropriate factor proportions, this last group argues, requires that production be reoriented toward a multitude of cheap items for mass consumption. This in turn requires a massive redistribution of income, which cannot be achieved without a social revolution. Hence the problem of inappropriate technology and inadequate job creation can only be solved in the context of a radical reform of society.

As Stewart sensibly concludes, elements of all three approaches are probably needed. The best evidence for the efficacy of radical reform comes from China. China has apparently found the social and technological solutions to permit her vast labor force to be employed more fully and productively than ever before. Chinese industry "walks on two legs"; it combines large-scale, relatively capital-intensive production units with smaller, more labor-intensive and decentralized plants. Large-scale public works projects, such as dams and irrigation channels, have been another important form of labor absorption. Finally, intensified agricultural technologies using much larger amounts of fertilizer and other modern inputs have absorbed more labor productively into China's massive agricultural work force. Appropriate technology is combined with strong production organization at the local level. The rural commune contrives to provide full employment for all its members in a combination of agricultural and nonagricultural activities.

Other socialist developing countries, by contrast, have sometimes had a hard time deciding just which way they want to go. Thus different conceptions of "African socialism" prevalent in Tanzania in the early 1970s stressed decentralized small-scale industry, increased processing of domestic raw materials, and creation of a modern, self-sufficient, state-run economy—not always consistently.

Nonsocialist governments are probably best advised to rely on a mixture of price incentives and judicious investment in research and development.

The Korean Institute of Science and Technology (KIST) provides an exam- **203**
ple of the kind of government-sponsored research, usually adaptive, that EMPLOYMENT
third-world countries should be conducting in greater amounts. POLICY

Other Employment Policies

Some theorists have argued that improvement in *income distribution* would
accelerate job creation. According to this argument, goods consumed by
poor people tend to be more labor-intensive than items consumed by those
who are better off, so redistribution of income in favor of the poor would
create a shift in the pattern of demand, which in turn would create employment. A number of simulation studies have tested the probable magnitude of
this effect.[15] Unfortunately, most of them have concluded that it is not very
great. A major stumbling block seems to be that while the goods consumed
by the middle- and upper-income groups are indeed more capital-intensive
than those consumed by the lower-income group, the better-off groups also
consume more services, many of which are almost pure labor, such as household services. Another factor is that goods consumed by the rich and poor
often use the same intermediate inputs, for example, steel. Thus a shift in the
pattern of final demand may have only a limited impact on the structure of
production.

An important goal for development planners is to look for investments
that complement labor rather than substitute for it. Such investment opportunities probably exist in every sector of the economy. In agriculture, for
example, mechanization of the planting and harvest functions may displace
massive quantities of labor, while investments in irrigation may actually
create employment by making it possible to cultivate the same land more
intensively and through a greater proportion of the year. A different kind of
complementary investment, discussed earlier, is training to fill skill
bottlenecks.

Despite our perception of low-income countries as capital-scarce, it has
been frequently observed that their existing stocks of capital equipment are
underutilized. Factories produce at only 30–60 percent of capacity, shift
work is unusual, tractors sit idle in fields, bulldozers rest by roadsides. If all
this idle capacity could somehow be put to work, there would be a sharp
upswing in the demand for labor, achievable in the short run, without having
to wait for new investments to be made and mature. This is an appealing
prospect, but not an easy one to realize. There are many possible explanations for unused capacity, including fluctuations in demand and inadequate
supplies of materials. Despite the scarcity of capital, distorted prices in some
developing countries may make it cheaper for firms to let their equipment
stand idle part of the time than to use it more intensively.

Generally speaking, small informal-sector establishments use less capital
and more labor to produce any given type of output than the larger formal-

---

15. A *simulation study* first models the behavior of a real world phenomenon, then tries to
measure how the outcome varies in response to changes in the one or more causal variables. In
the studies discussed here, the effects on employment of various possible income distributions
were measured.

sector firms. An important reason for this is that small firms face prices for labor and capital that are closer to their social opportunity costs. Minimum-wage laws, unionization, and payroll taxation all have little or no application to informal-sector firms. And not being preferred customers of the banks—indeed, often not dealing with banks at all—they have no access to rationed credit at artificially low interest rates. This situation has led many governments and international agencies to advocate special attention to small-scale industry.[16]

The employment-creation potentials of small-scale industry are not yet well understood. Normally the importance of small firms declines relative to that of large firms in the course of economic development. The conditions under which small-scale industry could progressively modernize itself and contribute to development, as it did in Japan, rather than stagnate and become a continuing drain on the exchequer as in India, have yet to be defined. Most third-world governments hamper the ability of small-scale industry to compete with large-scale domestic firms and with imports through a variety of policies and administrative procedures, ranging from exchange rate overvaluation and investment incentives available only to large firms to disruptively selective enforcement of tax and licensing requirements. Even if they are not sure exactly what to do to help small-scale, labor-intensive industry, third-world governments can at least desist from practices that harm it.

Small-scale industry is linked to the income distribution point made earlier. Since most of the products of small informal-sector units are consumed by the lower-income groups, income redistribution would strengthen the competitive position of these units. The characteristics and problems of small industry are discussed further in Chapter 20.

When all else fails governments may institute **food-for-work programs** to provide at least part-time or temporary employment to groups which are particularly distressed or in a particularly strong position to give the government trouble if their needs are not looked after. Many of these programs have been financed by foreign food aid, either by paying the participants with food or by selling the food and using the counterpart funds thus earned to help pay the cost of the program.

These programs offer the attractive prospect of combining construction of a socially useful facility with income redistribution to some of the poorest elements in society. It has been discovered, however, that these benefits have been attained only occasionally in the dozens of such programs that have been undertaken so far.[17] Many programs are plagued by bad management, and in some countries local elites have found ways to divert most of the benefits to themselves, sometimes even forcing the peasants to labor at low wages to provide a road or irrigation ditch that only increases the value of the

16. Besides being more labor-intensive, small-scale industry has also been thought to improve income distribution, promote democracy by widening participation in business, mobilize additional grassroots saving, and assist the spread of economic development to outlying areas.

17. J. W. Thomas, et al., "Public Works Programs in Developing Countries: A Comparative Analysis" (World Bank Staff Working Paper No. 224, February 1976).

landlord's property. Implementing an effective food-for-work program is a challenging task, best undertaken by governments (such as China's) that possess both a strong commitment to economic and social equity, and a capacity to enforce that commitment.

GOVERNMENT STRATEGIES

The desirability of accelerating the creation of productive employment, especially in countries hoping to combine a reasonable measure of equity with economic growth, should be evident. The feasibility of doing it is much less straightforward. Many different types of public policy impinge on employment creation. It is really not possible to draw up an "employment plan" for a developing country, only a general development plan stressing employment as one in a set of interrelated objectives.[18] The importance of employment as an objective of development policy and planning has received full recognition only in the last two decades. Planners and scholars alike are still learning what is involved in increasing productive employment in developing countries.

It is clear, though, that the context of the particular developing country—its size and economic structure—makes a difference for the kind of employment creation strategy to be pursued. South Korea and Singapore have been able to solve their employment problems by emulating the Japanese pattern of whirlwind industrialization based largely on the export market. Medium-sized, partially industrialized countries, such as Malaysia and the Philippines, may be able to follow a similar path, with modifications permitted by their richer natural-resource endowments. Larger, more agricultural countries will have to take a more balanced approach. At best they may be able to develop rapidly following a "continental" model, as Brazil seems to be doing. At worst, as in Bangladesh and the other very poor countries, a long period of reliance on job creation in agriculture and other rural activities will be required.

18. This has not prevented the ILO, under its World Employment Programme, from preparing a series of such plans through the use of visiting missions—for Colombia, Sri Lanka, Iran, Kenya, the Philippines, and the Sudan. While useful as a means of publicizing the goal of employment creation and as illustrations of how employment-oriented development planning can be carried out, these plans have not in any literal sense been implemented by the governments concerned.

Education

The previous chapter discussed labor as a homogenous resource in economic development, as a quantity of human power available to produce goods and services. But numbers of workers cannot tell the whole story. Attempts to attribute economic growth to growth in the factors of production always leave an unexplained residual. One important explanation for that residual is the improvement in the quality of human resources that leads workers to be more productive. Labor quality may be enhanced by education of either children or adults; by improved health and nutrition for children and working adults; by migration of workers to places with better job opportunities; and by fertility reduction.

Some of these activities are discussed in other chapters. At this point we want to stress their common characteristics. In each case someone—either the community as a whole, employers, the individuals concerned, or their parents—makes a decision to use scarce resources to improve the productivity, present or future, of human beings. In an influential presidential speech to the American Economic Association in 1960, Theodore Schultz suggested that such activities could be considered a process of accumulating capital, which could later be drawn upon to increase a worker's productivity and income. He called this **investment in human capital.** This form of investment, said Schultz, is every bit as important as investment in physical capital, but until his speech it had largely been neglected by academics and policymakers alike.[1] Subsequent work by Schultz and others elaborated the

1. See Theodore W. Schultz, "Investment in Human Capital," *American Economic Review* 51 (January 1961): 17.

idea of investment in human capital, applying it to all the human resource development activities mentioned above. A much better idea of what the concept implies should emerge from the discussion of it in the context of education later in this chapter.

Studies sponsored by the World Bank lend further support to the idea that human resource development has an important bearing on economic growth.[2] There is reason to believe that the relationship is two-way and mutually supporting. On the one hand growing economies can and do devote increasing resources to improvement of educational, health, and nutritional standards. But it is also apparent that investment in human resources helps to accelerate economic growth. It does this by increasing labor productivity, encouraging greater physical investment, and reducing the dependency burden of the population. These contributions to growth are especially evident in the case of education.

IMPORTANCE OF EDUCATION

Education can be defined broadly as all forms of human learning, or more narrowly as the process that occurs in specialized institutions called schools. It is unquestionably the most important form of human resource development, in several senses.

First, there is tremendous popular demand for education, particularly for schooling, in virtually all countries, developing and developed alike. Often in LDCs the number of people seeking admittance to schools far exceeds the number of places available. In Indonesia (see boxed example) there was a tremendous popular response when the government made primary schooling widely available. Obviously, people everywhere believe that education is beneficial for themselves and their children.

Education in Indonesia

In 1973, as he was working on his country's second five-year plan, the chairman of Indonesia's National Development Planning Board registered displeasure over statistics he had received from the Ministry of Education. The data showed that only 54 percent of 7–12 year olds were enrolled in primary school. Worse, the ministry's projections indicated that no rise in the percentage of children enrolled was likely over the next five years. The major reasons: too few of Indonesia's 60,000 villages had primary schools; trained teachers were in short supply; textbooks were scarce and expensive; and many poor rural households were unable to pay even the small fees charged to attend school. The chairman decided that something drastic had to be done.

The solution: a special program to improve the rural population's

2. See World Bank, *World Development Report 1980* (New York: Oxford University Press, 1980) and the working papers cited therein; also, George Psacharopoulos and Maureen Woodhall, *Education for Development. An Analysis of Investment Choices* (New York: Oxford University Press, 1985).

access to schools by cutting red tape and building primary schools in villages that did not yet have them. These new schools were then staffed with newly trained teachers and provided with millions of just printed library- and textbooks. Moreover, school fees were abolished at the primary level. The program was funded through loans from the World Bank and from the growing oil revenues that Indonesia was fortunately receiving during the 1970s. Would rural parents respond to the improved opportunity by sending their sons and daughters to school? They would. By 1983, after more than 60,000 new schools had been built and over 100,000 existing schools rehabilitated, about 95 percent of 7–12 year olds had signed up for school. The program was a great success.

But every development success brings new problems in its wake. Now the Indonesian government is struggling to cope with the rising tide of primary-school graduates who want to go on to secondary school and eventually university. Since the government cannot afford to build enough public high schools to accommodate all who want to attend them, and many parents cannot afford to send their children to private schools, enrollment in secondary and higher education is still restricted largely to the minority of students from better-off families who can afford to pay. Nor is it clear where the farmers of the future will come from, since virtually everyone who has completed primary school wants to get out of farming and seek a living elsewhere.

A second reason for believing that education is important is the frequently observed correlation between education and income at both the individual and the societal level. Figure 9–1 shows some typical patterns relating age, educational attainment, and earnings in two developing countries. Although not all high school graduates, for example, earn more than all who completed only primary school, the majority do, and on average their earnings are much higher. People the world over intuitively recognize this correlation, and base their desire to obtain the largest possible amount of schooling for their children on it.

Similarly, there is a strong correlation between national income levels and educational attainments. As Table 9–1 demonstrates, illiteracy is rife in the very poorest countries and diminishes steadily as one goes up the income scale. The reason is that mass education is still a relatively recent phenomenon in most parts of the world. When most adults now living were children, schooling was much less prevalent than it is today. Nevertheless, all but the very poorest countries are currently educating large fractions of their school-age populations (middle columns of Table 9–1), so the educational attainment of the adult population is rising fast.

It should be emphasized that the relationships shown in Figure 9–1 and Table 9–1 are averages. There are many contrary cases: of rich individuals and societies that have received little schooling, of well-educated individuals and heavily schooled societies whose incomes are relatively low. Some of the international variations are shown in Table 9–2. On average, however, the correlation between education and income is a strong one. But does this

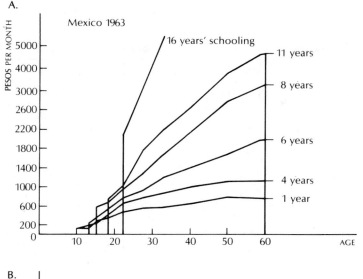

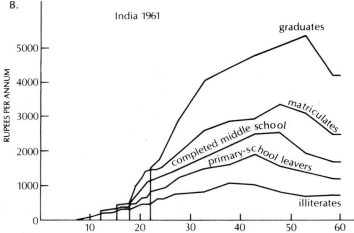

FIGURE 9–1   Age-Earning Profiles in Mexico and India. The lines on the graph represent mean earnings at different ages of people with varying amounts of formal education. On average, people who stay in school longer earn higher incomes. *Sources:* Martin Carnoy, "Rates of Return to Schooling in Latin America," *Journal of Human Resources* (Summer 1967): 359-74; M. Blaug, R. Layard, and M. Woodhall, *Causes of Graduate Unemployment in India* (Harmondsworth, England: Allen Lane, Penguin Press, 1969), p. 21.

mean that education really raises a person's, or a nation's, income? Or is it simply that richer countries and families spend more to acquire greater education? Or, finally, are higher income and education simply the common results of some unidentified third factor? These questions will be explored later in the chapter.

A third reason why education is important in developing countries is that large sums are spent to acquire it. Education is a major item in both household and national budgets. Because their people want it, and to some extent

TABLE 9-1   Educational Statistics in Relation to GNP Per Capita (1970s and early 1980s)[a]

| Income group | % of illiterate adults | Enrollment ratios[b] | | | | Approximate public expenditure dollars per pupil | | | |
| | | Primary school | | Secondary school gross | Higher education gross | % of GNP | 1st level | 2nd level | 3rd level |
		Gross	Net						
Below $300	64	61	50	13	1.7	3.0	40	270	3,100
$300–$500	37	70	54	19	1.7	3.0[c]	50	370	2,100
$500–$1,000	44	90	74	28	7.8	3.6	120	340	2,900
$1,000–$2,000	26	106	89	51	14.5	4.0	140	230	1,300
$2,000–$5,000	10	106	93	66	15.7	5.5	370	400	1,700
$5,000 or more	2[c]	102	89	77	24.0	6.2	1,800	2,200	5,500

Source: UNESCO Statistical Yearbook 1984 (Paris, 1984); World Bank, *World Development Report 1982 and 1985* (New York: Oxford University Press, 1982 and 1985).

[a] Year of most recent estimate available varies by country.

[b] Enrollment ratios express enrollment as a percentage of the school-age population. Gross enrollment ratios relate total enrollment of students of all ages to the size of the age group that normally attends that level of schooling; they can exceed 100%. Net enrollment ratios show the percentage of the pertinent age group that is enrolled.

[c] Rough estimate; many industrial countries with very high literacy rates no longer publish statistics on illiteracy.

TABLE 9-2   Educational Statistics for Selected Countries (1970s and early 1980s)[a]

| Country | % of illiterate adults | Enrollment ratios[b] | | | | Approximate public expenditure dollars per pupil | | | |
| | | Primary school | | Secondary school gross | Higher education gross | % of GNP | 1st level | 2nd level | 3rd Level |
		Gross	Net						
Brazil	24	96	76	33	12.0	3.8	90	280	1,330
Colombia	19	125	na	46	12.2	2.6	100	50	280
Bolivia	37	86	77	34	16.4	3.1	110	70	380
Peru	20	114	92	59	21.3	3.4	180	70	na
Chile	11	112	100	59	10.4	5.8	360	160	1,220
Kenya	53	104	72	20	1.0	6.5	50	110	2,350
Ghana	70	76	na	34	1.3	1.8	110	190	630
Tanzania	21	98	72	3	0.4	5.9	30	340	7,900
Indonesia	38	120	100	33	4.1	2.2	na	na	na
India	64	79	62	30	8.7	3.0	20	40	120
Pakistan	76	44	na	14	2.0	1.9	30	40	310
Sri Lanka	15	103	na	54	3.6	3.0	na	na	50
South Korea	7	104	100	86	21.0	4.3	100	80	170
Malaysia	40	92	na	49	4.6	7.6	240	220	2,880
Japan	1	100	100	92	30.0	6.0	1,340	1,490	1,720
Hungary	1	100	98	73	14.1	5.0	310	1,820	5,330
United Kingdom	1	102	95	83	19.4	5.7	1,500	980	3,630
United States	1	na	na	na	58.0	6.8	na	na	2,931

Source: UNESCO Statistical Yearbook 1984 (Paris, 1984); World Bank, *World Development Report 1982 and 1985* (New York: Oxford University Press, 1982 and 1985).

[a] Year of most recent estimate available varies by country.

also because they think it will stimulate development, LDC governments devote a substantial fraction of their resources to the creation and operation of school systems. As Table 9–1 (right-hand columns) illustrates, expenditure of 3–6 percent of GNP in public funds is typical; private expenditures on education, which are harder to measure, are left out. Some 15–20 percent of the government budget commonly goes for education. If we looked at education in less conventional terms as an industry, we would see that it is one of the largest industries in all economies, in terms of both value-added and employment.

TRENDS AND PATTERNS

The preceding discussion treated the terms *education* and *schooling* as if they were synonymous. Indeed this is probably the most common way of using these words in everyday parlance. Modern usage by specialists, however, tends to apply to the term *education* to a broader concept, akin to the notion of "learning." The purpose is to stress that there are different forms of learning that are important and can be seen as substitutes for each other in some circumstances. Usually three principal types of learning—education in the broad sense—are identified.

Types of Learning

Formal education takes place in institutions called schools. Its participants are usually young people who have not yet begun their working lives.

Nonformal education can be thought of as organized programs of learning that take place outside schools. Often the participants are adults. The programs are usually shorter and more narrowly focused than programs of formal education. Nonformal education may be concerned with occupational skills, or with other subjects such as literacy, family life, or citizenship.

Informal education is learning that takes place outside any institutional framework or organized program. People learn many important things in the home, on the job, and in the general community.

Although other definitions of the three terms can easily be found, these convey a reasonable idea of what is meant. Throughout the remainder of this chapter we will use them in the above senses.

Characteristics of LDC Education

School systems in most third-world countries have expanded with extraordinary rapidity over the last three to four decades. Countries that emerged from colonialism after World War II generally inherited narrowly based systems designed to educate only the local elite and a small cadre of literate clerks. Most colonial regimes distrusted the educated "native" and were terrified by the possible consequences of mass education. Even in Latin America, where most countries had obtained their independence during the nineteenth century, a rigid class structure confined schooling essentially to the better-off urbanites.

After independence, the political imperatives swung around strongly to favor rapid expansion of schooling. Pledged to change so many things in so short a time, new regimes found that one of the most popular things they could do relatively quickly was to build schools. Whereas a modern economy might be several decades, even a century or more away, a modern-looking school system could be built in just a few years.

As Table 9–3 shows, school enrollments at all levels in developing countries grew from about 100 million in 1950 to more than 600 million by 1980. The number of students enrolled more than doubled in the 1950s. In the 1960s and 1970s the growth rate of enrollment gradually declined, but the absolute number of students added each decade continued to rise.

In all countries enrollment growth proceeded in waves, hitting the primary schools first, then, as applications for secondary schooling swelled, high schools, and finally the universities, technical colleges, and other institutions of higher education. The spread of the system differed from country to country. A relatively westernized Asian country like Sri Lanka, which adopted a free schooling policy at independence in 1948, was able to achieve practically universal primary schooling in the 1950s and then press on rapidly with expansion of the higher levels until financial difficulties forced a slowdown of enrollment expansion in the 1960s. By contrast some countries in Latin America and elsewhere commenced rapid enrollment expansion at the higher levels long before universal primary schooling was attained. In some countries this pattern resulted from a concentration of political power which allowed the interests of the elite to be raised far above those of the general

TABLE 9–3   School Enrollment in Developing Countries,ᵃ 1950–1980 (millions)

	1950	1960	1970	1980
Primary				
Africa	7	17	30	59
Asia	71	164	234	319
Latin America	15	27	44	65
Total	93	208	307	443
Secondary				
Africa	—	2	4	14
Asia	6	12	66	123
Latin America	2	4	11	18
Total	8	18	80	155
Higher				
Africa	—	—	—	1
Asia	1	1	5	11
Latin America	—	1	2	5
Total	1	2	7	17
All Levels				
Total	102	228	395	615

Source: UNESCO Yearbook of Educational Statistics 1972 (Paris, 1973); UNESCO Statistical Yearbook 1981 (Paris, 1981); UNESCO Statistical Yearbook 1984 (Paris, 1984).

ᵃ North Korea is excluded from these statistics. South Africa and Japan are regarded as developed countries and are also excluded. Continents may not add to total because of rounding error and exclusion of a few small countries (— indicates less than 500,000).

population. Elsewhere, as in the more conservative Muslim countries, it was

a consequence of the low priority attached to education for girls.

Rapid expansion often created *teacher shortages* that led to increasing class sizes and use of less highly trained teachers. In some countries it proved possible to expand teacher training and overcome the worst of the shortages after a few years. In many places, however, teacher shortages persist to this day, particularly in the more remote areas where teachers, like other public servants, are reluctant to go.

As mentioned before, most LDCs were feeling strong budgetary pressures from the expansion of schooling by the 1960s, if not before. In oil producing countries, such as Indonesia (see boxed example), the crunch came later. But few LDCs have been able to satisfy all the "social demand" for education from public funds. The most common reaction to budgetary pressures was to put the brakes on enrollment expansion. Other possible adjustments, such as increasing the efficiency of educational expenditures and asking families to finance a larger share of schooling, were made less frequently. The latter adjustment sometimes took place by default as private secondary schools and colleges sprang up to offer places to disappointed applicants to the public institutions.

A major reason for the inefficiency of educational expenditures has been the high frequencies of **dropouts,** those who withdraw from schooling before completing an academically meaningful course of study, and **repeaters,** those who require more than the prescribed number of years to complete the program. Most educators believe that a child who fails to complete at least five or six years of school gains little from attendance, yet millions fail to do so. In large measure these problems result from poverty. The various costs of keeping a child in school become too heavy an imposition on the poor household after a while.

With all these problems of educational quality it is not surprising that many of the children who attend LDC schools fail to learn very much. A few years ago the International Association for the Evaluation of Education Achievement (IEA) administered standardized achievement tests to pupils in twenty-three countries, including three developing countries (Chile, Iran, and India). Although there is room for doubt about whether the tests were strictly comparable, it was evident that pupils in poor countries are likely to learn much less than their counterparts in rich countries. For example, final-year secondary school students in Iran and India scored far worse in a reading test than students from any of the developed countries, and the Chilean students also scored somewhat lower.[3] There is even evidence that those who do master specific skills in school sometimes lose them in later life through lack of use. Functional literacy is likely to be retained only by those who have access to written materials and are faced with daily incentives to read and write. Many third-world people have neither.

3. The shortfall of the LDCs was more noticeable when average scores were compared than when the scores of the top 9% of students were compared between rich and poor countries. This may reflect the wider quality variations among schools in poor countries as compared to richer ones. For discussion, see John Simmons, "How Effective is Schooling in Promoting Learning? A Review of the Research" (World Bank Staff Working Paper No. 200, March 1975).

Increasing interest in income distribution and equity after the late 1960s caused greater attention to be paid to the regional and social inequities that characterize most developing-country school systems. In many countries a child who lives in an urban area or who comes from a favored socioeconomic background is far more likely to receive schooling, and also more likely to receive high-quality schooling, than a student from a rural area or a more ordinary socioeconomic setting. To the considerable extent that education leads to a better job and a higher income, this pattern of educational provision worsens the distribution of opportunity and income. Some economists believe that an improved distribution of schooling could be a major force for achieving a more even distribution of income. Governments in the third world are just now beginning to address these problems and potentials.

One reason for the limited learning which seems to take place in third-world school systems is, in British scholar Ronald Dore's phrase, the "diploma disease."[4] According to some analysts, these systems are not primarily in the business of conveying knowledge and skills at all, but are principally concerned with "certification" or "credentialing." Dore's studies show that in late-developing countries there is a strong tendency to judge an individual's fitness for work by the academic credentials which he or she possesses. And of course successful completion of a given level of schooling is the main qualification for admittance to the next highest level. In most developing countries, nationwide examinations are given at particular stages in the schooling process to determine the student's fitness for educational advancement or employment. These exams take on tremendous importance, causing teachers to bend their classroom efforts to the task of preparing students for them, and often causing students to put in long hours outside of school cramming for the exam. Analysts such as Dore contend that this perverts the true purpose of education and escalates the cost of a selection process that might be carried out more cheaply in other ways.

Many nations that participated in educational expansion during the 1950s and 1960s found they had a problem of educated unemployment on their hands after a few years. India and the Philippines, two Asian pioneers in the expansion of secondary and higher education, acquired large pools of job-seeking graduates unable to find "suitable" employment. Sri Lanka, with its long-standing commitment to free schooling, found half its recent university graduates unemployed by the 1970s. A few lucky countries experienced a subsequent upswing in economic growth, which soaked up this pool of unemployed labor. Thus South Korea, which had had many frustrated out-of-work graduates in the late 1950s, moved to a position of shortage of educated workers by the 1970s. Even Sri Lanka began a growth spurt in the late 1970s after years of near-stagnation, and was thus able to work off some of its backlog. But in many countries educated unemployment seems to have become almost a permanent feature of society.

A lack of fit between what is taught in schools and what is needed on the job seems to aggravate the problem. Harvard University education expert

4. See Ronald Dore, *The Diploma Disease. Education, Qualification and Development* (Berkeley and Los Angeles: University of California Press, 1976).

Russell Davis reports that the employment exchange in Calcutta is daily thronged with college graduates (some of them "firsts"—recipients of top academic honors) in mathematics, English, and physics.[5] Yet employers who approach the same office seeking workers skilled in air conditioning, silk-screen printing, or plumbing, come away disappointed. In these circumstances, graduates must eventually accept work to which their education bears little relevance. Graduate taxi drivers are said to be common in Manila, as they are in some American cities. Employers then have to use on-the-job training to obtain the skills they need.

Nonformal education played little part in the inherited educational system. Significantly, however, many government departments that required technical skills conducted specialized training programs for their own staffs. This shows that the needed skills were not being supplied by the formal education system. Nor were they available through informal education, since the limited experience with modern economic activities meant that accumulated on-the-job learning was necessarily low.

EDUCATION'S ROLE IN DEVELOPMENT

Education is different things to different people. Besides the economic benefits already mentioned, education up to a certain level has often seen thought of as an inherent right. Education has also been promoted because it can socialize people. Through a common schooling experience, it has often been thought, people from different national, social, ethnic, religious, and linguistic backgrounds can be encouraged to adopt a common outlook on the world. Since many LCDs have diverse populations and must place a high premium on the attainment of greater national unity, this is often an important objective for them. Finally, education is also thought to confer civic benefits. Some political scientists believe that at least a minimal level of schooling is a prerequisite for political democracy.[6]

Thinking about the way in which education can be used to promote economic development has changed considerably over the years. During the 1950s much of the discussion centered on the need for trained manpower. The manpower-planning approach, outlined below, gained popularity as a way to analyze a developing country's manpower needs. The emphasis on middle- and high-level trained manpower implies that secondary and higher education are most in need of expansion. As we have seen, however, the 1950s was also a period of rapid growth in primary school enrollments. In 1959 a number of Asian governments subscribed to the **Karachi Plan,** which pledged them to provide at least seven years of compulsory, universal, and free schooling by 1980.

5. Russell Davis, "Planning Education for Employment" (Harvard Institute for International Development, Development Discussion Paper No. 60, June 1979).

6. Education, of course, does not guarantee the existence of democracy, as many examples of countries with educated populations but undemocratic governments attest. And there are examples of democratic systems in countries with relatively little education: India, Jamaica, Guyana, Colombia. So the relationship of education to democracy is not clearcut.

Disillusionment with this approach followed in the 1960s. Many governments found their budgets overstrained by the attempt to expand all levels of schooling simultaneously. Demand seemed unquenchable; expansion of capacity at one level of schooling only increased the demand for places at the next higher level. Paradoxically, the continuing boom demand for schooling was accompanied by an apparent decline in some of its benefits to the individual. The rise of unemployment among the educated caused politicians and officials to wonder whether more and more resources should be devoted to expanding the school system, just so people could be unemployed.

This cost-consciousness fit well with a new method of analyzing educational investments, introduced during the 1960s. Cost-benefit analysis, which was based on human capital theory, looked at both the costs and the benefits of education—unlike manpower analysis, which considered only the benefits. By the 1970s, however, disillusionment had spread to the human capital approach. A search for alternative concepts of education's role began, and is still underway. Education remains tremendously important in developing countries. Indeed, larger numbers of people and sums of money are involved than ever before. But there is no definite agreement on exactly how this burgeoning activity should be regarded.

Manpower Planning

In any economy there is a strong tendency for people with certain levels of education to hold certain types of jobs. For example, in developing countries nearly all people who have received a university education work at professional, technical, or managerial jobs, usually either in government or as independent professionals. People whose schooling ended at the secondary level tend to hold middle-level jobs in the clerical, sales, and service occupations. Half or more of the labor force in the typical developing country is made up of farmers and agricultural laborers who have received little or no formal education.

It is tempting to jump from these observable facts to the assumption that a certain level of education is required if a person is to fill a particular occupational role. If this assumption were valid it would follow that a growing economy, which is expected to undergo a shift in occupational structure towards more professionals, technicians, and industrial workers, must follow a defined pattern of educational development to obtain the kinds of trained people it will need.

Manpower planning is based on this assumption. It presumes that the economy's need for educated labor can be predicted, making it possible to plan the growth of the educational system to avoid both manpower shortages, which may slow down economic growth, and manpower surpluses, which waste educational resources and may lead to educated unemployment or "brain drain."

The starting point of manpower planning is therefore a prediction of manpower needs. There are various ways of obtaining such a prediction. A simple one is to survey employers, asking how much labor of various kinds they expect to employ, say, five years and ten years in the future. This is not a very good method for several reasons: employers often have no way of estimating future employment; different employers will probably use different assumptions in estimating their future demand for labor, so their replies cannot be aggregated consistently; enterprises to be started up in the coming five to ten years are left out of the calculation; and so on. A second possible method, if data for two historical dates are available, is to calculate past trends and then extrapolate them. A more sophisticated method, based on the work of Dutch Nobel Laureate Jan Tinbergen and the American economist Herbert Parnes, involves deducing the future employment pattern from a projection of GNP growth.

The Tinbergen-Parnes methodology predicts manpower needs through the following steps. (1) It starts from a target growth rate of GNP during the planning period, which must be at least several years long, since the training of middle- and high-level manpower takes time. (2) It then estimates the structural changes in output by sector of origin needed to achieve that overall growth rate. (3) Employment by sector is estimated, using some set of assumptions about labor productivity growth, or about the elasticity of employment growth relative to output growth, which is its inverse. (4) Next, employment by industry is divided into occupational categories using assumptions about the "required" structure in each industry; these are then summed across industries to get the economy's required occupation mix. (5) Occupational requirements are then translated into educational terms via assumptions about what sorts of education are appropriate for each occupational group.

These five steps lead to an estimate of manpower requirements in some future year. To project manpower supply in the same year, one first adjusts the current stock of manpower for expected losses through retirement, death, emigration, and withdrawal from the labor force. Then one projects increases to manpower supply resulting from outputs of the school system, immigration, and entry into the labor force by nonworking adults. The projected manpower supply is then compared to projected requirements. If a gap emerges, it is usually assumed that it must be closed through accelerated school enrollments. In some cases, other ways of increasing manpower supply, such as upgrading less skilled workers or bringing in foreign manpower, are considered.

This methodology will sound familiar to anyone who knows input-output analysis, since it involves the use of sets of fixed coefficients to derive input needs from output targets, as we saw in Chapter 6. The chain of deduction in the calculation of manpower requirements is as follows: GNP → industrial structure → total employment by industry → occupational structure of employment → educational structure of employment. Each arrow represents a set of fixed coefficients.

A major difficulty with the manpower planning approach is that in the real world these coefficients are often unstable and unpredictable. Labor productivity is affected by many factors, and often changes unexpectedly. The occupational mix also changes, for both exogenous (external) and endogenous (internal) reasons. For example, new technologies may be introduced, bringing a new set of occupational requirements. Or a change in relative wages might induce employers to hire a different mix of workers; such price adjustments are assumed away in the model. In the long run, in fact, changes in the coefficients tend to occur as a direct result of changes in the supply of educated labor. People with more schooling gradually do jobs that previously were done by less educated persons. This process is termed **educational deepening.**

Undercutting the logic of manpower planning is the fact that there is no unique education-occupation linkage. The knowledge required to do virtually any job can be acquired in any of several ways, through formal, nonformal, or informal education. Similarly, only a small fraction of what is learned in most educational programs is unique to a specific occupation; much more of it is applicable to a range of jobs.

Another problem with manpower planning is its failure to take account of the cost of education. Manpower "requirements" are assumed to be absolute, and the conclusion is always that any projected gap should be filled through educational expansion, generally of secondary and higher formal education. Yet these types of schooling are relatively expensive in many LDCs (right-hand columns of Table 9–1), and alternative, possibly cheaper, ways of dealing with the problem, such as nonformal education or on-the-job training, are seldom considered.

These objections, plus the emergence of the competing cost-benefit approach, have doomed manpower planning to limbo as far as most academic specialists are concerned. However, the approach is still used by practical planners to gain at least a rough idea of what a developing country's possible manpower problems are. Often its greatest support comes from politicians who find its apparent, but spurious, precision appealing. They like to be told, say, that the country needs to train 125 architects by 1995. As a matter of political economy, manpower planning is more likely to be influential when it projects deficits than when it projects surpluses. In the former situation it provides an apparently strong rationale for expanding a particular type of education. In many developing countries, however, schooling has expanded so much that few manpower deficits can be legitimately projected. In these circumstances, society's demand for education and the political pressures that go along with it generally ensure that the school system continues to expand at a much faster rate than would be indicated by manpower planning, which tends to be ignored.

Cost-Benefit Analysis

The hypothesis underlying human capital theory is that individuals, or their governments on their behalf, make expenditures on education, health, and other human services primarily for the purpose of raising their incomes and productivity. The added output and income that result in future years then become a return on the investment made. Application of this idea to formal education begins with a set of **lifetime earnings curves,** such as those shown in Figure 9–1. These curves, which show average earnings at various ages for people with particular amounts of schooling, have been calculated for many populations, and nearly all of them show some common characteristics.

First, given the amount of schooling, defined in terms of either years of
school or the highest level attained, earnings increase up to a maximum level that is reached around age forty or later, then level off or decline. Secondly, for those with larger amounts of schooling the curve is higher, and steeper in its rising phase; although people with more schooling start work a bit later in life, they usually begin at a higher earnings level than those with less schooling who are already working. Third, more schooling leads to later attainment of maximum earnings and to higher earnings in retirement. All three of these features can be seen in the curves for Mexico and India shown in Figure 9–1.

Estimating the Private and Social Rates of Return Cost-benefit analysis, introduced in Chapter 6 as a planning tool and used in Chapter 8 to analyze employment, is pertinent to both private and social calculations of the value of education. We take up the *private rate of return* first. We can begin by imagining a set of parents faced with a decision on how much schooling to provide a child. They have a rough idea of what the lifetime earnings curves look like and regard them as a prediction of what the child would earn at different levels of educational attainment. Although it may strain one's credulity, it is necessary to think of these parents as calculating the discounted present value of the future earnings stream attached to each level of schooling and comparing it with the cost of attaining that level of school.

The present value of prospective earnings in any future year can be defined as

$$V_o^t = \frac{E_t}{(1 + i)^t},\qquad\qquad [9\text{--}1]$$

where V_o^t = present value of earnings in year t, E_t = earnings in year t, and i = the rate of interest (opportunity cost of the parents' capital). The earnings are "discounted" to the present using the rate of interest, i.

The discounted present value of the entire stream of earnings until year n is therefore

$$V = \sum_{t=1}^{n} \frac{E_t}{(1 + i)^t}.\qquad\qquad [9\text{--}2]$$

This is the benefit side of the cost-benefit calculation. The private costs of schooling—that is, those costs borne by private households—are of two types, **explicit** and **implicit.** Explicit costs are those involving actual outlays of cash. Those most obvious type of explicit cost is tuition fees, but it it is important to recognize that even "free"—that is, tuition-free—schooling entails costs, both explicit and implicit. Cash outlays are often required for books, uniforms, transportation, and other purposes. Some type of explicit cost is almost always present, and can serve as an important barrier to school attendance for children from poor families. In addition there are implicit costs in the form of the forgone earnings or opportunity costs of students who could be working as wage-earners or as unpaid but productive workers in family farms and enterprises if they were not in school. In general these opportunity costs are most significant for older students and higher levels of schooling. But in settings where young children can work productively, they may be a factor even at the primary level, particularly for the poorer households.

The costs of schooling are incurred before its benefits are received. One way to determine whether a particular educational investment is worthwhile is to compare the discounted present values of the benefit and cost streams, as explained in Chapter 6. If the former exceeds the latter, using a relevant rate of interest to discount both streams, then the investment should be made. If discounted costs exceed discounted benefits, the investment is not worth making.

The more common method, however, involves calculating the *internal rate of return* on the investment. This, as we saw in Chapter 6, is the discount rate that equates the discounted present values of the benefit and cost streams. We can solve for the internal rate of return using the following equations.

$$\sum_{t=1}^{n} \frac{E_t}{(1 + r)^t} = \sum_{t=1}^{n} \frac{C_t}{(1 + r)^t} \qquad [9\text{--}3]$$

or

$$\sum_{t=1}^{n} \frac{E_t - C_t}{(1 + r)^t} = 0, \qquad [9\text{--}4]$$

where C_t = private costs (explicit and implicit) incurred in last year t, and r = internal rate of return. Using this approach, the family's rate of return on an investment in education would then be compared to the returns on other investments they might make. The educational outlay would then be made if it offered the highest return.

There is also a **social** or **economic rate of return,** which is calculated using a more comprehensive measure of cost: all costs of education, public as well as private, are now included on the cost side of the calculation. In other words, public-sector outlays that are not reimbursed by tuition are added in here. Properly speaking, income should be measured after payment of income taxes when the private rate of return is estimated, and before payment of income taxes when the social (economic) rate of return is estimated. This makes both benefits and costs higher in the social rate of return calculation than in the private rate of return calculation. Depending on the relative magnitude of the cost borne directly by the government and the income tax collected, the social (economic) rate of return to education can be either higher or lower than the private rate of return. In practice, however, calculations done for developing countries generally measure income before taxes in estimating both the private and the social rate of return. This is done partly because personal income taxes are less important in developing countries than in developed countries and partly because tax data are harder to obtain. If the same measure of benefits (income before taxes) is used in calculating both the private rate of return and the social rate of return, while a wider range of costs is included in the social rate of return calculation, it follows that the private rate of return must be higher than the social rate of return when this less satisfactory method of calculation is used (as in Table 9–4).

Country	Year	Social			Private[a]		
		Primary	Secondary	Higher	Primary	Secondary	Higher
Latin America							
Brazil	1970	na	24	13	na	25	14
Chile	1959	24	17	12	na	na	na
Colombia	1973	na	na	na	15	15	21
Africa							
Ethiopia	1972	20	19	10	35	23	27
Ghana	1967	18	13	17	25	17	37
Kenya	1971	22	19	9	28	33	31
Asia							
India	1978	29	14	11	33	20	13
Indonesia	1978[b]	22	16	15	26	16	na
Pakistan	1975	13	9	8	20	11	27
South Korea	1971	na	15	9	na	16	16
Developed Countries							
Japan	1976	10	9	7	13	10	9
United Kingdom	1978	na	9	7	na	11	23
United States	1969[c]	na	11	11	na	19	15

Source: George Psacharopoulos, "Returns to Education: A Further International Update and Implications," *Journal of Human Resources* 20, no. 4 (April 1985): 583–604.

[a] Income measured before payment of income taxes.

[b] Social rates refer to 1978, private rates to 1977.

[c] Private rates for secondary and higher education have declined since 1969; 1976 estimates are 11% and 5%, respectively. For social rates, no later estimates are available.

It should be stressed that social cost-benefit analysis of education is more comprehensive than private cost-benefit analysis only on the cost side. The various social benefits of education, all those which are not reflected in higher earnings, are excluded from both calculations. It would be better to include them, but is difficult to quantify benefits such as greater social cohesion and enhanced ability to participate in politics.

Analyzing the Rates of Return Many private and social rates of return to investment in education have been estimated for both developed and developing countries. Some representative results are displayed in Table 9–4. All the rates shown in the table are marginal rates. That is, they are rates of return on the *additional* investment needed to move from one level of educational attainment to the next higher level.

Three principal conclusions emerge from Table 9–4 and other similar calculations. First, rates of return to education in developing countries are generally high. In many cases they are higher than the rates of return earned on investments in physical capital. Therefore education looks like a good investment in most LDCs. Second, usually the highest social rates of return are earned on primary schooling. This is particularly true in countries where primary schooling is still far from universal. In countries where almost everyone has completed primary schooling, like the United Kingdom and the United States, the rate of return at the primary level becomes indeterminate because there is no lower level with which to compare it. Third, the spread between private rates of return (where income is measured before taxes) and social rates of return can be large because the government sometimes bears most of the costs. Examples from Table 9–4 are secondary education in the

United States and higher education in the three African countries. In other cases most of the costs of schooling are privately financed and the spread between the two rates of return is small.

Using the Analysis in Education Planning

Of what practical value are these calculations? The idea is that private rates of return can serve as guides to individual educational choices while social rates can inform public investment and policy decisions. But doubts surround the validity of both claims.

From the private point of view, the main problem is predicting what the structure of earnings will be in the future. The procedure outlined above implicitly assumes that the current structure provides an accurate guide to the future, but in fact relative earnings can change considerably for reasons originating either on the demand or the supply side of the labor market. In many LDCs in recent years the numbers of people possessing all kinds of academic credentials have increased much faster than the numbers of jobs traditionally held by people with these credentials. The result, discussed in Chapter 8, is that school leavers tend to be unemployed for a long period of time, following which they may accept lower salaries than their predecessors obtained. This process of educational deepening makes the incomes earned by previous school leavers a poor guide to the future since the rate of return to a particular level of schooling is likely to decline.

Despite this tendency, applicants continue to besiege the secondary schools and universities of most developing countries. How is this fact to be explained? Some observers interpret it as evidence that applicants for schooling are not motivated exclusively, or even primarily, by a desire for economic gains, but that they want more schooling mainly for social or psychological reasons. A different explanation is that when schooling is heavily subsidized by the government, the private rate of return remains reasonably high even as the social rate dips in response to educated unemployment and the continuing devaluation of academic credentials. This latter thesis has been used to explain the continuing strong demand for secondary and higher education in countries such as India and Sri Lanka. It suggests that education can be simultaneously a good investment for the individual and a bad investment for society.

In applying the cost-benefit approach to educational planning, the starting point is again data on lifetime earnings by level and type of education, along with information on the costs—explicit and implicit, private and public—of providing each level and type of education. The social rates of return on the various levels of education (primary, secondary, higher) and types of education (academic, vocational, nonformal, on-the-job) can then be calculated and compared. A rational government would expand those forms of education showing high social rates of return and cut back on those showing low rates of return.[7]

---

7. More precisely, activities showing a rate of return higher than the opportunity cost of capital (the return thought to be obtainable if the funds were invested outside the education sector) would be expanded and those with lower rates would be contracted.

There are, however, a number of questions that can be raised about this procedure. As with manpower planning or any other planning methodology, its results are only as good as its assumptions, and some of these can be questioned. Like the hypothetical parents discussed earlier, cost-benefit analysts must worry about how the structure of earnings may change in the future. In addition, they must make a number of assumptions about things that are of no concern to the private decision-maker.

If education is to be treated as an investment comparable to a road or steel mill, it must be justified in terms of its contribution to national output. From the social point of view, higher earnings are not sufficient justification unless they result from higher productivity. The usual way of linking earnings to productivity is to assume that wages are equated to the marginal product of labor through the workings of a perfectly competitive labor market. But if wages and salaries are more influenced by other factors (for example, the salaries paid to expatriates in colonial days—see Chapter 8), then wages or earnings are not necessarily equal to marginal product and thus become imperfect indicators of social benefits. In theory this problem could be dealt with by using shadow wages or opportunity costs (estimates of what wages would be under competitive conditions) instead of actual wages, but this adjustment has seldom been attempted.

A second and closely related issue is whether the relationship between education and earnings is truly causal. Up to now we have in effect assumed that differences in average earnings associated with differences in education are entirely caused by these educational differences. This is not strictly the case, since both education and earnings are also partly the results of other factors, such as individual ability and socioeconomic origin. People who are more able or who come from favored backgrounds may do better both in school and in the workplace. According to the "screening hypothesis," the main role of education is not so much to train people as to select those individuals who will do best in the job market.

Even if we agree that education does raise earnings, there is a question of how this works. Do schools teach skills that turn out to have economic value, or do they only socialize people to work better—to be punctual in their attendance and conscientious in completing their assignments? These issues have been much debated, but recent research appears to lend strong support to the view that underlies cost-benefit analysis of education: that skills learned in school, especially literacy and numeracy, account for much of the differential in earnings associated with higher levels of schooling.[8]

The cost-benefit approach implicitly assumes that educational categories adequately specify the types of labor relevant to the labor market. In other words, it assumes that there is perfect substitutability within each educational category. If categories are specified only by level (primary, secondary, higher) this assumption is obviously crude. Surely there are significant differences between graduates of academic and vocational high schools, or between graduates of medical and legal faculties. Separate calculations

8. See M. Boissiere, J. B. Knight and R. H. Sabot, "Earnings, Schooling, Ability, and Cognitive Skills," *American Economic Review* 75, no. 5 (December 1985): 1016–30.

should be made for these major different types of education, but even this leaves out the quality dimension. In the real world, graduates of the "best" schools, which may be best solely or mainly in terms of popular perceptions, earn far more than graduates of the "inferior" institutions. Finally, alternatives to schooling—nonformal education and on-the-job training—tend to get left out of the comparison altogether. If the Ministry of Education is responsible for educational planning but these programs are provided by other ministries, the tendency is to downplay them.

Like any planning tool, cost-benefit analysis can be used to provide information, but it cannot be used mechanically to dictate solutions. It can be used to measure the productivity of the existing pattern of investment in education. If, for example, the social rate of return to primary schooling is high, this suggests that investment at this level is likely to be socially remunerative. Similarly, large differences between private and social returns may help explain patterns of educated unemployment, as we have seen. But the value of these calculations is always limited by the assumptions on which they are based. It is particularly hard to determine how fast the social rate of return will decline as a particular variety of education is expanded. To know this we would have to calculate the elasticities relating earnings differentials to the relative supplies of different kinds of labor.

In spite of the attractiveness of its base in human capital theory—at least for those who admire neoclassical economic theory—the cost-benefit approach is of only limited use in practical educational planning. This brings us to the question of what alternatives might exist.

Alternative Viewpoints

Formal Modeling Most of the time in most developing countries, educational policy decisions are made pragmatically, responding to those political pressures that bear most strongly on the decision-makers at any particular moment. Manpower projections and cost-benefit analyses are undertaken from time to time, but they seldom have more than a small impact on what actually happens. Because of the intellectual limitations of the two analytical approaches outlined above, more elaborate and formal approaches have sometimes been suggested, but these have had even less influence. For example, several linear programming models of education and its relationship to the economy were constructed in the 1960s and 1970s but had little impact. Similarly, efforts have been made to synthesize the manpower and cost-benefit approaches. The latter may be a promising road to take, since the two well-known methodologies are really based on polar assumptions about the substitutability of labor with different types of schooling in particular types of jobs. Manpower planning assumes that particular levels and types of education are uniquely associated with particular occupations; no substitutability is possible. Cost-benefit analysis assumes that people completing particular levels and types of education earn a given wage regardless of the occupation they pursue; the implication is that there is perfect substitutability of labor across occupations within broad categories of educational attainment. Clearly these are polar assumptions and the truth lies somewhere in the middle. So far, however, neither type of modeling effort has had a dramatic influence on how education is planned in developing countries.

The Left Revisionists One group of economists and sociologists contends that the idea that education raises productivity is fundamentally erroneous. An element in their critique, mentioned earlier, is that education acts as a screen or sieve to select the fortunate few who are then "credentialed" to hold the elite positions in society. To this the more radical critics add that those who pass through the sieve and receive the prized credentials tend strongly to be the ones who started from privileged positions in life. The school system, they say, essentially reproduces the class structure from generation to generation. Those not destined for elite positions receive a form of education intended to make them more amenable to a subservient role in society. They are taught diligence, punctuality, and respect for authority. The solution to all this lies not in any conceivable reform of the school system within the framework of capitalist society, but in the radical reform of the social structure and economic system. Less conventional radical critics argue that efforts should be made to revamp schooling as we know it to permit true learning to take place or to use mass education as a means of raising the consciousness of the poor regarding their oppressed condition.[9]

In view of these criticisms and proposals, it is worthwhile to see how Communist regimes manage their school systems. They put strong emphasis on universal attainment of basic literacy and numeracy, then restrict secondary and higher education rather severely (or just higher education in the richer Communist states), heavily emphasizing the attainment of specific vocational skills. In the USSR and other East European Communist countries, as in the West, opportunities to obtain the more restricted types of schooling seem to go disproportionately to those with favored positions in society. The Communist regime most noted for radical reform efforts has been that of China, especially during the Cultural Revolution of the 1960s, but Chinese educational policy has subsequently returned to something much closer to the Soviet or Western model.

The Right Revisionists Meanwhile a diametrically opposed critique and reform proposal argues that educational planning has failed, that all proposed methodologies are inadequate, and that choices about what kinds of schooling to provide and whom to educate should therefore be left to the operations of the market. An obvious objection to this proposal is that if the market gives the wrong price signal it will only encourage people to respond in the wrong ways. As long as education is subsidized, people will tend to purchase too much of it relative to other goods and services. This problem could be dealt with by reducing the degree of subsidization and charging people something much closer to the actual cost of providing schooling. But this would only serve to strengthen another objection to the market solution: that it takes no account of equity considerations. Proposed means of rectify-

9. Iconoclastic analyses of education in developing countries include Ivan Illich, *Deschooling Society* (New York: Harper and Row, 1970); Paolo Freire, *Pedagogy of the Oppressed,* translated from the Portuguese by Myra Bergman Ramos (New York: Seabury Press, 1970); and Ronald Dore, *The Diploma Disease* (Berkeley: University of California Press, 1976).

ing this situation include liberal use of scholarships for the poor but deserving, or more far-reaching, creation of **educational vouchers,** a special currency that could be used to purchase any kind of schooling and could be distributed according to any criteria deemed equitable.

Like the radical reform proposals, those coming from the right have been discussed more than implemented. Most governments prefer to retain a much tighter grip on educational activities than this type of reform would permit. The main real-world use of the market in third-world education, as noted earlier, is to provide places for those who are unable to gain admittance to public institutions, and even this is permitted only in certain countries.

The Moderate Reformers A very old reform proposal is that education should be made more practical. This suggestion has usually led to the creation of agricultural, technical, or vocational schools intended to teach people useful skills. Some of these schools have succeeded and made valuable contributions to development, but many have failed. In a well-known article, University of Chicago educationist Philip Foster traced a series of unsuccessful experiments in Ghana going all the way back to the mid-nineteenth century. He attributed the persistent failure to "the vocational school fallacy," a tendency to think of certain types of skilled labor as needed for economic development, when in fact the structure of incentives strongly favors "impractical" academic training that opens the door to employment in the urban formal sector.[10] Added to this is the fact that many government-run vocational schools fail to provide the skills that are actually required by private employers. Yet when planned and administered properly, vocational schools can make a real contribution to development.

Another reform proposal is to give much greater emphasis to nonformal education.[11] The proponents of this approach argue that nonformal education compares favorably to formal education in terms of practicality, cost, flexibility, and ability to reach lower income groups. It is not clear to what extent these claims are justified. Certainly there have been many successful nonformal education projects in basic education (literacy and numeracy), family education (health, nutrition, child care, family planning), community education (cooperatives, community projects), and occupational training. It may be, however, that nonformal education is more usefully thought of as a complement to formal education, in terms of the skills taught and audience reached (mainly adults), than as its rival. A criticism of nonformal education is that, like vocational schools, it perpetuates a two-tiered social system. The favored class gets into the schools while the less favored have to make do with programs of nonformal education.

10. Philip J. Foster, "The Vocational School Fallacy in Development Planning," in *Education and Economic Development,* C. A. Anderson and M. J. Bowman, eds. (Chicago: Aldine Publishing Company, 1966), pp. 142–63.
11. Philip H. Coombs with Manzoor Ahmed, *Attacking Rural Poverty: How Nonformal Education Can Help* (Baltimore and London: Johns Hopkins University Press, 1974).

Health and Nutrition

Improving health conditions used to be a low priority of most LDC governments. It was regarded as something the governments would like to do if possible, but not at the expense of more directly productive expenditure categories. Development specialists generally took a similar view; as far as we know no previous economic development textbook includes a chapter on health and nutrition. Recently, however, more attention has been devoted to the relationship between health and development. One reason for this is the growing interest in equity-oriented development strategies for the basic human needs variety (introduced in Chapter 4), in which provision of basic health services necessarily plays an important part. A second reason is that health expenditures, like education expenditures, are increasingly regarded as investments in human capital.

The health-development relationship is a reciprocal one. As in Chapter 7's discussion of fertility decline, one can ask about the extent to which economic development itself leads to improvements in health status. Proponents of health-sector programs often deny that development alone can or will or do the job, arguing that special programs in nutrition, health care, and environmental sanitation are also needed. Sometimes these proponents go so far as to argue that development can be injurious to health, or that provision of appropriate health programs can do the job by itself, even in the absence of significant overall development. Opponents of this view reply that health status is generally related to income level, and specific health measures often fail to have much effect when the surrounding socioeconomic and physical environments are unfavorable to health. We will return to this debate later in the chapter. The other side of the reciprocal relationship between health and development involves the issue of how and to what extent health programs can promote economic development. This will be discussed after a presentation of basic facts and concepts.

HEALTH IN THE THIRD WORLD

What is "health"? How can one tell whether an individual, or a society, is healthy or sick?

The definition of health is surprisingly elusive. The World Health Organization (WHO), which is the United Nations agency responsible for programs to improve health standards, defines it as "a state of complete physical, mental and social well being," but this goes far beyond what is normally meant by health. For most people, health is simply the absence of disease and infirmity. But this can be a highly subjective definition. Conditions such as infection with intestinal parasites or first-degree (mild) malnutrition, which are seen as disease in countries with high health standards, may be so common in countries with lower standards that they are not even recognized as abnormal.

The health status of an individual can be determined through clinical examination by a qualified health professional. Since it is usually not practical to examine large groups of people, definitions of the health status of entire populations must rely on statistics. These are of two kinds: those covering **morbidity** (sickness) and those covering **mortality** (deaths). Aside from the lack of a clear-cut definition of sickness, many sick people, especially in poor countries, never enter a hospital, or even consult a doctor, as a result of which they often fail to come into contact with the statistical system. Mortality data are considerably better: death seldom goes unnoticed, and most countries now have reasonably complete official systems of death registration, although significant gaps remain in some cases. Death statistics are most useful for assessing the health status of a population when they include detailed information on the person who has died (age, sex, place of residence, and so on) and information on the cause of death. However, data on the cause of death are usually weak in low-income countries.

Patterns and Trends

In Chapter 7 we saw that mortality is negatively related to GNP per capita. The infant death rate falls from more than 100 per thousand live births to only 12 per thousand as one moves up the income scale from countries with less than $300 a year to countries with more than $5,000 per capita (Table 7–2). The crude death rate also falls, although less than one would expect because of the younger population structure in the poorer countries. Another way to look at the relationship between development and mortality in terms of **life expectancy.** Life expectancy is the average number of years

TABLE 10–1 Life Expectancy at Birth by Income Group, 1983[a]

Income group	Life expectancy
Below $300	53
$300–$500	64[a]
$500–$1,000	55
$1,000–$2,000	64
$2,000–$5,000	68
Above $5,000	75

Source: World Bank, *World Development Report 1985* (New York: Oxford University Press, 1985) pp. 174–75.
[a] Heavily influenced by the inclusion of China's life expectancy of 67; without China, life expectancy in the $300–$500 income group would be 53.

members of a given population are expected to live.[1] As Table 10–1 shows, children born in 1980 in the poorest countries could expect to live only 53 years on average, while children born in the same period in the richest countries were likely to live 75 years on average. This difference provides one measure of the effect of economic development of health.

The correlation between income level and mortality is high but by no means perfect. Table 10–2 shows life expectancy statistics for selected LDCs in 1960 and 1983. Some of the countries listed in this table have life expectancies far above the average for their income levels. Particularly notable in this regard are China and Sri Lanka (see boxed example on pages 232–33),

TABLE 10–2 Life Expectancy at Birth, Selected Countries, 1960 and 1983

Country	Life expectancy	
	1960	1983
Latin America		
Bolivia	43	51
Brazil	55	64
Chile	57	70
Colombia	53	64
Africa		
Ghana	40	59
Kenya	41	57
Tanzania	42	51
Asia		
China	na	67
India	43	55
Indonesia	41	54
South Korea	54	67
Malaysia	53	67
Pakistan	43	50
Sri Lanka	62	69

Source: World Bank, *World Development Report 1985* (New York: Oxford University Press, 1985), pp. 174–75.

1. We cannot, of course, know how long any particular individual will actually live. What we can do is predict the average longevity of a class of people (for example, males age three), using the recent mortality experience of the relevant group (in this case, all males) as a guide. Life expectancy at birth is the form of the statistic most often cited, as in Table 10–1, but the concept really refers to expected years of *remaining* life and can thus be applied to people of various ages, as in Table 10–3.

but the populations of Chile and Ghana also stand out as more long-lived than those other countries in their regions and income classes. Several of the countries listed in Table 10–2 increased life expectancy by ten years or more between 1960 and 1983.

The cross-section data in Table 10–1 reveal a pattern similar to what is believed to have happened through time in the industrial countries. Death rates fall as countries develop. Concurrently life expectancy rises; Figure 10–1 shows its historical trend in different groups of countries. As can be seen, the early-developing countries have experienced a slow, steady rise in life expectancy since around 1850. Japan, a later developer, was able to extend life more rapidly and reach a level close to that of the early developers by about 1960. Less developed countries have also been able to achieve rapid increases in life expectancy, particularly over the past forty years. However, these increases still leave them far below life expectancy in the rich countries (Table 10–1) and no better off in many cases than the developed countries were in the early twentieth century (see Figure 10–1). Moreover, there are signs that the rapid mortality decline experienced in the 1950s and 1960s slowed in the 1970s.

More of the reduction in mortality that has been achieved in the developed countries, and most of the difference in life expectancy between rich and poor countries in the world today, affects the very young. This fact is highlighted in Table 10–3, which compares male life expectancy at various ages in Sweden and India. It can be seen that these two countries differ enormously in life expectancy at birth. Yet for males who survive the early years of life, the differences in remaining life expectancy decrease. Whereas in Sweden and other countries with high health standards the expected years of further life decline steadily as a person ages, in Bangladesh a surviving five-

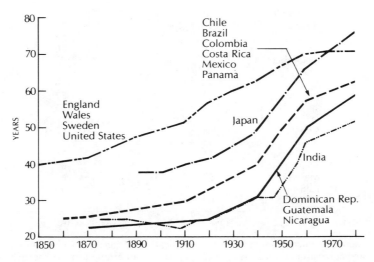

Figure 10-1 Trends in Life Expectancy in Selected Countries. Life expectancy rose gradually in Europe and the United States, more rapidly in Japan. It is rising rapidly in the LDCs, too, but they are still far behind the developed countries. *Source:* World Bank, *Health Sector Policy Paper* 2nd ed. (Washington, D.C., 1980), p. 10.

TABLE 10–3 Comparison of Male Life Expectancy in Bangladesh and Sweden

| | Additional years a male is expected to live if he is now: | | | | |
	newborn	age 1	age 5	age 15	age 65
Sweden (1976)	72.1	71.8	67.9	58.1	13.9
Bangladesh (1974)	45.8	53.5	54.4	46.3	11.6
Difference	26.3	18.3	13.5	11.8	2.3

Source: United Nations, *Demographic Yearbook, Historical Supplement* (New York, 1979), pp. 553, 558.

year-old can actually expect to live longer than a newborn. As Table 10–3 shows, life expectancy for males in Bangladesh in 1974 was 45.8 years at birth and 54.4 years at age five. Thus newborns on average would not reach their 46th birthdays, while five-year-olds could expect to live to age 59. This fact is testimony to the terrible extent of infant and child mortality in the poorest countries.

Causes of Sickness and Death

Interesting research by University of Pennsylvania demographer Samuel Preston has shown that the cross-section relationship between income and life expectancy is parabolic in form and has been shifting upward during the twentieth century (Figure 10–2).[2] That is, at any given level of real income per capita, people are tending to live longer as time goes by. However, the

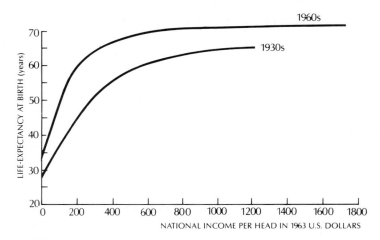

FIGURE 10–2 Relationship between Life Expectancy at Birth and National Income Per Head. In both decades, people in richer countries could expect to live longer. Between the 1930s and the 1960s, the curve shifted up; citizens of countries with given real income levels lived longer on average. Note also that the curve for the 1960s is flatter than the curve for the 1930s; except for very poor countries (below $500), per-capita income was no longer so important a determinant of mortality as it had been in the 1930s. *Source:* Samuel H. Preston, "The Changing Relationship Between Mortality and Level of Economic Development," *Population Studies* 29, no. 2 (July 1975): 231–48; adapted from p. 235.

2. Samuel H. Preston, "The Changing Relationship Between Mortality and Level of Development," *Population Studies* 29, no. 2 (July 1975): 231–48.

relationship between income and life expectancy has become looser in recent decades. Preston found that rising income accounted for only 10–25 percent of the rise in life expectancy between the 1930s and 1960s. Other factors accounted for 75–90 percent of the increase.

What could explain this loosening of the relationship between income and life expectancy? Increasing literacy and improved income distribution are possible influences, but the findings of Preston and other researchers are not consistent on this. Most likely, as Preston speculates, the international spread of health technology and a growing similarity of values regarding its application are factors contributing to the loosening of the relationship between income and life expectancy and the tendency for poor countries to acquire statistical life expectancies more similar to those of the rich countries.

Although the international spread of health technology has been a major factor in the worldwide decline in death rates and rise in life expectancy which has occurred since World War II, its effect has sometimes been exaggerated. A debated case is that of Sri Lanka (then still called Ceylon), where a fall in the crude death rate of 43 percent between 1945 and 1949 was originally attributed almost entirely to the control of malaria through the use of DDT. Later it was established that DDT was only part of the story, and that longer-run and more general factors such as rising income, wide-spread literacy, and the availability of low-priced foodstuffs were also influential.

Health in Sri Lanka

The small Asian country of Sri Lanka enjoys unusually good health and life expectancy compared to other countries at its approximate level of GNP per capita (only $330 in 1983). This favorable experience is attributable to a combination of good fortune and the policies followed in the period since independence in 1948.

A small island located on the trade routes between Europe and east Asia, Sri Lanka had early contact with Western colonialism. The British, who controlled the island after earlier periods of Portuguese and Dutch domination, began to introduce modern medicine in the early nineteenth century. Campaigns to eradicate smallpox and yaws began in 1802. Later a civil medical department was started in 1858, a Contagious Diseases Ordinance enacted in 1866, and a medical school opened in Colombo, the capital, in 1870. In the early twentieth century Ceylon's tea, rubber, and coconut plantations were required to provide medical care for their workers and their families, and a school health program was started. In the 1940s a network of rural hospitals was built. The compact, self-contained nature of the island supported these efforts, and when it gained its independence in 1948, Ceylon already had unusually high health standards compared to other Asian countries.

Credit for continued improvement since 1948 belongs primarily to the government of Sri Lanka, which has consistently accorded a high priority to improving the health of its people. From the start medical care was free to all. More important, efforts were made to extend the service network to all parts of the island. These efforts were continuously hampered by shortages of funds. Sri Lankan hospitals have always been crowded, and the provision of additional beds ran only marginally ahead of population growth between 1950 and 1980. There was some improvement in the availability of doctors, but efforts to train more doctors were offset in part by the emigration of physicians to countries where much higher incomes could be earned. The only dramatic change was in the supply of nurses and paramedics, which nearly tripled in relation to population between 1950 and 1980. This increase provided essential support for the extension of primary care to the rural areas.

Measures of mortality and morbidity show striking improvement in the past three decades. Epidemics have been eliminated and diseases such as typhoid, tuberculosis, and malaria have declined sharply as causes of death. Crude and infant death rates have fallen and life expectancy has climbed into the upper sixties. Sri Lanka has become, with China, one of the rare examples of a country with a poor but healthy population.

Not all this improvement is attributable to medical services. Sri Lanka is also unusually advanced in education, and its near-universal literacy is thought to have promoted improved health conditions. Another positive factor is the comparative rarity of malnutrition, which results from a relatively equal distribution of income and the policy of subsidizing basic foods. Although the average calorie intake is only average for countries at Sri Lanka's income level (see Tables 10–6 and 10–7), the calories are probably better distributed among the population than in most other countries.

Medical services in Sri Lanka form a colorful mosaic. The indigenous *ayurvedic* system coexists with Western medicine and receives some official support. Psychological disorders are treated by trance-dancers or exorcists in some cases, by Western-trained psychiatrists in others.

National statistics on causes of death, although weak, are good enough to permit clear-cut comparisons between rich and poor countries, and illuminate the historical pattern of death rate decline by cause. Rich and poor countries as groups have characteristically different cause-of-death patterns (Table 10–4). In poor countries, infectious, parasitic, and respiratory disease, mainly afflicting the young, account for nearly half of all deaths. Important examples of this category include the "diarrhea-pneumonia complex," malaria, whooping cough, polio, tetanus, and diphtheria. All these diseases are well controlled in rich countries. As Table 10–4 shows, their comparative prevalence accounts for over half (777 out of 1,100) the difference in number of deaths between the rich and poor countries.

Other causes of death are also less significant in developed than in less developed countries, except for cancer, which is more prevalent in rich countries because of the greater longevity of their populations. Again, the time-series and cross-section patterns are roughly similar. Diseases which in the twentieth century are known as "tropical diseases" were major killers in temperate Europe in earlier centuries.

TABLE 10–4 Numbers of Deaths by Main Causes in Typical Developed and Less
Developed Countries (annual deaths per 100,000 population)

	Typical LDC	Typical developed country	Difference
Infectious, parasitic, and respiratory diseases	874	97	777
Cancer	74	137	−63
Diseases of the circulatory system	296	290	6
Traumatic injury	70	61	9
All other causes	686	315	371
All causes	2,000	900	1,100

Source: Based on World Bank, Health Sector Policy Paper, 1st ed. (Washington, D.C., March 1975), p. 13.

Despite the unsatisfactory nature of morbidity statistics, it is all too easy to identify a number of endemic and epidemic diseases that affect large populations in the third world. Some of these diseases—tuberculosis, malaria, cholera—are prominent causes of death. Others may not kill large numbers, but they limit people's lives and may contribute to a premature death, which is officially ascribed to some other cause. One such category is parasitic conditions, which are all but universal in many areas. It has been estimated that perhaps one-fourth of the world's population has roundworms. Another is malnutrition, which is sometimes present in its easily recognized clinical form, but exists far more commonly at a lower level, where its effects, although destructive, are more subtle and difficult to detect.

EFFECTS OF HEALTH ON DEVELOPMENT

We have considered the effect of development on health. Now it is time to ask what better health can contribute to development. Can health expenditures really be regarded as a form of investment in human capital? Before addressing this question, it is important to recognize that the validity of health services as a developmental activity does not rest entirely on our ability to prove that health expenditures increase national output. Better health is also an important goal in its own right. Health increases the range of human potentialities of all kinds and is rightly regarded as a basic human need. Health is valued for its own sake. Everyone can benefit from better health in the present, and improved health for the young will lead to a healthier population in the future.

Like education, health services increase the quality of human resources, both now and in the future.[3] Better worker health can provide immediate benefits by increasing the workers' strength, stamina, and ability to concentrate while on the job. Better child health and nutrition promote future productivity by helping children develop into stronger, healthier adults. In

3. For a comprehensive statement of the case for regarding health expenditures as investment in human capital, along with some U.S. examples, see Selma Mushkin, "Health as an Investment," Journal of Political Economy 70, no. 5, part 2 (Supplement, October 1962): 129–57.

addition they supplement the acquisition of productive skills and attitudes   **235**
through schooling. It has been shown that healthy, well-fed children have   EFFECTS OF
HEALTH ON
higher attendance rates and are able to concentrate better while they are in   DEVELOPMENT
school.

Unlike education, health expenditures also increase the quantity of human resources in the future by lengthening the expected working life. In this way too they complement educational investment, since returns to education should be higher if people can be expected to work and earn for longer periods.

The returns to investment in health, however, are even harder to quantify and verify empirically than are the returns to investment in education. For one thing there is no simple measure, analogous to years of schooling, for the amount invested in the health of any particular individual. The economic effects of better health are also hard to measure. The quantitative effects (extended working life) can be gauged in additional years worked, but what valuation should be put on them? In a private cost-benefit analysis expected additional earnings can be used, but in a social cost-benefit analysis the marginal product of labor should be estimated to determine the value to society of extended working life. This opens up the complex question, already addressed in Chapter 8, of what the productivity of the marginal worker really is. In an economy in which marginal productivity is very low, the production benefits of extended working life are necessarily small. The qualitative effects of health expenditure (increased worker productivity and earnings) are also hard to measure, in the sense that the amount of any increase in productivity or earnings that is attributable to improvement in health may be difficult to identify.

Research to measure the effects of better health on labor productivity has so far yielded varying results. A study of Filipino road construction workers showed that nutritional deficiencies lowered their working time and level of effort, while a study of iron supplementation for Indonesian plantation workers was able to measure productivity benefits. Yet an ambitious attempt to determine the effects of controlling schistosomiasis (an infectious disease spread by snails) on the Caribbean island of St. Lucia could not find measurable effects and a study of the same disease in Egypt indicated that only severe levels of infection reduced productivity.[4] At present therefore, one cannot be sure how great the potential productivity gains from improved health and nutrition may be. It is possible that people find ways to adapt to wide ranges of ill-health and malnutrition without greatly reducing their productivity: they many not feel well, but they can still work. In this situation, improving health would not necessarily increase productivity. But it still would be desirable from a humanitarian point of view.

Besides increasing the quantity and quality of the human resource, health expenditures can also make available, or increase the productivity of, non-

4. See Barry M. Popkin, "Nutrition and Labor Productivity," *Social Science and Medicine* 12C (1978): 117–25; S. S. Basta and A. Churchill, "Iron Deficiency Anemia and The Productivity of Adult Males in Indonesia" (World Bank Staff Working Paper No. 175, April 1974); Burton Weisbrod and Robert E. Baldwin, "Disease and Labor Productivity," *Economic Development and Cultural Change* 22, no. 3 (1974): 414–35; and Nicholas M. Prescott, "Schistosomiasis and Development," *World Development* 7, no. 1 (1979): 1–14.

human resources. The most important example is the large tracts of land rendered uninhabitable or unusable by endemic diseases. Malaria and yellow fever blocked access to many parts of Latin America, Africa, and Asia before these diseases were brought under relatively effective control in the twentieth century. Even today schistosomiasis makes it unsafe for people to enter lakes and streams in sections in Africa, while trypanosomiasis (African sleeping sickness) restricts the range of the livestock industry. So far no chemical means of control has been discovered for either of these diseases. China, however, has made progress against schistosomiasis through mass campaigns aimed at ridding lakes and streams of the snails that transmit the parasite. Improved control of ankylostomiasis (hookworm) and other parasitic conditions would increase resource availabilities in a different way. The effective productivity of resources devoted to food production would be increased.

We have seen that the productive benefits of health expenditures, although easy to hypothesize, have proven difficult to verify empirically. But even the effects on health status are sometimes hard to measure. The main reason is the multiplicity of factors that go together to determine health status. For example, a study of the health effects of projects to provide safe water supplies to a number of villages in Lesotho found that, surprisingly, provision of a clean water source failed in many cases to lead to a significant reduction in the prevalence of water-borne and water-related diseases. One explanation was that water-borne diseases are also transmitted by other means, such as contaminated food, and the provision of a safe water source alone does not protect villagers from infection through other sources.[5]

Health improvement has one effect that could be considered a social cost: by reducing the death rate, it increases population growth. Admittedly, the decline in the death rate may in turn encourage a drop in fertility, which would reduce the overall positive impact on population growth; but studies indicate that the magnitude of this replacement effect, if it exists at all, is likely to be small. At this point, however, we confront a question of ethical values. Even if population growth is acknowledged to be injuriously high, universally espoused values make it unacceptable to reduce that growth by allowing persons already born to die when the means to save them are at hand. It follows that this "cost" should not be permitted to become an argument against health improvements and that other means should be found to limit population growth if this is considered to be an important social objective.

ENVIRONMENTAL HEALTH

The health planner, like the physician, should carefully diagnose before he prescribes. Health planning must address the real health problems found in the less developed countries. Some of the causes of sickness and premature death in the LDCs that deserve more careful examination are environmental

---

5. Richard Feuchem et al., *Water, Health and Development: An Interdisciplinary Evaluation* (London: Tri-Med Books, 1974), Chapter 9.

health problems, malnutrition, and lack of medical care of adequate quantity, quality, and type. We will analyze each of these problems in turn.

The principal problem of environmental sanitation in low-income countries is the contamination of the water supply, and sometimes also of food and soil, with human waste. This occurs in villages and cities alike. Although most urban residents have access to piped drinking water, the public water supply is often rendered unsafe by contamination in the distribution process as the result of a faulty or nonexistent sewage system. Few rural residents enjoy either piped water or decent sanitation. Table 10–5, although based on fragmentary data, gives some idea of the dimensions of the problem.

Many of the infectious, parasitic, and respiratory diseases that cause so much sickness and death in poor countries (Table 10–4) are water-borne. Typhoid, dysentery, and cholera are leading examples. Their prevalence results in much sickness among adults and frequent deaths among infants and malnourished children. A second type of environmental sanitation problem arises from housing with insufficient space, ventilation, and access to sunlight. This situation, which is more likely to occur in urban than in rural areas, promotes the spread of air-borne diseases such as tuberculosis.

Sanitation improvement programs primarily involve the problems of waste disposal and water supply, particularly the need to keep the one system from contaminating the other. In villages this means safe wells and properly constructed privies or latrines. Simple technologies are available for such improvements. In urban areas matters become more expensive and complex. It will be a long time before all third-world cities have decent sewage disposal and water supply systems, let alone adequate housing for their growing populations.

Historically, improvements in sanitation seem to be closely associated with reduction in diseases, becoming effective long before successful treatments have been discovered. So far in the contemporary third world the experience has been mixed. Some projects to improve water supply and waste-disposal methods have led to dramatic reductions in disease. Others, as noted earlier, have had no discernible effect.

**TABLE 10–5 Access to Drinking Water and Sanitation in Developing Countries, 1980[a]
(Percent of population)**

Region	Drinking Water			Sanitation		
	By house connection	By public standpoint	None	By sewer connection	Other	None
Urban Population						
Africa	29	37	34	11	43	46
Asia	—— 64 ——		36	—— 30 ——		70
Latin America	71	7	22	42	14	44
Rural Population						
Africa	—— 22 ——		78	—— 20 ——		80
Asia	—— 31 ——		69	—— 6 ——		94
Latin America	—— 20 ——		80	—— 20 ——		80

Source: World Health Organization, *The International Drinking Water Supply and Sanitation Decade. Review of National Baseline Data, as at 31 December 1980* (Geneva, 1984): 21.
[a] Covers fifty-one countries.

Malnutrition is a major source of ill health and premature death in the LDCs. Some data on nutritional standards appear in Tables 10–6 and 10–7. These tables give the most commonly cited nutritional statistic, average daily caloric intake, compared to the minimum daily requirement. The daily

TABLE 10–6 Daily Per-Capita Calorie Supply by Income Class and Region, 1982

	Total	As percent of requirement
Income Group		
Below $300	1,997	93
$300–$500	2,470	106
$500–$1,000	2,460	108
$1,000–$2,000	2,665	112
$2,000–$5,000	3,709	128
$5,000 and over	2,313	134
Region		
Africa	2,563	101
Asia	2,316	104
West Asia	2,792	116
South Asia	1,887	93
East Asia	2,564	110
Oceania and Indonesia	2,478	112
Europe	3,768	133
North and Central America	3,318	131
South America	2,638	109

Source: World Bank, *World Development Report 1985* (New York: Oxford University Press, 1985), pp. 220–21.

TABLE 10–7 Daily Per-Capita Calorie Supply for Selected Countries, 1982

Country	Total	As percent of requirement
Latin America		
Bolivia	2,158	90
Brazil	2,623	110
Chile	2,669	109
Colombia	2,551	110
Peru	2,114	90
Africa		
Ghana	1,573	68
Kenya	2,056	88
Tanzania	2,331	101
Asia		
China	2,562	109
India	2,047	93
Indonesia	2,393	111
Korea (South)	2,936	125
Malaysia	2,688	120
Pakistan	2,277	99
Sri Lanka	2,393	107

Source: World Bank, *World Development Report 1985* (New York: Oxford University Press, 1985), pp. 220–21.

average intake figures are normally compiled from **national food balance sheets,** a set of accounts which estimate human food consumption by taking the total supply of food (production plus imports) and subtracting other uses (exports; processing, spoilage, and rodent-infestation losses; livestock feed; and industrial uses). What remains must have been consumed by human beings. The resulting quantities of the various foodstuffs are then converted into nutrient values using standard equivalencies for the items concerned. Recommended daily consumption figures derive from an attempt to say how many calories and other nutrients a person would have to consume to maintain good health, given a certain body weight and at least a minimum level of daily activity.

According to these statistics there were caloric deficits in 1982 in countries with GNP of less than $300 per capita and in South Asia, while in other income classes and regions the actual intake was above the minimum required level. Even in the deficit countries things might not seem to be too bad. After all, the deficit in the poorest countries and South Asia was only 7 percent. However, these are tricky averages that understate the actual gravity of the situation for two reasons.

The first arises from the way the minimum standards are defined. If people do not receive the nutrition needed to maintain a given body weight and activity level, they adapt by weighing, and doing, less. Thus, the standards ("requirements") implied for the Asian regions in Table 10–6 are lower than the standards for other regions because Asians tend to be small. But their smallness is at least partially attributable to inadequate nutrition in the past. When Asians regularly get enough to eat, as the Japanese have since World War II and as have the Chinese and Koreans more recently, their average weight and height, and thus their caloric requirements, increase rapidly from one generation to the next.

The second reason these averages can be misleading is inequality of food distribution. Even in the least well-fed countries some people receive more than the recommended daily minimum. The difficulty is that while their extra consumption raises the average daily intake, it in no way diminishes the deficits experienced by those who cannot attain the recommended minimum. Averages computed for large and diverse populations are particularly likely to understate the nutritional problem by offsetting surpluses against deficits in this way.

Because of this problem, it may be more revealing to count malnourished people than to count calories. According to a recent estimate covering eighty-seven countries excluding China, 34 percent of the third world's population received insufficient calories for an active working life in 1980. Sixteen percent were so poorly nourished that their bodily growth was likely to be stunted and their health seriously endangered.[6] By far the largest number of malnourished people, 470 million, were found to be in South Asia, where 50 percent of the population received insufficient calories. In sub-Saharan Africa 44 percent of the population was malnourished and in Latin America 13 percent.

6. World Bank, *Poverty and Hunger: Issues and Options for Food Security in Developing Countries* (Washington, D.C.: World Bank, 1986).

The prevalence of malnutrition and its injurious effects is greatest among children. In the early 1970s the WHO estimated that three percent of third-world children were afflicted by severe (third-degree) malnutrition, which gives rise to clinical conditions such as kwashiorkor, a protein-deficiency disease marked by bloated bellies and glassy stares, and marasmus, a condition brought on by shortage of both calories and protein. Another 25 percent suffered from moderate (second-degree) malnutrition and a further 40–45 percent from mild (first-degree) malnutrition.[7] These conditions are indicated by substandard rates of physical development. Malnutrition is said to be present as a primary or contributing factor in more than half of all deaths among children under five in low-income countries. It can turn otherwise mild childhood diseases, such as respiratory problems, gastrointestinal difficulties, and measles, into killers.

Most of the malnutrition in the world today is of the type known as protein-calorie malnutrition (PCM). Conditions caused by deficiencies of specific nutrients—such as rickets, scurvy, and beri-beri—have generally diminished in importance. Among the remaining deficiency diseases the most important are vitamin A deficiency, which can cause blindness, and iron-deficiency anemia. At one time it was thought that shortage of protein

TABLE 10–8   National Average Daily Per-Capita Calorie Supply by GNP Per Capita and Region, 1960 and 1982

	Per-capita calorie supply (percent of requirement)	
	1960	1982
GNP Per Capita		
Below $300	93[a]	93
$300–$500	88	106
$500–$1,000	91	108
$1,000–$2,000	100	112
$2,000–$5,000	100	128
$5,000 and over	115	134
Region		
Africa	89	101
Asia	91	104
West Asia	90	116
South Asia	91	93
East Asia	91	110
Oceania and Indonesia	113	112
Europe	106	133
North and Central America	96	131
South America	97	109

Source: World Bank, *World Tables 1976* (Baltimore and London: Johns Hopkins University Press, 1976), pp. 517–21; World Bank, *World Development Report 1985* (New York: Oxford University Press, 1985), pp. 220–21.

[a]Heavily influenced by the inclusion of India's per-capita calorie supply of 95; without India, the below $300 income group would be 87.

7. See Alan Berg, *The Nutrition Factor: Its Role in National Development* (Washington, D.C.: Brookings Institution, 1973), p. 5.

was the principal nutritional problem of the third world, since protein is necessary for physical and mental development. More recently, however, it has been discovered that most of the children whose diets are deficient in protein also suffer from a deficiency of calories, and if protein is added to the diet while calories remain insufficient, development is little affected because the added protein is used up as energy. Accordingly, calories are now regarded as the limiting factor in nutrition, and most programs attempt to supplement calories first and protein, vitamins, and minerals only secondarily.

Aggregate data presented in Table 10–8 suggest that the extent of PCM may have lessened in recent decades. Average calorie and protein intakes appear to have increased during the 1960s and 1970s in all third-world regions. We must remember, however, the tendency of these averages to mislead. The upper half of Table 10–8 shows how average nutritional levels in different nations are closely related to GNP per capita. The same is true within countries: different income groups may have very different consumption levels. Where income distribution worsened during the 1960s and 1970s, the number of malnourished people could have increased at the same time as the average caloric intake went up.

Food Consumption

What causes malnutrition, and how could nutritional improvement contribute to economic development? The determinants of human nutritional levels can be analyzed using microeconomic consumption theory. The consumption of food, like that of other goods and services, can be thought of as determined by three elements: income, relative prices, and tastes. Engel's Law, as we saw in Chapter 3, says that households spend an increasing amount, but a decreasing proportion, of income on food as their incomes rise. Very poor households devote more than half their incomes to food and have relatively high income elasticities of demand for food; that is, a significant proportion of any additional income will be used to buy food. At higher income levels, the share of income devoted to food purchases falls to one-quarter or less, and the income elasticity of demand for food becomes quite low. Thus, income is an important determinant of food consumption levels, particularly at lower levels of household income.

Prices are also important, because of both income effects and substitution effects. For a poor household, a change in the price of a basic foodstuff, particularly of a staple food grain like rice, wheat, or corn, can have a significant effect on the household's purchasing power. If the household spends 30 percent of its income on rice and the retail price of rice increases by 20 percent, this amounts to a 6 percent cut in the purchasing power of an already poor household ($0.3 \times 0.2 = 0.06 = 6$ percent). For this reason staple food grain prices are a basic indicator of welfare levels among the poor, and of political stability, in many low-income countries.

Substitution effects can also be significant. Even when there are strong preferences for particular foods, large price differences can cause substantial substitution of cheaper foods for more expensive ones, especially among the very poor. Hence it was possible to induce large numbers of people in East Pakistan (now Bangladesh) to consume U.S.-surplus wheat instead of rice, the favored food grain, when there was a rice shortage during the 1960s. Similarly, desperately poor families are sometimes forced to "trade down" from the preferred food grain to a cheaper source of calories, usually either a hard grain like sorghum or a starchy root crop such as manioc (cassava).

A powerful argument for the influence of income on food consumption and nutritional status has appeared in recent discussions of famine. Most people associate famine with a precipitous drop in the overall food supply, usually as a result of crop failure, but the Indian economist A. R. Sen has shown that in several historical famines the total availability of food did not decline. The real problem, Sen argues, is likely to be people's **food entitlements:** the ability to obtain food, whether through purchase, rationing, or other forms of distribution.[8] Contemporary food policy analysts define their goal as **food security,** a situation in which all people, at all times, have access to enough food to permit them to lead active, healthy lives.

Both income and price influences apply to the consumption of food, but not directly to the consumption of nutrients. Although nutrition is derived from food, it is food that people consume, not nutrition per se. When people spend more on food, they may or may not obtain better nutrition. Some of the additional expenditure goes for a larger *quantity* of food, but much of it, especially above minimal income levels, goes for higher *quality*. Quality is defined in terms of people's tastes. Some of the foods regarded as higher in quality may have no nutritional advantages over less favored competitors. Indeed, foods of subjectively higher quality may even be nutritionally inferior. Every nutritionist can tell horror stories about deterioration in nutritional standards as development proceeds: carbonated beverages replace natural drinks, commercial infant foods replace mother's breast milk, various junk foods are increasingly consumed by children and adults. Statistics make it clear, however, that these cases run against the general pattern of improved nutrition in relation to increasing income, which is depicted in Figure 10–3. In general, people with higher incomes have both a higher caloric intake and a more varied diet, which is superior in nutritional quality.

Food beliefs and tastes can impede nutritional improvement. In every culture there are beliefs about the health effects of various foods that are not supported by modern nutritional science. Traditional feeding taboos for infants and new mothers are thought to be particularly injurious in many developing countries. In most human environments one can point to nutritional potentials which are underexploited for reasons of taste and habit. For example, soybean products provide a much cheaper source of protein than animal products, yet they are eaten in quantity only in East Asian countries where they are standard protein sources. Nutritionists can counter the economist's assertion that income is the main influence on nutritional status by demonstrating that even very poor households could eat nutritiously if they had the necessary knowledge and chose to do so.

8. Amartya Sen, "Ingredients of Famine Analysis: Availability and Entitlements," *Quarterly Journal of Economics* 96, no. 3 (August 1981): 433–64.

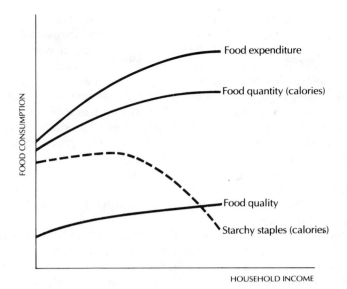

FIGURE 10-3   **Various Measures of Food Consumption Relative to Household Income Level.**
Food expenditure rises with income, but at a declining rate. Some of the rise goes for
improved quality, while consumption of starchy staples declines. *Source:* C. Peter Timmer,
Walter P. Falcon, and Scott R. Pearson, *Food Policy Analysis* (Baltimore: John Hopkins University Press, 1983), p. 57.

In conclusion, all three of the factors we have examined—income, prices,
and tastes—are significant contributors to the determination of nutritional
status. Emphasis on the role of each factor leads to a different approach to
nutritional policy, as will be seen.

The distribution of food within a family is another important aspect of
individual nutritional status. When food is scarce, children and older adults
tend to find their rations disproportionately reduced.[9] It is understandable
that in dire circumstances families channel food to the working adults on
whose continued health and strength the survival of all family members ultimately depends. This tendency makes it hard to devise programs to improve
the nutritional status of the more vulnerable family members, such as
infants and new mothers, since feeding programs aimed at them may create
consumption shifts within the family such that the breadwinner, rather than
the intended recipient, winds up with the extra food.

Nutritional Interventions

The first problem to be solved when designing a nutrition improvement program is selecting a target group.

9. Children with "high parity"—those born into families where there are several older sib-
lings—are particularly likely to suffer. Studies have shown that such children have higher mortality rates, presumably because large families strain supplies of income, food, and parental
attention.

Infants and children face the greatest nutritional problem in the third world. Infants are usually adequately fed through the breastfeeding stage, but they may suffer a nutritional decline after weaning. If not corrected this decline will reduce their energy levels and physical growth. This in turn may decrease their resistance to disease and impair their ability to learn in school. It has also been argued that malnutrition causes severe, even irreversible, retardation of mental development, but this assertion is now regarded as controversial at best. Even so, nutritional deficiencies among third-world children must be regarded as important because they are so widespread and have such serious consequences.

Pregnant and nursing women also merit special attention because of their relationship to the child nutrition problem. While carrying or nursing a child, a woman has especially heavy nutrition requirements because she is "eating for two," as the saying goes.

Whether working adults should be specially targeted for nutrition intervention is more debatable. Conceivably, improved nutrition for this group could have the most direct and immediate effect on economic growth, if its productivity were thereby increased. But we have seen that the evidence on whether their productivity is reduced by the degrees of malnutrition prevailing in most LDCs and whether it would be improved by nutrition intervention is mixed. In any case, since working adults tend to get favored access to whatever food is available, it is not clear to what extent their food supply is reduced when the family as a whole is short of food.

Several different types of nutrition intervention are possible. In the 1950s attention focused on the severely malnourished, who required hospital treatment. Later the emphasis shifted to treatment of milder cases outside hospitals. Supplementary feeding programs were instituted in a number of countries. Their most severe difficulty turned out to be that of reaching the intended beneficiary group at reasonable cost. School lunch programs can be helpful, but the worst nutritional deficiencies are likely to be among pre-school children. Even when the intended beneficiaries are reached and fed, evaluators of feeding programs suspect that substitution frequently takes place in the home: children are fed less to compensate for the school lunch and the net increase in the family's food supply thus goes to the adults rather than the children.

The best way to get supplementary food to infants and small children is to integrate food distribution with **maternal and child health** (MCH) programs. These programs aim to provide health services to mothers and infants through local clinics while also providing nutritional surveillance. The food offered can serve as an inducement for mothers to bring their children into an MCH center regularly for weighing, examination, and treatment if necessary. Persuasion and linkage with other services that may be desired, such as family planning, also promote these programs. Without such efforts, very few third-world mothers bring their babies in for examination by a health professional unless they are obviously sick.

Other conventional nutrition improvement programs include the promotion of **backyard gardens** to provide dietary supplementation and **nutritional education** conducted in schools, adult education courses, and the like. Since these programs are inherently limited in scope, there have been attempts to develop broader, more general types of programs. **Food supplementation** (fortification) programs have sometimes had dramatic results in overcoming specific nutritional deficiencies, such as through the addition of iodine to the salt supply in goiter-prone areas. Fortification of bread and other basic foodstuffs to increase their protein content has been attempted in several areas, with mixed results. Still less successful have been efforts, some of them widely heralded for a time, to develop commercially compounded **new foods** whose exceptional nutritional values would overcome the problem of malnutrition. The main problem with the new foods is that their high cost usually puts them beyond the reach of those low-income consumers who are likely to be malnourished.

Growing interest in malnutrition, coupled with the limited success of conventional approaches, has led to increasing attention to still broader programs, such as campaigns to increase national food production and food price subsidization for low-income urban consumers. There is no doubt that food-growing peasants, such as small-scale rice or corn producers, do eat better when their farms become more productive. Similarly, a price cut for staplefood items—made possible by higher farm production and greater supplies—can provide a substantial boost in both purchasing power and nutritional status for the urban poor, as we have seen. The main problems with staple-food subsidization programs are how to limit them to the intended beneficiaries, and forms of benefit, as well as how to finance them. Recipients of subsidized foodstuffs (or food stamps, as in the U.S. program) may sell them to buy other goods which they prefer. While this practice is consistent with the idea of consumer choice, it may defeat the purpose of nutritional improvement. Subsidy programs can be expensive, especially when their scope is broad. Egypt and Sri Lanka are two countries that have had food subsidy programs extending to nearly the entire population. In both cases subsidization of basic foodstuffs (wheat, beans, lentils, vegetable oil, meat, fish, and tea in Egypt; rice, wheat, and sugar in Sri Lanka) is credited with increasing the real income of the poor and improving their nutritional and health status. But the cost of the program grew to around 15 percent of government expenditure in both countries and came to be regarded as a contributor to fiscal instability. In both cases efforts to cut back on the subsidy bill led to political instability: riots in both countries, and in Sri Lanka the defeat at the polls of more than one government.

The cost-effectiveness of different approaches to nutritional improvement is a subject of current debate.[10] Targeted programs that deliver nutritional services to specific groups of beneficiaries—for instance, school lunch programs or baby-weighing programs—can involve high logistical and supervision costs per beneficiary served. More general programs, such as

10. Cost-effectiveness is a concept akin to the benefit-cost ratio, which was discussed in Chapter 6 (see footnote 7, page 138). But whereas in the benefit-cost ratio both benefits and costs are measured in money terms, cost-effectiveness uses a nonmonetary measure of benefits. In the case of a nutrition intervention, for example, greater cost-effectiveness would consist of achieving a larger amount of nutritional benefit for a given program expenditure. Alternatively, it could be defined as achievement of a given amount of nutritional benefit for less program expenditure.

fortification or food subsidies, may achieve a lower cost per recipient but entail a different kind of cost problem: leakage of program benefits to people other than the intended beneficiaries. The extension of nutritional programs, especially food subsidies, to large segments of the population can be costly, as the experiences of Egypt and Sri Lanka illustrate.

MEDICAL SERVICES

Most LDCs have too few health services, too poorly distributed. Public expenditures on health services are much smaller in developing than in developed countries, even as a percentage of GNP, as seen in Table 10–9. In terms of dollars per capita, these outlays are woefully inadequate. As Table 10–9 shows, governments in the poorer countries were typically spending two dollars per capita around 1980.[11] The inadequacy becomes clearer when we consider that in LDCs, in contrast to the United States, the public sector expenditure represents the bulk of the modern, Western-style medical and health services. Private doctors and hospitals are typically few and are patronized mainly by well-to-do urban residents. In most countries there are also indigenous practitioners of various kinds: herbalists, exorcists, acupuncturists. Typically the masses of people consult both modern and indigenous healers upon occasion, depending on the nature of the ailment and on their access to the various systems of medicine.

Low medical expenditures in the past have led to inadequate stocks of health facilities and manpower in most developing countries, as Table 10–9 indicates. Medical training in many of the poorest countries may not benefit society because doctors are highly mobile, and once trained, many emigrate

TABLE 10–9   Health Personnel, Facilities, and Expenditures (circa 1980)

Country's GNP per capita	Per 100,000 population			Public expenditure	
	Hospital beds	Physicians	Nursing persons	Percent of GNP	Dollars per capita
Below $300ᵃ	79 (76)	21 (11)	18 (16)	0.9 (1.4)	2 (2)
$300–$500ᵇ	190 (111)	52 (19)	57 (55)	0.7	2
$500–$1,000	117	19	45	0.8	6
$1,000–$2,000	398	80	125	1.5	26
$2,000–$5,000	860	246	626	1.1	33
$5,000 and above	859	188	673	3.7	402

Source: World Development Report 1985 (New York: Oxford University Press, 1985); International Monetary Fund, *Government Finance Statistics Yearbook 1984* (Washington, D.C., 1984); World Health Organization, *World Health Statistics Annual 1983* (Geneva, 1983).
ᵃ Figures in parentheses exclude India.
ᵇ Figures in parentheses exclude China; no data on health expenditures are available for China.

11. These figures are distorted by the extreme disparity in the pay of medical personnel, especially doctors, between rich and poor countries. A purchasing-power parity adjustment of the sort discussed in Chapter 3 would roughly triple the per-capita expenditure figures for the poorest countries and double those of the somewhat less poor. By any measure, however, the figures would remain abysmally low. See Frederick Golladay, "Health Problems and Policies in Developing Countries" (World Bank Staff Working Paper No. 412, August 1980).

to seek higher income elsewhere (see boxed example on Cuba). In many
cases, increasing the supply of nurses and other health auxiliaries may be a
better way to improve services.

247

MEDICAL
SERVICES

Health in Cuba

When the Castro forces took over in January 1959, Cuba was a middle-
income country with reasonably plentiful but poorly distributed health
care manpower and facilities. Average income was higher than in most
other Latin America countries, life expectancy at birth was over sixty
years, and the population was more than 50 percent urban. But inequalities were marked. Havana, with only 22 percent of the population, had
55 percent of the hospital beds in the country, while Oriente province,
one of Cuba's poorest regions, had 35 percent of the population but only
15 percent of the hospital beds. There were 6,300 doctors to care for a
population of eight million.

In the first three years after the revolution, 3,000 physicians left the
country, most emigrating to the United States. There is probably no prec-
edent in history for a country losing such a high percentage of its doctors
in such a short time. Massive training efforts were inaugurated to make
up this deficit. By 1971, 30 percent of all university students were studying medicine. By 1979, after more than twenty years of massive training
efforts, the ratio of doctors to population was finally restored to about
what it was in 1958, when Cuba then had about 9,000 doctors for a population of nearly 9.9 million.

Despite having to cope with this massive problem of medical manpower, Cuba has made major strides toward achievement of high health
standards for its entire population. It has done so largely by reorganizing
its health services and improving their distribution among social classes
and regions of the country. A new system of hospitals and clinics was set
up, stretching from provincial hospitals serving areas of about one million
people down to health centers serving communities of 25,000. Given the
initial disparities, new facilities were constructed primarily in the rural
areas. Thus while the number of hospital beds available in Havana
increased by only 8 percent in the first post-revolutionary decade, the
increases in Camaguey and Oriente provinces were 184 and 147 percent
respectively. Over half of the new health centers built were allocated to
rural areas which previously had no such facilities. Services in the new
system were provided virtually free, encouraging greater use by the
public.

Medical personnel participated in the planning and management of
health services, but the broad guidelines were laid down by the political
leadership, dominated by the Communist Party. After the introduction of
local elections in 1976, community participation in health care planning
increased.

Social and economic change have supported these improvements in
medical services. Economic growth was very slow in the 1960s but has

accelerated recently. Public policy has emphasized equitable distribution of basic necessities. Primary foodstuffs are rationed and price-controlled. Literacy is now estimated at 96 percent and elementary school attendance is universal (uniquely among Latin American countries). Housing problems have been chronic among Cuba's urban population, now 65 percent of the total, but are gradually being remedied by construction of apartment houses.

Mortality indicators for Cuba have improved from good to excellent. The infant death rate was only twenty per thousand in 1983 and the crude death rate was a miniscule six per thousand, thanks in part to the youth of the population structure. Life expectancy at birth was seventy-three years. The birth rate was seventeen per thousand, creating a low 1.1 percent rate of natural increase. Family planning is not officially promoted because the country is perceived as suffering from a labor shortage, but contraceptives are freely available to those who want them.

As well as being inadequately supplied, health services in poor countries are very unevenly distributed among the population. Capital cities, and urban areas in general, usually have several times as many doctors in relation to population as rural areas. Similar if slightly smaller disparities exist with respect to hospital beds and primary health workers.

The usual public health service is organized on a referral basis, so that in theory patients in rural areas suffering from acute medical problems are referred to better facilities in the towns and, if necessary, in the major cities, for care. Generally, however, the referral system does not work well in developing countries. The lower reaches of the system seldom provide easily accessible services to the whole country. For large parts of the population in the typical low-income country, even the most rudimentary public health facility may be so far away that, given the prevailing poor transportation systems, it is inaccessible. Those patients who can get to a government clinic or hospital often find that they have to wait many hours before receiving any attention at all. Even then the care they obtain may be slipshod and half-hearted. Managerial and logistical problems overwhelm some third-world health systems. Many of the vaccines administered, for example, have been rendered ineffective by age and exposure to heat, and sterile conditions for medical procedures are all but impossible to maintain.

A different aspect of the poor distribution of medical services concerns the relative degrees of attention and resources devoted to treating different types of ailments. In many countries large fractions of tight health budgets have been devoted to acquiring state-of-the-art medical technologies for hospitals in the capital city or at the local medical school. Does it make sense for a country that is not providing even rudimentary medical care to sick infants to acquire the capacity to do open-heart surgery? For the cost of a single complicated medical procedure, basic attention could be provided to hundreds of rural patients. Why then do so many countries opt for what appears to be a severe maldistribution of their scant health resources? One reason appears to be urban bias, the general tendency in developing countries for urban populations to benefit disproportionately from government expenditures and policies.[12] Urban bias in the provision of medical services has many causes, one of which is the fact that powerful national elites living in urban areas, especially the capital city, want good medical care for themselves and their families. A second reason is nationalism: "Our doctors are just as good as doctors in the advanced countries; they can do open-heart surgery, too." Yet a third reason is the technology-mindedness which many doctors share with engineers and other professionals. The medical area is often regarded as an outstanding example of the transfer of inappropriate technology from developed to developing countries. These three factors can interact, as when the self-interest of the elites prompts them to indulge the technology-mindedness of the doctors.

Still another shortcoming of public health services in most LDCs relates to the balance between preventive and curative services. Since, as we have seen, curing all the sick is a task beyond the means of many poor countries, it follows that the possibility that sickness and death can be reduced more cheaply through preventive measures deserves careful examination. Preventive actions such as inoculation campaigns, mosquito spraying, and rat killing have produced dramatic improvements in health conditions in some low-income countries, most notably in China. Many LDCs still spend too much on curative services relative to preventive activities.

It is thus evident that inadequate, maldistributed, and inappropriate medical services in poor countries are themselves contributors to sickness and premature death. What can be done about it?

Improved medical services depend on a better spread of coverage to reach the entire population, and on the development of service patterns more appropriate to the health needs and resource availabilities of a developing country. The greatest interest now is in reforming health systems along the following lines: (1) active and continuous promotion of community health, instead of intermittent treatment of specific conditions in individuals; (2) management of the system by nonphysicians; (3) training health-care auxiliaries recruited from the community to diagnose and treat simple ailments; and (4) limited referral of difficult cases.

The health care systems evolved by socialist developing countries, such as China and Cuba, are sometimes taken as models by those interested in similar reforms. In 1976 China reported spending over 60 percent of its health care budget in rural areas and sending half its medical school graduates to assignments in the countryside. Like other developing countries it has experienced difficulty in getting health professionals to live in rural areas. China has countered this tendency, however, and through its well-known system of health auxiliaries, it is providing—for the first time—decent health care to its enormous peasant population. As of 1976 official sources reported that there were 1.5 million "barefoot doctors" working in the country, doing preventive work, treating patients at home and in the fields, assisting with mass health and sanitation campaigns, and disseminating information on family

---

12. Urban bias has been defined and analyzed by Michael Lipton, *Why Poor People Stay Poor: Urban Bias in World Development* (Cambridge, Mass.: Harvard University Press, 1977).

planning and maternal and child health care. In addition there were reported to be some three million part-time health auxiliaries assisting in the same activities. These efforts have contributed to levels of health and life expectancy unusual for a country with China's still low income level.

Similar results have been achieved by other countries that have followed a basic human needs strategy. Table 10–10 contrasts two types of poor areas: one, including China and the Indian state of Kerala, in which a BHN strategy emphasizing the attainment of minimum acceptable levels of health services, education, and nutrition was pursued, and another type of area in which it was not. Although the countries in the first group are no richer than those in the second—indeed, they are substantially poorer than Iran, a member of the second group—they have achieved markedly lower mortality levels.

The development and dissemination of simple cures for widespread health problems must accompany the spread of medical services into the rural areas. For example, at present about ten percent of all children born in the developing countries die of diarrhea before reaching the age of ten. Yet there is a simple inexpensive technology that can prevent most of these deaths: oral rehydration therapy (ORT), which is nothing more than a solution of sugar and mineral salts in water. ORT counteracts dehydration, which is the direct cause of diarrhea deaths. A scientifically designed and tested ORT formula is being disseminated by organizations such as the United Nations Children's Fund (UNICEF), but even folk versions of the remedy, such as rice water and simple mixtures of sugar and table salt, may be effective. Sickness and early death among third-world children could be sharply curtailed by spreading knowledge and availability of this remedy throughout the third world, and developing others like it.

TABLE 10–10   Mortality in Two Groups of Areas, circa 1975

Area	Crude death rate	Infant mortality rate	Life expectancy at birth
Areas with Basic Needs Policies			
China	10	55	62
Sri Lanka	8	45	68
Kerala[a]	9	56	62
Areas without Basic Needs Policies			
Bangladesh	20	132	47
India	15	139	50
Iran	16	139	51
Pakistan	15	124	50

Source: James Kocher and Richard A. Cash, "Achieving Health and Nutritional Objectives Within a Basic Needs Framework" (Harvard Institute for International Development, Development Discussion Paper No. 55, March 1979): 19.
[a] A state in Southern India.

PART 3

CAPITAL RESOURCES

Capital and Saving

Of all of the approaches to development mentioned in Chapters 2 and 3, the emphasis on capital formation was perhaps the most influential and durable, for a number of reasons. First, relative to the other approaches, it had more respectable theoretical underpinnings—the simple but elegant Harrod-Domar model, discussed in Chapter 3. Properly viewed, the Harrod-Domar model provides insights into vital aspects of the development process, focusing as it does on the difficulties involved in meeting the investment requirements for assuring substantial and steady growth without high rates of inflation or unemployment. However, more mechanistic interpretations of the Harrod-Domar model postulated a lockstep relationship between growth in investment and national income. The view that capital formation was the key to growth, called **capital fundamentalism,** was reflected in the development strategies and plans in many countries. The development problem was viewed essentially as one of securing investment resources sufficient to generate some chosen target rate of national income growth. The implications of target rates of income growth for employment and income distribution were rarely examined, as it was widely assumed that faster growth rates would in and of themselves ameliorate both unemployment and extreme income inequality.

Second, capital fundamentalism resonated with the aims and approaches of foreign aid donors of the 1950s and 1960s, by furnishing a readily explicable, apparently clear-cut basis for the justifying aid "needs." Capital shortage was then widely judged to be the single most important barrier to accelerated economic development, and a heavy premium tended to be placed on framing development plans that reflected this point of view. The best-crafted of such plans, such as Pakistan's third five-year plan in the early 1960s, were able to show heavy initial capital requirements and a need for large early injections of foreign capital, especially foreign aid. Large initial contributions of aid, it was thought, would generate new flows of domestic savings, eventually reducing aid requirements in the long run.

Third, capital fundamentalism was durable because its framework was flexible enough to incorporate new economic ideas of the 1960s, especially the concept of human capital discussed in Part II of this book. The selective embedding of human capital considerations into the framework further strengthened the argument that capital formation was the linchpin of development. The incorporation of human capital into the framework was no minor embellishment, for the size of the human capital stock relative to the physical stock can be quite large. Recent estimates place the value of the human capital stock in the United States in the mid-1970s roughly equal to that of the stock of physical capital.

High levels of capital formation made possible by initial abundance of savings matter little for income growth—much less for employment creation and improving income distribution—when capital is deployed in projects of low productivity. These include the much-ridiculed, large-scale showcase steel mills and thousands of inefficiently small hydroelectric plants; in expensive higher education; and ultramodern cardiac care centers serving small elites in capital cities. Further, massive investment projects financed by foreign savings, however productive, may have little impact on income growth when host-country policies are poorly suited for capturing an equitable share of the returns from such projects. Particularly before the mid-1960s, there were several instances in which host countries, especially those with sizable natural-resource endowments, have ultimately had little to show from major foreign investment projects other than the scrap content of equipment left behind at the end. We return to this problem in Chapters 14 and 19.

INVESTMENT REQUIREMENTS FOR GROWTH

The critical role of savings and capital in creating income growth has been well established in industrial societies. For example, the sources-of-growth analysis introduced in Chapter 3 has been employed to show that expansion of physical capital inputs alone has been responsible for about half the growth in aggregate income of nine developed countries from 1960–1975. Many studies point to the very low investment rate in the United States in the 1970s and early 1980s as a prime reason, along with lagging productivity growth, for its low rates of per-capita income growth since 1970, relative to Japan and Western Europe. Indeed by 1983, gross domestic investment was but 17 percent of GDP in the United States, a ratio well below the 20 percent figure for 1965, and one of the lowest of all industrial countries.

Analyses of the relative contribution of capital to growth in developing countries are neither as numerous nor, owing to data limitations, as conclusive as those for the United States. However, the available sources-of-growth calculations suggest that the impact of capital formation on growth is considerable in those countries as well, particularly for the early stages of development; at higher levels of income, productivity growth appears much more important. Studies in middle-income nations such as Korea, the Philippines, and Mexico indicate that in recent years growth in the physical-capital stock, quite apart from growth in the stock of human capital, may have contributed from one-fourth to one-third of income growth, with estimates clustering toward the higher figure; the contribution is as much as one-half in poorer countries. None of these studies incorporate the contribution of human capital to income growth, so the results understate the role of capital formation, and therefore savings, in income growth.

In any case, while capital accumulation is no longer viewed as a panacea for poor countries, it is nevertheless clear that even mildly robust growth rates in incomes can be sustained over long periods only when societies are able to maintain investment at a sizable proportion of GDP. This proportion can rarely be much less than 15 percent and in some cases it must go as high as 25 percent, depending on the environment in which capital accumulation takes place and on what rate of income growth is deemed essential to allow progress toward basic societal goals. Growth aspirations probably do not vary as widely as did recorded growth performance between low- and middle-income countries from 1965 to 1983, where average growth in real per-capita income was only 2.7 percent in the former and 3.4 percent in the latter. (Refer to Table 1–2.) In general, if LDCs seek growth in real per-capita income that at least matches that for the middle-income countries from 1965 onward, then—given typical rates of LDC population growth of about 2.5 percent in the past decade (excluding China)—the requisite rate of aggregate income growth would have to be at least 6 percent per annum.

Effective Use of Capital

Given a goal of 6 percent growth in real aggregate income, annual investment requirements would then depend on both the volume of available savings and on the environment in which capital formation occurs. In developing countries where basic macro (economy-wide) prices (exchange rates, interest rates, wage rates) are approximately equal to scarcity values for factors of production, scarce capital is likely to be deployed where it can be applied most effectively with more abundant labor. In such circumstances a given addition to the capital stock can generate increments to output that exceed those in countries where production is more capital-intensive (see Chapter 3). Depending on the structure of basic macro prices such as interest rates and exchange rates and the orientation of public sector decision-makers, the ICOR may typically range from 1.0 to 4.0, with a median value for fifty-odd LDCs at between 1.0 and 2.5, as shown in Table 11–1. Consider the investment implications of an ICOR of 2.5 compared with an ICOR half as high—3.75. For countries with an ICOR of 2.5, a necessary, but not sufficient, condition for achieving sustained aggregate growth in output of 6.0

TABLE 11-1 Average Incremental Capital-Output Ratios, 1980–83 in Forty-six LDCs

Incremental Capital-Output Ratio (ICOR)	Number of Countries	Partial Listing of Countries
0.1–0.99	6	Bolivia, Sierra Leone, Uruguay, Zaire
1.0–1.49	12	Benin, Chile, Colombia, India, Pakistan, Senegal, Yugoslavia
1.5–1.99	7	Jamaica, Kenya, Zambia
2.0–2.49	9	Malawi, Philippines, South Korea, Thailand
2.5–2.99	2	Burma, Tanzania
3.0–3.49	2	Honduras
3.5–3.99	3	Jordan, Togo
4.0–4.49	3	Panama, Singapore
4.5–4.99	1	Venezuela
5.0 and above	1	Ivory Coast

Source: Derived from country tables in International Monetary Fund, *International Financial Statistics Yearbook, 1985* (Washington, D. C., 1985).

percent per year is securing capital resources equivalent to 15 percent of GNP. However, countries with an ICOR of 3.75 will need to invest 22.5 percent of GNP to attain the same rate of output growth. Thus efficient capital deployment can substantially reduce the savings effort required for sustained growth.

Capital-Intensive or Labor-Intensive Investment: A Hypothetical Case

In the presence of immobilities of productive factors of the type discussed at the end of this chapter, a pervasive pattern of capital-intensive production in capital-short countries leads to lower rates of income growth, strong suppression of consumption, or both. To illustrate, consider two countries that are initially identical in all important respects: per-capita income of $200 in 1980, population of five million, an investment ratio in 1980 of 15 percent, and similar patterns of exports, imports, agriculture, and industry. From 1970 to 1980, both followed essentially the same development strategies, resulting in an historic incremental capital-output ratio of 3.5. Both experienced real GDP growth rates of about 5 percent over the ten-year period.

In 1980 new governments in both countries altered past development policies. For the coming decade country A's government chose a strategy involving heavy outlays on large-scale, capital-intensive investments, such as oil refining, paper mills, and steel mills. As a result of this change, and supported by other government policies, the ICOR is expected to rise from 3.5 to 4. Country B, on the other hand, decided in 1980 to shift to a strategy emphasizing more labor-intensive investments in agriculture and industry, including textile mills, commercial firewood forests, coastal fisheries, and shoe manufactures. Decision-makers in country B expect the ICOR to decline from 3.5 to 3 as a result. These two capital-output ratios are well within the range for developing countries given in Table 11-1. In this example we overlook contributions of other factors to growth.

We assume that both countries faced similar constraints on investment finance during the period 1980–1985. For both, resources available for investment (from both domestic and foreign sources) are most likely to

expand by no less than 5 percent per year ("low") and by no more than 10
percent per year ("high"). The implications of these alternative investment
availabilities for GDP growth are presented in Table 11–2.

A striking implication can be drawn from Table 11–2. The table shows
that the efficiency with which capital is used can be much more important
for GDP growth than for raising the volume of investment. For the entire
five-year period, the ICOR of country A is only 25 percent higher than that
of country B. But after five years country B has a higher GDP than country
A, even when investment resources grow at twice the rate in country A as in
country B. At 5 percent growth in investment in country B, average annual
GDP growth is also 5 percent, while in country A even 10 percent growth in
investment leads to only a 4.2 percent average annual GDP growth. To
accomplish this, by the fifth year country A must find investment resources
equal to 19.7 percent of GDP. With an investment ratio of only 15 percent in
1985, country B can still grow faster than the maximum that is possible for
country A.

On the other hand, if investment resources available to both countries
were to grow at 10 percent per annum, aggregate income in B would be 6
percent higher than in A by 1985, even though they began at the same level.
While a 6 percent difference in total income after five years may not seem
large, when placed in proper perspective it can be quite significant. There are
few developing countries in the world that spend as much as 6 percent of
GDP on education, and no LDC spends as much as 3 percent on public
health. Merely because it uses capital more efficiently than country A, country B would, in the extreme, possess the capacity to more than double real
outlays for education, or triple expenditures on public health programs.

TABLE 11–2 GDP and Investment Under Two Different Strategies (millions of U.S. dollars)

	1980	Investment growth rate (%)	1981	1982	1983	1984	1985	Average annual growth (%)	1985 % of investment to GDP
Investment Availability									
I. Low	150.0	5.0	157.5	165.4	173.6	182.3	191.4	5.0	-
II. High	150.0	10.0	165.0	181.5	199.6	219.6	241.6	10.0	-
GDP Country A: Capital-intensive strategy (ICOR = 4)[a]									
I. Low	1,000	5.0	1,037.5	1,076.9	1,118.3	1,161.7	1,207.3	3.8	15.9
II. High	1,000	10.0	1,037.5	1,078.8	1,124.2	1,174.1	1,229.0	4.2	19.7
GDP Country B: Labor-intensive strategy (ICOR = 3)[a]									
I. Low	1,000	5.0	1,050.0	1,102.5	1,157.6	1,215.5	1,276.3	5.0	15.0
II. High	1,000	10.0	1,050.0	1,105.0	1,165.5	1,232.0	1,305.2	5.5	18.5

[a] To simplify presentation, the example assumes that all investment resources in any given year are available by the beginning of that year, and that there is only a one-year lag between the time investment resources are available and the time they begin to yield output.

Alternatively, if both countries place a high premium on national autonomy and are therefore apprehensive over foreign participation in their economies, it is much more likely that country B will satisfy this goal since it will have less need to resort to foreign capital to finance a substantial share of its development effort. An investment ratio of 15 percent is clearly much easier to support from domestic resources than the 20 percent required for country A to attain the same level of GDP growth.

Investment Ratios in LDCs

The heavy emphasis on capital-intensive investment often found in developing countries is to some extent the unintended result of government policies. But it may also be attributed to a pervasive belief that only capital-intensive technology is "efficient," and that in any case choice of technology is not sensitive to relative prices of labor and capital. Discussion in Chapter 8 casts significant doubt on the notion that choice of technique of production in LDCs is largely unaffected by price signals. Policies that result in underpricing of capital and overpricing of labor do seem to cause firms and government agencies to adjust by adopting techniques involving more of the former and less of the latter than would be the case in the absence of such policies. However, Chapter 8 also reminds us that wherever found, bias toward capital intensity in investment cannot always, or even usually, be fully explained in terms of distorted price signals, nor is it legitimate to assume that capital intensity always represents vice and that labor-using investment always denotes virtue. For example, those who would advocate a conscious, reverse bias in favor of labor-intensive methods of underground coal or tin mining have either never visited the hazardous labor-intensive facilities for these activities (for example, in Bolivia and Indonesia), or are unaware of the large surpluses available from capital-intensive mining that can be deployed for labor-intensive investments in other fields. Even in agriculture there are sound arguments, advanced in Chapter 18, for mechanization to increase both productivity and employment.

In the typical labor-surplus situation, 6 percent annual growth in real income cannot be sustained over extended periods in the absence of investment ratios of at least 20 percent (in the economies emphasizing more labor-intensive approaches) and 25 percent (in the capital-intensive strategies). Securing investment ratios of even 15 percent has proven a difficult task for many LDCs, and in particular some of the thirty-three nations (other than India and China) falling into the World Bank's category of low-income countries (see Table 11–3, first two columns). Nevertheless, all but four of the countries in this group did manage to increase the share of gross domestic investment to gross domestic product over the period 1960 to 1983. For this set of countries as a whole, investment's share rose from 19 percent in 1960 to almost 26 percent in 1980 (but from 13 to 18 percent with China and India excluded). The fifty-nine countries classed as middle income by the World Bank were on the whole able to increase investment shares but slightly from 1960 to 1983. However, the thirty-six lower middle-income countries did manage to expand investment shares by almost 50 percent

TABLE 11–3 Gross Domestic Investment and Gross Domestic Savings Rates, 1960–1983

Category[d]	Gross domestic investment[a] (as % of GDP)		Gross domestic savings[b] (as % of GDP)[d]		Resource gap[c]	
	1960	1983	1960	1983	1960	1983
Low-income countries[e]	19 (13)	26 (18)	18 (10)	24 (7)	−1 (−3)	−2 (−11)
Middle-income countries	20	22	19	21	−1	−1
Lower-middle-income	15	22	14	17	−1	−5
Upper-middle-income	22	22	21	23	−1	+1
High-income oil exporters	na	29	na	39	—	+10
Industrial market economies	21	20	22	20	+1	0
East European non-market economies	na	na	na	na	na	na

Source: World Bank, *World Development Report, 1985* (New York: Oxford University Press, 1985), pp. 182–83. World Bank, *World Development Report, 1984* (New York: Oxford University Press, 1984), pp. 226–27.

[a] **Gross domestic investment** is defined as all public and private sector expenditures for additions to the stock of fixed assets, plus the net value of inventory changes.

[b] **Gross domestic savings** includes both public sector and private sector savings. It indicates the volume of gross domestic investment financed by domestic sources. As given in this table, gross domestic savings is calculated as the residual after subtracting from gross domestic investment the deficit on current international accounts from gross domestic investment.

[c] Gross domestic investment minus gross domestic savings.

[d] Groups defined as in Table 1–1 (notes a–f).

[e] Figures in parentheses exclude China and India.

over the period. Investment shares in 1983 ranged from 7 percent of GDP in Bolivia to over 30 percent in Congo and Papua New Guinea. Among the upper middle-income countries, only Singapore, Malaysia, Jordan, Algeria, and Yugoslavia managed to reach or surpass 30 percent levels. Table 11–3 shows that both low- and middle-income countries had achieved, on the average, higher investment ratios in 1983 than even the advanced industrialized countries.[1] It is not surprising, then, that rates of growth in real GDP, at 5.0 percent for low-income nations and 4.7 percent for middle-income countries, were about twice as high as the average for the nineteen rich industrial countries from 1973 to 1983, which was but 2.4 percent.[2]

SOURCES OF SAVINGS

Developing countries, particularly the poorest thirty-five nations, were able to finance their higher investment-to-GDP ratios by intensified savings mobilization efforts directed at savings from various sources, both domestic and foreign, public and private. Before turning to an examination of recent patterns of investment finance it will be useful to consider a simplified taxonomy of savings.

Taxonomy of Savings

For a country, the total supply of available savings (S) is simply the sum of domestic savings (S_d) and foreign savings (S_f). Domestic savings may be bro-

1. The figures given in Table 11–3 have been weighted by the size of countries' GDPs. Thus the average for all industrial countries is dragged down substantially by the low investment rates of such large economies as the United States and the United Kingdom.

2. World Bank, *World Development Report 1985* (New York: Oxford University Press, 1985), Appendix Table 2, p. 112.

ken down into two components: government, or public-sector, savings (S_g) and private domestic savings (S_p). Government savings consists primarily of budgetary savings (S_{gb}) that arises from any excess of government revenues over government consumption, where public consumption is defined as all current government expenditure plus all capital outlays for military hardware. Examples of public-sector consumption include expenditure for food subsidies; for meeting recurring costs such as salaries for civil servants and police; for purchasing stationery, fuel, and arms; and for maintenance of roads and bridges, plus interest on the national debt. In focusing on this savings component, it is important to note that a country could still have positive public savings even when the overall government budget is in deficit, because budget expenditures include capital outlays, or investment, that represent uses of public savings. In addition, in some countries savings of government-owned enterprises (S_{ge}) have also contributed to public sector savings. Private domestic savings also arise from two sources: corporate savings (S_{pc}) and household savings (S_{ph}). **Corporate savings** is defined as the retained earnings of corporate enterprises (corporate income after taxes minus dividends paid to shareholders). **Household savings** (S_{ph}) is simply that part of household income not consumed. Household savings includes savings from unincorporated enterprises (single proprietorships, partnerships, and other noncorporate forms of business enterprise). In most LDCs unincorporated business enterprise is by far the dominant form of business organization.

Foreign savings also come in two basic forms: **official foreign savings** (S_{fo}) or foreign aid, and **private foreign savings** (S_{fp}), which may be broken down into two separate components. The first is **external commercial borrowing,** or *debt* finance, symbolized by S_{fpd}. LDC borrowers, including governments, agree to repay the amount of the loan (the principal) as well as interest on the loan, in accordance with prearranged schedules. The second major component of private foreign savings, **direct investment** represents *equity* finance, symbolized by S_{fpe}. Returns to equity are called dividends, and are paid only when profits are made.

To recapitulate, total available savings may be viewed in the first instance as

$$S = S_d + S_f = (S_g + S_p) + (S_{fo} + S_{fp}). \qquad [11\text{--}1]$$

For purposes of understanding savings patterns and policies, saving may be disaggregated further to

$$S = [(S_{gb} + S_{ge}) + (S_{pc} + S_{ph})] + (S_{fo} + S_{fpd} + S_{fpe}). \qquad [11\text{--}2]$$

Reliance upon different sources of savings differs greatly between developing nations, depending not only on factors such as the level of per-capita income, natural-resource endowments, and sectoral composition of GDP, but also on the nature of savings mobilization policies adopted by particular governments. The balance of this chapter identifies the determinants of domestic saving and its various components. Chapter 14 will examine foreign savings, its patterns, and the controversies surrounding it.

Domestic Savings

Relative to 1960, LDCs as a group had by 1983 greatly intensified their efforts to mobilize domestic savings. Although many relied heavily upon foreign savings as a source of investment finance, the rise in investment ratios depicted in Table 11–3 was accompanied by a nearly commensurate increase in the share of gross domestic savings in GDP. While these averages mask some major differences in the savings performances for countries within each category, the general picture is one of some success in mobilizing additional domestic savings since 1960, particularly in the low-income countries. Table 11–4 depicts the evolution of savings and investment ratios for a group of twenty-two LDCs in Asia, Africa, and Latin America, chosen to represent a wide range in per-capita income, natural resource endow-

TABLE 11–4   Domestic Savings Rates of Selected Developing Countries, 1960 and 1983

Country	Gross domestic savings as % of GDP 1960	1983	Gross domestic investment as % of GDP 1960	1983	Domestic savings as percent of domestic investment 1960	1983
Low-income countries[a, b]	18 (10)	24 (7)	19 (13)	26 (18)	95 (77)	92 (39)
Ethiopia	11	2	12	11	92	18
Bangladesh	8	2	7	17	114	12
Mali	9	−2	14	17	64	−12
Tanzania	19	8[c]	14	20[c]	136	40[c]
India	14	22[c]	17	25[c]	82	88[c]
China	23[d]	31	23[d]	31	100[d]	100
Ghana	17	5	24	8	71	63
Sri Lanka	9	14	14	29	64	48
Kenya	17	19	20	21	95	90
Pakistan	5	7	12	17	42	41
Middle-income countries[b]	19	21	20	22	95	95
Lower-middle-income	14	17	15	22	93	77
Senegal	15	3	16	17	94	18
Bolivia	7	−3	14	7	50	−43
Indonesia	8	20	8	24	100	83
Egypt	12	12	13	28	54	43
Philippines	16	21	16	27	100	78
Nigeria	7	19	13	19	54	100
Guatemala	8	9	10	11	80	82
Colombia	21	15	21	19	100	79
Upper-middle-income	21	23	22	22	95	105
Malaysia	27	29	14	34	193	85
Brazil	21	21[c]	22	21[c]	95	100[c]
South Korea	1	26	11	27	9	96
Mexico	18	28	20	17	90	165

Source: World Bank, *World Development Report 1985* (New York: Oxford University Press, 1985), pp. 182–83. World Bank, *World Development Report 1984* (New York: Oxford University Press, 1984) pp. 226–27.

[a] Figures in parentheses exclude China and India.
[b] Countries ranked in ascending order of per-capita income in 1983 (see Table 1–1).
[c] 1982.
[d] 1961.

ments, and ideological orientation. Among countries in this table, domestic savings rates in 1983 ranged from a negative 2 percent to a positive 31 percent. Table 11–4 underscores the significance of income levels for savings mobilization efforts. Among the low-income countries only China and India had savings rates of 20 percent or more in 1983, while among the middle-income group six of the twelve in the table have savings rates of over 20 percent. We would ordinarily expect a lower ratio of savings in poor countries relative to middle-income countries simply because there is less available for savings after subsistence needs are met.

It is also evident from Table 11–4 that the more prosperous LDCs tend to cover a larger share of their investment needs with local savings. Whereas seven of the poorer LDCs relied on foreign savings for more than one-third of investment finance by 1983, only three of the middle-income countries in the sample exhibited that much dependence on foreign savings. Indeed, in three of the middle-income nations domestic savings rates equaled or exceeded domestic investment rates. On average, the table also shows that although domestic savings rates have risen appreciably over the twenty-three years in both low- and middle -income countries, the share of domestic savings in total investment finance changed little. However, the strong savings performance of China and India in the group of low-income countries masks a serious decline in both savings rates and the share of investment financed locally in the other low-income nations included in Table 11–4.

But even Table 11–4 does not begin to portray adequately the diversity of savings performance across more than one hundred developing countries. In 1983, eight LDCs, besides Mali and Bolivia in the table, had negative rates of domestic savings; in Jordan, Lesotho, and Yemen, negative savings amounted to more than 15 percent of GDP. But in that same year, ten LDCs had positive savings rates in excess of 25 percent per year. This group includes, in addition to Malaysia, China, Korea, and Mexico in Table 11–4, such countries as Zaire, Cameroon, People's Republic of Congo, Algeria, and Singapore.

Government policies have had a major impact on the ability of developing countries to mobilize domestic savings. We will see in the next three chapters that in some countries, governments have actively sought to deploy policies, particularly fiscal and monetary policies, to encourage savings growth, and have utilized instruments well suited for that purpose. In still more countries governments have been no less concerned with the promotion of domestic savings but have relied on policy tools ill-suited for savings mobilization. Finally, in a small group of countries, government policies appear to have been designed with little or no regard for their implications for domestic savings. As might be expected, savings have generally responded positively to policy initiatives in the first group of countries, less so in the second group, and have tended to stagnate or decline in the third.

Government Savings

Where present, government savings have arisen almost wholly from an excess of total tax revenues over public consumption expenditures (S_{gb}). Chapter 21 shows that in very few cases do savings by government enterprises (S_{ge}) ever materially contribute to aggregate government savings. Given the very minor role for this component of public savings in all but a few countries, the discussion of government savings in this chapter is confined to budgetary savings.

During the 1950s and 1960s, one of the basic tenets of typical development strategies was that the investment expansion required for sustained income growth could not proceed in the absence of major efforts to increase the share of government savings in GDP. It was commonly held that growth in private savings was inherently constrained by such factors as low per-capita incomes and high private consumption propensities among wealthy families with the greatest capacity for savings. Limited availabilities of foreign savings also led planners, as well as aid donors, to stress the necessity of programs for mobilizing government savings. In almost all cases, the preferred means for achieving this goal was to raise the ratio of tax collections to GNP (the *tax ratio*), through significant reform of the tax structure if possible or via increases in existing tax rates if necessary. Underlying this view was a belief that the propensity to consume out of an additional dollar of income was substantially less in the public sector than in the private sector. In this view diversion of income to the government should increase national savings rates. This engendered a prevailing view among many LDC planners that rising tax ratios were associated with "successful" development strategies, a view reinforced by policies of foreign aid donors. In the 1950s and 1960s many donors, including the United States, utilized tax ratios and "tax effort" indices as prime indicators of national commitment to "belt-tightening" in recipient countries. Countries willing to suffer higher domestic taxes were seen as more "deserving" of aid, other things being equal.

It is not easy to increase tax collections in LDCs. Except for those countries blessed with valuable natural-resource endowments, developing countries in general would not be expected to have tax ratios nearly as high as is common in the industrial countries, if for no other reason than their much lower per-capita incomes, which allow a much smaller margin for taxation after subsistence needs are met. Whereas typical tax ratios in LDCs range between 14 and 20 percent, the ratio of taxes to GDP in 1983 in the twenty-one wealthy member countries of the Organization for Economic Cooperation and Development (OECD) averaged about 29 percent.[3]

Despite the difficulties involved, many LDCs have been able to raise shares of taxes in GNP since the 1960s. One study showed small advances in the average tax ratio for a group of forty-seven developing countries from 1950. For these nations as a group, the typical share of taxes in GNP hovered at about 11 percent in the 1950s. By 1972 to 1976 the average tax ratio had risen to 16 percent.[4] In more recent years, the average tax ratio for developing countries increased still further, to 17.5 percent (Table 11–5). That table

---

3. The range for 1983 tax ratios in the OECD countries went from a low of 26 percent in Spain to a high of 53 percent for Norway. International Monetary Fund, *Government Finance Statistics Yearbook, 1985.*

4. Alan Tait, Wilfred Gratz, and Barry Eichengreen, "International Comparisons of Taxation for Selected Developing Countries," *International Monetary Fund Staff Papers* 26, no. 1, (March 1979): 123–56.

TABLE 11-5 Tax Ratios in Eighty-two Developing Countries, Overall and by Type of Tax and Level of Income, 1977-1981

| Per-capita income | Total taxes as % of GDP (The tax ratio) | Taxes on foreign trade | Particular taxes as % of GDP | | | |
			Income taxes	Internal indirect taxes (sales & excise)	Social security taxes	Other taxes
Below $300	13.23	5.68	2.86	3.80	0.48	0.54
$300–$650	18.55	7.22	5.08	4.53	1.87	0.91
$651–$1,550	17.79	5.22	6.19	4.24	1.72	1.04
Above $1,550	20.63	4.00	8.02	5.13	3.06	1.10
Average all countries	17.55	5.53	5.54	4.43	1.78	0.90

Source: Vito Tanzi, "Quantitative Characteristics of Tax Systems in Developing Countries," in *Modern Tax Theory for Developing Countries,* David Newbery and Nicholas Stern, eds. In press.

Note: Tax information for most countries was for the years 1978–1980. However, for a few countries, data for the years 1975 and 1976 were utilized, because of gaps in more recent information.

also suggests that although the tax ratio tends to be much lower in very poor countries (below $300 per-capita income), tax ratios do not vary much with income beyond that level. Indeed, the countries where tax ratios were significantly increased in the latter period were not always those that have followed a conscious policy of savings mobilization through higher taxes, but those that were fortunate enough to benefit from fiscal levies on higher prices for oil and other natural resources from 1973 to 1982, such as Iran, Venezuela, and Indonesia. But while in some cases higher tax ratios may have advanced some important goals of development policy, in particular that of income redistribution, they did not guarantee more than transient success in meeting savings mobilization goals, except for those countries blessed with substantial export capacity in natural resources that can easily collect sizable taxes on those exports.

Higher taxes lead to higher savings only if the government's **marginal propensity to consume** (MPC) out of increased taxes is less than the private sector's propensity to consume out of the marginal income from which it pays increased taxes.[5] Government savings made possible through budget surpluses unquestionably played a major role in the early stages of Japan's economic development. But other success stories for savings mobilization through budget policy are difficult to find. Unfortunately, there is evidence that for LDCs in general, the government's MPC out of taxes has been sufficiently high that increased taxation may easily have resulted in less, not more, total domestic savings. This phenomenon has become known as the "Please effect," after Stanley Please of the World Bank, who first brought this phenomenon to widespread attention.[6] Whether or not the Please effect is widespread, we will see in Chapter 12 that higher taxes can and do displace

5. The marginal propensity to consume (MPC) refers to the amount of consumption out of each incremental (marginal) unit of income. Thus, if a government spends $80 out of each additional $100 in tax revenue on consumption, then the government's MPC is 0.80.

6. Stanley Please, "Savings Through Taxation: Reality or Mirage?" *Finance and Development* 4, no. 1 (March 1967): 24–32.

some household and business savings in the private sector.[7] And experience over most of the decades of the 1960s and 1970s does show rather strong consumption propensities on the the part of governments.

While tax ratios in LDCs typically rose marginally over the 1960s and through the 1970s, public-sector consumption expenditures expanded at rapid rates over the same period, generally in excess of GDP growth: in low-income countries, the share of public-sector consumption expenditures in GNP rose from 8 percent in 1960 to 12 percent in 1983, while in middle-income countries it rose from 11 to 13 percent.[8] This experience was widespread: in forty-eight developing countries the public-consumption share in 1983 surpassed that of 1965, even after nearly two decades of intensive efforts in most countries to mobilize savings through the government budget. In seventeen countries, however, the share of public consumption in GDP was actually lower in 1983 than in 1965.

It is worth emphasizing that in many countries much of the growth in public sector consumption has been intended to promote development. Some governmental salary adjustments have been meant to keep and attract qualified civil servants, and many governments have strengthened their efforts to maintain roads, schools, health facilities, communications networks, and the like. But when higher government consumption has been traceable to rapid buildup of military purchases (which we'll look at in the next chapter), to waste in government procurement of materials, or to upkeep of a large government vehicle fleet dominated by Mercedes or Bentleys, the effects have been unhelpful to national development.

Nevertheless, rapid growth in public-sector consumption in the 1960s and 1970s, coupled with only moderate increases in tax ratios, has meant that growth in government savings has not been a major source of investment finance in most LDCs. And it will be evident from Chapter 14 that while foreign saving has been a growing share of investment finance in many low-income countries since 1960, this was not so for LDCs as a group, particularly the middle-income nations. We may wonder, then, what was the source of the additional savings required to cover significantly higher investment ratios (see Table 11–3) over that period? To answer that question we now look to the private sector.

Private Domestic Savings

Until quite recently, economists, aid donors, and many LDC decision-makers tended to view private domestic savings as decidedly secondary to

7. Some analysts find a high degree of substitutability between government and private savings; others do not. See, for example, the exhaustive survey in Raymond F. Mikesell and James E. Zinser, "The Nature of the Savings Function in Developing Countries: A Survey of the Theoretical and Empirical Literature," *Journal of Economic Literature* 11, no. 1 (March 1973): 1–26. One article surveyed in this contribution indicated that an additional one dollar of government savings is associated with a fifty-seven cent decline in private savings. Another article indicates a positive relationship between public and private savings.

8. World Bank, *World Development Report 1985,* (New York: Oxford University Press, 1985), Appendix: Table 5 and World Bank, *World Development Report 1984,* (New York: Oxford University Press, 1984), Appendix, Table 5.

government savings and foreign aid as a source of investment finance. There is, however, some evidence that in many LCDs private savings have come to play a major role in supporting capital formation. Data compiled by the World Bank, summarized in Table 11–6, indicate that many LDCs have been able to restrain growth in private consumption over long periods, thereby expanding the pool of private savings. Among low-income nations, this was particularly true for India and China, where the share of private consumption in GDP declined from three-quarters to about one-third. This ratio rose marginally in other low-income nations and fell slightly in middle-income nations as a group. But here again, aggregate figures mask important differences between countries. Among twenty-four low-income countries for which data is available, the share of private consumption fell in nine and rose in fifteen. And among middle-income countries, the share of private consumption in GDP fell by more than ten percentage points in thirteen of the fifty-nine nations.

TABLE 11–6   Rates of Growth of GDP and Private Consumption, Shares of Private Consumption in Total GDP (Ninety-four Countries, 1965–1983)

| | Annual rates of growth (% per year) | | | | % share of private consumption in GDP^a | |
| | Real GDP^a | | Real private consumption^a | | | |
	1965–73	1973–83	1965–73	1973–83	1965	1983
Low-income countries (excluding China and India)	3.7	3.3	3.1	3.2	78	80
All low-income countries	6.0	5.4	3.5	4.8	75	68
Middle-income countries	7.1	4.7	6.8	4.8	68	66

Source: World Bank, *World Development Report 1985* (New York: Oxford University Press, 1985), pp. 176–77, 180–83.
^{a} Weighted average.

Although data on consumption growth are subject to large errors, the available evidence suggests that, except for a relatively small group of the poorest nations, growth in private consumption was held in check in most LDCs after 1965.

We have seen that the share of taxes in GDP rose only slightly in most LDCs over the 1960s and early 1970s. If higher taxes do not account for the drop in the share of private consumption in GDP, then the share of private savings must have increased. In any case, the most plausible source of a large share of finance for the rising investment ratios reported in Table 11–3 was private domestic savings. For LDCs in general, at least one of the components of private domestic savings must have risen at a fairly robust rate. But if so, it is difficult to determine which of the components played the most important role—household savings or business savings. In approaching an answer to this issue, and to gain further insights into fundamental relationships in the development process, it is useful to consider the economic theory of private-sector savings behavior.

Theories of household savings behavior were initially developed as part of the postwar Keynesian revolution in economic thought to explain savings patterns in industrial countries. Substantial focus upon household savings is justified by the fact that they are a large and increasing share of net savings in rich countries (50 percent in 1964 and 93 percent in 1981), and by indications that similar patterns may prevail in LDCs as well.[9]

Household Savings Behavior

All theories of household savings behavior seek to explain the following three observed patterns: (1) within a particular country at a given time, higher-income households tend to save larger fractions of their income than lower-income households; (2) within a particular country over time, household savings ratios tend to be roughly constant, more so in industrial than in developing nations; (3) across countries, household savings ratios vary with no clear relation to income. To help reconcile these "stylized facts" we will consider four alternative explanations of household savings behavior: the Keynesian absolute-income hypothesis; the Duesenberry relative-income hypothesis; the Friedman permanent-income hypothesis; and the Kaldor class-savings hypothesis.

Economists once widely believed in the general applicability of a simple income-savings relationship. Household savings were viewed as directly dependent upon current disposable income (household income after direct taxes). The propensity to save out of current disposable income was thought to rise with income. This was known as the **Keynesian absolute-income hypothesis,** after the famed British economist, John Maynard Keynes, who propounded the idea in the 1930s. In this view the savings-income relationship would be expressed as

$$S = a + sY^d, \qquad [11-3]$$

where S = savings, Y^d = current disposable income, a = a constant (a $<$ 0), and s = the marginal propensity to save ($0 < S < 1$). The constant "a" is generally taken to be negative, signifying that at low levels of income, savings will be negative. Under this formulation savings ratios (savings as a fraction of GDP) should be expected to rise over time in all countries where income is growing. But the historical record in both developed and developing countries provides very weak support for the Keynesian hypothesis.

At best the Keynesian formulation may depict savings behavior over the very short term, but it breaks down as a long-run proposition. The Keynesian formulation explains only the first household savings pattern, but not the second or third. To see why, consider Figures 11–1, 11–2, and 11–3. Figure 11–1 illustrates the Keynesian consumption function. It shows what households would consume and save at different levels of income during a period

9. World Bank, *World Development Report 1983* (New York: Oxford University Press, 1983) p. 22.

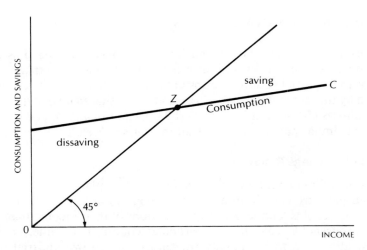

FIGURE 11-1 Short-term Keynesian Consumption Function. The consumption line plots Equation 11-3 with $C = Y^d - S = -a + (1 - s)Y^d$; because $a < 0$, $-a > 0$.

The 45-degree line shows all points at which consumption is equal to income. Point Z is the familiar break-even point. At income levels to the right of Z, saving is positive; to the left of Z, saving is negative.

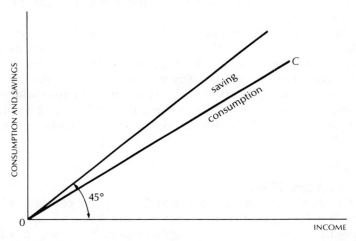

FIGURE 11-2 Long-term Consumption Function. This diagram is the same as in Figure 11-1, except that $a = 0$, so $C = (1 - s)Y^d$, and the consumption function goes through the origin.

such as a year. The graph shows that in the short run we would expect higher and higher ratios of saving to income at higher and higher income levels. However, over the longer run we observe that in most countries the consumption (savings) function appears as in Figure 11–2: the savings-income ratio tends to remain constant, as if the consumption function in Figure 11–1 goes through the origin.

The contradiction between the relationships depicted in Figures 11–1 and 11–2 is perhaps more apparent than real, once it is recognized that the Keynesian function describes a short-term situation. The apparent conflict

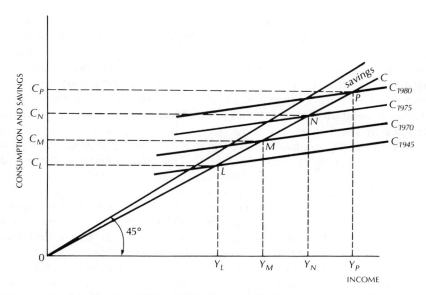

FIGURE 11-3 Consumption and Savings in the Short and Long Term. Four short-run consumption functions are shown for each of the years 1960, 1970, 1975, and 1980, representing what people would have spent at various levels of income in those years. The flatness of these curves reflects consumers' reluctance to change consumption habits in the short run. In each of these years, actual (current) income was Y_L, Y_M, Y_N, and Y_P respectively. Thus actual consumption in each of those years was C_L, C_M, C_N, and C_P. The points L through P trace out a long-term consumption function, with characteristics matching those of Figure 11-2: consumption, and thus savings, tend to be a constant proportion of income over time.

may be reconciled by consideration of an alternative view of the income-consumption relationship, the **relative-income hypothesis.** In its simplest form this hypothesis holds that consumption, and therefore savings, depends not only on current income but on previous levels of income and past consumption habits. One form of the relative-income hypothesis, called the **Duesenberry hypothesis** after the Harvard economist James Duesenberry who originated the concept in the late 1940s, may be expressed as

$$C_1 = a + (1-s)Y_1^d + bC_h, \qquad [11-4]$$

where C_1 = consumption in period 1, Y_1^d = income in period 1, C_h = previous high level of consumption, $0 < s < 1$, and $0 < b < 1$. Thus under the relative-income hypothesis, the short-run consumption (savings) function in an economy tends to ratchet upward over time. As income grows over the long term, consumers adjust their spending habits to higher levels of consumption. But in the short run they are reluctant to reduce—and slow to raise—consumption levels should income fall (or rise) temporarily. The relationship between the Keynesian absolute-income hypothesis and the Duesenberry relative-income hypothesis is depicted in Figure 11-3.

The Duesenberry hypothesis was formulated as an explanation of consumption-savings behavior for the United States. Later researchers argued that it may also be applicable to LDCs. Some have suggested that a "demonstration effect" operates to cause consumption in LDCs to ratchet upward as incomes grow. Internationally mobile and worldly-wise upper-income groups in LDCs are thought to emulate high consumption patterns of the wealthiest income groups in developed countries; successively lower income groups in LDCs tend to emulate the patterns of higher income groups, such that consumption in the society as a whole tends to be a high and stable function of income. Indeed, the British economist Nicholas Kaldor once estimated that if the richest families in Chile had the same consumption propensities as families at the same *relative* income position in developed nations (but at higher absolute levels of income), the Chilean savings rate in the 1950s could have been doubled.[10] The relative-income hypothesis explains all three of the observed savings patterns cited earlier.

Other approaches developed to explain consumption and savings behavior in developed countries have been applied to LDCs. The most influential of these has been the **permanent-income hypothesis,** first formulated by Milton Friedman at the University of Chicago in the 1950s. In the Friedman view income consists of two components: "permanent" income and "transitory" income. The basic idea is simply that because individuals expect to live for many years, they make consumption decisions over a horizon of many years. **Permanent income** is the yield from wealth, including both physical and human capital assets (education, and so on) at the disposal of the household. Friedman held that individuals can predict with a reasonable degree of assurance the magnitude of these flows over their lifetimes, and that they gear their consumption to what they perceive to be their normal, or permanent, income, which tends to be stable over time. Furthermore, in the most restrictive variant of the permanent-income hypothesis, consumption tends to be a constant proportion of permanent income, approaching 100 percent of permanent income. Thus any savings that occur will primarily be out of **transitory** income: unexpected, nonrecurring income such as those arising from changes in asset values, changes in relative prices, lottery winnings, and other unpredictable windfalls. In the most extreme version of the permanent-income hypothesis, individuals are held to save 100 percent of any transitory income. But econometric research since 1970 has called into question this assumption; some studies show a fairly high propensity to consume out of transitory income.

The permanent-income hypothesis may be expressed as

$$S = a + b_1 Y_p + b_2 Y_t, \qquad [11-5]$$

where S = savings, a = a constant, Y_p = permanent income, and Y_t = transitory income. As noted, in the most extreme version $b_1 = 0$ and $b_2 = 1$, so all savings arises from the transitory component of income and all of this component is saved. Modified versions of the permanent-income hypothesis hold only that saving out of permanent income is constant over a person's lifetime, but can be positive, and that while the propensity to save out of transitory income is high, all transitory income may not be saved. Equation 11-5 can represent this version with $0 < b_1 < b_2 < 1$.

10. Nicholas Kaldor, "Problemas Economicas de Chile," *El Trimestre Economico* 26, no. 102 (April–June 1959): 193, 211–12.

Several studies have sought to test the applicability of the permanent-income hypothesis to a variety of developing countries in Asia and Latin America. The results are far from conclusive, but in toto they do lend some support to the modified versions of the hypothesis: people do tend to save a higher proportion of transitory, as opposed to permanent, income. In general the permanent-income hypothesis explains all three observed savings patterns. Chapter 15 assesses the implications of modified versions of the permanent-income hypothesis in understanding the effects of fluctuating export income on growth.

One further model of household savings behavior merits attention: the **class theory** of the British economist Nicholas Kaldor. This approach views consumption (savings) habits to be sharply differentiated by economic class. Workers, who receive mainly labor income, are thought to have far weaker savings propensities than do capitalists, who receive primarily property income (profits, interests, rents). The class-savings hypothesis is represented as

$$S = s_w L + s_c P, \qquad\qquad [11-6]$$

where s_w = workers' savings propensities out of labor income, s_c = capitalists' savings propensities out of property income, L = labor income, P = property income, and $0 < s_w < s_c < 1$.

The class-savings hypothesis explains the first pattern and also explains the third pattern if factor shares (relative shares of labor and capital income) differ across countries. But the difference between the class-savings hypothesis and the permanent-income hypothesis may be more apparent than real. It is difficult to see why households, in their spending-saving decisions, treat labor income any differently than property income: a peso is a peso, a rupee of property income is no different than a rupee of labor income. However, property income of households, particularly that from unincorporated enterprises, tends to fluctuate more than labor income. The permanent-income hypothesis suggests that propensities to save out of variable income streams are higher than out of more stable streams. In addition property income is more concentrated in higher income groups. Thus studies of savings behavior based on the class model that show markedly higher savings out of property income may really be recording the effects of higher propensities to save out of higher fluctuating income.

All of the hypotheses discussed above view income, whether current, relative, or permanent, as the principal determinant of savings behavior. But income is by no means the only determinant of aggregate private-sector savings behavior, particularly in LDCs. As we will see in Chapter 13, the permanent income hypothesis concedes a role for interest rates in affecting savings behavior. Beyond that, many economists have stressed for years the effects of such explanatory variables as the age structure of a nation's population, location (rural vs. urban families), and, of course, subsistence expenditure as a proportion of per-capita GNP.

Changes in the age structure of a nation's population are often found to have significant effects on private savings in several countries. In general, the proportion of any increases in income saved tends to be less in younger households than in older ones. Younger families are rearing children and accumulating belongings, but they earn lower incomes. To illustrate, the average ratio of savings to income for older households in Chile in 1964 was found to be twice that of younger households.

There is a strong tendency around the world for rural households to save higher fractions of their incomes than urban households with comparable levels of income, a phenomenon observed in a number of countries, including both Korea and Yugoslavia in the early 1970s. This behavior is also consistent with the permanent-income hypothesis, because farmers' incomes are more variable than those of urban wage earners.

A high proportion of income spent on meeting basic subsistence needs implies low capacity for household savings. One recent study of seventeen countries indicates that total subsistence expenditure as a proportion of per-capita GNP falls sharply as GNP per-capita increases: from 62 percent at per-capita GNP less than $500, to 46 percent at per-capita GNP of between $1,000 and $1,500.

The relative-income hypothesis and the permanent-income hypothesis provide a basis for understanding the lack of strong correlation across LDCs between per-capita income and the ratio of private savings to GDP. The non-income factors (age structure of the population, rural-urban differences, and differences in subsistence ratios) help explain why private saving ratios do vary across countries, even at comparable levels of per-capita income.

Corporate Savings Behavior

We have seen that there is no shortage of hypotheses purporting to explain the determinants of household savings. There is, however, little consensus among economists as to the determinants of corporate savings, particularly in developing countries. Indeed there is little general agreement on the determinants of corporate savings even in developed countries. For example, in the United States a major question in research in business finance has been to explain why U.S. corporations pay such a high proportion of their after-tax income in dividends, despite strong tax and other incentives to retain earnings (save) within the firm.

In developed countries the share of corporate savings in total income is typically less than 5 percent, and the share of corporate savings in gross national savings is commonly less than 20 percent. For example, over the period 1972 through 1976, the United Nations reported that corporate savings was only 7 percent of gross national savings in Japan, 12 percent in Belgium, 18 percent in Australia, 13 percent in Germany, and 18 percent in Finland.[11] Such data are not available for large numbers of LDCs, but it is known that in only a few countries (Colombia, Pakistan, and Panama in the 1960s) has corporate savings represented a sizable share of total savings over any significant period.

Corporate saving in LDCs is relatively small primarily because the corpo-

11. United Nations, Department of Economic and Social Affairs, *Yearbook of National Accounts Statistics 1979* (New York, 1979), Table 12.

rate sector in most LDCs is relatively small. For a variety of reasons there are

fewer pressures and incentives in LDCs for doing business in the corporate form. The principal reasons for organizing as a corporation in the private sector are to limit liability of enterprise owners to amounts invested in a business and to facilitate enterprise finance through issue of equity shares (stocks). While these advantages are substantial in developed countries with well-developed commercial codes, civil court systems, and capital markets, they are less so in most LDCs, where collection of commercial claims (e.g., company debts) through courts is relatively difficult and where, as shown in Chapter 13, capital markets are poorly developed when they exist at all.

As usual, however, there are important exceptions to these generalizations. In some developing nations corporations are both numerous and quite large. For example in 1985, of the five hundred largest corporations outside the United States, ten were Korean and seven were Brazilian in origin.[12] Examples include conglomerates such as Bavaria (beverages and food processing) in Colombia and Hyundai (automobiles) in Korea, and enterprises such as Alpargatus (textiles and shoes) in Argentina, the diversified firm Tata in India, and Villares (steel products) in Brazil. But, except in Korea and Brazil, even in middle-income LDCs such corporations are not numerous, do not ordinarily account for a large share of private-sector business activity, and clearly do not provide a high proportion of domestic savings.

In all but a few of the highest income LDCs, the great bulk of private-sector farming and commercial and manufacturing activity is conducted by unincorporated, typically family-owned, enterprises, which will be discussed in Chapter 20. Some of these fall into the category of medium-scale establishments (from ten to ninety-nine workers). Very few are large-scale enterprises. The great majority are small-scale operations (having less than ten employees) which, in spite of their abundance, do not account for a sizable share of either value-added or savings.[13] Nevertheless the noncorporate sector manages to generate more than 50 percent of domestic savings in LDCs as a group, and this sector is the only consistent source of surplus in the sense that its savings exceed its investment. Even for a high-income country like the United States, with a large corporate sector, income from unincorporated enterprise in 1976 was about double the value of corporate profits (after taxes). For those closely held, largely family-owned and family-managed firms, enterprise profits become an important part not of corporate savings, but of gross household income.

The available evidence indicates, and economic theory suggests, that household savings accounts for the overwhelming share of private savings in LDCs, and that the chief source of household savings is probably household income from unincorporated enterprises.

12. *Fortune Magazine,* "World Business Directory," August 18, 1985.
13. One study for twenty-one LDCs in the 1960s shows that small-scale enterprises, while constituting 80 percent of industrial establishments, are responsible for an average of only 13 percent of industrial value-added. See Randev Banerji, "Small-Scale Production Units in Manufacturing: An International Cross Section Overview," *Weltwirtschafliches Archiv* 114, no. 1 (1978). See also Donald Snodgrass, "Small-Scale Manufacturing Industries [in Indonesia]: Patterns, Trends and Possible Policies" (Harvard Institute for International Development Discussion Paper no. 54, March 1979).

INTERNATIONAL MOBILITY OF CAPITAL AND DOMESTIC SAVINGS MOBILIZATION

This chapter has focused primarily upon patterns and determinants of domestic savings mobilization. The next two chapters examine policy options for mobilizing domestic savings, while Chapter 14 is concerned with issues in foreign savings. In practice, however, the distinction between "domestic" and "foreign" savings is rather more blurred than implied up to this point, to the extent that capital is mobile across national borders, particularly in the long run. The issue of the international mobility—or lack of mobility—of capital is one of the most important questions in economic policy; it is also one about which empirical evidence has been, at least until very recently, most scanty.

Short- and Long-run Mobility

"In the long run we are all dead." With this pithy remark, the British economist John Maynard Keynes closed his landmark volume, *The General Theory of Employment, Interest and Money.* In doing so, Keynes sought to jolt governments into undertaking demand-side policy measures that would have the desired short-term effects of pulling the world economy out of the deep depression of the thirties. The statement was appropriate at the time, but ever since the "long run" has had a bad press: Keynes' remark has been frequently employed as a verbal talisman against proponents of a longer-run focus on the effects of government policies on the economy. This has been particularly unfortunate in developing countries, inasmuch as it is the long-term effects of policies that are the most significant for growth and development. Furthermore, while it is indeed true that we are "all dead in the long run," when the long run is defined as sufficiently long, the long run in economic analysis is not always defined in terms of decades, or even years. The long run in some industries, such as mining of hard minerals, may be as long as ten years; in commercial chicken farming in the U.S., the long run may be defined in terms of *months,* for that is how long it takes for new firms to enter and exit the business in responses to changes in poultry prices.

In any case, the distinction between "short run" and "long run" is among the most fundamental in economic analysis. Not a small share of the unintended, and usually perverse, effects of economic policies are traceable to failure to recognize that the short-term results of policies may be very different from long-term results. The **short run** is defined as a period of time in which both capital and labor resources are locked into their present uses. The **long run** is defined as a period of time sufficiently long to allow economic agents—including resource owners—to adjust to changed circumstances, including economic policy changes that affect the returns to capital and labor. In the long run, resources may enter (or leave) an activity in response to higher (or lower) returns. Both capital and labor, then, tend to be much more *mobile* in the long run.

It is generally recognized that capital is particularly mobile across sectors of a given economy in the long run, even when highly immobile in the short run. For example, enactment of price controls on wheat in 1987 ordinarily will not lead to a movement of capital from wheat farming in 1987 (the short run) even if low, controlled prices result in negative profits in 1987. But if the controls are extended through 1989, we would then expect some proportion of capital invested in wheat farming to have left. The longer such a policy remains in place, the more capital will tend to flow to other domestic activities not subject to price controls.

275

INTERNATIONAL
MOBILITY OF
CAPITAL AND
DOMESTIC
SAVINGS
MOBILIZATION

But what of mobility of capital across national boundaries? The degree to which capital is **internationally mobile** is a topic of considerable debate, and has a profound bearing upon possibilities for success in all economic policies in any given country, particularly so for these geared toward mobilization of savings. This is most apparent in the case of private foreign savings. Private capital abroad, whether it arrives in the form of direct foreign investment or borrowings from foreign banks, is obviously *inwardly* mobile, from the LDC perspective. Foreign-source capital is also clearly outwardly mobile in the long run: foreign debts are eventually repaid by most countries, on the basis of prearranged schedules, and dividends on foreign equity investment return capital to overseas investors when direct investments turn out to be profitable.

International capital mobility, however, is a two-way street. Domestic savings in LDCs, like domestic savings in wealthy countries, may be highly mobile internationally as well, both in the short and in the long run. The degree of short-run outward mobility is exemplified by such episodes of massive capital flight as plagued Mexico in 1981 and 1982, and Indonesia in 1983 and early 1986, just prior to expected major currency devaluations in each country. In Indonesia in 1986, short-term capital flight reached nearly $100 million per *week* in a two-month period. Longer-term outward mobility is illustrated by the sizable outward migration of capital in Hong Kong in 1983 through 1985 and in the Philippines in 1985 and 1986. In the former, capital departed in response to uncertainties surrounding the 1982 announcement by the British of their plans to return the colony to Chinese sovereignty in 1999. In the latter, wealthy Filipinos sent capital abroad in large amounts as a hedge against the possibility of assumption of political power by opponents of the Marcos government. A high degree of international capital mobility, then, can be both a blessing and a curse for LDCs. Inward mobility expands opportunities for finance of domestic investment by foreign savings. But high *outward* mobility constrains the effectiveness of several policies intended to expand domestic savings mobilization. For example, in the short run, enactment of higher income taxes on corporations may allow a higher government savings. But if capital is internationally mobile, the long-run result may well be to encourage domestic, as well as foreign, capital owners to dispatch their funds to other countries to restore the rate of return prevailing before the taxes were increased.

Evidence of International Capital Mobility

In the distant as well as the more recent past, policymakers and economists have tended to overlook the *domestic* policy implications of international capital mobility. One reason for this oversight has been the widespread existence of domestic controls on international capital movements, and an equally widespread view that these controls were effective. It is true that official controls, both explicit and implicit, on capital flows abound in the world economy, particularly among LDCs. For example, in the five-year period 1978 to 1982, explicit controls on the international movement of capital existed in 72 percent of the 149 countries that are members of the International Monetary Fund (IMF) discussed in Chapter 14. Only 19 percent of IMF members had no explicit capital controls at all during the same period.[14]

Furthermore, even in those countries that employ no explicit capital controls, *implicit* controls may hinder international mobility of capital. These include institutional restrictions that act as barriers to investments outside the domestic economy. In the United States, examples include laws that prevent savings institutions from investing in real estate abroad, and state government rules on pension funds that preclude such institutions from investing in overseas assets. Most developing countries have adopted similar regulations for the portfolios of their financial institutions.

The pervasiveness of controls on international capital movements would seem to indicate that international capital mobility may be quite limited in both the short and the long run. There are, however, considerations that suggest otherwise. First, not all nations utilize explicit controls on capital movements. Indonesia, for example, abandoned all official foreign exchange controls in 1970. Britain followed suit in 1979, as did France in 1986. Second, controls may be evaded in whole or in part. There is no empirical evidence that capital controls are administered with anything close to 100 percent effectiveness, in either developed or developing countries, particularly in the latter.[15]

Third, there is a growing body of empirical evidence that suggests a fairly high degree of long-run international mobility of capital is sufficient to cause capital's real after tax return to converge toward about 7.5 percent in both rich and poor countries.[16] The significance of this finding is that in the *absence* of moderate mobility, rates of return would be far higher in low-income countries, where capital is relatively scarce, than in high income countries, where capital is relatively more abundant. Another 1985 study

14. Jeremy Greenwood and Kent Kimbrough, "Capital Controls and the World Economy," *Canadian Journal of Economics,* forthcoming.

15. Capital controls in such countries as Ghana (1963–1986) have been notoriously porous. Tight restrictions on the amount of dollars that could be removed from Ghana were easily evaded by several devices, including "over-invoicing" of imports: the importer merely requests the exporter abroad to place a higher value on the goods than the true price. The exporter, on receipt of payment, merely deposits the excess in the importer's bank account in the exporter's country. Long-standing controls in Colombia before 1968, Argentina before 1979, India, and numerous other countries did not prevent the buildup of large resident-owned foreign currency holdings outside these countries in the past. Presumed stringency of capital controls did not prevent Indian multinational firms from exporting substantial capital while becoming significant foreign investors in Southeast Asia before 1975.

16. Arnold Harberger, "Vignettes on the World Capital Market," *American Economic Review,* volume 70, no. 2 (May 1980): 331-37.

covered 115 countries, both developed and developing, and found significant evidence of a high degree of international capital mobility.[17]

In sum, while it is clear that capital is not perfectly mobile in or out of LDCs even in the long run, it is also clear that neither the design nor implementation of economic policies in LDCs may be based on the assumption that, given time, capital will not emigrate in response to policies that affect its return.

277

INTERNATIONAL
MOBILITY OF
CAPITAL AND
DOMESTIC
SAVINGS
MOBILIZATION

17. Larry Summers, "Issues in National Savings Policy" (Cambridge, Mass.: National Bureau of Economic Research, Working Paper no. 1710, September 1985).

12

Fiscal Policy

The next two chapters focus on policies to mobilize domestic savings and on the implications of such policies for income distribution, efficiency, employment, and price stability. Policies geared mainly toward foreign savings are discussed in Chapter 14. In mixed economies, fiscal and financial policies are, along with foreign exchange and agricultural policies, the principal tools available to governments to influence economic activity and stimulate development. In this chapter we focus on **fiscal policy,** alternatively called budget policy. Fiscal policy encompasses all measures pertaining to the level and structure of government revenues and expenditures. **Financial policies,** the subject of Chapter 13, include not only monetary policy, but a wide variety of policy measures affecting the growth and allocation of financial assets in an economy.

As the terms are used in this book, **government revenues** consist of all tax and nontax revenue flowing to the government treasury, including surpluses of public enterprises and domestic borrowing by the treasury. **Government expenditures** are defined as all outlays from the government budget, including those for current expenditures such as civil service salaries, maintenance, military costs, interest payments, and subsidies to cover public enterprise losses (which we'll encounter again in Chapter 21), as well as capital expenditures such as outlays for construction of irrigation canals, roads, and schools, and purchase of nonmilitary equipment owned by government.

Although our initial focus in this and the next chapter is on the role of fiscal and financial policy in the mobilization of domestic savings, it is important to recognize that these policies are generally expected to serve a variety of other important public policy objectives of developing societies. Subsequent discussion can be placed into perspective by a brief examination of Table 12–1, which lists the objectives developing countries commonly estab-

TABLE 12–1 Objectives and Instruments of Fiscal and Financial Policy in Developing Countries

Objective	Operational objective	Instruments
I. *Objectives common to both fiscal and financial policy*		
1. Promotion of economic growth	Expanded public- and private-sector savings; greater accessibility of savings	Fiscal: level of taxes; structure of taxes; restraint on government consumption Financial: interest rates; development of financial and other markets
2. Equity: reduction of income disparities between households and regions	Lower tax burdens on lower-income households than upper-income households; public provision of basic needs and primary education; promotion of employment	Fiscal: reliance on progressive taxes, avoiding regresivity; budget subsidies, primary education; revenue sharing Financial: measures to control inflation; interest rate reform
3. Promotion of economic stability	Reduction of inflation and unemployment	Fiscal: revenue-elastic taxes; restraint on government consumption Financial: interest rates; reserve requirements; credit controls;
4. Promotion of economic efficiency	Removal of fiscal barriers to efficiency; reduction in costs of tax administration and financial intermediation.	Fiscal: tax reform; training tax officials Financial: interest rates; financial reform
II. *Primarily fiscal-policy objectives*		
1. Increased host-country returns from natural-resource endowments	Capture of resource rents	Natural resource taxes
III. *Primarily financial-policy objectives*		
1. Promotion of socio-economic cohesion	Reduction in fragmentation of national markets; expand opportunities for disadvantaged groups	Financial reform; special credit programs

lish for both fiscal and financial policy, together with typical instruments employed to secure them. It will be evident from later sections that while these policy tools may be appropriate for promoting some of the objectives listed below, they are less well suited for achieving others.

Different societies place different weights on these policy objectives; indeed, not all countries pursue all of them. For example, some countries assign heavy importance to equity; for others, greater emphasis is given to economic efficiency. Nevertheless, the objectives are common enough through various LDCs to merit consideration here. Some objectives are served by both sets of policy instruments; for some purposes fiscal policy is more suitable; for still others financial policy is more appropriate.

Fiscal policy operates through both the tax and expenditure sides of the government budget. The locus of decision-making on fiscal policy in LDCs is typically split between two agencies: the Ministry of Finance (the Treasury Department) and the Ministry (or Board) of Planning. In most countries the Ministry of Finance is assigned primary responsibility for the design and implementation of tax policy and for decisions concerning current government consumption expenditures. The Ministry of Planning typically holds sway on decisions concerning government capital expenditures. This separation of responsibilities over budget policy is so common, and of such long standing, that many economists and policymakers tend to reserve the term *fiscal policy* for that which is done by the Ministry of Finance, and to term as *development policy* that under the ultimate control of the Ministry of Planning. This book accepts this convention, with reservations. Therefore this chapter focuses upon those aspects of fiscal policy dealing with taxation and government consumption expenditures, while public capital expenditures were considered in Chapters 5 and 6. But the distinction between public "capital" and "consumption" spending is essentially an arbitrary one, both in theory and in practice.

TAXATION AND PUBLIC SAVINGS

Growth in public savings (S_g) can be secured only by measures that expand budget savings (S_{gb}) and the savings of state-owned enterprises (S_{ge}). Because a substantial portion of Chapter 21 focuses upon savings mobilization through state-owned enterprises, here we deal only with budget savings, defined as the excess of government revenues over government consumption expenditures. Until quite recently, economists and policymakers alike have viewed the public savings problem as primarily a matter of raising tax collections. This approach has yielded disappointing results, as was seen in the previous chapter. Here we delve more deeply into the reasons why there are severe limits to the contribution taxes can make to increased saving.

Constraints on Taxation

We saw in Chapter 11 that the "average" tax ratio for LDCs in recent years has been on the order of 17 to 18 percent. But as is the case with virtually all summary statistics applied across over one hundred nations, this "average" ratio masks sizable differences between countries, even those at similar levels of per-capita income. For example, five LDCs—virtually all low-income nations—have tax ratios of less than 10 percent. At the other extreme, eight LDCs have tax ratios higher than 25 percent; in three the ratio exceeded that of the United States in 1983.[1]

Governments in countries with low tax ratios would ordinarily be expected to be more limited in their abilities to satisfy basic needs such as housing or public health, or to meet goals set for primary education and government investment. Over the past twenty years analysts have sought a basis for explaining why tax shares vary so markedly across countries. By 1985 the literature on this topic was voluminous. The search for determinants of tax shares has led researchers to consider factors ranging from economic explanations, such as differences in per-capita income, the role of natural resources in exports, the degree of industrialization, and the extent of "openness" (share of foreign trade in GDP), to a variety of demographic considerations, such as the dependency ratio, literacy rates, and the degree of urbanization.

An obvious reason for cross-country differences in the share of taxes in GNP would seem to be differences in per-capita income. In the poorest countries the margin between per-capita income and that part of income used for meeting basic subsistence needs is much smaller than in middle-income nations. One study of eighty-two countries for the late seventies found some significant correlation between tax ratios and per capita income. The correlation coefficient was significant and equal to 0.35.[2] Thus taxable capacity—and the share of taxes in GDP—should be greater in countries with higher per-capita income. It is true that the very poorest developing countries tend to have the lowest tax ratios: Bangladesh, Mali, India, and Ethiopia are all well below the average (see Table 12–2), but Sri Lanka is well above the average. However, excepting the group of very poor countries, there seems to be no strong relationship between per-capita income levels and tax shares, and much of any apparent relationship may be explained largely by factors other than difference in per-capita income. Specifically, some low-income countries display tax shares that are strikingly similar to those observed in upper middle-income countries, even though per-capita incomes are about four times higher in the latter.

Differences in the level and particularly the structure of foreign trade have long been thought to have a much more significant impact on tax shares among developing countries. For decades, analysts have hypothesized that the degree of **openness** in a particular economy—the relative share of imports and exports in a national economy—would significantly affect its ability to collect taxes. Countries with a higher ratio of exports or imports to

1. The "low" tax ratio countries are Bangladesh, Bolivia, Guatemala, Haiti, and Nepal. The eight countries with tax ratios near or in excess of that for the United States (27.2 percent) are Swaziland, Congo, Tunisia, Zimbabwe, Israel, Malta, Chile, and Portugal. IMF, *Government Finance Statistics Yearbook, 1985* (Washington, D.C.: IMF, 1986) p. 80.

2. Tanzi, "Quantitative Characteristics." In press.

TABLE 12–2   Tax Ratios, Per-Capita Income, and Mineral Exports, 1982

Per-capita income	Exports of oil and minerals less than 20% of total exports		Exports of oil and minerals more than 40% of exports	
	Country	Tax Ratio[a]	Country	Tax Ratio[a]
Low-income economies	Ethiopia	12.2	Zaire	16.5
	Mali	12.5	Togo	26.7
	Bangladesh	7.5		
	India	14.1		
	Sri Lanka	22.9		
Lower-middle-income countries	Honduras	13.5	Liberia	22.6
	Thailand	13.4	Bolivia	8.6
	Nicaragua	14.8	Indonesia	18.7
	Turkey	16.8	Cameroon	15.6
	Colombia	13.2	Peru	17.0
	Philippines	12.3	Tunisia	25.8
			Nigeria	20.6
Upper-middle-income countries	Brazil	23.2	Chile	25.6
	Argentina	21.3	Panama	20.9
	Uruguay	20.6	Mexico	13.9
	Korea	17.1	Gabon	20.9
	Cyprus	17.1	Venezuela	20.0
	Malaysia	21.5	Trinidad and Tobago	30.5

Source: World Bank, *World Development Report, 1985,* Appendix Table 10, and Tanzi, "Quantitative Characteristics of Tax Systems." In press. Tables 1 and 2.
[a] Tax ratio is typically for years 1978 to 1980. However, for some countries, ratios for 1977 and 1981 were utilized owing to data gaps.

GDP would be expected, other things being equal, to have higher tax ratios than those where foreign trade was relatively less important. The reason is that foreign trade, whether exports or imports, must normally pass through a bottleneck—one or more ports—where it can be relatively easily observed and taxed. Therefore, import duties and export taxes are imposed on tax bases that are fairly accessible to the tax administration. In contrast, taxes on income, wealth, and even domestic consumption depend upon bases that are far more easily concealed from tax officials. This holds with particular force for income and wealth taxes: administration of these levies requires administrative resources and skill levels in chronic short supply in developing countries. Even in much of Western Europe income tax evasion is fairly common, and tax avoidance is taken for granted; indeed, tax evasion has been on the rise in the United States since the early seventies.[3] Openness however, turns out only to be an important determinant of the share of import *duties* in GDP; openness plays almost no role in determining a country's total tax ratio.[4]

Much more significant than the degree of openness is the relative importance of natural resources in GDP and total exports. Virtually every study on

3. Evasion is distinguished from avoidance of income taxes in the sense that evasion encompasses activities to conceal net income or falsify tax deductions, or other illegal ploys to pay less taxes than due. Avoidance is merely the legal rearrangement of one's affairs to minimize tax obligations. Evasion is illegal, a punishable offense; avoidance is not.
4. Tanzi, "Quantitative Characteristics of Tax Systems." In press.

the determinants of tax shares indicates that countries with relatively large oil and mineral production, and consequently a high share of resources in exports, have substantially greater taxable capacity than countries at the same level of per-capita income and the same degree of openness, but with relatively small natural-resource production and exports. Some confirmation of this phenomena may be derived from the right-hand column of Table 12–2, where it can be seen that countries with the highest tax ratios tend to be those where natural-resource exports make up a high share of total exports.

For 1982 the average share of natural resource (fuels, minerals) exports in total exports in LDCs was about 40 percent. For the fifteen countries where mineral and oil exports exceeded 40 percent of total exports, the tax ratio averaged 20.3 percent. For the seventeen countries where the share of such natural resources in total exports was less than 20 percent, the average tax ratio was a mere 16.1 percent. Econometric investigations of the influence of mineral and oil exports, as well as other factors, on taxable capacity and tax shares have been carried out by several analysts. These studies focus not on the share of nonrenewable resources in exports but on their share in GDP, a closely related measure for LDCs. All confirm the key role of natural resources in the determination of taxable capacity: countries where mining and oil constitute a relatively rare share of GDP (usually more than 5 percent) have found it much easier to collect taxes, at least before the most recent decline in oil prices from 1982 to 1986.

Reasons for higher taxable capacity in such countries are fairly obvious. First, except for countries with large internal markets, such as Brazil, India, and China, about 95 percent of all hard minerals produced in LDCs is exported. And in LDCs with appreciable quantities of oil close to 80 percent of annual production is typically exported. For both minerals and oil the tax base is therefore easily accessible to the tax collector. In addition, from 1972 to 1982 oil and a few minerals were the source of high surplus returns, or rents, arising from high world prices. Such rents are not only tempting targets for taxation, but are particularly suitable for tax rates higher than those prevailing in the agricultural, industrial, or service sectors of most LDCs. This is partly because in virtually all LDCs, unlike the United States, property rights in natural resources are constitutionally vested in the state, not in private industry.

Finally, the hard mineral and oil sectors in many, though not all, LDCs are dominated by large multinational enterprises, which also tends to make mineral and oil revenues accessible to domestic tax collectors. It is not that multinationals are inherently more civic-minded in regard to their tax-paying obligations. Indeed, we shall see in Chapter 14 that such firms have at their disposal a wide array of devices that can be deployed to avoid LDC taxes. However, the multinationals are large, and being large have an internal need for much more detailed and accurate record-keeping than do small LDC enterprises. Further, substantial evasion of host-country taxes is a risky proposition for most multinationals which, after all, owe their presence in LDCs to the sufferance of governments. Successful tax evasion in the short run can lead to expropriation in the medium to longer term. For most large mining and oil multinationals, too much is at stake to make wholesale use of devices for escaping host-country taxes.

Some resource-rich LDCs, such as Algeria, Guyana, and Trinidad and Tobago before 1978, have utilized their high taxable capacity to bring the ratio of taxes collected to over 30 percent of GDP. Other relatively resource-rich nations, such as Indonesia, Mexico, and Bolivia, have had high taxable capacity but low or average ratios of taxes actually collected to GDP. Countries that intensively utilize their taxable capacity to attain high actual tax ratios are conventionally called **high tax effort** nations. Those that have made little effort to fully tap their taxable capacity are, conversely, termed **low tax effort** countries. There are several countries that, owing to low per-capita income, an absence of mineral and oil exports, and small industrial sector, have low tax capacity but relatively high tax ratios and thus high tax effort. These include Tanzania, Sri Lanka, Sudan, and Jordan.

By 1985 there was a wide consensus among developmental specialists that high tax ratios were not necessarily a virtue, nor low tax ratios a vice, in mobilizing domestic savings. Tax ratios reflect both opportunity and ideology. African countries, particularly sub-Saharan nations, tend to tax themselves more heavily relative to heir taxable capacities than countries in Asia.[5] Ideology may be a factor, but a high tax ratio may also reflect the fact that opportunities for mobilizing other types of savings, especially private savings, are limited because of poorly developed and organized financial systems. Latin American countries tend to dominate any list of countries with low tax effort. This may merely reflect the relatively greater ease with which private savings can be mobilized in Latin America. Since 1945, there has been relatively robust growth of organized financial markets in many Latin American countries, particularly in Mexico, Brazil, Argentina, Chile, and more recently in Colombia and Venezuela.

Tax Measures for Expanding Public Savings

A number of tax measures are available to LDCs for expanding public savings, including (1) periodic increases in rates imposed under existing taxes; (2) enactment of new taxes to tap previously unutilized sources of revenue; (3) improvements in tax administration that allow greater collection under existing taxes at present tax rates, by reducing tax avoidance and evasion; and (4) major reform of the entire tax structure, involving elements of options 1, 2, and 3. For many countries options 1 and 2 offer only slight hopes for increased collections. Options 3 and 4 are perhaps the most difficult to implement, but if feasible, are much more likely to achieve the desired results.

The first option, tax rate increases, is often the most favored, owing to a widely prevailing view among finance ministers, their advisors, and often aid donors, that there exists at any given time underutilized targets of opportunity for heavier taxation. The "slack" in the tax system is thought to make possible, say, a 10 percent increase in tax revenues simply by enacting

---

5. For the late seventies, the average tax ratio for African countries was 18.0 percent; that for Asia was but 15.0 percent (Tanzi, "Quantitative Characteristics of Tax Systems." In press.)

increases of 10 percent in existing tax rates, with no changes in underlying tax law or tax administration. We investigate the feasibility of increasing rates for the following taxes in turn: those on natural resources, other export taxes, import duties, income taxes, and sales and excise taxes.

Taxes on Natural Resources

The potential base for *taxes on natural resources* had been underutilized in many countries prior to the 1970s. In the short term, taxpayers in the natural-resource sector, particularly foreign-based multinational firms, are "captive" in the sense that production from existing mines and wells will not cease unless after-tax returns are very sharply curtailed. This "slack" in taxable capacity expands when world markets for minerals and oil strengthen rapidly, as in 1973 to 1974 and again in 1978 to 1979.

In general, governments have not overlooked this source of higher tax revenues for long, whether in developed or developing countries. Tax increases imposed by Middle Eastern oil nations in the 1970s are by now legendary examples. Among less wealthy LDCs, Jamaica in 1974 raised taxes on foreign-mined bauxite by over 700 percent. Indonesia succeeded in nearly doubling its tax collections from multinational oil firms between 1976 and 1978, even though its production was beginning to decline and world oil prices had been stagnant for three years. During the 1950s and 1960s Chile began extracting a steadily rising share of gross revenues from large copper multinationals. Gabon enjoyed some success in the early 1970s in extracting higher revenue on uranium from French enterprises.

This strategy works well in the short term, and carefully applied can be followed with some success in the long run, especially when world prices for natural resources remain high. Possibilities of higher tax collections from this source are not unlimited, however. The usual pattern of company response to very sharp increases in tax rates on their resource earnings is to continue production from existing facilities, but to postpone or cancel new investments in exploration, extraction, and processing. This occurred in both Indonesian oil in 1977 and 1978, and Jamaican bauxite in 1975–78. Within three years both countries found it necessary to grant partial rollbacks of the higher tax rates to induce the multinationals to resume investing. The oil firms reinstituted investment in Indonesia; aluminum companies did not do so in Jamaica. But where a developing country has a very strong position in the natural-resource market, major rollbacks have not been required. A good example occurred in Indonesia in 1978. Because of its relatively large and rich stands of tropical timber, Indonesia is the world's second-largest timber producer. Indonesia was able to double its export tax rates on logs that year, amidst little more than perfunctory outcries from international timber firms.

Outside of the natural-resource industries, attempts to increase tax rates are usually fraught with problems. In most LDCs, indeed most nations, prevailing tax structures are not generally of the type in which periodic increases in tax rates alone can be expected to fulfill all of the desired results. Slack is present in virtually all tax systems, but it usually cannot be eliminated merely by enacting higher tax rates on unchanged tax bases.

Taxes on international trade furnish only about one percent of tax revenues in the United States. Although reliance upon **taxes on foreign trade** has diminished in LDCs in recent years, tax-revenue structures in LDCs have historically depended heavily on this type of tax, particularly **import duties.** Poor and resource-poor LDCs, relative to middle-income or resource-rich LDCs, or both, still rely heavily on import duties (tariffs) as a revenue source. Even so, by 1982, taxes on foreign trade provided almost 25 percent of all LDC current revenue in low-income nations. Fourteen such countries rely on import tariffs for more than 40 percent of current government revenue.[6] Dependence on import duties is especially marked in Afghanistan, Sierra Leone, Gambia, Uganda, Rwanda, Sudan, Togo, and Yemen, where at least half of total government revenue comes from taxes on imports. Dependence upon import duties is much less marked in middle-income LDCs, which have developed alternative sources of tax revenue; for upper middle-income nations, import duties are typically about one-tenth of total current government revenue. The general patterns of dependence on import duties as a source of tax revenue are depicted in Table 12–3, for a sample of eighty-two countries for which recent data were available.

TABLE 12–3   **Dependence upon Import Duties as a Revenue Source, by Level of Per-Capita Income, 1975–1982, for Eighty-two Countries**

Level of per-capita income, 1979	Import duties more than 50% of total taxes	Import duties more than 20% of total taxes
Below $500 (31 nations)	Chad (48.3%) Gambia (68.6%) Lesotho (76.2%) Yemen (72.2%)	All 31 nations, excluding Mali, India, Sri Lanka, Tanzania, Indonesia, and Ghana
$500–$1,000 (18 nations)	Swaziland (61.6%) Botswana (57.0%)	All 18 nations, excluding Zambia and Guyana
$1,000–$1,500 (11 nations)	Jordan (64.2%)	All 11 nations, excluding Colombia, Jamaica, and Turkey
$1,500 and above (21 nations)	Bahamas (65.0%)	4 countries only, Fiji, Surinam, Cyprus, and Gabon

Source: Derived from Tanzi, "Quantitative Characteristics of the Tax Systems." In press.

6. World Bank, *World Development Report 1985,* Appendix Table 27.

Because imports, like exports, must be funneled through a small number
of ports, making them relatively easy to identify and tax, developing countries turned to this revenue source early in the development process and most have mined it to the limit. For most countries attempts to raise further revenues through higher duties is often infeasible. Later we will see that it is also undesirable, at least on economic grounds. Higher import duties intensify the incentive for smuggling or evading tariffs. Various studies have shown that for countries with already high duty rates, the incentive to smuggle increases disproportionately with further increases, so that a 10 percent rise in duty rates can result in an increase in smuggling activity by more than 10 percent (see the following boxed example). And in mountainous countries such as Afghanistan and Bolivia, or archipelago nations such as Indonesia and the Philippines, borders are especially porous to smuggled imports.

Tax Rates and Smuggling: Colombia

In Colombia before 1969, when the import duty rate on cigarettes was over 100 percent, it was virtually impossible to purchase duty-paid cigarettes. At such high rates import duty collections on cigarettes were nil and the market was flooded with smuggled foreign brands. In 1969 the duty rate was reduced to 30 percent. Cigarette smuggling on the poorly policed Caribbean coast of that country continued, but duty-paid packages began to appear in the mountainous interior, and duty collections on this product soared. Smuggling profits possible under a 30 percent duty were no longer high enough to compensate smugglers for the risks of arrest. Similar phenomena have been observed in Indonesia, Bolivia, and elsewhere.

Reliance on import duties for additional revenues may be infeasible for another reason. Except in open economies such as South Korea, Singapore, and Malaysia, the typical structure of import duties in LDCs is, as explained in greater detail in Chapter 16, heavily "cascaded": the highest rates of duty in virtually all countries are imposed on consumer durable goods, particularly "luxury" goods (appliances, cameras, and so on); lower rates are applied on such intermediate goods as cement and leather, with the lowest duty rates on capital goods and imported items viewed as basic "necessities" (food grains, fish, kerosene). When countries have sought additional revenues from tariffs, consumer goods already subject to high tariffs have been taxed even higher. Higher rates on necessities were considered inadvisable for reasons of income distribution, and higher rates on capital goods and intermediate goods were deemed unacceptable because it was believed that this would retard industrialization programs. But enactment of higher duties on consumer goods, particularly luxury consumer goods, generally did not produce higher revenue. The reason is simple: the price elasticity of demand is not zero for any consumer good, and for many already subject to very high duties, price elasticity is relatively high, in some cases — 2.0 or more. For an import already subject to a 150 percent duty, such as stereos, and with a price elasticity-of-demand − 2.0, a 10 percent increase in duty rates would actually decrease tax revenue on this item by about 2 percent.[7]

Taxes on International Trade: Export Taxes

Export taxes are constitutionally prohibited in the United States and are extremely rare in other industrial countries. But export taxes, distinct from income taxes that may be collected on export production, are not uncommon in LDCs, particularly in tropical Africa and Southeast Asia. Export taxes are ordinarily imposed not only on exports of raw materials such as timber (Ivory Coast and Liberia), tin (Malaysia), jute (Pakistan), and diamonds (Botswana), but on exports of foodstuffs, including coffee (Colombia), rice (Thailand), peanuts (Gambia and Senegal), cocoa (Ghana), and tea (Sri Lanka).

Fully twenty LDCs relied on export taxes for more than 10 percent of total tax revenue in the early eighties, but in only seven countries, primarily low-income African nations, do export taxes account for more than 20% of revenue (see Table 12–4). Export taxes are often imposed in the belief that they are "paid" by foreign consumers. That is, the taxes themselves are thought to be exported to consumers abroad, along with the materials. Chapter 19, however, shows that the conditions necessary for exporting taxes on exports to foreign consumers are rarely present in actual practice.

Export taxes are also employed to promote nonrevenue goals, including increased processing of raw materials within natural-resource-exporting LDCs. This is done by imposing high rates of export tax on unprocessed

---

TABLE 12–4 Dependence on Export Taxes as a Revenue Source by Level of Per-Capita Income, 1975–1981 for Eighty-two Countries

Per-capita Income, 1979	Export duties more than 20% of total taxes
Below $500	Ethiopia (23.3%) Rwanda (25.4%) Burundi (22.2%) Sri Lanka (36.2%) Ghana (30.2%)
$500–$1,000	El Salvador (28.4%)
$1,000–$1,500	Guatemala (22.4%)
Above $1,500	No countries

Source: Derived from Tanzi, "Quantitative Characteristics of Tax Systems." In press.

---

7. This result comes from applying the formula

$$\frac{dr/R}{dt/t} = 1 + \varepsilon \left(\frac{t}{1+t} \right),$$

where R = total duty collections on stereos, t = rate of duty on stereos, and ε = price elasticity of demand.

exports (cocoa beans or logs) and lower or zero rates of tax on processed
items fabricated from raw materials (plywood and tin ingot). In principle,
this form of export-tax use should increase local value-added on natural-
resource exports, thereby generating greater employment and capital income
for the local economy. Unfortunately, in many cases the result has been that
a government gives up more in export-tax revenues than its country gains in
additional local value-added, particularly when processed raw materials are
completely freed of export tax. In a study in progress of tropical timber processing in six southeast Asian and tropical African countries, for example,
one of the authors found that in all cases, the additional value-added gained
in local processing of logs into plywood was less than half the amount of
export taxes that would have been collected had timber been exported in the
form of logs. The reason for this unfortunate result was that in each case, the
local plywood mills established in response to the export tax on logs were
much less efficient than mills in Japan, Taiwan, and Korea. And in almost
every case, the prime reason for this inefficiency was the lack of competitive
pressure on the local plymills. The export tax incentive furnished very high
protection for these firms, since plymills abroad could secure logs as feed-
stock only by paying the high export taxes imposed by these six countries.

In other cases, high export taxes on raw materials have backfired on countries using them, and have ended up destroying or nearly destroying the local
export industry. This was clearly the case for the Chilean export tax on natural nitrates, imposed at high rates from 1890 through 1910, and for a Pakistan export tax on jute during the 1960s. In both cases, the tax was high
enough to promote the development of substitutes for these materials in
importing countries.[8]

Personal and Corporate Income Taxes

Harried ministers of finance, perceiving "slack" in personal and corporate
income taxes, often resort to rate increases in these taxes, with no change in
tax base. The results are usually disappointing, particularly for the personal
income tax. Indeed, in the early 1980s, the personal income tax accounted
for less than 20 percent of all tax revenues in all LDCs except five.[9]

Even in middle-income LDCs the base of the personal income tax reaches
only a very small proportion of the population. In the early 1970s the personal income tax covered no more than 2 percent of the population in
Ghana, Peru, and virtually all other developing countries save Burma,
Kenya, and Turkey. In contrast about half of the population in the United
States filed income-tax returns in 1980. Thus, few developing countries can
rely heavily on the personal income tax for revenues. Whereas the shares of
the personal income taxes in federal revenues in the United States is about
37 to 50 percent, rarely does the personal income tax account for as much as
10 percent of total central government revenues in LDCs.

---

8. See, for example, Robert Repetto, "Optimal Export Taxes," *Quarterly Journal of Economics* 86, no. 3 (August 1972): 396–407.
9. Personal income taxes were more than 20 percent of revenues only in Mauritania, Turkey,
Fiji, South Africa, and Bahamas. Tanzi, "Quantitative Characteristics of Tax Systems." In press.

In Colombia, for instance, the personal income tax is at least as well developed as in any LDC. Yet even though this tax is typically responsible for as much as 15 to 18 percent of national government revenues, a large share of it is paid by a small number of people: in the early 1970s the top 4 percent of households paid two-thirds of the total tax.[10] Furthermore, personal income taxes are largely paid by urban elites in LDCs. Not only are these groups usually the most vocal politically, but over the years they usually have developed such a variety of devices for tax evasion and avoidance that rate increases stand little chance of raising additional revenues.

Rate increases for corporate taxes are not usually productive, either. In only sixteen of eighty-two developing countries did the corporation income tax account for more than 20 percent of total taxes in recent years. And in most of these countries, corporate tax collections usually originated with foreign natural-resource firms. Except for several higher-income LDCs such as Argentina, Korea, Taiwan, and Mexico, the corporate form of doing business covers but a small portion of the private sector. To be sure, most state-owned firms are corporations, but Chapter 21 shows that few such firms outside the natural-resources sector earn sizable, taxable profits. Even fewer pay substantial income taxes.

Sales and Excise Taxes

A much more promising source of additional government revenue is internal indirect taxes, such as sales and excise taxes. **Sales taxes,** including value-added taxes, are broad-based consumption taxes imposed on all products except those specifically exempted, such as food, farm inputs, and medicine. Thirteen LDCs in the early eighties relied on general sales taxes for more than 20 percent of revenues, while in fourteen, excises accounted for more than one-fifth of revenues.[11] **Excise taxes** are also taxes on consumption, but these levies are imposed only on specifically enumerated items, typically tobacco, alcoholic beverages, gambling, and motor fuel.

Virtually every developing country imposes some form of sales tax. In most the tax is not applied to retail sales because of the burdensome administrative requirements of collecting tax from thousands of small retailers. In the past, as in Chile before 1970 and in some Indian states, the tax was often imposed as a gross "turnover" tax collected at all levels of production and distribution, with harmful implications for efficiency, income distribution, and virtually every other objective of tax policy cited in Table 12–1. In the LDC context, administrative problems in sales taxation are more tractable when the tax is confined to the manufacturing level: a much smaller number of firms is involved and output of manufacturers is far more homogenous than sales of retailers or wholesalers. For these reasons many LDCs utilize either the single-stage to the value-added form of manufacturer's tax, usually

---

10. Malcom Gillis and Charles E. McLure, Jr., "Taxation and Income Distribution: The Colombian Tax Reform of 1974," *Journal of Development Economics* 5, no. 3 (September 1978): 237.

11. Tanzi, "Quantitative Characteristics of Tax Systems." In press.

exempting very small producers. This kind of sales tax, however, involves more economic distortions than either a wholesale or a retail tax, and for that reason, as well as for revenue motives, more and more middle-income LDCs have turned to taxes at the retail level.[12]

Governments often resort to general rate increases in the national sales tax as the path of least resistance when public revenue must be increased. Except for those countries where the tax is riddled with exemptions or saddled with unenforceably high rates, this option has occasionally yielded desired results. But repeated resort to sales taxes ultimately leads to strong taxpayer resistance. Once rates of a manufacturer's tax begin to exceed 20 to 30 percent, as in many LDCs, incentives for evasion become irresistible.

Excise taxes might appear to represent an ideal source of additional tax revenue. Such taxes are typically imposed upon sumptuary items having relatively inelastic demand in both LDCs and industrial countries: tobacco and alcoholic beverages. When demand elasticity for such products is very low, as is the case for tobacco products, or is relatively low, as that for alcoholic beverages, an increase in excise tax rates will induce little reduction in consumption of the taxed goods. If price elasticity is as low as -0.2, as is not uncommon for cigarettes, then an additional 10 percent excise tax on this product would yield an 8 percent increase in tax revenues. Moreover, it is a hallowed theorem in optimal tax theory that taxes levied on items with inelastic demand and supply involve the smallest losses in economic efficiency or, what is the same thing, the least "excess burden," where excess burden is defined as loss in private welfare over and above the amount of government revenue collected from a tax.[13] Further, many agree—with much justification—that consumption of both tobacco and alcohol should be discouraged on health grounds.

All three considerations would seem to argue for very heavy reliance on such excise taxes in LDC tax-revenue structures. However, it is unfortunately true that in addition to low price elasticity, items such as tobacco and alcoholic beverages have low income elasticity. This means that such goods tend to be more important in the budgets of low-income than high-income households. It follows then that excise taxes on sumptuary items are decidedly regressive: poor people pay a higher proportion of their income in excise tax than do rich people, a serious matter when the sumptuary items constitute a substantial proportion of spending by poor people, as in most LDCs. In Indonesia, for example, the poorest 20 percent of Javanese households spent about 5 percent of total income on heavily taxed cigarettes in 1976, as opposed to 3.5 percent of income for persons with income more than five times as high. Thus each poorer family pays 60 percent more in cigarette taxes than their richer counterpart. This regressivity conflicts with one of the principal policy aims listed in Table 12–1.

---

12. For a complete discussion of the distortions involved in different forms of sales taxes, and particularly the manufacturers tax, see Malcolm Gillis, "Federal Sales Taxation: Six Decades of Experience," *Canadian Tax Journal* (January-February 1985): 46–59.

13. For a further discussion of optimal taxation and excess burden, see Figure 12–1 at the end of this chapter, and also Joseph Stiglitz, *Economics of the Public Sector* (New York: W. W. Norton & Co., Inc., 1985).

The second option for increasing public savings through taxation is that of tapping entirely new sources of tax revenue. In many LDCs, whether by accident, by design, or simply because of inertia, many sources of tax revenue may have been overlooked entirely. Many countries do not collect taxes on motor vehicle registration; some do not utilize urban property taxes as a significant source of revenue; many do not apply corporation income taxes to income of state-owned enterprises. Kenya, for example, does not seriously tax farm land, and a few, such as Indonesia until 1984, do not collect personal income taxes on salaries of civil servants.

The service sector furnishes other examples. Telephone service exists in all but the very poorest countries, and in many is fairly widespread but often untaxed. Some service establishments, such as restaurants and cabarets, are commonly taxed, but services of beauty shops, parking lots, tire recapping, photofinishing firms, modern laundries, and foreign travel are among the more common items excluded from the tax base. Not only is taxation of this category of spending attractive from a revenue standpoint, but in LDCs such services are typically characterized by relatively income-elastic demand: because families with higher incomes purchase proportionately more of these items, they would tend to bear the greater burden of taxation, consistent with the equity objectives of fiscal policy. However, these services constitute a small fraction of consumption, even for upper income groups, so their revenue potential is limited.[14]

Changes in Tax Administration

A far more significant option for increasing tax revenues than personal and corporate or sales and excise taxes is that of implementing changes in tax administration that permit more taxes to be collected from existing tax sources, even at unchanged tax rates. The potential for increased revenues from such action is very large in virtually all LDCs; rarely is this potential even partly realized. Shortages of well-trained tax administrators, excessively complex tax laws, light penalties for tax evasion, corruption, and outdated techniques of tax administration all combine to make tax evasion one of the most intractable problems of economic policy in LDCs.

Studies in Colombia indicate that in 1975 as many as 50 percent of small establishments did not file income tax returns, and that underreporting of income among professionals (lawyers, doctors) was as high as 70 percent. Evasion of sales taxes during the same period was between 40 and 50 percent. Still other studies suggest that widespread corruption remained in the Colombian Tax Service in the mid-1970s even after a decade of intensive effort to curtail such practices: for every peso of bribes paid to tax assessors the state lost about twenty pesos in tax revenue.[15] Similar, if not worse, pat-

14. In 1965 Colombia imposed no taxes on any of the services listed above. Malcolm Gillis estimated that if that country had enacted rather heavy taxes on these items in that year, total tax revenues would have been increased only by about 2 percent. Nevertheless, imposing taxes on them was desirable both from a revenue and an equity standpoint, and some were enacted.

15. Gillis and McLure, "Taxation and Income Distribution," p. 249.

terns have been reported in other countries. For Bolivia in the period from 1964 to 1966, it has been estimated that about 60 percent of property income was not reported to the tax administration, while in Argentina in the same period taxpayers succeeded in hiding over 50 percent of total income.[16] In Indonesia estimates suggest that as much as 80 percent of the personal income tax base goes unreported. For comparison, underreporting of total income amounted to about 13 to 15 percent in the United States and Canada in the 1960s.

Such figures suggest that even modest efforts to collect a greater share of taxes legally due could increase revenues by as much as 50 percent in some countries, without increasing tax rates. Nevertheless, there are few examples of even mild success in such undertakings, but many examples of unfulfilled expectations. Korea has been among the more successful. In 1966 it sought to increase tax collections by 40 percent through more effective enforcement alone. This ambitious target was not met, but in five years the Korean revenue service was able to reduce underreporting of nonagricultural personal income from 75 percent to slightly less than 50 percent. In 1974 Colombia, through swiftly implemented administrative changes, was able to make temporary inroads in the evasion problem; but by 1976 taxpayers had devised several new forms of evasion so that much of the earlier gains in revenue were eroded within three years. Virtually every serious study of the problem indicates that measures to curtail tax evasion in LDCs promise no "quick fixes" to the revenue problem. Rather, capacity for limiting tax evasion, like many other socioeconomic phenomena observable in LDCs, tends to follow a pattern of secular improvement associated with economic development.

Fundamental Tax Reform

The final policy option available for increasing tax revenues is the most difficult to implement, but the most effective when it can be done. Fundamental tax reform requires junking old tax systems and replacing them with completely new tax laws and regulations. Implementing tax reform engenders enormous technical and informational, not to mention political, difficulties in all countries. In general, governments resist genuine efforts to reform the tax structure until fiscal crisis—in the form of massive budgetary deficits—threatens. Even during a fiscal crisis, mobilizing sufficient political consensus to allow unpopular tax measures to pass is difficult. Tax policies that protect favored groups and distort allocation of resources did not just happen; more likely they are enacted at someone's behest, ordinarily the privileged and the powerful.

It is probably true that tax reform is a topic about which more has been said, to less effect, than almost any topic in economic policy. This is no less true for the United States than for fifty-odd LDCs where major tax reform efforts have been mounted since 1950. That the process is painful and slow is evident from the experience of several countries: in the United States the time lag between the birth of tax innovations (tax credit for child-care

16. Oliver Oldman and Daniel M. Holland, "Measuring Tax Evasion" (Paper presented at the Fifth Annual General Assembly of the Inter-American Center of Tax Administration, Rio de Janeiro, May 17, 1971), 33–37.

expenses, inflation-proofing of the tax system) and their implementation is usually at least fifteen years. If anything the lag may be slightly shorter in LDCs.

In spite of the difficulties involved, some LDCs have been able to carry through major reforms in tax structure and administration. The classic example is that of Japan in the 1880s, when that society began its transformation to a modern industrial power. Korea implemented a major tax-reform program in the early 1960s, as did Colombia (see following boxed example) and Chile in the 1970s and Indonesia in 1984. But also during the 1970s major tax-reform efforts went for naught in many more countries: Bolivia, Ghana, Liberia, and Peru, among others.

Lessons from Comprehensive Tax Reform

One of the most ambitious tax-reform programs ever undertaken in any developing country was that in Colombia in 1974. The Colombian experience illustrates both the potential payoffs and the difficulties involved in any serious tax reform effort.

In the last quarter of 1974 the new government of Alfonso Lopez Michelsen, acting in the midst of a national crisis, enacted a tax reform of very large magnitude. The reform, nearly a decade in the making, was engineered by an extraordinary group of officials as well versed in fiscal economics as any treasury department in the industrial countries. The reform package was comprehensive, involving nearly all tax sources. It was geared to all the fiscal policy objectives cited in Table 12–1: growth, equity, stability, and efficiency. The instruments employed were well-suited to the objectives sought. The reform contained measures to increase progressivity that are still absent in the tax systems of the United States and Canada. Numerous anomalies in the tax system that encouraged waste and inefficiency in the private sectors were eliminated. Innovations in tax administration and enforcement were introduced and were allowed to stand for a short time before they were struck down by the Colombian Supreme Court.

The reform's most striking initial achievements were its effects on tax revenue growth and income distribution. In the first year following the reform, tax revenues grew by 45 percent, or more than twice the growth rate in revenues in the years prior to the reform. The early impact on income distribution was just as striking: in its first year the reform served to shift as much as 1.5 percent of GDP away from the top 20 percent of the income earners, a rare feat.

Many of the achievements of the reform effort proved short-lived, however. The reform initially caught most powerful economic interests with their defenses down. But by 1976 groups injured by the reform were able to have many key measures watered down or repealed, and taxpayers began to develop defense mechanisms against the new law and to exploit loopholes uncovered by the best legal minds in the country. Also, the reform effort paid far too little attention to the practical problems of implementation and to the strengthening of tax-collection

procedures. Nevertheless many of the innovations introduced in 1974 **295**
survived relatively intact through 1980, such that by that time many reve- GOVERNMENT
nue-hungry and equity-oriented tax officials in other Latin American EXPENDITURES
countries still viewed much of the 1974 reform package as a model worth
detailed study.

GOVERNMENT EXPENDITURES

In the late 1800s, the German political theorist Adolph Wagner propounded his famous "law of expanding state activity." The thrust of Wagner's law was that the relative size of the public sector in the economy has an inherent tendency to grow as per-capita income increases. While few fiscal economists accept "Wagner's Law" without several qualifications, it is nevertheless true that poor countries do have smaller public sectors than rich ones, when size of the public sector is measured as the ratio of government expenditure to GDP. As may be noted from Table 12–5, this proportion rises steadily with per-capita income, from just above 16.0 percent in the lowest income LDCs to 30.1 percent in the high-income industrial market economies.

All categories of government spending tend to rise with per capita income, but those for health, housing, and social security grow at the most rapid rates, as may be seen in Table 12–5. Defense spending as a percent of GDP is only marginally higher in the richest nations than in the poorest, and the wealthiest countries actually spend a lower proportion of GDP on education than any other group save the very poorest LDCs. Hundreds of books and articles have been written on the reasons for these trends in government spending across countries and across time. Characterization of the research, much of which leads to conflicting conclusions, is not possible here. These trends, while clearly associated with income growth, do not seem to be related in any systematic way to population growth, but may be strongly influenced by other demographic factors such as urbanization. Defensible "laws" of growth of spending by particular governmental function remain to be propounded; clearly, careful additional research is required on this set of questions.

TABLE 12–5 Government Expenditures as a Percent of GDP by Function, 1982

Spending category	Developing Nations			Industrial Market Economies
	Low-income countries	Lower-middle-income countries	Upper-middle-income countries	
Defense	3.0	3.4	3.1	4.2
Education	0.9	3.3	2.9	1.4
Health	0.5	0.9	1.4	3.5
Housing and Social Security	0.8	1.6	5.6	12.2
Economic Services	4.1	5.6	5.5	2.9
Other	7.0	9.0	8.2	5.9
Total	16.3	23.8	26.7	30.1

Source: Derived from World Bank, *World Bank Development Report, 1985,* pp. 224–225.

The effects of government *capital spending* on growth were long viewed as unambiguously positive. Although critics of capital fundamentalism later succeeded in demonstrating that not all such investment has contributed to growth, much less development, there is still a pervasive believe that in any trade-offs between government capital spending and recurrent spending, the issue should be resolved in favor of investment, as recurrent outlays are still widely considered unproductive. Indeed, recurrent costs of development programs are by convention labeled as government consumption, implying that outlays for such purposes have no effect on increasing productive capacity. A number of analysts have sought to correct this misconception. They point out that while most governments focus their attention on new investments, they often do not make adequate provision for the recurrent operational and maintenance costs of previous investments.[17] This gives rise to wasteful underutilization of public-sector capital, and in some cases to its rapid decay.

These observations notwithstanding, it is also true that in many countries there may be some scope for expanding public savings by curbing growth of several types of recurrent expenditure: the Please effect discussed in the last chapter does have empirical support. We will examine the main categories of recurrent, or "consumption," expenditures of government to determine how wide this scope may be.

For many countries, the four most significant categories of recurrent expenditure are: (1) outlays for wages and salaries of civil servants and the military; (2) outlays on nondurable goods and services, including those for public-sector employees, maintenance, and all spending on military equipment; (3) interest payments on the government debt; (4) transfers to subnational government; (5) subsidies and other transfers to individuals.

Nondurable Goods and Services

In poorer LDCs, nondurable goods and services typically account for between half and three-quarters of total recurrent expenditure as illustrated in Table 12–6. The three principal items are: (1) salaries and benefits for civil servants and the military; (2) outlays on maintenance and repair; and (3) other military spending. In most LDCs, salaries and benefits account for more than half of total expenditures for goods and services.

The stereotypical image of public-sector bureaucracies in LDCs is one of bloated payrolls and inefficient, corrupt, even indolent performance. The basis for this view is essentially anecdotal, not systematic, evidence; reliable international comparisons of civil-service performance are almost nonexistent. It is easy to accumulate anecdotes involving bureaucratic snafus, stupidities, corruption, and short-sightedness in both developing and developed societies. No firm judgments can be made on the extent of overstaffing of public agencies or overremuneration of officials, or bureaucratic extravagance in LDCs relative to industrial countries: civil-service payrolls in Mas-

17. Peter Heller, "The Underfinancing of Recurrent Development Costs," *Finance and Development* 16, no. 1 (March 1979): 38–41.

TABLE 12–6 **Government Recurrent Expenditure, by type as Percent of Total Recurrent Spending[a] in Selected Developing Countries, 1982**

Country	Wages and salaries	Other purchases of goods and services	Interest payments on public debt	Transfers to subnational government	Subsidies and other transfers
Low-income countries					
Ethiopia[b]	41	49	4	na	5
Ghana	29	27	23	3	18
India	15	18	16	33	18
Kenya	35	30	15	5	16
Pakistan	66[c]		16	12	7
Sri Lanka	24	18	28	na	31
Sudan	13	35	9	na	43
Tanzania[d]	65	na	23	12	1
Zaire	36	38	15	6	6
Middle-income countries					
Argentina	34[c]		26	3	37
Bolivia	26	6	61	2	5
Brazil	12	8	16	12	52
Chile	32	13	2	na	53
Colombia[d]	30	15	6	26	22
Egypt	22	23	6	na	50
Indonesia	27	23	10	19	22
South Korea	18	33	8	29	13
Malaysia	36	23	15	3	23
Peru	41[b]	15	27	na	17

Source: International Monetary Fund, *Government Finance Statistics Yearbook, 1984* (Washington, D.C., 1984), country tables.
[a] Rows may not add to 100 because of rounding.
[b] 1979.
[c] Data not provided for breakdown between categories.
[d] 1981.

sachusetts and New Jersey may be as bloated as in many LDCs. And while there are examples of gross venality and blatant use of political patronage in public-sector hiring in segments of the civil service systems of some developing countries (and many U.S. cities), there are also examples of first-rate professionalism and codes of conduct that may rival many found in industrial countries, as in the Indian and Malaysian civil-service systems.

While there may be some countries in which the salary bill for civil servants would be compressed sufficiently to augment government savings, in others, like Bolivia and Kenya, civil-service salaries remain so low relative to those available in the private sector that it has been difficult to attract and hold the type of qualified public-sector managers, secretaries, and technicians essential for efficient government operation.

About the only safe generalization that can be made about civil-service systems in LDCs is that they appear more, or less, responsive to the socioeconomic changes that accompany development than any other group in society. In the 1950s it was almost impossible to discuss Latin American development without hearing repeated mention of the "antidevelopmental" effects of the famous *mordida* (bite) then commonly demanded by civil servants for doing what they should be doing as well as what they should not be doing. It was commonly believed then that such behavior was the result of both low-civil service salaries and unalterable cultural habits. In the early 1960s many Western and Korean social scientists felt that widespread corruption and inefficiency in the Korean government were immutable, owing both to practices that became acceptable under decades of Japanese occupation and to the "influence of the Confucian ethic." One hears much less of such claims today, whether for Latin America or Korea. While civil service reformers may not wish to use either the Colombian, Brazilian, or Korean experience as a model for other countries, there can be no mistaking the palpable verve and professionalism displayed by substantial numbers of civil servants in those countries by the 1980s, "cultural habits" notwithstanding.

If there is waste in government procurement in some areas, there are others where, for lack of funds, governments have been too miserly in appropriating funds, particularly with regard to maintenance costs for upkeep of the public-sector capital stock and for many vital operating expenses. The phenomenon is aptly characterized by Peter Heller:

> In Colombia, new tarmac roads have suffered rapid and premature deterioration for lack of maintenance. Throughout West Africa, many new schools have opened without qualified teachers, educational materials, or equipment. Agricultural projects are often starved for extension workers, fertilizer, or seeds. In the Sahel, pastoral wells constructed for livestock projects have fallen into disrepair. In Bolivia, doctors are often stranded at rural health centers for lack of gasoline for their vehicles.[18]

Underfinancing recurrent costs is pervasive across countries including the United States, where items such as bridge maintenance have been long postponed in many states. In LDCs, however, this pattern is exacerbated by the policies of aid donors, who strongly support capital projects, and as a matter of policy have been reluctant to support the recurrent costs of these projects. As a result, painfully accumulated public-sector capital stock tends to deteriorate rapidly, eventually requiring not incremental maintenance outlays but expensive new public works. Few countries are in a position to expand public savings by further compressing this category of recurrent expenditures.

Many social scientists in industrial countries believe that there is great potential for expanding public savings in LDCs through reduction of military or defense expenditures. Indeed for low-income developing countries as a group, military spending in 1982 was twice as high as government spending on education and health combined (Table 12–5). For middle-income LDCs, however, per-capita military spending was 78 percent of per-capita outlays on education and health or about the same ratio as for industrial countries. Here we can make no judgments about "appropriate" levels of military spending, whether in developed or developing countries. The fact remains that some countries, including developing countries, do perceive or actually face threats to their national security from time to time. It is also true that many countries, some LDCs included, maintain large, well-equipped military forces even in the absence of any short- or long-term external threats.

18. Heller, "Underfinancing Development Costs," 38.

A major budgetary cost for many LDCs is interest on government debt: in countries included in Table 12–6 this item ranges from no less than 2 percent to as high as 61 percent of total recurrent spending with a central tendency of about 20 percent. Since outside the OPEC countries recurrent costs run about 80 percent of total government expenditures in both the poorest and the middle-income countries, interest costs are typically about 10 percent of the budget, a figure not significantly different from that of the United States in the 1980s.

Interest obligations arise from past government budget deficits that are financed by either internal or external borrowing, or both. Interest payments on foreign borrowing grew rapidly in several LDCs from 1970 through 1984, owing to the surge in external commercial borrowings and to generally rising world interest rates from 1972 to 1982, both discussed in Chapter 14. Because interest on government debt reflects past decisions, both on deficit finance and external borrowing, this item of expenditure is difficult to reduce: even in the absence of further deficits and a moratorium on external borrowing over a several-year period, outlays for this purpose cannot be easily compressed in the short term except in countries that default on their international debt liabilities, as many threatened to do in the mid-1980s.

Subsidies

A variety of subsidies account for substantial shares of recurrent expenditures in LDCs: the proportion ranges from 5 to 43 percent in poor countries included in Table 12–6, and from 5 to 53 percent in middle-income countries, with central tendencies about 25 to 30 percent respectively. These figures do not include subsidies some governments classify, with reason, as capital expenditures.

Recurrent budget subsidies take a variety of forms. The most common are those for consumption of food. Like Indonesia, Sri Lanka provided heavy subsidies on rice consumption from 1960 to 1979; Colombia has at various times given substantial subsidies to consumers of food, as have Egypt and India. The usual mechanism is that of distributing price-controlled foods through state-owned entities and absorbing losses in food distribution through budgetary transfers to these entities. Another subsidy that was pervasive in oil-producing countries during the seventies was that on domestic consumption of refined oil products, discussed in a later section. Other items where budgetary subsidies have been common include those provided for rural electrification (Malaysia and Philippines), contraceptive devices (Indonesia), fertilizer (Indonesia and Sri Lanka), air travel (Pakistan, for travel between East and West Pakistan before 1971), bank interest payments on savings deposits (Indonesia), and urban bus services (Colombia, Indonesia, and others.)

In virtually all countries employing budgetary subsidies the stated purpose has usually been that of income redistribution. For foods, especially grains, the argument appears plausible, even if the ultimate effect is not always what was intended. On the other hand, heavy subsidies on fertilizer use in Indonesia had a very high payoff, in terms of rice production and rural incomes, at least through 1982. The role of many other subsidies in securing goals of income redistribution is less clear, however, as we shall see. Whatever the ultimate impact of budget subsides on income distribution, it is clear that in many countries substantial sums are involved, and that efforts to remove or reduce them in order to expand public savings meet with strong resistance virtually everywhere. Riots following reduction of food subsidies have occurred in Sri Lanka, Egypt, and Turkey and other countries. Severe social disturbances have followed reduction of subsidies on gasoline in Indonesia, Colombia, and Thailand when coupled with increases in urban bus fares. For these reasons governments often tend to view proposals for reducing subsidies with even more more reservations than proposals for tax increases.

Intergovernmental Transfers

Transfers from central to subnational governments are conventionally treated as recurrent expenditures, even though subnational governments (provinces, departments, counties, municipalities) may use the proceeds for capital formation such as construction of schools and hospitals. However, some countries, such as Indonesia, classify some transfers as capital spending and others as consumption. Note again the problem of making international comparisons when classification standards are not uniform across countries.

Table 12-6 shows that transfers to subnational governments (including revenue sharing) constitute a sizable proportion of recurrent spending in some countries (India, Colombia, Korea) and a very small share in others (Bolivia, Ghana, Malaysia, Zaire). In a few cases the small share of such transfers is due to the fact that subnational governments have access to very rich sources of revenue. This is true for Bolivia, where oil-producing provinces received large oil royalties before the decline in world oil prices after 1982, as well as the Federation of Malaysia, where the East Malaysian governments of Sabah and Sarawak earned substantial tax revenues from the export of tropical timber found there. In most unitary states, such as Chile, virtually all government affairs at all levels are run from the capital, and subnational units of government have few responsibilities to go with their small sources of local revenue.

Elsewhere, including many federal countries, transfers of funds from the central government to subnational units is essential because the center has monopolized the most productive sources of tax revenue. In most cases this monopoly is due to technical reasons: national governments impose income taxes because subnational governments lack the resources and skills required to administer such a complex tax, and could not do so effectively even given administrative resources because of the ease with which the income tax base can migrate within a country. Similarly, the major source of tax revenue for most countries—import duties—must necessarily remain a central government resource, since most countries have a very limited number of serviceable ports.

Evidently, then, there are few easy ways to reduce most types of recurrent expenditure to achieve higher public savings. Earlier we concluded that there

are also few easy ways in which tax revenues can be expanded to serve the
same purpose. Finance ministers are responsible for both and for many of
the macroeconomic prices that are crucial for development. Finance ministers who over extended periods have met with some success in holding the
line against rising current expenditures while securing robust revenue growth
and avoiding deep overvaluation of the exchange rate, tend to be as unpopular as they are rare. Indeed, in some countries over some periods an effective
finance minister may have contributed more to income growth than all the
formal development planning apparatus described in Chapters 5 and 6. The
far-reaching incentives and distributional and stabilization effects of fiscal
policy enhance the finance minister's key role in development.

TAXES AND PRIVATE INVESTMENT

Fiscal policy influences capital formation in the private sector in two main
ways: (1) by its effects on both the capacity and the incentive to save in the
private sector, and (2) by its effects on incentives to invest in private projects.
Taxes impinge more directly, but not necessarily more importantly, on both
sets of incentives than do government expenditures, and will be our prime
focus here.

Taxes and Private Savings

Taxation of households and firms is but one of many factors that affect their
savings decisions. A proper assessment of the role played by taxes requires an
understanding of other determinants of saving, including the level and vola-
tility of household income, the relative share of labor and capital income in
private-sector income, as well as the role of financial policy. In Chapter 11
we saw that various theories of savings behavior assist in sorting out the
prime determinants of household savings.

An increase in taxes on households will come partly out of consumption
and partly out of savings, but the relative effects of taxes in reducing consumption and savings is a matter of some dispute. Some studies of cross-
country savings behavior suggest that increases in taxes in LDCs merely
reduce private-sector consumption with little or no effect on savings. Other
studies conclude that there is a high degree of substitutability between private savings and taxes: one cited in Chapter 11 found that an additional dollar of public savings in LDCs tends to reduce private savings by at least fifty
cents. In this case the truth probably lies slightly closer to the latter
observation.

Different taxes will clearly have a differential impact on the *capacity to
save*. While heavy sales or excise taxes on highly price-elastic items of luxury
consumption will curtail rates of growth of consumption for such items,
heavy taxes on corporate income may come in large part at the expense of
business savings that might have been plowed back into company investment. Where upper-income groups have a high propensity to consume, as
has been often argued to hold for elites in many Latin American countries,
increased taxes on them may have little impact on private savings. But where

the same groups display strong accumulative characteristics, as many argue is true for some ethnic minorities in Southeast Asia, higher taxes may have relatively little effect on consumption and substantial effects on their savings. Further, heavier taxes on foreign natural resource firms will ordinarily have minimal negative impact on availability of private domestic savings unless such firms have local joint-venture partners and cut their dividends to them in response to reduced profitability.

There is less uncertainty concerning the effects of different *forms* of taxes on *incentives to save,* but even here offsetting considerations are present. Taxes on consumption probably impinge less severely on private savings than do taxes on income in most developing societies. Perhaps the only exception to this statement arises when households save primarily for later purchase of items subject to heavy consumption taxes. Some observers have argued that this motivation for saving is common in many low-income LDCs, where the nature of extended-family relationships makes household savings difficult. In some societies households with incomes above subsistence share resources with poorer households within the family group to help them meet subsistence needs. This pattern in characteristic of many African countries and of many parts of rural Asia. Under such circumstances household savings is largely devoted to the purchase of prized durable goods, such as transistor radios, bicycles, and sewing machines. In developed countries and middle-income LDCs these are typically viewed as consumer goods that are strong candidates for taxation. But it may well be that in some countries heavy taxation of such items also reduces incentives to save. It is even questionable whether products such as bicycles, sewing machines, and even small outboard motors should be viewed as consumer goods in many low-income societies. Purchasing a bicycle or a small outboard may allow a rural family to market garden produce and fish more easily; sewing machines are ordinarily bought to generate extra income for the household, not for the occasional fashioning of a prom dress or a Halloween costume.

On balance, consumption-based taxes are probably more favorable for growth in private savings than are income-based taxes. Virtually all LDCs implement aims of consumption taxation through such indirect means as sales and excise taxes. These levies, while not inherently regressive, are often perceived to be so. This perception has led many tax reformers to argue for direct taxes on consumption. Under a direct-consumption tax, taxpayers would annually report total consumption as well as income. Consumption below the level thought minimally necessary for an adequate living standard would be exempt, and any consumption above that level would be taxed at rates that rise progressively with total consumption. If such a levy could be administered it would stimulate savings, since a household could reduce tax liability by not spending. Direct-consumption taxes have been seriously proposed for the United States (1977), Britain (1978), Sweden (1976), and Australia (1976). Among LDCs they have been proposed for India, Guyana, and Sri Lanka, and actually enacted in India in the 1950s. The Indian experiment was short-lived, however, as the tax involved informational requirements beyond the capacities of the tax administration at the time; it proved impossible to administer. But in the 1980s the administrative problems, both real and imaginary, of direct consumption taxes are not so great as to preclude their consideration in many developing and industrial countries. And because inflation has so ravaged income taxation in most all countries, direct consumption taxes are likely to be adopted in many industrial countries before the next century.

Taxes can affect savings incentives in other ways. To the extent that national savings rates are responsive to the after-tax rate of return on savings (a question examined in the next chapter), heavy taxes on income from capital (dividends and interest) reduce the volume of private savings available for investment. Likewise, to the extent that people save mainly to finance retirement, social-security taxes can also reduce private and aggregate national savings if the social security system is financed on a pay-as-you-go basis (that is, from current revenues), as in the United States, Colombia, the Philippines, and India. Under a social security system financed in this manner, it is argued that individuals covered by the system will reduce their savings in anticipation of receiving future social security benefits. But there will be no corresponding increase in public savings because the social security taxes paid by those covered now are not set aside and invested, but rather are used to pay benefits to those already retired.

This is an important point, because many proposals have been made—and some enacted—for social security systems in Asia and Latin America intended to help increase the national savings rate. The argument that social security systems can foster domestic savings is correct only under two circumstances, both relatively uncommon in LDCs. First, social security systems that operate as true retirement funds can clearly help mobilize capital resources—provided the funds are invested in projects with an adequate social marginal rate of return. Under such systems, called the **provident-fund approach,** the taxes collected from those covered are invested by the government in assets that earn returns; payments are made to retirees out of these returns rather than from taxes collected by those still working, as under the pay-as-you-go system. Under this approach, used in Chile and for some workers in Malaysia and a few other countries, any decline in the private savings of those paying social security taxes is largely offset by a concomitant rise in public savings. But the provident-fund approach is not widespread.

Even the pay-as-you-go system can increase national savings rates in its early years of operation if benefits are denied to those who retired before the system was implemented, and if social security tax rates are set high enough to cover benefit payments for the first decade or so. This is because in the early years after establishment the number of workers covered is large relative to the the number of retirees, so that disbursement of benefits is small compared to inflow of revenues. Therefore a government seeking new temporary sources of public savings could enact a pay-as-you-go system for social security that would serve this purpose for a few years. Sooner or later, however, such a system would tend to reduce overall domestic savings, though not necessarily by as much as the social security taxes paid by covered workers.

If a country's tax system operates to reduce private savings, it will tend to curtail private investment. Beyond that effect, taxes can affect both the amount and allocation of private domestic investment undertaken out of any given volume of private capital available for investment.

We saw in Chapter 11 that in spite of exchange controls and similar restrictions, capital tends to be fairly mobile across international boundaries. If there are opportunities for earning returns abroad that promise higher after-tax returns than available in a particular developing country, domestic capital will tend to flow to these opportunities. Of course, a critical factor determining after-tax returns in a given country is the nature of taxes on capital there. Suppose, for example, that capital-owners in the Philippines can secure, on the average, before-tax returns equal to 15 percent of their investments and that capital income in that country is subject to a 50 percent tax. After-tax returns are then 7.5 percent. The same funds invested in well-developed capital markets in Hong Kong, where capital is less scarce, might obtain only a 12 percent return before taxes, but are taxed at only, say, 15 percent. The after-tax return in Hong Kong is therefore 10.2 percent. The difference of 2.7 percent in after-tax returns may be large enough to induce movement of Philippine savings to Hong Kong. In general, countries that attempt to impose substantially heavier taxes on capital income often experience outflows of domestic savings to countries employing lower tax rates on capital. This movement is quite distinct from the type of "capital flight" from developing to developed countries often observed in countries experiencing severe domestic political turmoil or exchange-rate uncertainties.

There is no shortage of low-tax foreign opportunities facing domestic savers in LDCs. "Tax havens" such as Panama and the Bahamas have been attractive to Latin American investors since the 1960s. Likewise, Hong Kong and Singapore financial markets garner substantial inflows of savings from other Asian countries. Until racked by civil war in the 1970s, Lebanon offered tax rates and financial services that induced many African and Middle Eastern savers to invest there, rather than at home or in Europe and the United States. Increasingly, enterprises from countries such as India, with relatively high taxes on capital income, have become major investors in other developing countries where after-tax returns are higher than at home.

Most countries have recognized that capital is fairly mobile across national boundaries and have sought to keep taxes on capital income from reaching levels much above those prevailing worldwide. This is evident from inspection of corporate income tax rates prevailing in most LDCs. In Latin America corporate tax rates are typically found in a band of from 25 to 40 percent, compared to 46 percent in the United States in 1986. In Southeast Asia corporate tax rates—other than those of Hong Kong—cluster in a narrow range of from 30 to 40 percent; the rate in Hong Kong is less than 20 percent.

Countries have sought to impede the outward mobility of capital through such devices as controls on movement of foreign exchange, imposition of domestic taxes on worldwide income of residents, and other devices. Flourishing business in tax haven countries, coupled with very large investment

holding of LDC citizens in the United States, Switzerland, Hong Kong, and
Singapore, are ample testament to the limited effectiveness of such controls.

Partly in order to stem capital outflow, and also to direct private invest-ment into priority areas, such as basic industry, exports, or backward regions, many LDC governments selectively offer substantial tax incentives to domestic investors. The two main types of incentives are income tax "hol-idays," wherein approved investments are exempted from income tax obli-gation for specified periods ranging from three to ten years, and tax credits for investment, wherein a government allows an investor to subtract some portion of initial investment (usually 20 to 25 percent) from his income tax liabilities. On rare occasions these types of incentives for domestic invest-ment have produced the desired results, but these devices suffer from a number of limitations, discussed more fully in Chapter 14. Because of their limitations, Indonesia in 1984 abolished all tax incentives, replacing them with the most effective tax incentive ever offered: lower tax rates for *all* firms.

INCOME DISTRIBUTION

As indicated in Chapter 6, a basic thrust of economic policy in many LDCs has been the mitigation of extreme income inequality. For decades devel-oped and developing countries alike have sought to use the fiscal system, particularly taxation, to redress income inequalities generated by the opera-tion of the private market. Social philosophers from John Stuart Mill and the eminent nineteenth-century Chilean historian Francisco Encina, to John Rawls in the 1970s, have sought to establish a philosophical basis for income redistribution, primarily through progressive taxes. Karl Marx also favored steeply progressive taxes in bourgeois societies, but for reasons other than income redistribution. Rather, in Marx's view, heavy taxes on capitalists were essential for speeding the decline of the capitalist state and its replace-ment by a socialist order.

There is no scientific basis for determining the "optimal" degree of income redistribution in any society. And across developing countries differ-ent views prevail as to the "ideal" distribution of income. But in virtually all countries the notion of "fiscal equity" permeates discussions of budgetary operations. In the overwhelming majority of countries fiscal equity is typi-cally defined materialistically, in terms of the impact of tax and expenditure policy upon the distribution of economic well-being. Progressive taxes, those that bear more heavily on better-off citizens than on poor households, and expenditures whose benefits are concentrated on the least advantaged, are viewed as more equitable than regressive taxes and expenditures. However, we shall see that the materialistic view of fiscal equity is not the only one that affects thinking on budget matters in developing societies.

Taxation and Equity

On the tax side of the budget, the materialistic conception of equity requires that most taxes be based on **ability to pay.** Ability to pay can be measured by income, consumption, wealth, or some combination of all three. Clearly, individuals with higher incomes over their life span have greater ability to pay taxes, quite apart from the moral question of whether they should do so. Indeed the redistributive impact of taxation is almost always expressed in terms of its effects on incomes. However, philosophers from the time of Hobbes have argued that consumption furnishes a better index of ability to pay than income; in this view tax obligations are best geared to what people "take out" of society (consume) rather than what they "put into" society (as measured by income).

In practice developing countries have relied heavily on both measures of "ability" in fashioning tax systems. Personal and corporate income taxes employ income as the indicator; sales taxes and customs duties are indirect assessments of taxes on consumption. But ability to pay is not the exclusive guide to assessment of taxes in all countries. Religious and cultural values often provide other bases for establishing tax liability. Nevertheless most societies do largely define equity in taxation as requiring taxation on the basis of ability to pay, and this is commonly interpreted to mean progressivity. At a minimum equity is usually assumed to require avoidance of regressive taxes whenever possible. There are a number of tax instruments that have been employed to secure greater progressivity in principle, if not in practice; all suffer from limitations to one degree or another.

Tax Equity and the Zakat

Consider, for example, the *Zakat,* a form of land tax levied in many Moslem or predominantly Moslem societies, including Pakistan, Malaysia, and formerly parts of Sumatra in Indonesia. According to a materialistic principle of tax equity, a land tax would be imposed on the basis of land value, or the value of income that a given parcel can produce. Therefore for two otherwise identical adjacent parcels, one irrigated and the other unirrigated, the owner of the former would pay more tax, as the greater productivity of his land gives him greater ability to pay. But as the *Zakat* is assessed in Pakistan, principles of equity in land taxes call for lower taxes on the irrigated parcel, on the reasoning that the owner of the unirrigated parcel directly owes any prosperity he may enjoy to rain sent by the Almighty, whereas the owner of the irrigated land owes his larger crops to his own labors in constructing irrigation canals and on that account should not be penalized with higher taxes. While by 1980 the *Zakat* was still a relatively minor source of tax revenue even in Pakistan, this illustration does serve to remind that the philosophical and theological underpinnings of economic policy vary across all societies, particularly those as diverse as those in the developing world.

Personal Income Taxes

The most obvious device for securing greater progressivity has been steeply progressive rates under the personal income tax. In some countries in some periods, nominal or legal marginal income tax rates have reached very high levels, even at relatively low incomes (less than $1,000 per household). Thus, for example, tax rates applicable to any income in excess of $1,000 in Indonesia in 1967 reached 75 percent, largely because tax rates were not indexed to rapid inflation; in Algeria in the 1960s marginal income tax rates on all income in excess of $10,000 was subject to marginal tax rates of nearly 100 percent; Tanzania imposed top marginal rates of 95 percent as late as 1981.

While in most LDCs marginal income tax rates are considerably lower than the examples above, some countries do attempt to impose rates that rival those of the United States before 1982, when the maximum marginal tax rate was 70 percent, since reduced to 50 percent. Although Egypt, Nigeria, and Zambia have progressive income taxes involving top marginal tax rates of about 75 percent, countries such as Brazil, Colombia, Malaysia, Mexico, Panama, Singapore, and Taiwan generally hold maximum marginal rates to 55 percent or slightly less, and the maximum income tax rate in Indonesia has been 35 percent since that country implemented tax reform in 1984.

If the tax administration machinery functioned well, and if capital were immobile among countries, the pattern of actual tax payments by high-income taxpayers would resemble the legal, or theoretical, patterns described above. In fact taxes actually collected as a percent of income (**effective tax rates**) in most countries fall well short of theoretical liabilities for several reasons.

Faced with high income tax rates, taxpayers everywhere tend to react in three ways: (1) they evade taxes by concealing income, particularly capital income not subject to withholding arrangements; (2) they avoid taxes by altering economic behavior to reduce tax liability, whether by supplying fewer labor services, shipping capital to tax havens abroad, or hiring lawyers to find loopholes in the tax law; (3) they bribe tax assessors to accept false returns.

For all of these reasons, achievement of substantial income redistribution through progressive income taxes has proven difficult in all countries, including the United States and also the three Scandanavian nations where tax rates are among the world's most progressive. Tax avoidance is the favored avenue for reducing tax liability in the United States, where use of the other methods can result in imprisonment. Indeed, heads of governments in both the United States (1971) and Sweden (1985) were found by the tax administration to have overstepped the bounds of propriety in avoiding taxes. But where tax enforcement is relatively weak, particularly where criminal penalties for evasion are absent (virtually all LDCs) and tax officials are deeply underpaid, as in countries such as Bolivia, Colombia, and Ghana, tax evasion and bribery are more commonly utilized. The scope for substantial redistribution through the income tax is thus even more limited than in the United States or Sweden.

Notwithstanding these problems, a significant share of the income of the wealthiest members of society is caught in the income tax net in many developing countries. Revenues from personal income tax collections in countries such as Colombia, Korea, and Chile have been as high as 15 percent of total taxes, and run between 5 and 10 percent of the total in a few others. In virtually all developing countries the entirety of such taxes is collected from top 20 percent of the income distribution. This means, of course, that the very presence of an income tax, even one imposed at proportional rather than progressive rates, tends to reduce income inequality. Income taxes, together with taxes on luxury consumption, constitute about the only feasible means of approaching income redistribution goals through the tax side of the budget.

Taxes on Luxury Consumption

In view of the difficulties of securing significant redistribution through income taxes, many countries have sought to employ heavy indirect taxes on luxury consumption as a means of enhancing the progressivity of the tax system. Efforts to achieve this goal usually center on internal indirect taxes, such as sales taxes, and on customs duties on imports. For reasons discussed earlier excise taxes on such sumptuary items as tobacco and alcohol are good revenue sources, but tend to be sharply regressive in virtually all countries save the very poorest, where pervasive poverty allows little indulgence in vices of any kind.

Several developing countries have found that, provided tax rates are kept to enforceable levels, high rates of internal indirect taxes on luxury goods and services, coupled with lower taxes on less income-elastic items, can contribute to greater progressivity in the tax system. For revenue purposes countries typically impose basic rates of sales tax on non-luxuries at between 4 and 8 percent of manufacturer's value. This is equivalent to retail taxes of between 2 and 4 percent because taxes imposed at this level exclude wholesale and retail margins. Food, except that consumed in restaurants, is almost always exempted from any sales tax intended to promote redistributive goals. In LDCs exemption of food by itself renders most sales taxes at least faintly progressive, given the high proportion (up to 40 percent in many middle-income LDCs) of income of poor households spent on food. Sales taxes involving a limited number of luxury rates of between 20 and 30 percent at the manufacturer's level have been found to be workable in many LDCs, including Colombia, Chile, Taiwan, and Korea.

The redistributive potential of sales tax rates differentiated in this way is, however, limited by the same administrative and compliance constraints standing in the way of heavier use of income taxation in LDCs. While sales taxes are not as difficult to administer as income taxes, they do not collect themselves. A manufacturer's sales tax system employing three or even four rates may be administratively feasible in most countries, even when the highest rate approaches 40 percent. Rates much higher than that, or reliance on a profusion of rates (over fifteen in Jamaica, over twenty in Chile from 1960 to 1970) in an attempt to "fine-tune" the tax, lead to substantial incentives and opportunities for tax evasion. In recognition of these types of problems, Indonesia adopted a flat-rate manufacturers tax in 1985: the tax applies at a rate of 10 percent on *all* manufactured items and all imports. The tax is nevertheless slightly progressive since it does not apply to items that do not go through a manufacturing process, including most foodstuffs consumed by low-income families.

While use of internal indirect taxes, such as sales taxes, can contribute to income redistribution goals without causing serious misallocation of resources, the same cannot be said for use of customs duties. Sales taxes are imposed on all taxable goods without regard to national origin, including goods produced domestically as well as abroad. Tariffs apply only to imported goods. Virtually all countries, developed and developing, utilize customs duties to protect existing domestic industry. Developing countries in particular employ customs duties as the principal means of encouraging domestic industry to produce goods that were formerly imported. This strategy, called "import substitution," is examined at length in Chapter 16.

Deliberate policies to encourage import substitution through the use of high protective tariffs might, under certain conditions, lead to results sought by policymakers. But accidental import substitution arises when tariffs are used for purposes other than protection, and this is unlikely to have positive results, except in rare instances. Many countries use high tariffs to achieve heavier taxation of luxury consumption. Often heavy tariffs are imposed on imported luxury items for which there is no intention of encouraging domestic production. Thus many Latin American and some Asian countries have levied customs tariffs of 100 to 150 percent of value on such appliances as electric knives, hair dryers, sporting goods, video-cassette recorders, and mechanical toys. For most countries these items are clearly highly income-elastic and are apt candidates for luxury taxation.

But efforts to tax luxuries through high customs duties leads to unintended—and almost irresistible—incentives for domestic production or assembly of such products. In virtually all countries save the very poorest, alert domestic and foreign entrepreneurs have been quick to seize upon such opportunities. By the time local assembly operations are established, they can usually make a politically convincing case that the duties should be retained to enable local production to continue, even when value-added domestically is as low as 10 percent of the value of the product. Such operations, if subject to any local sales taxes, usually succeed in being taxed at the basic tax rate, usually 5 to 10 percent. By relying on tariffs for luxury taxation, the government ultimately foregoes the revenues it previously collected from duties on luxury goods, as well as severely undermining the very aims of luxury taxation.

If, instead, higher luxury rates on imports are imposed under a sales tax collected on both imports and any domestic production that may develop, unintended import substitution can be avoided. The use of import tariffs for luxury taxation—indeed for any purpose other than providing protection to domestic industry—is one illustration of the general problem of using one economic-policy instrument (tariffs) to achieve more than one purpose (protection, luxury taxation, and revenues). Reliance on import duties for revenue purposes is subject to the same pitfalls just discussed: if it is desired to increase government revenues from imports, a 10 percent sales tax applied both to imports and any future domestic production will yield just as much revenue as a 10 percent import duty, without leading to accidental protection.

Income taxes on domestic corporations and property taxes are often mentioned as possible methods for securing income redistribution through the budget. It is true that corporate income is ultimately received, through dividends and capital gains, almost exclusively by the upper 5 to 10 percent of the income distribution. It is also true that ownership of wealth, which in many LDCs largely takes the form of land, tends to be even more concentrated than income. But, to a greater extent in developing than developed countries, efforts to secure significant fiscal redistribution through heavier taxes on domestic corporations and property are limited both by administrative and economic realities.

Administrative problems bedevil efforts to collect income taxes from domestic firms to at least as great an extent as for income taxes on individuals. Hence, in many countries such as China and Pakistan where corporate taxes on local firms have been important, as much as two-thirds to three-fourths of non-oil corporate taxes flow from state-owned firms, not from private firms owned by high-income individuals. Taxes on land should be subject to less severe administrative problems, since it is an asset that cannot be easily hidden. However, land valuation for tax purposes has proven difficult even in Canada and the United States; it is more difficult in developing countries. Other than Colombia, few LDCs have been able to assess property at anything approaching its true value.

Economic realities hinder efforts to achieve greater progressivity in the tax system through heavier use of corporate and land taxes, because of the tendency for taxation to unintentionally burden groups other than those directly taxed. This is the **incidence** problem. The incidence of a tax refers to its ultimate impact: it is not who actually pays the tax to the government, but those whose incomes are finally affected by the tax when all economic agents have adjusted in response to the tax. The point of incidence is not always the point of initial impact. Taxes on domestic corporations may reduce the incomes of capitalists, who in turn might shift their investment patterns to reduce taxation. The incomes of workers they employ and the prices charged to consumers may be affected as well. In the end taxes on land and improvement may not much reduce the incomes of landholders, but they may be reflected in higher prices charged to consumers. Ultimately, all taxes are paid by people, not by things such as corporations and property parcels.

The implications of incidence issues may be illuminated by a simple application of incidence analysis to the corporation income tax. Consider a profit-maximizing company that has no significant monopoly power in the domestic market. If taxes on the company's income are increased in 1988, then after-tax returns to its shareholders in 1988 will be reduced by the full amount of the tax. In the short term, as defined in Chapter 11, incidence of the tax is clearly on shareholders. Since shareholders everywhere are concentrated in higher income groups, the tax will be progressive in the short run. If capital were immobile, unable to leave the corporate sector, the long-term incidence of the tax would also rest on shareholders and tax would be progressive in the long run as well.

But in the long run capital can move out of the corporate sector. To the
extent that capital is mobile domestically, but not internationally, the corporate tax will also be progressive in the long run. Returns on capital remaining in the corporate sector will be reduced by the tax. Untaxed capital owners employed outside the corporate sector will also suffer a reduction in returns, because movements of capital from the taxed corporate sector will drive down the rate of return in the nontaxed sector. Because the corporate tax reduces returns to capital throughout the economy, all capital owners suffer, including owners of housing assets, and, in a closed economy, the long run incidence is again progressive.

However, no LDC is a completely closed economy; indeed, we saw in Chapter 11 that capital tends to be somewhat mobile internationally. To the extent that capital is mobile across national borders, and to the extent that higher returns are available in other countries, domestic capital will migrate to escape higher corporate taxes. But as capital leaves an economy, both new and replacement investment and, ultimately, output, will be curtailed, and the marginal productivity of workers will fall. Prices of products produced with domestic capital will therefore rise. In this way an increase in corporate taxes may be borne by domestic consumers, who pay higher prices for the reduced supply of corporate-sector goods. Similarly, domestic workers whose incomes are reduced when production is curtailed, may bear a part of the burden of corporate tax.

Hence the corporate tax may be regressive (worsen the income distribution) in the long run. The degree of regressivity will depend upon whether consumption by low-income groups is more or less capital-intensive, and on the relative position in the income distribution of workers losing their jobs or suffering declining real wages. In the end capital owners may suffer no significant decline in their incomes. While there are other plausible conditions under which an increase in the corporation income tax may not result in greater relative burdens on capitalists, the scenario outlined above is sufficient to illustrate that often the intentions of redistributive tax policy may be thwarted by the workings of the economy. Clearly, defending *a priori* assumptions that all taxes imposed on wealthy capital owners will ultimately be paid by them is difficult.

Limited Effects of Redistribution Policy

The foregoing discussion suggests that while some tax instruments may achieve income redistribution in LDCs, the opportunities for doing so are limited in most countries, a conclusion supported by a large number of empirical studies. With few exceptions these show that inability to administer personal income taxes effectively, failure to utilize the limited opportunities for heavier taxes on luxury consumption, overreliance on revenue-productive but regressive excise taxes, and the inclusion of food in sales taxes, all combine to reduce significantly the redistributive impact of LDC tax systems. By and large LDC tax systems tend to produce a tax burden that is roughly proportional across income groups, with some tendency for progressivity at the very top of the income scale. As a result the very wealthy do pay a somewhat greater proportion of their income in taxes than the poor, but the poor still pay substantial taxes: at least 10 percent of their income in many cases studied (Argentina, urban Brazil, Colombia, Jamaica, and six others).[19] This is the predominant pattern even in countries such as Colombia, Jamaica, Tanzania, and Chile before 1970 that have placed strong policy emphasis upon use of tax tools to reduce income inequality. One can only conclude that in the absence of such efforts, the after-tax distribution of income may have been even more unequal. This suggests that while difficult to implement and often disappointing in results, tax reforms intended to reduce income inequality are not futile exercises in LDCs, and they may serve the purpose of preventing taxes from making the poor worse off.

Expenditures and Equity

The limits of tax policy suggest that if the budget is to serve redistributive purposes the primary emphasis must be on expenditure policy. Indeed where redistribution through expenditures has been a high priority of governments the results have been generally encouraging. The effects of government expenditure on income distribution are even more difficult to measure than in the case of taxes. But both the qualitative and quantitative evidence available strongly indicate that in developing countries budget expenditures may transfer very substantial resources to lower income households, in some cases as much as 50 percent of their income. And the pattern of benefits tends to be progressive, contributing a much higher fraction of income to the poor households than to those in the upper reaches of the income distribution.

One study found that in Malaysia in the late 1960s the combined effect of taxes and recurrent government consumption expenditures was to transfer about 5 percent of GNP from the two highest income classes to the two lowest income groups, with more than three-quarters of the transfer going to the poor.[20] This figure understates the actual extent of the redistributive impact of expenditures since they do not include the effects of public investment, which was perhaps the most important tool of fiscal redistribution in Malaysia in 1968.[21] Another study found that in Indonesia in 1980 the tax system was only slightly progressive.[22] But the expenditure side of the budget, with its emphasis on food subsidies and primary education, markedly helped the poor; benefits from government expenditure were slightly more than 50 percent of the income of the poorest income group. Similarly, an exhaustive study of the net incidence of the Chilean budget for 1969 shows that while the tax system had virtually no effect on income distribution, government expenditures favored the poor: the lowest income groups received only about

19. Many of these studies have been summarized in Richard M. Bird and Luc Henry DeWulf, "Taxation and Income Distribution in Latin America: A Critical View of Empirical Studies," *International Monetary Fund Staff Papers* 20 (November 1975): 639–82.

20. Donald R. Snodgrass, "The Fiscal System of Malaysia as an Income Redistributor in West Malaysia," *Public Finance* 29, no. 1 (January 1974): 56–76.

21. Ibid.

22. Malcolm Gillis, "Micro and Macroeconomics of Tax Reform: Indonesia," *Journal of Development Economics* 19, no. 2 (1986).

Obviously not all government expenditures are effective in reducing income inequality. Some, like interest payments on government debt, have the opposite effect because interest income is concentrated in upper income groups. But it is not difficult to identify those categories of budget outlays that tend to have the most marked effects on the incomes of the poor. Public expenditures on primary, but not university, education tend strongly to reduce income inequality (Chapter 9). Government spending for public health programs (particularly water supply, sanitation, nutritional programs, and rural health clinics) also often has a clearly progressive impact (Chapter 10). Although many poor people live in huge cities such as Jakarta, São Paulo, Mexico City, Lagos, and Calcutta in most developing countries most of the poorest people tend to live in rural areas and wealthy people tend to live in urban areas. Hence programs that reallocate government spending to rural areas (irrigation programs, secondary roads, erosion control) may tend to reduce income inequality overall, particularly in the case of irrigation.

Irrigation and Equity

Many economists have long believed that government investments in irrigation in LDCs were bound to result in significant benefits for poor rural households, primarily by the effects of increased irrigation on agricultural productivity. However, this view was widely questioned by many analysts in the seventies. They claimed that irrigation tends to be adopted faster and more completely by large farmers at the expense of small farmers and landless laborers, because the large farmers are then more able to buy out the small ones and because the technology associated with irrigation is labor-saving.

Recent studies sponsored by the International Food Policy Research Institute (IFPRI) tend to confirm the older view: government investments in irrigation have not benefited the larger farmers more than small farmers and landless laborers. Rather, these studies find that the latter groups have made major increases in their income as a result of irrigation. This research was focused on ten project sites in Indonesia, Thailand, and the Philippines. It found no tendency to merge farms after the introduction of irrigation, and particularly in Indonesia, that the gains to landowners accrued primarily to small farmers. Further, gains to landless labor were substantial, however these are measured. This is primarily because of greater, not less, use of labor in the irrigated areas. The income of hired laborers was higher in all areas with irrigation. (Source: *IFPRI Report* 8, no. 1, January 1986.)

Subsidies for consumption of basic foodstuffs also can result in substantial redistribution, provided food subsidy programs are not accompanied by

---

23. Alejandro Foxley, Eduardo Aninat, and J. P. Arellano, *Redistributive Effects of Government Programs* (Oxford: Pergamon Press, 1980), Chapter 6.

oppressive price controls on production of food by poor farmers. Subsidies to subnational governments are often used to finance provision of basic human needs, such as water, sewerage, education, and health services, all of which have benefits concentrated in lower income classes. Housing subsidies favor the poor less frequently since many programs for housing subsidies (Indonesia, Ghana, Pakistan) are in reality largely confined to government employees, a group that in most countries is relatively well-off.

Finally, not all subsidy programs contribute to income redistribution even when redistribution is the announced goal. The most striking example has been that of subsidies for the consumption of petroleum products, particularly kerosene, in Bolivia, Colombia, Indonesia, Pakistan, and several other oil-producing countries. In all four cases mentioned, a principal justification offered for such subsidies was that of assisting low-income groups. In Bolivia through 1980, and in Colombia through 1974, this argument was extended to cover gasoline consumption, even though in both countries automobile ownership was largely confined to the upper 5 percent of the income distribution, and in both, urban bus transport was heavily subsidized. In Indonesia gasoline has been only lightly subsidized, but budget subsidies held prices of kerosene and diesel fuel at less than half the costs of production and distribution. While it seems plausible that kerosene subsidies strongly favor the poor, this is not the case. The poorest 40 percent of families consume only 20 percent of the kerosene sold. Therefore for every one dollar of subsidy to the poor, relatively high-income families received four dollars of benefit. And since kerosene can be substituted for diesel fuel, the subsidy program included it as well to prevent diesel users from switching. The result was that subsidies to kerosene and diesel fuel averaged about 5 percent of total tax revenues in Indonesia from 1979 to 1981, a figure exceeding total capital expenditures for education during the same period.

Fiscal policy to redistribute income must be viewed in perspective. It is not the only, and not always the most effective, instrument for redistribution in LDCs. Other chapters, especially Chapter 4, have drawn attention to the pivotal importance for income distribution of land tenure, the terms of trade between rural and urban areas, growth of employment, the relative prices of labor and capital, the openness and market orientation of the economy, and other factors. Taxation and government expenditures can affect most of those factors to some extent, but other, more direct policy instruments may have greater impacts on income distribution. Each of these instruments, some of which force radical changes in the economy, has its economic and political dangers. But a government determined upon a more equitable income distribution probably needs to employ all those measures—including progressive taxation and expenditure policies—to some degree.

ECONOMIC STABILITY

From the publication of Keynes' *General Theory* in 1936 until the 1970s, conventional wisdom in macroeconomics held that an active and deft use of fiscal policy in concert with monetary policy was, at least in principle, capa-

ble of combating economic instability in the form of inflation and recession.
The fiscal policy prescription was simple: when faced with inflation enact tax increases and cut government expenditures to reduce aggregate demand; in recession implement the same set of measures in reverse. Few macroeconomists now believe that the active use of fiscal policy is efficacious in combating moderate inflation or unemployment even in countries such as the United States. Studies of the effects of U.S. fiscal policy since 1960 do not suggest that the public responds to temporary changes in fiscal policy in ways predicted by analysts of an earlier era because such measures do not affect their "permanent income," the income variable on which, many economists believe, households base their spending decisions (see Chapter 11). In addition, members of an influential school of thought—the rational expectationists—argue that people do not respond in the manner expected because they have learned from past experience that governmental action with the announced goal of stabilization often fails to achieve that purpose.

Although framers of macroeconomic policy in many LDCs briefly flirted with Keynesian ideas of demand management in the early 1950s, active use of fiscal policy for countercyclical purposes has never been common in the developing nations. Of necessity, macroeconomic budget management has been focused not on cyclical variations of tax rates but on finding sufficient revenues to finance rapidly rising government expenditures without incurring large deficits. Given that unemployment has been of a type not easily remedied by simple demand expansion, and given the persistence of inflationary pressures arising from both the domestic and world economy, the task of macro stabilization policy in LDCs has usually been interpreted as one of restraining inflation. For fiscal policy this ordinarily has meant pursuit of a balanced budget. Adherence to the balanced budget rule is in many circumstances appropriate in light of national objectives. There are, however, three sets of circumstances in which it may be inadvisable to seek balanced budgets. One set of circumstances involves deficit spending; the other two require the overall government budget to be in surplus.

In situations where a society is prepared to accept the income distribution consequences of substantial inflation, and where the tax system has unwanted effects on the income distribution and cannot be easily reformed, a government may conclude that inflation represents a superior means of mobilizing resources for the public sector. Tax collections may be allowed to fall short of government spending; the government then covers the deficit by printing money. This accomplishes transfer of resources from the private to the public sector just as surely as government spending out of increased tax collections. Provided the resulting inflation can be held within moderate bounds (see Chapter 13), pursuit of the balanced budget goal under such circumstances may not be consistent with broader national objectives.

Of the two situations requiring surplus in the government budget, one is discussed in this chapter, the other in Chapter 19. In the present case we will assume that any further inflows of foreign savings are unwanted. We also assume that the government is unprepared to accept the ill effects of inflation on income distribution and employs a tax system that results in a distribution of the tax burden consistent with that society's redistributive goals.

In countries with relatively vibrant private sectors but where private savings are insufficient for financing private investment, maintenance of economic stability requires that the overall government budget be in surplus, i.e., government savings must exceed government investment. This can be seen from the use of the national income accounting identity:

$$Y = C_p + I + G + (E - M), \qquad [12\text{-}1]$$

where Y = gross domestic (or national) product; C_p = private consumption, or the demand for domestic goods by domestic residents in the private sector (personal consumption); I = total investment, *including* government investment; G = government consumption expenditures (recurrent expenditures); M = imports (domestic demand for foreign goods and services); and E = exports (foreign demand for domestic goods and services).[24]

Thus income is equal to total spending by domestic residents plus net exports $(E - M)$. Expressed in more detailed form we have

$$Y = (C_p + G) + (I_g + I_p) + (E - M), \qquad [12\text{-}2]$$

where I_g is government investment and I_p is private investment. The first term on the right-hand side of Equation 12–2 refers to total consumption, the second refers to total investment. Because our focus in this chapter is on domestic determinants of stability, we will assume that net exports are zero, or $E - M = 0$. From basic macroeconomics we know that if $E = M$, then economic stability requires that total planned investment must equal total planned savings, or $I = S$. Since with $E - M = 0$, there are two components of savings and two components of investment, we can write

$$I_g + I_p = S_g + S_p, \qquad [12\text{-}3]$$

where S_p = private savings and S_g = government savings.

Now suppose the government plans to run a balanced budget for the year, so

$$T = G + I_g, \qquad [12\text{-}4]$$

where T = total taxes. Since by definition

$$S_g = T - G, \qquad [12\text{-}5]$$

then from Equations 12–4 and 12–5,

$$I_g = S_g. \qquad [12\text{-}6]$$

As long as Equation 12–3 holds, stability will obtain. But now suppose that in the private sector, investors plan to invest more than savers plan to save. That is,

$$I_p > S_p. \qquad [12\text{-}7]$$

---

24. These definitions are consistent with those of the macroeconomic consistency model of Chapter 6 (Equations 6–7 to 6–11), except that consumption (C in Chapter 6) has been divided into private consumption (C_p) and government consumption (G), and investment (I in Chapter 6) has been divided into private and government investment $(I_p$ and $I_g)$.

We will use Z to denote excess demand: the excess of planned investment over planned savings in the private sector. Therefore,

$$I_p = S_p + Z. \qquad [12\text{--}8]$$

In this situation maintenance of stability requires an unbalanced budget: T must exceed G by an amount sufficient to offset Z. That is, $I_p > S_p$ is consistent with stability only of $S_g > I_g$ by the amount Z.

The savings shortfall could be made up either by compressing G or I_g by an amount equal to Z, or by increasing T by an amount sufficient to reduce C_p (private consumption) by Z or some combination of both measures. Because we saw earlier that a tax increase comes partly out of consumption and partly out of savings, T must be increased ordinarily by more than G to offset Z of any given size. The reduction in G or the increase in T would be taken to the point where once again Equation 12–3 is satisfied, i.e., where the excess of S_g over I_g just compensates for the shortfall of S_p that is necessary to finance I_p.

Therefore tax increases or spending cuts may sometimes be essential even when the government budget is not in deficit. More often LDC governments find that tax increases are essential in order to reduce deficits, because the tax system has failed to generate revenues at a pace consistent with development goals. This consideration implies that a high premium should be placed upon building features into the tax system that make it more responsive to economic growth, so that the government does not have to resort to periodic increases in tax rates to maintain economic stability and finance growing levels of government spending required for development. Such a tax system would have a high degree of **revenue elasticity**.

The revenue elasticity (ε_R) measures the responsiveness of the tax system to growth in GDP. It is defined as the percent change in tax collections divided by the percent change in GDP,[25] or:

$$\varepsilon_R = \frac{\Delta T/T}{\Delta Y/Y} \qquad [12\text{--}9]$$

If $\varepsilon_R > 1$, then the tax system is revenue-elastic and taxes rise proportionally more than national income. For example, if $\varepsilon_R = 1.2$, then for every 10 percent increase in GDP, tax collections rise by 12 percent. If $\varepsilon_R < 1$, the tax system is revenue-inelastic; if $\varepsilon_R = 0.8$, then with a 10 percent increase in GDP taxes rise by only 8 percent.

Governments are most concerned with fashioning tax systems that will be revenue-elastic at unchanged tax rates and unchanged definition of the tax base. This is termed **ex-ante elasticity** (i.e., the built-in response of the tax system to GDP growth). Few LDCs have been able to secure ex-ante revenue

---

25. In actual calculation of ε_R, the following formula should be used:

$$\varepsilon_R = \frac{T_1 - T_0}{(T_0 + T_1)/2} \div \frac{Y_1 - Y_0}{(Y_0 + Y_1)/2}$$

when the (0) and (1) subscripts on T and Y refer to the beginning and the end of the time period under consideration (usually one year).

elasticity equal to or greater than one. Because the observed elasticity of government spending in LDCs is typically greater than one (government spending tends to grow at rates faster than GDP), this represents a serious problem.

Some countries, however, have tax systems with **ex-post revenue elasticity** greater than one. Ex-post elasticity incorporates the built-in responsiveness of the tax system *plus* legislated changes in tax policy during the period under review. If ex-ante revenue elasticity is low, periodic tax increases designed to keep ex-post revenue elasticity at acceptable levels rapidly runs into diminishing returns, as we saw earlier.

A government can enhance the ex-ante revenue elasticity of the tax system by relying on taxes with income-elastic bases, that is, taxes for which the base grows at a rate faster than GDP. The tax bases for excise taxes on tobacco and alcohol are typically income-inelastic, except in very low-income countries such as Chad, Mali, and Haiti. For countries relying heavily upon import substitution as a means of rapid industrialization, the base for customs duties is income-inelastic.

The taxes with the most income-elastic bases are the income tax, sales taxes that exempt food but not services, and luxury-consumption taxes. The income taxes have income-elastic bases because as the economy develops, a growing proportion of income is earned in the modern sector and becomes more accessible to the tax collector. Use of progressive rates under the personal income tax accentuates the revenue elasticity of the tax, since with growth more income becomes taxable at the higher rates.

Sales taxes that exempt income-elastic food and tax income-elastic services are moderately revenue-elastic, even at unchanged tax rates. Luxury consumption is by definition income-elastic. It may be noted that virtually all measures taken to enhance the revenue elasticity of the tax system also contribute to the progressivity of the system. This is one of the rare cases in which one policy measure (enhancing ex-ante revenue elasticity) promotes two goals (economic stability and income redistribution).

ECONOMIC EFFICIENCY

Sources of Inefficiency

On the expenditure side of the budget, the tool we earlier called social cost-benefit analysis (Chapter 6) can be deployed to enhance efficiency (reduce waste) in government spending. On the tax side, promotion of economic efficiency is more problematic.

All taxes, save lump-sum levies (poll taxes), lead to inefficiencies to one degree or another. Lump-sum taxes are not realistic options for raising government revenues given their high degree of regressivity. The objective is therefore one of minimizing tax-induced inefficiencies consistent with other goals of tax policy. In most developing societies this objective largely reduces to the necessity of identifying examples of waste engendered by taxes and purging them from the system. If a particular feature of a tax system involves large efficiency losses, called "excess burden" in fiscal economics, and at the same time contributes little or nothing to such other policy goals as income redistribution, then that feature is an obvious candidate for abolition. A full discussion of those elements of tax systems that qualify for such treatment is properly the subject of an extended public finance monograph. We can do little more here than indicate some of the principal examples.

Quite apart from excess burden, discussed below, a major source of inefficiency in taxation not counterbalanced by positive gains in revenues, income redistribution, or other objectives of tax policy, is excessive costs of tax administration. In some countries and for some taxes these costs have been so high as to call into question the desirability of using certain taxes for any purposes. This is true for certain kinds of narrow-based stamp taxes widely used in Latin America to collect government revenues on documentation of transfer of assets, rental agreements, checks, and ordinary business transactions. Like a federal tax on playing cards used in the United States until 1964, many stamp taxes cost more to administer than they collect in revenues.

In some countries even broad-based taxes have had inordinately high costs of collection. For example, sales taxes in Chile and Ecuador in the 1960s cost one dollar in administration for each four dollars collected, as opposed to about one dollar per one hundred dollars for most state sales taxes in the United States. And because taxes on capital gains are so difficult to administer everywhere—including North America—costs of collecting this component of income taxes often exceed revenues in many LDCs.

Many LDCs, from Ghana in Africa to Colombia in Latin America and Indonesia in Asia, have offered substantial tax incentives to encourage investment in particular activities and regions. Many of these, particularly income tax "holidays" for approved firms, have proven very difficult to administer, and as shown in Chapter 14, few have led to the desired result. Given persistently pressing revenue requirements in most countries, the granting of liberal tax incentives may serve no purpose other than that of requiring higher rates of tax on taxpayers who do not qualify for the incentives. It is a dictum of fiscal theory that any economic wastes (inefficiencies) arising from taxation increase by the square of the tax rate employed, not proportionately. It is therefore not difficult to see that unsuccessful tax-incentive programs involve inefficiencies for the economy as a whole that are not compensated by any significant benefits. Largely for this reason, Indonesia abolished all forms of tax incentives in a sweeping tax reform in 1984.[26]

Finally, some features of major tax sources as utilized in many LDCs involve needless waste. From our earlier discussion of the use of import duties for luxury tax purposes it is clear that this is often a major source of inefficiency. The use of progressive tax rates in a corporation income tax (as in Colombia until 1974, Venezuela, Mexico, Brazil, Ghana, and a score of other countries) is another example. Progressive rates of corporate tax, where

---

26. The justification for abolishing all tax incentives in Indonesia may be found in: Malcolm Gillis, "Micro and Macroeconomics of Tax Reform: Indonesia," *Journal of Development Economics* 19, no. 2 (1986).

they cannot be enforced, do little to contribute to income redistribution, and where they can be enforced they lead to a variety of wastes. Two of the most important are their effects on fragmentation of business firms and their implication for inefficiency in business operation. The incentive for fragmentation is evident: rather than be subjected to high marginal rates of taxes, firms tend to split up into smaller units, losing any cost advantages of size. Where progressive rates are employed for company income, the tax will take a high proportion (say, 70 percent) of each additional dollar of earnings: therefore the incentive to control costs within the firm will be reduced. For example, for a firm facing a marginal tax rate of 70 percent, an additional outlay of $1,000 for materials will involve net costs of only $300, while taxes are reduced by $700.

Neutrality and Efficiency: Lessons from Experience

Experience around the world, both in developed and developing countries, seems to indicate that in societies where efficiency in taxation matters, efficiency is best pursued by reliance on taxes that are as "neutral" as possible. A **neutral tax** is defined as one that does not lead to material change in the structure of private incentives that would prevail in the absence of the tax. A neutral tax system then, is one that relies, to the extent possible, on uniform rates: an income tax on all income at a flat rate, a sales tax with the same rate applied to all foods and services. A neutral tax system cannot be an efficient tax system, nor can it be "optimal" tax system.

An **efficient tax system** is one that involves a minimum amount of **excess burden** for raising a required amount of revenue, where excess burden of a tax is defined as the loss in total welfare, over and above the amount of tax revenues collected by the government. Figure 12–1 demonstrates how the excess burden of, say, a commodity tax is the greater the more elastic is the demand or the supply of the taxed item. The right-hand diagram depicts the inelastic case, good a, while the left-hand diagram shows the elastic case, good b. Constant marginal costs *(MC)* are assumed in both cases, and at the same level for both goods, in order to more starkly portray the contrasts. Before the tax is imposed on either good, equilibrium price and quantity are P_a, Q_a for good a and P_b, Q_b for good b. Now impose a tax rate *(t)* on both goods. The new equilibrium (post-tax) magnitudes are P_{at} and Q_{at} for good a and P_{bt} and Q_{bt} for good b. For good a, the total amount of government revenue is the rectangle $P_a P_{at} cd$. The total loss in consumer surplus arising from the tax is the trapezoid $P_a P_{at} ce$. The excess of the loss in consumer surplus over the amount of government revenue is the conventional measure of efficiency loss from a tax, or excess burden. For good a, excess burden is the small triangle *cde*. By similar reasoning, excess burden in the case of good b is the larger triangle *fgh*. We may see that taxes of equivalent rates involve more excess burden when imposed on goods in elastic demand.

We can now see that efficient taxation requires neither uniformity nor neutrality, but many different tax rates on different goods, with tax rates higher for goods in elastic demand and lower for goods in inelastic demand. This is known as the **Ramsey rule** or the **inverse elasticity rule**. The problem is that a tax system on this rule would be decidedly regressive: the highest

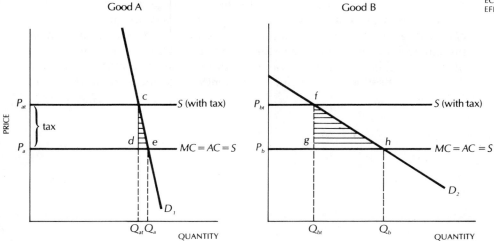

FIGURE 12-1 Taxation and Efficiency: Excess Burden of Commodity Taxes with Constant Marginal and Average Costs, under Competition. The shaded area in both panels represents the excess burden of equal tax rates imposed on different goods. The greater the elasticity, the greater the excess burden.

taxes would be required on foodstuffs, drinking water, and sumptuary items. Taxes would be lower on items such as clothing, services, and foreign travel, which tend to be both price- and income-elastic. **Optimal taxation** is closely related to "efficient" taxation, but is not identical.[27]

The principle of neutrality in taxation is not nearly as intellectually satisfying as a guide to tax policy as is efficient taxation or optimal taxation. Nevertheless, neutral taxation is to be preferred as one of the underlying principles of taxation, along with that of equity, until such time as analysts are able to identify optimal departures from neutrality—and uniformity in tax rates— in real-world settings, and until such time as administrative capacities are equal to the task of operating necessarily complicated structures of efficient or optimal taxes.

There is a paradox here. While neutral, uniform rate taxes are less suited for efficiency goals than perfectly administered efficient or optimal taxes, neutral tax systems probably are more likely to enhance efficiency in the economy than are the former systems, since neutral systems with uniform rates can be administered most easily, and are much less vulnerable to evasion. This is not to say that neutrality has ever been or should be the overriding goal of tax policy. Governments often undertake very deliberate departures from neutral tax treatment of certain sectors or groups of society, in order to achieve other policy goals. But in real-world settings, these depar-

27. An optimal tax system would be intended to pursue *both* equity and efficiency goals. Optimal tax analysis focuses on the tradeoff between equity objectives (avoiding regressivity) and the deadweight efficiency costs of raising a given amount of revenue. However, the informational and administrative requirements for imposing a set of "optimal" taxes across any economy are, under present technology, so great as to preclude its practical application. For a contrary view, however, see Newberry and Stern, *Modern Tax Theory for Developing Countries.* In press.

tures involve costs, not only in terms of tax administration, but often in both equity and efficiency terms as well. It is important that these costs be made as transparent as possible, so that policymakers may weigh them against expected gains from non-neutrality, including efficiency gains. Under present technology, major departures from neutrality in taxation are not likely to yield benefits commensurate with the costs. Neutrality in taxation may be the most advisable guide to efficiency in taxation for some time to come.

13

Financial Policy

A country's **financial system** consists of a variety of interconnected financial institutions, both formal (organized) and informal (unorganized). Except in a handful of countries (including Liberia and several Francophone African countries), a central bank lies at the core of the organized financial system, responsible for the control of the money supply and the general supervision of organized financial activity. Virtually everywhere, and particularly in developing countries, the commercial banking system is the most visible and vital component of the organized financial system, as acceptor of deposits and grantor of shorter term credit. Other elements of the organized financial system include savings banks, insurance companies, and in a few higher income LDCs, pension funds and investment banks specializing in long-term credit, as well as nascent securities markets. Coexisting with these modern financial institutions are the unorganized and largely unregulated systems of finance, including pawnshops, local moneylenders, trade credit, and other informal arrangements involving the borrowing and lending of money, such as intrafamily transfers and cooperative credit. In very low-income nations, or even in higher income LDCs with long inflationary histories, the unorganized financial sector may rival the organized system in size.

Financial policy embraces all measures intended to affect the growth, utilization, efficiency, and diversification of the financial system. In North America and Western Europe the term financial policy is ordinarily used as a synonym for monetary policy: the use of monetary instruments to reduce instability induced by cyclical fluctuations arising from either internal or external markets. In the United States these instruments include open-market operations, changes in both legal-reserve requirements of commercial banks and in central bank (Federal Reserve) lending (rediscount) rates to commercial banks; these terms are explained later in this chapter. As typically viewed in LDCs the term **financial policy** has a much broader meaning. Monetary policy is part of financial policy, but so are measures intended to encourage the growth of savings in the form of financial assets, to develop money and capital markets, and to allocate credit between different economic sectors.

Views on the Role of Finance in Development

For the first two decades of the post-World War II era, financial policy was not generally viewed as a significant instrument for promoting economic stability, much less for encouraging growth and development in LDCs. There were a number of reasons for this view. First, until after the Second World War there was a prevailing tradition in economics that monetary changes affected only prices and wages and had little impact on production and employment over the business cycle. Among other things, the Great Depression served to demonstrate that monetary factors could in fact have significant effects on both output and employment. Nevertheless the tradition died hard; many economists in the industrial countries and in LDCs in the 1940s and 1950s remained convinced that monetary factors had little influence on the business cycle and consequently downplayed the importance of that important subset of financial policy known as monetary policy.

Skepticism over the efficacy of monetary policy was perhaps more pronounced in LDCs, particularly those where a substantial portion of economic activity was conducted through barter and related informal transactions outside of the money economy. The **monetization ratio**—the proportion of the total of goods and services in an economy that are purchased with money—was relatively low in many LDCs, particularly low-income nations in Africa. Even in the 1970s it is likely that only three-quarters of all economic activity in Africa took place within the monetized sector, versus 90 to 95 percent in Asia, the Middle East, and in Latin America.[1] The effective use of monetary policy instruments for combating cyclical fluctuations is difficult enough in highly monetized countries such as the United States. In countries where as much as 15 to 25 percent of activity is outside the money economy it was thought that monetary policy would be even less effective in achieving stabilization goals.

Finally, postwar economic history to 1972 was a period in which fixed exchange rates prevailed virtually everywhere, including LDCs. It is well established in the literature on money and international trade that, given perfect capital mobility and fixed exchange rates, small countries will find monetary policy ineffective. Through the 1970s policy commitments to fixed exchange rates were relaxed in a few countries. Also, by the end of the decade there were few countries outside the twelve to fifteen poorest where the monetization ratio stood at less than 85 percent. And as we have noted in Chapters 11 and 12, the international mobility of capital is far from perfect. In light of these considerations there was by the early 1980s a growing number of adherents to the view that financial policy, when deftly applied, can contribute something to maintenance of short-term economic stability,

1. Anand G. Chandavarkar, "Monetization of Developing Economies," *International Monetary Fund Staff Papers* 24, no. 3 (November 1977): 678–79.

as shown by experiences in such countries as Indonesia (1967 to 1968 and 1974) and Argentina in 1985.

Less widely accepted, however, is the contention that financial policy can have an important influence over the long-term course of economic development. Earlier views of the role of finance in development held that the effect of financial policies on growth was benign at best and mildly restrictive at worst; in any case, financial policies were not thought to make much difference for higher living standards. More recently, analysts such as Edward Shaw and Ronald McKinnon at Stanford have argued that financial policies have important implications both for the accessibility of domestic savings to domestic investors and for the efficiency with which these savings are allocated to competing investment purposes.[2] We will explore those implications throughout this chapter.

THE FUNCTIONS OF A FINANCIAL SYSTEM

The financial system provides four basic services essential for the smooth functioning of an economy: (1) it provides a medium of exchange and a "store of value" called "money," which also serves as a "unit of account" to measure the value of the transactions; (2) it furnishes a vessel for mobilizing and allocating funds, and gathering savings from numerous savers and channeling them to investors, a process called **financial intermediation;** (3) it provides a means of transferring and distributing risk across the economy; (4) it provides a set of policy instruments for stabilization of economic activity.

Money and the Money Supply

An economy without money as a **medium of exchange** is perforce a primitive economy. Trade between individuals must take the form of high-cost, inefficient, barter transactions. In a barter economy goods have prices, but they are expressed in relative prices of physical commodities: so many kilos of rice for so many liters of kerosene, so many meters of rope for so many pairs of sandals, and so on. Trading under such circumstances involves onerous information costs.

Few societies have ever relied heavily on barter precisely because of the high costs implicitly in this means of exchange. At some point prices of goods and services begin to be expressed in terms of one or more universally accepted and durable commodities, like gold and silver, or even beads and cowrie shells. The rise of commodity money diminishes transaction and storage costs of trade, but still involves problems of making exchanges across space and time. Gold and silver prices do fluctuate, and the commodities are thus not fully reliable as **units of account.** As specialization within an economy increases, financial instruments backed by commodities appear. In the last century, with the rise of central banking all over the world, currency has evolved into **fiat** money: debt issued by central banks that is legal tender. It is backed not by commodities of equivalent value, but only by the full faith and credit of the central bank. As markets widen and specialization proceeds

2. Edward Shaw, *Financial Deepening and Economic Development* (New York: Oxford University Press, 1973) and Ronald I. McKinnon, *Money and Capital in Economic Development* (Washington, D.C.: The Brookings Institution, 1973).

apace, a need arises for still another financial instrument—**transferable deposits.** In the normal course of development, **checking deposits** appear first: deposits that may be transferred to any economic agent at the demand of the depositor. These are liabilities (debts) of commercial banks and ordinarily bear no interest. With further monetization still another financial instrument begins to grow in importance: **time deposits** which are not legally transferable on demand, but only after stated periods. Rising levels of economic activity require increasing needs for transaction balances; individuals will always maintain some balances in demand deposits to meet these needs, but will tend to economize on levels of such deposits if no interest is paid on them. Time deposits, however, do involve contractual interest payments; higher interest rates induce people to hold greater amounts of deposits in this form.

While checking (demand) and time deposits are **liabilities** (or debts) of commercial banks, they are **financial assets** to the persons who hold them. Both demand and time deposits are known as **liquid financial assets.** Unlike **nonfinancial assets** that can also be held by households and businesses (inventories, gold, land), demand and time deposits can be quickly and conveniently converted into their currency equivalents. Currency is, of course, the most liquid of all assets. The concept of liquid financial assets is an important one in any discussion of financial policy in developing countries. For most LDCs, movement of savers in and out of liquid financial assets may be the prime factor behind the success of failure of financial policy. We will see that secular shifts from tangible, or nonfinancial, physical assets to financial assets, particularly liquid assets, bodes well not only for economic growth but also for economic stability.

A country's **money supply** may be defined as the sum of all liquid assets in the financial system. While not all economists agree about what constitutes a liquid financial asset, most vastly prefer this money-supply concept to those commonly employed in early postwar monetary analysis. Formerly the money supply was conventionally defined as the sum of only two liquid financial assets: currency in circulation outside banks (C) plus demand deposits (D), which together are known as M_1 (narrow money). However, it has become clear that because depositors tend to view time deposits (T) as almost as liquid as demand deposits, the former should also be included in any workable concept of money supply, called M_2 (broad money). Thus,

$$M_1 = C + D. \qquad [13\text{--}1]$$

$$M_2 = M_1 + T. \qquad [13\text{--}2]$$

For most low-income LDCs and many middle-income countries, liquid financial assets constitute by far the greatest share of outstanding financial assets. But as income growth continues and the financial system matures, financial assets other than liquid assets assume progressively greater importance. These include primary securities such as stocks, bonds (issued both by government and firms), and other financial claims on tangible (physical) assets that are convertible into currency equivalents with only with some risk of loss to the asset-holder, and are hence less liquid than demand or time deposits.

The evolution of financial activity follows no set patterns across countries. Differing economic conditions and policy emphases may result in widely divergent patterns of financial growth. Nevertheless, the level of financial activity tends to increase relative to economic activity as per-capita income rises over time. M_1, the narrowly defined money supply, may be as low as 10 percent of GDP in very low-income countries, and tends to rise more or less steadily to between 25 and 30 percent of GDP in high-income LDCs and industrial countries. As income rises from very low levels, much of the growth in liquid assets tends to take the form first of growth in demand and then in time deposits. The ratio of M_2 to GDP can be taken as a measure of the real size of the banking system, a rough gauge of the flow of loanable funds in LDCs. In recent years this ratio has been typically no more than 12 to 15 percent in very poor countries, rising to an average of about 30 to 50 percent in middle-income nations and between 70 and 100 percent of GDP in such industrial countries as the United States, Canada, and France, and to 164 percent in Japan (see Table 13–1). But diversity in financial develop-

TABLE 13–1   Liquid Assets^a (M_2) as a Percent of Gross Domestic Product: Selected Countries, 1960–1983

	1960	1970	1979	1983
I. Developed countries				
Canada	33.8	52.2	71.6	66.9
France	47.6	62.6	74.6	70.5
Italy	59.9	86.8	100.6	81.6
Japan	66.6	92.8	143.5	163.5
United Kingdom	52.4	55.1	33.7	40.0
United States	63.5	70.0	72.6	63.9
II. Developing countries				
A. *Latin America*				
Argentina	—	30.6	35.0	33.0
Brazil	26.4	23.1	17.3	30.1
Chile	—	17.5	19.0	26.4
Colombia	17.6	19.8	26.5	34.2
Mexico	74.3	33.1	33.4	34.8
Peru	21.1	22.8	22.4	27.6
Uruguay	31.6	21.5	36.0	43.9
B. *Asia*				
India	27.8	27.3	40.4	42.9
Indonesia	—	10.0	17.6	26.2
South Korea	10.7	37.1	35.8	39.2
Malaysia	26.4	39.8	76.0	102.6
Philippines	20.0	23.4	24.9	31.1
Sri Lanka	29.5	29.3	36.5	39.7
Taiwan	17.0	44.9	98.2^b	—
Thailand	23.7	30.7	36.4	49.1
C. *Africa*				
Ghana	17.8	19.3	21.1	11.4
Kenya	—	31.4	36.9	40.7
Nigeria	12.6	17.5	25.1	43.4
Tanzania	—	24.8	37.1	40.9

Source: International Monetary Fund, *International Financial Statistics* (various issues, 1970–1986).
^a Liquid assets = money + quasi money + all deposits outside commercial bank (lines 34 + 35 + 44 + 45 of IMF tables).
^b For 1978.

ment is well exemplified by the fact that in some relatively high-income LDCs (Taiwan and Malaysia), the share of liquid assets in GDP is higher than in most industrial countries.

Liquid assets are not, however, the only source of financial growth. As financial markets widen with the spread of the money economy, they also tend to deepen as a greater variety of financial assets begins to appear. With rising incomes, a growing proportion of financial growth tends to come in the form of nonliquid financial assets, such as primary securities, suitable as a basis for the type of longer term finance that commercial banking systems cannot easily provide. The **financialization ratio** (the ratio of financial assets to GDP) tends to rise steadily from less than 20 percent of GDP in very poor countries, such as Haiti or Chad, to between 50 and 60 percent in higher income LDCs, such as Brazil, South Korea, and Venezuela. In very high-income developed countries, including Japan, Canada, and the United States, total financial assets are nearly twice as large as GDP. Here again, however, there is no evidence of immutable "laws" of financial development. Many very high-income industrial countries, including France and Holland, have financialization ratios that are less than half those of Japan and the United States. And many higher income LDCs, particularly those with long traditions of inflationary history (Uruguay, Chile, Argentina), display a lower ratio of financial assets to GDP than poorer countries such as India and Thailand.

Financial Intermediation

As financial structures become increasingly rich and diversified in terms of financial assets, institutions, and markets, the function of money as a medium of exchange, store of value, and unit of account, tends to be taken for granted except in the context of situations of runaway inflation, discussed later in the chapter. As financial development proceeds, the ability of the financial system to perform its second major function—financial intermediation—grows as well. The process of financial intermediation involves the gathering of savings from multitudinous savers and channeling them to a smaller but still sizable number of investors. At early stages of economic development a preponderant share of intermediation activities tends to be concentrated in one type of institution: commercial banks. As development proceeds, new forms of financial intermediaries begin to appear and gradually assume a growing share of the intermediation function. These include investment banks, insurance companies, and ultimately, securities markets. Plentiful intermediaries, however, do not always guarantee successful intermediation.

Financial intermediation activities are best measured through use of **flow-of-funds accounts,** which display the uses of finance by different economic sectors together with the sources of savings by sectors. These are akin to the flow matrix of input-output tables (see Chapter 6). Unfortunately, reliable flow-of-funds tables are available for only a few LDCs at present; therefore cross-country generalization about intermediation based on such tables is not yet possible. In the absence of information of the type available from flow-of-funds accounts, we will employ the liquid asset/GDP ratio as an approximate measure of financial intermediation.

Financial intermediation is best seen as one of several alternative technologies for mobilizing and allocating savings. The fiscal system discussed in Chapter 12 furnishes another alternative, and we will see in the next chapter that reliance on foreign savings constitutes still another. Further, we will observe in this chapter that inflation has also been employed as a means of mobilizing public-sector savings. Indeed a decision to rely more heavily upon financial intermediation as a means of investment finance is tantamount to a decision to rely less heavily upon the government budget, foreign aid and foreign investment, and inflation to achieve the same purpose.

Transformation and Distribution of Risk

Another major service provided by a well-functioning financial system is the transformation and distribution of risk. All economic activities involve risk-taking, but some undertakings involve more risks than others. Individual savers and investors tend to be risk-averse, i.e., the marginal loss of a dollar appears more important to them than the marginal gain of a dollar. But the degree of risk aversion differs across individuals. When risk cannot be diversified, or "pooled," across a large number of individuals, savers and investors will demand greater returns, or premiums, for bearing risk, and activities involving high risk will tend not to be undertaken. But high-risk activities may well offer the greatest returns to the economy as a whole. A well-functioning financial system furnishes a means for diversifying, or pooling, risks among a large number of savers and investors. The system may offer assets with differing degrees of risks. Financial institutions that specialize in assessing and managing risks can assign them to individuals having different attitudes toward, and perceptions of, risk. Indeed a perfectly functioning financial system can reduce all risk premiums to zero, except for those **systematic risks** that can never be diversified away from the domestic economy, such as those arising from national disasters like the 1985 earthquake in Mexico, and recessions in the world economy.

Stabilization

Finally, the financial system provides instruments for stabilization of economic activity in addition to those available under fiscal policy and direct controls. All economics experience cyclical changes in production, employment, and prices. Governments often attempt to compensate for these fluctuations through policies affecting the money supply. Because unemployment in LDCs is rarely of the type that can be readily cured by monetary expansion, use of financial policy for stabilization purposes generally focuses, as we shall see, on efforts to control inflation.

Inflation and Savings Mobilization

By the 1980s, **price inflation,** defined as a sustained increase in the overall price level, was generally regarded as a malady which in its milder forms was annoying but tolerable, and in its moderate form corrosive but not fatal. Runaway inflation, also known as hyperinflation, however, is always recognized as severely destructive of economic processes, with few offsetting benefits. Whereas a number of influential thinkers in the 1950s and 1960s advocated some degree of moderate inflation (e.g., inflation rates of between 8 and 12 percent) as a tool for promoting growth, few adherents of this view remain, for reasons discussed below. Many others did not actively advocate inflation, but tended to have a higher threshold of tolerance for a steadily rising general price level than is now common, on the grounds that development inevitably involved tradeoffs between inflation and unemployment, and that the wise course was to resolve the trade-off in favor of less unemployment and more inflation. Today few economists still believe in a fixed, long-term relation between inflation and unemployment; and many believe that restraining inflation may enhance, rather than retard, prospects for long-run growth.

Inflation in the LDCs: The Recent Record

Generalizations about inflation in developing countries are difficult to make. Inflationary experiences across countries are as diverse as their experiences in the fields of literacy, nutrition, and tax collection. Nevertheless, postwar economic history offers some interesting national and regional con-

TABLE 13–2   Inflation Outliers: Episodes of Cronic,[a] Acute,[b] and Runaway[c] Inflation among Developing Countries, 1950–1985

Country	Years of chronic inflation and average annual rate		Years of acute inflation and average annual rate		Years of runaway inflation and average annual rate	
	Years	Rate (%)	Years	Rate (%)	Years	Rate (%)
Argentina	1950–74	27			1974–76	293
					1981–85	400
Bolivia	1973–83	35	1952–59	117	1982–85	700
Brazil	1957–76	35	1978–80	72	1985	227
Chile	1952–64	32	1965–73	50	1971–76	273
	1978–82	44				
Ghana			1973–83	52		
Indonesia					1965–68	306
Mexico	1973–83	28				
Paraguay			1951–53	81		
Peru	1974–78	34	1950–55	102		
South Korea			1950–55	95		
Turkey	1973–82	42				
Uganda			1973–83	62		
Uruguay	1948–65	26	1965–68	83		
	1978–80	46	1972–76	77		
Zaire	1973–83	48.2				

Source: For years prior to 1977, all countries except Ghana and Zaire: adapted from Arnold C. Harberger, "A Primer on Inflation," *Journal of Money, Credit and Banking,* 10, no. 4 (1978): 502–21.
   For Ghana and Zaire and for all countries after 1977: *International Financial Statistics,* various issues.
   [a] Chronic inflation: annual inflation rates between 25% and 50% for three or more consecutive years.
   [b] Acute inflation: annual inflation 50% or more for three or more consecutive years.
   [c] Runaway inflation: inflation in excess of 200% for one year or more.

trasts in both susceptibilities to, and tolerances for, different levels of inflation.

Except for several inflation-prone countries in the southern cone of South America (Argentina, Bolivia, Brazil, Chile, Paraguay, Uruguay), the period prior to the early seventies was one of relative price stability in most LDCs. In the southern cone countries, however, in particular Chile and Argentina, and to a considerable extent Brazil, **chronic inflation** (inflation greater than 25 percent per year, but less than 50 percent, for three years or more) has been an enduring fact of economic life for much of the past four decades. The experience of these countries indicates that long periods of double-digit inflation does not necessarily lead to national economic calamity in all societies. Seven other countries also experienced chronic inflation from 1950 to 1983, as shown in Table 13–2.

However, a tolerable rate of inflation in one country may constitute economic trauma in another. This may be seen more readily by considering the next phase of the often progressive inflationary disease, called **acute inflation.** Acute inflation, defined here as inflation in excess of 50 percent for three or more consecutive years, was experienced by nine countries over the postwar period. For Brazil, the progression from chronic to acute inflation did not result in any noticeable slowing of that country's relatively robust economic growth, whatever it may have meant for income distribution. In Ghana, on the other hand, a decade of acute inflation coincided with a decade of negative growth in GDP per capita. While it may be tempting to attribute economic retrogression in Ghana to acute inflation, it is more likely that the same policies that led to sustained inflation were responsible for declines in living standards there.[3]

Although acute inflation has proven toxic to economic development in some settings and only bothersome in others, **runaway inflation** has almost always had devastating effects in countries where it has occurred. Inflation rates in excess of 200 percent per year represent an inflationary process that is clearly out of control: six nations have undergone this traumatic experience since 1950. The nadir of recent inflationary experience occurred in two southern cone countries: Bolivia and Argentina in 1985. In Bolivia in that year, the annual rate of inflation over a period of several months accelerated to a rate of nearly 5,000 percent. In Argentina the *monthly* rate of price increase was 30.5 percent in June alone; on an annual basis that would have been an inflation rate of 2,340 percent. In both Bolivia and Argentina for much of 1985, workers had little choice but to spend their paychecks within minutes of receipt, for fear that prices would double or triple over the next week.

The group of thirteen "outlier" countries in Table 13–2 is best viewed as falling into two special cases. In one group a succession of very large fiscal deficits (large relative to GDP) were financed by recourse to the banking system's resources (Chile, Indonesia, Argentina, Ghana). In another group

3. For a diagnosis of the causes of the Ghanian economic decline after 1962, see Michael Roemer, "Ghana, 1950 to 1980: Missed Opportunities," and Yaw Ansu, "Comments," both in *World Economic Growth,* Arnold C. Harberger, ed., (San Francisco: Institute of Contemporary Studies, 1984), pp. 201–30.

massive expansion of credit to the private sector beyond rates compatible with price stability was the major factor (Paraguay in the early 1950s, and Brazil and Uruguay before 1974.) Causes of inflation in these countries are not difficult to identify for the periods in question.

But this group of thirteen countries constitutes only a small fraction of LDCs. Through most of the postwar era most have restrained budgetary deficits to more manageable proportions, and few have allowed rates of credit expansion to the private sector to reach uncontrollable levels. Indeed aside from the countries listed in Table 13–2, the period 1952 to 1979 was one in which there were more years when inflation was marginally greater in developed than in developing countries. Only after the first oil-price shock in

TABLE 13–3   Average Annual Rates of Inflation Since 1952[a]

Country	Years 1952–66	Years 1967–72	Years 1973–81	Years 1982–84
A. *South and Central America*	10.5	8.9	24.2	21.3
Costa Rica	1.8	3.8	15.6	47.0
Dominican Republic	1.2	3.2	11.1	8.0
Panama	0.3	2.7	7.9	3.8
Paraguay	12.8	3.0	14.9	13.1
Venezuela	2.3	1.3	10.6	16.1
B. *Africa*				
Cameroon	(1963–66) 5.2	3.1	11.7	20.3
Ivory Coast	(1960–66) 3.1	3.6	14.7	3.4
Kenya	(1960–66) 2.3	2.4	13.7	10.3
Nigeria	(1954–66) 4.0	8.3	17.3	8.0
Senegal	na	3.4	11.1	9.5
C. *South Asia*				
Bangladesh	(1955–66) 4.3	4.8	19.7	21.5
India	4.8	3.7	9.5	14.4
Pakistan	3.8	4.0	14.2	13.1
Sri Lanka	0.8	5.6	10.9	17.4
D. *East Asia*				
Malaysia	−0.2	3.2	7.2	8.9
Philippines	2.7	8.5	14.1	14.3
Singapore	(1960–66) 1.1	1.0	8.7	8.5
Thailand	(1954–66) 2.7	2.2	11.9	7.6
E. *Middle East & North Africa*				
Egypt	1.4	3.3	11.1	17.7
Morocco	2.7	2.5	9.9	12.8
Syria	0.9	2.7	13.6	13.9
Tunisia	2.2	3.0	6.9	17.2
F. Range encompassing 80% of observations	0.9–10.5	2.2–8.3	7.9–14.9	7.6–17.7
G. World Inflation (OECD nations)[b]	2.2	4.5	9.9	6.5

Source: Developing Countries: *International Financial Statistics* (various issues), Consumer Price Index; OECD nations: *Economic Outlook* (various issues), Consumer Price Index.
[a] Selected developing countries excluding those with recent histories of chronic, acute, or runaway inflation.
[b] World inflation is the weighted average inflation rate for twenty-one OECD countries including the U.S., which fell steadily from 7.5 percent in 1982 to 4.2 percent in 1985.

1973 did inflation rates in LDCs (again, apart from the "outliers" in Table

13–2) tend to exceed those in developed countries. This pattern has been
documented by Arnold Harberger of the University of Chicago in a comparison of twenty-eight developing and sixteen industrial countries for the period
1952–1976, and also in Table 13–3 for a comparison of twenty-three developing countries and the twenty-one industrial countries of the Organization
for Economic Cooperation and Development (OECD).[4]

Another interesting observation can be drawn from Table 13–3. It is clear
from the last row that world inflationary history from 1952 through 1984
was characterized by four distinct periods. For convenience we will take the
weighted inflation rates in industrial countries of the OECD as our measure
of "world" inflation. In the first period, from 1952 to 1966, annual inflation
in both industrial countries and most LDCs was held to little more than 2
percent. In the second period (1967 to 1972) inflation almost everywhere
surged to nearly 6 percent. In the third period (1973 to 1981) the pace of
world inflation had accelerated strongly, rising to almost 10 percent by 1979.
Finally, in the fourth period, world inflation decelerated to 6.5 percent in
1982 to 1984, still well above the rates prevailing in the two decades after
1952. Inflation tended to be somewhat less in LDCs relative to industrial
nations in the first two periods and somewhat more in the last two periods.
However, what is more striking is the similarity of inflation rates within each
period between the more "typical" LDCs and the industrial countries, as
well as the significant change in the rhythm of inflation among the four
periods. It seems reasonable to conclude from these patterns that all countries were co-participants in a common process of world inflation, made possible until 1982 by a significant acceleration in the growth of the world
money supply (a weighted average of the growth rates of money supply in
different nations)[5] in a world of largely fixed exchange rates, or at best intermittent "dirty" floating rates.[6]

Virtually all LDC economies are **open economies,** i.e., they depend significantly on international trade. Given the acceleration of inflation in the
industrial countries from 1973 to 1981, we shall see that it is reasonable to
conclude that both imported inflation, as well as the homegrown variety, are
responsible for accelerated inflation in LDCs as a group since 1973.

4. Arnold C. Harberger, "A Primer on Inflation," *Journal of Money Credit and Banking* 10,
no. 4 (November 1978): 505–21.
5. The International Monetary Fund now computes and publishes figures on the "world
money supply," with weights assigned to different countries on the basis of relative size of economies. The annual growth in the world money stock rose from less than 3 percent in the fifteen
years before 1967, when world inflation was but 2 percent, to 12.5 percent in the period 1972 to
1976, when world inflation accelerated to nearly 10 percent.
6. Countries employing floating exchange rates allow the value of their currency to fluctuate
according to relative supply and demand for that currency in world markets. Countries employing a fixed exchange rate system establish a set value for their currency in terms of one of the
major currencies used in world trade, usually the U.S. dollar. Thus, Mexico's currency was
defined as 22 pesos to one U.S. dollar at the beginning of 1982. A fixed exchange rate will
usually be maintained for as long as a country can defend the rate. When that is no longer possible, a new exchange rate is chosen and fixed to some higher (or lower) value. For example, the
Mexican peso was devalued to a new fixed rate of 29 pesos to one U.S. dollar in February 1982,
and later (September 1982) to 60 pesos to one U.S. dollar.

Chapter 12 identified a number of problems involved in the use of conventional taxes, such as income and sales taxes, for mobilizing public-sector savings. One significant form of taxation available for this purpose was discussed only briefly: inflation. Governments from the time of the Roman Empire have recognized inflation as an alternative means of securing resources for the state. All that is required is that the stock of money be expanded at a sufficiently rapid rate to result in increases in the general price level, and that people be willing to hold some money balances even as the value of these holdings decline. Inflation then acts as a tax on money holdings. At 15 percent inflation the annual tax on currency is 13 percent, and at 40 percent inflation the tax is 29 percent.[7] These are higher annual tax rates than any country has ever managed to impose successfully on any physical asset, such as housing, automobiles, or equipment. Under extremely high rates of inflation, as in the German hyperinflation in 1922 to 1923 or the Bolivian inflation of 1985, households attempt to reduce holdings of money balances to virtually nothing. However, except during runaway inflation, because money is so convenient as a means of exchange and unit of accounts, people will always hold some money balances even if they must pay fairly heavy inflation taxes for the convenience.

Difficulties in collecting conventional taxes, the apparent ease of collecting inflation taxes, the convenience properties of money balances, and the view that inflation taxes are progressive (richer people hold higher money balances) have led many policymakers and economists to view inflation as a desirable means of development finance. During the 1950s and 1960s the influential United Nations Economic Commission for Latin America saw moderate inflation as a means of "greasing the wheels" of development, forcing savings from holders of money balances and transferring such savings to governments that were strapped for investment resources. Accordingly, much effort was expended in the search for what was viewed as an "optimal" rate of inflation for developing societies: the rate that maximizes tax collections, including both conventional taxes and inflation taxes.

Clearly implementation of such a forced-savings strategy will tend to curtail private investment, since some of the inflation tax will come out of money balances that would have been used for investment in the private sector. However, proponents of tax maximization through inflation assumed explicitly that the government's marginal propensity to invest out of infla-

---

7. Say the nominal value of money balances at the beginning of a year is M_n, equal to the real value, M_r. Now if price inflation proceeds at a rate, p per year, then after one year the real value of money balances M'_r would be

$$M'_r = M_r/(1 + p).$$

The tax on these balances is $T = M'_r - M_r$ and the tax rate is $t = T/M_r$. So

$$t = (M'_r - M_r)/M_r = \frac{1}{1 + p} - 1 = p/(1 + p).$$

If $p = 40$ percent, $t = p/(1 + p) = 29$ percent.

tion taxes exceeded that of the private sector, and that the government would invest in real assets as productive as the private investment it displaced. Therefore, it was thought, forced-savings strategies would never reduce total investment.

Two implicit assumptions lay behind the argument that the forced-savings strategy would improve economic welfare in LDCs. Collections of conventional taxes were believed to be highly responsive to inflationary growth, i.e., the revenue elasticity of the conventional tax system with respect to nominal income growth is greater than one. And efficiency losses from inflation taxes were thought to be less than efficiency losses from use of conventional taxes to increase government revenues. Indeed, it can be shown that under circumstances where (1) a government's marginal propensity to invest out of inflation taxes is unity or greater, (2) the revenue elasticity of the tax system is also unity or greater, and (3) the marginal efficiency costs of inflation taxes are less than those for explicit taxes, the growth-maximizing rate of inflation may be as high as 30 percent. However, a number of analysts have argued that these assumptions are so far divorced from economic realities in LDCs as to undermine severely, if not demolish, the case for forced savings through inflation.

First, there is little evidence that governments anywhere have a marginal propensity to invest out of inflation taxes that is near unity; recall Chapter 12's discussion of the Please effect. In order for tax-maximization through inflation to stimulate growth, governments' marginal propensity to invest would have to rise with inflation. Research by George von Furstenberg of the IMF and others finds no support at all for even the weakest form of this hypothesis. Second, the net result of even moderate inflation on a government's total revenues (conventional taxes plus inflation taxes) may actually be to decrease the government's ability to expand total investment. This may easily occur if the revenue elasticity of the tax structure is less than unity, as is the case in many, but not all, LDCs (see Chapter 12). In such cases growth in collections from conventional taxes lag well behind nominal GNP growth. Particularly in the early stages of an inflationary process, part of the higher inflation tax collections will be offset by a decline in the real value of conventional tax collections. Third, available evidence suggests that once inflation exceeds 2 percent per annum the incremental efficiency losses from inflation taxes tend strongly to outweigh those from conventional taxes.[8] And it is well to note that since 1973, typical inflation rates in LDCs have been far above 2 percent (Table 13–2).

At best then, government mobilization of resources through inflation is a knife-edged strategy. Inflation rates must be kept high enough to yield substantial inflation taxes, but not so high to cause holders of liquid assets to undertake wholesale shifts into real assets in order to escape the tax. Inflation rates must be kept low enough so that collections from conventional taxes do not lag far behind growth in nominal income and so that efficiency losses from inflation do not greatly exceed efficiency losses from higher conven-

8. George M. von Furstenberg, "Inflation, Taxes, and Welfare in LDCs," *Public Finance* 35, no. 2 (1980): 700–701.

tional tax revenues. Paradoxically, then, the inflation tax device can work best where it is needed the least: in those countries having tax systems that are most responsive to growth in overall GDP and which involve low efficiency costs. Countries with revenue-elastic tax systems do not need to resort to inflation in an attempt to finance expanded government investment. In this sense tax reform can be seen as a substitute for inflationary finance, but not the other way around.

Inflation as a Stimulus to Investment

The forced-savings doctrine was not the only argument employed in favor of purposeful inflation. For more than fifty years some economists have argued that even in industrial countries rising prices can act as a stimulus to private business enterprise, as inflation was thought helpful in drawing labor and capital out of declining sectors of the economy and into dynamic ones. If true for industrial societies then, it was reasoned, the argument might apply with special force in developing countries, where rigidities, bottlenecks, and immobilities were such that resources were particularly likely to be trapped in low productivity uses. Inflation, it was argued, would help to speed up the reallocation of labor and capital out of traditional or subsistence sectors into the modern sectors with the greatest development potential. Thus moderate inflation was not only seen as inevitable, but desirable: a progressive government would actively seek some target rate of inflation, perhaps as high as 10 percent, in order to spur development.

Experience with development since 1950 strongly suggests that some inflation is indeed inevitable in developing societies seeking rapid growth in per-capita income: factors of production are relatively immobile in the short run, and imbalances and bottlenecks in supply do develop in spite of the most careful planning. However, deliberate use of sustained inflation to spur development is likely to achieve the desired results only under a limited set of circumstances.

First, if inflation is the result of deliberate policy or can otherwise be anticipated, then in a sustained inflationary process the approaching rise in prices will cause individuals and firms to adjust their expectations of inflation. To the extent that the inflation is anticipated the supposed beneficial effects will never occur; people will have already taken them into account in their decision-making.[9] For industrial societies, it would be difficult, at least for an economist, to accept the idea that behavior does not ultimately adjust to expectations of inflation. In developing countries, where all markets, including that for information, tend to be more imperfect than in developed countries, it might be argued that firms and individuals are less efficient in collecting and using information, including that pertinent to formation of price expectations. Thus inflation may not be fully foreseen throughout the economy, and consequently rising prices may result in some stimulus to development in the short term. But it should be recognized that over the

---

9. This observation dates at least as far back as the early 1930s, to the Swedish economist Knut Wicksell. It contains the germ of the idea behind the rational-expectations school of thought of the 1970s and 1980s.

longer run a successful policy of deliberate inflation depends on people's not understanding the policy.

Second, the argument that deliberate inflation enhances private-sector performance overlooks the effects of inflation on risk-taking. Inflation increases the riskiness of all investment decisions. Suppose that businesses can anticipate inflation with a margin of error of plus or minus 20 percent of the actual rate. (If the margin of error is wider the effects about to be described will be more pronounced.) If inflation has been running at 5 percent per year, there may be a general expectation that it will settle within the range of 4 to 6 percent in the near future. But if inflation has been running at substantially higher rates, say, 30 percent, then expectations of future inflation may rationally be in the much broader range of 24 to 36 percent. The entrepreneur therefore faces far higher levels of uncertainty in planning investments and production. The more unsure he is concerning future returns and future uncertainties, the more he is likely to reduce his risks. Investments with long lives (long gestation periods) tend to be more risky than those with short lives. Thus inflation tends to reduce private-sector investment in projects with a long-term horizon, with the inhibiting effects rising with the rate of inflation. Unfortunately these are often precisely the types of investments most likely to involve high payoffs in terms of income growth for society as a whole.

Finally, inflation may severely curtail private-sector investment by constricting the flow of funds to the organized financial system if nominal interest rates are not allowed to rise as rapidly as the expected rate of inflation. As we shall see in the next sections, such situations are typical under strategies of shallow financial development.

In any case, many of the arguments developed in favor of deliberate inflation may have been little more than efforts to rationalize failure of many governments (particularly in Latin America from 1950 to 1975) to bring inflation under control. In most cases inflation in developed and developing countries has been a consequence of policy miscalculation or economic dislocations (oil prices shocks, agricultural disasters, and so on) than a consciously chosen instrument of economic growth. Some reflective observers of inflationary dynamics, such as Albert Hirschman, have maintained that inflation, in Latin America at least, is not usually the outcome of a systematic set of choices designed to promote growth and other policy objectives. Rather, inflation usually represents the consequences of governmental temporizing, of postponing difficult decisions that might shatter fragile consensus in governments with sharply divided constituencies.[10] Measures to increase collections from conventional taxes, or to reduce government spending on programs enacted at the behest of powerful vested interests, are examples of such difficult decisions. Avoiding such stabilizing changes is tantamount to choosing inflation, in the hopes that at some point in the future a more enduring coalition of constituencies can be assembled to directly confront difficult issues. Seen this way, inflation thus results not by design but by default.

10. Albert O. Hirschman, *Journeys Toward Progress: Studies of Economic Policy-Making in Latin America* (New York: Twentieth Century Fund, 1963), pp. 208–9.

The concept of real interest rates is central to the understanding of the implications of financial policy for growth and development. Interest rates may be viewed as prices of financial assets. The **nominal interest rate** on loans is the stated rate agreed between lender and borrower at the time of contracting a loan. The nominal rate of interest on deposits is the rate offered to savers at the time the deposit is made. The nominal rate is defined as an obligation to pay (on loans) or a right to receive (on deposits) interest at a fixed rate regardless of the rate of inflation. Currency, which is debt of the central bank but a financial asset for currency-holders, bears a *nominal* interest rate of zero. In some countries, such as Indonesia, Turkey, and South Korea, interest is paid on demand deposits, but typically this asset receives a nominal return of zero. Time deposits (including savings accounts) always bear positive nominal interest rates, ranging from as high as 30 percent in Indonesia in 1974 (for deposits committed for a two-year term) to as low as 4 percent in Ghana in the early 1970s. When an enterprise borrows from a commercial bank, the interest rate it agrees to pay is quoted in nominal terms, that is, independent of any changes in the general level of prices. Because costs are incurred in intermediating between savers and investors, the nominal lending rates must exceed nominal deposit rates or financial intermediaries will operate at a loss. However, in some countries, governments have, as a part of broader anti-inflationary programs, deliberately set lending rates below deposit rates and have subsidized banks to cover their losses, as in Korea (1960s) and Indonesia (1968 to 1980).

Nominal interest-rate levels—those quoted by banks on loans and deposits—are often subjected to maximum ceilings imposed by governments. For example, usury laws and conventions throughout much of the history of the United States limited nominal interest rates that could be charged on loans both to private citizens and the government. Similar laws have operated in developing countries. Also, several organized religions support limitations on nominal rates to limit usury, adding moral force to usury conventions.

Nominal interest rates are significant for financial development because the nominal rate governs the height of the *real* interest rate. The **real interest rate** is the nominal interest rate adjusted for inflation, or more precisely, the inflation rate expected by the public. Consider two depositors in different countries in otherwise identical circumstances, except that in one country the inflation rate is expected to be 5 percent and in the other 10 percent. If both receive nominal interest rates of 6 percent, then the real rate of interest in the first case is a positive 1 percent, and in the second case a minus 4 percent. The prospective value of the deposit will rise in the first and fall in the second.

Borrowers as well as depositors respond ultimately to real, not nominal, rates of interest. At sustained high rates of inflation, say, 30 percent per year, borrowers will be quite willing, indeed eager, to pay nominal interest rates of 30 percent per year, for loans then are costless: they can be repaid in money with purchasing power well below that at the time of borrowing. Where legal ceilings do not apply on nominal interest rates they will tend to adjust as expected inflation rises and falls. However, because ceilings on nominal interest rates are widespread and infrequently changed to reflect inflation, the inflation rate in any countries exceeds the nominal interest rate, and negative real interest rates result.

When expected inflation rates are relatively low, the real interest rate can be calculated by merely subtracting the expected rise in prices from the nominal interest rate. Thus for annual inflation (p) below, say, 10 percent,

$$r = i - p, \qquad\qquad [13\text{--}3]$$

where r = real interest rate, i = nominal interest rate, and p = expected inflation. (For all calculations of the real interest rate, we measure interest rates as decimal fractions, not percents—i.e., 0.12 instead of 12 percent.)

Reference to the real interest rate on deposits or other financial instruments can be misleading. At any given time there will be a number of different nominal deposit rates in force in any economy. Nominal interest rates on shorter term (say, three-month) deposits will generally be lower than those on longer term (say, one- or two-year) deposits. Of course the real rate can be computed for any class of deposit. In this chapter it will be convenient to speak of "the" real rate, meaning the one rate that has been selected as an indicator of the structure of deposit rates. And because of difficulties in quantifying the expected inflation rate, the typical surrogate for the expected rate is a weighted average of inflation rates over the recent past (two to four years). "The" real rate of interest on loans is determined in similar fashion: a representative nominal rate on loans is determined in similar fashion: a representative nominal rate on loans is chosen from the multitude of loan rates, and expected inflation is deducted to determine the real rate.

In economies experiencing high inflation and expectations of continued high price-increase rates, Equation 13–3 does not provide a reliable measure of real rates of interest. It then becomes necessary to employ a formula that more accurately recognizes that the corrosive power of inflation on nominal asset values works not instantaneously, but throughout a year:

$$r = (1 + i)/(1 + p) - 1. \qquad\qquad [13\text{--}4]$$

For example, inflation in Brazil in 1980 was near 100 percent but the nominal interest rate on one-year time deposits through most of the year was held to no more than 50 percent. Use of Equation 13–3 would indicate a real interest rate on deposits of a minus 50 percent, assuming that inflation was expected to continue at near 100 percent rates. However, correctly measured to reflect the steady, not precipitous action of inflation on nominal values, the real rate was a minus 25 percent, as calculated below:

$$r = (1 + 0.50)/(1 + 1.00) - 1$$

$$r = -25\%.$$

This means that depositors who placed their money in a time deposit on January 1, 1980, would by the end of the year have suffered a decline in asset value of 25 percent, even though nominal rate was a positive 50 percent. Put another way, depositors paid a tax of 25 percent on their interest-bearing money balances even if they paid no conventional taxes on their nominal interest income on bank deposits.

In cases where conventional income taxes are collected on interest income, the tax (at rate t) must also be deducted from the nominal rate in order to arrive at the real deposit rate net of taxes, r_n:

$$r_n = \frac{[1 + i(1 - t)]}{1 + p} - 1. \qquad [13\text{--}5]$$

Thus with only a 20 percent income tax on interest, Equation 13–5 shows that the real rate of deposit interest in Brazil would be a minus 30 percent.[11] Most countries impose taxes on interest income. A few countries, for example Indonesia and Chile (for some types of interest), do not impose taxes on such income. But most others do, including Colombia, Thailand, Philippines, and Korea.

The discussion of inflation and real interest rates brings us to the point where we may evaluate the role of financial policy in systematic fashion. We shall see that the real interest rate is critical in determining the extent to which the financial system will be able to *mobilize and allocate* savings for development finance. It is important to note that this is not the same thing as saying that higher real interest rates will induce households to save higher proportions of their income than would be the case at lower real interest rates. This would imply that the interest elasticity of savings is greater than zero. But if savings and consumption decisions are responsive to the real rate of interest, the effects of financial policy on income growth will be magnified.

INTEREST RATES AND SAVING DECISIONS

In evaluating the impact of financial policy on economic growth, it is important to distinguish between the implications of real interest rates for consumption-saving decisions on the one hand and for decisions about the uses of savings—including the channels through which savings flow—on the other. Debate over the first question revolves around estimates of the interest elasticity of savings (ε_{sr}); debate over the second is couched in terms of the elasticity of demand for liquid assets with respect to the real interest rate (ε_{lr}).

Where both elasticities are zero, financial policy can only have a minimal role in the development process. Where both elasticities are high and positive, the scope for growth-oriented financial policy can be substantial. Where ε_{sr} is small or zero but ε_{lr} is positive and large, financial policy may still have significant impacts on savings mobilization through the financial system. Virtually all economists can agree that the real interest rate has a significant impact on the demand for liquid assets; that is, with higher real rates, a higher proportion of savings will be channeled through the financial system.

11. Equation 13–5 may also be expressed as follows:

$$r_n = \frac{i(1 - t) - p}{1 + p}.$$

But as of the mid-1980s, there was no real consensus on the responsiveness

of total domestic savings to real interest rates; that is, on the extent to which
higher real rates may stimulate an increase in the ratio of savings to GNP,
although there is a growing body of evidence, based on empirical studies in
both the U.S. and Canada, that the interest elasticity of saving is not zero.

Theories of Saving

Many economists remain skeptical that interest rates, whether nominal or
real, have any significant impact on private-sector consumption behavior in
either developed or developing countries. Since saving is defined as not consuming, economists of this persuasion conclude that interest rates have little
impact on private-sector decisions to allocate income between consumption
and savings: the interest elasticity of saving is held to be zero or insignifi-
cantly small.

Economists in the Keynesian tradition, in both industrial and developing
countries, have been the leading elasticity pessimists. The standard Keynesian short-run consumption function was given in Chapter 11 (Equation
11–4) as

$$S = \text{a} + sY^d,$$ [13–6]

where S = savings, Y^d = current disposable income, a = a constant (a < 1),
and s = the marginal propensity to save ($0 < s < 1$). Neither this absolute-
income hypothesis, nor the closely related relative-income hypothesis of
Equation 11–5 provide any role for the interest rate as a variable affecting
savings behavior. (However, Keynes himself, in Chapters 8 and 9 of his
influential *General Theory,* did assign a minor role to the interest rate as well
as such demographic variables as the age structure of the population.) It was
not until the 1950s that hypotheses of private-sector saving behavior began
to appear in which interest rates figured as determinants of savings behavior.
These hypotheses were the life-cycle hypothesis and the closely related permanent-income hypothesis, both of which had, by the 1980s, been extensively applied in studies of saving in developing countries.

The life-cycle hypothesis, associated with Nobel laureates Franco Modigliani and James Tobin, is founded on the proposition that individuals save in
their working years in order to maintain a stable stream of consumption
during retirement years. According to the theory, net lifetime savings of individuals will be zero in static economies and positive in growing economies.
Under several variants of the life-cycle hypothesis the interest rate is given a
positive role in affecting savings decisions. It is interesting to note that in virtually all versions of the life-cycle hypothesis the level of absolute income (Y)
plays no role in explaining the ratio of saving (S) to income (Y). The life-
cycle hypothesis may be represented as

$$S/Y = \text{a} + b_1H + b_2U + b_3W + b_4D + b_5r,$$ [13–7]

where a = a constant, H = rate of growth of productivity, U = life expectancy
of older people, W = the real stock of non-human capital (wealth), D = the
dependency ratio (proportion of minors and aged persons in the total popu-

lation), and $r =$ the real rate of interest. We expect that b_1, b_2, and b_5 are positive, and b_3 and b_4 are negative. Thus rising productivity growth, life expectancy, and interest rates would all increase the saving ratio, while a rise in the stock of real wealth and a rise in the dependency ratio would decrease it.

The permanent-income hypothesis, first formalized by Milton Friedman, was introduced in Chapter 11 (Equation 11–5).

$$S = a + b_1 Y_p + b_2 Y_t, \qquad [13\text{–}8]$$

where $Y_p =$ permanent income, $Y_t =$ transitory income, and we expect that b_1 is positive but close to zero, and b_2 is less than, but close to, one. Thus most saving that does occur in an economy will come out of transitory income, such as might arise from an unforeseen boom in markets for exported goods. The parameter b_1, which governs the (small) fraction of saving out of permanent income, is in turn a function of several variables, including the real interest rate:

$$b_1 = c_1 \left(\frac{W}{Yp} \right) + c_2 N + c_3 r \qquad [13\text{–}9]$$

where $W/Yp =$ wealth as a proportion of permanent income, $N =$ socioeconomic variables such as family size, life expectancy, etc., and $r =$ real interest rate. The coefficients c_1 and c_2 are presumed negative, and c_3 is positive. Thus a rise in the real interest rate is hypothesized to raise the fraction b_1 of saving out of permanent income.

Research on consumption and saving in both industrial and developing countries has increasingly relied on variants of the permanent-income and life-cycle hypotheses. The results of these studies have conditioned many economists in both developing and developed countries to accept the notion of at least some positive interest elasticity of savings. Studies in the mid-seventies by Michael Boskin and Colin Wright using U.S. data indicate sizable elasticities of savings with respect to real interest rates, between 0.2 and 0.4.[12] Later research by Larry Summers at Harvard and by Canadian scholars suggests that the interest elasticity of saving may be as great as 1.0 or even higher.[13] However, even if these estimates ultimately gain wide acceptance for the United States and Canada, confirmation of similar relationships in the LDC context must await results of further econometric research.

12. Wright's work in 1975 concluded that the interest elasticity of saving was about 0.2, suggesting that a 50 percent increase in real interest rates (say, from 6 percent to 9 percent) would provoke an increase in savings of about 10 percent. Boskin's results, strongly challenged by some economists, suggest an interest elasticity of saving of twice as high, at 0.4. See Colin Wright, "Savings and the Rate of Interest" in *The Taxation of Income from Capital,* Arnold C. Harberger and Martin Bailey, eds., (Washington, D.C.: Brookings Institution, 1969); and Michael J. Boskin, "Taxation, Savings and the Rate of Interest," *Journal of Political Economy* 8b, no. 2, part 2 (April 1978): 3–27.

13. Summers calculated that the long-run interest elasticity of saving might be as high as 2.0. This result was based on simulation using a growth model. More recently, Beach, Boadway, Bruce, et al., found an interest elasticity of saving for Canada of 1.2. See Larry Summers, "Capital Taxation and Capital Accumulation in a Life-Cycle Growth Model," *American Economic Review* 71 (September 1981): 533–44, and Charles Beach, Robin Boadway, and Neil Bruce, "Taxation and Saving": Some Life-Cycle Estimates for Canada" (Ontario, Queens University Working Paper Series, August 1985).

We are left with the conclusion that real interest rates may be expected to have some positive effect on national savings ratios, but credible empirical estimates have yet to be made for developing countries.[14] Positive real interest rates result in somewhat higher savings ratios than negative ones, perhaps by a substantial amount, perhaps by very little.

Interest Rates and Liquid Assets

Whereas the role of the real interest rate in savings-consumption decisions is a matter of some dispute, the role of real interest rates in influencing the demand for liquid assets is rarely questioned, whether in developed or developing countries, by Keynesians or monetarists. Indeed there is evidence that the real interest rate paid on deposits plays an even greater role in liquid asset demand in LDCs than in industrial countries. Furthermore, experience with marked adjustments in real interest rates in Korea (1965), Indonesia (1968 to 1969, 1974 and 1983), Taiwan (1962), and a host of Latin American countries, strongly indicates the significance of real interest rates for growth in money holdings and demand and time deposits (M_2).

Liquid assets, or financial assets in general, represent one channel of savings open to those who have already saved out of past or current income. The demand for liquid assets in economies where nominal interest rates are not allowed to adjust fully to expected rates of inflation, as is true for most LDCs, is typically represented as a function of income, the real interest rate, and the real rate of return available on nonfinancial assets:

$$L/P = d + d_1 Y + d_2 e + d_3 r, \qquad [13–10]$$

where L = liquid asset holdings; Y = real income, i.e., money income deflated by the price level; P = price level; e = real return on nonfinancial assets, and r = the real interest rate on deposits; d is a constant, d_1 and d_3 are expected to be positive, and d_2 negative.

The values for the parameters in Equation 13–10 are readily understandable. As real income (Y) grows, the public will desire to hold more purchasing power in the form of cash, demand, and time deposits, the principal forms of financial assets available in LDCs. In particular, d_1 is positive because at higher levels of real income there will be greater need for higher real levels of liquid balances to carry out transactions and meet contingencies. Clearly, liquid-asset balances furnish a convenience service to asset-holders. In industrial societies with highly developed financial systems and securities markets, it might be reasonable to expect something like a proportional relationship between growth in income and growth in demand for liquid assets. However, in developing countries the demand for liquid assets may, given relative price stability, rise at a faster rate than income because of the paucity of other financial assets in which to hold savings. That is, in developing countries the income elasticity of demand for liquid assets may be expected to exceed unity. Indeed, even for fairly wealthy countries such as

14. For a recent critical discussion on the relationship between savings and the interest rate in LDCs, however, see Alberto Giovanni, "The Interest Elasticity of Savings in Developing Countries," *World Development* 11 (July 1983): 601–8.

Malaysia in the 1970s, the demand for liquid assets grew 1.6 times as fast as did real income. For many Latin American countries the long-run income elasticity of money demand is also often above unity. In such circumstances the rate of increase in the supply of liquid assets (M_2) can exceed the rate of income growth by a substantial margin and price stability can still be maintained.

The sign for d_2, the coefficient of the return on nonfinancial assets, is negative since liquid assets are not the only repository for domestic savings. A range of assets, including nonfinancial assets and, in higher income LDCs, nonliquid financial assets such as securities, is available to savers. Higher returns on these nonliquid assets relative to liquid assets will induce a shift of savings out of the latter.

The coefficient of the real deposit rate, d_3, has a positive sign, for at higher levels of real interest rates the public will be willing to hold larger liquid balances. Where r is negative, holders of all liquid assets pay hidden inflation taxes on their balances. Because higher rates of inflation tax are imposed on non-interest-bearing assets (cash and demand deposits) than upon interest-bearing time deposits, savers will be less willing to hold liquid assets.

TABLE 13–4 Nominal and Real Interest Rates[a] in Selected Asian and Latin American Countries, 1970–1982 (in percent)

	1970	1974	1978	1982
Asia				
Bangladesh	—	6.0	7.0	10.0
	—	(16.9)	(−8.9)	(2.3)
Malaysia	3.5	6.5	5.0	6.0
	(1.6)	(−10.9)	(0.1)	(−0.6)
Thailand	6.0	7.0	7.0	9.0
	(6.1)	(−14.7)	(−2.2)	(3.1)
Pakistan	4.2	6.1	7.6	7.6
	(−1.7)	(−9.3)	(0.7)	(0.4)
South Korea	22.8	14.8	16.7	8.0
	(12.6)	(19.2)	(4.5)	(4.3)
Latin America				
Argentina	8.0	14.8	215.0	221.0
	(−4.8)	(−7.0)	(−84.0)	(−104.0)
Brazil	26.4	23.8	27.0	50.0
	(3.0)	(−3.0)	(−9.3)	(−25.0)[b]
Chile	3.0	117.9	42.0	34.0
	(−22.7)	(−64.0)	(2.1)	(30.0)
Colombia	4.1	9.0	20.0	na
	(−2.5)	(−12.4)	(2.1)	
Peru	5.0	5.0	31.5	55.0
	(−0.7)	(−19.0)	(−22.3)	(−42.6)
Uruguay	6.0	10.5	22.8	24.2
	(−9.9)	(−37.6)	(−30.1)	(−24.9)

Sources: Korea before 1978: David Cole and Yung Chul Park, *Financial Development in Korea 1945–78* (Cambridge, Mass.: Harvard University Press, 1983); Thailand: World Bank, *Thailand: Industrial Development Strategy* (Washington, D.C., 1980), p. 57; Latin American countries before 1978: Vicente Gablis, "Inflation and Interest Rate Policies in Latin Ameria," *International Monetary Fund Staff Papers* 26, no. 2 (June 1977), Tables 1, 4, and 6; all countries after 1978: U.S. Department of Commerce, *Foreign Exchange Trends and Their Implications for the United States* (Washington, D.C., various issues).
[a] Deposit rates on savings deposits, or where rates on savings deposits unavalable, rates on shortest term time deposits. Real rates are in parentheses; na = not available.
[b] Denotes data for 1980, not 1982.

There have been numerous studies of the demand for liquid assets in a
variety of LDCs over the period 1965 to 1985. In these studies estimates of
the elasticity of demand for liquid assets with respect to real interest rates
vary according to differing economic conditions across countries. However,
in country after country the real interest rate has been found to be a powerful
factor in affecting liquid-asset demand. In Colombia, Indonesia, Taiwan,
and Korea, sharp increases in the real interest rate on time deposits (from
negative to positive levels) have resulted in dramatic growth in the volume of
such deposits. Marked increases in real interest rates were engineered
through increases in nominal rates in the mid-1960s in Korea, Taiwan and
Malaysia, and in the late 1960s and again in 1974 and 1983 in Indonesia,
and in Colombia in 1974. In all cases the share of liquid assets in GNP rose
strikingly. On the other hand, through 1979 most Latin American countries
and West African countries allowed real interest rates to remain negative
over long periods (see Tables 13–4 and 13–5). Consequently growth in
demand for liquid assets was minimal in these countries and in most, the
share of liquid assets in GDP either declined or remained constant (see Table
13–1) until after financial reforms were implemented in the early eighties.

TABLE 13–5　Real Interest Rates:[a] Eight West African Countries, 1976–1980[b] (in percent, end of period)

Country	Year				
	1976	1977	1978	1979	1980
Cape Verde	−1.3	−4.7	−6.8	−0.4	−3.5
Gambia	−13.8	−8.9	−5.2	−2.6	−1.8
Ghana	−48.6	−108.9	−61.1	−42.4	−38.1
Ivory Coast	−6.6	−21.9	−7.5	−11.1	−7.1
Liberia	−0.6	−1.3	−0.3	−3.6	−5.8
Mali	−4.8	−21.0	−29.2	na	na
Senegal	4.4	−5.8	2.0	−4.1	−1.3
Sierra Leone	−10.2	−1.4	−3.9	−13.2	−1.1

Source: Sergio Pereira Leite, "Interest-Rate Policies in West Africa," *International Monetary Fund Staff Papers* 29, no. 1 (March 1982): 48–76.
[a] Deposit rates.
[b] na=not available.

FINANCIAL DEVELOPMENT

Shallow Finance and Deep Finance

Policies for financial deepening seek to promote growth in the real size of the
financial system: the growth of financial assets at a pace faster than income
growth. In all but the highest-income LDCs private-sector financial savings
predominantly take the form of currency and deposits in commercial banks,
savings and loan associations, postal savings accounts, and, in some countries, mortgage banks. Thus for most LDCs growth in the real size of the
financial system is primarily reflected in growth in the share of liquid assets
in GDP. By contrast, under **shallow finance** the ratio of liquid assets to GDP

grows slowly or not at all over time, and typically will fall: the real size of the financial system shrinks. Countries able to mobilize large volumes of government savings or foreign savings can sustain high growth rates even under shallow finance policies, although even these countries may find deepening attractive for reasons of employment and income distribution. But for countries where mobilization of government savings is difficult and foreign savings scarce or unwanted, deep finance may be essential for sustained income growth. This is because growth in the share of liquid assets in GDP provides an approximate indication of the banking system's ability to increase its lending for investment purposes. We will see that the hallmark of deep financial strategy is avoidance of negative real interest rates; shallow finance, on the other hand, typically involves sharply negative real interest rates.

Growth in the real size of the financial system enhances its capacity for intermediation: the gathering of savings from diverse private sources and the channeling of these savings into productive investment. The need for financial intermediation arises because savings endowments do not necessarily correspond to investment opportunity. Those individuals with the greatest capacity to save are not usually those with the entrepreneurial talents required for mounting new investment projects. Except in very simple, rudimentary economies, mechanisms are required to channel savings efficiently from savers to enterpreneurs. In rudimentary economies, production in farming, industry, and other activities is small scale, involving traditional technologies. Producers can ordinarily finance most of their modest investment requirements from their current savings, or those of their families (self-finance). Small-scale enterprises employing traditional technologies have an important role to play in development (see Chapter 20). Yet at some stage improvement in productivity (and therefore living standards) in any economy requires adoption of newer technologies. These typically involve lumpy investments that are ordinarily well beyond the financial capacity of all but the wealthiest families. Where enterprise finance is restricted to current family savings, only very wealthy groups can adopt such innovations. Thus heavy reliance on self-finance tends to be associated with both low productivity and, usually, persistent income inequality.

Restriction to self-finance also guarantees that many productive opportunities involving high private and social payoffs will never be seized, because even the resources of the small number of very wealthy are not unlimited. Innovative, smaller-scale investors are not the only groups that fare poorly where financial intermediation is poorly developed; savers are penalized as well. Let us first examine the case where even the most basic financial intermediaries—commercial banks—are absent. Under these circumstances the domestic options open to savers are limited to forms of savings such as acquisition of gold and jewelry, purchase of land and consumer durable goods, or other relatively sterile forms of investment in physical assets. Alternatively, wealthier savers may ship their savings abroad. The common feature of all such investments is that the resources devoted to them are inaccessible to those domestic entrepreneurs who would adopt new technology, begin new firms, or expand production in existing enterprises. Savings in the form of physical assets like gold may be plentiful, as in France or

India, but this type of savings is effectively locked away from investors, or at
a minimum may be trapped in declining sectors of the economy, unable to flow to sectors with the brightest investment prospects.

However, even where financial intermediation is poorly developed, individuals have the option of holding some of their savings in the form of currency. Additions to cash hoards are superior to investment in unproductive physical assets from an economy-wide point of view, since at least this serves to curtail the demand for physical assets, reducing upward pressures on their prices, and thus moderating domestic inflation. Nevertheless, savings held in this form are still relatively inaccessible to investors.

There are now virtually no societies where financial systems are as rudimentary as those sketched above. All LCDs have financial institutions, however embryonic, to serve as intermediaries between savers and investors, even where these intermediaries are limited to commercial banks that accept checking (demand) and time (savings) deposits from savers, for purposes of relending to prospective investors at short term. Intermediation flourishes under deep finance, but under strategies of shallow finance intermediation is constricted and the financial system can contribute little to further the goals of economic growth. Later we will see that shallow finance may have unintended effects on employment and income distribution as well.

Shallow Financial Strategy

Shallow financial policies have a number of earmarks: high legal reserve requirements on commercial banks, pervasive nonprice rationing of credit, and most of all, sharply negative real interest rates. Countries rarely, if ever, have consciously and deliberately adopted strategies of shallow finance. Rather, the repression of the financial system flows logically from certain policies intended to encourage, not hinder, investment.

In developed and developing countries alike, policymakers have often viewed low nominal rates of interest as essential for expansion of investment. Indeed, so long as the supply of investible funds is unlimited, low interest rates will foster all types of investment activities, as even projects with low returns will appear more attractive to investors. In accordance with that observation, and in the belief that low interest rates are particularly essential to assist small enterprises and small farmers, governments have often placed low ceilings on nominal interest rates charged on all types of loans, quite apart from special credit programs involving subsidized credit for special classes of borrowers. Because financial institutions must ultimately cover costs (or else be subsidized by governments), low legal ceilings on nominal loan rates mean low nominal interest rates on deposits as well.

As long as inflation is held in check, low ceilings on nominal loan and deposit interest rates may not retard growth, even when these ceilings are set below the opportunity cost of capital. Indeed the United States over the period 1800 to 1979 managed rather respectable rates of income growth even in the presence of a set of archaic usury laws and other interest rate controls that (particularly before 1970) often involved artificially low, administered ceilings on interest rates. Even so, throughout most of the period before 1979 real interest rates in the United States remained positive; periods in which real interest rates were sharply negative were intermittent and confined to wartime (1812, 1861, 1917–1918, and 1940–1946).[15]

Usury laws and other forms of interest-rate ceilings have been common in developing countries as well, for all the reasons given above plus one more: financial officials in many LDCs, observing gross imperfections in financial markets, have concluded that the market should not be permitted to determine interest rates. Monopoly (or oligopoly) power in financial markets—particularly in commercial banking—does in fact provide ample scope for the banks and other lenders to exercise market power in setting interest rates on loans at levels higher than the opportunity cost of capital.

There are ample observations of gross imperfections in financial systems in LDCs. Barriers to entry into banking and finance often allow a few large banks and other financial institutions to possess an inordinate degree of control over financial markets, allowing them to exercise monopoly power in setting interest rates. Often these barriers are a direct result of government policies, as governments may have prohibited new entrants into the field, adopted such stringent financial requirements for entry that only the very wealthy could amass the needed capital, or reserved permission for entry to political favorites who were attracted to banking and finance largely by the monopoly returns available when entry was restricted.

In this way one set of government policies—entry restrictions—helps give rise to the need for extensive controls on price charged by financial institutions. Typically these controls take the form of interest-rate ceilings imposed to limit the scope for exercise of monopoly power in the financial system. Controls by themselves do not necessarily lead to shallow finance. It is the combination of rigid ceilings on nominal interest rates and inflation that impedes financial development and ultimately retards income growth.

Few economists believe that steeply positive real interest rates are essential for healthy growth in the real size of the financial system. In fact, the Chilean experience with very high real interest rates in 1981 to 1983 strongly suggests the opposite. Indeed there is no widely accepted answer to the question, What level of real interest rates is required for steady development of the financial system? Clearly the required real rate will differ across countries in different circumstances. In some, financial growth may continue even at zero or mildly negative real interest rates; for others, moderately high positive real rates at between 3 and 5 percent may be essential.

In an earlier section we saw that apart from a few Latin American countries and Indonesia, most LDCs were able to keep rates of inflation at or below 5–6 percent prior to 1973. Inasmuch as nominal deposit rates were typically between 3 and 5 percent, real interest rates tended to be slightly positive or only mildly negative. After 1973 inflation accelerated in all countries, including those accustomed to relative price stability, with typical rates (again except for several Latin American countries experiencing acute economic instability) varying from 8 to 16 percent. Because few countries made more than marginal adjustments in nominal deposit rates, real interest rates

15. Steven C. Leuthold, "Interest Rates, Inflation and Deflation," *Financial Analysis Journal* (January–February 1981): 28–51.

after the early 1970s turned significantly negative in many Asian and Latin American nations (see Table 13–4) and sharply negative in those with inflation rates exceeding 25 percent. Negative interest rates were even more common and enduring in some African countries in the period after 1975. Table 13–5 displays real interest rates for eight countries in West Africa. Of this group, only Senegal recorded positive real rates of interest over the period 1976 to 1980, and that was only for two years. And in Ghana the real rate was never more than a minus 42 percent in any year.

When real interest rates turn significantly negative—much more than a minus 3 to 6 percent—then maintenance of low nominal rates for purposes of promoting investment and income growth becomes counterproductive. Inflation taxes on liquid financial assets will bring real growth in the financial system to a halt. Sharply negative real rates lead to shrinkage in the system, as the demand for liquid assets will contract. This tendency is evident from a comparison of Tables 13–1 and 13–4. Countries where real interest rates were only mildly negative, or sharply negative for short periods of time, experienced little or no growth in the real size of their financial systems as measured by the ratio of liquid assets to GDP. These include the Philippines, Colombia, Turkey, Kenya, and India and Sri Lanka before 1977. But where real interest rates have been sharply negative over extended periods of time, as in Argentina, Brazil, Chile until 1976, Ghana, and Uruguay through much of the 1970s and early 1980s, the real size of the financial system has shrunk. Contraction in the real size of the financial system results in a reduction in the real supply of credit, and thus constricts investment in productive assets.

Under such circumstances nonprice rationing of investible resources must occur, and can take many forms. In most LDCs only those borrowers with either the highest quality collateral, the "soundest" social and political connections, or those willing to pay the largest under-the-table inducements to bank officers, will be successful in securing finance from the organized financial system. These criteria do not yield allocations of credit to the most productive investment opportunities.

Negative real interest rates make marginal, low-yielding, traditional types of investment appear attractive to investors. Banks and financial institutions find such projects attractive as well, since they may be the safest and the simplest to finance and involve the most "credit-worthy" borrowers. Thus such undertakings tend to move to the head of the queue of borrowers. Satisfying financial requirements of such investors constricts the pool of resources available to firms having riskier projects offering greater possibilities for high yields. Additionally, in the presence of substantial inflation, interest-rate ceilings discourage risk-taking by the financial institutions themselves, since under such circumstances they cannot charge higher interest rates (risk premia) on promising but risky projects. Also, negative real interest rates are inimical to employment growth, as they make projects with relatively high capital-output ratios appear more attractive than if real interest rates were positive. This implicit subsidy to capital-intensive methods of production reduces the jobs created for each dollar of investment, even as the ability of the financial system to finance investment is shrinking.

Negative real rates of interest tend to lower the marginal efficiency of investment in all of the ways described. In terms of the Harrod-Domar model described in Chapter 3, shallow financial strategies cause higher capital-output ratios. Consequently growth in national income, and therefore, growth in savings, tends to be lower than when real rates are positive. Therefore shallow finance retards income and employment growth even if the interest elasticity of savings is zero. And if savings decisions are responsive to real interest rates, then shallow finance will have even more serious implications for income growth, as the ratio of private savings to GDP will also contract.

Deep Financial Strategies

Deep finance as a strategy has several objectives: (1) mobilizing a larger volume of savings from the domestic economy, that is, increasing the ratio of national savings to GDP (where the interest elasticity of savings is thought to be positive and significant); (2) enhancing the accessibility of savings for all types of domestic investors; (3) securing a more efficient allocation of investment throughout the economy; (4) permitting the financial process to mobilize and allocate savings to reduce reliance on the fiscal process, foreign aid, and inflation.

A permanent move toward policies involving positive real interest rates, or at a minimum avoidance of sharply negative real rates, is the essence of deep finance. In turn this requires either financial liberalization that allows higher nominal rates on deposits and loans, curbing the rate of inflation, or some combination of both.

Given the difficulties involved in securing quick results in reducing inflation to levels consistent with positive real rates of interest, the first step involved in a shift from shallow to deep financial strategies is ordinarily that of raising ceilings on nominal rates for both deposits and loans. In some cases this has required nominal interest rates as high as 30 percent on time deposits (Korea in 1966, Indonesia in 1968 and 1974).[16] In extreme cases of acute inflation the initial step has involved raising ceilings on nominal deposit rates to as much as 50 percent in Argentina and Uruguay in 1976, and to nearly 200 percent in Chile in 1974 (where real interest rates nevertheless remained negative until 1976). As the real rate moves toward positive levels, savers strongly tend to increase their holdings of liquid assets, allowing a real expansion in the supply of credit to investors. Marked increases in flows of savings to financial institutions have been observed when nominal rates were increased substantially, as in Uruguay in 1976, Indonesia in 1968–1969 and 1983, Taiwan and Korea in 1965 (see Tables 13–1 and 13–4). Notable responses have also occurred in countries where mildly negative

16. Ceilings need rarely be increased to the point where they match the *current* rate of inflation. For example, in Indonesia in 1974 the nominal ceiling on two-year time deposits was raised to only 30 percent, even though inflation over the previous twelve months was 42 percent. The increase in nominal rates, coupled with a battery of other measures, convinced depositors that real rates would soon be positive. All that is required is that inflation expected by savers be reduced to levels closer to the nominal deposit rate.

real rates were moved closer to positive levels through increases in nominal
rates: these include India and Sri Lanka after 1977, and Turkey after 1980.

Available evidence suggests that countries that attempt to maintain modestly positive real interest rates over long periods tend to be among those with the highest rates of financial growth. Malaysia and Thailand both experienced steady increases in the real sizes of their financial systems over the period 1960 to 1982. For virtually the entire period real interest rates were positive in both countries, save for 1973 and 1974 when world inflation unexpectedly surged to double-digit numbers. Real rates have been positive in Taiwan almost every year since 1965, and over that span the ratio of liquid asset to GDP has risen to levels characteristic of industrial countries. Nevertheless, one can have too much of a good thing. This is as true for real interest rates as for smoked salmon. One factor contributing to sharply negative real GDP growth rates in Chile in 1982 and 1983 was the emergence of very high real interest rates in 1981 and 1982. The nominal interest rate on loans increased sharply, while at the same time there was a very large and unexpected drop in inflation: the real interest rate soared above 30 percent.[17]

Where finance is deep, inflation tends to be moderate; therefore savers are not subject to persistently high inflation taxes on liquid asset holdings. That being the case they will be less inclined to shift their savings into much more lightly taxed domestic assets such as gold, land, or durable goods, and foreign assets such as currencies or land and securities. Rather, financial resources that otherwise may have been utilized for these purposes flow to the financial system, where they are more accessible to prospective investors. Nonprice rationing of credit, inevitable under shallow finance, will diminish as well. As a result the capacity of the financial system to identify and support socially profitable investment opportunities expands: higher risk, higher yielding investment projects stand a far better chance of securing finance under deep than shallow finance. Growth prospects are accordingly enhanced.

The preceding discussion represents but a sketch of policies designed to promote financial deepening. The focus has been upon the real interest rate on deposits and loans when in fact a variety of other policies may be involved. These include central bank payment of interest on commercial bank reserves, and avoidance of high legal reserve requirements on commercial banks. That positive real interest rates tend to lead to growth in the real size of banking systems is now rarely questioned. Such a development substantially enlarges the real flow of short-term credit, the stock-in-trade of commercial banks. However, investment finance problems do not end with provision of a growing real flow of short-term credit. As economies move to higher levels of per-capita income the patten of investment shifts toward longer horizons. Longer term investment requires longer term finance.

17. Chilean real GDP growth was minus 13.2 percent in 1982, and minus 2.3 percent in 1983. For a comprehensive discussion of the Chilean economic debacle of 1982–1983, see Sebastian Edwards "Stabilization with Liberalization: An Evaluation of Chile's Experiment with Free-Market Policies 1973–1983," *Economic Development and Cultural Change* 27 (September 1985): 224–53.

Commercial banks everywhere are ill-suited for providing substantial amounts of long-term finance, given that their deposits are primarily of a short-term nature.

Therefore as financial and economic development proceeds the need for institutions specializing in longer term finance rises accordingly: insurance companies, investment banks, and ultimately equity markets (stock exchanges) become important elements in financial intermediation. Nevertheless the type of well-functioning commercial bank system that tends to develop under deep finance is almost always a necessary condition for the successful emergence and long-term vitality of institutions specializing in longer term investment finance. Where entry into financial activities is only lightly restricted, longer term financial institutions may appear spontaneously.

But earlier we observed that entry into the financial field is rarely easy, and other factors also often lead to gross imperfections in financial markets. In such circumstances many LDC governments have found intervention essential in order to develop financial institutions specializing in longer term finance. Intervention may take the form of establishment of government-owned development banks and other specializing institutions, to act as distributors of government funds intended as a source of longer term finance, as in Indonesia and Pakistan. In other cases, as in Mexico, Colombia, and Venezuela, governments have provided strong incentives for private-sector establishment of long-term financial institutions. Finally, in other countries governments have sought to create conditions favorable for the emergence of primary securities (stocks and bonds) markets, the source par excellence for long-term finance. In cases where these measures have been undertaken in the context of financial markets with strong commercial banking systems (South Korea, Thailand, Brazil, Mexico), efforts to encourage long-term finance have met with some success. In cases where commercial banking has been poorly developed as a consequence of shallow finance (Ghana, Uruguay before 1976), or where government has sought to "force-feed" embryonic securities markets through tax incentives and other subsidies (Indonesia, Kenya, Turkey), the promotional policies have been less effective.

Informal Credit Markets

The discussion of financial development has dealt with modern credit institutions, the formal market. But in many developing countries an **informal credit market** coexists with modern financial institutions. These markets arise in many forms. In rural India, village moneylenders make loans to local farmers who have no access to commercial banks. In Ghana and other West African countries, market women give credit to farmers by paying for crops in advance of harvest, and they assist their customers by selling finished goods on credit. In South Korea, established lenders literally make loans on the street outside modern banks, justifying their designation as the "curb" market. In much of rural Africa, wealthy family members make loans to less fortunate kin, while all over the developing world there are cooperative arrangements to raise funds and share credit among members. Even in modern economies, pawnbrokers and others give credit outside the formal credit system.

Informal credit is generally financed by the savings of relatively wealthy individuals, such as local landowners, traders, family members who have moved into lucrative jobs or businesses, and the pooled efforts of cooperative societies. But informal lenders may also have access to the formal banking system and borrow there, to relend to customers with no access to banks. How can they do this if the banks cannot? First, because they know their borrowers so well and may have familial, social, or other ties to them, informal lenders face lower risks than distant, large banks that might loan to the same borrowers. They also face lower administrative costs in making loans. Of course, moneylenders do charge very high interest rates, and this is the second reason they coexist with banks, which are often prevented by law from charging rates high enough to cover the risks and costs of loans in small amounts to very small firms and low-income borrowers. Third, and most basically, informal markets thrive in the early stages of development, before modern credit institutions spread much beyond the largest cities and the most creditworthy customers.

As modern credit institutions evolve, especially under deep financial policies, they draw customers and resources from the informal market. First, some of the largest and most creditworthy borrowers from informal lenders eventually qualify as borrowers in the formal market. Second, some moneylenders may themselves establish credit institutions within the informal system. Third, banks begin to attract savings from a wider group of households, some of which had previously directed their savings into informal channels. On all counts, the informal market is likely to shrink in size and coverage, though it is likely to exist in tandem for some time. The process may leave behind several kinds of borrowers, such as small farmers, traders, artisans, and manufacturers, who will still depend on the shrinking informal market for their credit. Competitive, efficient, and varied financial institutions—the kind encouraged by deep financial policies—will have incentives to integrate borrowers into the modern market, reducing the adverse impacts of financial development on those who once depended upon informal credit markets.

MONETARY POLICY AND PRICE STABILITY

We have seen that apart from a limited number of cases in Asia, prior to the 1970s double-digit inflation was largely confined to a few developing countries in Latin America. But by the 1980s inflation had become a serious problem across a wide variety of countries, not only in Latin America but in Africa and Asia as well.

Monetary Policy and Exchange Rate Regimes

Analysis of monetary policy issues cannot be divorced from the type of exchange rate regime used by a country. Exchange rate regimes form a continuum with **fixed exchange rate** systems at one end and **freely floating**

exchange rates (also known as **fully flexible exchange rates**) at the other. Under a fixed exchange rate system (also known as a **pegged exchange rate**), a country attempts to maintain the value of its currency in a fixed relation to another currency, say the U.S. dollar: the value of the local currency is *pegged* to the dollar. This is done through intervention by the country's monetary authorities in the market for foreign exchange, and requires maintenance of substantial **international reserves** (reserves of foreign currencies) usually equivalent to the value of six or more months worth of imports.

For example, consider a country such as Thailand. In September 1986 the Thai currency, the baht, was fixed at an exchange rate of baht 26 to one U.S. dollar. Because the exchange rate, if left to its own devices, would change from day to day to reflect changes in both the demand and supply of Thailand's exports and imports and in capital flows, the Thai government must be prepared to use the nation's international reserves to buy or sell dollars at an exchange rate of 26:1 in order to keep the exchange rate from moving. If, for example, a poor domestic rice crop caused Thailand to increase its food imports in October 1986, the baht/dollar exchange rate would tend to rise, absent any net sales of dollars from Thailand's international reserves.

Under freely floating rates, the authorities simply allow the value of local currency vis-a-vis foreign ones to be determined by market forces. Between the two ends of this continuum (see Figure 13–1) lie a number of intermediate options.[18] Closest to the floating exchange rate option is the **wider band** system, wherein the exchange rate of a country is allowed to float or fluctuate within a predefined band of values, say between twelve pesos to one U.S. dollar and ten pesos per dollar. But when conditions threaten to push the value of the currency beyond the band, the authorities intervene by buying or selling local currency as appropriate to stay within the band. Further along the continuum away from floating rates is the **managed float**, where

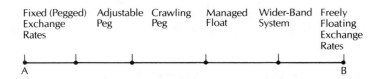

FIGURE 13–1   Continuum of Prototypes of Exchange Rate Regimes. As one moves from point *A* on to the left to point *B* on the right, both the frequency of intervention by domestic monetary authorities and the required level of international reserves tends to be lower. Under a pure fixed exchange rate regime (point *A*) authorities intervene so that the value of the currency vis-a-vis another, say the U.S. dollar, is maintained at a constant rate. Under a freely floating exchange rate regime, authorities do not intervene in the market for foreign exchange, and there is minimal need for international reserves; indeed, there can be no balance of payments deficit.

18. For a full discussion of these and other types of exchange-rate regimes, see John Williamson, *The Open Economy and the World Economy* (New York: Basic Books, 1983) pp. 238–41, or Anne O. Krueger, *Exchange Rate Determination* (New York: Cambridge University Press, 1983) pp. 123–36.

there is no particular exchange rate that the authorities are committed to defend, but where they nevertheless intervene continuously at their discretion. A country with steadily shrinking international reserves might, for example, allow the value of its currency to drift downward against the value of other currencies, i.e., allow the exchange rate against other currencies to rise.

Two other systems are closely related hybrids of fixed and floating rules. The **crawling peg,** used over a long period by Brazil and Colombia, involves pegging the local currency against some other currency, but changing this in gradual, periodic steps to adjust for any differential between the country's inflation rate and the world inflation rate. Closest to a fixed exchange rate system is the **adjustable peg,** involving a commitment by the monetary authorities to defend the local exchange rate at a fixed parity (peg), while reserving the right to change that rate when circumstances require.

The currencies of the major industrial countries have all floated vis-a-vis one another, with occasional intervention by national monetary authorities to prevent very sharp swings in rates. Most LDCs adhere either to the adjustable peg system or the crawling peg. Since in practice both systems are fixed-rate regimes, for purpose of analysis we will focus most of our attention on monetary policy issues arising under fixed exchange rates in small open economies.

Sources of Inflation

In open LDC economies with fixed exchange rates, the rate of monetary expansion is no longer under the complete control of domestic monetary authorities. Rather, countries with fixed exchange rates may be viewed as sharing essentially the same money supply, because the money of each can be converted into that of the others at a fixed parity.[19] Under such circumstances, the stock of money *(M)* is by definition the sum of two components: the amount of domestic credit of the banking system that is outstanding *(DC)*, and the stock of international reserves of that country *(IR)*, measured in terms of domestic currency. There is therefore a domestic and an international component of the money supply. Thus we have

$$M = DC + IR. \qquad [13\text{--}11]$$

Changes in the domestic money stock can occur either through expansion of domestic credit or by monetary movements that lead to changes in international reserves. That is,

$$\Delta M = \Delta DC + \Delta IR. \qquad [13\text{--}12]$$

Under fixed exchange rates a central bank of any small country can control *DC,* the domestic component, but it has only very limited control over *IR,* the international component. Under such circumstances LDCs that

19. This section draws substantially on recent syntheses of monetary and international economics by Arnold C. Harberger. See his "A Primer on Inflation," *Journal of Money Credit and Banking* 10, no. 4 (November 1978): 505–21; and his "The Inflation Syndrome" (paper presented in The Political Economy Lecture Series, Harvard University, March 19, 1981).

attempt to keep the rate of domestic inflation below the world inflation rate (through restrictive policies on domestic credit) will be unable to realize this goal. If, fueled by monetary expansion abroad (growth in the world money supply), world inflation initially is running in excess of domestic inflation, the prices of internationally traded goods will rise relative to those of domestic nontraded goods.[20] Imports will fall, exports will rise, and the balance of payments of the LDC will move toward surplus, causing a rise in international reserves. Thus the foreign components of the money stock will rise. This is tantamount to "importation of money" and will eventually undo the effort to prevent importation of world inflation. Again, a small country on fixed exchange rates can do little to maintain its inflation rate below that of the rest of the world. For very open LDCs with few restrictions on the movement of goods and capital into and out of the country, the adjustment to world inflation can be very rapid (less than a year). For less open countries with substantial restrictions on international trade and payments, the process takes longer, but the outcome is inevitable under fixed exchange rates.

The fact that financial policy for stabilization in LDCs under fixed exchange rates in heavily constrained by international developments is sometimes taken to mean that changes in the domestic component of the money stock have no impact on prices in LDCs adhering to fixed exchange rates. On the contrary, excessive expansion in money and credit will surely result in domestically generated inflation that, depending on the rate of expansion, can for a time be well in excess of world inflation rates. However, such a situation cannot continue for long, as excess money creation will spill over into the balance of payments via increased imports, leading to a drain on international reserves and, ultimately, inability to maintain the fixed exchange rate. As reserves dwindle the country can no longer defend its exchange rate and devaluation becomes inevitable.[21] Inflation can therefore be transmitted to LDCs through the working of the world economy or can be generated by domestic developments.

Very few developing countries have ever employed floating exchange rates (point B on the continuum in Figure 13–1). A floating exchange rate regime would allow countries to insulate themselves from world inflation. Under such a system, the rise in world prices attendant upon world inflation would initially favor exports from the country and discourage imports. As a consequence, the current account of the country's balance of payments would improve (see Chapter 15), international reserves would rise, and the exchange rate would soon appreciate (fewer pesos would be required to buy dollars, for instance). The appreciation in the country's exchange rate would cancel out external price increases, preventing the importation of world inflation.

Under any exchange rate regime, domestically generated inflation may result from excessive increases in domestic credit from the banking system to

20. The above is but one of several mechanisms that led to changes in international reserves sufficient to thwart efforts by LDCs to insulate themselves from world inflation. See Harberger, "A Primer" and "The Inflation Syndrome."

21. Imports controls are frequently used to stem the drain of reserves and avoid devaluation for a time. But import controls engender another set of distortions and inefficiencies—explored in Chapter 16—that eventually require more drastic measures, including devaluation.

either the public or the private sector. Budgetary deficits of the central government must be financed by borrowing. The embryonic nature of money and capital markets in most LDCs generally means that governments facing deficits must ordinarily resort to borrowing from the central bank, a process equivalent to direct money creation via the printing press. The result is a direct addition to the reserve base of the monetary system, an increase in so-called high-powered money. It is important, however, to recognize that not all budgetary deficits are necessarily inflationary. We have seen that a growing economy will be characterized by a growing demand for liquid assets, including money. Moderate budgetary deficits year after year, financed by the central bank, can help to satisfy this requirement without leading to inflation. In general the money stock may expand at least as fast as the growth in real income, with little or no inflationary consequences.[22]

For a country like Peru, where liquid assets are around 28 percent of GDP (see Table 13–1), even a small deficit can result in substantial inflation. For a country such as Malaysia, where the money stock is about 100 percent of GDP, a much larger deficit would be consistent with price stability. In Peru a noninflationary deficit might have to be as low as 0.5 percent of GDP; for Malaysia a budgetary deficit financed by bank credit might be as high as 2.5 percent of GDP with little inflationary consequences.[23] In general, deficits of around 1 percent of GDP or less are not inconsistent with price level stability in typical LDCs. But given a stable demand for liquid assets, much larger deficits will clearly be inflationary.

Use of bank credit to finance government deficits has not been the only source of inflationary monetary expansion in LDCs. Sometimes excessive growth of credit to the private sector has played the most significant role in domestically generated inflationary processes. Nevertheless, as a general rule, inflation rates for a particular LDC that are much in excess of world inflation have usually been traceable to budgetary deficits.

It is evident then that for LDCs attempting to maintain fixed exchange rates, efforts to avoid inflation rates in excess of world inflation must primarily be a matter of fiscal policy, not monetary policy. If budget deficits are not held to levels consistent with world inflation, even very deft deployment of monetary policy instruments will be unable to prevent rapid inflation, devaluation, or both. There is still a role for monetary policy in LDCs, but that role must be largely passive. Resourceful use of monetary policy can help by not making things worse, and also by moderating strong inflationary

22. Earlier we saw that liquid assets are normally between 35 and 50 percent of GDP in most LDCs, or equivalent to roughly four to six months of income. Thus the public is generally willing to hold this much in money balances. A deficit of 2 percent of GDP financed by money creation would add only marginally to the money supply, and may easily be accepted by the public. But a deficit of 8 percent of GDP would increase the stock of money by an amount equal to one more month of income, or by an amount more than the public would be willing to hold (unless nominal interest rates on deposits are greatly increased). The excess would spill over into the higher prices.

23. A deficit of 0.5 percent of GDP in Peru would, if financed by the central bank, cause the stock of money to grow by 1.8 percent, a rate well below the rate of real income growth in that country from 1960 to 1980. A deficit of that size could be financed, while still allowing substantial growth (5 to 6 percent) in credit to the private sector. A deficit of 2.5 percent of GDP in Malaysia, financed also by credit to the government, would also lead to growth in the money stock of only 1.5 percent, clearly well below expansion required to fuel inflation.

pressures until the budget can be brought under control, provided the latter is done fairly quickly.

We have seen that monetary factors are causes of inflation in both fixed and floating exchange rate countries. In the case of fixed exchange rates, both world monetary expansion and domestic monetary expansion generate inflation; in flexible exchange rate countries, inflation arises from domestic monetary sources. But thus far, no mention has been made of so-called non-monetary causes of inflation. It seems plausible that internal and external shocks, such as those arising from widespread crop failure in the domestic economy or a drastic increase in prices of imported energy, could have an important effect on inflation in countries suffering such shocks. This is true, but the mechanism whereby non-monetary factors may initiate or worsen inflation needs to be clearly portrayed.

Non-monetary disturbances may indeed precipitate policy reactions that lead to domestic monetary expansion large enough to accommodate higher relative prices of food or oil, and large enough to cause inflation. In the absence of accommodating monetary expansion in the face of such shocks, inflation can be contained, but at some cost. In practice failure to allow the money supply to expand to accommodate higher relative prices of important goods leads to increases in unemployment that most governments find unacceptable. Therefore, as a matter of course, governments in such cases usually do attempt to allow monetary expansion sufficient to avoid unwanted consequences for employment. But it is important to remember that however advisable monetary accommodation may be on social and employment grounds, expansion in the money stock is required to fuel inflation, whatever the external or internal factors may be that precipitated the expansion. But this truth, known for centuries, is often incorrectly interpreted to mean that non-monetary factors cannot "cause" inflation. They can, but only through expansion of the national, and international, stock of money, or both.

Controlling Inflation through Monetary Policy

The array of available instruments of anti-inflationary monetary policy in developed countries include: (1) open market operations,[24] wherein the central bank can directly contract bank reserves by sales of government securities; (2) increases in legal reserve requirements of banks, so that a given volume of reserves will support a lower stock of money (and reduce the credit expansion multiplier as well); (3) increases in rediscount rates, so that commercial bank borrowing from the central bank becomes less attractive; and (4) moral suasion, wherein the exhortations of monetary authorities are expected to lead to restraint in bank lending policies.

24. Open-market operations are used as an instrument of monetary policy in countries with well-developed financial markets. When the Federal Reserve System in the United States or a central bank in Europe wants to curtail the growth of the money supply, it sells government securities (bonds, bills) in the open market. When a buyer pays for the securities, the effect is to directly reduce the reserves of the banking system, since the funds are transferred from commercial bank deposits or household cash holdings to the account of the Federal Reserve. When the Federal Reserve wants to expand the money supply, it buys securities on the open market, directly adding to bank reserves.

For virtually all developing countries the first instrument—open market operations—is not available for inflation control. Securities markets are typically absent or not sufficiently well developed to allow exercise of this powerful and flexible instrument, although some countries, including the Philippines and Brazil, have utilized this tool to a limited degree. The other three monetary-policy instruments are employed, with varying degrees of success, in developing countries. In addition developing countries often resort to two other tools employed only infrequently in developed countries: (5) credit ceilings imposed by the central bank upon the banking system; and (6) adjustments in allowable nominal rates of interest on deposits and loans. Governments attempting to control inflation usually resort to all of these instruments, often together but sometimes separately, occasionally successfully as in Argentina in 1985 (see boxed example), and Indonesia in 1967 and 1968, and often unsuccessfully, as in Bolivia in 1985.

Successful Short-Term Financial Stabilization: The Role of Expectations

Governments do not always succeed in attempts to arrest inflation, whether of the chronic, acute, or runaway variety. Bolivia and Peru continued to struggle with runaway inflation throughout 1985, and Brazil unveiled new measures in February 1986 to curtail 227 percent inflation. The most recent country to enjoy marked short-term success in controlling hyperinflation was Argentina in 1985, where inflation was nevertheless still 675 percent for the year as a whole. But virtually all the inflation occurred in July 1985, before a new economics minister, Juan Sourrouille, conceived a bold stabilization program called the Austral Plan.

As in many previous Argentine stabilization programs, prices, wages, and the official exchange rate were frozen. In addition, the austral program involved a doubling of tax revenues and sharp cuts in spending. As a result, the Argentine Treasury experienced a rare surplus from August to October. But most important, President Raul Alfonsin vowed in July to print no more new money. Previous presidents had made the same promise over the past two decades; the difference in 1985 was that President Alfonsin and Mr. Sourrouille made themselves credible by taking difficult measures to slash the budget deficit. In other words, the government sought to reverse inflationary expectations.

The short-term results in Argentina were dramatic. Within three months, the annual rate of inflation fell sharply, from 2,340 percent in June to 27 percent in September. Whether or not short-term success in economic stabilization can be carried over to the longer term remains to be seen. However, once again it has been made clear that rampant inflation may be brought under control only when painful steps are taken to bring budgetary deficits, and hence money creation, under control. But for such bold measures to work, they must work fast, for few governments can withstand the pressures for relief from austerity for very long. The Argentine experience suggests such measures work fast only when the public views promises made by political leaders as credible.

All central banks require commercial banks to immobilize a portion of their deposits in the form of legal reserves that may not be lent to prospective customers. For example, legal reserve requirements for Indonesian and Malaysian banks in the late 1970s were expressed as 30 percent of deposits in domestic currency in the former and 20 percent of all deposits in the latter. Thus in Malaysia, for example, banks were required to add 20 units of currency to reserves for every 100 units of deposits. These figures are not too far out of line with legal reserve requirements in most industrial nations, where reserve ratios of 15 percent for demand deposits and 5 percent for time deposits are not uncommon.

Increases in reserve requirements can be used to help moderate inflation. An upward adjustment in reserve requirements works in two ways: it reduces the stock of money that can be supported by a given amount of reserves; and it reduces the money multiplier. The first effect induces banks to contract credit outstanding; the second reduces the growth in the money stock possible from any future increment to reserves.[25] Changes in legal reserve requirements are usually employed only as a last-ditch measure. Even small changes in the required ratio of reserves to deposits can have a very disruptive impact on commercial bank operations unless banks are given sufficient time to adjust.

Credit Ceilings

In some countries, particularly Indonesia from 1947 to 1983 and at various times Malaysia, Sri Lanka, and Chile, credit ceilings have been used as supplementary instruments of inflation control. Indeed the International Monetary Fund often requires countries seeking balance-of-payments support to adopt credit ceilings as a prerequisite for IMF assistance. General ceilings of domestic credit expansion represent a useful method of controlling growth in domestic components of the money supply. Credit ceilings, however, do not allow full control of money supply growth in the overwhelming majority of LDCs operating under fixed-exchange rate regimes, since the monetary authorities have no control over foreign components of the money supply. Nevertheless general credit ceilings can sometimes be usefully deployed in combating inflation in countries not experiencing major imbalances in external payments. Unfortunately ceilings work best where they are needed the least, since countries attempting to deal with chronic inflation are usually the same countries that are experiencing the most destabilizing changes in their international reserve positions. Finally, general credit ceilings are unlikely to have much effect on inflation unless the government simultaneously takes steps to reduce the budgetary deficits that—except in major oil

25. In its simplest form the money multiplier (m) can be expressed as:

$$m = c + 1/c + k$$

where c = the ratio of currency outside banks to deposits and k = the ratio of reserves to deposits. If k is raised, then m falls.

exporting LDCs—are typically the root causes of chronic, acute, and especially runaway inflation.

For example, consider the case of a country with a money supply to GDP ratio of 25 percent, in which inflation has recently surged to 30 percent per annum. In such a country the monetary authorities may have calculated that restriction of domestic credit expansion to 15 percent may be required to push the inflation rate down to 12 percent (the exact limit will depend on the income and interest elasticity of the demand for liquid assets, the projected growth in real income, and other factors). But suppose that for the coming year the budget deficit is projected at 3 percent of GDP, a level typical in developing countries experiencing chronic inflation. In order to finance this deficit, credit from the banking system to the government would have to increase by 3 percent of GDP. But an increase of credit to the government of 3 percent of GDP would, with a money to GNP ratio of 25 percent, translate into credit growth of 12 percent. Thus of the 15 percent limit on credit expansion, the government would take 80 percent of allowable credit expansion, leaving little for the private sector. In such instances government deficits are said to "crowd out" the private sector from credit sources. Initially the monetary authorities may be able to resist private-sector demands to increase the ceiling, but 3 percent growth in private credit in the face of even 12 percent inflation translates into a decline of nearly 9 percent in the level of real credit available. The consequences of adhering to a 15 percent ceiling would therefore be severe disruption in the private sector, including rising unemployment and low real income growth. Few governments anywhere are able to withstand such pressures for long, and inevitably the ceiling is raised to accommodate some or all of private-sector credit requirements. Therefore successful use of ceilings on credit expansion ultimately depends primarily on fiscal, not monetary, policy.

Countries often supplement general credit ceilings with specific ceilings on lending to particular sectors of the economy. Indonesia attempted to fine-tune credit controls in this way from 1974 to 1983, with poor results. The system of ceilings was so detailed and cumbersome that domestic banks were unable to come close to exhausting the ceilings. Excess reserves arose. The banks had little choice but to place their excess reserves in deposits overseas, primarily in banks in Singapore. As a result, many domestic firms in Jakarta were forced to seek credit from Singapore banks, which held well over a billion dollars of deposits from Jakarta banks that might have lent to domestic firms at a lower rate, in the absence of credit ceilings.

Interest Rate Regulation and Moral Suasion

In most industrial countries the central bank can influence interest rates by variations in the interest rate (the rediscount rate) charged on central bank lending to commercial banks. Otherwise interest rates on deposits and loans are largely left to market forces. Among developing countries very few, including Singapore and Chile (both since 1975) have left interest rate determination to market forces, although in 1981 both Brazil and Turkey experimented with freeing most interest rates from government controls and Indonesia allowed most interest rates to be market-determined from mid-1983.

However, for reasons discussed earlier few LDCs are willing to allow interest rates to be determined in the market, largely because money markets are not competitive.

In the large majority of LDCs where loan and deposit rates are regulated, the monetary authorities have sometimes enacted upward adjustments in regulated interest rates as part of an overall anti-inflationary package. Since 1973 use of such interest rate adjustments has been common in Latin America,[26] and increases in deposit rates and loan rates were major elements in stabilization programs in Korea and Taiwan in the mid-1960s, and in Indonesia in both 1968 and 1974. The objective in each case is twofold: to stimulate the demand for liquid assets and to discourage loan demand for marginal investment projects on the part of private-sector borrowers. The extent to which such measures can be successful depends on the interest elasticity of the demand for liquid assets and the interest elasticity of the demand for loans. In most of the cases cited above, and particularly in the three Asian countries, both sets of elasticities were evidently sufficiently high, as the stabilization packages did succeed to a large degree.

Moral suasion by the monetary authorities, sometimes called "open-mouth operations" or "jawbone control," is practiced no less extensively in LDCs than in developed countries. Warnings and exhortations to commercial banks to restrict lending or to encourage them to focus lending on particular activities have been quite common in Ghana and were used at various times in Malaysia, Singapore, Brazil, and elsewhere, sometimes prior to imposition of credit ceilings and often to reinforce pressures on banks to adhere to ceilings. In both developed and developing countries, however, moral suasion has proven credible only when accompanied by forceful use of more tangible instruments of monetary control.

26. See Vicente Gablis, "Inflation and Interest Rate Policies in Latin America, 1967–76," *International Monetary Fund Staff Papers* 26, no. 2 (June 1979): 334–65.

14

Foreign Savings: Aid and Investment

Countries that are unable to generate sufficient domestic savings to fuel their aspirations for economic growth have historically sought finance from other countries. The United States relied heavily on foreign savings, particularly during the antebellum period from 1835 to 1860. Likewise, Russia needed foreign savings to propel its development in the three decades before World War I and the communist revolution. Yet Japan, which has actively discouraged inflows of foreign savings and investment throughout its history, nevertheless became a modern nation during the period after the Meiji Restoration of 1868. Foreign savings can help development but is not essential for it.

It is useful to keep these examples in mind at a time when a majority of developing countries consider foreign savings to be an important ingredient in their development efforts, and when controversy surrounds both foreign aid and investment. This chapter examines the roles of foreign saving in development and explores some of these controversies.

CONCEPTS AND MAGNITUDES

Definitions

Before proceeding, some definitions are in order. **Foreign savings** include both official savings and private savings. Most **official savings** are on **conces-**

364

FOREIGN
SAVINGS:
AID AND
INVESTMENT
(Ch. 14)

sional terms; that is, they are made available either as **grants** (outright gifts) or as "soft" loans bearing lower interest rates and longer repayment periods than would be available in private international capital markets. Governments also make some loans on commercial terms, including export credits, equity investments, and "hard" loans from the World Bank and regional development banks. Concessional flows are technically called **official development assistance** (ODA), but are popularly called **foreign aid.** Aid can be further divided into **bilateral aid,** given directly by one government to another, and **multilateral aid,** in which the funds flow to an international agency like the United Nations, the World Bank, and the regional development banks (described below), which in turn grant or lend the funds to recipient developing countries. Finally, aid can be in the form of **technical assistance,** the provision of skilled individuals to augment national expertise; or **capital assistance,** the provision of finance or commodities for a variety of purposes discussed later in this chapter.

Foreign private savings consists of four elements. **Foreign direct investment** is made by nonresidents, typically but not always by multinational corporations, in the enterprises located in host countries; direct investment implies full or partial control of the enterprise and physical presence by foreign firms or individuals. **Portfolio investment** is the purchase of host country bonds or stocks by foreigners, without managerial control. This was a very important form of foreign investment in the nineteenth and early twentieth centuries, but is no longer so. **Commercial bank lending** to developing country governments and enterprises has supplanted portfolio investment in importance. Finally, exporting firms and their commercial banks offer **export credits** to importing countries as a way of promoting sales by permitting delayed payment for imports, often at commercial interest rates.

Recent Trends

Trends in the net flows of foreign savings (resources) by category are summarized in Table 14–1 for the period from 1960 to 1983. Total net resource flows in nominal terms in 1983 were twelve times the level in 1960. As relevant world prices increased by a factor of 3.6 over that period, real net resource flows more than tripled during that time.

Although no precise estimates are available, it can be estimated that the $98 billion of net resource flows in 1980 was equivalent to about 5 percent of gross domestic product for the low- and middle-income countries taken together. This compares to less than 4 percent in 1960. Foreign savings per capita in LDCs was roughly $26 in 1983. Table 14–2 gives foreign savings as a percentage of GDP for a representative sample of LDCs.[1] It shows some

---

1. Because Table 14–2 measures foreign savings on the basis of gross *domestic* product, its estimates are considerably lower than those for net resource flows given above and in Table 14–1, which are consistent with gross *national* product. In the latter, net resource flows include amounts necessary to finance net payments to foreign workers and to foreign capital (including interest payments). Gross domestic product *excludes* these outflows from foreign savings and, by implication, considers them part of domestic savings.

dramatic increases in the share of foreign savings in 1983 compared to 1960,
including GDP shares of 10 to 19 percent for Bangladesh, Mali, Tanzania,
Sri Lanka, Pakistan, Senegal, Bolivia, and Egypt.

Private flows contributed more to the growth of foreign savings to developing countries than did official flows: the share of private savings in the total flow rose from 38 to 51 percent over the twenty-year period. Within foreign private savings, commercial bank lending contributed almost 90 percent of the growth from 1970 to 1983 (Table 14–1). Direct investment, which is the most discussed category of foreign private investment, did not keep pace and dropped to less than a sixth of all private flows. Thus the tendency has been for capital on fixed, hard commercial terms to finance an increasing share of developing countries' net foreign resource flows.

This tendency has been intensified by the trends within official flow categories, because official finance on nonconcessional terms has grown more rapidly than aid (foreign aid in general). Although the nominal value of aid from all sources increased almost sevenfold from 1960 to 1983 (see Table 14–1), the real value rose by only 90 percent. Aid as a fraction of GDP in the third world actually fell during the twenty-three years, to 1.7 percent in 1983, or roughly $9 per person.

TABLE 14–1 Total Net Resource Flows (Disbursements) to Developing Countries from all Foreign Sources, 1960–1983 (in billions of U.S. dollars)

	1960[a]	1970	1983
Official flows: aid	4.94[b]	8.06	33.65[c]
1. Bilateral: DAC[d] countries	4.27	5.67	18.53
2. Bilateral: OPEC[e] countries	—	0.36	4.33
3. Bilateral: CMEA[f] countries	na	0.96	2.93
4. Multilateral agencies[g]	0.67	1.07	7.50
Official flows: nonaid[h]	na[b]	1.87	14.10
1. Bilateral: DAC countries		0.84	5.10
2. Bilateral: all others		0.32	2.00
3. Multilateral agencies		0.71	7.00
Private flows	3.01	9.08	49.80
1. Direct investment	1.88	3.69	7.80
2. Bond lending (portfolio investment)	0.67	0.30	0.50
3. Commercial bank lending	na[i]	3.00	36.00
4. Export credits	0.46	2.09	5.50
Total net resource flows	7.95	19.01	98.05

Source: Organization for Economic Cooperation and Development (OECD), *Development Cooperation: 1984 Review* (Paris 1984), pp. 64, 201, 235, 242; and OECD, *The Flow of Financial Resources to Developing Countries in 1961* (Paris, undated), Table 1.

[a] Data for 1960 covers only the countries of the Development Assistance Committee, consisting of seventeen industrialized aid donors of Europe, North America, Japan, Australia, and New Zealand.

[b] For 1960, non-aid official flows are included with aid flows.

[c] Totals do not add up because of the omission of $0.36 billion of aid from other bilateral sources.

[d] Development Assistance Committee of the OECD.

[e] Organization of Petroleum Exporting Countries.

[f] Council for Mutual Economic Assistance, including the Soviet Union and the countries of Eastern Europe.

[g] The World Bank and affiliates, plus the regional development banks.

[h] Loans and equity investments on commercial terms.

[i] Included under bond lending.

366
FOREIGN
SAVINGS
AID AND
INVESTMENT
(Ch. 14)

TABLE 14-2   Foreign Savings as a Share of GDP for Selected Developing Countries, 1960 and 1983

	Foreign Savings[a] as a Percent of GDP	
	1960	1983
Low-income countries[b]	1 (3)	2 (11)
Ethiopia	1	9
Bangladesh	−1	15
Mali	5	19
Tanzania	−5	12
India	3	3
China	1	−1
Ghana	7	3
Sri Lanka	5	15
Kenya	3	2
Pakistan	7	11
Middle-income countries[b]	1	1
Lower- middle-income	1	5
Senegal	1	13
Bolivia	7	10
Indonesia	0	4
Egypt	1	16
Philippines	0	7
Nigeria	6	0
Guatemala	2	2
Colombia	0	4
Malaysia	−13	5
Brazil	1	1
South Korea	10	1
Mexico	2	−11

Source: World Bank, *World Development Report 1985* (New York: Oxford University Press, 1985), pp. 182–83. World Bank, *World Development Report 1982* (New York: Oxford University Press, 1982), pp. 118–19.

[a.] Measured as the difference between gross domestic investment and gross domestic savings. Negative numbers mean the country was itself a net foreign investor.

[b.] Definitions same as for Table 1–1.

FOREIGN AID

Historical Role

Foreign aid as now conceived is a product of the post-World War II era. Its roots are in the Marshall Plan, under which the United States transferred $17 billion over four years—equivalent to about 1.5 percent of U.S. GNP—to help rebuild Europe after the war. Two elements of the Marshall Plan were believed at the time to have been crucial for its success: an influx of financial capital from the United States and coordinated plans to employ it productively to rebuild Europe's devastated physical capital stock. This early manifestation of capital fundamentalism was reinforced by the Harrod-Domar view of growth economics, which emerged during the 1940s and perceived capital and its productivity to be the critical factor responsible for growth (see Chapter 3).

The two decades after World War II saw the emergence of independent nations from Europe's colonies, especially in Asia and Africa. Encouraged by the success of Marshall Plan aid in rebuilding Europe, the United States took the lead in trying to help the newly emerging nations by providing that same element, capital, in the form of foreign aid, especially to countries that had development plans for investing the aid they received. Early aid programs also recognized that developing countries lacked certain kinds of skills and expertise, so technical assistance programs, which supplied foreign experts in fields from economic planning to engineering to construction, were also offered.

The motives behind the American aid programs of the postwar years were complex and ranged from the selfish to the generous. The security of the United States was the center of Congress's concerns in approving both the Marshall Plan and the "Point IV" program, under which President Truman began to shift U.S. attention and resources towards the less developed countries. This meant "containing communism" around the perimeter of the Soviet bloc as well as trying to ensure access to raw materials needed for U.S. industry. Prosperity of both the United States and its allies required expanding trade and investment, also promoted by aid. It was believed that development would serve both security and economic interests by reducing instability and giving the emerging nations a stake in the capitalist world order. U.S. aid policy was also intended to encourage the new countries to maintain or adopt democratic political institutions and private-enterprise-based economies in the U.S. image. But it has been argued that there was also a core of humanitarian concern for the welfare of the world's poor. Indeed the strength of the early aid programs depended upon this mixture of nationalistic and altruistic motives, which drew political support from a wide spectrum of opinion. Although the context has changed over thirty-five years and, as we shall see, the number of major donors has increased, the mixture of aims for all donors remains much the same in the 1980s: security, economic leverage, economic health, political evangelism, and humanitarianism.

Over time the size and composition of aid programs changed in important ways. Only half of the growth in aid flows came from the bilateral programs of the traditional donors of Western Europe and the United States. The real value of bilateral aid from these countries, who are grouped into the **Development Assistance Committee** (DAC) of the **Organization for Economic Cooperation and Development** (OECD), increased by about 20 percent from 1960 to 1983. Table 14–1 shows 15 percent of the increase in nominal aid flows came from the Organization of Petroleum Exporting Countries and 24 percent from the multilateral development agencies, led by the World Bank. However, most of the capital of the World Bank and the regional development banks originated in the DAC countries.

The DAC countries as a group disbursed $27.5 billion in aid in 1983, including both direct (bilateral) programs and their contributions to the multilateral aid agencies. This is less than a sixfold increase since 1960 and represents a 67 percent increase in real terms (Table 14–3). The United States, which in 1960 accounted for well over half of the DAC total, was responsible for only 29 percent in 1983. In that year U.S. aid represented just 0.24 percent of its GNP; only Austria and Italy had shares as low. All the other large contributors of the DAC, shown in Table 14–3, increased their nominal aid flows by at least fourfold over the twenty-three years and some by much

368

FOREIGN
SAVINGS:
AID AND
INVESTMENT
(Ch. 14)

TABLE 14-3   Net Official Development Assistance (Disbursements) from DAC Countries
to LDCs and Multilateral Agencies, 1960, 1970, and 1983

Source	1960 (million U.S. dollars)	percent of GNP	1970 (million U.S. dollars)	percent of GNP	1983 (million U.S. dollars	percent of GNP
Canada	75	0.19	337	0.41	1,429	0.45
France	823	1.35	971	0.66	3,815	0.74
Germany (West)	223	0.31	599	0.32	3,176	0.49
Japan	105	0.24	458	0.23	3,761	0.33
Netherlands	35	0.31	196	0.61	1,195	0.91
Sweden	7	0.05	117	0.38	754	0.85
United Kingdom	407	0.56	500	0.41	1,605	0.35
United States	2,702	0.53	3,153	0.32	7,992	0.24
Total DAC[a]	4,628	0.51	6,968	0.34	27,458	0.36
Indexes						
Nominal value	100		151		593	
Real Value	100		114		167	

Source: OECD, *Development Cooperation: 1984 Review* (Paris, 1984), p. 212; World Bank, *World Development Report 1981* (New York: Oxford University Press, 1981), Table 16 (for 1960, 1970)
[a] Total DAC columns include disbursements from other smaller DAC donor countries.

more. In 1983 France, Germany, and Japan together contributed 35 percent more than the United States; in 1960 the U.S. program had been more than double that of the other three combined. And six countries—Belgium, Denmark, the Netherlands, Norway, Sweden, and France—gave aid worth at least 0.6 percent of their GNP.

As the flow of aid and the number of donors expanded, the economic development rationale for aid changed as well. During the 1950s the main economic goal was rapid growth of output and incomes, to be achieved by increasing the amount of domestic and foreign savings available for investment. By the 1960s the two-gap model, described in Chapter 6, augmented the Harrod-Domar perspective and foreign exchange became as important as capital. Human capital received emphasis beyond the recognized role of technical assistance and aid programs spread into education, health, and other human services. During the late 1960s and the 1970s aid programs began to incorporate goals other than the promotion of economic growth: income redistribution, poverty alleviation, supply of basic needs, and rural development became motivators for the aid programs of most donors.

We saw earlier that in 1983 developing countries on average received aid equivalent to 1.7 percent of their GDP. However, there are major and moderately systematic variations around this rather low average, as Table 14–4 reveals. First, there is a strong tendency for aid to represent a higher fraction of GDP for poorer countries. All countries with GDP shares over 5 percent —and aid per capita levels over $15—had incomes per capita below $700 in 1983, while those with incomes over $700 generally have negligible flows of aid relative to GDP. This was not always true. In the early 1960s relatively prosperous Brazil and Colombia, for example, had large shares of the U.S. aid program. But the increasing scarcity of concessional resource flows, combined with growing emphasis upon the relief of poverty, have probably

Country	GNP per capita (dollars) 1983	Net Official Development Assistance		
		U.S. dollars (millions)	Percent GDP	Per-capita dollars
Low-income countries				
Ethiopia	120	251	6	6
Bangladesh	130	1,072	10	11
Mali	160	214	22	30
Tanzania	240	577	15[b]	28
India	260	1,722	1	2
China	300	659	*	1
Ghana	310	107	3	8
Sri Lanka	330	470	10	31
Kenya	340	397	8	21
Pakistan	390	722	3	8
Middle-income countries				
Senegal	440	314	12	51
Bolivia	510	166	5	28
Indonesia	560	739	1	5
Egypt	700	1,444	5	32
Philippines	760	424	1	8
Nigeria	770	47	*	1
Guatemala	1,120	73	1	9
Colombia	1,430	84	*	3
Malaysia	1,860	177	1	12
Brazil	1,880	98	*[b]	1
Korea (South)	2,010	8	*	0
Mexico	2,240	131	1	2

Source: OECD, *Development Cooperation: 1984 Review* (Paris, 1984), pp. 228–29 (for aid receipts); World Bank, *World Development Report 1985* (New York: Oxford University Press, 1985), Tables 1 and 3 (for GDP and population).
[a] Definitions are the same as for Table 1–1; includes ODA from DAC countries, multilateral organizations, and OPEC.
[b] 1982 (1983 GDP not available).
* Less than 0.5%.

intensified the tendency to aid very poor countries more than others.

The exceptions to this rule point to a second strong tendency. Among the countries in the table with incomes below $700 per capita, the three largest ones—China, India, and Indonesia—have very low aid levels relative to GDP or population, even though the dollar amounts going to these countries are quite large. Donors, faced with a choice of spreading their aid proportionally (to GDP or population) thus having scant impact anywhere, or concentrating it where they can make a larger impact, choose the latter. Small countries thus get greater relative amounts of aid, but also become more dependent upon the donors who provide it, than is true for large countries.

Finally, Table 14–4 includes some examples of countries that are favored for political and strategic reasons. Mali and Senegal benefit disproportionately, as do all Francophone African states—former French colonies—from France's generous aid program. Egypt, along with Israel, has been favored by the United States' efforts to reduce tensions in the Middle East. During the 1950s South Korea, Taiwan, Pakistan, Turkey, and other allied governments were favored recipients of U.S. aid. Although the manifestations of politically inspired aid are strongest in these cases, they are present to some extent in many other countries.

370 **Aid Institutions and Instruments**

FOREIGN
SAVINGS:
AID AND
INVESTMENT
(Ch. 14)

Bilateral aid donors usually plan and dispense loans and grants through an aid agency, such as the United States Agency for International Development (USAID), Britain's Overseas Development Ministry (ODM), the International Development Agencies of Canada (CIDA) and Sweden (SIDA), and others. Most development assistance agencies deal with a wide range of aid instruments, both technical and capital assistance. Most of the capital aid is disbursed against specific projects, such as a hydroelectric dam, a road, or a rural development project, and is called **project aid.** However, some bilateral agencies, including USAID, have made **program loans,** which finance general categories of imports and are conceived as broad support for the balance of payments, in the spirit of closing the foreign exchange gap of the two-gap model. Program loans were more important during the 1960s when large amounts went to countries like India, Pakistan, and Brazil, than during the 1970s, but made a comeback—largely as "structural adjustment loans" by the World Bank—during the period of extreme resource scarcity following the second oil price increase in 1979. **Food aid** is a kind of bilateral program loan since it provides commodities, mostly grains, that would otherwise have to be purchased with a country's own foreign exchange earnings.

The full range of motives of the donor countries, discussed above, is given fullest expression in bilateral programs, which can easily be treated as extensions of donors' foreign policy. The establishment of multilateral institutions to dispense aid and the provision of these international agencies with a growing share of aid resources, indicate that the donor countries give aid for reasons other than simple self-interest. Nevertheless it is true that the largest donors exercise greatest control over the World Bank and other multilateral agencies (though not over the United Nation's agencies: witness the struggle for control over UNESCO). Still the multilateral organizations are focused almost exclusively on development and shield recipients to a considerable extent from the foreign policy concerns of the industrial countries.

The main **multilateral aid** agencies and the amounts they disbursed in 1970 and 1980 are given in Table 14–5. The largest and most influential of these is the World Bank (International Bank for Reconstruction and Development, or IBRD), together with its affiliates, the International Development Association (IDA) and International Finance Corporation (IFC). Despite its leading role in the aid community, most of the capital supplied by the World Bank is not aid. The IBRD obtains its funds by borrowing on world capital markets at prevailing prime interest rates and relends to developing countries at slightly higher rates. It makes more capital available and at lower interest rates than could be obtained by the developing countries on their own. Its affiliate, the IFC, lends on commercial terms and takes small equity positions in support of private foreign investments. Only the IDA, which channels contributions from the richer member countries to the poorer LDCs on very soft terms, dispenses aid in the strict sense. Most of the World Bank's and IDA's loans are for projects, but program loans are also made. During the 1970s the World Bank became the world's leading center for research, information, and policy advice on economic development. In

Agency	Concessional flows		Nonconcessional flows	
	1970	1983	1970	1983
World Bank and related institutions[a]	163	2,383	576	5,283
Interamerican Development Bank (IDB)	224	364	84	957
African Development Bank	—	158	2	145
Asian Development Bank	1	222	15	549
Caribbean Development Bank	—	31	—	9
EEC/European Investment Bank	210	1,215	11	202
United Nations	498	2,739	—	—
OPEC (Arab members)	—	311	—	80
Total	1,096	7,423	688	7,225

Source: OECD, *Development Cooperation: 1984 Review* (Paris, 1984), p. 214.
[a] The World Bank Group includes, besides the World Bank, the International Development Association (IDA) which dispenses heavily concessionary aid, and the International Finance Corporation (IFC), oriented toward lending to the private sector.

1983 the World Bank group disbursed over $7.7 billion dollars, over half of the total for all multilateral agencies.

The word "reconstruction" in the bank's title stems from its origin, at the Bretton Woods (New Hampshire) conference in 1944, when its first task was to help finance the reconstruction of war-torn European countries. The other institution founded at the conference was the International Monetary Fund (IMF), whose main charge was to reestablish an international system of national currencies in stable relation to each other, in support of a rejuvenated world trade system. The IMF played a significant role in the unprecedented expansion of world trade during the 1950s and 1960s. Although not primarily concerned with promoting development, IMF practices and resources have had a major effect on developing countries, and the Fund is increasingly turning its attention toward assisting LDCs by offering balance-of-payments support in a variety of ways. IMF loans are conditioned on the adoption of short-term economic policies by recipient governments to stabilize their economies. The Fund's **conditionality** typically includes reductions in a government's budget deficit, a slower rate of money and credit creation —both to control inflation—and a devaluation of the exchange rate to correct imbalances in trade and other foreign transactions. IMF loans, called "stand-by facilities," and conditions have figured prominently in efforts of major debtor countries, especially in Latin America, to repay foreign loans. Such "stabilization packages" have come under heavy criticism in debtor countries for stifling economic growth.

Each of the third world's continents—Asia, Africa, and Latin America— has its own regional development bank. These each have separate "windows," or programs, that dispense hard and soft loans to member countries. Regional members and the major aid donors contribute to the capital of these banks, which also borrow on private capital markets to finance hard

372

FOREIGN
SAVINGS:
AID AND
INVESTMENT
(Ch. 14)

loans, and receive contributions from aid donors for their soft loan windows. Virtually all finance from the regional banks is for projects.

Two regional organizations are aid donors: The European Economic Community and the Arab OPEC states. The EEC originally concentrated its aid on former French colonies in Africa, but now spreads its assistance more widely, especially in Africa. OPEC, a new arrival on the aid scene, uses a part of its oil wealth to aid developing countries, with a concentration on Islamic states. Its role as a major aid donor is likely to decline with the fall in oil prices since 1985.

The United Nations has the largest concessional program of the multilaterals, $2.7 billion of mostly technical assistance in 1983. The focus of this effort is the United Nations Development Programme (UNDP), which makes grants to member countries. However, the "specialized agencies" of the U.N., such as the U.N. Industrial Development Organization (UNIDO), International Labor Organization (ILO), and World Health Organization (WHO), among others, execute the technical assistance projects financed by UNDP.

Almost 9 percent of the total aid flows given in Table 14–1 for 1983 are from the Soviet Union and its Eastern European allies. Two-thirds of this total is due to the Soviet Union's aid to Cuba, Mongolia, and Vietnam, the largest recipient. Only 13 percent went to non-communist developing countries. The political motive for eastern-bloc aid is evident.

Impacts on Development

In a Harrod-Domar world it would be easy to measure the contribution of aid and other foreign saving to development. In this model the role of foreign saving of all kinds is to augment domestic saving to increase investment and thus accelerate growth. If aid and other foreign saving added, say, 6 percent of GDP; if all of it went to additional investment; and the capital-output ratio were 3.0, then the growth rate would be increased by 2 percentage points.[2] A glance at Table 14–2 shows that for some countries—Bangladesh, Pakistan, Mali, Senegal, and others—foreign saving is a large fraction of GDP and could be contributing 4 to 6 percentage points to the growth rate in this simple model. For countries like India, China, Ghana, Mexico, and Brazil, foreign saving is a small fraction of GDP and cannot have much impact on growth.

In the slightly more complex world of the two-gap model, where aid and other foreign saving contribute either to greater investment or to greater imports (by supplying more foreign exchange), the story is essentially the same. If foreign exchange is the scarce factor, then aid's contribution to growth would be proportional to its contribution to additional imports. These contributions have been quite large for the more favored recipients of foreign saving shown in Table 14–2.

The fact that growth rates in the large aid-recipient countries have not been very high is one indication that the Harrod-Domar approach is faulty.

---

2. From Equation 3–4 of Chapter 3, $g = s/k$. Here, additional foreign saving adds a fraction, f, to GDP, all of which is saved, so $\Delta s = f$. Hence, $\Delta g = \Delta s/k = f/k = 0.06/3.0 = 0.02$ or 2%.

Developing countries may of course lack some important complementary
inputs to development, such as human skills, administrative capacity, infrastructure, economic institutions, and political stability, without which even high savings rates may not stimulate growth. But even if these barriers to growth were overcome, some economists have argued that foreign saving, especially aid, may not contribute much to additional saving or imports. Rather, suggest the doubters, foreign saving may substitute for—not add to —domestic saving, permitting increases in consumption instead of increases in investment and decreases in exports rather than increases in imports. The doubters are partly, but not entirely, right: economic theory suggests that aid should increase both consumption and investment.

Figure 14–1 helps us to understand why. A developing country, before it obtains aid, can produce consumption goods and capital goods along the production possibilities frontier PP. To simplify, the diagram ignores international trade. Community tastes are defined by a set of indifference curves, of which two, labeled I and II, are shown. Without aid the country's welfare is maximized if it produces and consumes at point A, where the indifference curve I is tangent to the frontier PP, with consumption at C_1 and investment at I_1. Now donor countries contribute an amount, AB, of aid. They intend that the full amount should be invested, raising total investment to I_2. However, the offer of aid AB in effect moves the production frontier outward from PP to $P'P'$. With these added resources the country maximizes its welfare by producing at point D, the tangency between $P'P'$ and indifference curve 2. It consumes C_3 and invests I_3. Of the aid amount AB, AE (equal to $I_3 - I_1$) has been invested, as intended by the donors, but BE (equal to $I_2 - I_3$) has been consumed. If the country's tastes favored consumption over investment even more, then it would reach equilibrium at a point along $P'P'$ to the southeast of D, and would convert even more of its aid into consumption.

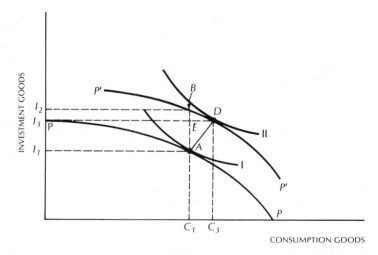

FIGURE 14–1 **Impact of Aid on Investment and Consumption.** Foreign aid totalling AB turns into actual investments of only AE, because the country maximizes welfare on the new production frontier, $P'P'$, at point D, not B. *Source:* Adapted from Paul Mosely, "Aid, Savings and Growth Revisited," *Oxford Bulletin of Economics and Statistics* 42 (May 1980): 79–91.

374
FOREIGN
SAVINGS:
AID AND
INVESTMENT
(Ch. 14)

The diagram demonstrates that the amount of aid actually used to increase investment rather than consumption will depend upon production possibilities, community tastes, and other variables, such as trade, left out of the figure. How can a country convert aid and other foreign saving, which is intended to be used for investment, into consumption? Some forms of foreign saving, such as program aid or commercial bank loans, are designed to provide finance for general purposes and thus deliberately give the recipient the kinds of choices demonstrated in Figure 14–1. Food aid, of course, is intended to increase or maintain consumption rather than investment. But even if all foreign saving were dispensed as project aid and targeted to specific investment projects, substitution would be possible. Project aid might, for example, be used for investments that the government or its private investors would have made even without aid. In that case resources are freed up for other purposes, including consumption. When aid finances projects that might not otherwise be implemented, government may simply cut back on its preferred projects because it wants to raise the share of consumption, for economic or political reasons. When substitutions of these kinds are possible, aid is called "fungible."

Perhaps more important, a host of subtle influences of foreign saving on relative prices may also contribute to substitution. More capital in general could conceivably mean lower returns on investments and hence a greater tendency to consume in the recipient countries, although this has never been documented. More foreign exchange tends to lower its price (i.e., to revalue the exchange rate; see Chapter 15) and cause greater demand for imports, as intended by donors, but also creates a reduced incentive to produce for export, which is not intended. And food aid has a similar effect, lowering food prices because it satisfies part of domestic demand, hence reducing the incentive for domestic farmers to produce foods. These influences could be overcome by countervailing government policies, but governments may not undertake such measures for a variety of reasons discussed in other chapters. In sum, the contribution of aid and other foreign saving to development is not that it provides specific amounts of additional investment, imports, or food. Rather, foreign saving provides additional purchasing power for the country and hence the possibility of increasing investment, imports, or food. Recipient countries will take advantage of such possibilities to varying degrees.

Considered in terms of substitution possibilities, aid is probably not very different from other forms of foreign saving, official or private. But in two respects aid makes a different kind of contribution to development. Obviously it comes on softer terms, thus reducing the burden of repayment in the future and increasing future net inflows of foreign resources, other things equal. A measure of this is the **grant equivalent** of aid. The grant equivalent of a loan is the difference between the loan amount and the discounted present value of loan repayments—principal and interest—expressed as a percentage of the loan's face value. The discount rate would be the interest rate obtainable in commercial markets. Thus the grant element of a commercial loan would be zero and that of a grant would be 100 percent. Soft loans, such as those made by the International Development Association, have grant elements over 90 percent. The grant elements for bilateral aid programs of the major DAC donors are all 90 percent or more, except for Japan.

The second difference between aid and private flows is that aid donors and other official sources of capital often try to use their assistance as a lever to obtain their own policy goals. Donors offer aid to reward political friends and military allies, and withhold it from those perceived as enemies. They tie aid funds to the purchase of goods and services in their own countries as a way of increasing their own markets for exports and of dampening the impact of aid on their own balance of payments. They channel it towards countries and institutions within countries that adhere most closely to the donor's own views of economics and politics. These are perhaps the crassest uses of aid and they are generally confined to bilateral donors.

Donors, both bilateral and multilateral, also use aid to induce LDC governments to change their development policies in what donors believe to be the country's own best interests. For reasons discussed in Part IV, donors offer aid in support of currency devaluation and liberalization programs. They make loans contingent upon changes in tax systems, adoption of new wage and income policies, adjustments in food and other agricultural prices, and many other policy actions. They change aid allocations to match shifts in development thinking, as for example toward rural development and away from industrial development during the 1970s. Donors supply technical assistance, much of which is truly technical in a narrow sense, but some of which involves foreign advisers whose aim is to change government policies in various ways or to alter budget and other resource allocations. To the extent that host governments acquiesce to such changes (and in many cases they may want to undertake them in any event), policy leverage may be as important a contribution of aid programs of development as the resource flows they finance. However, governments have ways of appearing to accept conditions, but then not implementing them fully, and donors have reasons to continue offering their aid even if conditions are not met. A summary judgment is that aid leverage generally is a weak and somewhat clumsy instrument, not difficult for host governments to evade if they choose.

FOREIGN INVESTMENT AND THE MULTINATIONALS

Foreign direct investment accounted for only 8 percent of the total foreign saving flows entering developing countries in 1983, a sharp drop from its 24 percent share in 1960 (Table 14–1). By the mid-eighties debate over foreign investment in LDCs had been eclipsed by controversy surrounding measures for dealing with the foreign debts of LDCs, an issue addressed later in this chapter. In 1986 debts—at one trillion dollars—are roughly five times larger than total foreign investment in LDCs. Yet direct investment still receives much attention, and attracts much controversy, when foreign resources flows are discussed in the literature or by LDC officials. There are two reasons for this. First, foreign investment comes in a package that may include not only equity finance, but often much larger amounts of loan finance,

376

FOREIGN
SAVINGS:
AID AND
INVESTMENT
(Ch. 14)

management expertise, modern technologies, technical skills, and access to world markets. The other elements of the package are perceived to be as important as the equity finance itself. Second, this package is controlled by multinational corporations, whose size and economic influence often match and sometimes outstrip that of the recipient country governments. An invitation to a multinational corporation raises the spectre of interference by, and dependence upon, foreign economic powers that seem beholden to a foreign government, or to no government. We shall examine the basis for these fears, and the potential benefits and costs of foreign investment, in this section.

Multinationals' Investment Patterns

The overwhelming proportion of direct foreign investment in third-world nations is done by **multinational corporations** (MNCs). A multinational is an enterprise that has significant productive operations in more than one nation and considers production abroad to be a central, rather than a peripheral, concern. Multinational enterprises come in all sizes and from all regions of the world, but a relatively small number are dominant. In 1980 roughly 10,000 MNCs were in existence, exercising control over nearly 90,000 foreign affiliates.[3] But only 500 firms accounted for 80 percent of the world's stock of direct foreign investment in that year.

A common misconception is that most foreign direct investment from industrial nations is located in developing nations. However, except for Japan, rich countries tend strongly to invest in one another, not in LDCs. Three-fourths of the MNC affiliates are located in the European Economic Community (EEC), Switzerland, and North America. The U.S. experience illustrates this pattern. Over the period 1966 through 1973, the years of the most rapid expansion by U.S.-based multinationals, only 18.7 percent of the flow of new investment by these firms was located in developing countries. While this proportion doubled to 36.4 percent in the subsequent period 1974 through 1980,[4] a very large share of U.S. direct investment flows to LDCs was directed toward the search for petroleum reserves in a few countries such as Indonesia[5] in those "oil crisis" years. Foreign investment by multinationals based in Britian, Germany, and France followed a similar pattern over the period 1966 to 1976. The developing country share in total flows of foreign investment from these countries was only 19 percent for Britain and barely 30 percent for West Germany and France. Only Japan ran counter to this pattern: 60 percent of Japanese direct foreign investment from 1960 to 1976 went to developing countries. And although the share of LDCs in the annual flow of direct foreign investment worldwide increased from 18 percent in 1967 to 27 percent in 1980 through 1983, the real value of these flows hardly increased at all, according to the *1985 World Development Report.*

3. John Stopford, *The World Directory of Multinational Enterprises 1982–83,* (Detroit: Gale Research Company, 1982), p. 2

4. Stopford, *World Directory,* p. 12

5. Between 1974 and 1980, foreign oil companies invested nearly $20 billion in that country's petroleum sector, most of which was exploration outlays by American firms. Malcolm Gillis, "Episodes in Indonesian Economic Growth," in *World Economic Growth* A. C. Harberger, ed. (San Francisco: Institute for Contemporary Studies, 1984) pp. 251–55.

Overall, the share of the cumulative stock of investment by all developed-

country MNCs in developing countries fell from 31 percent to 27 percent
from 1971 to 1980.[6] From Table 14–6 it is evident that foreign investment in
most LDCs, except for Brazil, has been a small proportion of that undertaken in most of the largest industrial-country recipients (Canada and the
United States).

Another common misconception is that most direct foreign investment
from rich to poor countries reflects an attempt by multinationals to shift
manufacturing activities to LDCs to take advantage of "cheap" foreign
labor. Some foreign investment in manufacturing is motivated by this consideration, and employment generation by MNCs is actively sought in many
LDCs. However, from 1965 to 1978 manufacturing investments were only
38 percent of total foreign investment flows from rich countries. Historically
a very sizable proportion of the flow of MNC capital to LDCs has been concentrated in the extraction and processing of natural resources, a highly capital-intensive activity that depends very little on the availability of low-cost
labor but very much on the presence of natural-resource deposits. Far more
MNC investment goes to relatively high-income, high-wage LDCs than to
very poor countries with "cheap" labor. By 1977 developing countries with
income per capita in excess of $1,000 had received 57 percent of all direct
foreign investment in LDCs.

It is also important to note that in virtually all LDCs, the stock of direct

TABLE 14–6   Stock of Direct Foreign Investment, in Developed and Developing Countries,
1978 (in billions of U.S. dollars)

I. *Total foreign direct investment in host countries*		$355.9
II. *Total foreign direct investment in developed market economies*		$251.8
Canada	42.9	
United States	37.2	
United Kingdom	33.0	
West Germany	29.2	
Italy	5.8	
Japan	1.9	
Netherlands	11.9	
All other developed countries	89.9	
III. *Total foreign direct investment in developing economies*		$104.1
Brazil	13.7	
Indonesia	6.6	
Mexico	5.1	
Nigeria	3.7	
India	2.4	
Singapore	1.8	
Venezuela	1.4	
South Korea	1.0	
Peru	1.0	
Philippines	1.0	
Colombia	0.8	
Ecuador	0.7	
All other LDCs	64.9	

Source: Derived from Tables 2, 3 and 4 in Stopford, *World Directory*, pp. i–ix.

6. Stopford, *World Directory*, p. 12

378

FOREIGN
SAVINGS:
AID AND
INVESTMENT
(Ch. 14)

TABLE 14-7   Stock of Direct Foreign Investment Compared to Stock of Outstanding External Debt of LDCs, 1983 (in billions of U.S. dollars)

	Stock of foreign direct investment (1983) (1)	Stock of outstanding external debt (1983) (2)	Total gross external liabilities (1) + (2) (3)	Foreign direct investment as percent of total external liabilities (4)
Seven Major Borrowers	59.6	350.1	409.7	14.6
Argentina	5.8	44.4	50.2	11.6
Brazil	24.6	88.0	112.6	21.8
Indonesia	6.8	30.4	37.2	18.3
Korea	1.8	38.9	40.7	4.4
Mexico	13.6	89.4	103.0	13.2
Philippines	2.7	23.9	26.6	10.2
Venezuela	4.3	35.1	39.4	10.9
Other	140.9	685.5	826.4	17.1

Source: Table items: David Goldsbrough, "Foreign Direct Investment in Developing Countries," *Finance and Development* March 1985.

Note: 1986 External Debt of LDCs = $1.01 trillion (estimate). *Source:* Press conference, March 26, 1986, Anne O. Krueger, Vice-President, World Bank.

foreign investment is a relatively small fraction of total external liabilities of the countries. Table 14–7 shows for 1983 that only in Indonesia and Brazil was the share of direct foreign investment as much as one-fifth the total. For non-oil LDCs in general, foreign direct investment was but 17 percent of the total.

Finally, investment activities of MNCs are not evenly distributed among different regions in the developing world. The *1985 World Development Report* indicates that Latin America and the Caribbean have received about half the flow from 1965 through 1983. Asia, principally Southeast and East Asia, received about a quarter of the total over the period, but the Asian share has been rising at the expense of Africa, which now receives about one-tenth.

Characteristics of Multinationals

The stereotypical image of a multinational enterprise is that of a very large, U.S.-based, private-sector enterprise. Modern multinationals are indeed typically very large, but they are no longer essentially American creatures, nor do all trace their lineage to the private sector. Indeed Chapter 21 identifies several state-owned MNCs that in recent years have begun to play a major role in international investments. Many multinationals have worldwide sales or assets that are large compared to the GDPs of some host country LDCs (see Table 14–8). Comparisons of multinationals' sales with GDP of developing countries are not, however, particularly instructive since GDP measures not total sales, but value-added. Comparisons of the relative size of MNC assets to those of LDCs would be revealing if data on the latter were available.

The perception that modern MNCs are essentially American carries over from the early postwar period when European firms were preoccupied with

TABLE 14–8 Comparison of Relative Size of Multinational Corporations and LDC Host-Country Economies, 1983 (in billions of U.S. dollars)

Largest LDC Market Economies	Total GDP 1983	
Largest (Brazil)	274.6	
Fifth largest (Nigeria)	80.9	
Tenth largest (Malaysia)	47.8	
Fifteen largest (Pakistan)	34.6	
Twentieth largest (Zaire)	25.9	
Largest U.S. MNCs in *Fortune 500*, 1984	Sales	Assets
Largest (Exxon)	90.9	63.3
Tenth largest (Standard Oil of Indiana)	26.9	25.7
Twenty-fifth largest (Dow Chemical)	11.4	11.4
Hundredth largest (American Cynamid)	3.9	3.3
Smallest MNC in Fortune 500 (Lukens)	0.4	0.3
Largest non-U.S. MNCs in *Fortune 500*, 1984	Sales	Assets
Largest (Royal-Dutch Shell—Britain, Holland)	84.9	69.1
Tenth largest (Hitachi—Japan)	18.5	20.5
Twenty-fifth largest (Fiat—Italy)	13.5	15.1
Hundredth largest (British Leyland)	4.5	2.6
Smallest (Norddeutsche Affinevig—Germany)	0.8	0.2

Source: Section I: World Bank, *World Development Report 1985* (New York: Oxford University Press, 1985), Table 3; section II: *Fortune* Magazine, April 29, 1985, pp. 280–90; section III: *Fortune* Magazine, August 19, 1985, pp. 165–230.

rebuilding war-damaged domestic markets. By 1967 U.S.-based firms accounted for about half of the total stock of foreign investment in the world (see Table 14–9) a figure that reached 57 percent by 1971. By 1980, the share of U.S.-based firms had fallen to 43 percent, owing to the very rapid growth of Japanese- and German-based MNCs. U.S., and to a lesser extent British, domination of foreign investment in LDCs has diminished as well. Over the period 1960 to 1976, U.S.-based multinationals accounted for barely 50 percent of total flows of foreign investment to LDCs. British and French firms

TABLE 14–9 Stock of Direct Foreign Investment from Developed Market Countries: 1967 and 1980 (in billions of U.S. dollars and current prices)

Country of Origin	1967		1980	
	Amount	%	Amount	%
1. United States	56.6	49.6	215.6	43.3
2. United Kingdom	17.5	15.3	74.2	14.9
3. West Germany	3.0	2.6	37.6	7.6
4. Japan	1.5	1.3	37.1	7.5
5. Switzerland	5.0	4.4	33.0	6.6
6. Netherlands	11.0	9.6	39.7	8.0
7. France	6.0	5.3	20.0	4.0
8. Canada	3.7	3.2	19.0	3.8
9. Sweden	1.7	1.5	7.2	1.4
10. Belgium-Luxemburg	2.0	1.8	6.9	1.4
11. Italy	2.1	1.8	6.9	1.4
12. All other (est.)	4.0	3.0	12.4	2.5
Total	114.1	100.0	497.5	100.0

Source: Stopford, *World Directory.*

380

FOREIGN
SAVINGS:
AID AND
INVESTMENT
(Ch. 14)

were responsible for 10 and 8 percent, respectively, while German and Japanese MNCs accounted for about 9 percent each.[7] The remaining 15 percent of foreign direct investment in LDCs was carried out by enterprises based in other Western European countries—and increasingly since 1970, over 1,000 multinational enterprises from developing countries such as India, Brazil, and Argentina.

Multinationals from developing countries have been investing in other LDCs for decades. Three Argentine-based firms had foreign subsidiaries before 1940. By the late 1970s MNCs from Asian countries such as Korea, Hong Kong, India, the Philippines, and Malaysia operated nearly seven hundred foreign investment projects, primarily in labor-intensive manufacturing investments and logging. Many of these are quite small, both in terms of total investment and in sales. But a few, such as India's Birla, Malaysia's Sime Darby, and Argentina's Bunge y Born, are among the largest privately owned firms in developing nations.

In sum, multinationals are now so varied in nationalities, production, ownership, and size that generalizations about their characteristics, much less their objectives and conduct, have become increasingly difficult to make.

The Multinational Investment "Package"

Today, foreign investment is valued, where it *is* valued, less for the additional capital it makes available than for other reasons. The successful multinationals have been able to assemble a distinctive "package" of resources attractive to host countries, developing and otherwise. Capital is an important part of the package, because the MNCs possess prodigious capacities for raising it. But MNCs have been able to bundle within the package other elements that are even more difficult for LDCs to secure: technology, management expertise, technical skills, and access to markets, all viewed as vital not merely for the process of industrialization but for coping with an increasingly complex, rapidly changing world society.

Technology often constitutes the core of the package, and is the element most jealously guarded by the MNCs because the maintenance of technological advantages increasingly determines the long-run survival of the firms. In some cases such advantages can vanish almost overnight, as in the early 1980s in the electronics industry when Japanese firms outraced U.S. enterprises in implementing successive innovations. The technological component of the multinational package is embodied in processes, such as in metallurgy or textile manufacture and equipment, as in steelmaking and communications. But it also encompasses the information and technological skills required to adapt, install, operate, and maintain processes and equipment. Occasionally these skills, but rarely the processes, can be lured away from the multinationals, or can be home-grown by developing countries, as Mexico has shown in certain lines of metallurgy and Hong Kong in textiles.

Another prime component of the package is managerial ability, without

---

7. K. Billerbeck and Y. Yasugi, "Private Direct Foreign Investment," *World Bank Staff Working Paper No. 348*(1979): pp. 4–5.

which access to technology is largely ornamental. To be sure, many LDCs

have gifted indigenous entrepreneurs and innovators. The market women in West African countries such as Ghana and Nigeria are prime illustrations, as are many representatives of such ethnic groups as the Batak and Minangkabau in Indonesia, or regional clusters of adaptive industrialists in such Latin American cities as Monterey, Medellin, and São Paulo. Nevertheless, few third world countries possess sufficient numbers of managers capable of organizing and operating large industrial projects such as those undertaken by MNCs, and virtually all are short of people with advanced training in management. For example, in 1980 Indonesia, with 147 million people, had less than thirty resident indigenous MBAs, and Ecuador, with eight million people, had but five; whereas IBM alone has perhaps one thousand. While an MBA diploma is not a guarantee of managerial competence, other trained personnel with technical backgrounds capable of assuming management tasks are also typically in short supply.

The final major component of the multinationals package is access to world markets. LDCs capable of producing at competitive costs often find it difficult to penetrate foreign markets. Many MNCs, particularly in natural resources, are part of vertically integrated, oligopolistic industries in which marketing is primarily a matter of intrafirm transactions. In the mid-1970s around half of all imports into and exports from Canada were intrafirm sales, while in the United States and United Kingdom about 30 percent of MNC exports were from parent multinationals to their affiliates.[8] In other cases MNCs have been able to develop preferential access to customers by fashioning and adhering to long-term contracts in standardized products, such as petroleum, or by acquiring a reputation for delivering a specialized product of satisfactory quality on a reliable schedule, as in construction and engineering. LDC efforts to overcome the marketing advantages of the multinationals often require years before a breakthrough is made, although Asian LDC textile firms have shown it can be done.

For much of the post-war era LDCs were generally forced to accept the entire multinational package or get none of it. The multinationals have been loath to allow any "unbundling" of the key ingredients, in the probably correct belief that the package as a whole is more profitable than the sum of its separate elements. Unbundling is also resisted because technological secrets might thereby be made more easily accessible to competitors, and because in some cases various elements of the package may have been inextricably linked, unable to stand alone.

The international oil industry illustrates the widespread resistance to unbundling. Large MNCs in petroleum have ordinarily preferred direct investment in overseas oil sectors, with equity funds forming a substantial part of the total investment. LDCs with prospective oil deposits face not only very large capital requirements in mounting exploration on their own, but even more fundamental technical and marketing barriers. Yet some host governments are reluctant to allow international petroleum companies to enter as equity investors, both because they reject any implication of foreign

8. Stopford, *World Directory,* p. 33.

382

FOREIGN
SAVINGS:
AID AND
INVESTMENT
(Ch. 14)

ownership of oil deposits and because equity investment entitles the oil companies to a portion of any future windfall gains from discovery and export of particularly attractive deposits. Consequently host governments, particularly in Latin America, have sought to induce oil companies to unbundle the package of resources at their disposal. Contractual devices such as service contracts are designed to limit MNC capital to debt, not equity, and to strip the companies of marketing functions, but at the same time to attract the technological and managerial skills so closely held by the MNCs. The companies would in effect perform a banking function on the one hand and act as vendors of technology and skills on the other.

The companies, however, have not perceived themselves as bankers, or as retailers of technological information, and tend strongly to resist any efforts toward unbundling. Although these and most other LDC efforts to break down the MNC package in oil and other fields have not been particularly successful to date, the potential benefits have appeared large to many governments. Nevertheless some knowledgeable observers of MNCs doubt whether the gains from unbundling would prove to be very great.[9] Although the Japanese have had some success in licensing technologies from multinationals without buying the whole package, they have also met stubborn resistance from multinationals. But the large size of the Japanese market gives them greater bargaining power. Also, the Japanese possess greater technical skills for adopting technologies to local conditions than do most, if not all, of the developing countries.

Benefits of Foreign Investment

Host-country legislation toward foreign investment reveals that those LDCs that do actively seek foreign investment expect a variety of tangible and intangible benefits from the infusion of resources provided by MNCs. Perhaps the most commonly stated objectives are those of job creation, transfer of usable technology and skills, and saving or earning foreign exchange. In addition many host countries seek foreign investment, particularly in natural resources, to help promote regional development objectives and to increase domestic tax revenues.

Employment Expansion The spotty empirical evidence on employment expansion from foreign investment is hardly convincing one way or another. Some observers maintain that displacement of local firms by multinationals may actually reduce local employment.[10] The argument hinges on the labor intensity of production techniques selected by foreign firms, a matter discussed below. The available evidence seems to indicate that host country hopes for significant employment gains from MNC investments are seldom realized. In very few LDCs has employment in multinationals' projects exceeded 1 percent of the labor force. Prominent exceptions include Brazil and Mexico, in which foreign-controlled affiliates compose half of the indus-

---

9. See, for example, Raymond Vernon, *Storm Over the Multinationals: The Real Issues* (Cambridge, Mass.: Harvard University Press, 1977), pp. 159–61.
10. Osvaldo Sunkel, "Big Business and Dependencies," *Foreign Affairs* 50 (1972): 518–19.

trial sector.[11] Other exceptions include such relatively small countries as Singapore (manufacturing and tourism), Jamaica (tourism and bauxite), and perhaps Cuba before Castro.

One reason for limited employment growth from MNC investments is that LDCs frequently permit entry of foreign firms only in highly capital-intensive sectors, such as minerals, petroleum, and chemicals. A five-hundred million dollar oil refinery may employ fewer than 300 people, and a one-billion dollar natural gas liquification plant ordinarily operates with even fewer workers. The share of multinational investments in LDCs devoted to natural-resource extraction and processing has been placed as high as 42 percent for the period 1965–1972.[12] In these industries investment costs per job created can be quite high. In 1976 it took $220,000 of investment to create one job in nickel mining in Indonesia, and $467,000 per job in pulp and paper in 1980, both sectors in which foreign companies are welcome. Yet in textiles, where they are no longer welcome, a job could be created for only $10,000 of investment.

Critics of multinationals allege that not only do these firms tend to invest in capital-intensive sectors (where the host governments usually want them to invest), but they also tend to utilize more capital-intensive technologies than do host-country firms in the same industry. There is conflicting empirical evidence on this question. One recent study found that subsidiaries of U.S.-based firms appeared to use technologies similar to those of locally owned firms, but operate in a more capital-intensive manner because as foreign investors they faced higher labor costs than local firms.[13] The study found that U.S. and Swedish multinationals do adapt to lower labor costs in LDCs by using more labor-intensive methods than the same firms use in industrial countries. Some researchers have found that some MNCs actually tend to use more labor-intensive technology processes than do domestic LDC firms in the same industry. Pack found this to be true in his study of forty-two foreign and local plants in the manufacturing sector of Kenya.[14] Pack's research was corroborated by a 1976 International Labor Office study on employment in Kenya. Yet other studies by Helen Hughes and You Pon Seng for Singapore, Steven Langdon for soap products in Kenya, and a study on Puerto Rico reached opposite conclusions.[15] Lawrence J. White cites a number of studies showing mixed results, but concludes that although MNCs may not be heroes of "appropriate" technology, they are far from the

11. C. Fred Bergsten, Thomas Horst, and Theodore H. Moran, *American Multinationals and American Interests* (Washington, D.C.: Brookings Institution, 1978), p. 355.

12. Billerbeck and Yasugi, "Private Direct Foreign Investment," Table SI-6.

13. Robert E. Lipsey, Irving B. Kraus, and Romualdo A. Roldan, "Do Multinational Firms Adapt Factor Proportions to Relative Factor Prices?" (Cambridge, Mass.: National Bureau of Economic Research, Working Paper #293, October 1978). For supporting evidence, see Byung Soo Chung and Chung H. Lee, "The Choice of Production Techniques by Foreign Firms in Korea," *Economic Development and Cultural Change* 29 (1980): 135–40.

14. Howard Pack, "The Substitution of Labor for Capital in Manufacturing," *Economic Journal* (March 1976): 45–58.

15. Helen Hughes and You Pon Seng, *Foreign Investment and Industrialization in Singapore* (Madison: University of Wisconsin Press, 1969), p. 193; Steven Langdon, *Multinationals in the Political Economy of Kenya* (New York: St. Martins Press, 1981) Chapter 4.

384

FOREIGN
SAVINGS:
AID AND
INVESTMENT
(Ch. 14)

villians painted by many critics.[16] Still other researchers have concluded that the origin of the investment—whether from multinationals or domestic firms—makes no decisive difference in technology selected for the project.[17]

But there is a growing body of evidence that developing-country multinationals employ markedly more labor-intensive practices than their developed country counterparts, even though the volume of their investments remains relatively small.[18] Their investments are more heavily concentrated in relatively labor-intensive industrial undertakings like textiles and simple consumer goods, such as umbrellas, kerosene lanterns, utensils, and several types of machinery. And the majority of the LDC firms depend on special production abilities on a small scale, attributes that are inherently labor-intensive.

Technology Transfer The second major benefit expected from foreign investment is the transfer of technology, skills, and know-how. This issue is best seen as only peripherally involving exotic processes and sophisticated equipment, as the fundamental problem is in the market for information, a market characterized by severe imperfections. Because much of the world's research and development activities have been undertaken within large firms in North America, Europe, and Japan, these firms are a potentially rich source of valuable information about new technology, new processes, new marketing methods, and managerial approaches. Smaller MNCs, particularly those from other developing countries, offer another kind of technological benefit: successful adaptation to LDC conditions of older technology from developed countries, and new, cost-savings innovations in small-scale manufacture. If this information can be transplanted to host countries, material increases in growth and productivity can result over the long term. The ability of an LDC to capitalize on such opportunities depends primarily on three factors: (1) the host country's capacity to absorb new information as defined by the skills of its people; (2) the willingness of MNCs to accommodate host-country desires for technological transfer; and (3) host-country policies toward technological transfer and information generation and dissemination in general, which is discussed in a later section.

The type of absorptive capacity required for successful transfer of technology from MNCs depends on the nature of the investment project. For some operations (such as logging), many manufacturing activities, and open-pit hard-minerals mining, acquisition of new information and methods by host-country workers requires only a basic educational background and a willingness to work in a modern, structured enterprise with clear standards for work schedules and work pace. But in other activities, particularly in natural-resource-based industries such as steelmaking, copper smelting, and chemi-

16. Lawrence J. White, "The Evidence on Appropriate Factor Proportions," *Economic Development and Cultural Change* 27 (October 1978): 27–59.

17. Sanjaya Lall and Paul Streeten, *Foreign Investment, Transnationals and Developing Countries* (Boulder, Colorado: Westview Press, 1977), pp. 104–6.

18. Prof. L. T. Wells of Harvard University has conducted a number of studies on MNCs from developing nations. See, among other examples of his work, "The Internationalization of Firms from LDCs," in *Multinationals from Small Countries,* Tamir Agmon and C. P. Kindleberger, eds. (Cambridge, Mass.: MIT Press, 1977).

cal manufacturing, absorptive capacity depends upon a locally available stock of more highly trained technical personnel such as chemical engineers, metallurgists, geologists, biologists, and industrial economists.

Some developing countries, such as India and Mexico, have trained relatively large numbers of technical industrial personnel and are capable of relatively rapid absorption of new technologies. Other countries, though not so well endowed with technical personnel, have made strong efforts to train them in order to take over important foreign-owned industries. For example, Venezuela has trained petroleum engineers and managers who now successfully run that sector; South Korea used its first chemical fertilizer plant, built and operated by a foreign firm, to train Koreans who now operate several other nationally owned fertilizer plants; and Malaysia has made itself capable not only of managing its own rubber industry, but of conducting its own research on new species and methods of cultivation. But for the most part developing countries do not have sufficient cadres of technically educated people to manage technologically complex industries. And as Chapter 9 suggested, it may be difficult to justify the large capital investments involved to train such personnel in sufficient numbers when substantial portions of the population have not even completed primary school. Further, many countries that have tried to educate a technical cadre have suffered from a "brain drain," as those with advanced educations are attracted by salaries and work conditions to emigrate to the industrial countries.

Perspectives on technology transfer differ markedly between multinationals and developing countries. The former view their investments in production of technology as a continuing process which should earn financial returns just as any investment would. Host countries, however, are concerned primarily with access to existing knowledge, and with some justification regard past MNC investments in the generation of technology as sunk costs not requiring reimbursement. Public goods theory, as well as casual observation, tells us that MNCs will withhold information on technologies when they would not otherwise be able to appropriate the returns. This is, according to some analysts, likely to be particularly true for the types of simple product technologies and unskilled-labor-using production techniques of most interest to LDCs.

Foreign Exchange Benefits A third objective of LDCs seeking foreign investment has been to save and earn foreign exchange. The impact of multinational investments on LDC balance of payments has been a source of some controversy. One study, published in 1973 and covering over one hundred MNCs, concludes that in the late 1960s net positive effects of multinationals on the balance of payments was negligible; indeed in perhaps half the cases firms were found to export more foreign exchange, through imports from abroad and profit repatriation, than they earned.[19] If this was indeed the case, it is unlikely that profit repatriation was the principal source of loss of foreign exchange. Total payments by non-oil developing countries

19. Paul Streeten and Sanjaya Lall, *The Flow of Financial Resources: Private Foreign Investment, Main Findings of a Study on Selected Developing Countries* (United Nations: Document TD/B/C-3 III, May 1973).

386

FOREIGN
SAVINGS:
AID AND
INVESTMENT
(Ch. 14)

on foreign direct investment were small in 1973 and have declined since then. Dividends and other forms of detectable profit repatriation were but 3 percent of the exports of such LDCs in 1973, and only 1.5 percent in 1983.[20] The controversy over the balance of payments impact of foreign investment does serve to underline a critical point concerning interpretation of foreign exchange benefits from any MNC project: the emphasis must be on net, rather than gross, foreign exchange earnings, in recognition of the fact that a sizable share of gross export earnings often does not represent retained value to host countries. As this issue—as well as the objectives of regional development and an increased tax base—is of central importance in natural-resources investments, we will postpone detailed consideration of these benefits until Chapter 19.

LDC Policies toward Foreign Investment

LDC governments use a wide range of restrictions and incentives intended to elicit desired behavior from multinational corporations. Of the four policy tools discussed here, three are restrictions: (1) performance requirements, (2) "saturation" laws, and (3) control over profit repatriation. The fourth tool is tax incentives.

Restrictions Performance requirements are generally tailored to fit each industry. MNCs entering the automobile assembly industry are often forced to increase annually the percent of local materials in each vehicle, for example, while those entering hard-minerals extraction may be required to commit themselves to future investments in domestic minerals processing. Performance requirements are most commonly established to serve the same LDC objectives already discussed: employment, transfer of technology, and, for export-oriented activities, foreign exchange earnings.

Policies requiring MNCs to utilize local personnel are also common. These measures are aimed not only at job creation but also at increasing absorptive capacity for the transfer of technology from multinationals. Provisions generally involve a time schedule with specific targets for employment of local labor and managers, with different targets established for different types of skills. For example, Indonesia typically requires MNCs in natural resources to fill all unskilled jobs with Indonesians after three years, but only 75 percent of skilled and supervisory jobs, and 50 percent of technical and managerial personnel.

LDCs have utilized a number of requirements intended to promote technology transfer. Many developing countries have imposed standards requiring MNCs to import only the most advanced capital equipment, and what amounts to the same thing, have prohibited the importation of used machinery. Such measures work against other LDC goals, however, because older used equipment is likely to be more labor-using, quite apart from being cheaper. This is but one example of widespread tendency to associate technological transfer with importation of equipment, rather than of information.

---

20. Goldsbrough, "Foreign Direct Investment," p. 32.

In addition some governments have imposed special taxes on MNCs to finance government research and development (Ecuador), or have required the firms to invest in local research and development (R&D) activities (India), or have otherwise pressured companies to undertake local R&D. One study cites eleven instances, primarily in Brazil and India, in which firms responded by establishing research and development facilities in the host country.[21]

A more widely used policy (particularly in Latin America and Southeast Asia), intended in part to yield greater transfer of technology, has been LDC insistence that foreign investors acquire local partners by forming joint ventures with local firms. These requirements are usually contained in what has become known as **saturation laws,** which make it mandatory for MNCs to sell a specified percent of equity, usually 51 percent, in each project to host-country citizens. The idea has been that the local joint-venture partners could, by virtue of their internal positions, somehow monitor incoming technology, appropriate it, and permanently embed it in the host economy. However, many local joint-venture partnerships are *pro forma* arrangements involving local elites close to the centers of political power with little interest in business matters. And parent MNCs often show even greater reluctance to allow diffusion of technology to joint ventures than to wholly owned subsidiaries.

Saturation laws requiring investment in the form of joint ventures clearly involve greater national presence and greater potential for host-country control over foreign investors' activities. Whether these devices also serve on balance to increase the income of local owners of equity capital and whether they involve net economic benefits to the host country are somewhat less certain. Indeed some analysts argue that such requirements may have little, if any, positive effects on the host country's national income because they divert scarce local resources to the multinational's sector, and also reduce the inflow of foreign capital.[22]

Other common restrictions include ceilings on repatriation of profits to the parent corporation and measures to increase reinvestment of profits in the host country, including stiff taxes on profits remitted to the parent firm abroad. Ceiling on profit repatriation are designed to reduce future outflows of resources from LDCs. Such limitations have been widely used by LDCs, particularly in Latin America and in India. In Colombia profits remitted by a firm to a parent abroad were limited to 14 percent of the firm's Colombian investments; Brazil has at time limited remittances to 10 percent of registered capital. In other countries, such as Argentina and Ghana, although no explicit percentage ceilings on profit repatriation may be established, repatriation is limited through the administration of the system of foreign exchange controls (see Chapter 16).

21. Jack N. Behrman and William A. Fischer, *Overseas R&D Activities of Transnational Corporations* (Cambridge, Mass.: Oelgeschlager, Gunn and Hain, 1980), pp. 107–9.

22. For example, Vernon stresses that if local buyers pay a price fully commensurate with the earnings they receive, all they will have done is export scarce capital to a foreign seller (Vernon, *Storm Over the Multinationals,* p. 168).

388

FOREIGN
SAVINGS:
AID AND
INVESTMENT
(Ch. 14)

Incentives For foreign investors able to meet performance requirements, most LDCs offer positive inducements: tax holidays and other tax incentives, monopoly rights in the local market, and covenants that investors will be allowed to repatriate profits. The latter inducement is rarely important in influencing investment decisions, since such covenants represent only good intentions on the part of the present government, not a guarantee that future governments will necessarily obey. Monopoly rights in the local market to a foreign investor do increase the incentive to invest, and such rights have long been sought by many multinationals wanting to invest in import-substituting industries in LDCs. Several countries have granted them. Kenya, Zambia, and Indonesia, for example, awarded monopoly rights to two of the world's largest tire manufacturers. Monopoly positions, however, reduce pressure on MNCs to hold prices down and keep quality up. Moreover, because they create higher domestic prices and profits, monopoly rights result in direct transfers from LDC consumers to the multinational's foreign stockholders.

Tax incentives are by far the most widely used inducements offered to multinationals. While the variety of such incentives is almost limitless, we will focus on the most common one, **income tax holidays** (income tax exemptions). Tax rates on corporate income in LDCs are typically between 40 and 50 percent. To attract foreign investment, LDC governments often offer to exempt the income of newly entering MNCs from corporate taxes for the first several years of operation, usually three to six years. During the heyday of these tax holidays, the postwar period through 1970, most MNCs investing in the third world received exemptions, usually for five-year periods. By 1980 tax holidays had virtually vanished for natural-resource investments, except in some former French colonies in Africa, and were becoming less common in other sectors as well. But there are still enough recent examples of tax holidays to arouse wonderment, if not dismay, among economists. Increasingly host countries have learned that where such incentives are valuable to MNCs, they may serve little purpose other than the enrichment of foreign shareholders and foreign treasuries, at the expense of local treasuries.

Tax holidays have been ineffective public policy instruments for several reasons. First, for most of the postwar era, tax holidays were of very limited value to multinationals from many of the major capital-exporting countries, including the United States, Japan, and West Germany. These and most other developed countries, excluding France, employ a "global" income concept: they tax all income of corporations based in their borders, whatever its source. If the income is earned abroad, the home-country income tax applies when the earnings are remitted. A multinational whose home country taxes global income can (except in Sweden) credit (offset) within limits the taxes paid on foreign income against income taxes due in the home country. Thus if the company pays zero or reduced taxes in the host country, it simply pays more taxes at home. For these investors the effect of tax holidays offered by developing countries is to transfer tax revenues from host LDCs to the treasuries of the industrial home country, a kind of "reverse foreign aid." With no host country income taxes to credit against home country taxes, the only benefit received by an MNC subsidiary is the deferral of home country taxes, since these are not due until income is repatriated. Figure 14–2 illustrates how tax holidays, alone and when coupled with other incentives, such as monopoly rights, have resulted in large benefits to foreigners, with little gain to host countries.

Consider a multinational firm that has received monopoly rights to manufacture automobile tires for an LDC market and has also received a five-year tax holiday. For simplicity, assume the monopolist can produce at constant marginal cost *(MC)* and hence constant average costs *(AC = MC)*. If the tire industry were a competitive industry consisting of many firms, then the supply curve of that industry would be identical to *MC = AC*. The price of tires would then be P_c, and the output of tires would be Q_c; equilibrium would occur at point *E*, where demand and supply schedules intersect.

A profit-maximizing monopolist, however, determines the level of output, Q_m, where marginal cost and marginal revenue *(MR)* are equal. Q_m, being smaller than Q_c, can be sold at a price of P_m, well above P_c. As a result, monopoly profits (rectangle $P_c DC P_m$) are generated, over and above "normal" (competitive) returns to capital. Consumers in the host country pay higher prices for fewer tires, and there is substantial economic waste (area *CDE*). Triangle *CDE* represents deadweight loss or excess burden. To interpret the meaning of triangle *CDE*, review Figure 12–1. When the monopolist repatriates his profits to the home country, the home-country treasury will take a proportion equal to the average tax rate (50 percent in the diagram). The monopolist is no better off with the tax holiday than without it. But for the five years of the tax holiday, host-country consumers will not only pay dearly for tires, they will also send contributions to governments in rich countries. After the tax holiday expires, tire consumers will continue to subsidize waste, but the host-country treasury will at least receive some taxes.

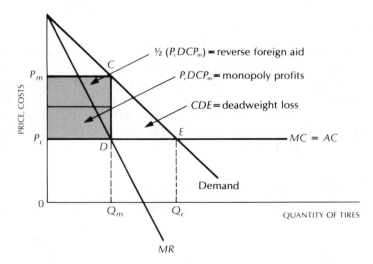

FIGURE 14–2 Interaction of Incentive Policies. Here we see the case of tax holidays for an MNC subsidiary with monopoly rights in the host country without tax-sparing. Consumers lose: they pay the monopoly price P_m rather than P_c. The host country loses, too: the taxes they do not collect flow to the MNCs' home country, resulting in reverse foreign aid. Yet the MNC gains nothing from the tax holiday because it now has to pay taxes to its home country.

390

FOREIGN
SAVINGS:
AID AND
INVESTMENT
(Ch. 14)

As the existence of reverse foreign aid began to be more widely recognized in the 1960s, LDC governments began demanding adjustments in home-country treatment of foreign-source income of MNCs. Eventually, many LDCs concluded tax treaties with industrial countries in which multinationals receiving tax holidays were, in effect, allowed to credit income taxes forgiven by LDCs (due to tax holidays) against income taxes due in the home country. These arrangements, known as "tax-sparing" clauses, have been granted by most capital-exporting countries, though not by the United States. Under tax-sparing, income taxes given up by the LDCs that award tax holidays benefit the foreign investor, not the home-country government.

Even though MNCs from certain developed countries other than the United States now receive the full benefits from LDC tax holidays, there remains substantial doubt that LDCs themselves receive full benefits commensurate with the costs of the tax revenues they forego. Study after study from locations around the world indicates that income tax holidays more often than not have only marginal effects on MNC investment decisions, rewarding them for what they would have done in any case.

One possible exception to this general rule is the investment decision on location of export-oriented, labor-intensive industries that make little use of domestic raw materials. A prominent example is the electronics industry, which utilizes large amounts of unskilled labor to manufacture chips, make integrated circuits, and assemble parts of products such as electronic calculators and computers. These firms operate largely in export processing zones in countries such as Malaysia, Thailand, and Ecuador. Electronics firms are primarily concerned with a stable source of low-cost, unskilled, and unorganized labor. They appear sensitive to differences in incentives offered by host countries, and LDCs have competed with each other in offering investment incentives and privileges to them. But even in this case inducements like tax holidays may play a secondary role in investment decisions. Malaysia and Indonesia, for example, have both offered similar tax incentives to semiconductor firms since 1970. But even though wage rates for unskilled labor were much higher in Malaysia, that country has been able to attract more than a dozen plants employing eighty thousand people, while in Indonesia, with a labor force three times as large, only five thousand people were employed in the two semiconductor firms that have located there. Clearly factors other than tax incentives were more important in influencing investment decisions, even in an industry where inducements should be expected to matter to foreign investors.

Objectives of Multinational Firms

Although the objectives of multinational enterprises may vary across firms even within the same industry, these various goals can perhaps be subsumed under two broad, related categories: the search for global profit and the drive for stability. The profit objective speaks for itself. Stability is sought because it moderates the risks and uncertainties that threaten long-term profits essential for enterprise survival. Uncertainty, whether stemming from the activities of competitors or from political instability in host countries, is anathema to enterprise managers.

The interplay between profit and stability is perhaps best depicted by reference to insights offered by an important field in economics: industrial organization. There, theory shows that even within one national market large firms in an oligopolistic industry do not necessarily seek to maximize profits at the level of the individual enterprise. Rather, firms may attempt to maximize the joint profits of the industry as a whole while maintaining stability to the extent possible. This is possible only when market power is concentrated in the hands of a few firms. Above all, maintaining stability requires discouraging new entrants into the industry, as well as any actions within the industry that might erode the market share of the firms in the oligopoly. New entrants are attracted by high profits; thus the existing firms in the oligopoly may not attempt to maximize profits in order to maintain stability in the industry. Therefore investment within a national market does not necessarily flow to the place where returns, as conventionally defined, are highest.

Similar observations apply at the level of international markets. Although concentration of economic power has been declining in many international markets since 1945, direct foreign investment is still dominated by firms in oligopolistic industries controlling a large share of the market for their products. Multinationals in international markets pursue profits as intensely as oligopolitsts in national markets, with one important difference. A project in a particular host country is evaluated not so much in terms of the potential profitability of the project viewed in isolation, but in terms of the effects of the investment on the global profitability of the MNC and upon the implications of that investment for enterprise stability. LDC policies that take into account this central aspect of multinational strategy are far more likely to obtain the desired results than those formulated on the assumption that the enterprises are involved in a single-minded, project-by-project hunt for profits as conventionally defined.

Balancing the goals of global profit and stability has led multinationals to undertake projects in LDCs that would otherwise appear inexplicable. Oil multinationals with reserves concentrated in one or two LDCs have accepted contractual arrangements from a host country involving lower returns than received by multinational competitors because they wanted to diversify reserves. A large tire manufacturer may agree to operate rubber plantations in a country not particularly suited to rubber cultivation simply to assure itself of adequate sources of raw material in times of market scarcity. A U.S.-based sulphur firm might enter copper mining in an LDC because it offers an opportunity to diversify activity and thereby better insulate the firm from the vagaries of the sulphur business. Another MNC in copper might respond to the sulphur firm's threat in the copper industry by accepting less favorable terms to mine copper in the same country, merely to protect its existing market share. Japanese firms often establish subsidiaries for producing in developing countries simply to protect the export markets they already have.

Such investments point to a fairly coherent pattern of defensive behavior by multinationals. Increasingly LDC negotiators have recognized the impor-

392

FOREIGN
SAVINGS:
AID AND
INVESTMENT
(Ch. 14)

tance of stability and other strategic considerations in MNC planning, which in turn has enhanced their abilities to play off one firm against others. In the process many host countries have been able to curtail, if not abandon, use of generous inducements to invest, particularly tax incentives.

Conflict and Conflict Resolution

The previous two sections make clear that just as the objectives of multinational investors and host LDCs often are not well matched, neither are their bargaining and administrative capacities. The reality, or even the perception, of poorly matched interests inevitably leads to conflicts between multinationals and host-country governments. Settlements of conflict range from the relatively amicable (Zambia's takeover of foreign-owned copper mines in the early 1970s) to the acrimonious (nationalization of the International Petroleum Company in Peru in the 1960s). Amicable resolution, or at least resolution without rupture, is the predominant pattern. Outright expropriation of MNC properties without compensation is now relatively rare. It was more widespread in the late 1950s and early 1960s after many LDCs in Asia and Africa first gained their independence. For the period 1960 to 1979, one analyst was able to identify 563 acts of expropriation in developing countries involving nearly 1,700 companies. But these companies represented only about 5 percent of the total value of MNC investments around the world.[23] Another study, for the period 1960 to 1976, found 511 cases wherein 1,535 foreign firms were forced to divest of their LDC direct investments, but few of the cases involved outright expropriations. Such acts of forced divestment, however, have been increasing: nearly three-quarters have occurred since 1970; 30 percent occurred in 1974 and 1975 alone.[24]

In an earlier era, the threat of expropriation was one of the few devices available to host countries dissatisfied with a multinational's performance. Leverage in conflict resolution, as well as prevailing philosophies concerning sanctity of contracts, was primarily on the side of the multinationals. MNCs were unaccustomed to dealing with LDC demands for redress, and orderly mechanisms for resolving conflict were lacking. Over time several factors have led to fundamental alterations in LDC–MNC relations, including those involving conflict resolution. First, the so-called doctrine of "sanctity of contracts" has been steadily undermined around the world, especially as industrial country firms began in the 1960s to abrogate or modify their own large international contracts, as happened with wool and dairy products in Japanese–Australian trade. Increasingly there developed a consensus, with reluctance by the multinationals, that some investment contracts in LDCs were too much the product of unequal bargaining positions and skills. By the 1980s there was a widespread view that changes in underlying conditions could justify changes in contract terms in favor of host countries. Second, the initial demonstration of market power by OPEC countries in 1973 sug-

23. *Business Week,* September 14, 1961, pp. 49–50.
24. Forced divestment is defined as the taking of foreign-owned property by nationalization, expropriation, forced sales and confiscation. See Stephen J. Kobrin, "Foreign Enterprise and Forced Divestment in LDCs," *International Organization* 34 (Winter 1980).

gested to other developing countries that more aggressive behavior in dealing with multinationals, short of expropriation, could on occasion succeed. Third, bitter memories of expropriation, rising "fiscal militancy" of host countries in general, together with the near-universal spread of saturation laws among LDCs, has served to convince many MNC managers of the tenuousness of their involvement in many developing countries. Many began to seek ways to moderate the scope for harsh conflict with host-country officials.

As a result, whereas even the word "renegotiation" was inadmissable in the MNC lexicon two decades ago, laws, contracts, and regulations governing multinational participation in LDCs now commonly contain provisions for periodic review of investors' activities to allow for orderly renegotiation of the original terms of entry. Further, new methods of arbitration have been devised for those conflicts that cannot be resolved by mutual agreement between the host country and MNC. Earlier, multinationals were generally unwilling to accept any provisions for arbitration other than those calling for ultimate settlement in the International Court for the Settlement of Industrial Disputes (ICSID) in The Hague. Increasingly host countries came to view this arbitration mechanism as an infringement of their sovereign powers and, particularly in Latin America, began to require MNCs to accept arbitration as prescribed by host-country laws.

By the 1980s the principal threat to MNC control over foreign subsidiaries was no longer that of forcible seizure of assets through outright expropriation, but what multinationals view as "creeping expropriation." This is said to result from stiffening requirements for local participation in joint ventures, growing restrictions on profit repatriation, and steadily rising host-country taxes on MNC operations. Both outright and creeping expropriation are important considerations in multinationals' growing efforts to insure themselves against political risk. One study indicates that in 1980 alone MNCs worldwide paid as much as $700 million in political-risk premiums to insuring agencies.

One of the major sources of conflict in MNC-LDC relations has been over the problem of **transfer pricing.** Because a substantial proportion of transactions by multinationals are internal to the firm (between affiliates of the same firm), such transactions may be assigned an arbitrary value to suit the enterprise's interests. Unlike transactions between unaffiliated firms, there are often no objective, market-determined, or "arm's-length" values that can be used to verify prices recorded in intrafirm and interaffiliate transactions. This being the case, MNCs can use transfer-pricing devices to change the location of reported income from countries with high taxes to countries with lower taxes, thereby maximizing after-tax profits of their global operations, or in some cases evading foreign exchange controls of host countries. For example, a multinational in cosmetics, headquartered in London with a subsidiary in Nairobi, could understate profits of its operations in Kenya by billing its Kenyan subsidiary for facial cream ingredients at twice the price it charges its affiliate in Hong Kong. Or an American MNC in forest products might attempt to underdeclare profits in the Philippines by overstating the

394

FOREIGN
SAVINGS:
AID AND
INVESTMENT
(Ch. 14)

costs of logging equipment it ships to its Philippine subsidiary or by under-stating the per unit-value of logs exported to still another subsidiary in Korea.

Critics of multinationals have long maintained that the companies have used intrafirm transfer pricing as a means of reducing LDC shares of gains from foreign investment for the benefit of the MNCs and home-country treasuries. MNCs also have strong incentives to underreport profits of sub-sidiaries in host countries that impose ceilings on profit remittances to the parent. And transfer-pricing devices may be employed for political reasons if the parent MNC believes that high reported profits in LDC subsidiaries increase the risk of contract renegotiation or expropriation.

The scope for transfer-pricing abuses is substantial, and some analysts believe it has grown in recent years. One study indicates that in 1977 fully one-third of all exports of developed-country MNCs from their home coun-try was to their own affiliates in other countries. There are, however, impor-tant differences between firms. The incidence of intrafirm transactions tends to be higher, the greater the proportion of sales of foreign subsidiaries to total sales of the enterprise. Further, firms in high-technology, high-research fields, such as electronics and chemicals, engage in intrafirm transactions to a greater degree than do firms in industries producing standardized products like textiles and food processing. U.S. firms, being generally more multina-tional in nature and more concentrated in high-research-intensity fields, engage more frequently in intrafirm transactions than their European counterparts.[25]

LDCs have responded to transfer-pricing abuses by attempting to tighten pre-existing controls and by intensive investigation of industries reputed to be notorious for transfer-price manipulations, such as the pharmaceutical industry. Given sufficient vigilance by host countries, transfer-pricing abuses can be curtailed easily enough in cases where intrafirm trade in standardized products is involved. Products such as copper concentrates, ammonium nitrate, and plywood have well-established world-market prices that can be used to determine whether an intrafirm transaction has been valued at arm's length. However, much of the intrafirm transactions of MNCs involve non-standardized products and services, for which arm's-length prices are not readily available. This is particularly true for goods shipped largely within vertically integrated MNCs (bauxite), and for payments made to parent firms by subsidiaries for technology, research, and overhead. Full resolution of the transfer-pricing issue to the satisfaction of LDCs appears unlikely in the near future.

COMMERCIAL BORROWING

The most rapidly growing source of foreign savings inflow to LDCs has been private loans from three sources: bond lending, commercial bank lending,

25. John Stopford, John Dunning, and James Haberich, *World Directory of Multinational Enterprises 1980* (Detroit: Gale Research Co., 1980) p. xxiii. For a summary of studies portray-ing transfer-pricing abuses, see Lewis D. Solomon, *Multinational Corporations and the Emerg-ing World Order* (London: Kennikat Press, 1978), pp. 79–83.

and export credits. **Bond lending** is one form of portfolio investment. The
other form, foreign purchases of equities (stock) in LDC enterprises, was never really important in most LDCs, except during certain periods of Argentine, Brazilian, and Chilean history. The international bond market has been used from time to time by such relatively prosperous LDCs as Mexico, Turkey, and Algeria. In this market, LDC governments (rarely private firms) borrow at long term (five to twenty-five years) by issuing bonds backed by the full faith and credit of the issuing government. Bonds are purchased by a variety of investors, normally from developed countries, operating through large brokers such as Kuhn-Loeb and Morgan Stanley (U.S.) or the Rothschild group (France, Britain).

The second, much newer, and much larger channel for capital transfers is **commercial bank lending,** both from the **Eurocurrency market** (Eurocurrencies are simply currencies on deposit at banks outside the country that issues the currency. Thus there are Eurodollars, Euromarks, Eurofrancs, and so on), and from ordinary lending abroad by banks using their own currency. The total stock of such loans outstanding at the end of 1984 was about $2.5 trillion, of which $2 trillion was in Eurocurrency loans. (Hereafter the sum of Eurocurrency borrowings plus domestic currency lending abroad will be called "total international lending.")

The Eurocurrency market dates from the early 1960s, when it developed in response to tax measures adopted by the United States government to protect the American dollar. Even by 1979 the total net size of this financial market was on the order of $475 billion. Eurocurrency credits or loans are typically made not by one bank but by syndicates of banks, each of which provides a share of the loan. Eurocurrency loans are typically granted for much shorter terms than those available in bond issues, at interest rates geared to rates charged by banks when they lend to other banks. The traditional rate employed for this purpose has been the London interbank borrowing rate (LIBOR), which fluctuates from period to period. The nominal LIBOR rate has ranged from as low as 6.5 percent in 1977 to 16 percent in 1980. In mid-1986, LIBOR hovered at between 6 and 8 percent for Eurodollar loans. Borrowers pay a premium over LIBOR depending on the market's assessment of risk. Since loans to LDCs are typically considered riskier propositions, the premium is usually higher for them than for developed-country borrowers. In recent years the premium was as low as five-eighths of 1 percent for some borrowers (Colombia in 1981) and as high as 2.5 percent for others (Panama in 1978, at the time of the Canal negotiations).

Prior to 1970 only a few developing countries borrowed on any significant scale for the Eurocurrency market, and they borrowed almost nothing in the form of ordinary domestic currency loans from foreign banks. Reported, or publicized, gross Eurocurrency credits (between a quarter and a third of such transactions are not publicized) to LDCs rose from virtually nothing in 1967 to almost $7 billion in 1973, and to over $42 billion by 1979, representing a compound growth rate of over 40 percent per year in just the latter six-year period. This remarkable growth was due in part to the commercial bank's need to find borrowers to "recycle" the enormous deposits by petroleum exports following the first oil price boom of 1973 and 1974.

396

FOREIGN
SAVINGS:
AID AND
INVESTMENT
(Ch. 14)

In some respects the rise of the Eurocurrency market and the rebirth of ordinary international lending as sources of foreign savings for LDCs has been a beneficial development, particularly for the middle-income countries that accounted for over 80 percent of such debt. Prior to the emergence of this market many LDC governments with an attractive list of domestic investment projects could secure finance for them only through requests for foreign aid from industrial country governments. Many countries found this to be unsatisfactory, not only because aid was often subject to conditions imposed by the donor country, but because procedures of many aid donors were so involved that even good projects were sometimes delayed for several years. International lending markets provided an alternative source of finance that involved few delays, no supplication to aid donors, and, in the eyes of many LDC officials, a channel of finance both more flexible and less intrusive on their economic independence.

External commercial borrowing is, however, very expensive relative to official aid for industrial countries. Until 1981, the weighted average interest rate of all foreign aid to LDCs was typically between 4 and 5 percent, and reached 7.5 percent only in 1983.[26] Interest rates faced by LDC borrowers on loans from private sources rose steadily from about 8 percent in 1975 to 1977, to 14 percent in 1981 before declining to about 11 percent in 1983, and to as low as 9.5 percent in 1986.

Further, the very rapid buildup of external commercial debt of LDCs from 1970 onward has resulted in serious debt service problems for many, as their export earnings available for paying interest and principal on debt have not grown at anything approaching the 40 percent rate of annual increase in commercial debt obligations.

THE LDC DEBT CRISIS

Prior to 1979 most countries, particularly the five major LDCs (Brazil, Mexico, Venezuela, Spain, Argentina), which together owed about half of total external debt in 1979 encountered no serious problems in meeting debt service requirements. However, by 1980 a number of LDCs, including Peru, Bolivia, Sudan, Turkey, Zaire, and Zambia, had experienced serious difficulties in coping with their debts. More ominously, there were indications even by the early 1980s that at least one of the large borrowers (Brazil) had reached or surpassed its capacity to service further debt, as a combination of doubling of import prices for oil, obligations from past external borrowings, and rising protectionism in the industrial countries left little foreign exchange to pay for imports.

By 1982 and 1983 concern over an impending crisis in LDC debts was pervasive, both in capital-exporting and capital-importing nations. The total value of outstanding LDC debts to commercial banks had nearly tripled from $160 billion in 1979 to almost $460 billion in 1983.[27] More and more countries each month experienced difficulties in servicing their debt. Many

26. World Bank, *World Development Report 1985*, p. 21.
27. *World Development Report 1985*, p. 115.

oil-importing LDCs had initially borrowed heavily in 1974 and 1975 and again in 1979 and 1981 to allow them to cope with the rise in oil prices from $3 per barrel to nearly $36 over that period. But with the onset of the deep world recession of the early eighties, and the rise of renewed protectionist policies in industrial countries, debt service capacity in those nations fell sharply with their exports. For all LDCs, the ratio of debt to exports had reached 131 percent and **debt service** (interest payments and repayments of principal) as a percent of exports was 19 percent. Oil exporters had only just begun to feel the pinch in 1982. Many, such as Indonesia and Nigeria, had borrowed heavily in 1978 through 1981, when oil prices peaked. As the world oil market softened gradually from 1982 through 1984, and then rapidly in 1985 and 1986, many such nations were beginning to face debt service difficulties as well.

A crisis atmosphere prevailed in 1982 and 1983; large debtor nations such as Argentina and Brazil appeared to be on the verge of default. The press was full of talk of an imminent collapse of several large American and European banks, not to mention the entire international monetary system. The so-called "crisis" appeared to abate in 1984 and 1985, with the recovery of the world economy and far-reaching structural changes in international financial markets. These served fundamentally to alter the future lending behavior of commercial banks and to blur the distinctions between banks and other financial institutions. The first change was the greater readiness of the banks to acede to postponement of scheduled debt repayments from debtor LDCs. Indeed, there was little alternative but to do so, since the only other option open to many LDCs was outright default on their loan obligations, as in fact many did during the Great Depression of the 1930s. By 1986, more than forty LDCs, including virtually every Latin American country, had been forced to postpone scheduled debt payments.[28] No country had yet defaulted outright, in spite of the onerous debt service burdens facing many: rather, the debts were rescheduled through negotiations, sometimes of a delicate nature. Still the burden remains of servicing an LDC debt (both commercial debt and official debt) that is estimated at $1.01 trillion in 1986 (Table 14-7), half of which is owed to private lenders. And by mid-1986, the debt service capacities of several formerly "safe" LDC oil exporters, including Indonesia and Nigeria, had weakened substantially, as noted earlier.

The "debt crisis" clearly worked severe hardships on a large number of LDCs. By 1986, a powerful "scissors" effect of escalating debt service ratios and declining capital inflows from new loans had developed. The outflow of foreign exchange required to service debt diverted savings that otherwise would have been available for domestic investment and for imports needed to support the recoveries of LDC economies. The outflow had become substantial by 1985: LDC debtor countries paid the equivalent of $50 billion in interest alone to overseas creditors in 1985; this was $22 billion more than the new loans they received in that year. The scissors effect was particularly damaging in Africa. *Net* external borrowing by sub-Saharan African coun-

---

28. Jeffrey D. Sachs, "The LDC Debt Crisis" (Cambridge, Mass. Paper presented at the Annual Research Conference of the National Bureau of Economic Research, in New York, October 7, 1986).

398

FOREIGN
SAVINGS:
AID AND
INVESTMENT
(Ch. 14)

tries fell from \$14 billion in 1982 to only \$2 billion in 1985. While most media attention has focused on the debt problems of Latin American countries, money experts believe that the impact of the debt crisis on *people* has been much more severe in Africa.[29]

Causes of the Crisis

There is disagreement concerning the basic causes of the debt crisis. Some, including many officials in LDCs, lay much of the blame at the feet of international bankers. It has been frequently observed that banking consortia, under pressure to find borrowers for growing deposits from oil exporting countries from 1973–1981 sometimes extended large loans to LDC governments with minimal analysis of the debt service prospects of the borrowing country. A major reason for inattention by bankers to debt-carrying capacity was that a very large share of the debt buildup was in the form of **sovereign debt** owed by LDC governments.

Unlike ordinary debt contracted between private parties, which is collectible by law, sovereign debt is above the law; service of such debt is not subject to external enforcement. Sovereign debt is debt that is backed by the full faith and credit of the debtor government. Except in cases of irreparable political disputes between nations, sovereign debt is—parodoxically to some —a much better risk for lenders since in the event of default, debtor government's access to future loans may be denied for a considerable time. Sovereign debt is an obligation of an entire country, and is not dependent upon the success or failure of any one activity financed by a loan. Prospects for repayment of non-sovereign debt, however, depend both upon the trustworthiness of borrowers and the success or failure of his or her business. The risk of default is therefore considerably greater for non-sovereign (or private) debt, even though these are collectible by law.

Basically then, many banks during the seventies and early eighties rushed to extend loans to LDC governments, often without much thought as to the prospects for debtor export earnings or much attention to the effectiveness of domestic management of fiscal, monetary, or foreign trade policies. The widespread, near-universal assumption was that "'sovereign debt always gets repaid." Unfortunately, many banks did not anticipate that the burden of servicing sovereign debt might become so harsh that living standards in debtor nations might have to decline sharply, thereby affecting the willingness of debtor countries to continue to make the sacrifice. The government of Peru, for example, declared in July 1985 that it would unilaterally limit payments on its \$14.3 billion foreign debt to 10 percent of its export earnings, or half that nation's 1983 debt service ratio.

Miscalculations or perhaps mismanagement of sovereign debt issues by lenders was not, however, the only or even the prime cause of the debt crunch of the mid-eighties. Global economic shocks and economic policies in many of the borrowing nations helped to bring on the crisis. Three global economic shocks were of particular importance: (1) the sharp run-up in

29. See for example several of the papers in *African Debt and Financing,* Carol Lancaster and John Williamson, eds. (Washington, D.C.: Institute for International Economics, 1986).

world oil prices in 1979 through 1981, from $13.50 per barrel to $36.00, and the even sharper drop in oil prices in 1985 and 1986 to as low as $10 per barrel; (2) the deep world recession that resulted in part from the 1979 to 1981 oil price rise; and finally (3) the sharp rise in world interest rates particularly in the years 1979 through 1983.

The implications of the extreme fluctuations in world oil prices for debt and debt service were discussed earlier. The deep recession depressed export earnings of many debtor countries to the point that many had no choice but to delay debt service. The sharp rise in real interest rates (see Chapter 13) in the U.S. and then around the world was clearly a critical factor in the onset of the debt crisis. The higher the real interest rate on external loans, the more real resources of LDC debtors are required to repay debts. What was behind this phenomena?

Before 1979 and 1980, monetary policy in the U.S. was geared to holding nominal interest rates to targets established by the Federal Reserve. After November 1979, U.S. monetary policy switched to targeting monetary aggregates, such as M_1 or M_2, as identified in Chapter 13. As a result, interest rates became much more volatile. Long-term nominal interest rates had fluctuated within a small band between 5.0 and 8.5 percent from 1965 to 1979. But after 1979, nominal rates rose swiftly to 10 and then nearly 15 percent (1981) before settling back in the 10 to 11 percent range in 1984 and 1985. In 1986 they began to recede toward pre-1979 levels, at least for a while.

At the same time as nominal rates began their upward climb in 1979, the rate of inflation in the U.S. and other OECD nations began to decelerate, from nearly 10 percent in 1975 to about 5.0 percent in 1984 and 1985. The implications for debtor countries were serious. As late as 1975, governments such as Brazil and Korea were able to borrow at essentially negative real interest rates (see Chapter 13). This is a powerful incentive for borrowing. The eagerness of foreign banks to accept sovereign debt, coupled with very low and negative real rates of interest, helped fuel the explosion in LDC borrowing in the seventies. But with the combination of the sharp rise in nominal interest rates after 1979 and the decline in world inflation after 1982 the real interest rate increased dramatically. By 1982, real interest rates in the U.S. were close to 7 percent, and had reached almost 8 percent in 1984. Because much of LDC external debt is "rolled-over" every six months, with the interest rate on that debt dependent upon the current level of rates around the world, higher interest rates in the U.S. and Europe are quickly reflected in rates charged to LDCs. Consequently, in 1980 through 1984, countries such as Brazil and Korea found themselves facing real interest rates on their external obligations of more than 10 percent.[30] The cheap external money of the mid-seventies had vanished. Loans became more expensive than at any time since the 1930s. Most countries lacked the export earnings to carry such expensive debt.

This very serious episode is a graphic demonstration of how the economic

30. *World Development Report 1985*, p. 32. The rise in real interest rates for these two countries was a consequence not only of rising nominal interest rates and a slowdown in U.S. inflation, but the marked appreciation of the U.S. dollar in 1979 through 1984.

400

FOREIGN
SAVINGS:
AID AND
INVESTMENT
(Ch. 14)

TABLE 14–10   Debt and Macroeconomic Indicators for Six Countries, 1975–1983

	Total debt (in billions of U.S. dollars at the end of 1983)	Debt to GDP ratios (percent)	GNP Growth (% per annum)			Inflation (% per annum)		
			1975–79	1979–82	1983	1975–79	1978–82	1983
Debt crisis countries								
Argentina	45.3	70.6	2.2	−3.4	3.0	215.9	121.5	343.8
Brazil	93.1	41.1	6.7	2.1	−3.2	44.1	95.2	142.0
Mexico	89.8	60.5	6.2	5.2	−4.6	20.0	37.0	101.9
"Successful" adjustors								
Indonesia	29.5	37.3	7.4	6.6	4.2	14.8	13.4	11.8
South Korea	40.1	53.5	10.2	3.1	9.5	14.5	18.7	3.4
Turkey	23.9	44.4	3.5	2.5	3.4	36.2	55.4	29.1

Source: Jeffrey D. Sachs, "The LDC Debt Crisis, *NBER Reporter* (Winter 1986): 15–16.

policies of industrial countries largely determine the economic climate in which LDCs must operate. But external shocks were not wholly responsible for the most recent debt crunch. Many analysts argue that poor economic management in many debtor countries contributed strongly to their debt problems. They point to the apparently successful adjustments to the initial external shocks by such nations as Korea, Indonesia,[31] and Turkey, all of which continued to enjoy relatively high GDP growth before and after 1979 and 1980. At least through 1985, none of these three "successful adjusters" had been forced to reschedule their external debts, and each had lower inflation in 1983 and in 1979. It is argued that the "crisis" countries delayed too long in undertaking measures that would have allowed them to cope with the unexpectedly severe debt crisis they faced through 1985. Argentina, Brazil, and Mexico were three such countries. In all three, economic growth after 1979 was much slower than before and inflation rates surged nearly out of control (see Chapter 13). All three had to undertake emergency debt reschedulings in the early eighties and have been denied access to new international borrowing at normal market terms. Table 14–10 summarizes the pertinent data for these six countries.

Avoiding Future Crises

International banks and international borrowers learned important lessons in 1980 through 1986. Some large international banks in the U.S. and Europe were severely weakened by the sharp rise in "non-performing" LDC loans in their portfolio. The U.S. stock market in 1984 significantly devalued the worth of outstanding stock of virtually all banks that were major participants in the frenzied international loan markets for sovereign debt of the late seventies and early eighties. The problems for many of these banks are far from over: several have large loans outstanding to domestic companies and

31. See case study in Chapter 19.

foreign countries that are major oil producers. Should the glut in the world oil supplies continue much past 1986, some banks may fail. If so, the international financial system will come under further stress. But it is unlikely to collapse as long as creditor and debtor countries, as well as international organizations such as the IMF and the World Bank, avoid inflexibility and continue to coordinate their activities.[32]

A few countries, however, face the possibility of years of economic deprivation whether they meet their rescheduled debt obligations or decide, like Peru, on unilateral measures to limit payment on debt. These include most sub-Saharan nations as well as Bolivia, Peru, Mexico, Argentina, the Philippines, and possibly Nigeria (see Chapter 19). Continued recovery in the world economy; sharp reductions in projected massive U.S. budgetary deficits, which help to keep real interest rates high; and an abatement of protectionism in industrial countries (see Chapter 17) would not only assist these nations in recovering from the debt crisis, but would help forestall future crisis. And we have seen that a country's ability to cope with external shocks is not independent of the domestic policies it follows. Domestic policies that curtail growth in domestic savings and hamstring agricultural development lead to critical needs for foreign savings, both to finance investment and to import foodstuffs. Domestic policies that lead to strongly overvalued exchange rates encourage imports and discourage exports, creating strong pressures to seek external loans to tide weak economies over until the next crisis.

In the meantime, external borrowing has contracted strongly, as wary lenders and wary borrowers reassess their situations. The "scissors" effect was very much in evidence by 1985, as LDCs as a group paid more in interest than the new loans they received. Many countries will not be willing or able to tap international financial markets for credit to finance projects with a high social payoff. External debt has developed a very bad name. This unfortunately may serve to obscure a fundamental truth about debt: debt contracted to finance "good" projects in well-managed economies is always "good" debt. The fact that the debt is foreign in origin is immaterial. When foreign loans with interest rates less than the domestic opportunity cost of capital are invested in domestic projects with returns higher than the interest rate paid, national income in the borrowing country will be higher than without the debt. Higher national income thus generated furnishes the capacity to service debt without economic deprivation in the borrowing country. Avoiding future debt crises is therefore just as dependent on good project selection (see Chapter 6) in borrowing countries as on any set of far-reaching proposals for reform on international finance that may be discussed in dozens of international conferences over the next few years.

32. International agencies have recognized that many of the most serious crisis countries are in Latin America. In March 1986, the World Bank announced intentions to extend $1.5 billion in new loans to Latin American nations, not to help them repay debt, but to enable their economies to recover. The new loans will be directed primarily toward Mexico, Colombia, Argentina, and Ecuador. (*New York Times,* March 24, 1986.)

TRADE AND DEVELOPMENT

Primary-Export-Led Growth

This and the following two chapters examine the interactions between developing countries and the world economy. This chapter begins by offering a perspective on international payments, trade, and comparative advantage. It then focuses on the dominant means by which developing countries earn foreign exchange, the export of **primary commodities,** which include food crops, agricultural raw materials, and minerals. Chapters 16 and 17 explore two industrialization strategies that turn on a country's trading posture: import substitution and outward-looking development. A fourth chapter—Chapter 19—returns to international trade issues as they bear on the role of natural resources in development.

THE STRUCTURE OF FOREIGN PAYMENTS

Foreign exchange, like capital, is a concept that can be understood on several levels. Most simply, it is foreign money that a country uses to conduct transactions overseas, a cash flow. Like any economic unit, the country must be careful to balance its payments of foreign currency against its income. To protect against shortfalls, countries keep stocks of foreign money in the form of international reserves. At another level, foreign exchange represents purchasing power over foreign resources of all kinds: goods (imports), transportation and other services, skilled manpower, and assets (investments) in foreign countries. Thus a country's ability to earn foreign exchange, by exporting goods and services and by attracting foreign capital, determines its command over the goods and services produced in the world economy.

Finally, foreign exchange can represent a factor of production. All countries, and especially those less developed, are unable to produce at acceptable cost certain goods or services that contribute to well-being and growth. In some countries consumers demand more food than can be produced; in others certain raw materials are not available; and most LDCs seek capital equipment and some technical and managerial skills from the industrial countries. These imports contribute as much to production and growth as do supplies of labor and capital, and like them are primary factors of production. Thus because foreign exchange represents purchasing power over factors of production, it can itself be considered in that light.

The availability of this resource is usually measured in terms of foreign currency. A country's **balance of payments,** like an accountant's ledger, measures the annual flows of receipts of foreign currency and compares these to annual payments, as shown in Table 15–1. To help keep items on the correct side of the ledger, remember that any payment *to* a country's government or its citizens is considered a receipt or credit, while any payment *by* the country's government or citizens to any foreign person or agency is a payment or debit. Thus although exports send goods out of the country, they earn revenues from overseas and are thus credits; while imports, which bring goods to the country in return for payments to foreigners, are debits. A loan from overseas, such as foreign aid or a line of credit with a foreign bank, is a receipt when the proceeds of the loan are given to a country, but is reflected on the debit side in later years when interest is paid and the principal is repaid.

TABLE 15–1   Balance of Payments for a Developing Country

PAYMENTS (debits)	RECEIPTS (credits)
Import purchases (including freight)	Export earnings
Nationals' travel abroad	Foreigners' travel in country
Remittances of income on foreign investment	Income from overseas investments (e.g., foreign reserves)
Interest on foreign debt	Remittances by nationals working abroad
Remittances by foreigners working in country	Grants from foreign governments
(−) Balance on Current Account (+) (typically negative)	
Investment abroad by nationals	Investment by foreign firms
	Long-term loans from foreign individuals and firms
Repayments of principal on foreign long-term debt	Long-term loans by foreign governments and multilateral agencies
(−) Balance on Long-Term Capital Account (+) (typically positive)	
Basic Balance = balance on current account + balance on long-term capital account	
Short-term loans abroad by nationals	Short-term loans from abroad (e.g., trade credits)
(−) Balance of Payments (+) = decrease or increase in foreign reserves	

All flows of goods and services, such as exports, imports, freight, interest, and so forth, are considered part of the **current account**; investment and loan flows—the foreign aid and private investment discussed in Chapter 14—are part of the **capital account.** The sum of these two is the balance of payments, which if positive equals the addition to foreign reserves and if negative is covered by drawing down reserves accumulated in the past. Once changes in reserves are included, the balance of payments must always balance: credits (including any fall in reserves used to finance a deficit) must equal debits (including any rise in reserves, the reflection of a surplus).

Governments do not have inexhaustible foreign reserves, so deficits cannot be run indefinitely. However, most developing countries, with the major exception of the petroleum exporters and some others, run chronic deficits on current account. Essentially, they import more than they export. Ordinarily the difference is financed by foreign investments and loans. The sum of these long-term capital inflows and the current account balance is often called the **basic balance.** As long as foreign investors and lenders, including aid donors, are willing to invest enough to cover the current account deficit, the country's foreign payments can be considered in balance. Indeed, standing the problem on its head, if a developing country is able to add to its resources by attracting foreign capital on favorable terms and investing it productively, then it should do so (see Chapter 14). To convert foreign capital into real resources—goods and services—for development, a country must import goods and services from abroad. Then the country necessarily runs a deficit on current account because imports exceed exports. But if a country runs a current account deficit that is not matched by an inflow of foreign capital, the country will eventually have to take steps to curb its imports or increase its exports, probably both.

Table 15–2 gives a broad view of the structure of foreign payments of the developing countries that are members of the International Monetary Fund; several socialist developing countries—China, North Korea, Vietnam, and Cuba—are not included in these data. The table shows that merchandise exports (measured at the country's border before shipping costs, which is called f.o.b.—freight on board) are responsible for over 60 percent of total receipts, whether oil exporters are included or not, while imports (measured with costs, insurance, and freight—c.i.f.—also at the country's border) cover about two-thirds of total payments. Clearly merchandise trade is the dominant source of foreign payments. Of the other items that receive most attention, private investment and aid (long-term capital in the table) contribute just over 10 percent to receipts, while the returns on past capital inflows— profits and interest on debt—constitute 11 to 13 percent of total payments.

The table also helps to place the developing nations in the world economy. By virtually any measure, such as export receipts, import payments, or total receipts and payments, developing countries are responsible for one-third of world totals (again, including only IMF members). For the non-oil countries the shares are just over one-fifth. These shares of trade and payments exceed developing countries shares of world GDP, which in 1983 was 22 percent for all LDCs and 20 percent when oil exporters are excluded.

TABLE 15–2   Developing Countries[a]—Aggregate Balance of Payments, 1983 (in billions of U.S. dollars)

	All developing countries		Non-oil developing countries	
	Receipts	Payments	Receipts	Payments
Current Account				
Merchandise exports, f.o.b.	514		338	
Merchandise imports, c.i.f.		538		384
Transport and travel	53	34	50	28
Investment income	48		19	
Profits remitted or reinvested		18		6
Interest on debt		74		67
Other services	55	90	45	41
Transfers	38	20	37	4
Total current receipts/payments	708	774	489	530
Balance on current account		66		41
Long-term Capital				
Direct investment	15	1	10	1
Private Loans	29		14	
Official loans	51	21	38	17
Total long-term capital	95	22	62	18
Basic balance[b]	7		3	
Short-term Capital (net)[c]		7		5
Total receipts/payments	803	803	551	553
Balance of payments[d]	0			2
As a percentage of world[a] *total*				
Exports/imports	32	32	21	23
Total receipts/payments	33	33	23	23

Source: International Monetary Fund, *Balance of Payments Statistics* vol. 29, part 2 (Washington, D.C., December 1984).
[a] Coverage includes members of the International Monetary Fund.
[b] Equals balance on current account plus balance of long-term capital items.
[c] Includes errors and omissions.
[d] Surplus of receipts (payments) equals the gain (fall) in reserves.

COMPARATIVE ADVANTAGE

Every country, regardless of size, ideology, or state of development, participates in international trade. Trade theorists have tried to explain why nations trade and how they benefit from it largely under assumptions of **static conditions** which hold all domestic factors of production (land, other natural resources, labor, and capital) in fixed supply. The resulting **theory of comparative advantage** is rich in its implications about the gains from trade, the following among them: (1) Any country can increase its income by trading, because the world market provides an opportunity to buy some goods at relative prices that are lower than those which would prevail at home in the absence of trade. (2) The smaller the country, the greater this potential gain from trade, but all countries benefit to some extent. (3) A country will gain most by exporting commodities that it produces using its abundant factors of production most intensively, while importing those goods whose production would require relatively more of the scarcer factors of production.

The first implication is a subtle one that requires elaboration. To simplify greatly, assume that two countries, which can be called Mexico and the

	Mexico	United States
Labor-days to produce:		
Vegetables (one ton)	5	4
Automobiles (one)	30	20
Relative price (tons of vegetables per auto)	6	5

United States, both produce only two products, vegetables and automobiles, and use only one factor of production, labor. Table 15–3 shows the labor days required to produce these products in each country.

Notice that in this example it takes more labor days to produce either product in Mexico. Despite this, it is to the advantage of the United States to buy vegetables in Mexico, even though they can be produced at home with less labor, and to sell cars to Mexico in return. In the United States labor costs dictate that an autombile sells for the equivalent of five tons of vegetables.[1] But if the United States sells one automobile in Mexico, it can buy six tons of vegetables for consumption. So if labor is shifted from farming to manufacturing automobiles, American consumers can eat more vegetables than if there is no trade with Mexico, while driving the same number of cars. At the same time Mexico, which has to produce six tons of vegetables to buy one car in the home market without trade, is better off to switch its labor into producing more vegetables and selling them to the United States, where it only needs to trade five tons of vegetables for a car, saving the other ton for its own consumption.

The important point of this example, and the core of comparative advantage, is that both countries can gain from trade whenever the *relative* prices of commodities in each country differ in the absence of trade. If the two countries do trade, then the relative price of vegetables in terms of automobiles would settle between five and six, the two relative prices prevailing before trade. The final trade price, which can be called the world price, will settle closer to the initial price in the market of the country whose economy is larger. Thus small countries benefit more from trade because the gains are greater the more the pretrade relative price differs from posttrade world price. To see this, consider an extreme case in which the U.S. economy is so large that the posttrade price settles at the U.S. price before trade. Then the United States cannot gain from trade (nor can it lose), while Mexico would gain to the full extent of the price difference.

The theory of comparative advantage is posed here in the very simple form developed by David Ricardo during the nineteenth century: two countries, two goods, and only one factor of production, labor. Some of the complexities of the real world can be incorporated into the theory, however. A trading world of many countries can be handled by taking the home country, say, Kenya, and treating the rest of the world as its trading partner. The com-

1. If each ton of vegetables requires 4 labor-days to produce, then it takes 5 tons of vegetables to absorb the same labor as one car, which uses 20 labor-days. This formula for calculating relative prices works in this oversimplified example because labor is the only input into production.

plexities of many goods will be addressed in the next chapter. The theory was expanded to deal with two factors, such as labor and capital, by the Swedish economists, Eli Heckscher and Bertil Ohlin, during the first half of the twentieth century. Under certain conditions the Heckscher-Ohlin theory can be extended to include more factors of production and to yield the third implication, that a country exports products which use its abundant factors of production more intensively and imports products which require relatively more of its scarce factors.

The implications of this more general approach to comparative advantage are encapsulated in Figure 15–1. It depicts a country, relatively well endowed with land and labor, that can produce labor- and land-intensive rice and capital-intensive cloth in amounts depicted by the production possibilities frontier. Its collective utility in consuming those goods is given by the community indifference curves (see Chapter 6). *Before trade* the country achieves its greatest utility by producing and consuming at *A*, the tangency of indifference curve *I* and the production frontier. The slope at *A* determines the domestic relative price of rice in terms of cloth. If the rest of the world is relatively better endowed with capital than with labor or land, then the relative world price of rice is likely to be higher than the domestic price. *After trade* the country can, by selling its rice at the higher world price (called the *terms of trade*), produce more of its abundant commodity, rice, and less cloth, settling at point *B* where the world price is tangent to the production frontier. It can also consume more of both goods at *C*, the tangency of the world price and indifference curve II, and hence is better off than before trade. The country exports *BD* of rice and imports *DC* of cloth, given by the *trade triangle, BCD*.

Any country, whatever its size and stage of development, can benefit from trade in the way shown in Figure 15–1, from small countries like Ghana or Belgium to large ones like China, India, and the United States. Large coun-

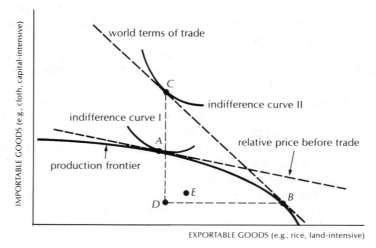

FIGURE 15–1 **Gains from Trade.** Before trade, a country both produces and consumes at a point like *A*. With trade, a country produces at a point like *B* and can increase its consumption of both goods, moving to a higher indifference curve at *C*.

tries and others whose exports command a large share of world markets, such as Zambia in copper or Sri Lanka in tea, may, in the process of expanding their trade, reduce the relative world price received for their exports. But even they still gain from trade if only their relative domestic prices would, in the absence of trade, differ from relative world prices.

Although every country can gain from trade, not all individuals or groups within each country share such gains. In the rice-cloth example of Figure 15–1, the producers of rice enjoy gains when trade is initiated because they sell more rice at a higher price. The consumers of cloth also gain from trade, because they can consume more at a lower price. But once trade begins, cloth manufacturers face competition from imports, hence sell less cloth at a lower price than before, while rice consumers must pay higher prices. Comparative advantage theory tells us that the gains outweigh the losses for the country as a whole, but that may be cold comfort to producers of cloth and consumers of rice. The losers from trade may share in the gains if suppliers of capital and labor to the cloth industry find it easy to shift into the production of rice, or if mechanisms exist to transfer income from the gainers to the losers. In most countries, neither condition holds to a sufficient degree, especially in the short to medium term. Therein lies the seed of political opposition to policies that promote freer trade, even though all countries gain from it. We shall return to this issue in Chapter 17.

EXPORT CHARACTERISTICS OF DEVELOPING COUNTRIES

When Chenery and Syrquin looked at cross-country patterns (see Chapter 3), they found that as incomes per capita rose from the neighborhood of $300 to $3,000 (in 1983 prices), the average export share of gross domestic product rose from 19 to 26 percent.[2] Size makes a considerable difference, however: for an average "small" country with a population of five million and income per capita of $700, exports of goods and services constituted about 24 percent of GDP, compared with half that level for an average "large" country with forty million people at the same income.

Some sense of the wide variety of individual country characteristics can be had from column 3 of Table 15–4, which shows the expected low export share of gross domestic product, 7 to 11 percent, for very large countries like Brazil, India, Mexico, and Pakistan; rather high ratios for the oil-rich countries of any size (including an extreme of 55 percent for Saudi Arabia); and a wide range for the smaller, non-petroleum-exporters, from an aberrant 8 percent for Ghana's collapsing economy, 11 percent for Colombia, where much foreign exchange is earned through illegal and unrecorded narcotics transactions, and 12 percent in Ethiopia, the poorest country in the world; to over 30 percent for such different countries as South Korea, an exporter of manufactures, Malaysia, a diversified primary exporter, and Zambia, which exports little other than copper.

---

2. Hollis Chenery and Moises Syrquin, *Patterns of Development, 1950-1970* (London: Oxford University Press, 1975). Their work used data from the mid-1960s in prices of 1964. We have converted per-capita incomes to 1983 prices by using a factor of 3.2, which is approximately the ratio of 1983 to 1964 price levels in the United States, to reflect world inflation during that nineteen-year span.

TABLE 15-4   Export Characteristics of Selected Developing Countries, 1983

Country	Population 1983 (millions)	GNP per capita 1983 (U.S. dollars)	Export[a] share of GDP 1982–84 (%)	Major primary exports[b]	Share of col. 4 in merchandise exports, 1982–84 (%)
Large countries					
Brazil	130	1,880	9[c]	Coffee, soy beans, iron ore	28
China	1,019	300	9[d]	—	47[e]
India	733	260	7[f]	—	40[g]
Indonesia[h]	156	560	25[c]	Petroleum	62
Mexico[h]	75	2,240	11[c]	Petroleum	58
Nigeria[h]	94	770	26[f]	Petroleum	96
Pakistan	90	390	11	Rice, cotton	21
Petroleum exporters					
Libya	3	8,480	39[f]	Petroleum	99
Saudi Arabia	10	12,230	55	Petroleum	100
Venezuela	17	3,840	28[c]	Petroleum	92
Other countries					
Bolivia	6	510	20[c]	Tin, gas, silver, zinc	91
Chile	12	1,870	20	Copper	46
Colombia	28	1,430	11	Coffee	51
Egypt	45	700	18	Petroleum, cotton	79[f]
Ethiopia	41	120	12	Coffee, hides	72[c]
Ghana	13	310	8[e]	Cocoa	46[f]
Guatemala	8	1,120	18[f]	Coffee, cotton, sugar, bananas	49[c]
Ivory Coast	10	710	38[c]	Coffee, cocoa, wood	53[c]
Jamaica	2	1,300	44	Alumina, bauxite, sugar	72
Kenya	19	340	26	Coffee, tea, petroleum	67
Korea	40	2,010	37	—	8[g]
Malaysia	15	1,860	54	Rubber, wood, petroleum, palm oil, tin	62
Peru	18	1,040	21[c]	Copper, petroleum, fish meal, silver, zinc, lead	65
Philippines	52	760	19	Sugar, coconut, copper, wood	30
Sri Lanka	15	330	28	Tea, rubber, coconut	50
Tanzania	21	240	11[c]	Coffee, cotton, sisal	52
Thailand	49	820	24	Rice, rubber, corn, tapioca, sugar	44
Zambia	6	580	32	Copper	89

Sources: World Bank, *World Development Report 1985* (New York: Oxford University Press, 1985), Tables 1 and 5—for columns 1 and 2; International Monetary Fund, *International Financial Statistics Yearbook 1985* (Washington, D.C.: 1985)—for columns 3 to 5.

[a] Exports of goods and services.

[b] Commodities accounting for at least 5% of merchandise export revenues.

[c] 1981–1983.

[d] World Bank estimate for 1983; excludes factor services.

[e] 1979–1981.

[f] 1980–1982.

[g] Primary commodity share of merchandise exports, 1982, as given by the World Bank; commodity breakdown not available.

[h] Could also be classified as petroleum exporters.

The advantages of trade are so compelling that even countries with a strong ideology favoring **autarky,** the absence of trade, participate in world markets. Despite their size, both the Soviet Union and China, whose Communist governments place a high value on self-reliance and independence from capitalist-dominated world markets, export in order to obtain food, sophisticated capital goods, and other commodities that are scarce in their economies. And since 1976 China has moved dramatically to increase its trade as a means of stimulating development: its export share of GDP tripled to 9 percent from 1965 to 1983. Cuba broke sharply with its former trading partners after 1959, but is no less dependent on its exports of sugar than before its Communist revolution; now those exports go to the Soviet Union.

Knowing the factor endowments of developing countries helps us explain the kinds of goods they export and import. Natural resources provide an obvious case and evoke images of the oil-rich countries of the Middle East and elsewhere; the copper exporters, Zambia, Zaire, Chile, and Peru; or timber exporters, such as Malaysia, the Philippines, and the Ivory Coast. Tropical climate may be considered a factor of production that helps to explain the exports of foods such as coffee, cocoa, bananas, and vegetable oils, and raw materials like rubber and cotton. Finally, abundant labor suggests the export of crops that can be produced efficiently with labor-intensive methods, such as coffee, tea, rice, and tobacco, and of labor-intensive manufactures such as textiles, clothing, and electronic components. The relative lack of both physical and human capital in developing countries indicates that they would gain by importing goods that use these factors intensively; such goods include most capital equipment and many intermediate products from the chemical, petroleum, and metals industries.

A standard description of a developing country would state that only one or a few primary commodities are responsible for most export earnings; many countries in Table 15–4 exhibit that characteristic. The extreme cases of export concentration include all the major petroleum exporters, Ghana in cocoa, Colombia and Ethiopia in coffee, Chile and Zambia in copper, and Jamaica in bauxite and alumina. Not surprisingly the very large countries show a much more diversified pattern. What may be surprising is that many of the primary-product exporters are highly diversified. In five of the cases shown—Bolivia, Malaysia, Peru, the Philippines, and Thailand—no one product dominates, and at least four commodities each account for 5 percent or more of total earnings.

However suggestive the theory of comparative advantage may be for developing countries, it is only the beginning of an explanation of development through international trade. The theory fails to explain growth and structural change because it excludes growth in the stocks of productive factors, as well as improvements in the quality or productivity of those factors. The theory thus provides no mechanism to explain how economies evolve over time and change the composition of their output, their consumption, and their trade. Extensions of the theory have been used to explain some facets of growth, but even these leave much unexplained.[3]

3. Gerald M. Meier summarizes these approaches in *The International Economics of Development* (New York: Harper & Row, 1968), Chapter 2.

In order to understand how trade and development interact, one affecting the other, it is preferable to adopt an eclectic approach, using trade theory where it is useful but reverting frequently to other kinds of analysis. The unifying theme is trade strategies: how different approaches to trade, favoring different types of exports and imports, lead to different kinds of economic development. The first such strategy, **primary-export-led growth** is examined in this chapter. As indicated by the summary balance of payments and the discussion of export characteristics, food and raw-material exports remain the principal means by which developing countries gain purchasing power over the imports that are essential to their development.

PRIMARY EXPORTS AS AN ENGINE OF GROWTH

Before the 1950s, it was conventional wisdom that the road to development could be traversed most rapidly by following comparative advantage, exporting foods and raw materials, raising per-capita income, and permitting structural change to take place as a consequence. The United States, Canada, Australia, and Denmark had become developed countries at least partly by following this path, and Argentina had gone quite far in that direction. Some countries in the third world, such as Colombia, Mexico, Ghana, Nigeria, Malaysia, and the Philippines, have undergone significant structural change as a consequence of primary exports, although these changes have propelled them only part of the way to development. Students of development, observing such cases, have noted three kinds of benefits to primary-export-led growth: improved utilization of existing factors, expanded factor endowments, and linkage effects.

Improved Factor Utilization

Static models of the gains from trade start with a country that is not trading and show what happens when it is opened to trade. An isolated country, shut off from world markets, might have substantial amounts of land that is either idle or used in relatively unproductive ways. Recall the land-abundant, capital-short country of Figure 15–1. In that case all factors of production are fully employed without trade. However, by reallocating resources—producing and exporting more land-intensive goods such as rice or cocoa, and importing more manufactures, such as cloth or chemicals—the country can consume more of both kinds of commodities and increase its welfare. The country moves along its production frontier, from A to B in Figure 15–1. Land, the abundant factor of production, is utilized more intensively with trade in the sense that its productivity (the yield per hectare) has risen as labor shifts from handicraft industries to agriculture or mining.

If, instead, the country has idle resources before trade begins, it can gain even more substantially from trade. This case is represented in Figure 15–1 by points D and E, within the production frontier. Trade may stimulate the economy so that all factors of production are utilized and the country moves towards its frontier, able to produce more of both goods.

This static model of the gains from trade can, with imagination and some judicious simplification, be applied to the development of several countries. In the nineteenth century the United States and Canada had abundant land in relation to their endowments of labor and capital. Much of this land was idle, so both countries produced at points within their production frontiers. British demand for cotton and wheat enabled North America to bring this land into production and move towards the production frontier by growing cotton and wheat for export, while importing the manufactured goods it could not produce as efficiently as Britain.

Burmese economist Hla Myint has observed that when parts of Africa and Asia came under European colonization, the consequent expansion of their international trade enabled those areas to utilize their land or labor more intensively to produce tropical foodstuffs such as rice, cocoa, and oil palm for export. Myint applies Adam Smith's term, **vent for surplus,** to these cases (as well as the cases of surplus land in the Americas and Australia).[4] The concept implies that some land or labor is idle before trade and that trade enables these economies to employ either land or labor more fully.

However, when underutilized land or labor was "vented" as a result of colonization, as was typical during the nineteenth century, the gains from trade were often purchased at high cost to the indigenous population. Land which may have been idle or utilized at low productivity was frequently alienated from its occupiers, whether these were American Indians, the Kikuyu and other peoples of East Africa, or Javanese farmers. Colonizers also used taxation and coercion to keep plantations and mines supplied with low-cost labor in many parts of Africa and Asia. And especially in British India, the movement along a production frontier toward greater production for export often resulted in cheap imports to compete with traditional handicraft industries, displacing artisans and workers. The questions about colonization—which cannot be answered in this text—are whether the distribution of gains from trade favored native populations enough to compensate them for the losses they bore and whether colonial economies propelled indigenous people towards development or retarded their eventual progress.

Expanded Factor Endowments

Once the profitable opportunities in tropical agriculture or natural resources become apparent, foreign investment is likely to be attracted to the country, first to exploit the country's comparative advantage and, perhaps eventually, to invest in other sectors. The influx of foreign investors has been the familiar story in all mineral exporting industries and in many tropical products industries in which plantation agriculture was the rule: Standard Oil in Venezuela, British Petroleum in Iran, Anaconda in Chile, Alcoa in Jamaica, Lever Brothers and Firestone in West Africa, and United Fruit in Central America are only some of the more visible of scores of examples. Capital has

4. Hla Myint, "The 'Classical Theory' of International Trade and the Underdeveloped Countries," *Economic Journal* 68 (1959): 317–37.

frequently brought migrant labor to the mines and plantations, as occurred in Southern and West Africa, Malaysia, Sri Lanka, and many other places. Both foreign investment and migrant labor were of course prominent features in the development in the "new lands" of the Americas and Australia in the nineteenth century. The emergence of new lines of export production is also likely to open up many new profitable outlets for investment that foreign capital will not completely satisfy, whether in the export sector itself or in related industries. These opportunities represent an outward shift of the demand for domestic savings and should induce some supply response, further increasing investment in the economy.

Thus the expansion of potential markets for primary products can lead to expanded supplies of foreign investment, domestic saving, labor, and skilled manpower to complement the fixed factors of production, land and natural resources. Not only does trade help an economy move towards its production frontier and then along it, but trade can also expand the frontier outward, enabling the economy to produce more of all goods than before.

Linkage Effects

The notion of export-led growth implies some stimulus to other industries that would not otherwise expand. When the growth of one industry, such as textiles, creates sufficient demand for some input, such as cotton or dyestuffs, it may stimulate domestic production of that input. Hirschman coined the phrase *backward linkage* for this stimulus.[5] Backward linkages, which were described in Chapter 3, are particularly effective when the using industry becomes so large that supplying industries can achieve economies of scale of their own, thus lowering their production costs and becoming more competitive in domestic or even export markets. The wheat industry worked this way in North America in the nineteenth century, creating sufficient demand for transportation equipment (especially railway rolling stock) and farm machinery that these industries became established in the United States. In Peru the rapid expansion of the fishmeal industry during the 1950s and 1960s led directly to the production of fishing boats and processing equipment. The boatbuilding industry became efficient enough to export fishing craft to neighboring countries, while the processing-equipment industry gave Peru a start on one kind of capital-goods production that can supply a wide range of food-processing industries.[6]

The linkage between food processing for export (rice, vegetable oils, tea) and a processing equipment industry might well be repeated in other developing countries over time. Three conditions would contribute to such linkages. Production should initially take place in small units that use simple technology, giving the fledgling equipment industry a chance to master production techniques and learn its trade by repetitive production. The export industry should grow steadily over time, promising a continuing market for

5. Hirschman, *Strategy of Economic Development,* Chapter 6.

6. Michael Roemer, *Fishing for Growth: Export-Led Development in Peru, 1950–1967* (Cambridge, Mass.: Harvard University Press, 1970).

its suppliers. And the export sector should be large enough to enable equipment manufacturers eventually to achieve scale economies. These conditions were met in fish meal and can be met in several agricultural fields. But they are generally not satisfied in mining, which typically requires complex equipment for large-scale investments that must be implemented in the shortest time possible, conditions under which domestic infant industries are unlikely to thrive.

Linkages may also develop indirectly through the demand by income recipients for consumption goods. The **consumption linkage** is most likely to operate if a large labor force is paid wages above previous levels, creating a demand for mass-produced consumer goods like processed foods, clothing, footwear, furniture, radios, packaging materials, and so forth. The North American wheat industry, with its extensive endowment of land, high labor productivity, and egalitarian income distribution based on family farms, successfully stimulated local consumer goods industries. Neither plantation agriculture in Africa, with its large labor force but low wages, nor mining industries, which pay high wages but employ relatively few workers, are able to generate adequate demand to stimulate local consumer goods industries.

The provision of overhead capital—roads, railroads, power, water, telecommunications—for the export industry can lower costs and otherwise open opportunities for other industries. The classic example is the railroad in the nineteenth-century United States, built to connect the East Coast with the grain-producing states of the Midwest, which lowered costs of transporting both inputs and outputs for manufacturing industry in the wheat-exporting region.[7] Harbors and rail and road networks built to facilitate the export of copper in southern Africa, cocoa and timber in Ghana, tea in India, and beef in Argentina have had similar effects on domestic manufacturing industry. Power projects that are made economically feasible by export industries, such as the Akosombo Dam in Ghana and the Guri Dam in Venezuela, provide cheap power that may encourage the domestic manufacturing industry. Primary export sectors may also encourage the development of local entrepreneurs and skilled laborers. The growth of the Peruvian fish-meal industry, with its many small plants, encouraged scores of new entrepreneurs and trained many skilled workers to operate and maintain equipment. These resources then became available for subsequent development. Rubber, palm oil, and tin production for export have encouraged entrepreneurs in Malaysia, and small-scale farming for export has proved to be an outlet for entrepreneurial talent in several African countries.

The best case for petroleum, mining, and some traditional agricultural crops is the fiscal linkage, which means simply that the large government revenues typically derived from these exports (as taxes or dividends) can be used to finance development in other sectors. Although a government is obviously better off with than without such a revenue source, its effective-

---

7. Albert Fishlow, *American Railroads and the Transformation of the Antebellum Economy* (Cambridge, Mass.: Harvard University Press, 1965), and Robert W. Fogel, "Railroads as an Analogy of the Space Effort: Some Economic Aspects," in *Space Program: An Exploration in Historical Analogy,* ed. Bruce Mazlish (Cambridge, Mass.: MIT Press, 1965).

ness in stimulating self-sustaining development in the rest of the economy depends critically on the kinds of programs and interventions that government undertakes.[8]

BARRIERS TO PRIMARY-EXPORT-LED GROWTH

Since the late 1950s some economists and many third-world leaders have argued that primary exports other than petroleum cannot effectively lead the way to economic development: markets for primary products grow too slowly to fuel growth; the prices received for these commodities have been declining; earnings are too unstable; and linkages do not work. We examine each of these arguments in turn.

Sluggish Demand Growth

In a world of balanced growth, exporters of primary products could expect their exports to expand at the same pace as national incomes of the countries that import primary products, and they could also expect their own incomes to grow at that rate. Faster income growth for primary exporters would require structural changes such as import substitution. The world is not balanced in this way, however, and economists skeptical of primary-export potential have cited structural shifts in the industrial world that seem to condemn third-world primary exports to slower growth than industrial world incomes.[9] It is a common observation, known as Engel's law, that the demand for staple foods and beverages grows more slowly than income (see Chapter 3). For the industrial world the income elasticity of demand for foods is probably below one-half. Thus even if the growth in production of foodstuffs in the industrial world fell short of income growth, there is a prima-facie case that its imports of foods would lag behind income growth. Technological change in manufacturing may also be working against the consumption of raw materials, as producers attempt to reduce costs by reducing wastage and otherwise raising the yield of finished products from a given input of raw material. Metal cans contain less tin, modern looms waste less cotton yarn, sawmills turn wood shavings into boards, and so forth. Concurrently, in affluent societies expenditures are expected to shift away

8. The impact of export industries on economic development through various forms of linkages is the focus of a body of literature called *staple theory,* which tries to explain differing impacts by differing characteristics of production technologies. For examples of the genre, see Robert E. Baldwin, *Economic Development and Export Growth: A Study of Northern Rhodesia, 1920–1960* (Los Angeles: University of California Press, 1966); Douglass C. North, "Location Theory and Regional Economic Growth," *Journal of Political Economy* 63 (1955): 243–85; Roemer, *Fishing for Growth;* and Melville H. Watkins, "A Staple Theory of Economic Growth," *Canadian Journal of Economics and Political Science* 29 (1963): 141–58. Perhaps the ultimate expression of production characteristics and linkages as determinants of development patterns is the essay by Albert O. Hirschman, "A Generalized Linkage Approach to Development, with Special Reference to Staples," in *Essays on Economic Development and Cultural Change,* ed. Manning Nash (Chicago: University of Chicago Press, 1977), pp. 67–98.

9. An early and articulate proponent of this view is Ragnar Nurkse, *Equilibrium Growth in the World Economy* (Cambridge, Mass.: Harvard University Press, 1961), Chapters 10 and 11.

from goods and toward services, further reducing the expected growth of material imports relative to income.

World Bank data show that the share of nonfuel raw material and food imports in total industrial country imports fell substantially, from 42 percent in 1960 to about 30 percent in 1973, just before the oil price rose.[10] Yet this took place during a period when the import growth in the industrial world was so rapid (over 8 percent a year) that imports of nonfuel raw materials and foodstuffs, valued in constant prices, appear to have grown about as fast as GDP in the industrial world, about 5 percent a year from 1960 to 1973. Over this period, admittedly one of extraordinary growth of trade and income in the industrial world, the balanced growth model seems to have prevailed. In the decade from 1973 to 1983, however, the growth of industrial countries' GDP slowed to 2.4 percent a year and their imports of non fuel raw materials and foods showed no real growth.[11]

Whatever the broad trends, there are likely to be encouraging prospects for some primary commodities and some primary-exporting countries. Many of the raw materials now prominent in world trade were hardly on the scene at the turn of this century and thus have undergone substantial growth. The demands for petroleum, rubber, copper, aluminum, newsprint, plywood, and vegetable oils received substantial boosts from technological innovation or from high income elasticities of demand, the very factors cited against raw material exports. Several commodities have experienced substantial export growth rates since 1960: exports of sorghum, corn, wheat, fish, soybeans, vegetable oils, oilseed cake and meal, alumina and aluminum, and nickel all grew by at least 5 percent a year from 1961 to 1982, valued at constant prices; timber exports and phosphate also grew rapidly until 1980.[12] Among the countries producing these commodities, several experienced moderately rapid economic growth, especially during the 1960s, including Jamaica, Jordon, Liberia, Malaysia, Mauritania, and Thailand. Several countries— including Cameroon, Costa Rica, the Dominican Republic, Guatemala, the Ivory Coast, and the Philippines, as well as Malaysia and Thailand—have used a diversified group of other traditional exports to stimulate growth.

The lesson is not that demand for primary imports in the industrial world will grow sufficiently to support rapid development in the third world. It is rather that some commodities will face brisk demand growth and some countries will benefit substantially from producing such exports. A prudent forecast of demand growth for primary commodities as a whole would, however, be lower than the postwar experience until the mid-1970s. With slower growth in industrial countries, the impact of Engel's law, and materials-saving innovations, it seems unlikely that the developed countries will import enough tropical foods and raw materials to fuel an era of rapid development for the third world as a whole during the rest of this century.

10. World Bank, *World Tables 1976* and *1980* (Baltimore: Johns Hopkins University Press, 1976 and 1980).

11. World Bank, *World Development Report 1985* (New York: Oxford University Press, 1985), Tables 9 and 11.

12. World Bank, *Commodity Trade and Price Trends,* 1983–1984 and 1985 editions (Washington, D.C.: 1983, 1985).

Primary-Export-Led Growth in Malaysia

When Malaysia achieved independence in 1957, it was close to the archetypical single-crop economy: rubber accounted for well over half of its export earnings and about a quarter of Malaysia's gross domestic product. The second largest export, tin, earned between 10 and 20 percent of total export revenues. Neither commodity faced a bright future: demand for rubber was constrained by the availability of cheap synthetic substitutes and the tin market was plagued by production exceeding likely demand. It would have been natural for the new country's planners to fall prey to the dominant export pessimism of the day and build a development strategy around import substitution.

But Malaysia enjoys a rich resource base with a relatively small population and its development strategy was based on its comparative advantage. The country invested in research to reduce the costs of growing rubber and maintained its competitiveness with synthetics. Measured relative to import prices, rubber export revenues did fall from 1960 to 1980, but only by 15 percent. At the same time, Malaysia invested in planting oil palm and this new export grew by 16 percent a year in volume from 1960 to 1984. Exports of logs and timber also grew briskly for two decades and petroleum exports grew by a steady 8 percent a year. Consequently, from 1960 to 1984 Malaysia's export earnings deflated by import prices (i.e., its income terms of trade—see next section) grew by 5.7 percent a year. Its oil reserves also spared Malaysia from the full impact of rising import costs during the 1970s.

As a consequence of its investments in primary exports, Malaysia has sustained rapid economic growth, 6.3 percent a year from 1965 to 1983. Its per capita income of $1,800 puts Malaysia on a par with Brazil, Argentina, and South Korea, even though in the mid 1960s its average income was close to that of Zambia and El Salvador and well below Jamaica. Although still dependent on exports for over half its GDP, Malaysia's diversified export base, efficient production, and high income provide the resources for continued rapid development.[13]

Declining Terms of Trade

An influential school of thought, led by Argentine economist Raul Prebisch and Hans Singer of the University of Sussex,[14] has argued that not only will primary exports face sluggish growth of demand, but prices received for these commodities will fall on world markets relative to the prices of LDC imports of manufactures from developed countries. The most commonly used measure of these relative prices is the commodity or **net barter terms of trade,** T_n. T_n is a ratio of two indexes: (1) the average price of a country's

13. Data are from the World Bank, *World Development Report 1985* (New York: Oxford University Press, 1985) and the International Monetary Fund, *International Financial Statistics Yearbook 1985* (Washington, D.C.: 1985).

14. United Nations (Raul Prebisch), *The Economic Development of Latin America and its Principal Problems* (Lake Success, New York: 1950); Hans W. Singer, "The Distribution of Trade between Investing and Borrowing Countries," *American Economic Review* 40 (May 1950): 473–85; an excellent review of these arguments appears in Meier (1968), Chapter 3.

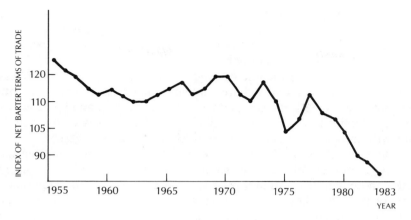

FIGURE 15-2 Commodity Terms of Trade for Non-Petroleum Exporting Developing Countries, 1956–1979 (1975 = 100). The net barter terms of trade have both fluctuated and declined considerably since 1970. Measured from 1955, the decline has averaged 0.9 percent a year to 1983. *Source:* International Monetary Fund, *International Financial Statistics Yearbook 1984* (Washington, D.C.: 1984), pp. 116–19.

exports (P_x), which can be approximated by dividing an index of export volume into an index of export revenue, and (2) the average price of its imports (P_m), determined for imports by the same method as P_x. The commodity terms of trade rise if export prices rise relative to import prices.

Postwar data on the terms of trade of the less developed countries are summarized in Figure 15–2. The figure illustrates what a regression analysis can prove: there has been a downward trend in the terms of trade of non-petroleum exporting LDCs since the mid-1950s, about 0.9 percent a year. These countries have thus required export growth of almost one percent a year merely to maintain their purchasing power over imports. Of course, petroleum exporters enjoyed substantial improvements in their terms of trade, which more than quadrupled from 1960 to 1983.

However, the net barter terms of trade tells us little about income or welfare, which ought to be the basis for judging changes in world trade conditions. A better measure of the income effect of price changes would be the **income terms of trade,** T_i, which measures the purchasing power of exports by comparing an index of export revenues to an index of import prices. This is equivalent to the net barter terms of trade multiplied by the volume of exports (Q_x), or $T_i = P_x Q_x / P_m = T_n Q_x$. If, for example, Zambia increases its copper exports and causes the world price to fall, but less than proportionately to the volume increase (that is, the absolute value of the demand elasticity for Zambian copper is greater than one), then copper revenue would increase and, in the absence of import price changes, the income terms of trade would rise. Assuming the resources shifted into copper production could not have produced goods or services of equal value in other sectors, Zambia would be unambiguously better off than before. For any single country, the elasticity of demand for a particular export is likely to exceed 1, even if the elasticity of world demand for this export is below 1.

Similarly, an increase in Zambia's copper production due to higher productivity may cause world copper prices to fall. But if the price decline is less than the percentage rise in the productivity (Z_x) of all factors engaged in production for export, the factors engaged in copper mining would be better off than before. The **single factoral terms of trade**, T_s, measures factor income relative to factor inputs and import prices, or $T_s = (P_x/P_m) Z_x = T_n Z_x$. Note that a rise in either the income or single factoral terms of trade implies an improvement in income or welfare relative to that country's previous situation. But if, as is often the case, either index rises less than export volume, this also implies that exporting countries are sharing part of the potential gains with importing countries, as Prebisch and Singer suggest.

Is there any theoretical reason to expect the decline in LDC's terms of trade to continue? The reasons given in the previous section for sluggish growth in demand for primary products can also be used to argue that the terms of trade for these commodities will decline over time. More fundamentally, to the extent that developing countries increase their output of primary exports as a means of growing faster than the industrial countries, prices of their exports may be expected to fall relative to those of industrial country exports, simply because the supply of LDC primary exports will be increasing faster than the demand for them.

It is even possible that such export-based growth can lead to a decline in a country's welfare. If a country that already has a large share of the world market and thus faces an inelastic world demand for its major export invests heavily in expanded production, it may force its terms of trade down far enough so that total export earnings and hence import volume decline. In Figure 15–1, the production possibilities frontier would be pushed so far outward to the right that the country ends up on a lower indifference curve, consuming at a point to the southwest of C. Jagdish Bhagwati, a prominent trade theorist, has called this "immiserizing growth."[15] Primary-export expansion would lead to reduced welfare only in extreme cases, seldom if ever realized in practice. But the possibility reinforces the arguments in favor of diversifying a country's export base by producing nontraditional exports, including manufactures.

Ghana—A Case of Arrested Development

At independence in 1957, Ghana was probably the richest country in black Africa, with a per capita income close to $500 (in prices of 1983). In 1983, its per capita income had fallen to $310, below that of Kenya, Sudan, and Pakistan. Many things went wrong for Ghana in that quarter century, but the failure of export policy was crucial.[16] Like Malaysia, Ghana was a one-export country in the late 1950s: cocoa earned almost 60 percent of export revenues and represented almost a fifth of GDP. But in contrast to Malaysia, Ghana under its charismatic leader, Kwame Nkrumah, turned sharply away from its export base to invest in import substituting industries. In this it failed. Had export agriculture, forestry,

---

15. Jagdish N. Bhagwati, "Immiserizing Growth: A Geometrical Note," *Review of Economic Studies* 25 (1958): 201–5.

16. On Ghana's development policies, see Tony Killick, *Development Economics in Action: A Study of Economic Policies in Ghana* (London: Heinemann, 1978).

and mining been maintained, Ghana might have earned sufficient revenues to make a gradual transition into import substitution. But so abrupt was the disinvestment in primary exports that cocoa exports halved in volume from the early 1960s to the early 1980s, when export earnings accounted for less than 10 percent of GDP, compared to almost 30 percent two decades earlier.

Ghana's failure to utilize its generous export base is made more vivid by the rapid growth of its next-door neighbor, the Ivory Coast. With virtually the same resource base, the Ivory Coast invested enough to maintain its coffee exports and then diversified into cocoa (just as Ghana was disinvesting), wood and other primary products. For two decades, export growth averaged 6.7 percent a year and per-capita GDP grew to more than twice that of Ghana, despite substantial immigration from less prosperous neighboring countries.[17]

Fluctuating Export Earnings

Not only do the net barter terms of trade show a secular decline, they also fluctuate considerably, as is evident in Figure 15–2. If the underlying source of instability is export supplies, there is likely to be considerably less variation in export revenues than if the problem is unstable world demand for a country's exports, as illustrated in Figures 15–3 and 15–4.

Whether the principal source of instability is demand or supply, or a combination of both, a second question remains: What kinds of exporting countries suffer most from instability? The usual expectation is that export instability will be most serious among less developed countries whose export earnings are concentrated in one or a few products, especially if those products are primary commodities, and among countries whose markets are concentrated in a few importing countries. However, not all of this specification stands up to empirical testing. Two thorough studies, one by Alisdair Mac-Bean using data from the 1950s and a second by Odin Knudsen and Andrew Parnes that extends the data through the mid-1960s, reach several conclusions. First, developing countries as a group do have more unstable export earnings than industrial countries, although the difference between the two groups is not great. Second, although not all studies agree, commodity concentration does seem to be a significant cause of fluctuations in export earnings. However, there appears to be little or no association between export instability and the geographic concentration of export markets or the fraction of a country's export that consists of primary commodities. In fact manufactured goods may be subject to earnings instability as great as primary commodities.[18]

The truly surprising empirical result in these studies is that even if devel-

17. For an early contrast of Ghana and the Ivory Coast, see Elliot J. Berg, "Structural Transformation Versus Gradualism: Recent Economic Development in Ghana and the Ivory Coast," in *Ghana and the Ivory Coast: Perspectives on Modernization,* Philip Foster and Aristide R. Zolberg, eds. (Chicago: The University of Chicago Press) 1971, pp. 187–230.

18. Alisdair I. MacBean, *Export Instability and Economic Development* (London: George Allen and Unwin, 1966), pp. 34–52; Odin Knudsen and Andrew Parnes, *Trade Instability and Economic Development* (Lexington, Mass.: Heath Lexington Books, 1975), pp. 19–30.

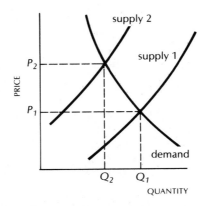

FIGURE 15–3 Variable Export Supply. If export supply is unstable, as for most agricultural exports, the supply curve shifts along the demand curve. A decline in output from Q_1 to Q_2 causes a rise in price from P_1 to P_2. Consequently any decline in revenues, PQ, is dampened.

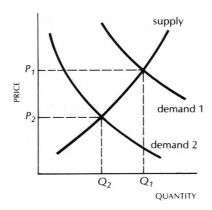

FIGURE 15–4 Variable Export Demand. In contrast to Figure 15–3, if export demand is unstable, typical of markets for metals like copper, the shift of the demand curve along the supply curve causes both price and quantity to fall (P_1 to P_2 and Q_1 to Q_2). The decline in revenue is greater than the change in either price or quantity.

oping countries suffer more export instability, their investment and economic growth may not be hurt by it. Conventional wisdom has generally held that the instability in export earnings would be transmitted to the domestic economy, making domestic demand unstable and rendering investment more risky. Uncertain access to imported materials, caused by fluctuating export earnings, intensifies investors' risks. Consequently, investment is discouraged and economic growth retarded. The econometric tests of these propositions either fail to support them or prove the opposite: export instability seems positively correlated with investment and growth. However, there is some controversy over the validity of these findings. Observations on the structural characteristics of nonfuel minerals exporters—especially their heavy dependence on one or two mineral exports for government revenue—suggest that these countries may be severely hampered by earnings fluctuations.[19]

Knudsen and Parnes have advanced the permanent income hypothesis to explain why fluctuating earnings might not retard development. Income earners (and by extension, countries) count on some level of relatively certain annual income and try to maintain consumption patterns based largely on that "permanent" income. More of the uncertain, fluctuating component of income tends to be saved than is true for the "permanent" component. The more unstable total income is likely to be, the larger the fraction that income earners will save. Under this hypothesis about behavior, greater export instability forces residents (and governments) to save more than they otherwise would, hence to invest more.[20]

Most individuals and presumably most governments prefer situations of greater stability, other things being equal. If, as suggested by the permanent income hypothesis, greater variance of export economies leads to faster growth, then the preference for stable earnings (reduced variance) may force governments to choose slower growth as well, as depicted in Figure 15–5. Something like this model could explain the efforts expended by many developing-country governments to stabilize export earnings through pro-

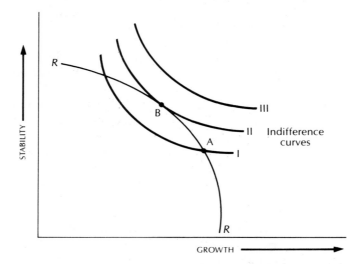

FIGURE 15–5 Trade-Off between Export Stability and Economic Growth. The curve *RR* represents achievable combinations of growth and stability. It can be viewed as a production possibilities curve. Countries will prefer points like *B*, on a higher indifference curve, to points like *A*, even though growth is higher at *A*.

19. The work of F. G. Adams and J. R. Behrman, *Commodity Exports and Economic Development: The Commodity Problem and Policy in Developing Countries: An Integrated Econometric Investigation* (Lexington, Mass.: D. C. Heath, 1982), points to a negligible effect of export instability on growth. Gobind Nankani, "Development Problems of Non-fuel Mineral Exporting Countries," *Finance and Development* 17, no. 1 (March 1980): 6–10, provides structural reasons for believing that fluctuating export earnings do harm the development efforts of these countries.

20. Knudsen and Parnes, *Trade Instability,* 81–128. Savings and the permanent-income hypothesis is treated in Chapter 11 of this text.

ducer price controls, international buffer stocks, or compensatory payments schemes, despite the implications of the permanent-income hypothesis.

Curve *RR* represents the trade-off between export stability and economic growth in an economy, analagous to a production frontier with two "goods," stability and growth. Indifference curves show the country's preference for lower variability and higher growth. A primary exporting country might be at *A*, with high growth but high instability of export earnings. By reducing both instability and growth, shown as a move from *A* to *B*, the country could achieve a higher indifference curve, thus considering itself better off.

Commodity Agreements to Raise Prices

Developing countries have made several attempts over the past two decades to raise the prices of specific export commodities. One of the proposals of the 1974 United Nations resolution on a "New International Economic Order" (NIEO) called for international **commodity agreements** that would both stabilize commodity prices and raise them. In order to raise export prices it is necessary either to restrict output (that is, to shift the supply curve to the left) or to impose a common export tax. If world demand for the commodity is inelastic (i.e., the price elasticity is between −1 and 0) as is true for most tropical food exports, then restricting supply causes a more than proportional increase in price and an increase in total revenues to exporters. If, however, world demand is elastic, as may be true for meat and for many manufactured goods, then supply restrictions raise prices less than proportionally and revenues fall.

Output restriction works best when large majorities of both producing and consuming nations participate. The International Coffee Agreement, which was first negotiated in 1960, has been a notably successful example. Export quotas are allocated to all producers, while most Western consuming nations agree to buy only from producing members of the agreement. Exporters can sell to nonquota markets, such as Eastern Europe and most developing countries, but at market prices that can be substantially lower than in participating countries.

However, under certain conditions producers may be able to restrict demand and raise prices without the agreement of consumers. Among many unsuccessful attempts to accomplish this looms the one dramatic success, the Organization of Petroleum Exporting Countries (OPEC). From 1972 to 1982, OPEC raised oil prices from under $4 a barrel to over $30, a real increase (allowing for international inflation) of 240 percent. The slippage of OPEC prices since 1982 and the collapse in 1986 suggests the limitations of producer agreements, but does not detract from its dramatic accomplishments of the 1970s. This example has stimulated exporters of other commodities—especially minerals—to form their own **cartels,** as price-raising agreements among commodity producers may be called.

Attempts to raise world prices for primary exports are akin to a **zero-sum game** in which the gains of one group of countries (producers) are offset by the losses of another group (consumers and the foreign owners of capital).

Even when developing country exports are the object of price-raising agreements, potential losers include other LDCs that import these commodities. Developing-country importers of petroleum were among the hardest hit by OPEC's price-fixing cartel. There has been little consumer-country support for the price-raising features of the NIEO and the debate has instead centered on price stabilization, which can benefit both exporting and importing countries.

Commodity Agreements to Stabilize Prices

Following the 1974 United Nations resolution on the New International Economic Order, the United Nations Conference on Trade and Development (UNCTAD) developed an "Integrated Programme for Commodities," which became the pivotal proposal in NIEO discussions. Under this integrated program a common fund was to be established by agreement among both exporters and importers. The fund would be used to purchase stocks of commodities, called **buffer stocks,** that would be used to stabilize the prices of eighteen commodities that are among the most important LDC exports: bananas, bauxite, cocoa, coffee, copper, cotton, hard fibers, iron ore, jute, manganese, meat, phosphates, rubber, sugar, tea, timber, tin, and vegetable oils.

To stabilize commodity prices in world trade it is necessary for some central authority—a large company, a private cartel, a single government, a cartel of producing countries, or an international agency—to intervene in the market, buying the commodity when prices are falling and selling from their stocks when prices are rising. To do this the authority must control a buffer stock and must have access to funds that can be used to increase that stock when necessary. The principle of stabilization is easy, but the application is fraught with difficulty. First, the buffer stock authority must have a reliable forecast of the commodity's price trend over a long period, because intervention is intended to reduce fluctuations about that trend. If predictions of future prices turn out to be higher than the actual average price, the authority will on balance buy more for the buffer stock than it sells and eventually may be unable to finance further purchases. Conversely a low prediction results in excessive sales, depleting the buffer stock.

Second, even if price forecasts are accurate, the authority must set floor and ceiling prices that it can maintain, given available finance and the size of the buffer stock. Once speculators sense that the authority's resources are too limited they can bid the price up or down, depending on whether stocks or finance are in short supply, to break through the ceiling or floor and make a certain profit. Finally, if buffer stocks lead to higher inventories of a commodity than would otherwise be held, this represents a real resource cost to someone. In the NIEO proposals the industrial nations were to finance the stocks and would thus have borne this cost, estimated to be over $10 billion. Thus the eventual success of negotiations depend not only on whether the technical problems can be overcome, but also on the assessment of consuming nations about the costs to them of continued price fluctuations.

Stabilizing world commodity prices is not necessarily the same thing as stabilizing a particular country's export earnings. As suggested above, if pro-duction is itself unstable because of variable weather, strikes, or other disruptions, then a stable world price can increase the variability of earnings, although studies by University of Pennsylvania economist Jere Behrman suggest that this would not be a serious problem in the UNCTAD scheme.[21] An alternative with considerable appeal is to compensate directly for earn-ings fluctuations rather than to stabilize prices. Two such schemes are in existence: the Compensatory Financing Facility of the IMF and the Stabex scheme operated by the EEC under the Rome Convention. Under the IMF facility countries can borrow to finance balance-of-payments deficits which are partially caused by a drop in export revenues below a five-year moving average. The EEC scheme permits borrowing if a country's particular com-modity export revenues, earned from the Community, fall below a four-year average. During 1984 the IMF lent $1.25 billion under its facility.

Ineffective Linkages

An export sector may grow satisfactorily, enjoying favorable and steady prices, yet still fail to stimulate development if linkages fail to materialize. From the previous discussion of linkages it would appear that the petroleum industry and, with a few exceptions, the mining industry, generally remain **enclaves,** remote from other centers of production and ill-adapted to link with them economically. Neither backward linkages to suppliers of produc-tion materials and equipment nor consumption linkages are likely to work. In some instances railroads and ports built for the mines do aid other indus-tries by lowering costs and stimulating investment, but examples of remote or specialized overhead capital can also be found: Liberia's rail and harbor link with its iron mines is poorly placed to stimulate agriculture or other industry, and the pipelines and tanker ports of the petroleum industry have no uses outside that sector. Some agricultural export sectors, particularly plantations in colonial Africa, also had few effective linkages. But generally the smaller scale and greater labor intensity of agriculture make possible more linked development than is true for minerals.

The **fiscal linkage,** which can channel resource wealth to finance develop-ment in other sectors, is too often used to avoid the difficult choices required to launch development. A typical pattern is represented by Zambia, whose copper wealth has allowed it to invest in highly protected, inefficient indus-tries with no potential market outside the country and to avoid the difficult problem of stimulating small-scale African agriculture in a sector dominated by large-scale European farmers. The petroleum exporters face similar choices: whether to use oil revenues in employment and welfare programs, unrelated to increased productivity among its farmers and industrial workers; or to resist this temptation and invest in agriculture and industry

---

21. Jere R. Behrman, *Development, the International Economic Order and Commodity Agreements* (Reading, Mass.: Addison-Wesley, 1978). Chapter 3 provides an analytical treat-ment of commodity agreements and summarizes the conditions under which stable prices will stabilize or destabilize revenues. On pages 87–90 he reports his conclusions that UNCTAD's scheme would either stabilize revenues or have no impact on their variability.

that will eventually be able to compete in world markets, thus diversifying the economy.

The choice is made more difficult by the high wages typically paid in capital-intensive petroleum and mining sectors, which often provide high wage standards for union bargaining and government minimum wage-setting in other sectors. As wages rise, the prospects for development based on abundant low-cost labor diminish. The dualistic structure (see Chapter 3) is perpetuated, with a small but relatively high-income work force in modern employment and a large, low-productivity work force of farmers and marginal urban workers, the latter mostly in casual employment and petty services.

An even more pervasive bar to generating linkages from mineral enclaves and certain other primary-export sectors is the impact of abundant export revenues on the exchange rate. Figure 15–6 shows what happens when minerals like petroleum and copper or tree crops like cocoa and coffee dominate the supply of foreign exchange revenues for a country. In this diagram of a foreign exchange market, the quantity along the horizontal axis is the amount of foreign exchange, while the price along the vertical axis is the exchange rate, expressed as units of local currency per unit of foreign currency, e.g. pesos per dollar.

The demand curve is a *total revenue curve,* giving the quantity of imports times the price of imports—i.e., the amount of foreign exchange demanded by importers—as a function of the exchange rate. The total supply of foreign exchange is the horizontal sum of the supply of (a) traditional mineral or agricultural exports, abundant but fairly inelastic, and (b) nontraditional

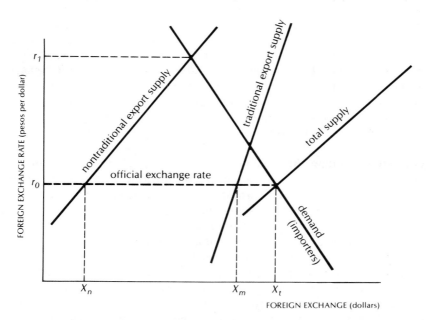

FIGURE 15–6 Foreign Exchange Market in a Resource-Rich Economy. Without intervention, the exchange rate will settle at r_o, a rate which most non-traditional exporters will find too low to allow them to cover costs.

exports, with much higher unit costs than traditional exports. The market-determined exchange rate would be r_o, the intersection of total supply and demand. At that rate, traditional exports (X_m) would dominate total exports (X_t). Nontraditional exports (X_n) would be small because the local currency yield of a dollar's worth of exports (the exchange rate, r_o) is low relative to the cost of producing these exports. (The nontraditional export supply curve could include import substitutes, which also contribute to the supply of importable goods.) If traditional exports were suddenly to disappear, the exchange rate would devalue to r_1, stimulating a marked rise in the production of nontraditional exports (and import substitutes) and forcing a marked decline in imports.

For nontraditional export (and import-substituting) industries the exchange rate is **overvalued,** because the dollar price of the currency is too high (and the local currency price of the dollar is too low) to make production profitable for most suppliers of these goods.[22] Overvalued exchange rates, together with high wages, discourage the development of new industries and thus prevent diversification of the economy. These adverse impacts of rich natural-resource deposits are not confined to developing countries. The exploitation of off-shore oil and natural gas reserves has had a similar effect in the Netherlands, damaging once-competitive export industries, from which observers coined the term **Dutch disease.** (In Chapter 19 we explore Dutch disease and some country cases in more detail).

Several policy interventions have been used to raise the effective price to nontraditional industries and thus to encourage their development. **Taxes on primary exports,** whether for fiscal revenue or to restrict supply and thus raise world prices, move the traditional (and total) export supply curve of Figure 15–6 to the left, effectively devaluing the exchange rate (i.e., raising the peso-per-dollar rate). This makes it more profitable to produce and export nontraditional goods, moving upwards along the non-traditional export supply curve. The same effect could be obtained with a **split exchange rate.** The central bank would pay a higher peso-per-dollar rate for receipts for nontraditional exports (and require importers to pay this rate also), but pay a lower peso-per-dollar rate for traditional export receipts. To accomplish this, however, authorities must prevent exporters of traditional commodities from selling foreign exchange to importers or other exporters, who would pay more than the official rate on traditional exports. This may be virtually impossible to police, especially over the long term. Finally, **import tariffs and quotas** are used in most countries to raise the local price of imports, thus protecting import-competing industries and stimulating their development. This policy is explored at length in Chapter 16.

Natural-resource exporters, recognizing the need to diversify their economies and raise productivity, have turned towards the processing of their exports as a vehicle for development. If petroleum and mining industries create few backward linkages, they can generate *forward linkages* to industries whose principal input is the export sector's output. Thus Venezuela is using its iron ore, natural gas, and hydroelectric power to produce steel,

---

22. For a more complete definition of an overvalued exchange rate, see Chapter 16.

partly for export in place of the iron ore and partly for domestic use. If, and only if, the domestic steel is cheaper than imported steel, it may stimulate further forward linkages to steel-using industries like construction, transport equipment, processing equipment, and even oil derricks, one of those undeveloped linkages to the petroleum industry. Other mineral and timber exporters are trying to exploit forward linkages and either substitute processed exports for raw materials or divert part of their raw materials into inputs for domestic industry.

These **resource-based industrialization strategies** may succeed in expanding the industrial base and increasing the economic benefits derived from a natural resource. However, resource processing is no panacea for development. Most of the mineral-processing industries share with mining the characteristics of large scale, capital intensity, sophisticated technology, and high wages, so they tend to be extensions of the export enclave, generating little employment and realizing few linkages to the rest of the economy. Nor would they represent much diversification if the processed product is mostly exported in place of the raw material.

We are left with the conclusion that primary exports can be effective leading sectors for development if the nature of the natural resource and of the production process is conducive to linkages. Where these characteristics are absent, the task is more difficult and requires enlightened, forceful, and sustained government intervention to channel revenues into productivity-raising investments elsewhere in the economy.

Import Substitution

Whatever the relative merits and drawbacks of primary-export-led growth, most governments have pushed their economies full-speed in other directions. There have been exceptions: Malaysia, Thailand, the Ivory Coast, Guatemala and a few others, have used their primary exporting base to generate growth, while the petroleum exporters simply followed their overwhelming comparative advantage. For most of the rest, development has become synonymous with industrialization. This has been pursued by a strategy called **import substitution,** which is the substitution of domestic production for imports of manufactures. A few countries have followed a very different path, emphasizing the export of labor-intensive manufactures. This chapter examines the first of these strategies; Chapter 17 describes the second, then attempts a synthesis among the various trade-and-industrialization approaches to development.

THE STRATEGY OF PROTECTION

Import substitution is a well-trod path to industrialization. It was taken during the nineteenth century by most of the currently industrial countries as they followed the pathbreaker, England, into the Industrial Revolution. In the newly independent United States, Alexander Hamilton's 1791 *Report on Manufactures* argued for tariffs to protect American manufacturers from cheap British imports, and President Jefferson unintentionally boosted American manufacturing by the politically inspired Embargo of 1807. Friedrich Lizst, the German economist, espoused protective tariffs as an instrument to industrialize Germany in the mid-nineteenth century. All the major European powers, including Russia both before and after the Communist revolution, and Japan, marched down the road of protectionism to develop manufacturing as it became apparent that military strength depended on industrial strength.

In the third world, import substitution was first explored by Latin American countries when their primary export markets were severely disrupted, first by the Great Depression of the 1930s and subsequently by the breakdown of commercial shipping during World War II. Emerging from the war with fledgling industries, countries like Argentina, Brazil, Colombia, and Mexico began systematically to sustain these manufacturers by erecting tariffs and other barriers to competing imports from the United States. The export pessimism chronicled by Prebisch, Singer, and others reinforced protectionist sentiment, and Latin America developed import substitution regimes with a multitude of protective techniques that were later emulated by other developing countries. A few Asian countries, such as India and Turkey, also began to industrialize before World War II. But in most of Asia and Africa independence was the stimulus that induced countries to embark on the path of import substitution. By the 1960s import substitution had become the dominant strategy of economic development.

The underlying concept of import substitution is simple. First, identify large domestic markets, as indicated by substantial imports over the years. Then ensure that the technologies of production can be mastered by local manufacturers or that foreign investors are willing to supply technology, management, and capital. Finally, erect protective barriers, either tariffs or quotas on imports, to overcome the probably high initial cost of local production and make it profitable for potential investors in the target industries. This approach has generally meant that consumer goods industries—especially processed foods, beverages, textiles, clothing, and footwear—became the first targets for investment. Not only are these products manufactured with relatively standardized technologies easily accessible to LDC producers, but it was also believed that consumers could bear the higher costs of local production without disrupting development. The only other major category of manufactured import before industrialization began was capital goods. Increased investment was essential to development, however, and it was believed that higher costs of capital equipment would discourage investors.

Infant Industries

Economists find much to criticize in the protective structures of both developing and industrial countries, as this chapter will make clear. But there are valid arguments in favor of protective tariffs as a tool of development, centering on the concept of an infant industry. A country wishing to develop through industrialization may see opportunities in several lines of manufacturing to begin the process. (A similar argument could be made in terms of diversifying agriculture by introducing new crops.) With little experience in these new lines of production, domestic capitalists, managers, technicians, workers (and farmers) are likely to be relatively inefficient compared to producers in more advanced industrial countries and are likely to remain so for several years. Eventually, as the new industries "learn by doing," the productivity of all factors of production will rise. The new enterprises may become able to compete at home against imported goods without tariff protection or may even be able to export. Until these producers gain the necessary experience, however, they cannot manufacture (or grow new crops) profitably and sell at the price of competing imports. So unless the government either subsidizes these fledgling industries or protects them from competing imports by imposing tariffs or import quotas, the infant industries have little chance of being born, let alone maturing into efficient competitors.

To justify protection or a subsidy, an infant industry must eventually be capable of competing against imports in the home market, or, a stronger condition, as an export sector. This suggests a temporary tariff, one that declines towards zero as productivity increases and costs fall, or a declining subsidy. The subsidy has the advantage of clearly identifying the costs of starting the new industry, but the disadvantage of an additional burden on the government's revenue system. Most governments find it easier to impose tariffs, which make domestic consumers bear the cost instead. Even a temporary tariff or subsidy may not be justified if the eventual benefits to society of establishing the new industry, suitably discounted as explained in Chapter 6, do not exceed the costs of protection.[1] All too often these conditions are not met. The industrial landscape is littered with infants that never grew up and require protection indefinitely, from the petrochemical industry of Colombia to the textile industry of Kenya.

The infant industry argument can be extended to include several industries at once and even to include all manufacturing. For example, a balanced growth strategy of developing many industries simultaneously (see Chapter 3) might be started with a uniform protective tariff, declining over time. This is a third approach to the problem discussed at the end of Chapter 15, diversification of the economy away from dependence on a few primary-product exports. There we discussed taxing the primary exports or imposing a split exchange rate in order to raise the prices facing other industries. A uniform protective duty on competing imports would have the same effect on non-traditional industries, although the costs of protection would be distributed differently. Ideally all these interventions in the market share three characteristics: they are intended to diversify the economy towards a new but efficient structure; they are necessary because the market, left alone, would not achieve this desirable result in a reasonable time; and they should be temporary measures with declining impacts if the diversification strategy is successful. As we will see, the protective structures used to promote import substitution deviate from this ideal in crucial ways.

Protective Tariffs

In the early stages of import substitution, when a protective tariff is placed on competing consumer good imports, not one but two significant aids are

---

1. For a complete specification of the infant industry argument, see Harry G. Johnson, "Optimal Trade Interventions in the Presence of Domestic Distortions," in *Trade, Growth and the Balance of Payments*, R. E. Caves et al., (Amsterdam: North Holland, 1965), pp. 3–34.

provided simultaneously to the potential manufacturer. First and obviously, the domestic price of the good, say cloth, will be raised above the world price. For the importing country the world price of imported cloth is the cost of the cloth landed at the port of entry, the c.i.f. or "border" price. With no tariff, the domestic price of cloth would settle at the world price. When a tariff is imposed the domestic price must rise above the world price. If the home country's demand for imports does not affect world prices (i.e., the world supply is perfectly elastic) and if the tariff does not preclude imports altogether, then the domestic price will rise by the full extent of the tariff. Any potential manufacturer can charge anything up to the tariff-supported domestic price and still compete with imports, assuming his quality is comparable and domestic consumers do not prefer imports simply because they are foreign.

This effect of increased domestic price is called **nominal protection** and is depicted in Figure 16–1. At a world price P_W (equal to the border price, c.i.f.), consumers demand Q_1 of cloth and local producers find it profitable to produce only Q_2; the balance, $M_1 = Q_1 - Q_2$, is imported. If an *ad valorem* (i.e., a percentage) tariff t_o is imposed on imports competing with domestic cloth and if world supply is perfectly elastic, then the domestic price rises to P_d, reducing demand to Q_3 and increasing domestic production to Q_4. Imports are thus reduced to $M_2 = Q_3 - Q_4$. The **protective effect,** given by the increase in domestic output from Q_2 to Q_4, entails a rent or **producers' surplus,** given by trapezoid *a;* and a **resource cost,** given by triangle *b,*

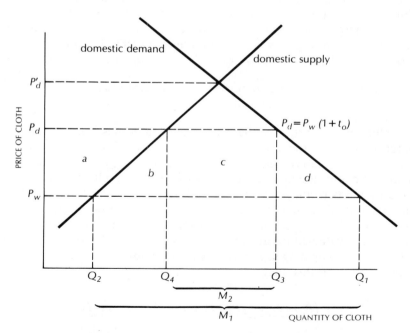

FIGURE 16–1 Nominal Tariff Protection. The imposition of a protective tariff, t_o, causes the domestic price, P_d, to rise above the world price, P_w. Domestic production therefore increases. The resulting loss in consumers' surplus ($a + b + c + d$) is offset by the gain in producers' surplus (a) and in tariff revenue for the government (c). The remaining areas b and d represent deadweight losses.

because factors of production are diverted from more productive uses into import substitution for imported cloth. The government's tariff revenue is represented by rectangle $c = t_o P_w(Q_3 - Q_4)$. Consumers pay for protection by the loss of **consumer surplus,** equal to area $a + b + c + d$, generated by both the higher price and reduced consumption. Area $b + d$, two triangles representing welfare losses that are not compensated by gains to anyone, is called the **deadweight loss.** A prohibitive tariff would raise the domestic price to P'_d, at which point domestic demand equals domestic supply and no cloth is imported.

The second aid to domestic manufacture is that tariffs are typically *not* raised on the imported inputs required for production. If the textile manufacturer is to import cotton that he will spin into yarn and weave into cloth, then his concern is not only with the price of the cloth but with the margin between the cost of imported cotton (and other imported inputs, such as chemicals and dyes) and the sale price of finished cloth. It is within this margin that he must pay wages, rents, and interest on borrowed capital and from which he must extract his profit. The greater that margin, the more room there is to accommodate higher factor costs and the higher is the potential profit. This margin is the *valued-added* measured *in domestic prices.* It can be increased either by raising tariffs on competing imports of finished products, lowering tariffs on imported inputs, or both. This dual effect of the tariff structure is called **effective protection.**

To measure the concept of effective protection, it is necessary to compare two margins: first, the margin between the domestic, tariff-determined prices of inputs and outputs, or value-added measured at domestic prices; second, the same margin, but measured at world or c.i.f. prices, which is called **value-added at world prices.** The fraction by which the first margin exceeds the second is called the **effective rate of protection,** abbreviated ERP:

$$\text{ERP} = \frac{\text{value-added (domestic prices)} - \text{value-added (world prices)}}{\text{value-added (world prices)}}. \quad [16\text{--}1]$$

To refine this further, note that value-added at domestic prices (V_d) is the difference between the potential domestic price (P_d) and the potential domestic cost of material inputs per unit of output (C_d). Further, the potential domestic price is equivalent to the world price (P_w) plus the increase permitted by the percentage (or *ad valorem*) tariff on competing imports (t_o), while potential domestic cost equals the cost at world prices (C_w) plus any increase permitted by the *ad valorem* tariff on imported inputs (t_i). The denominator, value-added at world prices (V_w), is the difference between the world price of competing imports and the cost of inputs, also valued at world prices (C_w). Given this, then,

$$\text{ERP} = \frac{(P_d - C_d) - (P_w - C_w)}{P_w - C_w} = \frac{P_w(1 + t_o) - C_w(1 + t_i) - (P_w - C_w)}{P_w - C_w}. \quad \begin{array}{l}[16\text{--}2]\\[16\text{--}3]\end{array}$$

$$\text{ERP} = \frac{P_w t_o - C_w t_i}{P_w - C_w}.$$

As a last refinement, Equation 16–2 can be put in terms of a dollar of output

by dividing the fraction through by P_w. The cost of an input for a dollar's worth of output, C_w/P_w, can then be designated a, an input coefficient. If we then allow for several inputs, each with its own input coefficient, a_i, and its own tariff, t_i, then the formula can be written:

$$ERP = (t_o - \Sigma a_i t_i)/(1 - \Sigma a_i). \qquad [16–4]$$

This formula can also accommodate subsidies on competing outputs and on inputs by treating them as negative tariffs.[2]

To illustrate the workings of effective protection, assume, using Equation 16–3, that $100 of cloth, valued at world prices, would require $60 of material inputs, such as cotton and chemicals, also valued at world prices. Value-added is $40 at world prices. If the government has imposed a uniform duty of 20 percent on both competing imports and imported inputs, then

$$ERP = \frac{100(.20) - 60(.20)}{100 - 60} = 0.20.$$

A uniform tariff, 20 percent in this case, yields an effective rate of protection of the same amount. If, however, in order to encourage investment in the textile industry, the government were to permit textile firms to import cotton and chemicals duty-free, then $t_i = 0$ and

$$ERP = \frac{100(.20)}{40} = 0.50.$$

Effective protection is 50 percent, or 2.5 times the nominal rate of 20 percent. Similarly, if the input duty stayed at 20 percent but competing cloth imports were taxed at 32 percent, the ERP would also be 50 percent.

The implication in the second and third examples is that, even though only modest nominal protection is provided, the domestic manufacturer enjoys a large margin of 50 percent over value-added at world prices. If the local manufacturer takes advantage of the effective protection afforded by the tariff structure, he can earn extremely high profits, pay high wages, or simply accommodate inefficiencies and high costs substantially above those of foreign competitors. The higher the effective protection, the greater the potential for inefficiencies, high input costs, or profits, and hence the greater the likelihood that the industry will be established in the country.

Tariff structures in most countries, including most industrial countries, are like those in the latter two textile examples: duties tend to escalate from low rates on imported industrial inputs to higher rates on imports of finished goods that compete with domestic manufactures. In fact the levels of protection in this hypothetical example are modest by world standards. It is common to observe effective protection of 100 percent or more in several industries in countries strongly pursuing import substitution. Not only is the level high, but there is a wide range of protective rates that result in severe

2. For a complete, although advanced, treatment of effective protection, see W. M. Corden, *The Theory of Protection* (London: Oxford University Press, 1971), especially Chapters 2 and 3.

discrimination against particular kinds of investment. The fairly typical pattern of protection is illustrated by the data in Table 16–1 for Bangladesh in 1984 and Brazil and the Philippines in the mid-1960s.

TABLE 16–1   Effective Rates of Protection

Sector	Bangladesh (1984)	Brazil (1966)	Philippines (1965)	Norway (1954)
Agriculture	13	46	33	34
Mining	—	−16	−9	−7
Manufacturing	114	127	53	9
Consumer goods[a]	na	198	72	29
Intermediate goods[a]	na	151	45	9
Machinery	10	93	24	18
Transport equipment	na	−26	−3	−6

Sources: Thomas L. Hutcheson and Joseph J. Stern, "The Methodology of Assistance Policy Analysis," (Harvard Institute for International Development: Development Discussion Paper No. 226, April 1986)—Bangladesh; Bela Balassa, et al., The Structure of Protection in the Developing Countries (Baltimore: Johns Hopkins University Press, 1971), p. 55 (other countries).
na = not available.
[a] Aggregates for consumer goods and intermediate goods are simple, unweighted averages of constituent industry data.

The average level of effective protection for manufacturing as a whole ranges from moderate (Philippines) to high (Brazil). However, the structure within manufacturing is widely skewed. Consumer goods are highly protected, at considerable cost to consumers of manufactures, and intermediate goods are comfortably protected, though at lower rates. The capital-goods industries, however, receive less protection because tariffs on capital goods are thought to discourage investors; rates are especially low in Bangladesh for machinery and in Brazil and the Philippines for transport equipment (which does not include automobiles, a consumer durable). As a consequence the incentive to invest in capital-goods production is less than in other manufacturing and the development of this sector typically lags behind the others. More damaging in terms of many development objectives, manufacturing as a whole enjoys a substantial advantage over agriculture, which faces effective rates of protection ranging downward from 46 percent to only 13 percent in these examples. In many countries, agriculture has negative effective protection.[3] These biases against investment in agriculture and in capital-goods industries are characteristic of import substitution regimes and have been partly responsible for the failure of import substitution to stimulate self-sustaining development. This biased protective structure is not unique to developing countries, as demonstrated by the figures for Norway in Table 16–1.

---

3. A negative effective rate of production can have two meanings. If the rate is small, it means that the industry faces high taxes on either its inputs or its own outputs, as is likely to be true for many primary-exporting industries. Alternatively, a very high negative ERP usually indicates that the industry is so inefficient that its inputs cost more in foreign exchange than its outputs are worth at c.i.f. prices; i.e., value-added is negative if measured at world prices! Then the denominator of Equation 16–3 or 16–4 becomes a small negative number.

However, extremes like the Bangladesh structure, especially the severe bias
against agriculture, do seem confined to the third world.

A closely related measure, the **domestic resource cost** (DRC), also compares value-added in domestic and world prices. However, it measures domestic value-added as the *actual* payments to factors of production—wages, rent, interest, depreciation, and profit—in local currency units such as pesos or rupees. This contrasts with the ERP measure, which is usually (though not necessarily) based on the *potential* domestic value-added created by the tariff structure, as measured in Equation 16–3. The denominator of the DRC, value-added at world prices, is the same as that for the ERP, only it is designated in foreign currency. Thus,

$$DRC = \frac{\text{value-added at domestic prices in local currency}}{\text{value-added at world prices in foreign currency}}. \quad [16–5]$$

This measure has some potential wrinkles that make it useful. First, domestic value-added can be measured, not at the private costs paid by firms for factors of production, but at the actual value to society, the opportunity cost or shadow price of these factors (see Chapter 6). Second, the denominator can allow for payments to foreign capital and other foreign currency costs, so that the DRC becomes a measure of the domestic cost of earning or saving foreign exchange. Third, linked industries can be incorporated into this measure, which can therefore cover either the textile industry or the textile industry and cotton farming together. (The ERP could be adjusted to incorporate actual value-added at domestic prices and to allow shadow prices and linkages. However, in that form the ratio no longer measures the impact of the tariff and subsidy structure, as it was designed to do.)

The DRC has dimensions of local currency per unit of foreign exchange; for example, rupees per dollar. If for a particular investment this ratio is below the official exchange rate, it implies that the country could save or earn foreign exchange through this project, convert the dollars into rupees at the official rate, pay the factors of production, and still retain a surplus in local currency. Such a project is obviously desirable. In order to reach its development goals a country may have to undertake projects for which the DRC is above the official exchange rate. This indicates that the official rate is not set at a level consistent with development goals; it is "overvalued," in a sense explained below. Projects can be ranked in ascending order of DRC and this ranking used to select the most efficient projects for investment.[4]

A sample of Indian industries ranked by their DRCs is shown in Table 16–2. At a time when the official exchange rate was 7.50 rupees per dollar, all industries except food-grain production required at least 10 rupees to save $1 of foreign exchange. Without considerable protection, these sectors could not compete with imports. Note the wide range of estimates: the DRC for

4. For a comparison of the DRC and ERP as measures of efficiency, see Michael Bruno, "Domestic Resource Costs and Effective Protection: Clarification and Syntheses," *Journal of Political Economy* 80 (1972): 16–33; and Bela Balassa and Daniel M. Schydlowsky, "Domestic Resource Costs and Effective Protection Once Again," *Journal of Political Economy* 80 (1972): 63–69.

TABLE 16–2   Efficiency Indicators for Selected Industries: India, 1968–1969

Rank	Industry	Domestic resource cost (rupees/dollars)[a]
1	Food grains	7.5
2	Timber	10.7
3	Cement	10.8
4	Cotton	11.5
5	Transport equipment	12.1
6	Wood products	14.2
7	Electrical equipment	16.5
8	Leather footwear	16.9
9	Leather	17.1
10	Metal products	17.5
11	Vegetable oils	18.0
12	Iron and steel	18.9
13	Paper and products	20.4
14	Cotton textiles	24.3
15	Fertilizer	42.1
16	Mill products	46.6
17	Petroleum products	47.6

Source: Jagdish N. Bhagwati and T. N. Srinivasan, *Foreign Trade Regimes and Economic Development: India* (New York: Columbia University Press,1975), pp. 179–81.
[a]The official exchange rate, 1968–1969, was 7.50 rupees per dollar.

petroleum products is over six times that for food grains. The pattern is consistent with the tendency towards escalating tariff rates. Industries with low DRCs are agricultural products and capital goods, while manufacturers of consumer and of intermediate goods have high resource costs.

Import Quotas

The protective effects of tariffs can also be achieved through restrictions on imports, known as **quantitative restrictions** (QRs), **quotas**, or **import licensing**. For both the government and domestic manufacturers, import quotas have the advantage of permitting a known quantity of imports. With tariffs the quantity of imports depends on the elasticities of supply and demand, which are generally not known in advance. A quota that limits imports to the same quantity as a tariff would have most of the same effects. To see this, refer back to Figure 16–1. Instead of the tariff t_0, assume the government limits imports of cloth to the quantity, $M_2 = Q_3 - Q_4$. As with the tariff, the domestic price would still rise to P_d; domestic production would rise from Q_2 to Q_4, causing a resource cost measured by triangle b; and consumption would fall from Q_1 to Q_3, adding the area of triangle d to the deadweight loss. But in two important respects the effects of import quotas differ from those of tariffs.

The first difference is that the government no longer collects tariff revenues. Instead the government issues licenses to a limited number of importers, giving them the right to purchase imports of cloth up to a total of M_2 in Figure 16–1. If the government were to sell these import licenses at auction, potential importers would be willing to buy these licenses for as much as $P_d - P_w$ per unit of imports. Then they could purchase each unit of

imported cloth for P_w, the world price, and break even by selling it at the
domestic price, P_d. In that case the auction price for import licenses would
just equal the tariff, t_o, that would have led to the same quantity of imports.
Also, the government would collect the same revenue as under a tariff, rectangle c in Figure 16–1, in the form of fees for import licenses.

However, most governments do not auction import licenses, but give
them free to a limited number of those importers who apply for them. Then
although the importers pay only P_w for their imports, they can sell them at
the domestic price, P_d in Figure 16–1, and keep for themselves a windfall
profit, or *rent,* of $P_d - P_w = t_o$. This rent—often called a **quota premium**—
can be substantial, so import licenses are valuable to their recipients. Much
effort is expended and large bribes are offered to obtain import licenses, with
profound consequences discussed later in this chapter.

The second difference between quotas and tariffs is that quotas can convert a single domestic manufacturer into a monopolist who can charge whatever price maximizes his profits. Figure 16–2A depicts the market for a
single domestic producer who is protected by a tariff, t. Imports are available
at the world price, P_w, plus the tariff, tP_w. With infinitely elastic world supply,
domestic consumers can buy all they want at the world price plus tariff, P_d
$= P_w (1 + t)$. The domestic producer, despite being the only local supplier,
must compete with this price, which becomes his marginal revenue schedule,
so long as P_d is below the intersection of the marginal cost and demand
curves. Consumers purchase Q_c while the domestic producer offers Q_p, an
output that equates his marginal revenue and marginal cost (point A). The
balance, $Q_c - Q_p$, is imported. Figure 16–2B depicts an alternative means of
stimulating domestic production. Here, a quota replaces the tariff, as the
government uses licensing to hold imports to the previous $Q_c - Q_p$, leaving
the domestic manufacturer with a residual demand (which must be drawn
through the same point A) that can only be met from domestic production.
With no further competition from imports, the firm now faces a marginal

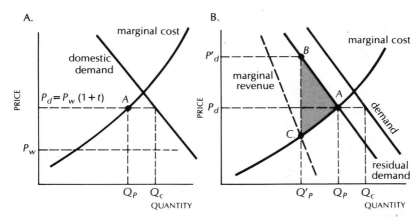

FIGURE 16–2 Protecting Domestic Monopoly: Tariff versus Quota. Panel A depicts a
monopolist protected by a tariff. The monopolist produces at the point (A) where marginal
revenue equals marginal costs. The balance demanded is supplied by imports. In panel B a
quota is imposed to hold imports to the same level as in panel A. The domestic price rises
and the economy suffers a deadweight loss.

revenue curve that is below the residual demand curve. It equates marginal revenue with marginal cost at point C, producing only Q_p and charging P'_d in the captive residual domestic market. Hence, output and consumption fall, price rises, and society faces a deadweight loss (reduction of consumers' plus producer's surplus) given by shaded area ABC. Clearly, it matters a great deal whether protection is granted through tariffs that are not prohibitive or through equivalent import quotas.

Overvalued Exchange Rates

A third prop of the import substitution regime, the one that clarifies the biases of the entire system, is the **overvalued exchange rate.** There have been several definitions of the term "overvalued" in this context, but for purposes of understanding import substitution a simple explanation will do. In Figure 16–3, the schedules representing exporters' supply of and importers' demand for foreign exchange are total revenue curves, as in Figure 15–6. In the absence of tariffs or quotas an exchange rate of r_e would just clear the market and thus be an equilibrium. If tariffs are imposed on imports, the demand curve shifts downward because importers are then unwilling to offer as much foreign exchange per unit imported. This lowers the peso-per-dollar rate for equilibrium to r_t. Often, however, the official exchange rate, r_o, is below both those levels. Because the peso price of the dollar is so low, import demand is high (M_d) and export supply is low (X_s), creating a potential deficit in the current account of the balance of payments. To reduce this deficit, governments typically resort to import quotas and controls over all foreign exchange transactions. The rate, r_o, is considered *overvalued* in the sense that

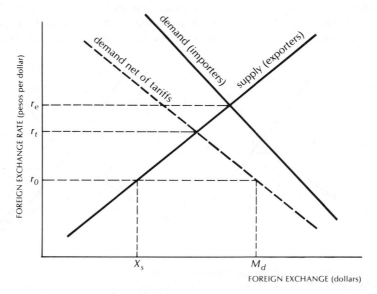

FIGURE 16–3   Overvalued Exchange Rate. The exchange rate r_o represents a common problem: it is too high in dollars per peso, or too low in pesos per dollar, to balance the demand for foreign exchange with the supply of foreign exchange without high protective tariffs, import quotas, and restrictions on other foreign exchange transactions.

the dollar price of pesos (the reciprocal of that shown in the diagram) is too high to maintain equilibrium without controls and high tariffs; the peso rate, r_o, is therefore too low.

Exchange rates become overvalued for a variety of reasons. The genesis of the problem is sometimes an abundant supply of primary exports, which tends to support low (peso to dollar) exchange rates and thus to discourage investment in nontraditional industries (see Chapter 15). As incomes rise and import demand increases at any exchange rate, devaluation is required to stimulate the production of import substitutes and nontraditional exports, and thus to maintain equilibrium in the balance of payments. Domestic inflation, which causes domestic prices and costs to rise faster than the world average, also requires devaluation to maintain exports and restrain imports. For most of the period after World War II, however, most governments maintained fixed exchange rates and were reluctant to risk the destabilizing political effects of devaluation. The exchange rate is one of the most pervasive prices in the economy, perhaps affecting more transactions than any other single price. To change it, especially by the large amounts sometimes required, means changing the relative wealth of influential segments of the population. Not only are the relative prices of imports raised, but in order to prevent domestic prices from rising as much as the currency is devalued, wages and other incomes must be restrained by government policy. Frequently it is the politically powerful who would lose by these measures, especially urban workers, middle-class professionals, civil servants, the upper classes, and others whose consumption depends substantially on imports. For these reasons governments resist devaluation, and when they do undertake it, often devalue by too little in the face of growing demand and continuing inflation. Hence there has been a tendency for exchange rates to remain overvalued in the third world.[5] This tendency has been alleviated by the greater flexibility in exchange rates since 1971, but controlled rates at overvalued levels remain common in the third world.

A glance at Figure 16–3 shows that the overvalued exchange rate discourages exports. It does so by reducing the local currency payment for any given dollar amount of exports, hence reducing revenues to domestic exporters in the currency that matters to them, the home currency. But overvalued rates also encourage imports by keeping the peso payments lower than they should be and this in turn is detrimental to import substituting industries. How then is the overvalued rate consistent with import substitution regimes?

The answer lies in the triumvirate of exchange rates, tariffs, and quotas. Because the exchange rate is so low, import-competing industries depend heavily on high effective tariff protection and on quotas to shield them from cheap imports. Industries without such protection are unlikely to find it profitable to produce for either the home or foreign market. Recall, then, the highly skewed protective structure presented in Table 16–1: consumer goods and intermediate goods manufacturing can overcome the overvalued exchange rate with their high effective rates of protection or with additional

---

5. The economic and political difficulties of devaluation make selective tariffs and quota restrictions even more appealing to governments, despite the allocative inefficiencies such measures entail.

help from import licensing. But agricultural and capital goods manufacturing are exposed to import competition at the low local currency prices engendered by the overvalued exchange rate. Even import quotas on capital goods do not help much because these tend to be variable, depending on the state of the balance of payments.

Outcomes and Problems

Import Substitution in General Equilibrium

The process of import substitution is represented in Figures 16–4, 16–5, and 16–6. Figure 16–4 depicts the imposition of uniform protective tariffs, say in 1960, when the country produces at point A and consumes at C under world terms of trade favorable to its export. Imposition of the tariff, presumed here to be a uniform one on all imports, swings domestic relative prices in favor of importable goods. Production moves towards point B where more of the importable and less of the exportable are produced. If the country is relatively small and does not affect world prices, trade can take place at the same terms of trade as before, so that consumption settles somewhere, such as point E, along line BD, drawn parallel to the terms-of-trade line. Consumption of both goods is lower than before the tariff, so consumers' well-being has been reduced. Both imports and exports have also fallen, as indicated by the line segment, BE (the hypotenuse of the trade triangle—see Figure 15–1), which is shorter than AC. Initially, this shift from free trade necessarily reduces both trade and consumers' welfare.

If protection successfully stimulates investment in infant industries and subsequent growth is substantial, the production frontier will be pushed outwards, as in Figure 16–5, and after several years consumer welfare will have

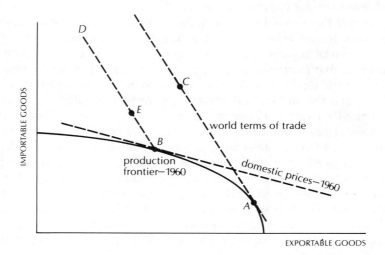

FIGURE 16–4 Imposition of Protective Tariff (situation in 1960). A protective tariff increases the relative domestic price of importables, inducing a rise in their production from point A to B. At first, consumption of both goods falls from point C to E.

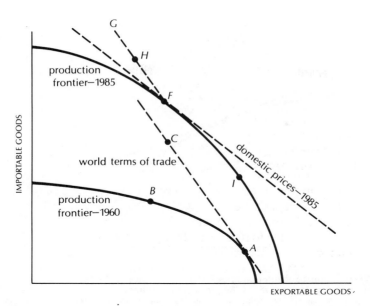

Figure 16–5 Import Substitution after Twenty-five Years of Rapid Growth, 1985. After twenty-five years of successful import substitution, the production frontier has been shifted outward sufficiently to enable the country to produce at point F and to consume at point H, on a higher indifference curve than at a point C before the imposition of a tariff.

increased. Over time, as more import substitutes become available, their relative domestic price is likely to fall, even if the protective tariff is maintained. So the 1985 domestic price line is drawn with a steeper slope than the 1960 line in Figure 16–4. In 1985, then, production takes place at a point like *F*, where the domestic price line is tangent to the new frontier, and consumption can take place at a point like *H*, somewhere along line *FG*, drawn parallel to the original world terms of trade (which are presumed not to have changed since 1960). In 1985 consumers are better off at *H* than they had been in 1960 at *C*, since they are on a higher indifference curve (not shown). There is also less trade than in 1960 (*FH* is shorter than *AC*). However, once the production frontier has been expanded, consumers' welfare could be improved still more by removing tariffs and reverting to the world terms of trade. Producers would then move along the 1985 frontier to point *I*, permitting consumption at a point to the northeast of *H*, on a still higher indifference curve. Trade would be increased compared to the situation a point *F*. This is the desirable result that attracts advocates of import substitution.

Too often, however, slow or arrested growth is the outcome of protective policies, as we shall see. In that case, shown in Figure 16–6, trade and consumer welfare may never reach their former levels. With slow growth, producers reach point *J* on the 1985 frontier, but consumption, at a point like *L*, remains below the original point *C*. Trade is reduced from its 1960 level. Here again consumption of both goods could be increased if the country reverted to world prices and moved production from *J* to *M* on the new frontier. Note that once import substitution has taken place, a return

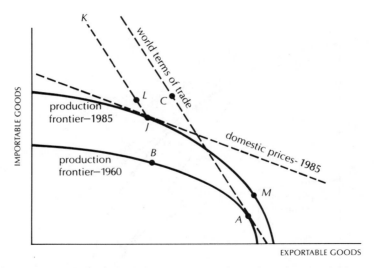

FIGURE 16–6   Import Substitution after Twenty-five Years of Slow Growth, 1985. If, instead, import substitution does not move the production frontier outwards as substantially as in Figure 16–5, production will take place at a point like *J* and consumption, at *L*, will remain on an indifference curve lower than at the starting point, *C*.

towards free trade can always improve welfare compared to both the protected position and the initial free trade position.

Import Levels and Structure

In both Figures 16–5 and 16–6, the *ratio of imports to national product* declines from 1960, before the tariff is imposed, to 1985.[6] This suggests that we use the ratio of imports to national product as an indicator of import substitution. But Figure 16–7 shows how ambiguous such an indicator can be. The import ratio declined in only six of the thirty-eight countries represented in the figure and showed almost no change for five others. (Major petroleum exporters other than Mexico have been omitted, because their import ratios increased markedly). Of these eleven, only six—Mexico, Paraguay, Kenya, Malawi, Colombia, and Tanzania—grew at close to 5 percent a year or more and might therefore be considered to have generated substantial growth through import substitution as depicted in Figure 16–6. Zambia, and especially Ghana, grew very little despite large reductions in their import ratios, examples of the case depicted in Figure 16–6. In contrast, the import ratio rose substantially for several countries that pursued determined import substitution policies during at least part of the period, including India, Pakistan, Turkey, and the Philippines. Others with increasing import ratios, including Argentina, Brazil, and Chile, went through earlier periods of sustained import substitution.

These results do not necessarily mean that import substitution has failed to replace imports with domestic production. The level of imports is probably determined more by the levels of exports and capital inflows than by any

6. For this to be unambiguously true, national product must be measured at domestic, rather than world, prices. Since measures of national product are virtually always in domestic prices, this presents no problems in what follows.

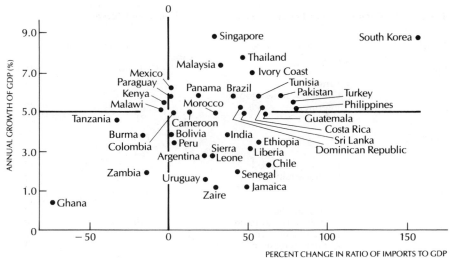

FIGURE 16–7   Growth and Import Substitution in Thirty-eight LDCs, 1960–1983. A success-ful import-substituting country ought to have reduced its ratio of imports to GDP over the twenty-three years and thus lie to the left of line 00 drawn from the horizontal axis; and simultaneously ought to have grown relatively rapidly and thus lie above the 5.0 percent a year line drawn from the vertical axis. Only two countries—Kenya and Malawi—fill these conditions, while only four others—Mexico, Paraguay, Colombia, and Tanzania—come close. *Sources:* International Monetary Fund, *International Financial Statistics Yearbook 1985* (Washington, D.C.: 1985): World Bank, *World Tables* (Baltimore: Johns Hopkins University Press, 1983). Three-year terminal averages were used as end points to measure the change in the ratio of imports to GDP. For countries where GDP fluctuated considerably in the 1980s, a three-year average was used to replace 1983 GDP.

other factors. Thus import ratios may rise despite import substitution if a country is fortunate in expanding its primary exports (despite the adverse incentives of import substitution regimes) or in obtaining rising export prices. Chile, Indonesia, Ivory Coast, Malaysia, Nigeria, and the Philippines are countries that may have import substituted in several sectors while increasing their primary export earnings and thus their capacity to import. If import substitution in some industries stimulates rising incomes that are biased towards imported goods, or if import-substituting industries require imported inputs themselves, then part of the reduction in the import ratio would in any case be cancelled. Chenery and Syrquin observe that as incomes (in 1983 prices) rise from $300 per capita to $3,000, there is a grad-ual but steady tendency for the import ratio to rise, from 22 to 26 percent, apparently despite import substitution in manufacturing.[7] Moreover, Figure 16–7 reflects the overriding tendency for both imports and exports to rise rel-ative to GDP for all countries. The diagram encompasses a period when imports expanded faster than GDP on average for all groups except the low-income countries and when many third-world governments recognized that expanding exports were important for sustained growth, even though import substitution was being pursued simultaneously.

Whatever happens to imports as a whole, one trend is clear: as import sub-

---

7. Chenery and Syrquin, *Patterns of Development,* p. 37.

TABLE 16–3   Composition of Imports: Brazil, Ghana, Pakistan, and Turkey

Country	Category of import	Share of total imports (%)	
Brazil		1946–48	1960–62
	Wheat	6	13
	Other consumer goods	15	9
	Intermediate goods	41	49
	Capital goods	38	29
Ghana		1956	1969
	Consumer goods	54	30
	Intermediate goods	31	47
	Capital equipment	15	23
Pakistan		1951–52	1964–65
	Grains and flour	0	13
	Cotton yarn and cloth	29	0
	Iron and steel products	7	17
	Capital equipment	9	33
Turkey		1961	1970
	Consumer goods	23	15
	Raw materials	41	62
	Investment goods	36	23

Sources: Brazil—Joel Bergsman, *Brazil: Industrialization and Trade Policies* (London: Oxford University Press, 1970); Ghana—J. Clark Leith, *Foreign Trade Regimes and Economic Development: Ghana* (New York: Columbia University Press, 1974), p. 176; Pakistan—Stephen Lewis, *Economic Policy and Industrial Growth in Pakistan* (London: George Allen and Unwin, 1969), p. 6; Turkey—Anne O. Krueger, *Foreign Trade Regimes and Economic Development: Turkey* (New York: Columbia University Press, 1974), p. 127.

stitution proceeds through finished consumer goods towards producer intermediates, the *composition of imports* shifts noticeably. Table 16–3 presents indicative data from four countries that underwent substantial import substitution. All show a marked decline in imports of nonfood consumer goods. There is no clear trend for capital goods, although given the protective bias against their production we would not expect to find the sharp declines in share evident in Brazil and Turkey. The marked increase in food-grain imports in Pakistan is testimony to its bias against agriculture: in the mid-1960s, the effective rate of protection for agriculture was only 19 percent, compared to 188 percent for manufacturing.[8]

Once the structure of imports has been transformed from a concentration on consumer goods and capital goods to a greater share of materials and intermediate goods, the economy is in some ways more vulnerable to disruptions in trade. In times of drought, falling export production, or falling export prices, nonfood imports must be reduced. Whereas these cuts would primarily affect the less essential consumer goods in the past, they must now be absorbed by intermediate and capital goods. Because industrial production and employment depend on imported inputs and continued growth depends on imported investment goods, swings in export earnings have a direct impact on output, employment, and growth. *Import dependence* has not been reduced, although its form has been changed.

8. Balassa et al., *The Structure of Protection*, p. 55.

Kenya is one of only two countries in Figure 16–7 whose GDP grew by more than 5 percent a year from 1960 to 1983 while its import-to-GDP ratio fell. This small, open economy provides an example of both the potential power and the structural difficulties of import substitution. Kenya's population of 19 million generated GDP of $340 per capita in 1983, giving Kenya a total domestic market about 3 percent the size of India's and 16 percent the size of Colombia's internal market. Kenya exports 25 percent of its GDP, down from 31 percent in 1965. Thirty percent of its GDP and nearly 60 percent of its exports come from agriculture, which has been relatively favored by policy compared to other African countries and to most import-substituting regimes.

Yet Kenya pursued import substitution as a means of industrializing both before and especially after independence in 1963, utilizing high protective tariffs, quotas, and outright bans on competing imports to attract investors. Effective rates of protection ranged from slightly negative, especially on agricultural processing industries, to levels of 100 to 500 percent for chemical industries based on simple last-stage mixing and for the assembly of vehicles and consumer durables. After substantial liberalization in the early 1980s, about a third of imported items— many of them potential competitors with local industry—remained under highly restrictive import licensing. In 1960, Kenya imported over a third of its GDP; in the early 1980s, imports were down to 28 percent of GDP. From independence in 1963 to 1984, GDP grew at 6.1 percent a year, with manufacturing leading the way at 9 percent a year. From 1972 to 1983, the leading industries, with annual growth exceeding 10 percent, were canned vegetables, clothing, footwear, paper, printing, petroleum refining, rubber products, plastic products and vehicle assembly, all but the first being typical first-stage import substitution leaders. Also typical of import substitution, the import share of machinery and equipment more than doubled from 11 percent in 1965 to 24 percent in 1983, while the share for non-food consumer goods fell from 18 to 7 percent.

By the end of the 1970s, it became generally recognized in Kenya that import substitution had run its course. The domestic market was too small to attract many more industries, manufacturing costs were generally too high to make manufactured exports feasible, and further backward integration into intermediate goods would mean even higher costs for user industries. During the early 1980s, economic growth slowed to just over 4 percent a year after its spurt of almost 8 percent a year from 1965–1973. Since 1980, Kenya has been shifting towards a more outward-looking policy for industry, along the lines described in the next chapter, and has been actively reducing the disparities between wages and profits earned in industry versus those in agriculture, and between profits in manufacturing for export versus those in import substitution.[9]

9. Data are from Central Bureau of Statistics, *Economic Survey 1985* (Nairobi: May 1985); World Bank, *World Development Report 1985* (Washington, D.C.: 1985); and unpublished reports.

Import substitution regimes establish a series of interrelated effects that over the long run reinforce import dependence and retard structural changes required for self-sustaining development. Underlying the regime is a set of incentives that reward political astuteness and "rent-seeking" (described in Chapter 5) more than economic competitiveness. Probably the most important determinants of a manufacturer's profit rate are the tariff and quota treatment bestowed upon him by government. Protective duties and access to low-cost inputs create the import-substituting firm. Should costs of production rise or world prices of competitive imports fall, the natural reaction is to return to government for enhanced protection. This blunts the competitive instincts of entrepreneurs, who might otherwise work to raise productivity to increase or protect their profits in the face of changing conditions. Thus the most effective market restraints on increased costs operate in muted fashion, and industry tends to become and remain high cost by world standards. The infant-industry argument, which could justify a temporary protective tariff, fails to hold. Instead of facing reduced protection over time, the entrepreneur can look forward to rising protection, as needed, if he minds his political fences.

In this environment of government intervention the most successful managers are those who have political skills, who can bargain effectively with— or simply bribe—officials who administer import quotas and determine tariff rates, or who have close ties with the political and bureaucratic elite. It is no accident that manufacturers usually have their top executive, if not the plant itself, located in the capital city, nor that he spends much if not most of his time seeing government officials. Thus the wealthy and powerful succeed best and become reentrenched in their wealth and power. These tendencies exist in most political-economic regimes, but the adverse economic impacts seem accentuated in many import substitution regimes.

Because import-substituting industry typically produces at high cost, it has little potential to penetrate export markets in the absence of large subsidies. Export subsidies have been part of several import substitution regimes: in Pakistan bonus vouchers were paid to exporters of nontraditional goods, giving them access to licensed imports that carried large quota premiums; in Colombia exporters were granted certificates entitling them to income tax reductions; in Ghana cash subsidy payments were offered; and in several countries exporters of nontraditional products have received access to controlled imports, tariff reductions on inputs, access to cheap credit, and so forth. In a few cases, notably Pakistan and Colombia, manufactured exports did respond to incentives. But for the most part these were weak measures. In the face of much stronger incentives to produce for the domestic market and of bureaucratic requirements that made it difficult to realize the proffered export incentives, such incentives often had only a marginal impact on exports. Moreover the price incentives that work against agriculture discourage that potentially important source of new exports. Export diversification and growth are really not consistent with the biases of an import substitution regime, but represent a very different approach to development, as will be seen in the next chapter.

Import substitution regimes also have a tendency to limit backward-linked industrialization. Once consumer goods industries have been started it is natural to seek further import substitution by producing at home the intermediate goods used by the consumer industry. Because the domestic market for such intermediate goods as chemicals and metal products is frequently smaller than for consumer goods, and for some producer-goods industries economies of scale are large (see Chapter 20), there is a natural barrier to investment in these sectors. This could be overcome by protection, but that would drive up the costs of inputs to already established manufacturers whose profits depend both upon protection for their products and upon low duties on their inputs. Since established manufacturers have already proven their political adeptness in establishing their industries and keeping them profitable, they now turn these skills towards preventing tariff increases on their imported materials, effectively discouraging investment in backward-linked industries.[10] This is not an absolute barrier to backward integration, as attested by casual observation of many chemical, fertilizer, and steel plants in the third world. And in large countries such as Brazil and India, the ability to achieve scale economies can mitigate to some extent the high costs of backward integration. However, especially for small countries, these barriers do exert a tendency to slow down industrial development once most consumer industries have been established.

The *foreign exchange gap,* introduced in Chapter 6, has evolved from these characteristics of import substitution. The bias against agriculture that prevents food supplies from keeping pace with population and income growth; the shift towards imported inputs for industrial production; continued dependence on imported capital goods for investment; and the blockages, or at least retardation, of backward integration in manufacturing—all combine to make it essential that import levels continue to grow about as rapidly as the national product. Yet the rapid growth of nontraditional exports required to finance growing import bills is stifled by price incentives that condone inefficiency, favor industrial production for the home market, and frequently work against agriculture (see Chapter 18). Any attempt to accelerate growth thus faces increased imports beyond the likely growth of exports. The country must either borrow abroad or restrain its ambitions to develop. The level of foreign investment and aid then determines how fast the economy can grow.

In addition to these structural problems, import substitution incentives also lead to potentially severe misallocations of national resources. The most serious of these affects foreign exchange. The overvalued exchange rate encourages use of imported inputs, especially those on which duties are also low, further widening the foreign exchange gap. If imported materials are cheap, users have less incentive to adopt practices or technologies that conserve their use and in this sense scarce foreign exchange may be wasted. When the imports in question are capital equipment, on which duties are

10. This phenomenon is described by Albert O. Hirschman, "The Political Economy of Import Substitution," *Quarterly Journal of Economics* 82 (1968): 1–32, who also notes that if the owners of initial import-substituting industries are capable of running the backward-linked industries themselves, the barriers to backward integration may be lower.

typically very low, investment is encouraged to be more capital-intensive than is desirable, hence raising capital-output ratios and reducing the growth realizable from a given amount of saving. This effect is reinforced by the habit of constraining interest rates, discussed in Chapter 13. The motivation for low interest rates has little to do with trade strategy. However, the combined effect of low rates and relatively cheap capital-equipment imports, typical of import-substituting regimes, can reduce the cost of capital substantially below its relative scarcity in most developing countries.

Concomitant with excessive use of imports and capital, labor is not used intensively in import-substituting manufacturing and hence employment does not grow as rapidly as it might. One characteristic of these regimes has been high labor costs, as governments legislate minimum wages, add social benefits to these wages, and protect the employed worker by limiting firms' freedom to dismiss workers. As explained in Chapter 8, these measures have been legislated or decreed to protect workers' incomes and not for any purpose of trade policy. But they happen to reinforce the anti-employment bias of protectionist policies. Facing high wages and relatively inexpensive capital, investors—who are in any case insulated from competitive forces by protection—have little incentive to seek and use labor-intensive technologies, even though labor is relatively abundant. Domestic policies alone are not to blame for this. The capital goods readily available on world markets were developed mostly for use in labor-scarce economies, and third-world investors often have to make special efforts to obtain labor-intensive technologies. But such technologies do exist (see Chapter 20) and domestic policies discourage the effort needed to find them. Furthermore, to the extent that agriculture is more labor-intensive than industry and export industries more labor-intensive than others, the price biases against these kinds of activity further reduce the potential employment generated by economic growth. It is too much to say that the employment problem endemic to developing countries can be blamed entirely on import substitution strategies, but they have certainly contributed to it.

Several of these characteristics combine to suggest that import substitution strategies may intensify the tendency, noted in Chapter 4, for income distribution to worsen in the early stages of development. Two effects are probably critical in this respect. First, limited employment generation reduces the access of two of the poorest groups in society, landless rural workers and the urban underemployed, to the benefits of industrialization. Policies such as minimum-wage legislation, intended to protect workers' incomes, typically worsen income distributions because they protect only workers employed in modern establishments (the formal sector) and exclude others. Second, in economies characterized by small-holder agriculture, as in much of Asia and Africa, one of the most effective instruments for equalizing incomes is to improve the prices facing farmers, who tend to be among the poorest groups in society, relative to the prices of goods produced in urban industry. Yet protection does just the opposite. The problems of income distribution cannot be solved by a choice of trade strategy alone. Land and other asset distribution, the ethnic composition of society, access to education, and other factors are probably more important than the trade regime. But the tendency of import substitution is in the wrong direction.

This catalogue of woes has become a familiar one, shared by economists and many policymakers in the third world. Import substitution, though still widely practiced, is viewed more skeptically now than twenty years ago and disillusioned policy-makers are seeking alternative paths to development. Export substitution, described in the next chapter, is the most promising of these. However, to preview the concluding lessons from Chapter 17, it has not been import substitution as such that has been responsible for the disappointing performance of manufacturing in many countries. Rather the distortions of import substitution can be traced to the policies that accompanied and promoted it. A less doctrinaire form of import substitution, promoted by more moderate, market-oriented pricing policies, could well be a successful mode of development in the future.[11]

11. Two excellent articles summarizing the experience of import substitution are John H. Power, "Import Substitution as an Industrialization Strategy," *The Philippine Economic Journal* 5 (1966): 167–204; and Henry J. Bruton, "The Import Substitution Strategy of Economic Development," *The Pakistan Development Review* 10 (1970): 123–46 (excerpts reprinted in *Leading Issues in Economic Development,* G. M. Meier, ed., 3d ed. [New York: Oxford University Press, 1976], pp. 747–52).

17

Outward-Looking Development

For countries that are resource-poor and have relatively small domestic markets, the trade strategies based on primary exports or on import substitution provide scant hope for sustained development. Four countries in Asia—Taiwan, South Korea, Hong Kong, and Singapore, sometimes called the "Gang of Four"—have pursued an alternative strategy that has gone by different names, but is basically to export manufactures that intensively use their most abundant resource, labor. Gustav Ranis of Yale University has termed this strategy **export substitution,** in the sense that exports of labor-intensive manufactures replace exports of labor-intensive agricultural products.[1] Other authors have called this an **outward-looking** strategy, in contrast to the **inward-looking** strategy of import substitution.

THE STRATEGY OF EXPORT SUBSTITUTION

Although the Asian model of export substitution has hinged on labor-intensive manufactures and services (construction, tourism, finance, and so on), a more general specification would be the promotion of nontraditional exports, whether these happen to be labor- or land-intensive, manufactured or agricultural products, or services. The common denominator is the pursuit of any exports in which the country has a potential comparative advan-

1. Gustav Ranis, "Industrial Sector Labor Absorption," *Economic Development and Cultural Change* 21 (1973): 387–408.

tage, that is, whose production costs are or could become relatively low by world standards. The distinguishing characteristic is a thoroughgoing application of pricing policies that closely reflect both world commodity prices and the scarcities of domestic factors of production. This definition would exclude several countries, such as Pakistan, Ghana, and Colombia, for which export promotion has been a limited part of a trade regime that remained overwhelmingly protectionist.[2]

The Exchange Rate and Related Policy Instruments

To oversimplify only a little, a useful prescription for export substitution policies is to do everything that the import substitution regime avoids. First, a necessary condition is to maintain an exchange rate that helps make it profitable for domestic producers to sell their crops, manufactures, and services on world markets. The export-substituting country must undertake periodic devaluations, initially to approach an equilibrium, market-clearing rate and subsequently to maintain that rate relative to inflating domestic prices and costs. South Korea entered its phase of export substitution in the early 1960s with two large devaluations, of 104 and 65 percent, respectively, and maintained the resulting rate relative to domestic prices by continuing devaluations in succeeding years. Brazil began to emerge from its postwar import substitution phase with a 100 percent devaluation in 1964, then continued to devalue over the next several years to overcome the effects of rapid domestic inflation.

Second, it may be necessary to subsidize some exports to induce manufacturers and farmers to invest in capacity for the export market. Breaking into export markets entails more risk than producing behind protective barriers for the domestic market. Cost competitiveness is greater, quality standards are higher, and marketing is more demanding. Once a producer learns how to cope with these factors, however, he may enjoy a large, profitable market. Compensation in the form of tax relief, import duty rebates, reduced interest rates, cash payments, or a variety of other means can help make it more attractive for a potential exporter to overcome these barriers to entry. This case for export subsidies is analogous to the infant-industry argument for a protective tariff. One advantage of subsidies over tariffs is that, except for preferential interest rates, the cost is borne by the government's budget. Fiscal pressures sometimes limit the size and duration of the subsidy, more closely approximating the desirable phase-out of an infant-industry tariff.

Third, if governments want producers to turn towards world markets, they must reduce the relative attractiveness of production for the domestic market. This implies reduction of high protective tariffs for favored industries and the avoidance of quantitative restrictions on imports. Because investors are likely to seek the most profitable opportunities, profits in import substi-

2. For detailed studies of the trade regimes of ten countries, see the volumes by Anne O. Krueger, *Foreign Trade Regimes and Economic Development: Liberalization Attempts and Consequences,* and Jagdish N. Bhagwati, *Foreign Trade Regimes and Economic Development: Anatomy and Consequences of Exchange Control Regimes* (Cambridge, Mass.: Ballinger 1978) and the companion country studies.

tution must be kept in line with those in exporting. This means that tariff protection should be no higher than export subsidization and should also be fairly uniform for all commodities. The biases in effective protection, illustrated in Table 16–1, must be reduced if not eliminated. South Korea's protective regime provides a contrast to those shown in that table. During the late 1960s, when the shift into export substitution was most intense, the effective rate of protection for agriculture, 18 percent, was not only modest but higher than for manufacturing, minus one percent. And the bias between exports and domestic sales was reversed: allowing for subsidies, exports had an effective rate of protection-cum-subsidy of 12 percent, compared with a −9 percent for domestic sales.[3]

Effective Exchange Rates

The combined incentive effect of the exchange rate, subsidies, tariffs, and quota premiums can be captured by a very useful concept, the **effective exchange rate** (EER). The EER corrects the nominal (i.e., official) exchange rate to measure the actual amount of local currency paid for a dollar's worth of imports, or received for a dollar's worth of exports, by allowing for average duties, subsidies, and quota premiums. There may be as many EERs in an economy as there are goods traded. Generally, however, two effective exchange rates are measured: one for exports,

$$\text{EER}_x = r_o(1 - t_x + s_x) \qquad [17\text{–}1]$$

and another for imports,

$$\text{EER}_m = r_o(1 + t_m - s_m + q_m). \qquad [17\text{–}2]$$

In these equations, r_o is the official exchange rate, t is the average duty or tax rate on exports (subscript x) or imports (m), s is the average level of subsidy, and q_m is the quota premium (see Chapter 16) averaged over all imports.

One way to differentiate an outward-looking regime from an inward-looking one is to compare the EERs for exports and imports within each country. Table 17–1 does this for eight countries studied by the National Bureau of Economic Research. Only in South Korea, which has had the most thoroughgoing export substitution policy of all countries listed, does an exporter receive more local currency (won in this case) per dollar of foreign exchange than an importer must pay. That is, in Korea the bias favors production for export over import substitution. In Egypt the exchange regime was neutral, while all other countries showed a bias in favor of import substitution, listed in ascending order in the table. None of the countries with a bias favoring import substitution was able to diversify its exports substantially in favor of

---

3. Charles R. Frank, Jr., Kwang Suk Kim, and Larry E. Westphal, *Foreign Trade Regimes and Economic Development: South Korea* (New York: Columbia University Press, 1975), pp. 195–200. However, the effective rate of subsidy was exceptionally high for two important export sectors, plywood and cotton fabrics, indicating inefficiencies in the export sector. See Anne O. Krueger, *Studies in the Modernization of the Republic of Korea, 1945–1975: The Developmental Role of the Foreign Sector and Aid* (Cambridge, Mass.: Harvard University Press, 1979), Chapter 5.

TABLE 17–1   Effective Exchange Rates[a] (local currency per U.S. dollar)

Country	Year	EER$_x$	EER$_m$
1. *Pro-export bias:*			
South Korea	1964	281	247
2. *Negligible bias:*			
Egypt	1962	43.5	42.9
3. *Pro-import bias:*			
Chile	1965	3.31	3.85
Brazil	1964	1,874	2,253
India	1966	6.79	9.23
Philippines	1970	5.15	8.70
Ghana	1967	0.84	1.50
Turkey	1970	12.9	24.0

Source: Krueger, *Foreign Trade Regimes and Economic Development,* p. 73.
[a] Following devaluation in year shown.

manufactured goods. (Brazil began to export manufactures only after it changed its trade regime; see page 462.)

It is not enough, however, to offer a pro-export bias in the effective exchange rate for short periods. Investment for export will depend on government's demonstrated willingness to maintain the incentive in favor of exporting over long periods despite domestic inflation. To the extent that domestic prices (and costs) rise more rapidly than foreign prices, the exchange rate is eroded and becomes increasingly overvalued. As demonstrated in Table 17–2, devaluation is then necessary to restore exporters'

TABLE 17–2   Effects of Inflation and Devaluation on Exporters' Profits

Today: Exchange rate = 12 pesos (P) per dollar.

1. Exporter sells goods worth	$ 100,000;
2. For which exporter receives local currency of	P1,200,000;
3. If exporter's costs—all domestic—are	P 900,000;
4. Then exporter's profits are	P 300,000.

Three years later: Cumulative domestic inflation has been 33%.[a]

1. Exporter sells same goods, still worth	$ 100,000;
2. For which exporter receives	P1,200,000;
3. But exporter's costs are now 33% higher	P1,200,000;
4. So exporter now earns no profit	P 0.

Three years later: If currency was devalued by 33%, to 16 pesos per dollar, then;

1. Exporter sells goods worth	$ 100,000;
2. For which exporter now receives	P1,600,000;
3. With costs of	P1,200,000;
4. Profits are	P 400,000.
5. Which, deflated by 33% to year 1 prices,[b] have been restored to	P 300,000.

[a] Assume for convenience that there is no inflation in the economies of trading partners. Alternatively and more realistically, the home country's cumulative inflation is 33% more than in its trading partners' inflation.
[b] P400.000/(1 + 0.33) = P300,000.

TABLE 17–3 Index of Effective Exchange Rates,ª South Korea and Brazil

Year	South Korea IEER$_x$	IEER$_m$	Year	Brazil IEER$_x$(mfgs)
1960	104.9	71.2	1963	73.2
1964	100.0	87.9	1964	100.0
1965	99.9	96.2	1967	85.0
1970	101.1	85.4	1970	98.0
1975	94.9	85.8	1972–73	107.9

Source: Kwang Suk Kim and Michael Roemer, *Studies in the Modernization of South Korea, 1945–75: Growth and Structural Transformation* (Cambridge, Mass.: Harvard University Press, 1979), p. 73; William G. Tyler, *Manufactured Export Expansion and Industrialization in Brazil* (Tubingen, W. Germany: J. C. B. Mohr, 1976), p. 220.
ª All indexes, for exports and imports, based in IEER$_x$ = 100 in 1964.

profits. To measure the effective exchange rate over time, index numbers are substituted for actual values in Equations 17–1 and 17–2 and price indexes are added, as follows:

$$\text{IEER} = R_o T P_w / P_d, \qquad [17\text{–}3]$$

where IEER is the index of the *price-deflated EER*, R_0 is an index of the official exchange rate, T is an index of one plus the average rate of nominal protection (tariffs plus quota premiums less subsidies),[4] and P_w and P_d are indexes of world and domestic prices, respectively. The formula can be used for either exports or imports, with appropriate substitutions, and can be calculated separately for specific commodities or groups of commodities. If domestic prices rise more rapidly than world prices the index falls, indicating that the exchange rate has become overvalued; that is, the peso to dollar rate is now too low or the dollar to peso rate too high.

One element in South Korea's rapid growth of manufactured exports, detailed later in this chapter, has been the government's willingness and ability to adjust the exchange rate, tariffs, and subsidies, both to maintain the effective exchange rate for exports over time and to prevent the import rate from slipping above the export rate. Table 17–3 shows the movement of EERs from 1960 to 1975, with the export value in 1964 taken as 100 and the import index adjusted to show its level relative to exports. Notice the fairly steady level of the export rate, which was also maintained above the import rate throughout the period. This performance has required a series of devaluations and subsidy adjustments, as Korean domestic inflation was considerable throughout the period.

Brazil, which also promoted manufactured exports successfully, shows a similar pattern (Table 17–3). From 1968 onward Brazil adopted a policy of small, regular currency devaluations that for a time kept pace with domestic inflation. Concurrently, tax relief and other export incentives were increased from an average of about 18 percent of domestic prices for equivalent goods sold in Brazil to 40 percent in 1973. The combined effect was to raise substantially the effective exchange rate for manufactured exports after 1967. Also, effective tariff protection for import-competing manufacturers was

4. That is, $T_m = (1 + t_m + q_m - s_m)/(1 + t_m^0 + q_m^0 - s_m^0)$, where the superscript, "0", denotes the base year.

reduced from 180 percent in 1966 to only 47 percent in 1973, narrowing or eliminating the differential between the import and export effective exchange rates.

Factor Prices and Government Support

To work effectively, outward-looking regimes must also maintain the relative prices of domestic factors of production at levels reflecting their scarcity. The underlying principle is to export those products that use most intensively the productive factors that are most abundant in the economy. To ensure that enterprises, whether private or public, make investment and production decisions consistent with this principle, the relative prices they pay for labor, capital, and land should not be very different from the prices that would be established by competitive market forces, given the supplies of and demands for these resources. If labor is abundant its wage and other costs should be low, while scarce capital should be costly to investors. Then not only will firms and farms substitute labor for capital where possible, but those lines of production that use labor more intensively will be more profitable than capital-intensive ones. The four Asian exporters all avoided artificially high wages. Their interest rate policies were not so exemplary, although South Korea and Taiwan did undertake monetary reforms that raised interest rates to scarcity levels for a period.

Governments determined to diversify their exports do not depend on market prices to accomplish the task alone. The successful ones are, like governments pursuing import substitution, interventionist. But they intervene by helping fledgling exporters to find markets and by pushing reluctant producers towards world markets. These governments provide market information, and to some extent market access, by establishing trade offices overseas, sometimes attached to diplomatic missions. They place a high priority on port facilities, transport networks, and communications infrastructure. Commercial and government banks are encouraged to favor exporters in their lending policies, and credits may be offered to foreign customers if necessary to help exporters compete. Political favors are part of life in every country, but in export substitution regimes they are used to encourage exporting. In South Korea, for example, tax authorities bear less heavily on those who export successfully. Market inducements and political power, both working obviously in the direction of export growth and diversification, can be an irresistible combination.

Stabilization and Structural Adjustment

Attempts to move from inward- to outward-looking strategies have frequently been assisted by international aid agencies, particularly the IMF and the World Bank. The IMF's stand-by credits are generally associated with *stabilization* efforts to correct the macroeconomic imbalances in an economy. These programs aim to slow inflation, trim large budget deficits, bring the money supply under control, and bring foreign payments into balance. Higher taxes, reduced subsidies, higher interest rates, reduced growth of wages, and exchange rate devaluation are the policy tools typically employed. The IMF makes successful implementation of these policies a condition for disbursement of its credits.[5]

Although the primary motivation of stabilization programs is to bring the macroeconomy into balance, they also can be seen as an essential first step in restructuring an economy towards an outward-looking posture. Action on interest rates, wages, and exchange rates is an integral part of the outward-looking strategy described above. Further steps—continuing flexible management of the exchange rate, removal of quantitative restrictions on imports, tariff reform to reduce effective protection and make it more uniform, the relaxation of price and other market controls—cannot be effective until economic balance has been restored. In recent years, the World Bank has been making *structural adjustment* loans to support governments carrying out these and similar policies beyond stabilization towards fundamental liberalization of the economy. These loans finance general imports, rather than projects, and are thus a form of balance-of-payments support similar to the IMF stand-by credits.

OUTCOMES AND LIMITATIONS

Export Achievers

Only a handful of countries—now called **newly industrializing countries** (NICs)—have followed the export substitution path to industrialization. The five most prominent of these—Hong Kong, Singapore, South Korea, Taiwan, and Brazil—are featured in Table 17–4. In all five, GNP per capita, manufacturing value-added, and exports grew significantly faster than for the average middle-income country; Korea's exceptional performance and Brazil's more limited experience are described in case studies.

TABLE 17–4   Growth in Five Outward-Looking Economies, 1965–1983

Country	Average annual growth (% per year), 1965–1983, in:			Manufactured exports as share of commodity exports 1982
	GNP per capita	Manufacturing Value-Added	Exports	
Hong Kong	6.2	8.3[a]	10.9	92
South Korea	6.7	15.8	22.0	92
Taiwan[b]	6.5	11.7	16.7	85[c]
Singapore	7.8	12.9	11.2	58[d]
Brazil	5.0	7.3	9.0	39
Average for all middle-income countries	3.4	6.8	2.4	42

Source: World Bank, *World Development Report 1985* (New York: Oxford University Press, 1985).
[a] Includes utilities and construction.
[b] From World Bank data tape.
[c] Estimate from late 1970s.
[d] Excludes processing of minerals and fuels, which accounts for 30% of Singapore's exports.

5. The effectiveness of IMF "conditionality" in support of stabilization efforts has been explored in two collections: John Williamson, ed., *IMF Conditionality* (Washington, D.C.: Institute of International Economics, 1983) and Tony Killick, ed., *The Quest for Economic Stabilization: The IMF and the Third World* (London: Heinneman Educational Books, 1984).

The market incentives and political support of the South Korean government from 1961 onward led to a remarkable sustained growth in exports that averaged 24 percent a year for twenty-three years, from 1960 to 1983. During the same period, Korean GNP per capita grew by 6 percent a year, one of the highest rates in the world. It has been estimated that, allowing for both the direct effects of export industries and the indirect effects of other industries stimulated by exporters' demands for inputs, exports were responsible for 33 to 40 percent of the growth in national product from 1955 to 1973. During that interval exports rose from only 3 percent of GNP to 28 percent, almost three times the average for a "typical" country of Korea's characteristics (according to Chenery and Syrquin's regressions). To achieve this, Korea depended almost entirely on its manufacturing sector, whose share of exports grew from 17 percent to over 80 percent by the mid-1970s. Diversification and structural change accompanied growth. All manufacturing sectors developed rapidly. The producer-goods industries, which accounted for only 15 percent of manufacturing value-added in the early 1960s, grew sufficiently rapidly to account for 39 percent by the mid-1970s, indicating industrial diversification as backward linkages were developed. Since this occurred under competitive conditions, some of the new producer-goods industries were later able to export.

Although exports were mostly labor-intensive manufactures in the early years of growth, principally clothing, textiles, and footwear, by the mid-1970s South Korea was also exporting steel plate, electrical machinery, ships, and construction services, and by the 1980s was beginning to export cars. International competitiveness and the realization of backward linkages were further enhanced because, by depending on the world market rather than the limited domestic market, firms could achieve economies of scale without creating domestic monopolies. The benefits of this developing capacity to produce a variety of products efficiently were realized as Korea struggled to overcome the oil price increases of the 1970s, the world recession of the early 1980s, and growing protectionism against the very kinds of manufactures produced by Korea. These problems have slowed Korea's export growth to 15 percent a year from 1974 to 1983, a rate exceeded only by Jordan, and still sufficient to propel growth of 7.4 percent a year in GDP. By 1983, Korea was considered to be a "newly industrializing country": it generated 39 percent of its GDP through industry, compared to 42 percent in Japan and 32 percent in the United States.

New employment was created rapidly enough—12 percent a year in manufacturing during the 1960s and 9 percent a year in the 1970s—so that by the late 1960s rising Korean real wages indicated a probable end to the labor surplus condition that had characterized the economy until then. Credit for this performance is due to several factors including the rapid growth of labor-intensive manufactured exports and the policy toward wages and interest rates that made it attractive to utilize more labor and less capital wherever possible.

Both South Korea and Taiwan, another successful export substituter, enjoy relatively equal income distributions, especially by third-world standards. The principal causes of equality are thorough land reforms, equal access to education, and at least in Korea, homogeneity of the population. However, a case can be made that rapid export growth based on labor-intensive industries and the resulting employment creation played a role in stimulating development without substantially worsening the distribution. As the labor surplus became absorbed and real wages began to rise, it was also possible to raise farm prices so that all elements of the population benefited from growth.[6]

Brazil

Brazil provides a less dramatic story of manufactured export-led growth. After the military took power in 1964, the government went through a stabilization process to control inflation. The ensuing reduction in domestic demand, helped by devaluation, induced manufacturers to seek export markets for their output. Although Brazil had protected its manufacturing as heavily as most import substitution regimes, many firms had costs low enough to make export feasible. Brazil's relatively large domestic market, which in many industries permitted several firms to attain economies of scale, undoubtedly worked to reduce costs, as did the long period during which Brazil had undergone import substitution. From 1968 to the early 1970s a policy of small but regular devaluations and larger incentives for exports, together with reduced import protection, steadily improved the relative incentive to export (recall Table 17–3).

In response, the volume of commodity exports grew by 9.0 percent a year from 1965 to 1983. But manufactured exports grew twice as fast, reaching 39 percent of the total. Agriculture still dominates Brazil's exports despite its substantial diversification into manufactures. Because Brazil's economy is three times larger than Korea's, the contribution of exports to growth was less dramatic. Exports of goods and non-factor services rose only modestly as a fraction of GDP from the mid-1960s to the early 1980s, starting at under 7 and reaching 8 percent of GDP, while GDP expanded by 6.7 percent a year. Manufactured exports accounted for under 5 percent of manufacturing output in 1972, compared with 24 percent in Korea, and for about 6 percent of employment in manufacturing. Nevertheless, the rapid growth of exports helped manufacturing to expand by over 9 percent a year from 1965 to 1983.

Thus the picture in Brazil is one of rapid export growth, but within a small segment of a large economy. Because the impact of exports on income growth and employment creation was inevitably limited and contained within the advanced sectors of the economy, it did not con-

6. For full treatments of South Korea's modernization, see Frank, Kim, and Westphal, *Foreign Trade Regimes and Economic Development;* Paul W. Kuznets, *Economic Growth and Structure in the Republic of Korea* (New Haven: Yale University Press, 1977); Kim and Roemer, *Studies in the Modernization of South Korea;* and Krueger, *Studies in the Modernization of the Republic of Korea.*

tribute noticeably to ameliorating Brazil's sharply unequal income distribution. Indeed, it has been argued that the wage containment policies required by this strategy may have contributed to a worsening income distribution since 1964.[7]

Thus in smaller economies, the outward-looking policies of export substitution can have remarkable success in stimulating the growth of new export products and diversifying the economy; in stimulating industrialization and growth of national income; and in distributing the benefits of growth widely through employment creation, rising real wages, and rising agricultural prices. In large economies like Brazil, however, export substitution is unlikely to have such widespread structural effects. Given its success in Asia, is export substitution a strategy for all countries? Probably not, for reasons both domestic and international.

The four Asian countries promoted manufactured exports because they had no place else to go. Lacking abundant natural resources, unable to feed themselves (except Taiwan), and recognizing the limitations of their domestic markets, these countries had to turn outward to generate self-sustaining growth. Resource- and land-rich countries, with opportunities to sell raw materials and foods on world markets, may still find it advantageous to do so and relatively costly to develop manufactured export industries. If agriculture can be organized on smallholder principles, primary-export activity can be at least as egalitarian as industrially oriented export promotion. Although lacking natural resources, the Asian exporters were relatively richly endowed with human resources, especially entrepreneurs and a large, well-educated labor force. Countries with lesser endowments of these resources will find Korea's kind of diverse, small-unit, internationally competitive manufacturing sector more difficult to develop, even with the right incentives.

The Political Costs of Transition

A final caution is the potentially great cost—economic, social, and political —of the transition from an entrenched regime of import substitution to one of export promotion. The shift in relative prices of imports versus exports and of agricultural goods versus manufactures; the broadened access to imports and credits; rises in real interest rates; and reduced growth of real wages in the protected sectors—all hit groups in society that have been most successful in realizing their claims on rising incomes: successful manufacturers and traders, strong labor unions, civil servants, and most critically, the officer corps of the army. Any change, but most especially liberalizing change, will be resisted by these groups, which have the most to lose from them. The potential beneficiaries—small farmers, rural laborers, small manufacturers, the unemployed and underemployed—are generally politically impotent and count for little in the urban-based struggle to maintain existing income shares.

7. For full treatments of Brazil's export promotion strategy, see William G. Tyler, *Manufactured Export Expansion and Industrialization in Brazil*; and Richard Weisskoff, "The Growth and Decline of Import Substitution in Brazil—Revisited," *World Development* 8 (September 1980): 647–76.

Compounding these difficulties, there is likely to be a lag of several months to a few years before the clear advantages of liberalized, outward-looking policies become evident. Those investors waiting in the wings have based plans on the old prices; it takes time for them to adjust their expectations and their investment plans to fit the new conditions. Some existing producers may respond immediately by shifting to export markets, but the needed massive growth of exports is likely to take a few years in many economies. Until that happens it may be necessary to maintain some controls on imports, restricting supplies.

This kind of fundamental transition, in which the powerful are hurt and the beneficiaries, weak to start with, do not realize their gains for some time, is a passage of great danger for any government. In Ghana such a transition was attempted by a democratic government in late 1971, followed by a military coup early the next year. In Korea, despite some rocky passages in the early 1960s, and in Brazil, successful transition was accomplished by strong regimes, backed by the military, which repressed political opposition. Colombia went through a moderate transition (though not to a completely outward-looking regime) with a democratic government, but a popular one that shared power with the opposition. Sri Lanka has been attempting one under a democratic government since 1977 and Kenya under an elected government since 1980.[8]

Whatever the government, it is safer to navigate this passage when economic conditions are favorable, harvests good, unemployment low, and the balance of payments strong. Paradoxically, that is the least likely occasion to induce governments to change things. But if a crisis is awaited, the government's position is likely to be weakened and its prospects for success dimmed.

PROTECTION IN THE NORTH

As a group, the developing countries have become significant suppliers of manufactured goods to consumers in the industrial world. In 1982, the developing market economies exported $71 billion of manufactures to the industrial-market economies, representing almost a sevenfold expansion in export volume (i.e., at constant prices) from the 1965 level (see Table 17–5). Although textiles and clothing were the leading exports, products such as wood paneling, machinery, electronics, chemicals, and even automobiles were also exported to industrial countries. Asian exporters, led by the Gang of Four, were responsible for 60 percent of these manufactured exports. LDC exports of manufactures doubled their share of total imports into developed countries from 1965 to 1982, but still accounted for only 13 percent. In tex-

8. John Sheahan discusses the connection between outward-looking strategies and political repression and suggests some compromises that might avoid repression, in "Market-oriented Economic Policies and Political Repression in Latin America," *Economic Development and Cultural Change* 28 (January 1980): 267–92. Joan Nelson deals with the closely related problems of managing economic stabilization programs in "The Political Economy of Stabilization," *World Development* 12 (October 1984): 983–1006.

TABLE 17–5 Exports of Manufactures from Developing Countries to Industrial Countries[a]

	1965	1983
A. *Value* of exports (in billions of U.S. dollars)		
1. All exports (0–9)[b]	26.0	312.0
2. Manufactures (5–8)	3.8	71.0
a. Chemicals (5)	0.2	5.2
b. Machinery[c] (7)	0.1	17.4
c. Other (6 + 8)	3.5	48.4
1) Textiles (65)	0.7	5.3
2) Clothing (84)	0.3	13.9
B. *Quantity index* of exports (1980 = 100)		
1. All exports (0–9)	55	80
2. Manufactures (5–8)	18	122
C. *Share* of industrial country imports (%)		
1. All commodities (0–9)	20.4	26.4
2. Manufactures (5–8)	6.7	13.4
a. Chemicals (5)	3.2	5.8
b. Machinery[c] (7)	0.4	5.8
c. Other (6 + 8)	9.7	16.9
1) Textiles (65).	12.1	17.5
2) Clothing (84)	16.0	44.5

Source: United Nations, *Yearbook of International Trade Statistics 1983* vol. 1 (New York: 1985), Special Tables B and C.
[a] Market economies only, excluding socialist Asian and Eastern European countries and Cuba. (Socialist Asian countries are: China, North Korea, Vietnam, Mongolia, Cambodia, and Laos.)
[b] Figures in parentheses give the standard industrial trade classification (SITC) for each group of commodities.
[c] Includes transport vehicles.

tiles, LDC exports accounted for 18 percent of total industrial country imports and in clothing the share almost tripled from 1965 to 1982, when it reached 45 percent.

The "New" Protectionism

The success of the newly industrializing countries of Asia and Latin America in penetrating northern markets, together with Japan's export dynamism, has engendered a reaction popularly called the "new" protectionism. There is not much new about the motives behind this reaction: the northern countries are trying to stop the decline of aging industries that can no longer compete in world markets. In the United States and Europe industries such as textiles, clothing, footwear, chemicals, steel, and automobiles face increasing competition from less costly imports, often products of high quality, produced in Asia and Latin America. Lower wages in the newly industrializing countries are no longer matched by proportionately lower productivity; managers have learned how to operate productive industrial units; and in the case of steel and other resource-based products, some LDCs have ready access to raw materials that were exhausted long ago in the industrial countries. In these and other ways, comparative advantage has shifted towards the developing countries for a range of labor-intensive and resource-based manufactures once produced more efficiently in the industrial countries.

All countries would gain, in the manner described in Chapter 15, if production in these products moved to the south, while the north concentrated on temperate-zone farm products, more technologically sophisticated and more capital-intensive exports, and financial and other services. But although all countries would gain in the long run, the readjustments require disinvestment from declining industries in the short run, which in turn means temporary unemployment for workers in those industries. Here is a classic example of the general good—widespread benefits among all consumers and the owners and workers of new export industries—being thwarted by the concentrated interests of a narrow range of losing groups—owners and workers of textile and steel mills, and clothing, footwear, and car factories. In the United States, the affected groups lobby their congressmen, often contributing generously to election campaigns, and in Europe they work through labor-based political parties to write the protection of their specific interest into national policy. Any attempts to open world markets to freer trade must contend with this pervasive and effective political force.

The motives for the "new" protectionism, then, are really both old and universal. It is the methods that are considered new. During the 1930s, protectionism was even stronger and more damaging than during the 1980s, but the dominant method was high import tariffs. A series of negotiating "rounds" after World War II reduced the tariffs on most trade to very low levels, although tariffs on goods traded among industrial countries were cut more than goods exported principally by developing countries. In the United States, average tariffs, about 50 percent of import value in the 1930s, had been reduced to only 5 percent by 1985, about the same level as in Europe and Japan. The General Agreement on Tariffs and Trade (GATT) was established as a mechanism to negotiate and then to monitor multilateral tariff reductions. Tariffs under GATT are based on the **most favored nation** principle (MFN): all trading partners enjoy the lowest duty rate an importing country accords to any one of its trading partners.

With low tariffs and GATT rules, it became difficult to protect declining industries. Instead, starting in the 1960s, the United States and the EEC began to negotiate "voluntary" agreements with trading partners, especially Japan and the newly industrializing countries, to restrict the export of sensitive goods such as cars, textiles, and steel. This new mechanism was added to more traditional non-tariff barriers (NTBs) that are practiced by all countries, especially unilateral restrictions on the quantities of imports, as well as regulations affecting quality standards, packaging, labeling, health inspection, and so forth, established ostensibly to protect consumers but frequently utilized to protect competing domestic manufacturers.

Both tariff and non-tariff barriers have been used extensively to protect northern agriculture as well as industry. The EEC and the United States unilaterally restrict imports of sugar to protect their inefficient beetsugar producers, while they and Japan limit beef imports. The World Bank estimates that restrictions on sugar and beef imports cost developing country exporters over $12 billion in foreign exchange in 1983, more than half of the total value of all industrial countries' aid programs. Cherno Sar of Senegal, introduced in Chapter 1, faces strict quotas on peanut exports to the United

States to protect his much wealthier competitor, John Johnston of Georgia. However severe the impact of NTBs in agriculture, the liberal use of subsidies throughout the industrial world may be even more damaging. EEC subsidies on dairy products and wheat, for example, not only protect its own domestic market but capture export markets elsewhere that might otherwise be won by developing countries.

Partly, then, the newness of the "new" protectionism springs from the proliferation of non-tariff barriers. The World Bank estimates that in 1983, 20 percent of all LDC exports to the industrial countries faced non-tariff barriers. However, it is not so much the extent of protectionism as the vehemence with which it is being espoused, especially in the United States in the mid-1980s, that makes it potentially dangerous to the export aspirations of third-world countries. To a considerable extent this is related to the overvaluation of the dollar from 1983 to 1986, which has made import competition much more fierce than it should have been. But underlying the clamor for protection in the United States and Europe is the more fundamental, long-lasting need for transformation from aging industries into new ones. The pressure for protection will not disappear with the overvaluation of the dollar.

The Costs of Protection

It is easy to generalize about the costs of protection: the theory of comparative advantage tells us that any divergence from free trade causes a loss to both trading partners. More specifically, the losses to an economy from tariff protection of a single industry were illustrated in Figure 16-1 as the deadweight loss, the area of triangles *b* plus *d*. If the industry is protected by voluntary export restraints, the loss to the importing country can be greater. Recall in Figure 16-1 that under tariff protection, area *c* represents revenue to the government, which is not a loss to the country. But under voluntary export restraints, such as the Multifiber Arrangement protecting northern textile manufacturers or Japan's voluntary restriction on car exports to the United States, low-cost exporting firms can capture much or all of this revenue rectangle. Restrictive arrangements make it easy for exporting countries and firms to agree among themselves to share the protected export markets and to charge the higher domestic market prices, P_d in the diagram, even though they can export profitably at the lower world price, P_w. This helps explain why such agreements are "voluntary": the exporting countries and their firms can gain benefits otherwise accruing to the governments or consumers of the importing countries. Moreover, the result is a less competitive market in which exporters' profits are more stable. These agreements typically exclude potential new exporters, particularly those aspiring to follow the strategy of the newly industrializing countries.

Attempts have been made to estimate the cost to the United States and Canada of protecting jobs in the textile and clothing industries.[9] The estimate for the United States incorporates only the costs of tariff protection, i.e. the area of the two triangles, *b* plus *d,* in Figure 16-1. In 1977, this cost was

---

9. World Bank, *World Development Report 1984*, p. 40.

$80,000 per job saved. In both countries most workers who lose jobs in these industries find alternative jobs within a year and draw unemployment compensation while out of work. The net loss to these workers averaged $5,600 per person. Hence society paid $14 in higher-than-necessary costs and prices for every $1 of benefit to the workers whose jobs were saved. In Canada, where the estimate incorporated the higher costs of non-tariff barriers, the ratio was $70 of costs to society for every $1 of net income saved by workers who held their jobs. It would have been highly advantageous for the United States and Canada to import textiles freely and to use a small portion of the resulting benefits to compensate the workers who lost their jobs.

But even these costs do not capture all of the losses to importing countries from their own protection. Tariffs or NTBs reduce the volume of imports and keep the exchange rate at higher (overvalued) levels, thus making export industries less competitive in world markets. Reduced exports mean fewer jobs in those industries and some economists believe the net gain in jobs may be negligible. If so, the costs per job saved may, literally, approach infinity. In the United States during the mid-1980s, protection contributed to the overvaluation of the dollar which, in turn, made it more difficult to export farm products and to compete with Japan in electronics, thus helping to put many farmers out of business and probably reducing potential employment in electronics. One can only marvel at the political strength of entrenched interests that convince governments to protect their industries despite the astronomical costs to everyone else.

The costs to developing countries are also high. Protection limits their gains from trade and reduces potential growth for all the reasons that outward-looking strategies have proved superior to inward-looking ones. If Japan, Korea, and Brazil find they cannot expand their exports because of protection in the north, then India, Peru, Kenya, and others will be discouraged from attempting to utilize exports to stimulate development. Countries facing large debt burdens will be unable to generate the foreign exchange to repay their loans, which will probably reduce the capital available to all developing countries (see Chapter 14). With the potential losses so high on both sides, it would seem natural that a way would be found to avoid protection and liberalize trade.

Trade Reform

The various postwar negotiations to reduce tariffs were tedious and difficult, but successful. Negotiations to halt the new protectionism will be much more difficult. Voluntary export restrictions, for example, may be defended not only by importing countries but also by those exporters, usually the newly industrializing countries, lucky enough to have gained the largest market shares with their attractive rents. Removal of other non-tariff barriers has always been difficult to negotiate because NTBs cover so many different kinds of actions, can be difficult to monitor, and because many of them deal with legitimate concerns such as health regulations.

At the heart of the negotiating process will be the acceptance by all countries, north and south, of the need for structural adjustment of their econo-

mies. In the industrial countries, the interests of exporters and consumers
will have to prevail over those of declining import-competing industries. This task will be easier if there are obvious gains to be made in exporting those items in which industrial countries now appear to have comparative advantage, especially some temperate-zone farm products, manufactures based on advanced technology, and services like finance and management consulting. But in these areas the southern countries themselves—especially the NICs—become protectionist. Brazil, aspiring to build its own capabilities, makes it difficult for American firms to bid on telecommunications projects. Banking is one of the most protected industries throughout the world, while most countries favor their own nationals whenever professional services are considered. These are, of course, legitimate means to develop, adding to human and technical capabilities by learning through doing. But trade is necessarily reciprocal. If northern countries are to show the political will to overcome the special interests favoring protection, southern countries will have to become more open markets for many products and services in which they are not efficient and which they have been protecting. This is, of course, the essence of the outward-looking strategy of development.[10]

INTEGRATION IN THE SOUTH

The developing countries, frustrated by their inability to gain wider access to industrial-country markets or to improve their terms of trade with these markets, have exhorted each other to form larger and more meaningful regional trade groups. In essence groups of developing countries would try to stimulate development by granting preferential access to each other's exports, placing relatively less emphasis on access to industrial-country markets. Table 17–6 shows that trade among developing countries more than doubled from 1965 to 1982, when developing countries sold 30 percent of their exports to other third-world countries; for manufactured exports the share was 37 percent. Proponents of regional trade groups hope that greater economic integration among developing countries would further increase the importance of intra-LDC trade to the benefit of all participants.

Three systems of trade arrangements can be defined, in increasing degree of economic integration. **Free-trade areas** eliminate tariffs among member countries, but each member is permitted to set its own external tariff for imports from the outside world. The European Free-Trade Association was a prominent example before it was largely absorbed in the European Economic Community. The Latin American Free-Trade Association is the largest current example. Because members are typically free to set their own external tariffs, free-trade associations represent minimal cooperation and integration and have generally not been very effective. **Customs unions** eliminate tariffs among members, but go beyond free-trade areas by erecting a common external tariff against imports from the rest of the world. This is

10. For a review of trade-reform issues, see Jaleel Ahmad, "Prospects of Trade Liberalization Between Developed and Developing Countries," *World Development* 13 (September 1985): 1077–86.

TABLE 17-6   Trade Among Developing Market Countries[a]

	1965	1982
1. *Value* of exports (in billions of U.S. dollars)		
A. All exports (0–9)[b]	7.9	145.0
B. Manufactures (5–8)	1.7	43.5
2. *Quantity index* of exports (1980 = 100)		
A. All exports (0–9)	47.0	105.0
B. Manufactures (5–8)	14.0	125.0
3. *Share of intra-LDC in total LDC exports*[c] (%)		
A. All exports (0-9)	21.0	29.8
B. Manufactures (5–8)	28.0	36.5

Source: United Nations, *Yearbook of International Trade Statistics 1983* (New York, 1985), Special Tables B and C.
[a] Excludes Cuba and socialist countries in Asia.
[b] Figures in parentheses are SITC numbers for each group of commodities.
[c] By current market value.

sometimes a stated aim of trade groupings, such as the Andean Pact among countries along the west coast of Latin America, but it is often difficult to achieve. The Preferential Trade Area of eastern and southern African countries, which began in 1984 to reduce internal tariffs for selected commodities, is intended to become a full-fledged customs union by the 1990s.

Common markets move several steps closer to full integration. In addition to free trade among members and a common external tariff, common markets either eliminate or substantially reduce restrictions on the movements of labor and capital among member states. They may go further to promote coordinated fiscal, monetary, and exchange-rate policies and may cooperate in many other ways. The European Economic Community (EEC) is the most integrated group in the world today. Both the Central American Common Market and the East African Community had achieved important elements of economic integration until political differences among members destroyed each grouping.

Static Gains

Customs unions (which we use here as a shorthand for all regional preferential trading arrangements) may benefit their members by conveying **static gains** in the form of a one-time improvement in resource allocation, and by offering **dynamic gains**, stimulating investment in production for export and linked industries. The traditional analysis of the static gains from customs unions makes the distinction between **trade creation** and **trade diversion.**

Trade is created when a new customs union, which lowers the duty on imports from all member countries, permits some member, say, country A, to export more to another, country B, by displacing production of country B's own industries. The import-competing industry in country B was presumably able to sell in the home market because the protective duty shielded it from the exports of more efficient, lower-cost industries in other countries. When the customs union lowers the duty on exports from other member countries, more efficient industries in those countries can then compete with country B's firms in their own markets. More is traded than before, hence

the term trade creation. Although some producers in country B are disad-
vantaged by the change, presumably there are others that benefit from the
lower duties in other member countries' markets, and of course consumers
benefit from lower prices and wider selection. Gains from trade creation are
analogous to gains from the opening of trade (see Chapter 15) except that
they take place in the limited world of the customs union.

Because customs unions also discriminate against outside countries, they
may divert trade by permitting member country A to export more to country B by displacing imports previously bought from a nonmember country. If
before the union country B had a most-favored-nation tariff, i.e., all other
nations were treated equally, then the outside country's exports must have
been cheaper than those of country A, or else country B would have
imported from country A in the first place. Once the union is formed, consumers in country B will buy from producers in country A at a lower cost to
the consumers, because of the preferential tariff, but at a higher cost in foreign exchange to the country as a whole. Part of the revenue previously
earned on imports from nonmember countries is now paid to exporters in
country A, who are less efficient producers than their outside competitors.

From each member country's standpoint the customs union is beneficial
if trade creation outweighs trade diversion. This is more likely to be the case
if customs union partners have different relative resource endowments or
their consumers have different tastes, so that the members have a comparative advantage in the export of different commodities. For example, if Mexico, with a comparative advantage in vegetables and petroleum, were to join
in a customs union with Colombia, with a comparative advantage in coffee
and textiles (to oversimplify greatly), trade is likely to be created and both
countries would benefit. But on the whole neighboring developing countries
tend to export goods that are more similar than different and there is a pre-
sumption that trade diversion would be large. In the East African Community, for example, much of the trade in manufactured goods came from
industries, such as tire manufacturing in Kenya, that could not compete with
the outside world and for which Tanzania and Uganda had to pay higher
c.i.f. prices than if they had purchased from outside the market. Note that
even if, on balance, trade creation within the union exceeds trade diversion,
so long as there is some diversion nonmember countries are losers.

Dynamic Gains and Risks

Most advocates of customs unions among developing countries would argue
that the major gains are not static, but dynamic. Customs unions widen the
market for industries in all member countries, with the attendant benefits
noted by Adam Smith. Economies of scale may be realized by some industries whose output would be too small if confined to the home market. This
broader market especially benefits infant industries which are not ready to
compete in world markets. If the larger protected market helps them achieve
scale economies, they may reduce the time it takes to learn to become competitive in world terms. One potentially important, if largely unimple-
mented, feature of the Andean Pact and the Association of Southeast Asian

Nations (ASEAN) is the **complementation agreement**, under which large-scale infant industries are allocated to member countries so that each can benefit from, while each shares the costs of, starting industries such as petrochemical, fertilizer, pulp and paper, vehicle manufacture, and basic metals.

Customs unions also increase competition among producers in the member countries and reduce the perverse effects of protection, discussed in Chapter 16. This effect can be especially important for large-scale industries that would otherwise monopolize home markets at efficient levels of output. But it can have a much more pervasive effect, sharpening entrepreneurial and managerial performance in all industries. The bracing winds of competition are thought to have played a major role in stimulating European growth after the formation of the EEC and may have contributed to the temporary success of the Central American Common Market as well. One manifestation of increased competition is a characteristic pattern of trade in customs unions: much increased trade is in similar or even identical products. Members will export canned foods, shoes, clothing, or steel products to each other. To some extent this represents specialization in fine detail, one textile firm narrowing its products to concentrate on the few things it does especially well. To some extent it may represent more efficient subregional patterns of trade, a realignment to reduce transport costs once borders no longer serve as barriers. But a lot of the trade in similar goods may just reflect greater competition and a wider range of choice for consumers. In any event it certainly belies the trade creation approach, which predicts that countries will gain only if they export dissimilar goods. Trade in similar goods is good evidence that dynamic gains are more important than static ones.

These dynamic effects act over the long run to induce greater investment and hence accelerated growth within the customs union, and to restructure the economy toward exports of all kinds and toward industries that might otherwise have a difficult time getting started. Given these advantages, why are there so few examples of successful customs unions in the third world? One major problem has been the distribution of the gains, whether static or dynamic. The East African Community illustrated this point. When it was functioning well, both Tanzania and Uganda believed that Kenya benefited most from the resulting development of manufacturing. Kenya, which had moved faster to industrialize, was better able to take advantage of the customs union and exported more to its neighbors than it imported. (Indeed, Kenya kept its trade close to balance primarily because of this; it generally ran a deficit with the outside world.) Once Kenyan industries began to export, more investment flowed into Kenya to take advantage of the industrial infrastructure and the central location of Nairobi. Thus Kenya, and in particular Nairobi, acted as a growth pole for the whole East African market. Growth poles are often considered desirable in developing countries, but not when the pole is outside one's own borders. The increasing concentration of gains in the more advanced members of common markets causes the less advanced partners to resist integration, to avoid becoming "backwaters." This contributed to the demise of the East African experiment and has helped to dampen the ardor of countries like Bolivia and Ecuador for the Andean Pact.

The concentration of gains—real or perceived—in the more advanced member countries leads to political tensions that sometimes exacerbate the political problems among neighboring countries. Conversely, political disagreements among neighbors, which are probably inevitable, become much more dangerous when those neighbors are tied together in customs unions or other economic arrangements. Each partner, but especially the economically less advanced one, can use participation as a whip to threaten other partners if decisions are not taken in its favor. The rise of Idi Amin and the tensions between Tanzania and Kenya eventually destroyed the East African Community. Chile withdrew from the Andean Pact over political disagreements with Peru and other countries. The potential for such schisms always exists and substantially increases the risk a country takes when it enters an integration scheme. Certainly the country can reap substantial economic benefits from integration with its neighbors. But to achieve these gains it must develop its economy in ways that do not make much sense in the absence of a customs union. Malaysia might invest in a fertilizer plant intended to serve the ASEAN countries. But if the free-trade area does not develop, or if political arguments make it ineffective, Malaysia has considerably more fertilizer capacity than it can use, especially if it remains a high-cost producer. This kind of example, multiplied over several industries, could lead to serious dislocation and stagnation if the customs union breaks up.

Will the developing countries move towards greater trade with each other? The potential advantages are great, but so are the risks. To be successful any integration plan must bring the promise of substantial additional investment in the foreseeable future and must provide for a broad and equitable distribution of the benefits of union. Member countries will have to be governed by strong leaders who recognize common interests and work harmoniously together. Even this cannot rule out the risk of political change and future disagreements that cripple the union. It would seem that the conditions for successful integration schemes are no less stringent than those for successful outward-looking strategies of development. The political risks are reduced, however, the wider the membership of any union, so that no single country can destroy the arrangement by withdrawing. Thus the newly emerging Preferential Trade Area of eastern and southern Africa has a better chance of avoiding crippling political conflicts than did the East African Community.

TRADE STRATEGIES: A SYNTHESIS

What general rules can be derived from experience with the three major trade strategies—primary export-led growth, import substitution, export substitution—since World War II? First, pragmatism and eclecticism should rule over any doctrinaire, single-purpose approach. Although it is comfortable to think in terms of import substitution or outward-looking development, our understanding of these strategies has been enhanced by identifying and analyzing their components. In the future it would be better to avoid labels and to construct strategies from the components that seem to have worked. Whether the resulting product mix is import-substituting or export-led should not matter if the strategy effectively leads the country towards its development goals.

What elements seem to work best? Import substitution has gone awry in its excessive protection and its divorce of production decisions from market conditions, while an orientation towards world markets has been crucial for successful export substitution. If, for whatever reason, one or several import-substituting industries appear advantageous at a particular stage of development, they should be encouraged, not with high and continuing tariffs or restrictive quotas, but with moderate tariffs or subsidies. And either of these should be phased down on a predetermined schedule to force the infant industries to mature into efficient adulthood. Some longstanding tariffs are part of every trade regime. In most developing countries tariffs are a necessary source of government revenue (see Chapter 12) and in some resource-rich LDCs tariffs may support diversification away from dominant primary exports (see Chapter 15). But permanent tariff protection should be modest and uniform, covering all imports, including capital goods, and avoiding the disincentives to backward linkages previously mentioned. Import-substituting industries that grow up under these conditions are likely to avoid the worst excesses of protracted inefficiency and eventually become capable of exporting.

Resource-rich countries should, of course, exploit their natural advantage by exporting primary products. The task for them is to avoid the sharp dualism that infects such economies. Export taxes on primary products can be used to control profits and supplies, while the exchange rate supported by modest protective tariffs can be used as an incentive for efficient import substitution and export diversification. The tendency for wages to rise in the nonresource sectors needs to be resisted so that these can be developed in labor-intensive ways.

To the extent that investment is left to private market forces, then the price signals generated in reasonably open economies should lead to efficient investments that promote development goals. If governments prefer to plan industrial and agricultural investment, then cost-benefit analysis, linear programming models, or computable general equilibrium models (explained in Chapter 6) can be used to select projects for implementation, not according to some predetermined criterion such as import substitution, but for their ability to satisfy national development goals. In some situations these may yield a preponderance of import substitution industries; in others primary or manufactured exports could predominate. The nature of this outcome should be secondary to the ability of the package to propel a desirable kind of development. Once the investment package is set, the market environment must be carefully designed, avoiding large distortions and exposing producers to the discipline of competition. This outcome holds for private or public companies. "Getting prices right" is not a panacea for development, but getting them wrong has been a proven formula for failure.

These prescriptions apply with less force to large countries than to small. The distinguishing characteristic is the size of the potential domestic market. The massively populated countries, China and India, qualify by sheer weight of numbers. Countries with smaller populations but higher incomes per capita, such as Brazil and Mexico, can also provide large enough internal markets to temper some of the demands of trade-oriented strategies. Indonesia, Nigeria, and South Korea are borderline cases. For the very large countries, trade is a significantly lower share of national income and affects domestic market conditions less than in smaller countries. Strategic options, such as concentrating on one kind of manufacturing, are more limited, and balanced growth of industries and agriculture is virtually essential. Indeed, any attempt to depend too heavily on trade is likely to affect world-market prices and turn the terms of trade against the large country. With large internal demand it is possible to attain economies of scale, even in some producer goods industries, without establishing monopolies. The benefits of competitive, efficient industrial and agricultural development can, with good economic management, be captured within the domestic economy.

Nevertheless, trade can help even the very large countries to promote efficient, equitable growth. Imports can be used, especially in the early stages, to quell any tendency for pioneering firms to act like monopolists. Similarly, the potential for export can help fledgling firms achieve scale economies and produce more efficiently for home use as well. Any outward-looking foreign exchange regime will encourage competitive behavior, keeping prices of goods from straying very far from world-market levels.

For small countries there is no way to avoid the implications of these trade strategies. With large fractions of total supply deriving from imports, the choice is either to tie the economy to world prices through outward-looking policies or to accept the costs of inward-looking, protective regimes. For the small country these costs can be very high, severe enough to retard development for long periods. Whether the small country is successful is likely to depend upon its acceptance of the outside trading world more as an opportunity than as a constraint on development.

PART 5

SECTORS

Agriculture

Understanding the nature of agriculture is fundamental to understanding development. The labor surplus and neoclassical models presented in Chapter 3 dealt primarily with the nature of the relationship between the industrial and agricultural sectors. The problem of income distribution or extremes of poverty within developing nations discussed in Chapter 4 is substantially a question of how to do something about the rural poor. Nutrition, the subject of Chapter 10, is a question of food production and distribution. And the contribution of exports to development, as treated in Chapter 15, is for many countries a question of creating agricultural exports.

Much of this book has been about **rural development,** a term that refers to all those activities that affect the well-being of rural populations including the provision of basic needs, such as food, and the development of human capital in the countryside through education and nutrition programs. This chapter concentrates on problems that have a direct bearing on raising agricultural production and farmers' incomes. Indirect measures treated elsewhere in this book, even those as crucial as rural education, will be dealt with only in passing.

In a sense agriculture is simply one industry among many, but it is an industry with a difference. To begin with, the agricultural sector in a country at an early developmental stage employs far more people than all other industries and sectors put together—60 to 70 percent and more of the total work force are in agriculture in many of the poorer LDCs, including China and India. By contrast, agriculture in developed economies typically employs less than 10 percent of the work force (only 3 percent in the United States). Second, agricultural activities have existed for thousands of years, ever since mankind gave up hunting and gathering as its main source of food. Because of this long history the rural economy is often referred to as **tradition bound.** Generating electric power or manufacturing automobiles can only be done by means based on modern science and engineering, but crops are often grown using techniques developed hundreds or even thousands of years before the advent of modern science. And the rural societies in which traditional techniques are used often develop customs and attitudes that reinforce older ways of doing things, thus making change difficult.

A third characteristic of agriculture that separates it from other sectors is the crucial importance of land as a factor of production. Other sectors use and require land, but in no other sector does land play such a central role. The availability of cultivable land, whether relatively plentiful in relation to population, as in the Americas, or scarce, as in much of Asia, fundamentally shapes the kind of farming techniques that can be used. Closely related to the central role of land is the influence of weather. No other sector is as subject to the vagaries of the weather as is agriculture. Land, like the weather, differs from place to place so that techniques suitable in one place are often of little use elsewhere. The manufacture of steel must also adjust to differences in the quality of iron ore from place to place, and similar problems occur in other industries; but the basic techniques in much of manufacturing are similar, at least within and often between nations. In agriculture differences in soil quality, climate, and the availability of water lead to the production of different crops and different ways of raising a particular crop, not only within countries, but even within provinces or counties of a single country.

Finally, agriculture is the only sector that produces food. Mankind can survive without steel or coal or electric power, but not without food. For most manufactured products, in fact, there are substitutes, but there is no substitute for food. Either food must be produced within a country or it must be imported.

Agriculture's Role in Economic Development

Agriculture's role in economic development is central because most of the people in poor nations make their living from the land. If leaders are seriously concerned with the welfare of their people, the only ways they can readily improve the welfare for the majority is by helping to raise their productivity in growing food and cash crops, and by raising the prices farmers receive for those crops. Not all increases in farm output benefit the majority of rural people, of course. The creation of mechanized, large-scale farms in place of small peasant farms may actually make the majority of the population worse off. Although it is a necessary condition, raising agricultural output is not by itself sufficient to achieve an increase in rural welfare. We shall return to this problem later.

Most developing countries must rely on their own agricultural sectors to produce the food consumed by their people, although there are exceptions.

Nations with large natural-resource-based exports, such as Malaysia or Saudi Arabia, have the foreign exchange necessary to import much of their food. But most developing nations cannot rely so heavily on foreign-exchange earnings to feed their populations.

Farmers in developing nations must produce enough to feed themselves, as well as the urban population. Hence, as the proportion of the urban population rises, the productivity of farmers must also rise. If productivity does not rise (and in the absence of food imports), the models in Chapter 3 make it clear that the terms of trade will turn sharply against the industrial sector, thus cutting into profits and eventually bringing growth to a halt.

The agricultural sector's size is the characteristic that gives agriculture such an important role in the provision of factor inputs, notably labor, to industry and to the other modern sectors. With 70 percent or more of the population in agriculture, the rural sector is virtually the only source of increased labor power for the urban sector. Importation of labor is possible, and there is usually population growth within the urban sector itself, but neither of these sources is likely to be sufficient for the long-term needs of economic growth. If there are restrictions on the movement of labor out of agriculture, economic development will be severely crippled. Serfs in Russia through the mid-nineteenth century, for example, were tied to their lord's land by law and hence were not free to move to the cities and into industry. Thus Russian industry did not begin to grow rapidly until after the serfs were freed. Today such feudal restrictions are increasingly rare, but heavy indebtedness by a farmer to a landlord-moneylender often has the same effect of tying an individual to the land and making him unavailable to modern industry.

The agricultural sector also can be a major source of capital for modern economic growth. Some writers have even suggested that agriculture is the main or even the sole source of capital in the early stages of development, but this overstates agriculture's role. Capital comes from invested savings and savings from income. However, even in the poorest countries the share of agricultural income in national product is typically less than half of gross domestic product. Over half of GNP is therefore provided by non-agricultural sectors (industry and services), and these sectors are often important contributors to saving and hence to investment. Furthermore, whereas imports of labor seldom provide a large portion of the domestic labor force, imports of capital, whether in the form of aid or private investment, sometimes do contribute a substantial share of domestic capital formation. Thus it is possible for a nation to achieve a high rate of capital formation without drawing on the agricultural sector at all. South Korea is a case in point where capital formation in the early years of rapid growth was provided mainly by foreign aid and in later years was increasingly paid for from the profits of the industrial sector.

If one treats foreign exchange as a separate factor of production, agriculture has an important role to play in the supply of this factor as well. As indicated in Chapter 15, developing countries' comparative advantage usually lies with natural resources or agricultural products. In only a few cases is the export of manufactures or of services the principal source of foreign exchange for a nation in the early stages of modern economic growth. Thus, unless a nation is rich in natural resources, such as petroleum or copper, the agricultural sector will play a key role in providing foreign exchange with which to import capital equipment and intermediate goods that cannot be produced at home.

Finally, the farming population of a developing nation is, in some cases at least, an important market for the output of the modern urban sector. The qualification "in some cases" must be added because farm populations in some poor countries purchase very little from modern industry. This is particularly likely to be true where the distribution of income is extremely unequal, with most of the nation's income, land, and other wealth in the hands of a small urban and rural upper class. In that situation the rural population may simply pay taxes and rents to wealthy urban residents and subsist on whatever is left over. Even cheap cloth from urban factories may be beyond the means of a very poor rural population. If income is less unequally distributed, however, the rural sector can be an important source of demand for industrial products. If a large rural market exists, industries can continue to grow after they have saturated urban demand for their product without turning to foreign markets until they are better able to compete.[1]

Self-Sufficiency and Dwindling World Food Supplies

One important aspect of agriculture's role in development typically gets a great deal of attention from economic planners: the degree to which a nation wishes to achieve **food self-sufficiency.** Food self-sufficiency can take on several different meanings. At one extreme is the view that any dependence on foreign trade is dangerous to a nation's economic health, and dependence on food imports is simply one part of this broader danger. More common is the view that food is a basic or strategic good, not unlike military weapons. If a nation is dependent on others for food and hence for its very survival, the suppliers of that food will be in a position to bring the dependent nation to its knees whenever it suits the supplier nations' purposes. Others argue that population growth is rapidly eating into the world's food surpluses, and nations relying on food imports will soon find themselves paying very high prices in order to get what they need from the world's dwindling surplus.

The national defense argument for food self-sufficiency may be valid under certain specific circumstances. Since discussion of these circumstances would divert us into an analysis of complex international security issues, suffice it to say that the national defense argument is frequently used to justify policies that have little relationship to a nation's real security.

The issue of a dwindling world food surplus cannot be dealt with so easily. History does not support the view that world supplies of exportable food are steadily diminishing. Data on world grain exports are presented in Table

---

1. There are a number of good studies that treat the role of agriculture in development, including John Mellor, *The New Economics of Growth* (Ithaca: Cornell University Press, 1976), and his *The Economics of Agricultural Development* (Ithaca: Cornell University Press, 1966); Bruce Johnston and Peter Kilby, *Agriculture and Structural Transformation* (London: Oxford University Press, 1975); and Lloyd Reynolds, *Agriculture in Development Theory* (New Haven: Yale University Press, 1976).

TABLE 18-1   World Grain Exports (million metric tons)

Year	Exports
1962	85.34
1964	103.23
1966	114.11
1968	102.25
1970	113.34
1972	130.89
1974	149.05
1976	167.50
1978	191.20
1980	216.10
1983–1984	204.70

Source: FAO, *Trade Yearbook 1972* (p. 122); *1976* (p. 105); and *1978* (p. 109) (Rome: 1973, 1977, and 1979); International Grain and Feed Markets Forecast and Statistical Digest 1981 (London: 1981), p. 12; and *Milling and Banking News* 63, no. 16 (June 19, 1984): 48.

18–1. What these and other data indicate is that while the world grain export surplus and the corresponding size of the deficit in importing nations fluctuates, the overall surplus is growing, not declining. In 1972, for example, bad weather struck a wide part of the globe, including the Soviet Union, China, India, and Indonesia. The resulting surge in demand for grain imports drove prices up sharply in 1973, but prices fell again when production in these deficit areas recovered. The 1972 to 1973 "crisis" was not significantly different in magnitude from other weather-induced fluctuations of the past. After 1973 grain exports rose substantially and prices fell.

Those who speak of an impending world food crisis are implicitly or explicitly forecasting the future. Continued population growth is rapidly pushing people out onto the world's diminishing supply of arable land. In places like Africa's Sahel agriculture may already have developed beyond the capacity of the land to sustain it. The real issue, however, is not whether the world is running out of surplus land—it is—but whether yields on existing arable land can be raised fast enough to meet the needs of an increasing population with rising per-capita incomes. The problem is not one of biology. Research in the plant sciences has shown that yields per acre could be higher than even those of such advanced agricultural systems as Japan's. And most of the world produces food at levels per acre nowhere near those of Japan. While there is some biological limit to the capacity of the planet earth to produce food, the planet is not remotely close to that limit today.

The real danger of a long-term food crisis arises from a different source. From a scientific point of view, the nations that could expand food output dramatically may not do so because of internal social and economic barriers to technical progress in agriculture. At the same time, because of economic reasons, the world's few food-surplus nations may not be able to continue to expand those surpluses. Thus it is possible that the world could face growing food deficits in importing nations that are not matched by rising surpluses in exporting nations. Under such circumstances, food prices would rise sharply, and only nations with large foreign-exchange earnings could afford to continue to import sufficient food. Some of the poorest nations, including those where food imports make the difference between an adequate diet and severe malnutrition, may not have the foreign exchange earnings needed to maintain required imports. One must emphasize, however, that while the potential for a disaster of this kind is present, it is not today a reality; many economists believe it will never become a reality. A possible future world food crisis is a weak basis for a nation's economic planners to give a high priority to the development of agriculture.[2]

LAND TENURE AND REFORM

Before we focus on agricultural production, it is best to explore the problem of land, and the way it is owned and organized. Conditions of land tenure set the context within which all efforts to raise agricultural output must operate.

Patterns of Land Tenure

Land tenure and **land-tenure relations** refer to the way people own land and how they rent it to others to use if they choose not to cultivate it themselves. In Europe during the Middle Ages, for example, a local lord owned a piece of land that he allowed the local peasants to cultivate. In exchange for cultivating that land, the peasant family had to deliver a part of the harvest to the lord, and members of the peasant family had to perform labor services in the lord's castle. In most cases the peasant could not freely leave the land to seek work in the cities or with another lord. Peasants did flee, but the lord had the right to force them to return if he could catch them. Serfdom, as this system is sometimes called, was only a modest step up from slavery.

Serf-like land-tenure relations prevail today in only a few remote and backward areas of the globe. The patterns that do exist, however, are diverse, as the following incomplete listing makes clear.

Large-scale modern farming or ranching usually refers to a large crop- or cattle-raising acreage which uses some hired labor but where many of the activities are highly mechanized. Many such farms are found in the United States, while much of Latin American agriculture is characterized by large modern farms that exist alongside small peasant plots.

Plantation agriculture is a system in which a large piece of land is used to raise a cash crop such as tea or rubber, usually for export. Cultivation is by hired labor who are paid wages, and the plantation is run either by the owner or more frequently by a professional manager.

Latifundia is a term used in Latin America and Europe to refer to large estates or ranches on which the hired labor still have a servile (master-servant) relationship to the owner.

2. Works on the food self-sufficiency issue are numerous on both sides of the argument, including R. Barker, E. Bennagen, and Y. Hayami, "New Rice Technology and Policy Alternatives for Food Self-Sufficiency," in *Economic Consequences of the New Rice Technology,* International Rice Research Institute (Los Banos, Philippines 1978), pp. 337–61; Richard Goldman, "Staple Food Self-Sufficiency and the Distributive Impact of Malaysian Rice Policy," *Food Research Institute Studies* 14, no. 3 (1975): 251–93; Lester Brown, *By Bread Alone* (New York: Praeger, 1974).

Family farms or **independent peasant proprietors** own plots of land (usually small) and operate them mainly or solely with their own family's labor. This type of tenure is dominant in Asia and Africa and is important in Latin America as well.

Tenancy usually refers to a situation where an individual family farms a piece of land owned by a landlord to whom the farmer pays rent. Much of Asian agriculture is made up of either individual peasant proprietors or tenants.

Sharecropping is a form of tenancy in which the farmer shares his crops with the landlord.

Absentee landlords, who are particularly important in Asia and Latin America, tend to live in cities or other places far away from the land they own. Landlords who do live near their land may have little to do with it except to collect rents. Some resident landlords provide seeds and certain kinds of capital to tenants.

Communal farming is practiced in parts of Africa, where villages may still own some of their land jointly. Individuals and families may farm plots on communal land, gaining access by custom or by allocation from the community's leaders. Europe in an earlier period also had such common lands that were used, among other purposes, as pasture for the village cows.

Collectivized agriculture refers to the kinds of agricultural systems found for the most part in the Soviet Union, China prior to 1981, and parts of Eastern Europe. Land, except for small family plots, is owned by a cooperative whose members are typically all or part of the residents of a single village. Management is by a committee elected by the villagers or appointed by government authorities, and members of the cooperative share in output on the basis of the amount of labor they contribute to it.

There are numerous variations within and between these categories, but this list gives some idea of the great range of land-tenure systems that exist in the developing world. The kind of land-tenure system existing in any given country or region has an important bearing on economic development for several reasons. To begin with, prevailing land-tenure arrangements have a major influence on the welfare of the farm family. A family farming only one or two acres of land that must turn over half of its main crop to the landlord will not have much left over to feed itself or to invest in improvements. Such a heavy rent burden may seem harsh, but half and more of the farmers in some major countries, such as China and Korea before land reform and parts of Latin America and India today, labor under comparable conditions or worse.

A second important impact of the land-tenure system is on the prevailing degree of political stability. Families that own the land they cultivate tend to feel they have a stake in the existing political order, even if they themselves are quite poor. Because they possess land they have something to lose from turmoil. Landless farm laborers and tenants who can be pushed off the land at the will of a landlord have no such stake in the existing order. The history of many nations with large landless rural populations is often one of periodic peasant rebellions. One such rebellion played a major role in bringing the

Communists to power in China. Much of the history of modern Mexico has also been shaped by revolts of the landless.

Tenure and Incentive

Land-tenure systems also have a major impact on agricultural productivity. An individual proprietor who owns his land knows that increased effort or skill that leads to a rise in output will also improve his income. This result does not necessarily follow if the land is owned by someone else. Under sharecropping, for example, the landlord gets a percentage share, typically a half of any increase in output. If a tenant's rent contract is only a year or two in length, a rise in output may cause the landlord to threaten eviction of the tenant so that all or much of the increase in production can be captured through a rise in the rent. In some countries landlords have had to draw up land-rental contracts of many years or even a lifetime's duration, precisely because tenants otherwise would have no incentive to invest in improvements or even to maintain existing irrigation and drainage systems.

Farms with large numbers of hired laborers have an even more difficult incentive problem, compounded by a management problem. Farm laborers are paid wages and typically do not benefit at all in any rise in production. One way around this difficulty is to pay on a **piece-rate basis,** that is, to pay workers on the basis of the number of bushels of cotton or tea leaves they pick. But although this system works at harvest time, it is virtually impossible to pay on a piece-work basis for the cultivation of crops. A laborer can be paid by the acre for planting wheat, but it will be many months before it will be possible to tell whether the planting job was done well or carelessly. In a factory, elaborate procedures can be set up by management to check on the pace and quality of work performed. But work in a factory is much easier to reduce to a routine that can be measured and supervised than is work on a farm. There are a thousand different tasks that must be performed on a typical farm; and supervision, even in the hands of a skilled manager, is seldom a good substitute for a farmer motivated by knowledge that his or her extra effort will lead directly to a rise in income.

Incentives under communal farming suffer in a different way. Because the land is owned in common, each individual family has an incentive to use the land to the maximum extent possible, but no one has much of an incentive to maintain or improve the land because the benefits of individual improvement efforts will go not mainly to the individual but to everyone who uses the land. Economists call this the **public goods** or **free-rider** problem. Everyone agrees that a fire department is necessary if a town is to avoid conflagration, but few people would voluntarily pay what the fire department is worth to them. Instead they would pay little or nothing in the hope that their neighbors would pay enough to maintain the department, but of course their neighbors would not pay enough either. The usual solution to this problem is to turn payment over to the town government and allow that government to assess taxes on everyone in town on an equitable basis. Similar solutions are found in communal agriculture. Certain dates can be set aside when everyone in the village is expected to show up and work on a particular land improvement, such as repair of a fence with a neighboring village. But the incentive to work hard in a common effort relies heavily on community social pressure plus the inner goodwill of each individual. If farmers were saints, goodwill would do the job, but for better or worse, farmers are like the rest of us.

Collectivized agriculture has some of the incentive and management problems of both plantation and communal agriculture, but with important differences. Because the land is owned in common, the free-rider problem is present, but its impact is modified by paying everyone "work points" on the basis of the amount of work they actually do. At the end of the year the total number of work points earned by collective members is added up and divided into the value of the collective's output, thereby determining the value of each work point. The individual therefore has a dual incentive to work hard. More work means more work points, and indirectly it leads to higher collective output and hence a higher total income for that individual.

The incentive issue posed by collective agriculture is whether the work-point system is an adequate substitute for the motivation provided on a family farm where increased output benefits a farmer's own family and only that family. The main problem with the collective system is that an individual can sometimes earn work points by saying he or she worked hard, when in fact that person was off behind a tree sleeping or leaning on a hoe. The solution to the leaning-on-a-hoe problem is to have the leadership of the collective check up on how hard members are working, but that can introduce the supervision or management problem found in plantation labor—namely, that it is extremely difficult to supervise many agricultural activities. In general both the incentive and managerial problems worsen as the collective unit gets larger. In a unit of twenty or thirty families, the size of the Chinese production team in the 1970s, families can supervise each other and penalize laggards. But in a unit of several thousand families, the size of the Chinese commune in the late 1950s, family members have little incentive to pressure laggards to work harder because no single individual's work, however poorly done, will have much impact on the value of a neighbor's work points. If everyone in the collective thinks this way, of course, the output of the collective will fall. By 1981 the Chinese leadership had decided that even the twenty- to thirty-family collective unit created incentive and managerial problems, and they introduced reforms that returned Chinese agriculture to a system of family farming.

From an incentive and management point of view, therefore, the family-owned farm would seem to be the ideal system. The analysis so far, however, has left out one very important consideration: economies of scale. In agriculture economies of scale may exist because certain kinds of machinery can be used efficiently only on large farms. On small farms tractors or combines may be badly underutilized. Such considerations help explain why many Latin Americans feel that large-scale farming is the most appropriate way to increase agricultural production and exports. Economies of scale may also exist because large collective units are better at mobilizing labor for rural construction activities than are individual family farms. We shall return to the question of scale economies later. Here all we can conclude is that the question of the ideal type of rural land-tenure system has not been completely resolved.

Land Reform

The reform of land-tenure systems can assume many different forms. Typical measures found in many reforms, starting with the least radical, include:[3]

Reform of rent contracts ensures the tenure of a tenant farmer. Many tenants farm at the will of the landlord and can be easily removed at the end of a season. Laws requiring long-term contracts that restrict the landlord's right to remove a tenant can markedly improve the tenant's willingness to maintain and invest in the land, and also introduce a degree of stability into the family's life.

Rent reduction typically involves a ceiling on the percentage share of the crop that a landlord can demand as rent. If the percentage share is substantially below what prevailed in the past, the impact both on tenant welfare and the tenant family's surplus available for investment can be substantial.

Land to the tiller (the former tenant) **with compensation** to the landlord for loss of his land is a measure that can take many different forms. A government can pass a law setting a ceiling on the number of acres an individual can own, forcing that individual to sell all land over that limit. Or the reform law can state that only those who actually till the land can own it, and all other land must be sold. A key issue in this kind of reform is whether the former landlord receives full or only partial compensation for the land he has been forced to sell.

Land to the tiller without compensation involves the most radical transformation of rural relations, except for the further step of collectivization. All land not cultivated by its owner is confiscated, and the former landlord receives nothing in return. Frequently in such reform the landlord may lose his life as well as his land.

The Politics of Land Reform

The main motive for undertaking land reform is usually political, not economic.[4] The politics that lead to reform is of two types. A society with a large tenant and landless laborer population that is controlled by other classes may find itself faced with increasing rural unrest. To keep this unrest from blowing up into a revolution, land reform bills are passed to reduce the burden on the peasantry and to give them a stake in continued stability. In the second type, land reform takes place after a revolution supported by the rural poor has occurred. The main purpose of reform in this case is to consolidate support for the revolution among the rural poor and to eliminate the

3. There are numerous studies of land reform. One of the best known practitioners was Wolf Ladejinsky. See *Agrarian Reform as Unfinished Business: The Selected Papers of Wolf Ladejinsky,* ed. Louis J. Walinsky (London: Oxford University Press, 1977).

4. Elias Tuma, *Twenty-six Centuries of Agrarian Reform: A Comparative Analysis* (Berkeley: University of California Press, 1965.)

economic base of one of the classes, the landlords, that was most opposed to the revolution.

The motive behind the Mexican land reforms of the twentieth century, for example, has been largely of the first type. Prior to the Mexican Revolution of 1911, land in Mexico had become increasingly concentrated in large haciendas ranging in size from 1,000 acres to over 400,000 acres. While the revolution of 1911 was supported by those who had lost their land and other rural poor, those who took power after the revolution were largely from upper income groups or the small middle class. This new leadership, however, had to deal with the continuing rural unrest that was often ably led by men such as Emiliano Zapata. To meet the challenge of Zapata and people like him, the Mexican government has periodically redistributed some arable land, most recently under the government of President Echeverria in the 1970s. Mexican land-tenure relations, however, continue to be characterized by large estates existing alongside small peasant holders. Reform eliminated some of the more extreme forms of pressure for more radical change, but Mexican agriculture still includes a large, poor, and not very productive rural peasant class.

The Chinese land reform of the 1940s and early 1950s under the leadership of the Communist Party was a reform par excellence of the second type. The Communist revolution had been built primarily on the rural poor, and the landlord class was one of the main pillars of support of the existing Kuomintang government. Prior to the reform some 40 percent of the arable land had been farmed by tenants who typically paid half of their main crop to the landlord as rent. The landlord, whether resident in the village or absentee, contributed little or nothing other than his land. After the reform, and prior to collectivization of agriculture in 1955 to 1956, land was owned by the tiller and the landlord received no compensation whatsoever. In fact many landlords were tried publicly in the villages and either executed or sent off to perform hard labor under harsh conditions.[5]

The Japanese land reform that followed World War II was different in important respects from the Chinese experience. Land reform in Japan was carried out by the American Occupation forces. The Occupation government believed that the landlord class had been an important supporter of the forces in Japanese society that brought about World War II. Small peasant proprietors, in contrast, were seen as a solid basis on which to build a future democratic and stable Japan. Since the Americans had won the war, Japanese landlords were not in a position to offer resistance to reform, and a thoroughgoing reform was carried out. Compensation of landlords was provided for in legislation, but inflation soon had the effect of sharply reducing the real value of the amounts offered. As a result Japanese land reform also amounted to confiscation of landlord land with little compensation.[6]

A second feature of land-reform efforts is that land-reform legislation is

5. Among the many studies on Chinese land reform are John Wong, *Land Reform in the People's Republic of China* (New York: Praeger, 1973); and William Hinton, *Fanshen* (New York: Vintage Books, 1966).
6. There are many studies of Japanese land reform, including R. P. Dore, *Land Reform in Japan* (London: Oxford University Press, 1959).

extremely difficult to enforce in the absence of a deep commitment from the government. Most developing countries have some kind of land-reform legislation on the books, but relatively few have experienced real reform. In some cases no serious effort is made to enforce the legislation. In other cases the legislation is enforced but has little effect because of legal loopholes.

India provides examples of both kinds of problems. In the Indian state of Bihar the government has awarded substantial tracts of land to the *harijan* (former untouchable) caste. But Bihar is a state where much of the real power rests in the hands of so-called "higher castes" that include many landlords, and these higher castes have forcibly prevented the *harijans* from taking over the land the government awarded to them. Elsewhere in India a law limiting the amount of land that can be owned by a single person has been enforced, but has had limited real effect. An individual with more land than allowed by law registers the extra land in the name of trusted relatives or associates. For truly enormous landholdings subterfuges of this kind may be impossible, but most landlords in India possess only several tens or a few hundred acres of land.

Land Reform and Productivity

The impact of land reform on agricultural productivity depends on what kind of system is being reformed as well as the content of the reform measures. Land reform has the greatest positive impact on productivity where the previous system was one of small peasant farms, with high rates of insecure tenancy (for example, one-year contracts) and absentee landlords. Under such conditions reform has little impact on cultivation practices since farms are small both before and after reform. Elimination of landlords also has little effect on productivity because they have nothing to do with farming. On the other hand, turning tenants into owners provides them with a greater incentive to invest in improvements. The Chinese, Japanese, and South Korean land reforms of the 1940s and 1950s were all essentially of this kind.

At the other extreme are reforms that break up large, highly efficient modern estates or farms and substitute small, inefficient producers. In many parts of the developing world, such as Mexico, Kenya, and Malaysia, large, highly mechanized estates using the most advanced techniques have grown up over time. The incentive problems inherent in the use of hired farm labor are at least partially overcome by the use of skilled professional estate managers. Often these estates are major suppliers of agricultural produce for export, and hence a crucial source of the developing country's foreign exchange. If land reform breaks up these estates and turns them over to small peasant proprietors who know little about modern techniques and lack the capital to pay for them, the impact on agricultural productivity can be catastrophic. But there are also examples, as in the Kenyan highlands, where the breakup of large estates into small peasant holdings actually increased productivity, mainly because the small holdings are farmed much more intensively than the large estates. In between these two extremes are a myriad of variations with different impacts on productivity, both positive and negative.

Land Reform and Income Distribution

491

TECHNOLOGY
OF AGRICUL-
TURAL
PRODUCTION

Land reform will have a major impact on the distribution of income in rural areas only if land is taken from landlords without compensation, or at least without anything close to full compensation. If former tenants are required to pay landlords the full market value of the land received, the society's distribution of wealth will be the same as before. The tenant will receive land together with a debt exactly equal to the value of the land, and hence the change in net wealth of the former tenants will be zero. The former landlord will surrender land but will acquire an asset of equal value in the form of a loan to the former tenant. Reform with full compensation may still be desirable on productivity grounds because of the advantages of owner rather than tenant cultivation, but initially at least the new owner will be just as poor and the new landlord just a rich as before. On the other hand, if the landlord is compensated with bonds paid for out of general tax revenues, the former tenant's income share may rise provided that the taxes to pay for this do not fall primarily on him. The best known successful land reforms have commonly involved little or no compensation for confiscated assets of landlords. Such was the case in Russia after 1917 and China after 1949, as well as in the Japanese and South Korean reforms after World War II.

This discussion of land-tenure relations and their reform sets the scene for the discussion of agricultural production and how it can be raised. Much of the analysis that follows will deal with subjects like agricultural research or the uses of chemical fertilizer. But it must always be kept in mind that behind the use of better techniques and more inputs there must be a land-tenure system that provides farmers with the incentive to introduce those techniques and inputs, and then use them efficiently.

TECHNOLOGY OF AGRICULTURAL PRODUCTION

The popular view of traditional agricultural systems is that they are made up of peasants who have been farming the same way for centuries. The implication is that traditional farmers are bound by custom and incapable of making changes that raise the productivity and efficiency of their efforts. Custom in turn is reinforced by values and beliefs often closely tied to religion. Change thus becomes doubly difficult because to make a change may involve rejection of deeply held religious beliefs. In this case only a revolution that completely overturns the traditional society and all it stands for holds out real hope for agricultural development.

Traditional Agriculture

Tradition-bound societies of this type do exist in the world, but the description does not fit the great majority of the world's peasant farmers. A great accumulation of evidence suggests that these farmers are efficient, that they have already made sensible—sometimes complex and subtle—adaptations to their environment, and that they are willing to make further changes to increase their welfare if it is clear that an improvement will result without an unacceptable increase in the risk of crop failure and hence starvation.[7]

When traditional agriculture is described as "efficient," the word is used in the same way as it has been used throughout this book. Given existing technology, traditional farmers get the most output they can from available inputs or they get a given level of output with the smallest possible use of inputs. Foreign advisors, regardless of their background, have often had to relearn this fact, sometimes at considerable cost. With a little reflection it is hardly surprising that traditional agriculture tends to be efficient within the limits of traditional techniques. The central characteristic of traditional technology is that it changes very slowly. Farmers thus are not in a position to constantly respond to changing agricultural methods; instead, they can experiment over long periods of time with alternative techniques until just the right method for the given technology is found. Long periods of time in this context may refer to decades or even to centuries. If a slightly deeper method of plowing or a closer planting of seeds will raise yields per acre, for example, one or two more venturesome farmers are eventually going to give such methods a try. At least they will do so if they have plows capable of deeper cultivation. If the techniques work, their neighbors will observe and eventually follow suit. Given several decades or a century all farmers in the region will be using similar methods.

This example brings out a closely related characteristic of traditional agriculture. In addition to being efficient, traditional agricultural techniques are not stagnant; they have evolved slowly over time. That peasant farmers in a traditional setting are willing to change if the benefits from a change are clearly perceived has been demonstrated over and over again. Some of the best evidence in support of this willingness to change is that provided by responses to changes in prices. Time and again as prices of cotton or tobacco or jute have risen relative to other farm prices, farmers—even in some of the poorest nations in the world—have rushed to increase the acreage of these crops. And the reverse has occurred when prices have fallen.

Change in traditional agriculture has involved much more than responses to fluctuations in relative prices. Long before the advent of modern science and its application to farming, there were fundamental advances in all aspects of agricultural technology.

Slash-and-Burn Cultivation

One of the most fundamental changes, of course, was the conversion of society from groups of hunters and gatherers of wild plants to groups of settled farmers who cleared and plowed the land. Initially settled farming often involved **slash-and-burn** methods of cultivation. In slash-and-burn agriculture, trees are slashed and fire is used to clear the land. The burnt tree stumps are left in the ground, and cultivation seldom involves much more than pok-

7. One of the clearest statements of this point has been made by Theodore W. Schultz, *Transforming Traditional Agriculture* (New Haven: Yale University Press, 1964). A classic field study making the same point, based on the author's work in Guatemala, is Sol Tax, *Penny Capitalism* (Chicago: University of Chicago Press, 1963).

ing holes in the ground with a digging stick and dropping seeds into the holes. The original nutrients in the soil plus the nutrients from the burnt ashes make respectable yields possible for a year or two, after which most of the nutrients are used up, weed problems increase, and yields fall off drastically. Farmers then move on to slash and burn a new area, perhaps returning to the first area twenty or thirty years later when the land has regained a sufficient level of plant nutrients. Slash-and-burn agriculture is thus often referred to as a form of **shifting cultivation** or **forest-fallow cultivation.** This system requires a large amount of land to support a small number of people. Today the system exists mainly in remote, lightly populated areas, such as in the mountains of Laos and in parts of Africa and the Amazon.

The Shortening of Fallow

The evolution from slash-and-burn agriculture to permanent cultivation in which a crop is grown on a piece of land at least once every year, can be thought of as a process of gradually shortening the period that land is left fallow. The term **fallow** refers to the time that land is left idle to allow the soil to reaccumulate the nutrients essential to successful cultivation. In Europe the shortening of fallow gradually took place during and after the Middle Ages, and annual cropping did not become common until the latter part of the eighteenth century. In China the evolution to annual cropping occurred at least a thousand years earlier. In both Europe and China the driving force behind this evolution was increased population pressure on the land.[8]

The elimination of fallow did not occur automatically or easily. Farmers had to discover ways to restore nutrients in the soil by rotating crops and by adding fertilizers such as compost and manure. Ploughs had to be developed to cultivate the land each year yet prevent it from being taken over by grasses. Each of these changes was at least as fundamental as many that have occurred in agriculture in the twentieth century. The difference is that these earlier changes took place over centuries rather than years.

Farming within a Fixed Technology

Once fallow was eliminated, increases in agricultural production could be obtained either by increasing yields on annually cropped land or by expanding onto previously uncultivated land. Where population pressure was particularly severe several centuries ago, grain yields reached levels per hectare higher than those found in many parts of the world even today. In China, for example, two crops a year of rice or of rice and wheat were common before the sixteenth century. By the mid-nineteenth century in both China and Japan average rice-paddy yields per acre over large areas had passed 2.5 to 3 tons per hectare, while in India and Thailand as late as the 1960s average rice yields were under 1.5 tons per hectare. Hence, traditional agriculture was capable of achieving high levels of productivity per unit of land.

8. Ester Boserup, *The Conditions of Agricultural Growth: The Economies of Agrarian Change and Population Pressure* (Chicago: Aldine, 1965), and Dwight H. Perkins, *Agricultural Development in China, 1368–1968* (Chicago: Aldine, 1969).

What separates traditional from modern agricultural development, therefore, is not the existence of technological progress or the sophistication of the techniques used. Traditional agriculture experienced substantial technological progress, and the techniques used in highly populated areas at least were as sophisticated as many so-called modern techniques found today. The difference between traditional and modern agriculture is in the pace and source of change. In traditional agriculture change is slow, while in modern agriculture it is rapid. And in modern agriculture scientific research produces most of the new techniques used, while in traditional agriculture new techniques were sometimes the result of the tinkering of individual farmers. At other times new inputs, such as improved seeds, were accidents of nature that led to a variety that produced higher yields or required a shorter growing season.

The principal problem of traditional agriculture, therefore, was that farmers worked most of their lives within a technology that changed very slowly. They could spend their energies raising the efficiency with which they used that technology, but the gains from higher levels of efficient use of a stagnant technique were limited. The improvements in technique that did occur happened over too long an interval of time to have anything but a marginal impact on rural standards of living.

Modernizing Agricultural Technology

Traditional agriculture can be modernized in two ways. The first is technological: specific inputs and techniques can be combined to produce higher agricultural production. Technological modernization deals with such issues as the role of chemical fertilizer and the relationship of fertilizer's impact to the availability of improved plant varieties and adequate supplies of water. These technological issues are the subject of this and the next section. The second approach to modernization concerns the mobilization of agricultural inputs and techniques in developing countries. How, for example, does a nation mobilize labor for rural public works or create institutes that will develop new techniques suitable to local conditions? These issues of mobilization and organization are the subject of the following part of this chapter.

There is no universally best technology for agriculture. All agricultural techniques must be adjusted to local soil and climatic conditions and to local factor endowments. Even in industry technology must be adapted to local conditions, but an automobile assembly plant in Ghana will look much like one of similar size in Indonesia. In agriculture, local conditions are fundamental, not secondary. Students from a developing country can be sent to advanced nations to learn how to develop improved plant varieties suitable to their country, but only occasionally will the plant varieties in the advanced country be directly transferable.

Still, generalizations can be made about the characteristics of modern agricultural technology. The technological development that occurs will differ markedly depending on whether a nation has a large area of arable land and a small declining rural population, or whether it has a large rural population on a very limited amount of land. The problem in the former is to get the most output possible out of its limited rural labor force. While the latter nation must also raise labor productivity, the key to success depends primarily on achieving rapid increases in the productivity of the land.[9] The fundamental difference between these two strategies can be illustrated with a simple diagram, Figure 18–1. As the figure makes clear, the United States and Japan have pursued fundamentally different agricultural strategies, and most other nations fall somewhere in between. In the United States labor productivity is extremely high but yields per hectare are well below those of many nations, including more than a few in the less developed category. In contrast, Japanese labor productivity in agriculture is only a fraction of that in the United States, but land productivity is several times that of the United States.

The difference between the two strategies involves basically different technologies. These different technologies are often called the mechanical package (of technologies) and the biological package. The **mechanical package** refers to the use of tractors, combines, and other forms of machinery primarily as substitutes for labor that has left the farm for the cities. The **biological package** refers to the raising of yields through the use of improved plant varieties such as hybrid corn or the new varieties of rice developed at the International Rice Research Institute in the Philippines. Because of the dramatic effect on yields of some of these new varieties, the phenomenon is often

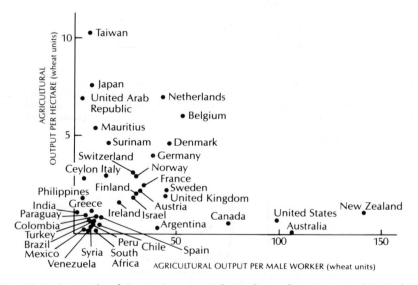

FIGURE 18–1   International Comparison per Male Worker and per Hectare of Agricultural Land. The dot for the United States indicates that American grain output per farm worker was nearly 100 tons of wheat or its equivalent but American yields per hectare were only about 1 ton. Mauritius, in contrast, had over 5 tons of output per hectare but little more than 10 tons per worker. Output data in the diagram are 1957–1962 averages; and labor and land data are for the year closest to 1960. *Source:* Yujiro Hayami and Vernon W. Ruttan, *Agricultural Development: An International Perspective* (Baltimore: Johns Hopkins University Press, 1971) p. 71.

9. The point is that innovation is induced by perceived needs. See Hans P. Binswanger and Vernon W. Ruttan, *Induced Innovation: Technology, Institutions and Development* (Baltimore: Johns Hopkins University Press, 1977).

referred to as the **Green Revolution.** But these new varieties raise yields only if they are combined with adequate and timely water supplies and increased amounts of chemical fertilizer. The basic production functions that describe these two packages therefore are fundamentally different. The isoquants of a production function representing the mechanical package indicate a high degree of substitutability (Figure 18–2), while the isoquants for the biological package are drawn in a way to indicate a high degree of complementarity (Figure 18–3). The L-shaped isoquants in Figure 18–3 indicate complementarity because only a limited number of fertilizer and water combinations will produce increases in grain output. Continual increases of only one input, such as fertilizer, will run into diminishing returns and then, where the curve flattens out, zero returns. Even with the biological package there is some substitutability but less than in the case of the mechanical package.

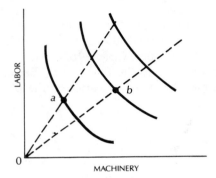

FIGURE 18–2   The Mechanical Package Production Function. The isoquants in this production function represent increases in agricultural output as one moves out from the point of origin (0). Movement from point *a* to point *b* represents a shift to the use of more machinery, which also involves a rise in agricultural output because machinery is a good substitute for labor.

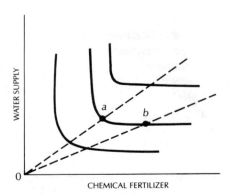

FIGURE 18–3   The Biological Package Production Function. The isoquants in this production function also represent increases in agricultural output as one moves out from the point of origin (0), but these isoquants, unlike those in Figure 18–2, indicate that there is little substitutability between inputs. An increase in fertilizer from point *a* to point *b*, for example, does not lead to a rise in agricultural output because the required increase in water supply to make the fertilizer effective has not occurred.

The Mechanical Package

497

TECHNOLOGY
OF AGRICUL-
TURAL
PRODUCTION

To someone familiar with the cornfields of Iowa or the wheat fields of Nebraska and the Dakotas, mechanization means the use of large John Deere tractors and combines, metal silos with mechanical loading devices, and numerous other pieces of expensive equipment. With such equipment a single farmer with one assistant can farm hundreds of acres of land. But mechanization can also occur profitably on farms of only a few acres. As labor becomes more abundant and land less so, the mechanical package becomes less important in relation to the biological package, but mechanization has a role to play even in poor, labor-intensive agricultural systems.

Mechanization of agriculture in labor-abundant developing nations is primarily a substitute for labor, just as in the labor-short American Midwest. Even in nations such as China or India there are periods when the demand for labor exceeds its supply. When two rice crops are grown each year, for example, the first crop must be harvested, fields prepared, and the second crop transplanted, all within a matter of a few weeks. Transporting the harvest to market also takes an enormous amount of labor if goods must be brought in on carts hauled by men or animals, or head loads by women, as is still the case in much of the developing world. One driver with a truck can do in a day what might otherwise take dozens of men and women several days to do. Nor can humans or animals working a hand pump or a water wheel move much water to the fields, however hard they work. A small diesel pump can move more water to higher levels than a large number of oxen turning wheels, and oxen cost more to feed than the pump costs to fuel.

Even when labor is extremely inexpensive, therefore, it can be economical to substitute machines for labor in some operations. Over the years manufacturers in Japan and elsewhere have developed whole lines of miniaturized machinery such as hand tractors and rice transplanters to meet this need, and these machines are in widespread use in the developing world. Not all mechanization in the developing world has been economic, however. Frequently tractors and other forms of farm machinery are allowed to enter a country duty free (when other imports have high tariffs) or are subsidized in other ways. Large farmers thus sometimes find it privately profitable to buy tractors and get rid of hired labor when, in the absence of subsidies, they (and the country) would be better off economically by using laborers.

The Biological Package and the Green Revolution

The main impact of the biological package is to raise yields. There is nothing new about using improved plant varieties in combination with fertilizers and pesticides to raise yields of rice or corn. The use of modern scientific laboratories to develop the new varieties dates back a half century and more. Only in the 1960s and 1970s, however, have the methods so successful in the industrialized countries been applied throughout the developing nations. The founding of the International Maize and Wheat Improvement Center (CIMMYT)[10] in Mexico and the International Rice Research Institute

10. The acronym refers to the name in Spanish, *Centro Internacional de Mejoramiento de Mais y Trijo.*

TABLE 18–2   Estimated Area Planted to High-Yielding Varieties of Wheat and Rice in Asia (in thousands of hectares)

Year	Wheat	Rice	Total
1965–66	9[a]	49[a]	59[a]
1967–68	4,123[a]	2,654[a]	6,777[a]
1970	11,098	36,718	47,816
1983	39,163	74,260	113,423

Source: Dana G. Dalrymple, *Development and Spread of High-Yielding Varieties of Wheat and Rice in the Less Developed Nations*, U.S. Department of Agriculture, Foreign Agricultural Economic Report No. 95, 1976, p. 108; and Dana G. Dalrymple, "Development and Spread of High Yield Varieties of Wheat and Rice in Less Developed Countries," U. S. Agency for International Development, eighth edition (forthcoming) as reported in Jack R. Anderson, "International Agricultural Research Centers: Achievements and Potential," Part III, consultations group on International Agricultural Research, August 1985, pp. 23–26.

[a] These figures exclude China.

(IRRI) in the Philippines marked the beginning of a truly international effort to develop high-yielding varieties of grain suitable to the tropical conditions found in so much of the developing world. National efforts preceded these international centers, and other international centers devoted to the problem of arid and semi-arid developing areas have followed. The result has been a steady stream of new, high-yielding varieties of wheat and rice that have found increasing acceptance in Asia (see Table 18–2) and Latin America, and to a lesser degree in Africa. (See Chapter 16.)

A rapid increase in the use of chemical fertilizers in the developing world had accompanied the increased use of high-yielding and other improved varieties (see Table 18–3). Prior to World War II, modern chemical fertilizers were virtually unknown in the less developed nations. By the 1970s they were in widespread use from Brazil to India. Unlike machinery, chemical fertilizers can be purchased in quantities of almost any size, and even very small amounts help yields. Thus, chemical fertilizers are within reach of even quite poor peasants. The principal limitations on the greater use of chemical fertilizer have not been the conservatism of the peasants or their poverty, but the availability of supplies and the price at which these supplies have been sold. We shall return to the price question later in this chapter.

TABLE 18–3   Consumption of Chemical Fertilizer in Less Developed Countries (in 1,000 metric tons of nutrient)

Year	Latin America	Far East	Near East	Africa
1948/49–52/53 (annual average)	116.5	617.2	93.8	32.5
1961/62–65/66 (annual average)	609.7	1,839.3	379.3	192.2
1966/67	877.5	1,605.5	470.0	274.7
1969/70	1,171.7	3,546.3	693.9	398.5
1976/77	5,402	6,358	2,409	1,047
1979/80	6,720	9,473	2,831	1,142
1983/84	5,708	12,269	4,259	1,475

Source: Food and Agricultural Organization of the United Nations, *Production Yearbook, 1970* and *Fertilizer Yearbook, 1984* (Rome: FAO, 1985), p. 121. The Far East excludes Asian centrally planned economies but includes all of South Asia and the FAO classification.

A key component of the biological package is water. Improved plant varieties using more chemical fertilizer lead to dramatically higher yields only when there is an adequate and timely water supply. In much of the American Midwest rainfall provides all the water required and at the right time. In many parts of the developing world rainfall is often inadequate or comes at the wrong time. In much of India the difference between a good crop and a harvest failure still depends primarily on when the monsoon rains arrive and in what amount. As a result, efforts to raise yields in the developing world have often focused on measures to extend irrigation systems so that crops are not as dependent on the vagaries of the weather.

Extending the irrigated acreage has often been seen as primarily a financial and an engineering problem. If a nation had enough money in the 1950s and 1960s (from aid or its own resources), it hired a group of engineers to build a dam to create a reservoir and canals to take water to the fields. As one dam project after another was completed, however, it became increasingly apparent that the irrigation potential of these systems was badly under-utilized. Engineers could build the dams and the main canals, but they could not always get the farmer to build and maintain the feeder canals to the fields. Who should do the work, and who would reap the benefits of these canals, became entangled in the conflicting interests and local politics of rural society. Irrigation extension was as much a social, as an engineering and ecological, question.

More than anything else, the increased use of inputs from this biological package has made possible the steady, if unspectacular, expansion of agricultural output that has kept the food supply even with or a bit ahead of the rise in population (see Table 18–4). In the future, further development of improved varieties and expansion of irrigation systems, together with increased chemical fertilizer production, will remain the major contributors to higher yields. The main function of the mechanical package, in contrast, remains freeing labor from the burden of producing food so that it can do other, hopefully more productive, tasks. Whether those tasks will in fact be more productive depends on what is happening in the rest of the economy.

TABLE 18–4   Food Production Per Capita in Developing Countries (Indices, 1969 to 1971 = 100)

Year	All developing countries[a]	Latin America	Far East[b]	Near East	Africa
1955	91	95	90	92	98
1960	95	95	95	98	102
1965	95	99	93	100	99
1970	101	102	102	99	100
1975	104	102	104	106	94
1980	108	108	105	104	89
1984	106	106	121	93	84

Source: FAO, *Production Yearbooks* (Rome, 1971, 1980, 1981, 1984).
  [a] For 1955–1965 the figures are for all nations in Latin America, the Far and Near East, and Africa, except for Asian centrally planned economies.
  [b] The Far East in this table does not include Asian centrally planned economies but does include South Asia.

While the technology of increasing agricultural output is well understood, the ways in which the relevant inputs can be mobilized are both complex and much less well understood. Some of the problems have already been touched on, both in the discussion of difficulties in expanding irrigation and in the earlier presentation of the relationship between land-tenure systems, individual incentives, and management difficulties. Here we shall discuss some of these issues further in the context of the agricultural production function. In brief the question is: What are the alternative ways a rural society can supply itself with the necessary amounts of labor, capital, and improved techniques?

Rural Public Works Projects

Mobilizing labor to raise crops is primarily a question of individual and family incentives. The main determinants of these incentives are the land-tenure system, and the prices paid and received for agricultural inputs and outputs (treated later in this chapter). Mobilization of labor to create rural capital—roads, irrigation systems, and other parts of the rural infrastructure—is the topic of this section.

Creation of a rural infrastructure through the mobilization of rural labor has long been the dream of economic planners in the developing world. The idea is a simple one. In the off-season, labor in the rural sectors of developing nations is unemployed or underemployed. Therefore the opportunity cost of using that labor on rural public works projects is zero or near zero (although food consumption may go up for people doing heavy construction work).

To use this labor in factories the factories must first be built, and that requires use of scarce capital equipment. Furthermore, this equipment will lie idle when the rural workers return to the fields to plant and harvest their crops. No such problems exist, however, when off-season unemployed labor is used to build roads or irrigation canals. There is no need to buy bulldozers and other heavy equipment. If there is enough labor, shovels and baskets to carry dirt can accomplish much the same purpose, and farmers already have shovels and baskets or can easily make them. In the ideal situation, therefore, unemployed workers can first be put to work making crude construction tools, after which they can begin to create roads and canals. The end result is a major expansion in the rural capital stock at little or no cost to society other than the reduced leisure time of rural workers.

Effective implementation of rural public works programs using seasonally unemployed labor, however, has proved extremely difficult. The community development programs of India and elsewhere are widely perceived as failures. Time and again international aid agencies have started pilot public works projects, only to see the projects die quietly when aid money ran out. Of all the problems connected with the mobilization of unemployed rural labor, the most basic has been the lack of connection between those who did the work and those who reaped most of the benefits.

When an irrigation canal or a road is built, the main benefits that result take the form of higher yields on land near the canal or easier access to the market for crops grown on land near the road. Land distant from the canal or road receives fewer benefits or none at all. If the people who own the nearby land are also those who did the work constructing a road or canal, then there is a direct relation between effort and reward. Unfortunately, more often than not the people who do the work reap few of the rewards. The extreme case is when the land serviced by the new canal or road is owned by absentee landlords. Absentee landlords are never mobilized for rural public works projects. It is landless laborers and tenants who do all the work, while the landlords benefit in the form of increased rents. Workers on such projects must be paid wages, and these wages tend to be higher than is justified by their productivity. Rural construction with crude tools is, after all, very low productivity work. If the wages paid exceed the benefits of the project, it is hardly surprising that these projects come to an end when government or aid-agency subsidies run out.

Labor Mobilization in Chinese Communes

Even when land is owned by those who cultivate it there is a problem of matching effort and reward. A typical project may require the labor of an entire village or several villages, while the benefits go primarily to farmers in only one part of the village. The Chinese solution to this problem was to collectivize agriculture by forming People's Communes.[11] An entire village owned its land in common. People who participated in public works projects received work points based on the amount of effort expended just as if they had spent their time cultivating crops. When the project was completed the land in a part of the village would be more productive, but the higher productivity benefited the entire village. The gap between work and reward in effect had been closed.

The Chinese Commune did make possible the more or less voluntary mobilization of large amounts of underemployed rural labor. Hills were leveled to create new fields, new reservoirs dotted the countryside, and roads reached deep into the countryside where only footpaths had existed before. But the Chinese ran into the work-reward problem in a different form. As the rural works projects became larger and larger, it became necessary to mobilize labor from two dozen villages, even though the benefits of the project went largely to only one or two of those villages.

The initial solution to this problem was to pool the land of all two dozen into a single commune. Then increased productivity on the land around a single village would be shared by all twenty-four villages, and workers in those villages once again had an incentive to participate in the project. This larger commune, made up of two dozen villages, however, immediately ran into all the incentive and managerial problems common to large collective units. The result was that despite all of the construction

---

11. When China first collectivized agriculture (1955 to 1957) the Chinese called their rural collectives producers' cooperatives, but to simplify the discussion we refer to them as communes.

activity, or even because of it, Chinese agricultural output fell; and small collective units called production teams replaced the large communes as the basic agricultural management unit, although the latter continued to exist and to perform some functions.

Clearly the problem of mobilizing unemployed labor to build rural infrastructure is more difficult than economists and others first thought.[12] The complexity of successfully sharing the benefits is such that rural public works, though possible, are not the universal solution to the problem of rural development that some once thought them to be.

Rural Banks and Credit Cooperatives

A second approach to the problem of providing rural areas with sufficient capital for development is to establish rural banks or credit cooperatives that will lend to farmers. In traditional agriculture a farmer has only two sources of credit: members of his family and the local moneylender. Since the interest rates charged by moneylenders typically range from 30 or 40 percent to over 100 percent a year, a farmer goes to a moneylender only when desperate. Peasants do not borrow from moneylenders in order to buy more fertilizer or a new pump. Only rarely will such investments be productive enough to make it possible to pay off loans with exceedingly high interest charges.

There are numerous reasons why urban commercial banks do not move in and take over from the moneylenders. Because of their location, urban banks lack the knowledge and skills necessary to operate effectively in rural areas. On the other hand, local moneylenders know the reliability of the people to whom they are lending and the quality of land put up as collateral. Individuals without land, of course, have difficulty getting money even from local moneylenders. Women in particular may have difficulty when they farm land registered in the name of an absent husband, a frequent occurrence in Africa and elsewhere.

Credit cooperatives set up by the small farmers are one potential solution to this problem. The idea is that each farmer is capable of saving a small sum, and if these sums are pooled, one or two farmers can borrow a substantial sum to buy a new thresher or pump. The next year it will be another farmer's turn, and so on. In the meantime those who put their money in the cooperative will draw interest, thus encouraging them to save more. But this approach has flaws. Farmers' savings tend to be small, and hence the cooperatives tend to be financially weak. More seriously, farmers in developing nations have little experience relevant to the effective operation and management of the cooperatives. In addition, economic, social, and political conflicts within the village may make it impossible to decide something as simple as who will get the next loan.

Because of these and other problems, the establishment of rural credit

---

12. For a discussion of these problems in a number of developing economies, see S. J. Burki, D. G. Davies, R. H. Hook, and J. W. Thomas, *Public Works Programs in Developing Countries: A Comparative Analysis* (World Bank Staff Working Paper No. 224, February 1976).

institutions usually requires significant injections of both money and personnel from outside the village, usually from the government. The entry of the government, however, does not necessarily or even usually solve the underlying difficulties. A common occurrence is for a rural credit institution to be set up with funds from the central government's budget. These funds are then lent to local farmers at rates far below those charged by private credit sources. Since the rates are low and the credit institutions are run by government personnel, local farmers with political clout have both the incentive and the means to grab the lion's share of the financing available. Corrupt bank officials may also skim off some of the funds, and corrupt officials are seldom among the poorer elements in the village. Equally or more serious is the fact that these loans are often never paid back, so that the new credit institution must be constantly resupplied from the central budget or go out of business. Too frequently the government personnel running the local bank or cooperative lack the will or the authority to make their clients live up to their contracts.

The problems involved in setting up effective rural credit operations can be overcome. Nations with well-trained banking personnel and a strong government administration capable of drawing up sensible procedures and enforcing them are certainly able to make rural credit institutions work. The problem is that well-trained personnel and effective government administrators are in short supply in a great many developing nations.

Extension Services

If one key to rapid progress in rural areas depends on the introduction of new inputs and new techniques, it follows that some of the most important rural institutions are those responsible for speeding the transfer of these new techniques to the farmers. **Extension services,** as these institutions are usually called, provide the key link between the research laboratories or experimental farms and the rural population that must ultimately adopt what the laboratories develop.

The key to the effectiveness of the extension worker is contact and trust. Rural education helps to increase the channels of contact, because if farmers can read, contact can be made through the written as well as the spoken word. Trust is necessary, because even if there is contact the farmer may not believe what is read or heard. Trust, of course, depends not only on the extension worker's honesty or personality, but fundamentally, on his competence and that of the research system. Giving a farmer bad advice that leads to crop failure is likely to close the channels of communication for some time. Making contact and establishing trust is further complicated because extension workers are usually men while those doing the farming, particularly in parts of Africa, are women.

These remarks are common sense, but they get at the heart of the failure of extension services in many developing countries. Frequently, training for the extension service is seen not as a way of learning how to help farmers but as a way of entering the government bureaucracy and escaping from the rural areas. Some extension workers are government clerks living in town and just as averse to getting their hands dirty as their colleagues in the tax collection bureau or the post office. Even when they do visit the farmers they are supposed to be helping, they know so little about how farmers really operate that they are incapable of pointing out genuinely useful new methods. Too often the extension worker visits the village, tells the farmers what is good for them, and departs, leaving the farmers to guess as best they can whether the gain from using the new idea is worth the risk of failure.

At the other end of the spectrum are extension workers who are well trained, and who live in the villages and work closely with the farmers when new techniques are being introduced. Chinese communes in the 1960s and 1970s, for example, sent one of their members off for training on the condition that the individual would return to work for the commune. The same can happen in villages where family farms predominate, although the absence of the authoritarian controls found in China makes it more difficult in many places to guarantee that the individual sent will return. Another variation on this theme, tried by CIMMYT among others, is for the basic research to be carried out on farmers' fields rather than in separate experimental stations.

There is much that we do not yet know about the spread of advanced technology in agriculture, but an effective extension service is only a part of the picture. To a large degree, farmers learn from their neighbors. If one local farmer owns thirty acres that he farms with a large tractor and his neighbors farm only five acres without tractors, the smaller farmers may feel they have little to learn from the experience of their larger colleague. More evidence is required, but technology appears to travel more rapidly when neighboring farms in a country or region are much alike. Extremes of inequality thus may impede technological progress as well as being undesirable on equity grounds.

As this discussion of mobilization of rural labor and capital and of accelerating the rate of technical advance makes clear, agricultural development in the less developed countries is not solely a scientific or an engineering problem. It also depends on the quality of government administration at both central and local levels.[13]

The Development of Rural Markets

One common theme in the preceding chapters has been the importance of avoiding major distortions in the structure of prices. Nowhere is an appropriate price structure more important than in the agricultural sector. But in agriculture as in other sectors there must first be a market before prices can have widespread effects. And in the rural areas of developing countries the existence of an effectively operating market cannot be taken for granted.

There are virtually no areas of the world today where subsistence farming in its purest form still exists. All farmers specialize to some degree and trade their surplus output on some kind of market. Economic development is usually accompanied by the increasing size and sophistication of this rural

13. A major study of these issues in the African context is by Uma Lele, *The Design of Rural Development: Lessons from Africa* (Baltimore: Johns Hopkins University Press, 1975).

marketing network, and in turn that improved network has an important impact on productivity in agriculture. The key to an increasing role for the market is specialization, and specialization depends on economies of scale, low-cost transport, and acceptable risk.

Economies of scale are at the heart of specialization. If everyone could produce everything they needed at the lowest possible cost, there would be no need to turn over certain tasks to others. In fact economies of scale are pervasive. In the most advanced agricultural sectors such as the American Midwest, farmers grow only one or two crops and rely on the market for all their other needs. In developing countries the single greatest barrier to taking advantage of these economies of scale is transport costs. The absence of good roads or of trucks to run on them can mean that it can cost as much to move a bulky commodity fifty miles as to produce it in the first place. In the United States wheat is turned into flour in large mills, and farmers buy bread in the local supermarket like everyone else. In developing countries only wheat destined for urban consumption is processed in large mills. In rural areas wheat is processed at home or in village mills, because to take the wheat to a large distant mill would be prohibitively expensive. In large parts of southern Sudan, to take an extreme but not uncommon example, there are no all-weather roads at all, and large regions are completely cut off from the outside world during the rainy season. Regions such as this cannot readily specialize on crops for sale in the cities or for export abroad.

In large parts of the developing world, therefore, improvements in the transport system and hence in marketing can have a major impact on agricultural productivity. Construction of an all-weather road system in South Korea in the 1970s, for example, made it possible for millions of Korean farmers to increase dramatically their emphasis on vegetables and cash crops destined for urban and export markets. Even the simple device of building paved bicycle paths connecting to the main road made it possible for Hong Kong farmers to expand their vegetable acreage. In the absence of refrigerated transport many vegetables spoil quickly, and hence it does not pay to raise them if too much time elapses between the harvest and their sale on the market. Furthermore, enormous amounts of labor are required if the vegetables must be carried every day on human backs across muddy fields. The ability to move the vegetables along a paved path on the back of a bicycle can make the difference between growing vegetables or concentrating on rice, which has to be moved to market only once a year.

Even when the transport system is adequate, farmers in developing countries may limit their dependence on the market because of the risk it entails. While cash crops can fail due to bad weather or pests, the principal risk from market dependence is that the price of the crop being raised will fall sharply by the time the farmer is ready to sell. For large farmers in advanced economies a fall in price of their main crop leads to a reduction in their income. If the fall is large enough, that farmer may be forced to borrow from a local bank to tide him over until prices rise again. Or he may merely have to draw from the family's savings account. In developing countries a fall in the price of a cash crop, particularly if food prices are rising simultaneously, may lead to a drop in a farm family's income to a level below that necessary to survive.

Credit may tide the family over, but interest rates will be so high (30 to 40 percent a year and more) that once in debt, the farmer may never be able to pay off his creditors and will lose the land he put up as collateral. Most farmers in developing countries avoid becoming dependent on a single cash crop and instead devote part of their land to meeting their family's food requirements. Their average income over the long run might be higher if they planted all their land to cotton or tobacco, but they might not live to see the long run if one or two years of depressed prices wipe them out.

Governments can take measures to reduce both transport costs (by building roads) and risks (by guaranteeing prices and other similar measures), and thereby develop more efficient markets. But governments also can, and often do, take measures that inhibit the development of rural marketing. Governments around the world have seldom had a real understanding of the role of rural traders, of the numerous middlemen who make a marketing system work. Middlemen are seen as exploiters who get between the producer and consumer; they drive the price paid to the producer down and that charged to the consumer up, while they reap huge monopoly profits. In response to political pressures from farmers, governments have often moved to take over the rural marketing system in order to improve its operation and eliminate the monopoly profits.[14] The temptation for governments to take this step is particularly strong where the middlemen are of a different race from the majority of the population, as is the case in much of Southeast Asia, where Chinese play a major role in marketing, and in East Africa, where descendants of nineteenth- and early twentieth-century Indian immigrants now control wholesale and retail trade.

While occasionally government involvement improves rural marketing, more often such involvement is based on a wrong diagnosis of the problem. The price at which a farm product is sold in the cities is markedly higher than the price paid to the farmer, but the difference has little to do with monopoly profits. The real cause is the high cost of transport and a generally rudimentary system of distribution and marketing. It is not that rural traders get paid so much, it is just that it takes so many of them to get the goods to market. When the government takes over it does not change this basic situation. For a high-cost, private rural trading network the government often substitutes an even higher cost bureaucratic control of the movement of goods.

Agricultural Price Policy

This discussion of agricultural development has stressed the central role of institutional change such as land reform and the creation of effective rural credit, marketing, and extension systems. It has also emphasized the importance of government investment in infrastructure, notably in agricultural research. But the creation of new rural institutions can take a long time.

14. The problems created by too much government interference in agricultural marketing in Africa are discussed in Elliot Berg et al., *Accelerated Development in Sub-Saharan Africa* (Washington, D.C.: The World Bank, 1981).

Needed changes in the land-tenure system, in particular, can be blocked by powerful interests for decades and even longer. Nor can an agricultural research system be created in a few years' time. New plant varieties suitable to local conditions may take a decade to develop. If the plant scientists needed to carry out the research have not yet been trained, the process can take longer.

The Multiple Role of Prices

There is one area, however, where government intervention has an immediate and often profound positive or negative impact. Most governments in both industrialized and developing countries intervene in agricultural markets to set prices both for the rural producer and the urban consumer. How they intervene can have a profound effect both on agricultural production and on consumption. Specifically, the prices at which grain and other agricultural produce are bought and sold play three, and sometimes four, vital roles: (1) The prices paid to farmers, and the relation of those prices to prices farmers pay for key inputs, such as fertilizer, have a major impact on what and how much that farmer can produce. (2) The prices paid to farmers, together with the quantity of produce sold, are the primary determinants of farmers' cash income. (3) The prices at which agricultural products are sold in the cities are major determinants of the cost of living of urban residents in developing countries. (4) Prices of agricultural products, particularly in many African countries, are often controlled by government marketing boards that manipulate them to earn profits for the government, a slightly disguised form of taxation.[15]

Prices have a profound impact on agricultural production because most farmers, even in very poor countries, are interested in maximizing their income. While some hold that peasants grow particular crops or use particular inputs because that is the way their grandfathers did it, study after study has shown that when prices change, peasant farmers respond much like any profit-maximizing businessman operating in a world fraught with uncertainty.[16] If the price of cotton rises relative to, say corn, farmers will grow more cotton even in very traditional societies.

The most important price relationship from the standpoint of agricultural production is that between farm outputs and purchased inputs, notably chemical fertilizer. From the farmer's point of view it makes sense to use more chemical fertilizer so long as it increases the value of farm output by more than its cost. (This is simply a manifestation of the profit-maximizing rule that the use of a factor of production should be increased as long as the factor's marginal revenue product exceeds its marginal cost.) One of the simplest and most effective ways of increasing rice yields is either to raise the

15. For a full discussion of the multiple role of prices, see C. P. Timmer, W. P. Falcon, and S. R. Pearson, *Food Policy Analysis* (Baltimore: Johns Hopkins University Press, 1983).

16. The literature on farmer price responsiveness is large. See, for example, Hussein Askari and John Cummings, *Agricultural Supply Response: A Survey of the Econometric Evidence* (New York: Praeger, 1976), and Raj Krishna, "Agricultural Price Policy and Economic Development," in H. M. Southworth and B. F. Johnston, eds., *Agricultural Development and Economic Growth* (Ithaca, N.Y.: Cornell University Press, 1967).

price of rice or to lower the price of chemical fertilizer, or both. As studies of rice production in Asia have shown, there is a clear relationship between the rice yield per acre in a country and the rice-fertilizer price ratio.[17] Other elements are also at work, but the role of prices is a primary influence. This basic point is illustrated with the diagrams in Figure 18–4.

Panel A is a simple one-input-one-output production function. The production function is drawn to reflect diminishing returns. If we know the prices of both fertilizer and rice, we can easily derive the marginal cost and marginal revenue curves facing the individual farmer as is done in panel B.

If the price of fertilizer is lowered, the marginal cost curve will fall from MC_1 to MC_2 and rice production will rise from q_1 to q_2 as farmers maximize their profits at point b instead of point a by increasing the use of fertilizer. Similarly, a rise in the price from P_1 to P_2 while holding fertilizer prices constant will increase rice output from q_1 to q_3.

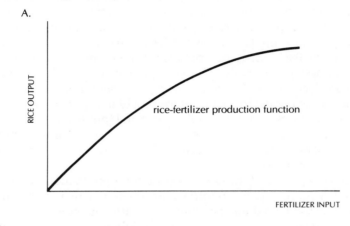

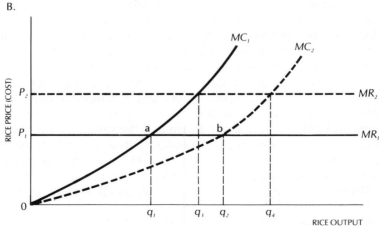

FIGURE 18–4   Rice Production and the Rice Fertilizer Price Ratio.

17. Walter Falcon and C. P. Timmer, "The Political Economy of Rice Production and Trade in Asia," in *Agriculture in Development Theory,* L. Reynolds, ed. (New Haven: Yale University Press, 1975).

One of the most persistent problems facing planners and politicians in the developing world is the conflict between urban consumers and rural producers over appropriate agricultural prices. Since food purchases account for at least half of the budget of urban consumers in most developing nations, a substantial increase in the price of food will cut sharply into the income of all but the richest urban people. Even governments indifferent to the welfare of their poorer urban residents cannot ignore the political impact of major increases in food prices. From Japan in the 1920s to Egypt in the 1970s, food price rises have triggered massive rioting that has threatened the very existence of particular regimes. (This phenomenon is closely akin to—and often part of—the politically dangerous transition from controlled to liberalized economies discussed in Chapter 17.) Because political leaders themselves live in urban areas, and because urban residents are in a better position than rural villagers to threaten governments, many nations attempt to hold food prices down even during periods of general inflationary pressure. The result is depressed prices for farmers that reduce both farm income and farm output.

Especially in some (but not exclusively) developed nations the political power of the farmers is such that governments raise farm purchase prices in order to gain rural support. Democracies that still have large or politically powerful rural populations are particularly likely to respond to these pressures. The United States and Japan in the 1950s and 1960s, the EEC in the 1960s, and South Korea in the late 1960s and early 1970s are examples. The result is prices that are favorable to higher yields, but the income and production benefits of the higher prices may not be equitably distributed. In some countries it is richer farmers who market a high percentage of their output and hence gain most from high prices. Small subsistence farms market little and hence gain little. In other nations, however, all farmers market a high percentage of their crop and hence all gain from higher prices.

Where both urban and rural residents have considerable political influence governments have sometimes tried to maintain both low urban food prices and high farm purchase prices. Japan since World War II and South Korea and Mexico in the 1970s all pursued this dual goal. Since the government must pick up the resulting deficit arising from selling food at prices below what it cost to purchase, only governments with large resources or those willing to forego other high-priority goals can afford this policy. Thus there is no single right answer to how high prices to farmers should be. Ultimately the decision turns on political as well as economic judgments.

One common way to subsidize grain marketing is for the government to absorb the often substantial costs of moving grain from the farm to the urban retail market. Who benefits from this process depends on how the subsidy is handled. Several of the possibilities are illustrated in Figure 18–5, in which marketing costs are represented by the vertical distance between the farmer's grain supply curve and the retail supply curve facing urban residents. These costs are assumed to be a constant amount per unit of grain marketed. On a free market without subsidy, the retail price of grain on the urban retail market would be p_1 and the price received by farmers would be p_2. As this dia-

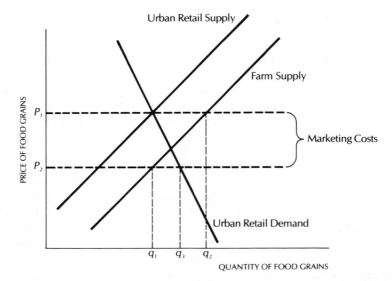

FIGURE 18-5 Effect of a Marketing Subsidy on Supply and Demand for Food Grains. If farmers receive the marketing cost subsidy, P_1P_2, then the farmer's price rises to P_1 and farm output rises from q_1 to q_2. Since food-grain supply now exceeds demand, the excess must either be stored or exported. On the other hand, if urban consumers are given the entire P_1P_2 subsidy, then the price paid by these consumers will fall to P_2 and their demand will rise from q_1 to q_3. The excess in demand will then have to be supplied from imports or the government will have to ration the allocation of food grains to urban consumers. *Source:* This diagram is a modified version of that in Timmer, Falcon, and Pearson, *Food Policy Analysis,* p. 198.

gram indicates, if the subsidy goes to farmers, the result can be either a rise in grain storage or exports. If the subsidy goes to urban consumers, on the other hand, the excess demand will lead to a rise in imports.

It is not just foreign trade in grain that is affected by these subsidies. The cost of marketing must be borne by someone and in these cases it will most likely be an expenditure item in the government's budget. Or the grain marketing authority may borrow from the central bank to cover its costs, but without the ability of ever paying the loan back. The macroeconomic effects of these subsidies can be substantial, particularly in countries where a large portion of marketed agricultural produce is subsidized.

Overvalued Exchange Rates

Because the high cost of large subsidies to government marketing boards becomes increasingly obvious to policymakers over time, steps are usually taken to eventually bring these costs under control even though the political cost can be high. There is another way of subsidizing urban consumers or rural producers, however, that has a less obvious effect on the government budget but a profound effect on the economy: the use of an *overvalued exchange rate* (see Chapter 16). The impact of an overvalued exchange rate on the grain market is illustrated in Figure 18-6. If, at an equilibrium

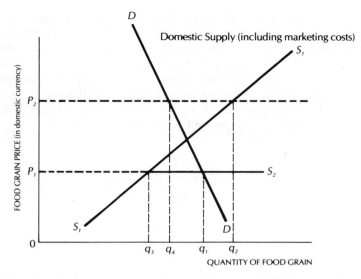

FIGURE 18–6 The Grain Market with an Overvalued Exchange Rate. If the world price of grain is P_2, then domestic demand (DD) will be q_4, and domestic supply ($s_1 s_2$) will be q_2, resulting in excess stocks for storage or export. With an overvalued exchange rate, represented by P_1, however, domestic demand (q_1) exceeds domestic supply (q_3), requiring imports or rationing.

exchange rate, the world price of grain is P_2, then domestic demand, represented by the curve DD, will be $0q_4$, and domestic supply of grain will exceed demand by the amount $q_4 q_2$. This excess could be either stored or exported. But if this nation's currency becomes overvalued, the world price of grain expressed in terms of domestic currency will fall from P_2 to P_1. Domestic food-grain supply, in this case, will fall to q_3 and the excess of demand at this price, $q_3 q_1$, will be made up with imports or by restricting urban demand through rationing. Thus, while this method of subsidizing urban consumers does not show up as an expenditure item in the government budget or a loss for the grain marketing board, it has a large negative impact on domestic agricultural production. Domestic agricultural production would fall from q_2 to q_3.

An undervalued exchange rate, of course, will have a positive impact on farm output, but poor urban and rural purchasers of food grain may be forced by high prices to reduce substantially their intake of food, leading to malnutrition and worse. In developing nations the poor spend a high proportion—over 50 percent—of their budget on food. A price increase for food thus represents a sharp drop in income for these people. They can try to maintain food consumption by cutting back on other items in their budget, but these are usually necessities as well.

Agricultural price policies, therefore, have a profound effect on both agricultural production and on the standard of living and even the basic health of the poorer segments of a country's people. Since agricultural prices and the exchange rate are usually set by the government in developing countries, it is technically a simple matter to change these prices to reflect the objectives of the government. Price changes involve few of the institution-building or implementation problems connected with building an effective extension system or mobilizing labor for public works projects. Price changes, however, do involve readily apparent costs to those on the receiving end of higher prices. If these people are in a position of influence, the political barriers to effective price policy can be formidable.

Natural Resources

This chapter focuses on LDC endowments of energy, mineral and tropical timber resources, and policies toward their utilization. Time figures heavily in the discussion. In the tropical forests of the developing world, between fifty and one hundred years is required for a tree to reach maturity. Nature requires almost unimaginable spans of time to build up accumulations of oil and mineral resources in forms usable by humankind. Consider, for example, the complete sequence necessary to generate oil and gas in sedimentary basins, such as the giant fields in Alaska's Prudhoe Bay or Indonesia's Minas field in Sumatra. The geological processes involved last between 10 and 100 million years, and they are so intricate that if any one of the six basic essential ingredients is missing, sizable accumulations of oil and gas are impossible. For this reason when a commercial accumulation of oil and gas does occur, it can be considered a natural anomaly. Other geological processes have, over eons, resulted in the buildup of scattered concentrations of such hard minerals as nickel, iron, copper, and tungsten. Where these minerals are found in minute concentrations, as is ordinarily the case, they are merely rock. In the infrequent instances where these accumulations are both sizable and sufficiently concentrated, they are called **ores.**

Through such processes nature has provided a stock of **natural capital** that, from the point of view of the short history of human existence relative to that of the planet, must be considered as nonrenewable. This does not mean that the available stock of natural resources is a quantity that remains fixed from decade to decade or century to century. Rather, higher prices that increase the value of reserves or technological improvements that lower extraction costs can and do convert rock into ore, and marginal sedimentary basins into commercially attractive fields that oil companies may spend billions of dollars to bring into production. But in a zinc deposit once mined, or an oil field once depleted, the extracted resources can not be renewed by nature in the next thousand millennia, if ever. Until recently, the world presumed that tropical hardwoods were fully renewable. Now, this is not so clear. In what follows, we discuss the special public policy problems and opportunities presented by largesse or paucity of nonrenewable natural resources.

OWNERSHIP OF NATURAL RESOURCES

Systems of property rights can and do have significant effects on the way a society uses resources, including nonrenewable resources. The United States is one of the few nations in the world in which property rights in minerals and natural forests can be vested in private individuals. In all states, the owner of rights to surface land generally owns the title to subsoil rights as well. The federal government, however, is a major landowner itself, particularly in the western states. Federal lands are thought to contain 20 percent of the nation's oil, 30 percent of its natural gas, and 40 percent of its coal. Still, most of the present known reserves of natural resources in the United States remain in private hands and in lands owned by state governments.

The situation is different in the overwhelming majority of developing countries. There, subsoil rights are ordinarily separate from surface rights and may not be vested in individuals or private business firms. Rather, natural-resource deposits in most LDCs are defined, whether by constitutional or other legal means, as part of the national patrimony, wherein the state acts as either the trustee for, or the actual owner of, all natural-resource endowments. Countries in which property rights in subsoil deposits are vested entirely in the state include Bolivia, Brazil, Chile, Indonesia, Malaysia, Peru, and Thailand. In some countries, such as Colombia, Ghana, and Pakistan, limited private or tribal ownership of resource rights is allowed in certain regions, but the central government nevertheless holds property rights to most oil and mineral resources, as well as tropical forest rights.

Among other differences, the pattern of property rights in minerals in most LDCs leads to much greater direct government involvement in natural-resource development than is the case in the United States. The federal government is relegated to an essentially passive role for resource exploitation projects on privately owned land in the United States. Once the landowner or the mineral company has satisfied environmental requirements, the only federal stake in the project is in potential income tax revenues. In contrast, governments play a far more active role in resource development in LDCs, functioning not only as tax collector, but as seller (or lessor) of mining or drilling rights, gatekeeper for the entry of foreign firms, and often as a business partner in resource projects with private domestic and foreign firms. Indeed in many countries, government have decided to exploit their natural-resource endowments directly by creating large, government-owned mineral or oil enterprises.

Mineral Resources and Growth

Mineral and energy resources in the ground are, contrary to views often expressed by oil ministers, of little value to a society.[1] Only upon extraction can natural capital be converted into capital usable by humans. We saw in Part III that for most nations capital accumulation involves a slow, and often painful, process involving austerity in domestic consumption, substantial inflows of foreign savings, or both. Many countries, however, have been favored by geological anomalies that have left sizable endowments of natural capital in the form of nonrenewable resource deposits. Such diverse countries as the United States, Canada, Australia, Kuwait and Saudi Arabia, Venezuela, and Chile have found sufficient natural capital within their borders to enable them to short-cut the usually laborious and ordinarily lengthy processes of capital accumulation. This can be done by capturing the potential surpluses from natural-resource endowments and utilizing them to diversify and otherwise strengthen the economy.

Many, but by no means all, countries with significant resource endowments do have something to show from decades of extracting nonrenewable natural wealth, in the form of higher stocks of physical and human capital. Over at least the period 1973 to 1983, before the sharp drop in oil prices in 1985 and 1986, several oil-producing countries outside the large Mideast oil exporters managed to secure high income growth through resource exports. These include Ecuador, Indonesia, and Malaysia, in all of which real GDP grew at a 6 percent annual rate or better. In general, middle-income oil-exporting LDCs grew at a slightly *faster* rate (4.9 percent) than did middle income oil-*importing* countries (4.5 percent), in the decade 1973 to 1983 (see Table 19–1). Even the high-income oil exporters of the Middle East grew at a rate marginally higher (5.2 percent) than did oil-importing nations.

On the other hand, the postwar history of countries such as Bolivia, Zambia, and Zaire suggests that relatively rich natural-resource endowments constitute no guarantee of national prosperity. Even before the marked weakening of world non-oil commodity prices after 1974, this latter group of countries encountered little success in deploying mineral earnings in ways that foster diversified, and hence more sustainable, economic growth. In fact, Table 19–2 shows that nonfuel mineral exporters tended to grow substantially more slowly than low-income nations in general, and among middle-income, nonfuel mineral exporters, only Morocco grew as rapidly as middle-income nations in general. But disappointing results from resource-led growth is not exclusively a recent phenomenon. Chile, for example, by

---

1. This statement applies in almost all real-world circumstances, except during those infrequent periods (e.g., 1973 to 1975 and 1978 to 1981) when the value of a known deposit (oil) appreciates at a rate faster than the interest rate.

TABLE 19-1   Dependence on Oil Exports, and Real GNP Growth, 1973–1983: OPEC Countries and Mexico

	Oil exports as percent of total (1981)	1973–1983 Real GDP growth (percent)
Middle-income capital-importing, developing OPEC countries		
Algeria	98	6.5
Ecuador	56	5.2
Gabon	88	3.2
Indonesia	82	7.0
Iran (1970–1980 only)	98	2.5
Iraq	99	12.1
Nigeria	95	1.2
Venezuela	93	2.5
Mexico	75	5.6
All LDCs		
All middle-income developing oil exporters	(90)	(4.9)
All middle-income developing oil importers	(0)	(4.5)
High-income capital-surplus OPEC members		
Kuwait	84	1.4
Libya	100	3.0
Qatar	94	—
Saudi Arabia	99	6.9
United Arab Emirates	75	—
All high-income oil exporters	(97)	(5.2)

Source: For OPEC countries' oil exports: Organization of Petroleum Exporting Countries, *Facts and Figures: A Comparative Statistical Analysis* (Vienna: 1981), p. 17; for other countries, World Bank, *World Development Report, 1985* (New York: Oxford University Press, 1985), Table 2 and Appendix Table 11

1975 had little to show for nearly a century of large-scale activity in her mining sector, first in extraction of natural nitrates and later in copper, and Bolivia in the early 1980s was still one of the poorest countries in Latin America after more than three centuries as a mining country *par excellence.*

Dependence upon nonrenewable resources for export earnings is marked in the case of major oil exporters. Table 19–1 shows that many of the relatively populous middle-income developing countries, including Algeria, Nigeria, Iran, and Venezuela, are no less dependent on petroleum earnings than are such very wealthy, thinly populated, OPEC member countries as Saudi Arabia, Libya, and Kuwait. For exporters of nonfuel minerals, listed in Table 19–2, hard minerals have typically accounted for more than 10 percent of GDP, more than 50 percent of total merchandise exports, or both.

Thus we have to reject the conventional wisdom of the 1950s and 1960s, which held that countries with relatively rich natural-resource endowments should ordinarily be expected to achieve higher rates of economic growth than less well-endowed nations. Neither the great abundance of foreign exchange nor the greater ease of raising tax revenues in resource-exporting countries guaranteed rapid growth when oil prices were high in 1973 to 1982. And many oil countries highly dependent on oil exports paid a heavy

Country	Share of mining in GDP (1970–81)	Share of minerals in total merchandise exports (1974–76)	1973–1983 Real GDP growth rates (percent)
Low-income countries			
Guinea	13.9	70	3.1
Sierra Leone	12.8	11	1.9
Togo	9.1	66	2.3
Zaire	17.1	97	−1.0
Average annual real growth, all low-income countries	—	—	(4.6)
Middle-income countries			
Bolivia	10.1	74	1.5
Chile	7.7	66	2.9
Guyana	15.1	26	1.5
Liberia	23.0	70	0.2
Mauritania	17.0	87	2.5
Morocco	5.3	56	4.7
Peru	9.9	37	1.8
Zambia	18.9	97	0.2
Average annual real growth, all middle-income countries	—	—	(4.7)

Source: World Bank, *World Tables 1983* (Baltimore: John Hopkins University Press, 1984)

price for their dependence in 1984 through 1986. The fact that LDC oil exporters have in general not grown much more rapidly than oil-importing LDCs is considerably easier to explain than the relatively low growth rates experienced by mineral exporters. We defer this discussion until later in the chapter, when we consider a broader set of problems associated with resource exports.

Minerals: Endowments and Utilization

Although relative resource abundance furnishes no guarantee of material prosperity, countries with significant natural-capital endowments clearly enjoy advantages not available to resource-poor ones. The more accessible the natural capital is, the easier is accumulation of physical and human capital. Resource endowments often provide a basis for resource-based industrialization (see Chapter 15), particularly given the savings in transportation costs made possible by resource processing. Taxes on domestic industrial and agricultural incomes may be lower, and public spending on infrastructure and social amenities may be higher, because a nation possesses readily accessible resource deposits. Resource abundance, particularly in energy resources, may help insulate a country from unstable sources of resource supply, enabling it to continue normal growth while less fortunate countries strain to adjust to sharply higher prices when critical resource imports are relatively scarce. Whatever problems accompany resource abundance—and clearly there are some—fall into the category of "good" problems, in contrast to "bad" problems, such as persistent drought in the resource-poor African Sahel, about which little can soon be done.

Several nineteenth-century developing countries that are now classified as industrial-market economies, including Canada, Australia, the United States, and Norway, have encountered and largely solved the "good" problems associated with relative resource abundance. Notwithstanding widely held perceptions, few of the far more numerous countries now classed as "developing" have had sufficiently large resource endowments to be faced with the "good" problem of natural resource abundance.

Energy Reserves

Energy from nonrenewable resources includes that derived from oil, coal, natural gas, and uranium. Because nuclear power obtained from enriched uranium is an unimportant source of power for all but a very few LDCs, it will not be discussed in any detail in this chapter. Other sources of **commercial** energy are renewable or inexhaustible in nature; in order of their relative importance in LDCs in 1980, they include hydroelectric power, geothermal energy, solar power, and wind power. Of this group, only water power was a significant source of commercial energy in LDCs in the early 1980s, particularly in countries such as Brazil, China, Colombia, Ghana, and Zimbabwe. Indeed, studies by the World Bank indicate that about 45 percent of electric power consumed in LDCs in 1980 was produced in hydroelectric plants, rather than in oil- or coal-fired generating facilities.

While virtually all energy consumed in transportation, electric power generation, and for residential and commercial use in the developed countries comes from commercial energy sources, developing countries also make substantial use of **noncommercial** energy sources, including animal dung, agricultural waste, and fuel wood. In large countries such as India, and even OPEC-member Indonesia in the mid-1970s, noncommercial energy use was almost as important as commercial energy. The share of noncommercial energy in overall LDC energy utilization has, however, been declining steadily since 1960, and this decline is expected to continue as nations develop. For this reason, and because cross-country information on non-commercial energy usage is scanty, the remainder of the discussion focuses upon commercial energy sources.

A **resource reserve** is an identified deposit known to be recoverable with current technology under present economic conditions. Total world *proven* recoverable reserves of any resource are merely the sum total of all known deposits that can be recovered with reasonable certainty. Reserve figures are never precise, even for a particular deposit in a particular country, and published reserve figures by country often differ significantly according to whether they are derived from industry or government sources. Further, and more significantly, reserve estimates can change abruptly as resource prices change; at higher oil prices, for example, reserves are higher, as formerly submarginal deposits are converted into commercially attractive ones.

Table 19–3 portrays the distribution of proven hydrocarbon (crude oil, natural gas, coal) energy reserves between five groups of nations. Of these

TABLE 19–3 Proven World Reserves of Energy in Oil, Natural Gas, and Coal, 1984 (in billions of barrels of oil equivalent)

	Oil Reserves	%	Natural Gas Reserves	%	Coal Reserves	%	Total Reserves	%
Developed market economies	68.0	10.0	97.8	19.6	1,624.2	51.3	1,790.0	41.2
Centrally planned economies	84.3	12.4	299.3	60.0	1,229.5	38.8	1,613.1	37.2
High-income OPEC nations	283.7	41.9	42.3	8.4	1.0	0.0	327.0	7.5
Developing-country oil exporters	214.2	31.6	44.7	9.0	13.5	0.1	272.4	6.3
Developing-country oil importers	27.5	4.1	14.7	3.0	297.1	9.3	339.3	7.8
TOTALS	677.7	100.0	498.8	100.0	3,165.3	100.0	4,341.8	100.0

Source: British Petroleum, *Statistical Review of World Petroleum* (London: British Petroleum Co., June 1984).
Note: Percentages may not add to 100 because of rounding.

three energy resources, oil is most prized, primarily because it can be transported most easily, through pipelines on land and in tankers plying the oceans. In its original state, natural gas can be shipped only via pipeline, and it can be shipped across oceans by tanker only when liquified in very expensive liquified natural gas installations. But gas burns more cleanly than oil, while oil ordinarily involves fewer pollution problems than coal. Coal, a resource with a high ratio of bulk to heat content, is also expensive to transport, particularly to overseas export markets.

In 1984 proven oil reserves were heavily concentrated in high-income OPEC countries, while most natural gas reserves were, and are, located in centrally planned economies. Developed market economies had respectable shares of both oil and gas reserves, but the ninety-odd oil-importing countries were virtually bereft of these energy resources. Proven world coal resources are heavily concentrated in developed market economies and centrally planned economies. In terms of barrels-of-oil equivalence (barrels of oil required to yield the same heating equivalent), the coal resources were 2.3 times greater than combined oil and gas reserves. When coal is considered, the energy futures of present energy-importing LDCs as a group appears somewhat brighter. Counting coal, they held almost 7 percent of total world energy reserves. Altogether, developing countries, including those non-OPEC nations that now export oil, had about 8 percent of the world's commercial energy reserves, excluding water and geothermal power.

Energy Production and Consumption

Two of the world's three largest petroleum and gas producers are not members of OPEC, and no developing country is a major coal producer. The world's first-ranking oil producer in 1984 was the Soviet Union, followed by the United States and Saudi Arabia, which could at any time produce more than the United States if it so desired. Outside the broad expanses of the U.S. and USSR, the known geological anomalies that yield oil deposits have tended to occur in lightly populated countries in the Mideast, where annual production in high-income OPEC members commonly exceeded 300 barrels (bbl) per capita per year, valued at $10,200 per capita given 1982 oil prices, but only at $3,300 per capita at 1986 oil prices. For middle-income LDCs, oil riches are relatively modest, even among developing-country OPEC members. Per-capita production of oil in Canada was four times as high as in OPEC member Nigeria, and U.S. production per capita is four times that of OPEC member Indonesia. For developing-country oil producers not included in Table 19–4, per-capita production is ordinarily less than 0.5 bbl per year, but most developing countries produce no appreciable amounts of oil or natural gas.

Over the long run improvements in living standards within a country require steady advances in labor productivity. In turn enhanced productivity ultimately requires replacement of human and animal power by electric power obtainable from such primary energy sources as oil and gas. World consumption of commercial energy across countries is even more skewed than world reserves and world production. The four billion people in low- and middle-income developing countries (including China) constitute about four-fifths of the world's population, but use only three-tenths of the annual world production of commercial energy. The nation with the highest per-capita consumption of energy, Canada, uses thirty-two times more energy per person per year than the average in low-income LDCs, and about twelve times more than the average for middle-income LDCs.

Although the U.S. has been the second leading oil producer since 1983, it is one of the largest importers of oil and oil products. U.S. dependency on

TABLE 19–4   Major Producers of Crude Oil, 1984

	Yearly Production (million barrels)	Per-Capita Yearly Production (barrels)
OPEC Countries		
Saudia Arabia	1,807.1	167.3
Kuwait	358.8	199.3
Libya	426.0	121.7
United Arab Emirates	444.6	370.5
Iraq	420.5	27.7
Iran	789.9	18.0
Nigeria	515.7	5.3
Venezuela	628.2	35.5
Indonesia	503.7	3.2
Ecuador	92.3	11.0
Gabon	54.8	78.2
Western Countries		
United States	3,216.0	13.6
Britain	904.8	16.1
Canada	511.0	20.4
Developing Countries		
Mexico	1,017.3	13.3
Malaysia	147.8	9.7
Trinidad-Tobago	59.5	54.1
Egypt	266.5	5.8
Soviet Union	4,494.6	16.4

Source: Oil and Gas Journal 83, no. 30 (July 1985): 95.

foreign petroleum, which peaked at 45 percent of total oil consumption in 1980, has been a source of continuing concern for reasons of national security and economic stability. However, the U.S. has diversified sources of energy in coal, natural gas, and hydro and nuclear power. Imported oil and gas account for only 17 percent of total energy consumption. But there are sixty-four LDCs that depend on imported oil alone for more than 75 percent of their total commercial energy, a share that makes the U.S. energy problem pale in comparison.

Nonfuel Minerals

Although often considered to be a critical source of minerals, in 1983 the developing countries' share of annual world production exceeded 50 percent in only four metals: cobalt, chromite, copper, and tin. All except copper are relatively minor items in world trade when compared to petroleum and tropical timber. LDCs are also the leading producers of phosphate and bauxite. (See Table 19–5.) For these minerals, developed nations, such as the United States, Canada, and Australia, still account for one-third or more of annual world production. Developed industrial countries are the leading sources of world supply for six other minerals: potash, sulphur, phosphate, iron ore, nickel, and zinc. And for nine of the sixteen minerals in the table, centrally planned economies, principally the USSR and China, have a larger share in world production than developing countries.

Within developing countries, production of nonfuel minerals tends to be concentrated in less than a dozen nations. Brazil is far and away the leading producer of iron ore and is an important source of manganese and asbestos. Bolivia is a leading producer of both tin and tungsten, Indonesia is the world's third-ranking producer of both tin and nickel, and Zaire and Zambia

TABLE 19–5   Percentage Share of World Production of Sixteen Nonfuel Minerals, 1983: Developed, Centrally Planned, and Developing Countries

Mineral	Developed countries	Centrally planned countries	Developing countries
Asbestos	25.8	57.6	16.6
Bauxite	37.2	17.7	45.2
Chromite	5.8	41.1	53.1
Cobalt	25.3	13.5	61.2
Copper	25.2	21.1	53.7
Iron ore	39.2	33.8	27.0
Lead	57.9	31.3	10.8
Manganese	28.4	45.8	25.8
Nickel	38.0	30.0	33.1
Phosphate	32.3	30.0	37.7
Potash	55.3	41.9	2.8
Silver	29.2	40.0	31.0
Sulphur	54.6	37.0	9.4
Tin	7.3	24.2	68.5
Tungsten	28.9	45.2	25.9
Zinc	51.6	25.1	23.3

Source: *Engineering and Mining Journal* (March 1985): 43–130.

are the two principal sources of cobalt. After Chile, Zambia is also the second leading source of copper among LDCs. Over 80 percent of LDC production of bauxite comes from four developing countries—Jamaica, Guinea, Guyana, and Surinam—but even so, developed countries produce almost as much as these four.

The years following the 1973 and 1974 commodity boom were not good ones for LDC hard-minerals producers. Not only did real world prices of most of the minerals in Table 19–4 (particularly copper, nickel, and bauxite) decline over that period, but multinationals' search for stability (see Chapter 14) led large mining companies to shift much of their exploration efforts to developed countries, particularly the United States, Canada, and Australia. Plans for new mining capacity in copper were cancelled in several LDCs, and large known deposits of nickel and bauxite have remained untouched in countries as diverse as Indonesia, Brazil, and Bolivia, while copper mines in Zambia and Zaire sold their ore at prices below extraction costs from 1978 through 1982.

TROPICAL TIMBER RESOURCES

World trade in tropical hardwood timber is very substantial; every log harvested and exported came from the natural tropical forests of developing countries in Asia, Africa, and Latin America. At the peak of world demand in 1979, the total value of LDC exports of tropical timber exceeded $5 billion. Two countries dominate this market: Malaysia and Indonesia. In the early eighties, both Indonesia and Malaysia by themselves exported more tropical timber than all of Africa and Latin America combined.[2]

The Economic Value of Tropical Forests

Timber in general is ordinarily viewed as a renewable resource. This is clearly evident for the great beech forests of Germany and the vast stands of pines found all over North America. Tropical hardwood logs are also renewable in principle; left alone a cut-over tract will ultimately yield new adult stems, although not necessarily of the same species extracted. But although tropical *timber* may be renewable, it is not altogether clear that natural tropical *forests* are renewable.[3] At recent rates of utilization of the tropical forests in LDCs, the world runs a serious risk of a future shortage of tropical forests, even though there is not in any sense a present or potential world-wide shortage of *wood*. This is a serious issue not so much for reasons of future supplies

2. Malcolm Gillis, "Malaysia: Public Policies Resource Management and The Tropical Forest in Sabah, Peninsular Malaysia and Sarawak," forthcoming in *Public Policy and the Misuse of Resources,* Malcolm Gillis and Robert Repetto, eds. (New York: Cambridge University Press, 1987).

3. It is not even clear that tropical *timber* logs should be treated as a "renewable" resource like pine, oak, or beech. Several factors have led many forest specialists to classify this resource as semi-renewable. These factors include: (1) the long growing cycle (40–150 years) for most species of logs harvested; (2) the fragile ecology of the tropical forest; and (3) except for teak, the widespread lack of success in inducing regeneration of harvested species.

of hardwood logs for furniture, plywood, and wood chips, but because unlike oil and hard mineral deposits, stands of virgin tropical timber have economic values well in excess of the value of the resource that might be extracted.

The tropical forest is first an important source of nonwood products, in addition to the economic value of the commercial logs. Valuable fats, medicinal herbs, aromatic herbs, oils, barks, flowers, and chemicals are available in the tropical forest; they may be removed without cutting down the trees. In Indonesia, the value of nonwood products from the forest in 1981 and 1982 was about one-eighth the value of the wood taken for logs. The income from nonwood products is an important source of income for local indigenous rural populations. In addition, the virgin tropical forest has been a major source of fruit trees. Many commercial fruits important in world markets were native to the tropical forests of Asia and Africa. Cinchona bark, so critical as a source of quinine for malaria control in the last century, comes from trees in the tropical forest. In the future, the tropical forest will be an extremely important source of genetic material, both plant and animal. More than half the world's species of plants, animals, and insects are native to the tropical forest.

The wood and nonwood values of the tropical forest are clearly tangible. But the tropical forest is also a source of vital protective services. These include protection of soils, climate, animal habitat, and species diversity from the effects of erosion, salinization, fire, and floods. The economic value of these services is no less tangible, but far less measurable, than those flowing from the production of wood and nonwood forest products. But the protective services provided by these vast, but steadily diminishing, tracts of natural forest are in immediate danger. The reason for this threat is that historically there has been stress upon using the wood and land in tropical forest stands for production of logs and, after forest clearing, plantation products. Government policies in virtually all countries have been geared away from maintaining the economic value of the forests' protective function and of sustaining the forests' capabilities for producing nonwood products.

The problem, then, is not simply the clash of *economic* with broader *social* values. Rather, we find conflict at a more elementary level: conflict between the economic value of wood and plantation products, and the economic value of nonwood products and the forests' productive services. The conflict has been consistently resolved in favor of the former.

Dimensions of the Problem

The bad news concerning the future of tropical forests is that deforestation rates have been high and are rising throughout the world, particularly in Asia and Africa. By 1984, Ghana was almost fully bereft of virgin forest; Haiti is essentially deforested. Thailand, of all places, now imports teak, its majestic teak forests having succumbed to loggers and commercial agriculture. Even so, annual deforestation rates in LDCs are *not yet on the average* disastrously high: about 0.6 percent of the world's tropical forests vanished each year in the early eighties. But in several countries, including Malaysia, the rate has been three to four times as high, and in the Ivory Coast, the deforestation rate in the early eighties was at 7.0 percent per year, ten times that for LDCs in general. In Indonesia, more than 100 percent of the productive forest area had been awarded to logging concessionaires by 1984. Fire in the moist rain forest in logged-over areas in Indonesia burned an area the size of Belgium in 1983 alone, as well as an almost equally vast area in neighboring East Malaysia.

Even the good news is not good: deforestation rates in such important forest nations as Zaire and Gabon have been very low through 1985. But the reasons have been political instability in Zaire, precluding any major foreign investments in logging and plantations there, and inaccessibility to most of Gabon's timber stands. At least in Gabon this situation will change dramatically upon the completion of the multi-billion dollar trans-Gabon railway in 1987. A major purpose of the railway is to get at the timber.

Rapid deforestation rates in particular countries have ben associated with long-term drought (Haiti), flooding of downstream communities when catchments have been cut over (Thailand, Malaysia), and major forest fires (Malaysia, Indonesia). Usually not taken into account is the permanent loss of nonwood product capacities and the loss of numerous species of birds and insects, and the heavy silting of formerly perennial rivers (Indonesia).

Causes of Deforestation

In the early seventies, environmental groups focused most blame for excessive rates of deforestation in tropical forests upon large multinational timber firms. While these enterprises did contribute to deforestation in a few countries for a few years, the accusations were largely incorrect, and served for over a decade to divert world attention from the basic causes of the problem. The truth is that large multinationals were responsible for a very small fraction of logging in the tropical forests of Asia, Africa, and Latin America. Local firms dominate logging in Malaysia, the Philippines, Indonesia, and Ghana. In 1981 there was not a single large multinational wood products company operating in Indonesia, then the world's biggest producer. Although logging activities by local firms have been a significant source of deforestation in the tropical forest, they are by no means the most important.

There are four basic causes of rapid deforestation of the world's tropical forest. They are, in descending order of importance: poverty; ignorance; the nature of property rights in the virgin forest; and commercial use of the forest, by loggers and for conversion of natural forests to other uses (rubber and palm oil plantations in Asia, cattle ranches in Latin America).

A recent exhaustive survey by the United Nations Food and Agricultural Organization (FAO) has made it abundantly clear that in most LDCs, the prime cause of deforestation is the practice of **shifting cultivation.**[4] Shifting

---

4. Comprehensive surveys of deforestation were undertaken by dozens of people under the FAO project. The surveys have been published for each region (Asia, Africa, and Latin America). Titles are FAO, *Forest Resources of Tropical Asia* (Rome: United Nations, 1981); FAO, *Forest Resources of Tropical Africa* (Rome: United Nations, 1981); and FAO, *Forest Resources of Tropical Latin America* (Rome: United Nations, 1981).

cultivation involves a variety of activities that, when carried out on the scale of the past fifteen years, are immensely destructive to both the productive and protective values of the forest. A common form of shifting cultivation is slash-and-burn agriculture. (See Chapter 18.) The forest is cut down, burned, and the exposed soil planted with food crops until exhausted, usually within two or three years. In virtually all countries, the principal driving force behind shifting cultivation is *poverty.* Where rural incomes are very low, as in much of Africa, it is most widespread; where rural incomes are relatively high, as in Penisular Malaysia (Malaya), shifting cultivation practices are uncommon.

The world scientific community, not to mention the world body politic, has extremely limited information about the fragile ecology of tropical forests, so that there are still wide zones of *ignorance* on many critical issues. Even in places where scientific information on regeneration, fruiting, transplantation and soils is fairly extensive, as in Malaysia, much of the information is site-specific, of little value in the husbandry of forest stands elsewhere. Characteristics of tropical forests not only differ from region to region and from country to country, but often *within* countries. The natural tropical forests of Peninsular Malaysia are different from the forests of Ivory Coast or Ghana, but they are also different in many important respects from the forest endowment of East Malaysia (Sabah and Sarawak). Research on tropical forest biology has probably been even more limited in the past twenty years than it was fifty years ago. Much of the research that has been done is inaccessible to scientists who might utilize it. Further, forest husbandry methods developed for the temperate forests of North America and Europe are largely irrelevant to the world's tropical forests. For all of these reasons, policymakers have little or no idea of the long-term consequences of their decisions on use of the forest for logging, plantations, or resettlement programs.

According to the recent comprehensive assessments of the FAO, over 80 percent of the **closed forest** area (the largest share of the still largely undisturbed forest area) are public (government-owned) lands.[5] In most countries, access to this land is largely unrestricted. These conditions constitute fertile ground for the phenomenon known as the "tragedy of the commons."[6] Because property rights to the natural forest are vested in governments, the forests tend to be viewed as common property, owned by no one in particular. When this is so, and when access to the forest is open, incentives to maintain and preserve the economic and social value of the forest are virtually absent. Since no one has a vested interest in preserving these values, the resource endowment tends to deteriorate rapidly. These tendencies are exacerbated by governments which, when assigning logging rights in the forest, restrict the number of years of the license to a period (typically ten years)

---

5. **Closed forests,** found in humid and semi-humid regions, are those in which tree crowns and other growth are so thick that sunlight cannot reach the ground, preventing the development of grass cover. **Open forests** are typical in drier regions, such as in many African nations. As the name implies, light can reach the ground, allowing grass cover to develop.

6. The term comes from the experience in many countries, including Colonial New England, with common pastures for grazing of animals. Because property that belongs to everyone belongs to no one, the commons were soon overgrazed and unfit for their intended purpose.

well below the growing cycle of trees remaining in the forest (typically sixty to eighty years). Consequently, loggers have no incentives to avoid needless destruction of smaller trees during the harvest, since their rights to the trees will expire long before the trees mature. As a result, damages to stands in cut-over tracts in several Asian nations have been in excess of 50 percent of the unlogged trees left by loggers.[7]

In a very few countries, **commercial utilization** of the tropical forest has been the principal cause of deforestation. Commercial utilization embraces land-clearing for plantation crops and cattle ranching (agro-conversion) as well as logging. Conversions to agriculture have been particularly important in the Amazon Basin and Malaysia. In Penisular Malaysia, such conversions were responsible for 89 percent of total deforestation from 1976 to 1981, according to the FAO.

Logging per se has not been an important cause of deforestation in very many countries. However, logging activities play a significant indirect role in deforestation: logging roads and land-clearing by logging firms make the forest much more accessible to the shifting cultivators that are the prime cause of deforestation around the world.

Remedies

While containing valuable fiber and non-fiber products not found elsewhere, the forests are also an important regulator of the world's climate, and the home of most plant and animal species of the planet. Subsidies to curtail exploitation, paid by high-income industrial countries to low-income LDCs with tropical forest endowments, may be in order. This is because the entire world, not just forest countries, has a major stake in the continued existence of large areas of tropical forest. Implementing such subsidies involves political and negotiating skills that, up to now, have not been much in evidence anywhere.

One proven method of at least slowing down the rate of deforestation is by making it more expensive. Higher taxes on log exports and fewer government subsidies on agricultural conversions represent two important ways to make world consumers bear higher costs for degradation of tropical forest endowments. These policies are under the control of LDC governments.

Until very recently however, LDC policies provided very strong signals for very rapid utilization of tropical forest resources. A recent study (sponsored by the World Resources Institute) of over a dozen LDCs with major endowments of tropical forests, concluded that governments, as owners of forest resources, systematically sold the resources at excessively low prices. Although some improvement was noted for the period after 1978, it remains true that government taxes on forest products are too low to compensate for the social costs involved in rapid deforestation. It also remains true that many governments continue to offer heavy direct and indirect subsidies to developers of plantation agriculture and cattle ranches, particularly in Latin America. Both activities require forest clearing on a massive scale. It can be

7. Gillis, "Malaysia: Public Policies Resource Management," pp. 79–82.

shown without doubt that these subsidies, particularly for cattle ranching in the cleared forest, are, while privately profitable for the developers, socially unprofitable: without the subsidies, the lands would not have been cleared. Many of the lands thus deforested have been sold or abandoned, even as new lands are cleared for the tax benefits they offer.

In sum, long-term salvation of the world's valuable tropical forest endowments must necessarily involve support from consumer countries, perhaps including subsidies for forest preservation. But in the short to medium term, policy reform in nations with tropical forest endowments is essential if the economic and social values of these natural assets are to be maintained at anything near their present levels.

RENTS AND RETURNS IN NATURAL-RESOURCE PROJECTS

Resource Rents

Commercial accumulations of nonrenewable resources within the borders of any country are particularly valuable to that country because they involve potential surplus value over and above the costs of labor and capital used to find and extract them. In resource economics this surplus value is called **rent.** While advanced resource economics treatises show that resource rents depend on a complex set of relationships involving the time path of extraction, rate of interest, and risk considerations, we present here a more prosaic, but still serviceable, view of the rent concept. There are actually three types of rent associated with commercial resource deposits. First, there is a **scarcity rent,** defined as any return accruing to any production factor in inelastic supply. Scarcity rents are not confined to natural resources; they can be received by sports figures blessed with extraordinary strength or speed, or by concert violinists possessing an unusual combination of musical skills and dexterity. Like natural resources, such talents are also scarce and in inelastic supply. Lacking these rare talents, the sports figures and violinists might be qualified only as security guards and music teachers. The earnings they receive in excess of salaries for security guards or teachers are called rents.

Geological processes do not produce large numbers of readily accessible deposits, nor do soil and climate conditions everywhere favor the rise of dense forests. Thus resources are scarce. Indeed, at any given time a particular natural resource is in perfectly inelastic supply. And ignoring exploration costs to keep the presentation simple, the cost of a resource in the ground is zero, as it was left by nature at no cost to society. Because in the typical LDC situation government owns the natural resource, it may dispose of it as it sees fit. Natural-resource firms will be prepared to bid for rights to extract the resource.

To understand the nature of scarcity rent, let us consider a mineral to be called monzanium. Assume initially that there is only one use for monzanium, say, in making ball bearings, and also assume that all monzanium deposits are of uniform size and quality (i.e., they are homogeneous). Then, assuming a competitive market, the demand curve for monzanium deposits (*DD* in Figure 19-1) is the value of the marginal product schedule of mon-

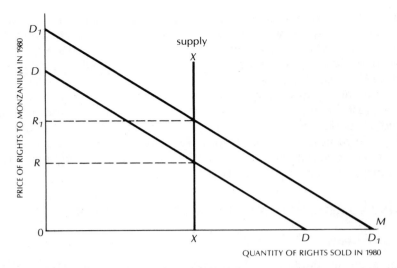

FIGURE 19-1 **Scarcity and Differential Rent for Monzanium Deposits.** Scarcity rent is depicted by *OR*, and the differential rent (for higher quality deposits) is *OR₁* minus *OR*.

zanium in ball-bearing production. If, in 1980, monzanium deposits are very plentiful and easily accessible, then (ignoring exploration costs) OD_1 deposits will be employed, and the government will receive no rents from firms that might bid for mining rights. But if monzanium is scarce relative to demand for it, and also in inelastic supply as shown by the supply curve in Figure 19-1, then each of the OX deposits available in 1980 will earn a "scarcity" rent equal to OR.

In the real world, however, resource deposits are not homogeneous; some deposits are of higher quality, or can be more cheaply mined. Bidders for rights to extract monzanium will pay more for rights to the deposits of better quality. Let us assume two deposit qualities, indicating demand for poorer deposits as DD and demand for better deposits as D_1D_1. With supply of monzanium still at XX, then OR_1 is the rent paid to each deposit of high quality and the lower-quality deposit will receive OR in rent. The rent OR may be viewed as a scarcity rent, while the excess of OR_1 over OR may be called **differential resource rent,** reflecting the differential value of the higher quality deposit.

Two types of rent are therefore depicted in Figure 19-1: **scarcity rent** due to the limited inelastic supply of a resource, and **differential rent,** due to the higher quality or lower extraction costs of some deposits relative to others. A third type of rent is often associated with natural-resource activities: **monopoly** (or **oligopoly**) **rent.** Historically, natural-resource extraction has been dominated by large multinational firms, several of which have had sufficient market power to affect world resource prices. For example, INCO of Canada until recently controlled enough of the international nickel market to set nickel prices. DeBeers of South Africa controlled virtually all the world's supply of uncut diamonds for nearly fifty years and clearly exercised monopoly power. Although the monopoly power of the natural-resource multinationals has eroded in recent years, there are still enough barriers to entry in modern, highly capital-intensive mineral and petroleum extraction to generate some monopoly rents, as shown in Figure 19–2.

Suppose that mining of monzanium is dominated by a single profit-maximizing monopoly firm, or, almost the same, by a small group of oligopolists who attempt to maximize joint profits of firms in the industry. If, for a monzanium deposit in any particular country, the resource can be extracted at constant marginal costs (a simplifying cost assumption), then average costs will also be constant, as represented in Figure 19–2 by horizontal curve *TT*. As in any average cost curve depicted in microeconomics, included in *AC* is a "normal" return to capital, or simply the opportunity cost of capital.

If demand for monzanium is given as *DD*, we know that associated with any straight-line demand curve such as *DD* is a marginal revenue curve *MR* having exactly twice the slope of *DD* (which is merely an average-revenue curve). Under these conditions then, the monopolist (or the joint profit-maximizing oligopolists) will produce *0H* units of monzanium. This is the level of production that maximizes profit, since only at *0H* production does *MC* of producing monzanium equal *MR* from sales. Each unit of monzanium will sell for *0E*. Economic profit per unit is *0E-0T*, or the excess return over per-unit average cost inclusive of a normal return to capital. Total economic profit is the shaded rectangle *TEFG*. This is identical to monopoly rent, defined as a surplus return over and above the costs of labor and capital used to extract the resource.

Rents, whether scarcity, differential, or monopoly, have a very special characteristic. By definition a rent is a return in excess of that required to attract factors of production to an activity. There are no laws, economic or otherwise, that can specify who has a "right" to rents arising from natural

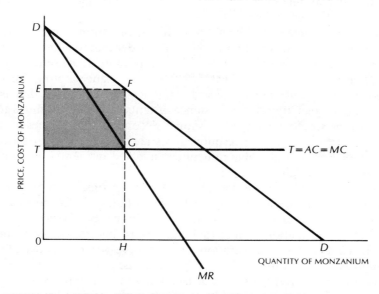

FIGURE 19–2 Monopoly or Oligopoly Rent in the Monzanium Industry. The shaded area *TEFG* represents economic profit, or the monopoly or oligopoly rent for monzanium.

resources. The rents may accrue to investors in LDC resource projects; if they are multinationals, the rents will flow to stockholders abroad. Alternatively, the host LDC government may take steps to capture the rents through taxation or through direct involvement in the project. The central point, however, is that full capture of rents by the host country will not affect the behavior of the extractive firm, be it national or foreign. Only when government efforts go beyond extraction of rents and impinge on the "normal" return to capital invested by the firm will the firm consider shutting down operations. That is, the government, through taxes or other devices, could appropriate 50 or 100 percent of the rents represented by the shaded area *TEFG* in Figure 19–2 without affecting either the price or the production of the firm.

Public Policy and Rent Capture

If capture of rents in natural-resource activities in LDCs were as simple a matter as depicted above, many resource-rich countries would be substantially wealthier than at present. In fact rents turn out to be easy to describe, difficult to identify in any given setting, and almost impossible to capture fully. They are difficult to identify with any precision for several reasons. First, modern extractive activity is a highly complex undertaking, both in an engineering and a managerial sense. Second, an accurate assessment of rent in oil and hard-mineral projects requires accurate delineation of reserves. Inasmuch as these are not always easily verifiable even with modern technology, magnitudes of potential resource rents in any project are never fully knowable. Rents are impossible to capture fully because many steps that a government may take to appropriate rents may, and often do, induce extractive firms to conceal them, whether by transfer pricing or other devices described in Chapter 14.

Nevertheless, there have been enough lessons from natural-resource investments in enough countries in the past few decades to allow one or two safe generalizations about rent and rent capture in an LDC setting, or, for that matter, in Alaska or the North Sea. First, experience around the world has shown that public policy toward nonrenewable resources that is not based on an appreciation of the existence of rents is *perforce* inimical to the interests of the society owning the resource. Second, public policies purporting to secure full capture of resource rents are not to be taken seriously, owing to the very considerable difficulties involved in identifying and collecting rents in any given project.

By now dozens of countries have learned these lessons, often only by trial and error. Over the period 1960 to 1980, the attitudes of LDC governments toward rent capture have evolved steadily, and this has been reflected in both the design and execution of their policies toward natural-resource endowments. It is only a slight exaggeration to say that the prime objective of natural-resources policy in most LDCs only two decades ago was a very simple one: secure for the host country at least some share of resource rents from exploitation of natural resources by the large multinational firms that then dominated the world resource picture. Attaining that modest goal depended almost entirely on tax policy. Employment, regional development, and other expected benefits from natural-resource development have historically been relatively insignificant in most LDCs, primarily because of the marked capital intensity of most extractive activity. (See the discussion of linkages in Chapter 15.) By the end of the 1960s, emphasis in many LDCs had shifted toward efforts to minimize the returns of the multinationals, and by the close of the 1970s, to the much sounder objective of maximizing net host country returns, by no means the same thing as minimizing multinationals' profits, given the type of risk considerations (both geological and market risks) always present in natural-resource exploration.

531

RENTS AND
RETURNS IN
NATURAL-
RESOURCE
PROJECTS

Even by the mid-1970s the changes in tax policy and tax administration sketched earlier had, in a number of LDCs, converted the natural-resource sectors into very significant revenue producers. Natural resources furnished between 5 and 15 percent of total central government receipts in Thailand, Colombia, Honduras, Panama, Peru, and the Philippines, between 15 and 25 percent in Chile and Malaysia, in excess of 25 percent in Ecuador, Mexico, Jamaica, Liberia, Zaire, and Zambia, and well in excess of 50 percent in Bolivia, Indonesia, Gabon, the Malaysian state of Sabah, Papua New Guinea, and New Caledonia.

Recent measures for facilitating host country capture of resource rents include "windfall" or "excess" profits taxes and transfer of "free" equity shares in natural resource projects to the governments involved. The measures have met with a considerable degree of success. The percentage share of host country taxes in the value or resource production or in resource profits has been typically half again—and sometimes twice—levels common in the early 1960s, except, in general, for uranium. Host country exceptions are former French colonies such as Gabon, Niger, and Chad. This indicates a very marked tightening of terms available to investors.

Rising host countries' shares have been particularly evident in the case of oil. Host countries' shares of profits in oil were never much more than 10 to 15 percent before 1930. But by 1980 there were numerous instances in which this share had surpassed 80 percent. In 1980 Malaysia had managed to capture 80 percent of production and 98 percent of the profits in oil production. By 1980 even in countries that do not employ windfall profits taxes or windfall royalties in oil, the government's share in the value of oil produced was close to 70 percent. For many other non-OPEC producers, as well as some OPEC members like Indonesia, host countries' shares of between 75 and 85 percent of value and 80 percent and 90 percent of profits were common before the sharp decline in oil prices after 1983.

Substantial changes also occurred in taxation of tropical timber, but not until the latter part of the 1970s, after decades in which host governments seemed to overlook the presence of rents in timber. Tax adjustments by Indonesia and the Malaysian state of Sabah, the two dominant producers, in 1978 to 1980 resulted in sizable increments in revenues. The share of taxes in gross value of timber exports doubled to 29 percent in Indonesia and to 53 percent in Sabah.

Another measure of host country benefits from natural-resource projects is provided by the concept of **retained value,** used in several studies focusing on the division of benefits from foreign investment in hard-minerals extraction. While the measure by no means represents a perfect method of assessing host country benefits from such activity, movements in the ratio of retained value to gross natural-resource exports are indicative of host country performance in capturing larger shares of resource rent over time. Simply put, retained value is defined as the total of all revenues from natural-resource projects retained in the host country, as shown in Equation 19–1:

$$RV = W_d + C_d + DP(1 - Z) + K_d + T_d + Q_d, \quad [19\text{–}1]$$

where RV = retained value; W_d = labor income for host country workers employed in natural resources projects; C_d = proportion of income of expatriate workers spent locally; DP = domestic procurement of goods and services for natural resource projects; Z = percentage import content of DP; K_d = capital income for domestic shareholders (including governments) in natural resource projects; T_d = taxes, royalties, and other fiscal receipts received by host country government; and Q_d = miscellaneous payments received in host country.

Retained value is itself a fraction of total proceeds *(R)* gained from the sale of natural-resource production, where R is broken up into components as given in Equation 19–2:

$$R = M + I + L + P + W_f + U + RV, \quad [19\text{–}2]$$

where M = cost of imports: I = interest cost on external loans and credits; L = loan repayments; P = profits remitted abroad; W_f = salaries of expatriates accruing abroad; U = unidentified items; and RV = retained value as defined in Equation 19–1 above.

The proportion RV/R was, prior to the mid-1960s, typically less than 50 percent in many LDCs with significant foreign investment in natural resources. For example, for Peruvian copper mining in 1960 to 1965, retained value was but 30 percent of gross export proceeds in large projects operated by foreign enterprises. In this instance, foreign firms received one or more forms of special tax incentives, usually in the form of income tax holidays of five years or more. The capital and import intensity of modern mining generally means that the nontax components of retained value are relatively small, and that efforts to secure significant increases in retained value must of necessity focus on tax policy. Peru managed to increase substantially the ratio of retained value to total copper exports from 30 percent in 1960 to 1965, to 50 percent in 1966 to 1972, primarily through higher taxes obtained in renegotiation of its agreements with foreign firms. In the latter period taxes accounted for just over 60 percent of retained value in the largest Peruvian copper project. In the mining industries of both Bolivia and Sierra Leone, taxes were responsible for over 45 percent of retained value, and in the West African tropical forestry in the early 1970s, taxes accounted for as much as 75 percent of retained value in forest projects mounted by multinationals. In Indonesian tropical timber in the late 1970s, very substantial increases in export taxes and other fiscal levies resulted in a very sharp increase in retained value, from less than 20 percent of gross timber-export earnings in 1975 to perhaps 50 percent by 1982.

Many of the resource tax adjustments depicted in the foregoing section were undertaken in the belief that the burden of higher taxes on LDC natural-resource exports could be easily shifted to foreign consumers. Indeed, tax increases have often been seen as the preferred tool for securing the aims of the various attempts to form "commodity cartels" discussed in Chapter 15. Such efforts were heavily influenced by OPEC's apparent success in inflicting higher prices for oil upon foreign consumers in the 1970s.

Taxes on nonresidents are popular with governments everywhere. In the United States in the mid-1970s, New Mexico and Montana drastically increased taxes on uranium and coal, respectively, largely out of a conviction that since virtually all production of these resources was exported out of state, the taxes imposed upon them could be fully exported as well. Nearly all of Jamaican bauxite is exported. In 1974 that government increased taxes on bauxite by 700 percent, also in the belief that foreign consumers would pay. Indonesia and the Malaysian state of Sabah more than doubled taxes on timber exports with the same intention.

To what extent can expectations of tax exporting be realized? Attempts to export natural-resource taxes to foreign consumers can be successful, even in the short run, only under certain rarely satisfied conditions. And even when the taxes can be fully exported to foreign consumers in the short run, this might not be in a country's long-term interests. With care, however, resource taxes may be exported to foreign stockholders and may have little effect on resource investment in the host country, provided the taxes do not go beyond full taxation of rents.

To illustrate, let us consider a hypothetical case involving the small mythical country of Binaro. This nation is a significant producer of the mineral monzanium, the value of which typically exceeds $100 million per year. All monzanium produced is exported by large multinationals operating in monzanium mining. In 1980 Binaro faced a budgetary crisis involving a projected deficit equal to 3 percent of GDP, or U.S. $5 million. The country had for years imposed a tax of $2 per pound on monzanium, which was about 1 percent of the export value. With an additional $10 tax per pound the budget deficit would be covered, provided the tax did not reduce monzanium output. The Minister of Finance enthusiastically recommended that the president approve the quintupling of the tax, on grounds that foreign consumers would bear the entire burden in the form of higher prices. Our task is to determine whether this expectation was justified.

Five basic factors determine whether a country like Binaro can expect short-run success in attempts to export taxes on monzanium, or any other resource, to foreign consumers. They are, in order of importance: (1) Binaro's monzanium should have a high share in the relevant export market; (2) the elasticity of supply of Binaro's monzanium should also be high; (3) the elasticity of supply of monzanium from other monzanium-producing countries should be low; (4) the overall elasticity of supply of monzanium for all producers in the relevant market should be high; and (5) the price elasticity of demand for monzanium in the world market should be low.

Given the relevant elasticities, we can find the fraction of Binaro's $10 per pound tax that will be exported by using Equation 19–3:

$$T_c = \frac{E_s}{E_s + E_d} \cdot \frac{ae_{st}}{ae_{st} + (1 - a)e_{sn}}, \qquad [19\text{–}3]$$

where T_c = the percentage share of Binaro's additional $10 per pound tax shifted to foreign consumers in the form of higher prices for monzanium; E_s = overall elasticity of supply for monzanium (all producers) in the relevant market; E_d = the price elasticity of demand for monzanium in the relevant market, taken as a positive number; a = the share of Binaro's monzanium in the relevant market; $(1 - a)$ = the share of other producers in the relevant market; e_{st} = the elasticity of supply of monzanium from Binaro; and e_{sn} = the elasticity of supply of monzanium from other producing nations. Subscript "t" stands for taxing country and "n" for non-taxing country.

Suppose that in the case at hand the relevant short-run elasticities and market shares are as follows: $E_s = 1.5$; $E_d = -0.2$; $e_{st} = 1.0$; $e_{sn} = 2.0$; $a = 25\%$; and $1 - a = 75\%$. These elasticities are typical for resources such as oil, coal, tin, and uranium. Then,

$$T_c = \frac{1.5}{1.5 + 0.2} \cdot \frac{0.25(1.0)}{0.25(1.0) + 0.75(2.0)} = 12.6\%.$$

In this case, then, Binaro would be able to shift only 13 percent of the tax to foreign consumers in the short term.[8] This result does not necessarily mean that the increased export tax was contrary to Binaro's interests. The portion of the tax not shifted to foreign consumers (87 percent) must be paid by someone. In fact the unshifted taxes will reduce rents received by any or all of several affected parties: (1) the owner of the deposit; (2) labor in the Binaro monzanium industry; (3) shareholders in firms extracting monzanium in Binaro.

To the extent that any of these economic agents are not residents of Binaro, that portion of the tax not shifted to foreign consumers could also reduce their returns, thereby exporting the burden of the tax in this manner. But we have seen that in most LDCs the government itself is the owner of the property right to the resource, and in virtually all LDCs labor policies heavily favor the use of domestic, not foreign, labor. In such circumstances significant tax exporting, if it is to occur at all, must take the form of reduced returns to foreign shareholders of foreign extractive firms.

Not all countries, however, are as poorly situated to export taxes to foreign consumers as in the case of Binaro. Equation 19–3 can be used to verify that the greater the market share (a) of the taxing country, the greater the proportion of export taxes that may be shifted to foreign consumers. Dominance by the taxing nation, i.e., the share of the market taken by the nation's resource, turns out to be the critical factor in exporting taxes to consumers. Even if the

8. Strictly speaking, any result derived by use of the formula is valid only for relatively small taxes imposed in situations where no taxes applied before. But it is indicative of the results obtained under typical real-world conditions. See Charles E. McLure, "Market Dominance and the Exporting of State Taxes," *Natural Tax Journal* 34, no. 4 (December 1981).

Binaro would still be unable to export a sizable fraction of the export tax to foreign consumers, since T_c can never exceed (a), Binaro's market share, which is only 25 percent. This is because Binaro's market share determines the extent to which it (as opposed to all producers of monzanium) faces elastic or inelastic demand for the resource. On the other hand, if elasticity or demand for monzanium were at unity, five times greater than in the first example, and Binaro's market share were at 75 percent, only three times as high, then Binaro would be able to export almost 36 percent of its export tax to foreign consumers, given the same supply elasticities as used earlier.

There are real-world examples of short-run success in exporting taxes on mineral or agricultural products; there are not many examples of long-run success. For a time during the 1960s Pakistan managed to export substantial taxes on jute. Over time the higher prices for Pakistani jute led users to switch to synthetic substitutes and at the same time encouraged vastly expanded plantings of jute in other countries, notably Thailand.[9] That is, in the long run, both E_d and E_s for jute were high. By 1970 the Pakistani jute industry was in a perilous situation, from which it has never fully recovered.

DUTCH DISEASE

Three populous LDCs—Nigeria, Mexico, and Indonesia—provide typical examples of what has become popularly known as **Dutch disease,** an affliction (outlined earlier in Chapter 15) of the relatively affluent large- and middle-size nations exporting large quantities of oil, natural gas, or both. For virtually all of the postwar period until 1975 the Netherlands enjoyed remarkable prosperity in almost all respects. Inflation rarely exceeded 3 percent per year, GNP growth rarely dropped below 5 percent, and unemployment fluctuated around 1 percent of the labor force, very low by U.S. standards. Much of Dutch prosperity was due to the fact that the traditional export sector of this very open economy was highly competitive with the rest of the world. This was particularly true of the Dutch agricultural sector, which accounted for a third of all its merchandise exports from 1950 to 1975.

In the early 1960s substantial reserves of natural gas were found in the Netherlands. By 1975 gas exports had risen to about 10 percent of total exports, and the Netherlands enjoyed a surplus (on current account) of 4 percent of GNP. The proceeds of taxes on gas were used to fund drastically increased government spending, particularly welfare spending, but even higher taxes from gas proved insufficient to finance them. One result was a surge in inflation rates, from 2 percent in 1970 to 10 percent in 1975, tapering gradually to 4 percent in 1980. From 1973 through 1978 the inflow of foreign exchange from gas exports bouyed up the exchange rate, as the Dutch guilder appreciated by about 30 percent relative to its major trading partners. As a result traditional exporters were faced with a double blow: ris-

9. Robert Repetto, "Optimal Export Taxes in the Short and Long Run: Pakistan's Jute Export Policy," *Quarterly Journal of Economics* 86, no. 3 (August 1972): 396–406.

ing domestic costs coupled with drastically lower guilder earnings from each dollar's worth of exports. Unemployment rose sharply from 1973 through 1978 as the relatively labor-intensive export sector stagnated, and GNP growth dropped from the 5 percent rates of the 1960s to 1 to 2 percent by the end of the decade. Clearly the gas "bonanza" brought mixed blessings to the Netherlands, just as the oil bonanza did for several large LDCs, including Mexico, Nigeria, and Indonesia.

Oil-Fired Development: Three Case Studies

Nigeria

Before the first oil boom in 1973 and 1974, Nigeria's economy was one of the most prosperous in Africa, with agriculture as the leading economic sector. The nation was a major exporter of cocoa and a leading supplier of other very labor-intensive, smallholder agricultural products, such as palm oil and groundnuts. Strong export performance in these commodities and in cotton and rubber keyed major increases in rural incomes in a large country with a rapidly growing population just behind Brazil's. The manufacturing sector grew rapidly as well, rising from a very small base before independence to 5 percent of GDP by 1964 and 9 percent of GDP by 1976, just after the beginning of the first oil boom. Throughout the 1960s, even through a costly civil war ending in 1969, domestic inflation was held to an average rate of less than 3 percent, and growth in governmental expenditure was held closely in check. By 1980 Nigeria's per-capita GDP, at $1,010, was the fourth highest in sub-Saharan Africa, having grown at 4.1 percent per year since 1960.

If growth in per-capita income were the only measure of improved national well-being, Nigeria's record from 1960 to 1980 would appear to be one of unmitigated prosperity. But surface appearances can be deceiving. By 1980 the labor-intensive agricultural sector lay nearly in ruins. The share of agricultural exports in total exports had fallen from 90 percent in 1960 to only 8 percent in 1980, while the share of agriculture in GDP dropped precipitously, from almost two-thirds in 1960 to one-fifth by 1980. Nigeria, a net food exporter in the 1960s, spent almost $3 billion on food imports in 1980. Inflation surged to an annual rate of 18 percent for the decade ending in 1980, as government spending grew at roughly double the rate of GDP growth just in the period 1972 to 1977. Throughout the whole period, the government allowed the exchange rate to *appreciate* gradually against the dollar, as the value of the Nigerian naira rose from U.S. $1.52 in 1973 to $1.88 in 1981.

When the world oil market softened after 1981, the exchange rate did begin to depreciate in nominal terms, falling from 1.88 naira to the dollar in 1983 to naira 1.31 in 1984. But domestic inflation continued at a rapid pace relative to the rest of the world. While the Consumer Price Index in the U.S. increased by 2.3 times over the period 1973 through 1984, it rose by 7.3 times in Nigeria. As a result Nigerian exports became increasingly less competitive: the *real* exchange rate *continued* to appreciate even as the nominal rate declined slowly. (The real exchange rate is equal

to the nominal rate times the Nigerian Price Index over the U.S. Price Index.) By 1984, the naira real exchange rate was 2.7 times higher than at the beginning of the first oil boom in 1973.

This sharp rise in the real value of the naira placed tremendous pressure on local producers, and led to declining values of the only remaining significant agricultural export (cocoa) as well as industrial production. Real GDP per capita in 1983 was over 20 percent lower than in 1977. The government refused to devalue the naira until a new government took over in a coup in early 1984, and only then by 20 percent, and economic conditions continued to worsen in early 1986. The external public debt stood at $24 billion and inflation remained unchecked.

Mexico

Mexico enjoyed vibrant growth across virtually all economic sectors from 1960 to 1970, and observers began speaking of the "Mexican model" in glowing terms. Real GDP grew by over 7 percent per annum over this period because of very strong performance in both the agricultural sector (3.9 percent growth) and in industry (9.3 percent growth). By 1976 growth in Mexican GDP had slowed somewhat, to 5.5 percent, and large increases in public spending had led to deficits that pushed inflation from annual rates of 4 percent in the 1960s to close to 20 percent for the period 1971 to 1976. These developments led to a devaluation of the peso of over 50 percent in 1976. Shortly thereafter Pemex, the state oil enterprise, confirmed rumors of truly major oil discoveries in the states of Tabasco and Chiapas, with expected 1980 production capacity in excess of 3 million barrels per day, a rate of output that would place Mexico in the elite company of such OPEC members as Venezuela and Iraq, and ahead of Nigeria and Indonesia. Oil exports, just one percent of total exports in 1973, were by 1978 over 30 percent of exports. Thus in 1978 Mexico seemed poised to return to its previous high growth, and perhaps to enter several decades of vigorous oil-fired development sufficient to propel it into a position as the third wealthiest in the western hemisphere by the end of the century, just after the United States and Canada.

But by 1982 the bright promises of five years earlier had faded badly even though oil exports had risen to 70 percent of exports by then. The beginnings of Mexico's oil boom touched off an explosion in spending by government-owned enterprises, much of which was financed not by oil-export earnings but by foreign borrowing. Mexico's external public debt rose from $15.6 billion in 1976 (U.S. $251 per capita) to a 1982 figure reported to be as high as $66.7 billion (U.S. $1,146 per capita), the largest amount of outstanding debt any developing country had incurred up until that time. Inflation, nearly tamed in 1977 and 1978, had by 1980 surpassed 30 percent and by late 1981 threatened to move above 50 percent per annum in the subsequent year. Worse still, unemployment rose strikingly in the midst of the oil boom. According to several published reports, nearly half of the labor force was either unemployed or underemployed.

From 1976 through 1981 the exchange rate remained near 22 pesos to the dollar in spite of rapid inflation, and the current account deficit reached $13 billion, or 7 percent of GDP, in 1981. Finally, in early 1982, the government devalued the peso by 30 percent. The step turned out to be too little, too late, and in August and September the peso was devalued again. By the end of the year, between 60 and 80 pesos, depending on the transaction, were required to buy one dollar, and the government reluctantly sought emergency help from the IMF.

As in Nigeria, the situation continued to worsen through 1985, after an aborted recovery in 1984. Even before the calamitous earthquake in Mexico City in September 1985, Mexico's economic position was becoming desperate. Capital flight accelerated as wealthy Mexicans shifted their assets to the United States and elsewhere. In 1985, although Mexico allowed the peso to depreciate by 50 percent, most of the beneficial effects were negated by a domestic inflation rate of 64 percent for the year. With a government deficit apparently out of control even before world oil prices fell by a further 50 percent after October 1985, the outlook for Mexico in 1986 was even bleaker than five years earlier. By March of 1986, Mexico had little choice but to turn to substantial outside assistance, in the form of very large loans for reconstruction, from the World Bank and in the form of further debt reschedulings with foreign banks. Years may be required for the country to recover from the economic and natural disasters of recent years.

Indonesia

In 1972 Indonesia had just completed the first stages of economic reconstruction, following a disastrous hyperinflation from 1965 to 1967, after which almost the entire social and economic infrastructure of this densely populated, primarily rural nation lay in shambles. Economic growth, and in particular agricultural production, had rebounded smartly by 1971, and even after a 10 percent devaluation in mid-year, inflation had been reduced to less than 5 percent per annum. When the first oil boom began in late 1973, following the quadrupling of oil prices by OPEC, the country appeared to be well-placed for a decade of very strong economic growth. The ensuing five years were indeed high-growth years, but as in Mexico and Nigeria, the quality of that growth was poor: the income distribution worsened and employment growth stagnated. Inflation spurted to an annual rate of 40 percent in the six months after the first oil shock, returned to a 10 percent rate after a stabilization program in April 1974, and then proceeded at a 20 percent clip through 1977.

By mid-1978, idle capacity in the manufacturing sector was widespread and manufactured exports were virtually nonexistent as rapid domestic inflation, coupled with a constant nominal exchange rate from 1971 to 1978, had made exporting decidedly unprofitable. The combination of inflation and a constant nominal exchange rate had even more depressive effects on the large, much more labor-intensive, agricultural export sector, particularly in rubber, the source of more employment than any other commodity except rice. Still, the country had ample foreign exchange reserves to defend the value of the rupiah, and the business community viewed devaluation as unthinkable.

Nevertheless the Indonesian rupiah was devalued by 50 percent in November 1978, not to protect a precarious foreign exchange reserve situation but primarily to encourage labor-intensive manufactured and agricultural exports. The measure had the desired effects. Although domestic inflation remained at a relatively high 22 percent in 1979, manufactured exports enjoyed explosive growth over the subsequent two years, with some categories growing at annual rates of 300 to 500 percent, albeit from a small base. Although 1979 and 1980 saw still another oil boom, this time taking world oil prices from less than $14 to $38 per barrel, agricultural exports, including rubber, surged as well.

Partly as a consequence of well-timed policy measures such as the 1978 devaluation, partly because of the oil booms, and partly because of remarkable growth in rice production in this heavily rice-consuming nation, the economy grew at an unprecedented annual rate of 7.6 percent over the decade ending in 1980, while inflation dropped to an annual rate of just below world inflation in 1980 and 1981. The nation entered 1982 with a foreign debt one-third as high as that of less populous Mexico, and had developed a sizable economic cushion, in the form of over $10 billion in exchange reserves to cope with any future weakness in the world oil market.

The cushion proved necessary. Slow weakening of oil prices in the next fifteen months threatened to exhaust reserves quickly. Policymakers moved decisively again in 1983, enacting six major economic reforms, including a major devaluation and sweeping tax and financial reform. The measures met with considerable success. Inflation remained under control, non-oil exports expanded sharply, and real economic growth recovered to five percent in 1984. But even the reform package of 1983 may prove insufficient to insulate the economy from the effects of the 50% drop in world oil prices in the first half of 1986 or from major losses in rice production—the major staple—due to insect infestation in that year. The Indonesian experience suggests that even the most deft economic management is not always sufficient in the face of large, unexpected external or internal shocks.

The symptoms of Dutch disease have faded with the decline of world oil prices in recent years, but the after-effects remain. When world oil prices eventually recover, exporting countries may be better able to cope with this malady, having suffered so from 1974 to 1986. In cases of Dutch disease, the resource-exports "tail" wags the "dog" of overall growth and development. Nigeria, Mexico, and Indonesia are not the only countries that suffered from Dutch disease in the 1970s and early 1980s. Ivory Coast, Cameroon, Gabon, and Venezuela are other examples. In some countries with major oil exports and very small populations, the phenomenon takes an extreme form, known as the "Kuwait effect."

An understanding of the Kuwait effect provides insights into diagnosis and treatment of Dutch disease. In Kuwait and other very small oil-exporting nations, such as Qatar, per-capita export earnings from oil, at about $14,000 in both countries in 1982, were large enough to provide every family with a high standard of living, quite apart from any income from labor and capital. In terms of Figure 15–6, the available supply of foreign exchange from oil was so great relative to the demand for foreign exchange that the exchange rate steadily appreciated. In such extreme cases of oil riches, a free market rate of foreign exchange (relative to, say, the U.S. dollar) would tend to be so high that almost nothing else produced in the economy could be profitably exported. Indeed, in such economies practically everything tends to be imported, because the heavily appreciated exchange rate makes imports appear unusually cheap.

In countries like Kuwait most of the labor force was foreign in 1981, and in Qatar 80 percent of the population consists of expatriates who have migrated to do work that Qataris find unattractive. There were clearly no employment problems for Kuwaiti or Qatari nationals in the early eighties, even though many of them may choose not to work. But, as we have seen, in more populous, diversified economies with far less oil wealth per capita, large export earnings from an enclave sector, such as oil or gas, can be a mixed blessing, both in developed countries like Holland and in developing countries like Nigeria and Mexico.

But if there is a "Dutch disease" why is there no "Japanese disease" from equally dramatic expansion in automobile and electronic exports, or no "Singapore disease" when exports of manufactures grow at better than 30 percent for several years, as they did in the early 1970s? The answer lies partly in the enclave nature of oil and gas production. But part of the answer depends on the fact that a far greater proportion of the value of oil and gas exports accrues to government treasuries than is the case for manufactured exports from Singapore or agricultural exports from the Netherlands, Indonesia, or Nigeria.

Unlike the case for enclave oil and gas sectors in Indonesia, Nigeria, or even in the Dutch economy, the manufacturing sectors of such important manufacturing and exporting economies as Korea, Taiwan, or Singapore, are tightly linked with the rest of the economy, and with the external sector as well. If, for whatever reason, inflation in, say, Korea began to run at a rate faster than world inflation, then the exchange rate—whether fixed or freely floating—must soon adjust toward depreciation, or growth in manufactured exports would cease because the double squeeze of higher domestic costs and constant domestic currency earnings per unit of exports would make exporting unattractive (see Chapter 17).

The situation is very different for an enclave-export sector such as oil, because of the presence of easily taxed rents in oil and the weak linkages of most natural-resource sectors with the rest of their economies. Particularly in developing countries, oil exploration, production, and processing uses very little domestic labor or materials. When, for whatever reason, inflation in economies like Indonesia's or Nigeria's exceed world inflation, costs in the oil enclave are affected only slightly. Thus when world inflation is 10 percent, inflation of 20 percent in Taiwan can rapidly ruin its export-oriented manufacturing sector unless the exchange rate is allowed to depreciate. But in an oil-exporter like Indonesia, inflation of even 30 percent will have little impact on the profitability of exporting oil, even if the exchange rate is left untouched. International reserves can then continue to build up in an oil-exporting country, even as non-oil exporters in these countries lay off workers or close their doors in bankruptcy.

Finally, the rents from oil and gas exports make them particularly attractive sources of government revenue. Indonesia depended on oil for over two-thirds of its taxes from 1979 to 1981, Nigeria about 65 percent, Mexico about half, and the Netherlands over 20 percent, with as much as 85 percent of the value of net oil or gas exports siphoned off as taxes. Note that such taxes do not depress household or business spending or income in the same way that higher income or sales taxes would. The deployment of a sudden flood of oil tax revenues plays the pivotal role in cases of Dutch disease. If a high proportion of oil taxes are "sterilized"—not spent on domestic goods, services, or transfer payments—and are kept in overseas government deposits, or are spent on additional imports to diversify the economy, the worst symptoms of Dutch disease may not appear. But increased government spending of a large proportion of oil taxes on items such as drastically increased civil service salaries or—as in the Dutch case—on welfare payments, results in large, direct additions to the money supply that sooner or later lead to accelerated inflation. And with oil revenues propping up the value of the currency in the face of domestic inflation, the by now familiar signs of Dutch disease are soon manifested in higher unemployment and stagnation of the non-oil economy.

Dutch disease is not the inevitable outcome of sudden increases in oil-export earnings. The foregoing discussion suggests two prophylactic measures that LDCs may take: the first is restraint in government spending out of unexpected natural-resource revenues, a particularly appropriate prescription for countries such as Indonesia, Qatar, or Ecuador, where depletion of present oil reserves is likely before the end of the century.

But given that virtually all governments with sizable oil income face very strong pressures to spend most of it, the second remedy is perhaps more realistic, though more difficult: a systematic policy of gradual depreciation of the exchange rate, in the fashion of the "crawling peg" (discussed in Chapter 13), so that inflows of oil revenues and subsequent government spending are not allowed to maim or destroy other export sectors, or to artificially cheapen imports. Such a policy can be best implemented by a series of periodic "mini-devaluations" of the domestic currency against the dollar at intervals of a year or less. This policy allows a country to avoid the inevitable trauma of a major devaluation when a populous oil-exporting country goes for long periods at constant nominal exchange rates (Indonesia and Mexico), or even worse, allows the exchange rate to appreciate over a decade (Nigeria).

Figure 19–3 portrays the essence of policy choices involved in coping with the problems of resource largesse and dependency. The diagram is based on work by C. P. Timmer of Harvard Business School, and involves simulations of the economies of three Pacific Basin oil exporters (Indonesia, Malaysia,

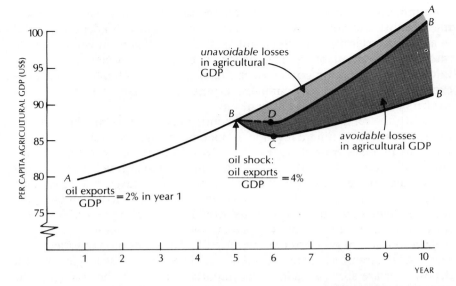

FIGURE 19-3 Effects of Alternative Exchange Rate Policies on Agricultural Growth in Oil-Exporting Economies. The lower, more heavily shaded area shows losses in agricultural production that could be avoided through appropriate devaluations in the exchange rate. The upper, lightly shaded area represents unavoidable losses. *Source:* C. Peter Timmer, "Energy and Structural Change in the Asia-Pacific Region: The Agricultural Sector." (Paper prepared for the 13th Pacific Trade and Development Conference, Manila, January 24–28, 1980, Figure 6.)

Mexico). It shows what may be expected to happen to agriculture in an oil-exporting economy where oil exports are initially (year 1) 2 percent of GDP and then, after five years, rise to 4 percent of GDP as a consequence of a doubling of oil prices. Curve *AA* shows the predicted path of GDP per capita in the agricultural sector in the absence of the doubling of oil prices in year 5. Curve *BCB* shows the path of GDP per capita in the agricultural sector (GDP_{AG}) from year 5 to year 10, when the oil-exporting country *fails* to devalue the exchange rate in the face of significant inflation, over and above world inflation. Curve *BDB* shows the path of GDP_{AG} when, before the end of the sixth year, the oil-exporting country devalues its exchange rate.

In the absence of the oil price-rise, agricultural GDP would grow at a rate of 2.9 percent per year, a healthy rate by international standards. When oil prices double in year 5, agricultural GDP is bound to *fall* in any case. But it falls *less* in the case of an immediate exchange-rate devaluation (*BDB*) than in the absence of devaluation (*BCB*) and then grows at a more rapid rate (4.1 percent per year) than before the oil price increase. By the tenth year, GDP_{AG} is nearly as high with the positive oil shock as it would have been without it. But if the oil-exporting country fails to devalue, the growth rate is only 1.6 percent in year 7.

The lightly tinted area under curve *AA* shows the unavoidable loss over time in agricultural GDP caused by the oil shock. The darker area shows the additional and needless loss in agricultural GDP caused by avoiding devaluation. In four years' time the needless loss reaches 2.5 times the unavoidable loss. Note that the loss compounds over time, suggesting that the longer devaluation is postponed, the worse the effects for the agricultural sector.

Even for relatively oil-rich, populous nations, the type of smothering of the agricultural sector resulting from policies that yield curve *BCB* is not likely to be good for long-run development. This is true even if overall GDP growth remains high, as agricultural stagnation is likely to lead to acute maldistribution in income distribution, accelerated rural-to-urban migration, and heightened future vulnerability to shocks in the world food-market as well.

The principal lesson of this section is that maladies like Dutch disease can be contained by sensible economic management, even when full remission of the disease is impossible. In this way, countries may enjoy more of the benefits and fewer of the problems of resource abundance. When properly used, exchange rate adjustments are important tools of national economic management even when problems arise from the natural resource sector. And even though devaluation in LDCs often leads to more egalitarian income distribution—since it transfers income from the urban sector to the ordinarily poorer rural sector—this policy is often resisted. This has been particularly true in Latin America, according to some analysts. This is because urban workers tend to have, in the words of one, more "political muscle" than do rural dwellers.[10] This urban bias has been much less pronounced in many Asian nations, and may help account for their stronger economic performance since 1960.

10. Sachs, "The LDC Debt Crisis," p. 17.

Industry

The concept of development and the process of industrialization have often been treated as synonymous, ever since the Industrial Revolution enabled Britain to raise its industrial production by 400 percent over the first half of the nineteenth century.[1] From then until the present the dominant criterion for development has been the rise in per-capita incomes brought about largely by industrialization. Earlier chapters, especially those in Parts I and IV, have focused on the relation between development and industrialization. This chapter emphasizes aspects not covered in depth elsewhere.

INDUSTRY AS A LEADING SECTOR

From Chapter 3's discussion of cross-country patterns, we know that higher shares of gross domestic product generated by industry are closely associated with rising income per capita. Figure 20–1 shows this pattern for manufacturing value-added in 1983 for twenty-two large countries (with populations over 25 million) and twenty-one small ones. The trend remains clear: on average for large countries, as income quadruples from $250 to $1,000 per person, manufacturing value-added rises from 14 to 19 percent of GDP. For an average country with per-capita income growing at 3 percent a year, this transition would take forty-six years.

But wide variations are evident. The regression lines in each scatter-dia-

1. E. J. Hobsbawm, *The Pelican Economic History of Britain*, vol. 3, *Industry and Empire* (Baltimore: Penguin Books, 1969).

A. Large Countries

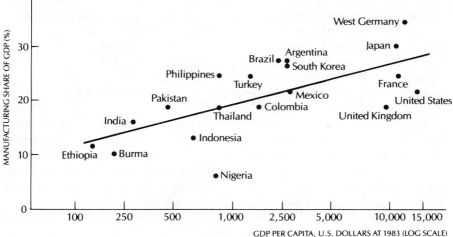

B. Small Countries

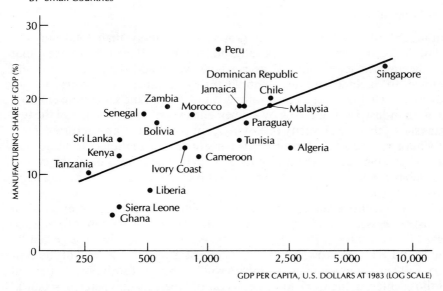

FIGURE 20-1 Manufacturing Share of GDP, Large and Small Countries, 1983. There is a strong tendency for manufacturing value-added to rise as a share of GDP as average income rises, both for large countries (populations over 25 million) and for small ones. But there is considerable variation among countries with different resource endowments and development strategies. *Source:* World Bank, *World Development Report 1985* (New York: Oxford University Press, 1985).

gram explain less than half the variation in country experience.[2] The heavy dependence of Nigeria and Liberia (and of Saudi Arabia, not shown) on mineral exports is evident from their very low manufacturing share, but

2. The association of manufacturing value-added and GNP per capita is not as close as between GNP per capita and *industry* value-added, defined to include manufacturing, utilities, often construction, and sometimes mining.

mineral-rich countries like Bolivia, Zambia, Jamaica, and Peru lie above the regression line, at least partly because they process their minerals before export. Both import substituters (the Philippines, Turkey, and Argentina) and export substituters (Korea and Brazil) are substantially above the regression line. Note the vertical scatter of the five industrial countries, with manufacturing shares ranging from 18 percent for the United Kingdom to 36 percent for West Germany: there is no convincing evidence here that the manufacturing share must eventually decline as countries reach very high per-capita incomes.

Cross-country patterns imply that value-added in manufacturing ought to grow more rapidly than GDP in the typical developing country. This prediction is borne out by World Bank data. For the middle-income countries as a whole, over the period from 1965 to 1983 manufacturing grew by 6.8 percent a year, compared to 5.8 percent a year for GDP. This average pattern is observed in most individual countries, too: of thirty-eight LDCs for which data are available over 1965 through 1983, manufacturing grew faster than GDP in twenty-five countries and lagged behind GDP in only five.

Employment Growth

Although industrial employment grows more rapidly than total employment, it does not grow as fast as value-added. World Bank data indicate that for the low-income countries as a whole, value-added in industry (here defined to include mining, manufacturing, utilities, and construction) advanced at 7.1 percent a year from 1965 to 1983. At the same time employment in industry was growing by 4.3 percent a year. A comparison of the two rates shows that the elasticity of employment growth in manufacturing, the η of Chapter 8, was 0.6: for every 10 percent rise in manufacturing output, manufacturing employment rose by 6 percent. The other side of the coin is that **labor productivity** in industry, the ratio of value-added to employment, rose by 2.7 percent a year.

As 13 percent of the labor force in low-income countries is engaged in industry, the sector adds jobs for about 0.6 percent of the labor force each year (4.3 percent $\times$ 0.13 = 0.6 percent). With the labor force projected by the World Bank to grow at about 2.0 percent a year for the rest of the century, industry in low-income countries will be able to absorb only 30 percent of those entering the work force each year (0.6 percent/2.0 percent = 0.30).[3] Clearly in these poorer countries agriculture and services must continue to bear the major burden for job creation. Similar calculations show that middle-income countries will not do much better, creating industrial jobs for only 36 percent of their new job seekers.

Industrial Structure

Chapter 3's discussion of patterns of industrialization and Chapter 16's discussion of import substitution suggest that the process of industrialization

---

3. Labor force data are from the World Bank, *World Development Report 1985* (New York: Oxford University Press, 1985), pp. 214–15.

Share (%) of GDP for Manufacturing Branches at Different Levels of Income
(by GNP per capita in 1983 dollars)

| Branches | Large Countries | | Small Countries | | | |
| | | | Manufacturing-oriented[a] | | Primary-oriented | |
	$500	$1,300	$500	$1,300	$500	$1,300
1. Simple consumer goods (early developing)[b]	7.7	8.6	7.7	9.6	7.3	8.5
2. Producer goods and consumer durable[c]	9.4	18.9	7.9	17.2	4.7	9.7
3. All manufacturing[d]	17.0	27.0	15.3	25.5	12.1	18.0

Source: Vinod Prakash and Sherman Robinson, "A Cross-Country Analysis of Patterns of Growth" (World Bank, draft of July 1979).

[a] Small countries are considered "manufacturing-oriented" if they export a higher fraction of manufacturing than an average country of the same population and income per capita.

[b] Food, textiles, clothing, and leather.

[c] Wood, paper and printing, chemicals and rubber, minerals, basic metals, metal products, and miscellaneous.

[d] Estimated from a regression equation; *not* a total of the above figures.

requires the **backward integration** from predominantly consumer goods industries towards producer goods industries. This progression is evident in cross-country comparisons of the value-added shares among *branches* within the manufacturing sector. The study summarized in Table 20–1 shows that by the time an "average" country has reached per capita income of $500 (in 1983 prices), the GDP share of the "early developing" branches of manufacturing—food, textiles, clothing, and leather—will change only moderately with further growth. Beyond $500 per capita, most of the above-average growth is supplied by the producer goods (and consumer durable) branches, including the so-called basic or *heavy industries:* pulp and paper, chemicals and rubber, basic metals, and metal products.

Recall from Chapter 16 the problems that protectionist import-substituting countries have in integrating backwards from consumer goods industries. Obviously, "typical" countries—both large ones and small ones that tend to be oriented towards manufacturing—are eventually able to overcome these barriers to backward integration.[4] But the time span represented by the increase in GDP per capita incorporated in Table 20–1 is forty-five years for a country with per-capita income growing at 3 percent a year.

Linkages

If manufacturing generally and early developing branches of manufacturing in particular are to lead economic development, they ought to have more *backward linkages* than other sectors, in the sense described by Albert Hirschman and introduced in Chapter 3. There have been several attempts to measure Hirschman's linkages. Among the several formulas proposed to

4. Small countries are considered "manufacturing oriented" if they export a higher fraction of manufactures than an average country of the same population and income per capita.

measure linkages, those used by Pan Yotopoulos and Jeffrey Nugent seem as easy to understand and useful for our purposes as any.[5] Not surprisingly, linkage formulas depend upon input-output tables, which are constructed to display linkages within an economy. A **direct backward linkage** for any industry, j, is measured as

$$L_{bj} = \sum_i a_{ij}, \qquad [20\text{–}1]$$

where L_{bj} is the index of backward linkage, and a_{ij} is the Leontief (input-output) coefficient defined in Chapter 6. Thus a measure of backward linkage for any industry is simply the sum of its domestic input coefficients. If, for example, the textile industry adds value equal to 30 percent of its output, and imports inputs equivalent to another 15 percent of output, its backward linkage index, L_b, would be 55 percent, the share of domestically purchased inputs ($100 - 30 - 15 = 55$).

Those who recall Chapter 6 will immediately recognize that this index captures only the direct links. But if textile production stimulates cotton growing, might not cotton in turn stimulate fertilizer production? It is easy to incorporate these indirect effects by summing the direct plus indirect coefficients of the Leontief inverse, designated r_{ij},[6] to get

$$L_{tj} = \Sigma r_{ij}, \qquad [20\text{–}2]$$

where L_{tj} is an index of direct plus indirect or **total backward linkages** from the jth industry.

There is an analogous simple measure of **direct forward linkages,**

$$L_{fi} = \sum_j X_{ij}/Z_i, \qquad [20\text{–}3]$$

where L_{fi} is the forward linkage index for the ith industry, X_{ij} is the output of the ith industry that is purchased by each jth user industry (the row of the input-output table), and Z_i is the production of good i for both intermediate and final use.

Yotopoulos and Nugent have used input-output tables for five developing countries (Chile, Greece, Mexico, Spain, and South Korea) to measure the linkage indexes for eighteen industries. The results are shown in Table 20–2. For leather, the next-to-last column tells us, for example, that for each additional dollar of leather goods produced, production of all inputs must rise by $2.39. A high index indicates that expansion of the industry will stimulate production in other sectors of the economy. Manufacturing industries dominate the upper ranks of Table 20–2 on the basis of both direct and total backward linkages. The early-developing sectors—leather, clothing, textiles, and food and beverages—represent four of the first five branches ranked by total backward linkages. Primary industries, utilities, and services are low on both

5. Pan A. Yotopoulos and Jeffrey B. Nugent, "A Balanced-Growth Version of the Linkage Hypothesis: A Test," *Quarterly Journal of Economics* 87 (May 1973): 157–71; reprinted in their text, *Economics of Development: Empirical Investigations* (New York: Harper & Row, 1976), pp. 299–306.
6. The Leontief inverse matrix is explained in footnote 2 of Chapter 6.

TABLE 20–2 Sectoral Linkage Indexes and Rankings in Five Less-Developed Countries[a]

	Direct forward linkage index (L_f)	Rank	Direct backward linkage index (L_b)	Rank	Total backward linkage index (L_t)	Rank
Leather	0.645	4	0.683	2	2.39	1
Basic Metals	0.980	1	0.632	5	2.36	2
Clothing	0.025	18	0.621	6	2.32	3
Textiles	0.590	8	0.621	7	2.24	4
Food & Beverage Manufactures	0.272	16	0.718	1	2.22	5
Paper	0.788	3	0.648	3	2.17	6
Chemicals & Petroleum Refining	0.599	7	0.637	4	2.13	7
Metal Products & Machinery	0.430	13	0.558	9	2.12	8
Wood, Furniture	0.582	9	0.620	8	2.07	9
Construction	0.093	17	0.543	10	2.04	10
Printing	0.508	10	0.509	12	1.98	11
Other Manufactures	0.362	15	0.505	13	1.94	12
Rubber	0.453	12	0.481	14	1.93	13
Minerals (non-metallic)	0.870	2	0.517	11	1.83	14
Agriculture	0.502	11	0.368	15	1.59	15
Utilities	0.614	6	0.296	16	1.49	16
Mining	0.638	5	0.288	17	1.47	17
Services	0.378	14	0.255	18	1.41	18

Source: Yotopoulos and Nugent, "A Balanced-Growth Version of the Linkage Hypothesis," *Quarterly Journal of Economics* 87: Table 2, p. 163.

[a] Chile, Greece, South Korea, Mexico, and Spain.

lists. Hence an unbalanced growth strategy should, to stimulate investment in other sectors, begin with the early developing industries and then move to chemicals and metal products. Advocates of import substitution strategies find sustenance in these findings.

But what do these indices really mean? Should a country base its development strategy on them, even if rapid growth is the principal goal? These particular measurement formulas have been attacked for several reasons, many of them sound ones. But alternative and more complicated formulations give similar rankings anyway. The real issue is whether a mechanical summing up of input-output coefficients for one country really tells us anything about the dynamic processes of growth in another country. The textile industry, which ranks high in Table 20–2 according to its total backward linkage coefficient, may well require inputs of cotton and of synthetic fibers. But whether this additional demand will lead to new investment in farming and chemicals depends on many conditions, none of them reflected in the index. Can cotton be grown in the country at all and if so, at what cost? It might remain cheaper, and to the country's advantage, to import cotton and use the land to grow more profitable crops. If cotton is already being grown and exported, can output expand to accommodate the textile plant or would it simply divert exports? Reduced exports would of course cancel the backward linkage effect.

The potential linkage back to synthetic fibers raises additional issues. Petrochemical industries are subject to substantial economies of scale (discussed later in this chapter) and it would take a considerable expansion of the textile industry to justify the very large investment in petrochemicals. If protection is used to keep out imports of synthetic fibers, the textile industry itself would suffer higher costs and perhaps lose its impetus to expand, as explained in Chapter 16. However, it is also possible that some infant supplier industries may have the potential to reduce costs over time—learning by doing—if they are given a chance.

The requirements for effective forward linkages from manufacturing are even more stringent. To continue the example, textiles have a large forward linkage index, primarily to the clothing industry. But does domestic cloth stimulate the clothing industry? It can if textiles can be produced at costs below the world price of imported cloth. Otherwise the user industry is better off importing its input. If clothing manufacturers are forced, through tariffs or import controls, to take more expensive domestic cloth, this would discourage, rather than stimulate, the forward linkage.

The static linkage indices can help direct attention to potential linkages, but detailed studies are required to consider all the relevant conditions and to pinpoint the ways in which investment in one industry will lead to investment in others. These studies may well show that some manufacturing sectors can lead growth in certain countries. But some of the references cited in Chapter 15 demonstrated that certain primary sectors also generate effective linkages, and there is no overwhelming case favoring manufacturing on this ground.

Urbanization

Since the Industrial Revolution, urbanization and industrialization have moved in tandem. England started the nineteenth century with 30 percent of its people living in cities and ended the century with an urban population share over 70 percent.[7] The trend towards urbanization with industrial development is evident today in cross-country comparisons, depicted in Figure 20–2. Although there is considerable variation among countries at any income level, the association between development and urbanization is nevertheless unmistakable.

What causes this apparently inexorable urban growth as industrialization proceeds? Several **external economies** (see Chapter 5) benefit manufacturing firms in urban settings. Large populations reduce the firms' cost of recruiting labor of all kinds, but especially skilled workers and technicians. Moreover, in cities workers usually find their own housing, so firms do not have to provide it, as they might in rural areas or small towns. **Infrastructure,** including industrial sites, electricity, water, sewage, roads, railroads, and in many cases ports, is provided by government in the cities at costs that reflect substantial scale economies. Health and education facilities are also more highly developed in the cities.

Each firm also benefits from the **economies of agglomeration** that result from the presence of many other firms, because a wide range of necessary inputs and services becomes available. Manufacturers can reduce transport

7. Hobsbawm, *Industry and Empire,* Figure 13.

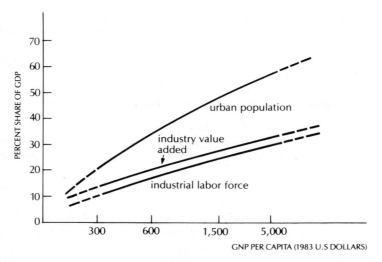

FIGURE 20–2 Industrialization and Urbanization: Cross-Country Comparisons, 1965. Cross-country comparisons indicate that as GNP per capita rises from $300 to $1,500 in 1983 prices, on average industrial value added grows from 14 to 28 percent of GDP while the urban population increases its share of total population somewhat faster, from 20 to 51 percent in a typical country. *Source:* Chenery and Syrquin, *Patterns of Development,* pp. 36, 50, and 55.

costs and shipping delays if they locate near their suppliers. They also benefit from the proximity of repair and other industrial services. Financial markets cluster in cities where domestic and international communication facilities are available and cheap. Manufacturers need access to banks and other financial institutions. They also need the city's communications to stay in touch with distant suppliers and markets, especially export markets. When the city in question is a national capital, manufacturers may locate there to gain ready access to government officials who control investment licenses and incentives, import allocations, and a myriad of other policy and administrative devices that affect the profitability of the firm. Finally, the strong preferences of capitalists, managers, and technicians for the amenities of large cities can be a significant reason for locating there.

Once a city is established, its large market creates reinforcing attractions. Distribution costs are minimized when the firm locates near its largest market. If the costs of shipping output weigh heavily in a firm's costs, and especially if they are more important than the costs of transporting inputs, firms will be pulled towards cities. This attraction is particularly strong in developing countries, where intercity and rural-urban transport networks are sparse. In developed countries, where transport networks are dense and efficient, manufacturing tends to be more footloose, seeking out advantages like cheap labor with less regard for transport costs.

But urbanization has its costs, as the residents of every large city in the world observe daily: overcrowding, unsanitary conditions, displacement of rural migrants, crime. These too have been features of industrialization for two centuries. During the first half of the nineteenth century, London and the other growing cities of Britain were dismal places:

Smoke hung over them and filth impregnated them . . . the elementary public services—water supply, sanitation, street-cleaning, open spaces, and so on—could not keep pace with the mass migration of men into the cities, thus producing, especially after 1830, epidemics of cholera, typhoid and an appalling constant toll of the two great groups of nineteenth-century urban killers—air pollution and water pollution, or respiratory and intestinal disease. . . . New city populations . . . pressed into overcrowded and bleak slums, whose very sight froze the heart of the observer.[8]

Migrants to the large cities of the third world probably do not have to put up with conditions as bad as those of early nineteenth-century London, but cities like Calcutta, Lagos, and São Paulo contain large slums with many of the same kinds of problems.

Although urban infrastructure can be provided at lower cost than the alternative of providing the same services in small, scattered towns, infrastructure is still the largest direct cost of urbanization. A study of cities and towns in India conducted in 1967 estimated that the capital cost of infrastructure provided for manufacturing industry was $820 for every $1,000 of incremental value-added in manufacturing, or about $1,300 per employee (converted to 1983 prices) in a city of one million. Only about a quarter of this is due to construction in the industrial area itself. The balance serves the residential area, so can generally be interpreted as the capital cost of supporting workers in the city. If capital costs are amortized at 10 percent a year and maintenance costs ($600 per employee) are added, it would appear that cities provide manufacturers with annual infrastructure services costing 13 percent of the value-added in manufacturing.[9]

Industrializing cities become magnets for rural workers seeking jobs at higher wages, a pervasive third-world phenomenon explored in Chapter 8. In the cities the presence of migrants in large numbers aggravates congestion, with its attendant ills: crowded and unhygienic living conditions that cause disease and malnutrition; overburdened schools, crime, social disorientation, and political unrest. Despite the risks of unemployment and the poor living conditions, urban life may still be attractive to many rural dwellers, relative to the opportunities available at home. The costs of congestion are external diseconomies: each new migrant will benefit on average, but in so doing he reduces the well-being of all others, even if only slightly. The social costs are high, however, because this marginal reduction in well-being must be added up for all residents of the city.

No government feels comfortable with crowded cities and many have attempted to stem the flow of migration. Over the long run this can best be done by encouraging rural development as actively as industrialization, using the wide range of land tenure, investment, price, incentive, and other policies described in Chapter 18 and elsewhere in this text. A complementary approach is to encourage the dispersal of new industries to smaller cities through provision of infrastructure, incentives, and controls over location. Spreading investment reduces congestion and may also reduce the cost of

8. Hobsbawm, *Industry and Empire*, p. 86.
9. Stanford Research Institute et al., *Costs of Urban Infrastructure for Industry as Related to City Size in Developing Countries: India Case Study* (Stanford Research Institute: Menlo Park, Calif., 1968). The costs per worker are converted from 1967 to 1983 prices using a factor of 3.0

migration. Migrants will have shorter average distances to travel, so more of

them can search for jobs without a commitment to permanent residence in
cities remote from their homes. Decentralization of industry also has complementary benefits for agriculture, distributing urban markets and manufactured supplies more widely among the farming population.

Industrial dispersion does have costs, however. Infrastructure costs may be
greater in small towns, which have not provided as much of the basic facilities as large cities. The study of urban infrastructure in India cited earlier (see
footnote 9), showed that in a town of 50,000, infrastructure for industry
costs 13 percent more than in a city of one million, allowing for both capital
and recurrent costs. No measurements were made for larger cities, in which
economies of scale are evidently exhausted and congestion may well raise the
unit cost of infrastructure. To this must be added the higher costs of transport and other infrastructure required to connect dispersed industrial
locations.

Even with this wider network of transport and communications in place,
private firms—and society—incur higher costs of hauling freight (both their
material inputs and their final outputs) if they do not locate in the most efficient place; of communicating with suppliers, customers, and financial institutions, not to mention government officials; and of waiting with idle
facilities while parts and repair specialists from distant places arrive to fix
broken equipment. Whether the benefits of dispersal justify the costs will
depend on the circumstances. Costs will be lower if the population is already
dispersed, if several urban centers and connecting infrastructure already
exist, and if the new sites have obvious advantages, such as nearby raw materials or abundant water.

Industry is guilty of another external diseconomy that has received much
attention in the past decade: **pollution,** especially of urban environments. In
the developed world environmental protection has been one of the important forces determining the costs and location of investment in the heavy
industries (chemicals, metals) and energy-producing industries (refineries,
power plants). Some have seen growing environmental concern as an opportunity for third-world countries to move more rapidly into heavy industries
and transform their exports of raw materials into semifinished products.
Whether or not this is a real opportunity depends upon two factors. First,
pollution can be controlled by installing equipment that raises investment
costs. These costs would tend to push investments toward the third world
only if they outweigh the existing cost advantage of industrial countries,
something that cost-benefit analysis can reveal.

Second, the only way developing countries can realize any potential cost
advantage conferred by anti-pollution devices is to forego the devices and
accept the pollution. Because they start with less industry, some LDC environments have been less damaged and may be better able to accept some
additional pollution, at least to a point. But some LDCs have already suffered environmental damage from copper smelters, steel mills, pulp mills,
fishmeal plants, and other resource-based industries. For the others the
acceptance of polluting industries becomes a political choice: Is the spur to
industrialization and income growth worth the reduction in the quality of

life implied by pollution? It cannot be presumed that all developing countries would answer affirmatively.

INVESTMENT CHOICES IN INDUSTRY

Chapter 3 introduced the proposition that, because factors of production can be substituted for one another in many production processes, economies were able to conserve capital and get more growth out of a given amount of saving. Chapter 8 used the same analytical device—the neoclassical production function—to demonstrate that policies to make labor less expensive and capital more expensive could move producers towards investments that employ more labor and less capital for a given level of output. But is there enough variance in production techniques to make such policies effective in conserving capital and creating more employment for a given amount of production? For industry, the answer is yes.

Choice of Technique

Table 20–3 illustrates the choice of technology for a single industry, textile weaving. Three alternative technologies are included: an older, semi-automatic loom (T1); a more modern, fully automatic, high-speed loom (T3); and an intermediate technology (T2). More alternatives could have been

TABLE 20–3   Choice of Technology in Textile Weaving

A. *Inputs* (per million yards of shirting)	Alternative Technology[a]		
	T1	T2	T3
1. Equipment cost ($1,000)	80.0	200.0	400.0
2. Labor (person-years)	22.0	11.0	5.0
3. Other costs ($1,000/year)[b]	11.4	9.3	6.7

B. *Factor costs*	Rich Country		Poor Country
1. Real interest rate (% p.a.)	5.0		10.0
2. Present-value factor (20 years)[c]	12.46		8.51
3. Wages ($1,000/year)	15.0		1.5

C. *Present value of costs* ($1,000)[d]	Alternative Technology		
	T1	T2	T3
Rich country			
1. Capital charges	80	200	400
2. Wages	4,112	2,056	935
3. Other costs	142	116	83
4. Total	4,334	2,372	1,418
Poor country			
1. Capital charges	80	200	400
2. Wages	280	140	64
3. Other costs	97	79	57
Total	457	419	521

Source: Adapted from data in Howard Pack, "The Choice of Technique and Employment in the Textile Industry," in *Technology and Employment in Industry,* ed. A. S. Bhalla (Geneva: International Labour Office, 1975), pp.153–174.

[a] Technologies are: T1—semi-automatic loom; T2—intermediate technology; T3—fully automatic, high-speed loom.

[b] Includes cost of space, power, and wastage of yarn, all of which vary depending on the technology. Excludes the common cost of yarn in the finished product.

[c] Present value of $1 per year for 20 years at the interest rate shown in B1.

[d] Wages and other costs discounted at appropriate interest rate over 20 years using present-value factor in B2.

shown, including traditional handloom weaving, which is still used in some Asian countries. As expected, the three technologies show increasing capital intensity, in the sense that the ratio of capital to output rises, and decreasing labor intensity. The treatment of Chapter 8 has been augmented by consideration of other operating costs, including rental of space, power, and differential wastage of the main input, yarn. In many cases, modern equipment conserves both energy and material inputs, lowering production costs.

Analysis of the choice of technology is conveniently done using project analysis as described in Chapter 6. Revenues and costs, including the cost of investment, can be discounted over the life of each technology and the technology with the highest net present value chosen as the most economic. In Table 20–3, it is assumed for simplicity that all techniques produce cloth of equal quality and value, so revenues are not brought into consideration. Instead, the present value of costs is minimized.

Part B of the table presents indicative factor costs for a rich country and a poor one: workers in the rich country are paid ten times the wage of those in the poor one, while the real interest rate in the poor country is twice that of the rich one. Under those conditions, investors in the rich country would minimize costs by choosing the most modern looms, largely because these require so much less labor. Investors in the poor country should select the intermediate technology. However, should the annual wage in the poor country be $1,000 a year instead of $1,500, which is a realistic possibility, the oldest and most labor-intensive technology would minimize costs. Figure 20–3 represents these technological choices as a production isoquant similar to those of Figures 3–2 and 8–3, only in a form more realistic for alternative technologies in single industries.

The range of technologies represented in Figure 20–3 is realistic for the weaving industry in a developing country. The scope for technological choice in this industry can be indicated by the range of capital-labor ratios from the most to the least capital-intensive technology. The capital-output ratio of technology T3 is 22 times that of technology T1. The study from which these figures are taken gives a similar range for cotton spinning, while cement block-making in Kenya alone exhibits a ratio of 11:1.[10]

Even if the scope is narrowed to a choice between the appropriate technology (T2 for the poor country in Figure 20–3) and the most capital-intensive alternative (T3), there is a wide range of technologies available in several industries; for shoe manufacturing, the most capital-intensive technology has a capital-labor ratio 2.8 times that of the appropriate technology; for cotton weaving the ratio is 4.3; for cotton spinning, 7.3; for brickmaking, 13.8; for maize milling, 3.3; for sugar processing, 7.8; for beer brewing, 1.5; for leather processing, 2.3; and for fertilizer manufacturing, 1.1.[11]

The cumulative impact of the choice of more labor-intensive technologies can be considerable. In one indicative experiment, Howard Pack, an Ameri-

10. Howard Pack, "The Choice of Technique and Employment in the Textile Industry," p. 169, and Frances Stewart, "Manufacture of Cement Blocks in Kenya," p. 221, both in *Technology and Employment in Industry*, ed. A. S. Bhalla (Geneva: International Labour Office, 1975).

11. Howard Pack, "Aggregate Implications of Factor Substitution in Industry Processes," *Journal of Development Economics*, Vol. 11, no. 1 (August 1982): 7.

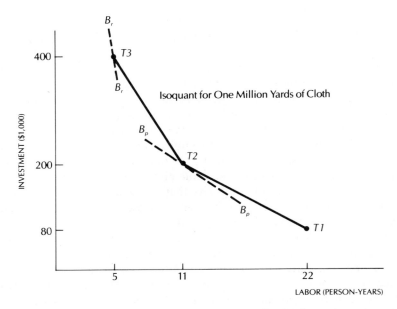

FIGURE 20–3 **Technological Choice in the Weaving Industry.** Three alternative weaving technologies, T1, T2, and T3, are taken from Table 20–3. Each represents a different ratio of capital to labor. Because the industry, or even a single firm, is able to use any combination of technologies, production could take place at all combinations of labor and capital along *T1T2* and along *T2T3*. Thus an isoquant can be traced from *T1* to *T2* to *T3*. The slopes of the budget lines, B_rB_r and B_pB_p, represent the ratios of wages to capital charges for the rich and poor countries, respectively. They indicate that costs will be minimized for the rich country by using the most capital-intensive technology, *T3*, while the poor country should use intermediate technology *T2*. Were wages in the poor country only slightly lower relative to capital costs, it might well find the most labor-intensive technology, *T1*, to be optimal.

can economist who specializes in the choice of technology, assumes that each of the nine industries listed in the previous paragraph receives $100 million of investment. If all of this were spent on the most capital-intensive technology, it would generate employment of 58,000 and value-added of $364 million a year. But if invested in the appropriate technology instead, the same investment would create over four times the employment (239,000) and 71 percent more value-added ($624 million).[12]

Despite the advantages to be gained in both output and employment from using appropriate, more labor-intensive methods in developing countries, we observe many industrial plants using processes that are too capital intensive. Several possible explanations for this were given in the discussion of the employment problem of Chapter 8 and elsewhere in this text: market prices of productive factors typically do not reflect true factor scarcities (opportunity costs or shadow prices) and so distort technology choice; more labor-intensive methods are usually embodied in older models of equipment, frequently available only in used machinery, which may be difficult to learn about, obtain, and maintain; newer equipment may manufacture products

12. Pack, "Aggregate Implications," p.10.

of higher quality and value; or managers may not be skilled in handling large labor forces. These factors are often exaggerated. In any case, most of them can be incorporated in present value calculations that reveal least-cost technologies.

These factors probably do not explain the wide range of technologies, many of them apparently inappropriate, that can be observed in a single country or in similar countries. There may be two further explanations for this. First, different firms can face different factor prices. Foreign firms usually have access to cheaper capital than domestic companies can obtain, so their optimal choice of technology is more capital intensive. (However, this may be countered by the multinational firm's greater knowledge of and easier access to machinery using older techniques, some of which may be in use in older plants of the same company.) Among domestic companies, small firms, with limited access to formal capital markets, may have to pay more for their capital than large firms. Similarly, small firms may escape both unionization and minimum-wage laws, and so are able to employ workers at lower costs. In Indonesia, economist Hal Hill observed four textile-weaving technologies in operation, with a capital-output ratio for the most modern looms over 200 times that for traditional handlooms. Two of these technologies represented least-cost choices for their firms. Surprisingly, these were the two most capital intensive. But when shadow prices were used, only the more labor-intensive of the two techniques remained appropriate.[13]

Second, investors may purchase inappropriate equipment because they and their managers have a strong bias towards the most modern machinery and the highest possible quality of output, with less emphasis on profitability and other economic considerations. Harvard management expert Louis Wells has called this the behavior of "engineering man."[14] If the characteristics of management constrain the choice of technology, the selection may be technique T3 in Figure 20–3, even though the budget line indicates the choice of technique T2. Such non-economic behavior is more likely to prevail in highly protected, monopolistic situations, where a decision to produce at less than minimum cost will not threaten the firm's existence. State-owned enterprises, which are further analyzed in the last chapter, are particularly prone to inefficiencies of this type.

Economies of Scale

In decisions about alternative technologies, **economies of scale** may be a crucial consideration. It has been observed by economists at least since Adam Smith that for many kinds of production, larger facilities may be able to produce at lower unit costs than small ones. For example, steel produced in a

13. Hal Hill, "Choice of Technique in the Indonesian Weaving Industry," *Economic Development and Cultural Change*, Vol. 31, no. 2 (January 1983): 337–54.
14. Louis T. Wells, Jr., Economic Man and Engineering Man: Choice of Technique in a Low-wage Country," in C. P. Timmer, et al, eds., *The Choice of Technology in Developing Countries* (Cambridge, Mass.: Center for International Affairs, Harvard University, 1975), pp. 69-94.

mill designed for two million tons a year might cost 15 percent less than steel produced in a mill designed for only one million tons. As the scale of output rises, the potential average cost falls. (However, if the larger mill produces only one million tons, its average cost is likely to be higher than the small mill, because the small one was designed for lower output and the large one was not.) Readers familiar with the theory of the firm will recognize the concept of **long-run average cost**, the potential unit cost of output when plant size is variable. If the long-run cost curve declines over a range of output relevant to the plant in question, as depicted in Figure 20–4, there are economies of scale.

Scale economies arise for a number of reasons. (1) Some costs, such as research and design efforts or start-up costs, may be fixed over a wide range of output. (2) The amount and cost of materials used in capital equipment will rise with output, but not always in proportion. For example, the capacity of a boiler is related to its volume, which for a sphere varies as the cube of its radius, while the material used to build it is related to its area, proportional to the square of the radius. (3) The amount of inventories and other working capital does not rise proportionally to output. (4) Greater scale permits greater specialization of both workers and equipment (the point emphasized by Adam Smith), which in turn permits higher productivity. (5) Larger production runs reduce the number of times equipment must be set up or readjusted for each run. For example, a plant that produces two or more products with one machine, such as metal cans of different sizes, could be run more efficiently once it has enough volume to produce each on a separate machine, reducing set-up costs. (6) Larger producers may be able to obtain quantity discounts when they procure inputs. These economies all apply to individual plants. At the level of the firm, further economies may arise in management, transport, marketing, and finance as more plants are added.

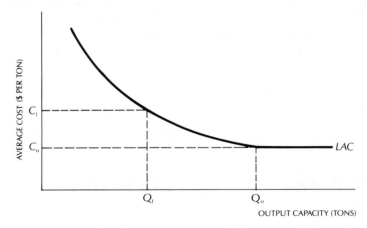

FIGURE 20–4 Economies of Scale. The long-run average cost curve LAC shows the average cost for plants designed to produce at any capacity. Average cost falls as capacity rises up to Q_0, sometimes called the *minimum efficient scale* (MES). Q_1 is half of Q_0. The percentage by which C_1 exceeds C_0 is a measure of the economies to be gained by building plants to a larger scale.

These cost savings can be quite important in manufacturing certain products. Table 20-4 presents data on the scale economies measured for several industries in the United Kingdom in 1969. The **minimum efficient scale** (MES) is defined as a plant large enough so that no further economies can be gained by building a larger facility, Q_0 in Figure 20-4. The first column of the table gives the percentage by which average costs would be greater if a plant were built to only half the MES, compared to a plant built at the MES, or $100 (c_1 - c_0)/c_0$ from Figure 20-4. In practice, if the largest plant in existence does not exhaust potential scale economies, investigators often take that output as the MES until a larger plant is built and its costs measured.

Some of the cost increases in column 1 (for plants half of MES) are significant: 8 to 22 percent for bread, beer, dyes, cement, steel, electric motors, and domestic appliances. However, this is not very meaningful unless we know how large an MES plant is relative to the national market. In the cases of bread and beer in Britain, the second column shows that economies of scale are exhausted at outputs that are very small relative to total consumption, so it is possible to have many plants of sufficient scale. For dyes, steel, electric motors, and automobiles, however, a plant of minimum efficient scale would (in 1969) have met at least half of British demand. This suggests that as manufacturers of these products pursue profits through cost savings, output is likely to become concentrated in a few firms, even in markets as large as Britain's.

No developing country has an internal market as large as Britain's. In 1983 the total gross national product of the largest LDC, China, was less than 60 percent that of the United Kingdom; Brazil's GNP was less than half of Britain's and India's only 37 percent. The largest African economy is

TABLE 20-4 Economies of Scale in Manufacturing in the United Kingdom, 1969

Product	% increase in average cost for plant capacity = half the MES[a,b]	MES[a] as % of UK market
Bread	15	1
Beer	9	3
Footwear	2	0.2
Dyes	22	100
Sulphuric acid	1	30
Polymers	5	33
Cement	9	10
Steel (integrated)	8	80
Machine tools	5	100
Electric motors	15	60
Automobiles (one model)	6	50
Bicycles	small	10
Diesel engines	4	10
Domestic appliances	8	20

Source: C. F. Pratten, *Economies of Scale in Manufacturing Industries* (Cambridge: Cambridge University Press, 1971).
   [a] Minimum efficient scale defind as the output beyond which average costs cease to decline (Q_0 in Figure 20-4) or beyond which no larger plants have been built.
   [b] As a percent of the average cost of production for a plant producing at minimum economic scale.

Nigeria's with a GNP one-seventh that of Britain; even oil-rich, pre-revolutionary Iran had a GNP only a third that of Britain.[15] For medium to large third-world economies, then, only industries with negligible scale economies (footwear, sulphuric acid, and bicycles in the table) or with a very small MES (bread, beer, and footwear) can be accommodated efficiently in a competitive domestic market. For the other industries in the table, large size and significant cost savings imply that plants built to serve the domestic market will either have no domestic competition, produce at high cost, or both.

The characteristics of these large-scale industries shed light on the industrialization process. All are producer goods or consumer durables. The industries in which small countries face the greatest disadvantages, those with large economies at large outputs, are in chemicals (dyes and, to a lesser extent, polymers), basic metals (steel), capital equipment (electric motors and, to a lesser extent, machine tools), and consumer durables (automobiles and appliances). Thus the non-durable consumer-goods industries develop early at least in part because economies of scale are not much of a barrier, except in the very smallest countries. And the barrier to backward integration, noted in discussing import substitution (Chapter 16), can also be blamed in part on economies of scale.

Despite the existence of scale economies it may be efficient to build small plants in developing countries. A steel plant, for example, should be built when it can produce at a cost below the price of imported steel. This may happen long before the market grows to accommodate a steel mill of minimum efficient scale. Economic size is only one of the factors that bears on efficiency. All the others mentioned earlier in this text—productivity, opportunity cost of capital and labor, availability of raw materials and complementary inputs, managerial skills, market organization—also affect the outcome and may outweigh the effects of scale economies. Techniques such as project appraisal (Chapter 6) and domestic resource cost (Chapter 16) can be employed to analyze the impact of all these elements on profitability.

Moreover, the domestic market is not the only possibility. The "virtuous circle," through which export markets make it possible to attain scale economies, which in turn increase export competitiveness, was one of the forces behind Britain's Industrial Revolution. Indeed if a domestic industry in a small LDC were efficient enough to compete with foreign plants at any given output, then scale economies would not matter: the home industry could export enough to achieve any scale desired. Developing countries like South Korea and Brazil have achieved scale economies, even in industries like steel and automobiles, with the help of export markets. Economic integration among developing countries may help other countries to do the same.

Small-Scale Industry

Despite economies of scale in many industries, developing countries still have a choice between large- and small-scale firms in producing a number of

15. Gross national product is only a rough approximation of market size, especially for specific products. Both income per capita, which helps to indicate the per-capita demand for individual commodities, and population, should be included separately in a more comprehensive measure of market size.

the most widely consumed manufactured products, including grain flour, clothing, footwear, wood products, cement blocks, bricks, and many simple metal products. Throughout the postwar era of rapid industrialization, third-world advocates have promoted small-scale industry as either a complementary or an alternative development to large-scale modern manufacturing. India, which has probably been the post-independence leader in planning for large-scale industrialization, has also pursued small-scale development with vigor, a legacy of Gandhi's famous advocacy of smallness. China's use of small-scale rural industry in support of local self-reliance is equally well known. Throughout the developing world there are probably very few development plans that have not paid homage to small industry. It is hoped that small workshops and factories will generate more employment, permit greater decentralization, promote income equalization, and mobilize latent entrepreneurs.

In a moment we will assess the potential of small industry to accomplish these goals, but first we need to define "small industry." Many competing systems of classification have been suggested and no sharp distinction between small and large is possible. For our purposes an approximate tripartite classification will do. At one extreme, **traditional small-scale industry** includes handicraft industries, artisans, workshops, and household-based industry, a collection of overlapping categories sometimes fuzzily called "cottage industry" or "the informal sector." The distinguishing characteristics of these operations are their smallness—they usually employ less than five, or at most ten, workers—and their use of traditional techniques (handloom weaving or manual working of metal, for example) to produce traditional products (cotton cloth or small cookers). These are the village industries of which Gandhi spoke and the urban informal sector identified by the International Labour Office.[16] Further up the hierarchy are **small, modern factories,** employing perhaps ten to fifty or one hundred workers in the manufacture of modern products, such as wood products, plastic goods, paints, or metal goods. The division between small and **large factories** must be elastic. In large countries or small industrial ones, a plant employing two hundred would be considered small.

How important are small firms in developing countries? One source showed that for twenty-one developing countries during the 1960s, a mean of 79 percent of all manufacturing establishments has less than ten employees—probably qualifying as traditional industries—and were responsible for 31 percent of the workers and 11 percent of the value-added in manufacturing. Firms of up to fifty employees constituted 91 percent of the total in manufacturing for this sample, employed 52 percent of the workers and produced 24 percent of the value added.[17] Details for selected countries are shown in Table 20–5.

The case that small-scale industry can *generate more employment* than large factories is based on the observation that small firms generally use

16. International Labour Office, *Employment, Incomes and Equality: A Strategy for Increasing Productive Employment in Kenya* (Geneva: 1972).

17. Ranadev Banerji, "Small-scale Production Units in Manufacturing: An International Cross-section Overview," *Weltwirtschaftliches Archiv* (114) 1978: 62-82.

TABLE 20–5   Importance of Small Industry in Manufacturing, Selected Countries, 1960s

Country (year)	% share of employment in manufacturing firms employing:		% share of value-added in manufacturing firms employing:	
	1–9	1–49	1–9	1–49
Brazil (1960)	16	35	10	26
Colombia (1968)	22	36	10	20
Iraq (1964)	37	49	25	40
Lebanon (1964)	39	66	29	63
Malaysia (1968)	20	57	11	33
Mexico (1965)	24	37	8	20
Peru (1963)	24	43	4	15
South Korea (1967)	14	38	7	23
Taiwan (1966)	13	36	14	28
Thailand (1963)	68	80	12	28
Turkey (1964)	54	60	19	28
Japan (1971)	16	41	8	26
Norway (1963)	13	38	10	31
United States (1967)	2	12	3	14

Source: Ranadev Banerji, "Small-Scale Production in Manufacturing: An International Cross-Section Overview," *Weltwirtschaftliches Archiv* 144 (1978): 62-82.

more labor and less capital per unit output. Data gathered from several studies by the World Bank generally support this conclusion.[18] In Japan, for example, capital-labor ratios rise from an index of 30 for firms with less than thirty employees to over 100 for firms employing over three hundred. And the capital-output ratio rises from an index of 53 to 100 (except that very small firms with less than ten workers have an index of 64, indicating less efficient use of capital than somewhat larger enterprises). The rise in capital-output ratios with firm size was also evident in India, Malaysia, Mexico, Pakistan, and the Philippines during the late 1960s.

The average indices may mask variations not only in the use of labor and capital but also in the products manufactured. Perhaps small enterprises tend to manufacture those products that are more labor-intensive, but use the same capital-output and labor-output ratios as large firms in the same industries. To sort this out we need factor ratios by product and by size of firm. Ranadev Banerji has compiled data on labor productivity for his sample of twenty-one developing countries.[19] For each of seventeen branches of manufacturing, whether we consider firms of one to nine workers or of one to forty-nine workers, the labor-output ratio averaged across all countries is higher than in large firms in the same branch. However, for some of the individual countries in Banerji's sample, there are examples of lower labor-output ratios in small enterprises than in large ones of the same branch, contradicting expectations. This surprising result is partially supported by

18. World Bank, *Employment and Development of Small Enterprises: Sector Policy Paper* (Washington, D.C., 1978), pp. 65-67.

19. Banerji, "Small-Scale Production Units in Manufacturing," p. 80.

detailed studies of India by P. N. Dhar and H. F. Lydall and of Ghana by

William F. Steel.[20] Both found several industries in which capital-output ratios are lower for larger firms. Dhar and Lydall suggest that traditional industries of fewer than ten employees may be more labor-intensive than all modern firms, large and small. But among modern firms, economies of scale determine that larger firms use less of both capital and labor per unit of output.

If Dhar and Lydall are right, then employment goals can be pursued through small industry only if: (a) traditional and informal sector, rather than small modern, enterprises are encouraged or (b) small modern factories are encouraged, but are likely to use more of both labor and capital. In either case, small industry would generate more employment at the expense of either modernization and widening consumer choice or at the expense of rising productivity and efficiency. This would be a serious indictment. But the issue is an empirical one: the available data give no clear answers and more research is needed before we rule out the small industry approach.

It is argued that small enterprises can lead to **decentralization** of industry because they do not require large markets for their output and thus do not have to locate in big cities. Here it is important to make the distinction between traditional and modern small-scale industries. As Dhar and Lydall point out, the traditional industries are already in the rural areas. Their encouragement may help to increase rural incomes and employment, but does not draw industry away from congested cities. Modern small factories, on the other hand, are not so easily located in rural areas. Firms serving rural consumers and farmers and those using local raw materials may be drawn to rural locations. But suppliers of producer goods need to locate near the large urban manufacturers they serve, and most small producers need access to intermediate material inputs, which favors locations near ports and transport facilities. Perhaps more critically, small modern industries benefit from being near urban growth centers in which entrepreneurs and skilled workers are located.

To the extent that small enterprises can generate more employment per unit of output and can locate in small cities and towns, they will **promote greater income equality** among families, among regions, and between rural and urban areas. Workers in small firms generally earn incomes between those paid by large enterprises and those earned in agriculture. If small factories either augment the production of large ones or substitute for the output of larger firms and employ more workers, the benefits of industrialization are more widely distributed. If traditional industries are encouraged, then rural family incomes are directly augmented. Whether small industry can promote equity without reducing growth hinges on the empirical issues of its productivity relative to large firms and to the additional costs of dispersed industry.

20. P. N. Dhar and H. F. Lydall, *The Role of Small Enterprises in Indian Economic Development* (New York: Asia Publishing House, 1961), p. 14; and William F. Steel, *Small-Scale Employment and Production in Developing Countries: Evidence from Ghana* (New York: Praeger, 1977), p. 107.

Rural Small Industry in China

The Chinese have done what appears to be difficult in market econo-mies: they have established modern small factories in rural centers to supply farm inputs, equipment, and consumer goods to communes and other rural consumers.[21] Several conditions encouraged the emergence of local factories. China's rural transport and marketing system is poorly developed, isolating rural communities from urban centers of produc-tion. The central planning and control of industrial goods intensifies this isolation, because communes wanting fertilizer or trucks must apply to authorities located in urban centers, a process that entails long delays and may not be successful. It is in the communes' interest for their regions to become self-reliant in agricultural inputs to avoid these delays, and it is also in the planners' interests if local materials, capital, and labor can be used, so that other industrial priorities are not sacrificed. Local industry has the additional advantages of bringing modern technology directly to the countryside, and of helping to narrow the economic and social gap between farm and city.

Despite the success of the small-industries program, Chinese planners apparently have only limited goals in mind. The program is not conceived as a generator of off-farm employment; rather, there is concern that rural factories will draw needed workers away from the communes. Nor is rural industry expected to replace modern, urban industry. "Walking on two legs" means that both must be pursued, and self-reliance implies that rural factories must not divert resources from large-scale, urban ones. Self-reliance also suggests that regional equality is not a prime goal of the program, because wealthier regions with more resources, espe-cially savings, are likely to do better than poor ones. However, rural-urban equality is probably served by the program. Finally, it should be recognized that China is a large, densely populated country. The rural counties in which self-reliant factories are based have populations greater than many of the countries in the third world. And the "small" factories—of fifty to six hundred employees—are also large by the stan-dards of most developing countries.

Small-scale manufacturing has a clear advantage in **mobilizing potential entrepreneurs.** Most societies have latent or actual entrepreneurs in retail trading, farming, transportation, and other small-scale activities. Small-scale manufacturing represents a feasible step for these entrepreneurs, who would be blocked from entering manufacturing if large amounts of credit and the ability to manage large-scale enterprises were essential. Small industry also permits imitation of more advanced entrants and so requires less innovative entrepreneurs.

Accepting, as most governments do, that small industries ought to be encouraged, how should this be done? Positive measures of encouragement

---

21. This account is based on the report of the American Rural Small-Scale Industry Dele-gation, *Rural Small-Scale Industry in the People's Republic of China* (Berkeley: University of California Press, 1977), Chapter 1. Dwight Perkins was chairman of the delegation.

may not be as important as removing the discouragements that plague small industrialists in most countries. The price distortions and controls described in earlier chapters generally benefit the large-scale firm at the expense of the small. Tariffs tend to favor goods manufactured by large producers with the political influence to obtain protection. Import licenses for industrial inputs are most easily obtained by the same large-scale manufacturers, who have the time and the money to spend obtaining favors from officials. Controls over interest rates and credit allocations push the small firm onto the informal money market where interest rates are much higher. The only control that may help small operators is minimum wages, since they can often circumvent wage regulations and gain a competitive advantage in labor costs.

If governments aim to encourage small industries in markets where they have a competitive advantage over large firms, then a reduction of controls and a greater dependence on markets should help. It has been proposed that governments go further than this by protecting small firms from large-scale competition. This could be done by controlling large-scale output, restricting investment in big firms that would compete with small ones, applying excise taxes to large manufacturers only, or subsidizing small-scale producers. In a system with controls that discriminate against small firms these measures may have some merit as an antidote to the handicaps under which they operate. But in a liberalized regime protection of the small would introduce a new distortion that should be unnecessary if small industry really has the advantages claimed for it.

Even in a liberalized economy, however, small industry may need special help from government to overcome some of its initial handicaps. A fairly standard package has emerged to provide this assistance. It includes credit, made available though small industry development banks or similar institutions; technical advice, organized along the lines of an agricultural extension service; training of managers and skilled workers; help in setting up procurement and marketing channels; and industrial estates that provide sites with infrastructure and a focal point for the assistance package. The idea behind this package is to help inexperienced entrepreneurs over their early hurdles, to introduce them to regular market channels, and eventually make them self-reliant. However, this package is expensive and often ineffective. It requires government agencies to make contact with individual entrepreneurs to offer assistance tailored to the needs of each and thus draws heavily on government's limited managerial and technical resources. Because of its expense and complexity, the package typically reaches only a small fraction of its target firms. Nor is it clear that government agencies have the skills and nimbleness required to help small entrepreneurs deal with market situations. Thus this approach is no substitute for general economic policies that benefit small operators.

INDUSTRY AND DEVELOPMENT GOALS

This and previous chapters, which have examined industry from several perspectives, point towards a consensus on the role that industry can be expected to play in development. Industrialization is not a panacea for underdevelopment. But two of its strengths are essential for any development program. As suggested by the Lewis-Fei-Ranis two-sector model (Chapter 3), greater productivity in industry is a key to increased per-capita income. And manufacturing provides a much larger menu of possibilities for efficient import substitution and increasing exports than is possible with primary industries alone.

Industrialization and rural development must proceed in tandem. Industry can supply agriculture with inputs, especially fertilizer and simple farm equipment, that raise farm productivity. If outward-looking policies have been followed and manufacturing is efficient, these inputs may be supplied more cheaply than imports. The relationship is reciprocal, because agriculture supplies raw materials for manufacturing, such as cotton and other fibers, rubber, or tobacco. Agricultural and industry also provide reciprocal consumer-goods markets. If agricultural incomes grow in egalitarian fashion—which may require land reform and broad-based rural development—then manufacturing will enjoy a wide and growing market for its consumer goods, one that may enable it to achieve scale economies in both production and marketing. Similarly, the growth of urban incomes, stimulated by industrial expansion, should provide a continuing stimulus to agricultural output and productivity through increasing demand for food. The key to growing food demand is expanding employment and improved urban income distribution.

Industry cannot by itself generate sufficient jobs to absorb the growing number of workers or to equalize income distribution, especially in the poorest countries. Liberalized economies, with reduced controls and market prices closer to scarcity values, can help to arrest the tendency towards capital intensity and inappropriate, modern technologies in manufacturing and thus to raise job creation in industry. Renewed emphasis on small industry may also help. Moreover, to the extent that intermediate or innovative technologies are needed to save capital and create more jobs relative to output, an innovative, efficient capital-goods industry is an essential part of a development strategy. But in the final analysis much of the burden for employment creation and income equalization will lie outside industry, in agriculture and the services.

Industry has rightly been seen as a key to another goal of many developing countries: reduced *dependence*. If a country wants the capability of doing without imports of essential commodities, it must develop both an integrated industrial structure and a productive agriculture. If it wishes to exclude foreign political and cultural influence, it must learn to operate its manufacturing plants without foreign help. Much of the discussion about reduced dependence really is about increasing autarky or self-sufficiency, implying that a country must produce everything it needs. But an alternative goal suggests the capability of producing a wide variety of goods efficiently enough to trade them on world markets and obtaining some goods overseas when it is advantageous to do so. This leads to the outward-looking strategy discussed in Chapter 17.

Behind these considerations lurks a hidden development goal: industrialization for its own sake. Despite advice from many quarters to temper their protective and other industrial policies and instead to promote greater efficiency, employment, and equity, many governments continue to establish the most modern, capital-intensive industries available. This cannot be attributed entirely to misguided policy. The desire to have modern industry may be as great for a country as the desire for a radio or car can be for an individual. To the extent that modern manufacturing is a goal in itself, the best that development economists can do is to point out how much could be accomplished with alternative policies and measure the costs of industrialization in terms of other goals that remain to be achieved.

21

Public Enterprises

In the United States one has to look hard to find state-owned enterprises, such as municipally owned electric utilities, the Tennessee Valley Authority, Conrail, and such exotic activities as uranium-enrichment plants. The situation is very different in Europe, as we are reminded by denationalizations in England and France since 1975. In most developing countries, from socialist Tanzania and Cuba through market-oriented nations such as Brazil and Korea, state-owned enterprises are common and known variously as **public enterprises** or **parastatals.** In this chapter we will see that the activities of these enterprises can have far-reaching implications for development.

The label **state-owned enterprise** (SOE) means different things to different people. To some the label has a very broad meaning, applying to all government entities that supply goods and services to the general public. In this view entities such as disaster-relief agencies, agricultural extension services, and police and fire protection agencies would qualify as state-owned enterprises. A far narrower view would reserve the label for government-owned entities created primarily for the purpose of profit-making and that, once established, were substantially free to operate in much the same fashion as private firms.

Neither the broad nor narrow definition is serviceable in approaching the study of modern state enterprises. There is an immense variety of such enterprises. A definition is required that is broad enough to encompass this variety, but at the same time narrow enough to enable sharp focus on the major issues peculiar to the stockholder and the managers in the state-enterprise sector. For purposes of this chapter an enterprise qualifies as a state enterprise if it meets three criteria:

1. The government is the principal stockholder in the enterprise, or is otherwise able to exercise control over the broad policies followed by the enterprise, and to appoint and remove enterprise management. This does not mean that the state must necessarily be involved in the day-to-day operations of the enterprise. Nor is majority ownership essential, because the state may effectively control an enterprise with a minority share of its equity, depending on the distribution of ownership of the other shares, and on any agreements between the government and the private partners.

2. The enterprise is engaged in the production of goods or services for sale to the public, or to other enterprises, private or public.

3. As a matter of policy the revenues of the enterprise are supposed to bear some relation to its costs. State enterprises for which profit maximization is not the prime stated objective may still qualify if they are expected to pursue profitability subject to constraints implicit or explicit in social functions assigned the enterprise by the state.

In the absence of the first criterion, an enterprise qualifies as a private enterprise. In the absence of either conditions 2 or 3, a governmental entity would not be viewed as a state enterprise, but as an ordinary public agency.

The Growth of State Enterprises

Through the first decade of the postwar period, state-owned enterprises in LDCs were largely confined to the so-called natural monopolies (decreasing-cost public utilities), to small-scale monopoly producers of sumptuary products (liquor, beer, tobacco) and basic necessities (salt, matches), and to transportation (railroads, airlines); in some cases to banks, which were also government-owned (Indonesia, Mexico). But, except for Turkey from 1930 onward and China from 1949 onward, there were few examples of significant state ownership of productive facilities extending much beyond these areas. However, in the last two decades an entirely different pattern of public enterprise has emerged. The present section provides a thumbnail sketch of the extent of state enterprise participation in the economies of developing countries, while a subsequent section focuses upon some of the reasons for the establishment of SOEs.

By whatever standard employed there has been a marked expansion in the relative size of state-owned enterprise in LDCs. With few exceptions the reasons for this expansion have little to do with ideology. By the early 1980s the role of SOEs in such market-oriented countries as Bolivia, Brazil, Chile, Indonesia, Korea, and Taiwan was as significant as in India, Bangladesh, Sri Lanka, and Egypt, countries where interventionist traditions have historically been stronger. Contrary to the pattern of the early twentieth century, SOEs are now common, and sometimes dominant, in manufacturing, construction, services, natural resources, and even agriculture. Although public enterprises prior to 1960 were typically small-scale undertakings in most LDCs, many are now among the largest enterprises in their countries, and some are among the largest enterprises in their fields anywhere in the world. A handful are multinational enterprises in the truest sense of that word. Even by 1978, of the largest five hundred industrial corporations outside the United States, thirty-four were state enterprises from LDCs (primarily natural resource-based industries in Brazil, Venezuela, and Korea).[1] By size of assets, the three largest firms in Brazil are state-owned, as are two of the three largest Mexican enterprises and the nine largest domestic firms in Indonesia. In terms of sales, twelve of the largest sixteen Korean enterprises are state-owned. Developing-country SOEs that merit the multinational label include Petrobras (oil) and CVRD (mining) in Brazil, the National Iranian Oil Company, two construction firms from Indonesia, and an Indian engineering company.

State-owned enterprises have come to dominate large segments of many LDC economies. In countries as diverse as Bangladesh, Bolivia, and Mexico, the share of SOEs in annual gross investment outside of agriculture has been upward of 75 percent, while it is close to 50 percent in India and Turkey, and it has hovered between 25 percent and 33 percent in Korea and Brazil. Public enterprises have in recent years contributed about 40 percent of GDP in Bolivia, about 20 percent in Chile, 25 percent in Pakistan and Ghana, 12 percent in India, and 11 percent in Korea. In Bangladesh, Turkey, and Syria, SOEs account for at least 60 percent of total industrial value-added, and over 80% in Egypt. In Nepal and Sri Lanka this ratio is about one-third, in India one-fifth, and Korea one-sixth. For Latin American nations the output of public enterprises is typically estimated at between 5 and 25 percent of national industrial output, depending on the country in question and the nature of the definitions applied to SOEs.[2]

Nowhere is the much-expanded role of SOEs more evident than in the natural-resources industries. In hard minerals large-scale state enterprises are responsible for more than two-thirds of annual value of output in Bolivia, Chile, Guinea, Guyana, Indonesia, Zambia, and Zaire. In hydrocarbons and energy the dominance of SOEs is complete in some countries, including Mexico and Pakistan, and nearly so in numerous others, including Bolivia, Brazil, Indonesia, Malaysia, India, Turkey, Colombia, and Iran.

Few countries have experienced growth in SOE operations as dramatic as that in Tanzania, Pakistan, and Sri Lanka, where the number of public enterprises in all fields doubled in the decade after 1964. Yet the figures cited above provide ample indication of strong growth in government ownership of productive facilities in a wide array of fields in developing countries.

The emergence of rapidly growing LDC state-enterprise sectors has important international implications as well. In a variety of fields developing

---

1. "Directory of the 500 Largest Industrial Corporations Outside the U.S.," *Fortune,* Aug. 13, 1979: 193*ff.*

2. Raymond Vernon, "The State-Owned Enterprise in Latin American Exports," in *Trade Prospects Among The Americas,* Werner Baer and Malcolm Gillis, eds. (Urbana, Ill.: National Bureau of Economic Research and University of Illinois Press, 1981), pp. 98–114.

country SOEs have increasingly come to represent substitutes for, or competitors to, private multinationals—certainly in the home markets of the state firms and potentially in the markets of other countries. This has already begun to occur in mining, steelmaking, petroleum refining, and petrochemical manufacturing and to a more limited extent in the shipbuilding, textile, and construction fields. To finance this expansion, state enterprises from developing countries have become major users of international credit markets. Flows of external commercial debt contracted by such firms rose by nearly 350 percent over the period 1975 to 1978 and accounted for nearly one-third of total LDC commercial borrowings for all purposes.[3] The expanded flows of international debt capital to SOEs was the prime factor in the buildup of large, potentially troublesome, stocks of external debt in Indonesia, Brazil, Peru, Zaire, and Zambia during the 1970s and again in the early 1980s.

RATIONALES FOR ESTABLISHING SOEs

It is not always easy to identify with any clarity the basic reasons why particular enterprises have been created in particular countries. In many cases the passage of time has obscured the original rationale; in other cases governments may have announced one set of justifications while intending the enterprise to serve other goals. It is often thought that most of the motives are grounded in socialist ideology. Among the LDCs this has been true for only a few socialist countries, such as China, Burma, Tanzania, Algeria, Cuba, and, in certain periods, India. For most other developing countries the establishment of public enterprises has usually had little to do with socialist ideology, or for that matter, any other ideological framework. Otherwise it would be extremely difficult to explain the existence of very large public-enterprise sectors in countries such as Brazil, Bolivia, Indonesia, Kenya, or Korea, none of which is socialist.

The reasons for creating public enterprises can be grouped into three separate but inextricably related categories: primarily economic and sociopolitical motives, and mixed motives. The compartments are by no means watertight, and often many nuances are ignored.

Economic Reasons

Savings mobilization has been one of the longest-standing and most frequently employed rationales for creating public enterprises. Even when decisions to establish state-owned enterprises have hinged primarily on sociopolitical considerations, savings mobilization has often been mustered as a supplementary argument. The argument runs as follows: domestic capitalists in LDCs generate too little savings because they are conspicuous con-

---

3. Figures on borrowing by LDC-based SOEs are computed on the basis of data presented in the World Bank, Financial Studies Division, *Borrowing in International Capital Markets* (Washington, D.C., 1978).

sumers. Moreover those savings that are generated by domestic capitalists are often invested abroad. Public savings cannot adequately finance capital formation because low levels of per-capita income and weak public administration make it particularly difficult to raise tax revenues. In the face of these and other difficulties in mobilizing savings, many LDC governments turned hopefully to state enterprises, whose surpluses could be used to finance investment. Earnings of SOEs would not, it was hoped, be dissipated in low-priority consumption, and since they accrue to government directly, would be more readily accessible for financing both physical and human capital formation. SOE surpluses would also reduce the need for administratively difficult and politically unpopular tax reforms.

Employment objectives have often been important in the establishment of public firms. In most instances the goal has been defined as the creation of new jobs as the economy and the firm expand. In other cases the focus has been upon job preservation, as large, ailing, private firms (**sinking sands** enterprises) have been taken over by the government in order to avoid the unemployment consequences of potential bankruptcies. This rationale has been present in nationalization decisions ranging from textile companies in India to cement plants and bicycle factories in Bolivia.

Capital lumpiness has been an argument for public enterprise in countries where money and capital markets are not well developed, so that private domestic firms have been unable to mobilize the volumes of capital necessary to mount large, capital-intensive projects. This is particularly true in the minerals sector, where today the average size of projects around the world runs over U.S. $200 million, and billion-dollar projects are not uncommon. In most developing countries only the state or foreign enterprises have the resources to mount such projects. And if foreign participation has been precluded, responsibility for undertaking large projects with "lumpy" capital requirements falls to the state, which may respond by assigning the task to an existing public enterprise, as has often been the case in mining in Peru, Brazil, and Panama, or by creating an entirely new one, as for example in the huge Asahan hydropower and aluminum smelting project in Indonesia. The large scale of these projects tends to make them especially risky. In many LDCs private investors are highly risk-adverse, and public-sector involvement is essential if large projects are to be carried out at all.

Sociopolitical Reasons

The **commanding heights** is a term applied to sectors of the economy that are so strategic and generate such important linkages that they cannot, it is argued, be left in private hands, whether foreign or domestic. Rather, to guarantee socially responsible performance from these commanding heights of the economy, it has been thought that the state must control such industries. The commanding heights can be a rather elastic concept, but generally includes basic industries, such as mineral extraction and processing, iron- and steel-making, chemical manufacturing, electricity generation, rail service, and crucial services such as banking. The preferred means of exercising

state control over the commanding heights has been to turn these sectors
over to government-owned enterprises. At various stages in the development of postindependence India, as well as for certain periods in Sri Lanka and under the Bhutto administration in Pakistan, the commanding heights rationale was used as the prime justification for creating state enterprises in the steel, shipping, coal, electric power, fertilizer, and banking industries, and several other fields. This reasoning also appears to have been the basis for the largely amicable nationalization of foreign mining interests in Zaire and Zambia in the 1970s. One hears less of this argument today, perhaps because of the lack of any firm evidence that the enterprises thus created could, in the absence of any stronger economic rationale, remain viable without substantial government aid over long periods of time.

Decolonialization is closely related to the commanding heights motive. Many countries formerly under the domination of a colonial power have viewed the continued presence of colonial industrial interests as a bitter reminder of the past and a major impediment to development. Thus, particularly in the late 1950s and early 1960s, both socialist and non-socialist developing countries nationalized foreign interests. In virtually all instances the shortage both of capital and of trained indigenous managers has meant that ownership of the nationalized enterprises could not immediately pass to the domestic private sector, but rather devolved to the state.

This rationale accounts for perhaps three-quarters of the nearly two hundred central government-owned enterprises now operating in Indonesia, primarily expropriated from Dutch interests in 1957 and British interests in 1962; for a large number of Egyptian SOEs created in 1957 when, after the Suez War, Nasser nationalized important foreign firms; and for a significant share of public enterprises in Ghana and Algeria. In Peru, Mexico, and Chile, nationalization was undertaken in response to a perceived economic neocolonialism from the United States rather than from the former colonial occupying power.

In many LDCs state-owned enterprises have been created to serve **social goals;** many other state-owned firms that owe their existence to other reasons have been assigned such goals. These include income redistribution and the correction of imbalances in regional growth; employment creation, an economic goal, also has social aspects.[4] In many countries pursuit of such objectives is second nature to public-enterprise managers. In Bolivia the managers of large mining SOEs commonly stress the "social content" of all basic enterprise decisions; managers of state-owned banks in Indonesia cite the broader "development mission" to which their activities are oriented; the operations of SOEs in Bangladesh are expected to help reduce income differentials over time. Although few public enterprises owe their existence entirely to government's social or equity goals, in recent years a number of enterprises have been established principally for purposes of rectifying imbalances between social groups and between regions of a country.

4. For an alternative, and longer, list of such goals, see Armeane M. Choksi, *State Intervention in the Industrialization of Developing Countries: Selected Issues* (Washington, D.C.: World Bank, 1979).

Concentration of economic power in the hands of a small number of families has been significant in such countries as Pakistan, Chile, and Peru. On occasion governments have moved to reduce the scope for abuse of such power by nationalizing private domestic firms. The desire to curb drastically the influence of Pakistan's dominant "twenty-two" families was clearly a significant factor in actions taken by the Bhutto government in 1974, when many banks, insurance companies, industrial firms, and agricultural interests were nationalized. From 1971 to 1973, the Allende government in Chile justified seizure of a variety of textile, banking, publishing, and industrial concerns on grounds of excessive concentration of ownership in the hands of a small number of individuals. Bolivian capitalists have long avoided rapid growth in domestic market shares for their enterprises, or the appearance of such growth, on grounds that largeness sooner or later invites expropriation.

Preferences of some foreign aid donors have reinforced the tendency to create state-owned enterprises in a number of countries. The World Bank, particularly since 1967, and the Asian, African, and Latin American development banks have preferred to channel large portions of their resources through SOEs rather than through ordinary government agencies or private enterprises in LDCs. This was not always the case. Originally the World Bank favored private enterprise in mining and manufacturing, since there were substantial reservations about the capacity of the public sector to execute projects in these industries. But in many countries the private sector seemed too weak to undertake large projects. In addition countries such as India, Egypt, and Indonesia had decided that "strategic" or "basic" industries in any case would be in the hands of the state.[5] By the mid-1970s the World Bank's emphasis in mining and manufacturing had shifted strongly to the public sector. Independent, state-owned enterprises were favored over ordinary government agencies because the World Bank saw significant advantages in fostering decentralized decision-making in areas involving the production and distribution of basic industrial and agricultural goods. At the same time both the bank and many LDC officials viewed existing governmental departments as either too inefficient or too corrupt to execute large-scale projects effectively. Under this stimulus new SOEs were created and existing ones expanded to execute major projects. Examples include holding companies in shipping, investment banks, and fertilizer plants in Indonesia, development finance institutions in Colombia, a state-owned mining bank in Bolivia, and a wide variety of SOEs in several fields in African countries.

IMPACT ON DEVELOPMENT

Until very recently little comparative information of any kind was available on the activities of state-owned firms. Although this situation has changed

---

5. The discussion of the evolution of the World Bank's attitude toward SOEs draws heavily on Berti Walstedt, "State Manufacturing Enterprises in a Mixed Economy" (unpublished manuscript; Washington, D.C., August 1978).

for the better since the early 1970s, large gaps remain. Enough data are available, however, to permit some generalizations on savings mobilization, efficiency, employment, and a few measures of the "social" activities of the enterprises.

Savings Mobilization

While public-sector enterprises have contributed materially to overall savings mobilization efforts in a few socialist developing economies such as China and Yugoslavia, they have not performed as well in mixed LDC economies. Indeed for some avowedly socialist LDCs, such as Tanzania under Nyerere, Ghana under Nkrumah, Sri Lanka under Mrs. Bandaranaike, and Indonesia under Sukarno, large state-enterprise sectors persistently ran deficits that had to be financed from general government revenues. At times even single enterprises have accumulated losses and external debt obligations large enough to cripple developmental efforts across all fields of government activity. This was the case for Comibol, the state-owned tin mining enterprise in Bolivia, from 1957 to 1972, and from 1972 to 1976, for Pertamina, the state-owned petroleum enterprise in Indonesia, which accumulated over $10 billion in debt before 1976, as well as for state mining enterprises in Zaire and Zambia from 1974 through 1978. The severe tribulations of the Turkish economy in the 1970s, culminating in massive devaluation and debt rescheduling in 1979, were due primarily to problems originating in debt-ridden state enterprises.

Generally, public enterprises have not been a net source of savings but a net user of savings in developing nations. In sixteen of the seventeen LDCs in Table 21–1, state-owned enterprises experienced overall deficits in the latter half of the 1970s; in some cases (Guinea, Ivory Coast, Burma, India, Korea, and Taiwan), these deficits exceeded 5 percent of GDP. These deficits had to be financed either by capital transfers from the parent government, or by borrowing, including foreign borrowing.

Savings-mobilization performance by LDC state enterprises, however, has not always been uniformly disappointing. In Korea before 1972,[6] Uruguay from 1975 to 1976,[7] India in 1970–1972, Pakistan in 1972–1974, and Indonesia in 1976–1978, the savings of state enterprises generated as much as 10 to 15 percent of gross domestic investment finance.

Why have efforts to mobilize savings through state-enterprise activities had relatively disappointing results? There are, after all, some reasons for expecting some state enterprises to yield larger surpluses than would be the case for business enterprise in general. First, virtually all of the largest state enterprises in developing countries are concentrated in natural-resources industries, and would normally be expected to generate very substantial profits from the rents present in natural resource activity (see Chapter 19), particularly after 1973, when prices of commodities other than copper began to surge upward. In fact some natural-resource enterprises do show sizable

6. Leroy Jones, *Public Enterprise and Economic Development* (Seoul: Korea Development Institute, 1976), p. 8.

7. World Bank, *Economic Memorandum on Uruguay* (Washington, D.C., 1977), p. 15.

TABLE 21-1   Overall Deficits[a] or Surpluses of Public Enterprises as Percent of GDP, Selected LDCs, 1978–1980

		Surplus (+) or Deficit (−) as % GDP	
	Latest Period of Data	Latest Period	Next Latest Period
Africa			
Botswana	1978–80	−0.6	−4.7
Guinea	1978–79	−23.4	−8.0
Ivory Coast	1978–79	−8.4	−3.5
Malawi	1978	−2.7	−2.5
Senegal	1974	+2.2	—
Tanzania	1974–75	−2.8	−2.6
Asia			
Burma	1978–80	−10.6	−1.2
India	1978	−6.2	−6.3
Korea	1978–80	−5.2	−5.4
Taiwan	1978–80	−5.5	−7.3
Thailand	1978–79	−2.0	−1.1
Latin America			
Argentina	1976–77	−3.1	—
Bolivia	1974–77	−4.4	−3.4
Brazil	1980	−1.7	—
Chile	1978–80	−0.4	−0.2
Mexico	1978	−3.7	−3.9
Uruguay	1978–80	−0.8	+1.0

Source: R. P. Short, "The Role of Public Enterprises: An International Statistical Comparison" (Washington, D.C.: Working Paper of the International Monetary Fund, Fiscal Affairs Department, May 17, 1983), Table 4.

a. The overall deficit here is defined as the difference between (a) the current plus capital expenditure of SOEs, and (b) SOE revenue plus receipts of current governmental and nongovernmental transfers.

profits, but most do not. Indeed, three major LDC state-owned natural-resource firms (Turkiye Petrolerri of Turkey, Ecopetrol of Colombia, and Zambia Industrial and Mining) ranked, along with British Steel and ENI (hydrocarbons) of Italy, among the twenty largest money losers of all state enterprises in the world in 1978.[8]

Second, many state enterprises enjoy monopoly privileges in their respective markets, privileges not as readily available to private firms. These monopoly privileges extend well beyond those traditionally granted to state-owned producers of sumptuary items (tobacco, beer, spirits) and to public utilities (electric power, telephones). State-owned monopolies are also pervasive in other fields, including fertilizer and steel manufacture in Indonesia; distribution of refined petroleum products and management of domestic airline service in over thirty LDCs; the export of cocoa products in Ghana and Bolivia; peanut export in Senegal; and match manufacture in Bolivia. Where state enterprises do not enjoy full monopoly positions, they often operate in the most concentrated markets where the potential for receipt of monopoly or oligopoly rents is substantial. (See Chapter 19 on monopoly rent.)

For example, Leroy Jones of Boston University reports that for Korea in

8. "Directory of the 500 Largest Industrial Corporations Outside the U.S.," *Fortune,* Aug. 13, 1979: 193*ff.*

1972 only 10 percent of value-added in the public sector was marketed under competitive conditions, and that public enterprises either dominated or played a leading role in all mining and manufacturing industries that might be considered strategic.[9] For Ghana, Tony Killick of Britain observes that in 1979 state enterprises accounted for all output in six industries, and that 83 percent of total output of all state enterprises was produced in industries where state firms were responsible for more than 75 percent of output.[10]

Given that substantial market power is characteristically available to SOEs almost everywhere in developing countries, it might be expected that most state-owned firms would show profits and that these profits would tend to be reflected in enterprise savings. However, financial profitability is not a common characteristic of LDC state-owned firms, whether monopoly power is present or not. For some public-enterprise sectors, operating losses, as distinct from overall deficits, are a chronic condition.[11] This has been particularly true for Egypt, Congo, Ghana, Zambia, Turkey, and to a lesser extent Bangladesh, Sri Lanka, Argentina and Mali. In other countries, such as Brazil, Indonesia, Chile, Uruguay, and Thailand, the results are mixed: generally more major firms show accounting profits than show losses. But the state-enterprise sectors in Korea, Taiwan, and Singapore enjoy relatively strong reputations for generating accounting profits.

This relatively poor profit and savings performance can be attributed to three factors: (1) "inefficiency" in operation, (2) government-imposed controls, particularly price controls, and (3) often the financial burden of social responsibilities assigned to SOEs.

Efficiency

Virtually everywhere the stereotypical image of state-owned firms is one of an inefficient economic unit. To the extent that inefficiency refers to a failure to minimize costs, or **X-inefficiency,** state enterprises are likely to be less efficient than private firms. The notion of X-inefficiency, developed by Harvey Leibenstein, can be understood in terms of the isoquant diagram shown in Figure 21–1.[12]

The diagram is similar to Figure 8–3 except that in all cases, output levels are constrained to one level, at Q. Points along isoquant Q_1, such as a and b, use the minimum amounts of labor and capital (l_a, k_a or l_b, k_b) and so are *technically efficient*. Points like c, to the southeast of the isoquant, are infeasible: output level Q cannot be produced with the level of inputs implied by

9. Jones, *Public Enterprise and Economic Development,* pp. 190–94.

10. Tony Killick, *Development Economics in Action* (New York: St. Martins Press, 1978), pp. 220–22.

11. Operating losses are losses incurred by enterprises before subtracting depreciation and before subsidies from the parent government. Operating losses are typically smaller than the overall deficit for state-owned firms.

12. For a full discussion, see Harvey Leibenstein, *Beyond Economic Man* (Cambridge, Mass.: Harvard University Press, 1976). For a condensed presentation of these factors, see Leibenstein, "X-Efficiency, Intrafirm Behavior and Growth," in *Lagging Productivity Growth: Causes and Remedies,* Schlomo Maital and Sidney Meltz, eds. (Cambridge, Mass.: Ballinger Press, 1980).

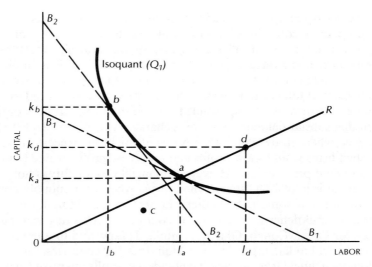

FIGURE 21–1   Allocative and X-Inefficiency: Production Function. Points a and b are technically efficient, point d is possible but not efficient, and point c is infeasible as an alternative
for producing the given level of output Q_l. Correct price signals may lead society to a point
like a, in which case allocative efficiency is achieved. "Incorrect" price signals may lead to
allocative inefficiency, with cost minimization, as at point b. But even with correct price signals, a firm may not minimize costs (point d). This is X-inefficiency.

point c. Suppose that market forces determine the relative prices of labor (w)
and capital (r) such that w/r represents the relative opportunity cost of the
two factors (see Chapter 6), and that w/r = 2. Then isocost (or budget) line
B_1B_1, with a slope = 2, shows the combinations of labor and capital that
could be purchased for a given total cost. A producer who wants either to
minimize his cost for a given output, Q_l, or to maximize his output for a
given cost of inputs, B_1B_1, would produce at point a on the isoquant. Not
only would the firm be producing efficiently, but because the firm's costs
represent the society's opportunity costs, this would be a point of allocative
efficiency for the society as well. Note that all points along $0R$ indicate production using identical *ratios* of labor and capital use, with **no** distortions.

Suppose instead that the government controls interest rates to subsidize
capital and enacts minimum wages that raise labor costs. This would lower
the relative price of capital and increase the slope of the isocost line, yielding
a budget line such as B_2B_2 in Figure 21–1. Now a profit-maximizing firm
would produce Q with capital-labor combination indicated at point b, which
is technically efficient, but is not allocatively efficient: the factor price distortions have caused the firm's factor use $(1_b, k_b)$ to diverge from the social optimum, which remains $1_a, k_a$, but the firm still produces Q, of output, and is
minimizing costs given the price signals he fares.

A firm may, however, face a correct set of price signals, represented by
B_1B_1, yet not produce at an allocatively efficient point. It might, for example,
produce the same quantity Q, by using too much of both capital and labor
even though it is using both factors in the correct proportions (as at point d,
which also lies on ray $0R$, going through the origin). This depicts Leiben-

stein's **X-inefficiency:** despite correct price signals, the firm does not minimize costs and is not allocatively efficient.

Any firm, public or private, could be X-inefficient for a variety of reasons. Managers may lack motivation to minimize costs, either because they are satisfied with less than maximum profits or because there are alternative ways to earn high profits, as is true in the import substitution regimes described in Chapter 16. Or managers may be skillful and motivated but unwilling to expend the effort to adopt new productive techniques to achieve minimum costs. They may make the judgment that somewhat lower costs and higher profits are not worth the often intangible costs of convincing their peers to change, motivating middle-level managers to greater efforts, or overcoming workers' resistance. Finally, changes in method do not always lead to certain outcomes, and this risk may discourage efforts to minimize costs. Whatever the reasons, firms and their managements are subject to "inert" regions, in Leibenstein's phrase, or gray areas in which they do not act as cost minimizers, but may accept less than optimal outcomes without taking action.

Although both private and public enterprise managements are subject to such inert zones, there is reason to believe that public firms, as well as private monopolies, may act less forcefully than private competitive firms to mini- mize costs.[13] Private enterprise must eventually meet a market test or go out of business. Cost control, if not cost minimization, is vital if the private firm is to make profits and survive in a market environment. But cost control is not nearly so essential to the survival of state-owned enterprises, for two rea- sons. First, governments are prone to protect their own enterprises from competition, either domestic or foreign, and thus to confer monopoly power on them.

Second, governments, the principal and often only shareholder, are loathe to permit their firms to die a natural death, to "sink beneath the sands." This is true in both industrial and developing countries: witness the loan guaran- tees to Lockheed and Chrysler in the United States and any number of take- overs of ailing firms by European governments (Rolls-Royce, British Leyland, and so on). This reluctance may stem from the fear of lost employ- ment, as in the case of cement plants in Bolivia, much of the textile industry in India, the state gold mines in Ghana, and the French steel mills; the desire to preserve national prestige, as in the case of Rolls-Royce in Britain; or gov- ernment's large financial stake in the firm as a result of past salvage opera- tions, as in the cases of British Leyland and any number of SOEs in Italy. Rather than permit bankruptcy, it is more common for a government to pump new funds into troubled firms or, under dire circumstances, to reor- ganize them and change managements. Thus public-enterprise managers, with a large cushion between themselves and ultimate test of market forces, have much less incentive than private firms to minimize costs, and there is greater scope for X-inefficiencies to go unchecked.

13. For evidence that private enterprises that enjoy monopoly power (e.g., regulated electric utilities) are also susceptible to this type of inefficiency, see W. J. Primeaux, "An Assessment of X-Efficiency Gained through Competition," *Review of Economics and Statistics* 59, no. 2 (June 1977): 516–17.

But X-inefficiency in SOEs is not due exclusively to any inability or unwillingness of managers to minimize costs. Pressures for X-inefficiency also arise from the external environment in which state firms operate. These include faulty incentive structures for workers and managers, such as the rigid limits on compensation that are decreed by government agencies; governmental insistence that SOEs hire unneeded workers, whether for patronage or to relieve unemployment problems; and government-imposed requirements to purchase materials from specific sources, whether to realize potential backward linkages or to reward political favorites.

Two other common causes of poor profit performance in SOEs also have their origin in the external environment: price controls and social responsibilities. State enterprises producing items regarded as basic necessities or key services are typically subjected to rigid and infrequently adjusted price controls for their products, reducing both revenues and profits. In many cases the enterprises are monopolies because private firms could not survive under price controls. Thus in Indonesia eight of nine items subject to price controls are produced by SOEs; food grain and kerosene distribution are handled by state firms in Colombia, Bolivia, India, and Sri Lanka because price controls make private participation impossible; and urban bus services are operated by public enterprises in many countries because of chronically low government ceilings on fares.

Finally, many SOEs record low profits or continuing losses because the government-as-stockholder has decreed that the enterprises must perform certain social functions normally carried on by ordinary government policy instruments. These are discussed in the next three sections.

Employment

Many SOEs have been established because they were thought to be more effective than private firms in creating new jobs for rapidly expanding labor forces. State enterprises do employ large numbers of workers: 1.5 million in India, 0.7 million in Indonesia, and nearly 0.5 million in Bangladesh. However, in very few countries does the proportion of employment in public firms to total employment outside of agriculture reach much above 10 percent, and for most countries with important SOE sectors the share is less than 5 percent.

In many LDCs the state enterprise sectors' share in total investment over comparable periods has been at least 30 percent, and in some countries over 50 percent. So it would appear that SOEs have not had remarkable success in creating new jobs in the past decade or so. This performance seems all the more perplexing in light of the pervasive tendency toward overstaffing state enterprises in most all developing countries.

The principal reason is traceable to the marked capital intensity of state-enterprise investment relative to private-sector investment in the same economy. This pattern has been documented in studies for such countries as Korea, Ghana, Brazil, India, Bolivia, Algeria, Colombia, Indonesia, and numerous others. One observer goes so far as to say that in Brazil and India "it is almost as if industries were divided between public and private enterprise according to their capital intensity," and that "public enterprise in Algeria is focused in capital intensive methods with little or no regard for chronically high rates of unemployment."[14] For Korea it has been demonstrated that the public-enterprise sector is more than three times as capital intensive as the Korean economy generally.[15] Another analyst has tracked a very marked bias toward capital intensity in a wide variety of Ghanaian SOEs, ranging from agricultural estates to sugar factories, footwear, fishing firms, and glass and canning factories.[16]

How does one explain an apparent anti-employment bias on the part of the public sector in countries where governmental commitments to expanded employment are written so large in national plans? There is a tendency for public officials and managers to favor capital-intensive projects, but the preference is not necessarily an active one. Rather it stems from a variety of market and nonmarket pressures toward capital intensity across a wide range of countries. The capacities, training, and orientation of governmental bureaucracies appear to operate in subtle ways that induce them to prefer capital- over labor-intensive projects.[17] There is also evidence that the terms and conditions upon which foreign aid is channeled to projects involving SOEs serve to heighten incipient biases toward capital intensity.[18]

There are a variety of economic considerations that help to explain why so much of SOE investment is more capital-intensive than would be the case if investment decisions were based upon scarcity values for both labor and capital. First, SOEs tend to be more heavily represented in concentrated industries than their private-sector counterparts. Biases toward capital intensity in investment are stronger where monopoly or oligopoly power can be exercised, a phenomenon observed in a growing number of studies on this subject.[19] The more competitive (the less concentrated) the environment in which firms operate, the greater the pressures for cost minimization, forcing firms to adopt more appropriate technology.

Second, a substantial share of SOE investment is concentrated in sectors, such as mineral extraction and heavy industry, that would tend to be capital intensive in any case, whether the investor is private, public, domestic, or foreign. And state enterprises dominate in other inherently capital-intensive sectors because private enterprises have been unwilling or unable to enter

14. John B. Sheahan, "Public Enterprise in Developing Countries," in *Public Enterprise: Economic Analysis of Theory and Practice,* W. G. Shepherd, ed. (Lexington, Mass. Lexington Books, 1976), p. 211.

15. Jones, *Public Enterprise and Economic Development,* p. 123.

16. Killick, *Development Economics in Action,* pp. 228–30.

17. For a cogent discussion of such subtle biases in capital intensity in public investment, see C. P. Timmer, "Public Policy for Improving Technology Choice" (manuscript prepared for Alternative Technology, Inc., September 1979), pp. 16–24.

18. A classic example dealing with rice milling is discussed in C. P. Timmer, "The Choice of Technique in Indonesia," in *The Choice of Technology in Developing Countries,* Timmer et al. (Cambridge, Mass.: Harvard University Center for International Affairs, 1975), pp. 1–30.

19. For Indonesia, see Wells, "Economic Man and Engineering Man," in *The Choice of Technology in Developing Countries,* pp. 71–90. On Thailand, see Donald J. LeCraw, "Choice of Technology in Low-Wage Countries: A Non-Neoclassical Approach," *Quarterly Journal of Economics* 93 (November 1979): 631–54. See also R. A. McCain, "Competition, Information and Redundancy: X-Efficiency and the Cybernetics of the Firm," *Kyklos* 28 (1975): 286–308.

them. These are activities characterized by substantial economies of scale (e.g., public utilities) and high risk.

Third, both public and private enterprises are subject to the price distortions—low interest rates, high wage rates, and overvalued exchanged rates discussed in Chapters 8 and 16—that make capital cheap and labor expensive. But additional pressures for capital-intensive choices apply to SOEs. In some countries (Colombia until 1974, for example) state firms are exempt from all tax obligations, including customs duties on imported capital equipment. SOEs also tend to pay a lower price for loan capital than do their private-sector counterparts because their debt is guaranteed, explicitly or implicitly, by the parent government, and therefore involves less risk of default to the lender. In countries where the banking system is also dominated by SOEs (Indonesia, Pakistan, Mexico), lower interest costs to SOE borrowers are often the result of conscious policy enforced by the government. Moreover SOEs often view equity capital as costless, because governments normally do not place a price upon it by insisting that dividends be paid. Under such circumstances decisions by managers that involve wasteful use of capital may not reflect lack of concern for the cost of capital, but may instead reflect an accurate reading of, and rational response to, highly distorted price signals from governments.

State enterprises may have had a greater impact on preserving jobs when private firms are about to fail, although usually at a substantial continuing cost to the government. Governments' reluctance to permit their enterprises to fail was discussed in the previous section. In many cases this reluctance can be traced to the fear that bankruptcies will lead to unemployment and its political consequences. Nowhere has this fear been more evident than in Bolivia. Under Bolivian law and tradition it is virtually impossible for a firm to go out of business. Because it is also virtually impossible to dismiss workers, for whatever reason, many private investors over the years have, after experiencing continuing losses, merely walked away from their enterprises, leaving them, as it were, on the government's doorstep. In other cases labor groups have pressed government to assume ownership prior to this stage and have met with some success. As a result perhaps half of the over fifty firms owned by the Bolivian central government belong in the "sinking sands" category, as do the majority of Indian textile SOEs.

Social Responsibilities

While available evidence does permit some tentative generalizations concerning the impact of SOEs on savings mobilization and employment, there is very little basis for assessing their contribution to other common societal goals. These include income redistribution, provision of basic services, training of managers, rectifying long-standing societal imbalances (ethnic or otherwise), breaking domestic monopoly power, and promoting national independence through counterbalancing or entirely displacing the influence of multinational enterprise. Still, it is instructive to examine this set of issues briefly.

Large segments of the poor, particularly the urban poor, have direct day-

to-day contact with state-owned enterprises in many lines of activity, such as
food distribution, electric power transmission, water supply, and bus transportation. Given the nature and extent of this contact, and given the limited short-term effectiveness of tax and expenditure policies in reaching the poor, many economists advocate the use of the state-enterprise sector as a prime tool to advance income redistribution goals through subsidized prices for items of basic necessity. We have already seen that in one important respect —job creation, especially for the poor—SOEs have been singularly unsuccessful in improving income distributions.

Results from a variety of countries indicate that a well-designed subsidy system can contribute significantly to redistribution, provided two conditions are met. First, items eligible for subsidy must be those that are important in the budgets of the poor, and not in the budgets of the nonpoor. If the relatively well-off are also major consumers of the item, a little redistribution may be secured at relatively great cost.[20] Second, the subsidy scheme must be structured to avoid incentives for waste and inefficiency in the operation of the affected state enterprise. Otherwise, as experience in a number of countries shows, the enterprise almost inevitably becomes incapable of fulfilling its social function effectively. This outcome is particularly likely when the enterprise itself is required to absorb losses from the operation of the subsidy program. The public enterprise manager is then inclined to attribute all problems to the necessity of meeting its social obligations, a pattern that has been repeated in Indonesian and Bolivian SOEs in banking (subsidized loans to farmers), Pakistani SOEs in fuel distribution, and Colombian SOEs in food distribution. There is almost no way in which such claims can be disputed. If, on the other hand, the enterprise is directly reimbursed by the government for the difference between the costs of acquiring the subsidized item and the selling price, subsidy schemes directed to the poor can work reasonably well and the enterprise cannot plead extenuating circumstances in explaining large losses. Examples include rural electrification efforts in Malaysia, where the state electricity enterprise is reimbursed for the higher cost of serving distant villages, and rice distribution in Indonesia, where the cost of the subsidy is borne by the government budget and not the state firm involved.

Several countries have established regional development banks and corporations designed to assist "lagging" regions to catch up with more prosperous parts of the country. Some, like the Guyana Development Corporation in Venezuela, are quite large and well endowed. Others, including several regional development corporations in Bolivia and regional development banks in Indonesia, operate on far more modest budgets. But in general these entities are expected to operate on commercial principals, even if they do not attempt to maximize profits. This merely reflects recognition of the fact that financially viable firms are better able to contribute to social objectives.

Malaysia and Indonesia have both established a number of public enterprises in the financial sector intended to promote greater participation by

20. See the example of Indonesia's kerosene subsidy discussed in Chapter 12.

economically weak groups, largely the Malay majority *(bumipatra* or *pribumis),* in the development process. In Indonesia an enterprise has been created in order to channel more equity capital and technical assistance to economically weak entrepreneurs in the small- and medium-scale industrial sector. Another enterprise has been charged with the responsibility of providing finance for the "Indonesianization" of equity in foreign investment projects. While both SOEs were established primarily to promote a social goal, both are expected to maintain long-term commercial viability without the need for large government subsidies.

SOEs and Multinational Investments

In much of the developing world, particularly in Latin America, public enterprises are viewed as an essential means of counterbalancing or harnessing the economic power of multinational firms based in industrial countries. Until recently this goal was generally promoted through the nationalization of the domestic operations of foreign firms and the subsequent transfer of all assets to state-owned enterprises. This approach has been particularly common in natural resources, as illustrated in Mexico, Peru, Indonesia, and Argentina in oil, and in Chile, Peru, Zambia, Zaire, and Indonesia in mining. Although in a few cases, such as Mexico and Peru, nationalization has been undertaken subsequent to heated domestic outbursts of nationalistic, anti-imperialist sentiment, governments have by and large selected enterprises to be nationalized with clear criteria.[21] In Chile, Zambia, Zaire, and a variety of other countries, nationalization was merely the end product of a long series of measures designed to assert more national control over natural-resource endowments, coinciding with what host countries perceived to be declining national needs for foreign capital, technology, and market access.

By the late 1970s a new pattern emerged as many LDCs began to utilize state enterprises in a somewhat different fashion to counter the influence of the multinationals. New SOEs were created and existing ones rapidly expanded to move into markets previously (or still) dominated by multinationals. Examples of the former type include nearly a half dozen new firms engaged in the mining of uranium (Bolivia and Colombia), fishery projects (Indonesia), and natural resources processing (Bolivia and Indonesia). Among the SOEs that have undergone dramatic expansion in markets where multinationals have predominated are CVRD and Petrobras of Brazil, Ferrominera of Venezuela, and Pemex and Cananca of Mexico.

In virtually all of these countries, and in parts of Africa, a relatively new form of multinational involvement has evolved: joint ventures between the multinationals and domestic SOEs, particularly in the natural resources area. In earlier days the project undertaken would likely have been mounted exclusively by foreign private interests or, more recently, by foreign private interests in cooperation with private domestic interests. Rising nationalism and dissatisfaction with the economic and social outcomes of direct foreign

21. Vernon, "The State-Owned Enterprise in Latin American Exports," p. 5.

investment have curtailed the former, and disappointment with the results of
earlier private joint ventures have led many governments increasingly to favor arrangements in which the state itself, through one of its public enterprises, is the joint-venture partner. Recent examples include mining projects in Brazil and Peru, fisheries and natural-resource-processing projects in Indonesia, and a host of agreements recently concluded in Latin America in uranium. All of these involved the creation of new state enterprises in the host country, or at a minimum, rapid expansion of pre-existing enterprises owned by the state.

Strong forces have been at work to expand the number of this new breed of public enterprise. From the point of view of foreign investors the arrangement is often very attractive. It involves a venture in which the partner (the government) is also the dispenser of favors (tax relief, insulation from competition, and so on), which is perceived as a means of reducing the political risks of operating in a foreign country. From the government's point of view this type of arrangement is often seen as the best way to protect national interests from potential damage by commercially oriented, profit-seeking enterprises with little long-run stake in the country's future. In particular it is often viewed as a way to prevent "sophisticated" foreign investors from taking advantage of inexperienced private, domestic joint-venture investors who are thought unable to exploit their bargaining positions. And finally, the increasing reliance on state-owned joint-venture partners may in some cases represent a governmental reaction against the "sham" types of joint ventures so often concluded at the height of the "joint-venture movement" of the 1960s and early 1970s, in which the main domestic effect may have been to enrich small elites in the private sector without resulting in any significant transfer of technology, know-how, or meaningful managerial control to the host country.

Bibliography and Additional Readings

CHAPTER 1. INTRODUCTION: WORLDS APART

World Bank, *World Development Report* (New York: Oxford University Press, annual).

———, *World Tables* (Baltimore: Johns Hopkins University Press, 1983).

CHAPTER 2. STARTING MODERN ECONOMIC GROWTH

Obstacles to Development
Alexander Gerschenkron, *Economic Backwardness in Historical Perspective* (Cambridge, Mass.: Harvard University Press, 1962).

———, *Europe in the Russian Mirror* (Cambridge, Mass.: Harvard University Press, 1970).

Entrepreneurship
Everett Hagen, *On the Theory of Social Change: How Economic Growth Begins* (Homewood, Ill.: Richard Dorsey, 1962).

Bert F. Hoselitz, *Sociological Aspects of Economic Growth* (Glencoe, Ill.: The Free Press, 1960).

David McClelland, *The Achieving Society* (Princeton: Van Nostrand, 1961).

Joseph Schumpeter, *The Theory of Economic Development* (Cambridge, Mass.: Harvard University Press, 1934).

Paul Baran, *The Political Economy of Growth* (New York: Monthly Review Press, 1957).

Celso Furtado, " 'The Brazilian Model' of Development," in *The Political Economy of Development and Underdevelopment,* Charles K. Wilber, ed. (New York: Random House, 1979) pp. 324–33.

Keith Griffin and John Gurley, "Radical Analyses of Imperialism, the Third World, and the Transition to Socialism," *Journal of Economic Literature,* 23, no. 3 (September 1985).

J. A. Hobson, *Imperialsim—A Study* (Ann Arbor: University of Michigan Press, 1965).

Alan Hodgart, *The Economics of European Imperialism* (New York: W. W. Norton, 1977).

V. I. Lenin, *Imperialism, The Highest Stage of Capitalism* (Moscow: Progress Publishers, 1975).

Karl Marx, *Das Kapital* (1867).

Robert I. Rhodes, ed., *Imperialism and Underdevelopment: A Reader* (New York: Monthly Review Press, 1970).

Historical Heritage and Economic Development

Keith Hart, *The Political Economy of West African Agriculture* (New York: Cambridge University Press, 1982).

Albert O. Hirschman, "Ideologies of Economic Development in Latin America," in *A Bias for Hope* (New Haven: Yale University Press, 1971).

Anthony G. Hopkins, *An Economic History of West Africa* (New York: Columbia University Press, 1973).

E. S. Mason et al., *The Economic and Social Modernization of the Republic of Korea* (Cambridge, Mass.: Harvard Press, 1980).

D. H. Perkins, ed., *China's Modern Economy in Historical Perspective* (Stanford: Stanford University Press, 1975).

CHAPTER 3. GROWTH AND STRUCTURAL CHANGE

The Harrod-Domar Model

Evsey Domar, "Capital Expansion, Rate of Growth and Employment," *Econometrica* (1946): 137–47.

———, "Expansion and Employment," *American Economic Review,* 37 (1947): 34–55.

Roy F. Harrod, "An Essay in Dynamic Theory," *Economic Journal* (1939): 14–33.

The Changing Structure of Output

Hollis B. Chenery, *Structural Change and Development Policy* (London: Oxford University Press, 1979).

Hollis B. Chenery and Moises Syrquin, *Patterns of Development, 1950–1970* (London: Oxford University Press, 1975).

Hollis B. Chenery and Lance J. Taylor, "Development Patterns: Among Countries and Over Time," *Review of Economics and Statistics* (November 1968): 391–416.

Irving Kravis, Alan Heston, and Robert Summers, *International Comparisons of Real Product and Purchasing Power* (Baltimore and London: Johns Hopkins University Press, 1978).

Simon Kuznets, *Economic Growth and Structure* (New York: W. W. Norton, 1965).
———, *Modern Economic Growth* (New Haven: Yale University Press, 1966).
W. W. Rostow, *The Stages of Economic Growth: A Non-Communist Manifesto* (Cambridge: Cambridge University Press, 1961).

Two-Sector Models

J. C. Fei and Gustav Ranis, *Development of the Labor Surplus Economy* (Homewood, Ill.: Richmond and Irwin, 1964).
Dale W. Jorgenson, "Testing Alternative Theories of the Development of a Dual Economy," in *The Theory and Design of Development,* I. Adelman and E. Thorbecke, eds. (Baltimore and London: Johns Hopkins University Press, 1966).
W. Arthur Lewis, "Economic Development with Unlimited Supplies of Labor," *The Manchester School,* 22 (May 1954): 139–91.

Balanced versus Unbalanced Growth

Albert O. Hirschman, *The Strategy of Economic Development* (New Haven: Yale University Press, 1958).
Ragnar Nurkse, *Problems of Capital Formation in Underdeveloped Countries* (New York: Oxford University Press, 1953).
Paul N. Rosenstein-Rodan, "Problems of Industrialization of Eastern and Southeastern Europe," *Economic Journal* (June–September 1943), reprinted in *The Economics of Underdevelopment,* A. N. Agarwala and S. P. Singh, eds., (New York: Oxford University Press, 1963).

CHAPTER 4. DEVELOPMENT AND HUMAN WELFARE

Concepts and Measures

Gary S. Fields, *Poverty, Inequality and Development* (Cambridge, England: Cambridge University Press, 1980).
Charles R. Frank, Jr. and Richard C. Webb, eds., *Income Distribution and Growth in the Less-Developed Countries* (Washington, D.C.: Brookings Institution, 1977).
Arnold Harberger, "Basic Needs versus Distributional Weights in Social Cost-Benefit Analysis," *Economic Development and Cultural Change* 32, no. 4 (April 1984): 455–77.
Morris David Morris, *Measuring the Condition of the World's Poor. The Physical Quality of Life Index* (New York: Pergamon Press for the Overseas Development Council, 1979).
Dudley Sears, "The Meaning of Development," in *The Political Economy of Development and Underdevelopment,* Charles K. Wilber, ed. (New York: Random House, 1973).
Amartya K. Sen, *On Economic Inequality* (New York: W. W. Norton, 1973).
———, "Three Notes on the Concept of Poverty" (International Labour Office, World Employment Programme Research Paper No. 65, January 1978).
Richard Szal and Sherman Robinson, "Measuring Income Inequality," in *Income Distribution and Growth in the Less-Developed Countries,* (Washington, D.C.: Brookings Institution, 1977), pp. 491–533.

Patterns of Inequality and Poverty

Irma Adelman and Cynthia Taft Morris, *Economic Growth and Social Equity in Developing Countries* (Stanford, Calif.: Stanford University Press, 1973).

* Irma Adelman and Sherman Robinson, *Income Distribution Policy in Developing Countries. A Case Study of Korea* (Stanford, Calif.: Stanford University Press, 1978).

Montek S. Ahluwalia, "Income Inequality: Some Dimensions of the Problem," in *Redistribution with Growth,* pp. 3–37.

———, "Inequality, Poverty and Development," *Journal of Development Economics* 3 (1976).

International Labour Office, *Poverty and Landlessness in Rural Asia* (Geneva: ILO, 1977).

Simon Kuznets, "Economic Growth and Income Inequality," *American Economic Review* 45, no. 1 (March 1955).

World Bank, *Prospects for Developing Countries, 1978–85* (Washington, D. C.: World Bank, November 1977).

Theories of Inequality and Poverty

William R. Cline, "Distribution and Development: A Survey of the Literature," *Journal of Development Economics* (1975): 359–400.

Strategies for Growth with Equity

Hollis Chenery et al., *Redistribution with Growth* (London: Oxford University Press, 1974).

International Labour Office, *Employment, Growth and Basic Needs: A One-World Problem* (New York: Praeger Publishers, 1977).

John Mellor, *The New Economics of Growth: A Strategy for India and the Developing World* (Ithaca, N.Y.: Cornell University Press, 1976).

CHAPTER 5. PLANNING, MARKETS, AND POLITICS

Plans and Markets

Oskar Lange, "On the Economic Theory of Socialism," in *On the Economic Theory of Socialism,* B. Lippincott, ed. (Minneapolis: University of Minnesota Press, 1938).

I. M. D. Little, *Economic Development: Theory, Policy and International Relations* (New York: Basic Books, 1982).

Planning Process

Graham T. Allison, *The Essence of Decision: Explaining the Cuban Missile Crisis* (Boston: Little, Brown, 1971).

Everett E. Hagen, ed., *Planning Economic Development* (Homewood, Ill.: Richard D. Irwin, 1963).

* G. M. Heal, *The Theory of Economic Planning* (Amsterdam: North Holland, 1973).

Tony Killick, "The Possibilities of Development Planning," *Oxford Economic Papers* 28, no. 2 (1976): 161–84.

David K. Leonard, "The Political Realities of African Management" (Binghampton, N.Y.: Institute for Development Anthropology, September 1985).

* Daniel P. Loucks, "Planning for Multiple Goals," in C. R. Blitzer et al., eds., *Economy-wide Models and Development Planning* (London: Oxford University Press, 1975).

* Asterisks denote more advanced readings.

Michael Roemer, "Planning by Revealed Preference," *World Development* 4, no. 9
(1976): 775–83.
Albert Waterston, *Development Planning: Lessons of Experience* (Baltimore: Johns Hopkins University Press, 1965).
Louis J. Walinsky, *The Planning and Execution of Economic Development* (New York: McGraw-Hill, 1963).

Implementation
Robert H. Bates, *Markets and States in Tropical Africa* (Berkeley: University of California Press, 1981).
Anne O. Krueger, "The Political Economy of Rent-Seeking," *American Economic Review* 64, no. 3 (1974): 291–303.
Jeffrey L. Pressman and Aaron Wildavsky, *Implementation: How Great Expectations in Washington are Dashed in Oakland* (Berkeley: University of California Press, 1973).
Donald Warwick, "Integrating Planning and Implementation: A Transactional Approach," in *Planning Education for Development,* vol. I., R. Davis, ed. (Cambridge, Mass.: Center for Studies in Education and Development, Harvard University, 1980).

The Resurgence of the Market
World Bank, *Accelerated Development in Sub-Saharan Africa: an Agenda for Action* (Washington, ·D.C.: 1981).

CHAPTER 6. PLANNING MODELS

Keynesian Growth Models
* Jere Behrman and James Hanson, *Short-term Macroeconomic Policy in Latin America* (Cambridge, Mass.: National Bureau of Economic Research, 1979).
* Hollis Chenery and Alan Strout, "Foreign Assistance and Economic Development," *American Economic Review* 56 (1966): 679–733.
* Ronald McKinnon, "Foreign Exchange Constraints and Economic Development," *Economic Journal* 74 (1964): 388–409.
* Lance Taylor, "Theoretical Foundations and Technical Implications," in *Economy-wide Models and Development Planning,* C. R. Blitzer et. al, eds. (London: Oxford University Press, 1975).
*_____, Macro Models for Developing Countries (New York: McGraw-Hill, 1979).
Jan Tinbergen, *Economic Policy: Principles and Design* (Amsterdam: North-Holland, 1956).
_____, *Central Planning* (New Haven: Yale University Press, 1976).

Interindustry Models
Hollis Chenery and Paul Clark, *Interindustry Economics* (New York: Wiley, 1959).
* Kemal Dervis, Jaime de Melo, and Sherman Robinson, *General Equilibrium Models for Developing Countries* (Cambridge, England: Cambridge University Press, 1982).
* Robert Dorfman, Paul Samuelson, and Robert Solow, *Linear Programming and Economic Analysis* (New York: McGraw-Hill, 1958).

* Asterisks denote more advanced readings.

Graham Pyatt and Erik Thorbecke, *Planning Techniques for a Better Future* (Geneva: International Labour Office, 1976).

Project Appraisal
*Arnold Harberger, *Project Evaluation: Collected Papers* (Chicago: Markham, 1974).
* I. M. D. Little and James A. Mirrlees, *Project Appraisal and Planning for Developing Countries* (New York: Basic Books, 1974).
Michael Roemer and Joseph J. Stern, *Cases in Economic Development* (London: Butterworths, 1981).
————, *The Appraisal of Development Projects* (New York: Praeger, 1975).
* United Nations Industrial Development Organization (P. Dasgupta, S. Margolin, and A. Sen) *Guidelines for Project Evaluation* (New York: United Nations, 1982).

CHAPTER 7. POPULATION

A Brief History of Human Population
Lester R. Brown, *In the Human Interest* (New York: W. W. Norton, 1974).
Carlo Cipolla, *The Economic History of World Population* (Harmondsworth, England: Penguin Books, 1962).

The Demographic Future
Thomas Frejka, *The Future of Population Growth* (New York: Population Council, 1973).

The Causes of Population Growth
* Gary Becker, *A Treatise on the Family* (Cambridge, Mass.: Harvard University Press, 1981).
John C. Caldwell, "Mass Education as a Determinant of Fertility Decline," *Population and Development Review* 6, no. 2 (June 1980): 225–55.
Richard Easterlin, "Modernization and Fertility: A Critical Essay," in *Determinants of Fertility in Developing Countries,* vol. 2, R. Bulatao and R. Lee, eds. (New York: Academic Press, 1983), pp. 562–86.
Michael S. Teitelbaum, "Relevance of Demographic Transition Theory for Developing Countries," *Science* 188 (May 2, 1977): 420–25.

Analyzing the Effects of Rapid Population Growth
Ester Boserup, *The Conditions of Agricultural Growth* (Chicago: Aldine, 1965).
Colin Clark, "The 'Population Explosion' Myth," *Bulletin of the Institute of Development Studies* (Sussex, England, May 1969).
————, "The Economics of Population Growth and Control: A Comment," *Review of Social Economy* 28, no. 1 (March 1970).
Ansley J. Coale and Edgar M. Hoover, *Population Growth and Economic Development in Low-Income Countries: A Case Study of India's Prospects* (Princeton: Princeton University Press, 1958).
Geoffrey McNicoll, "Consequences of Rapid Population Growth: An Overview and Assessment," *Population and Development Review* 10, no. 2 (June 1981): 177–240.

* Asterisks denote more advanced readings.

Mark Perlman, "Population and Economic Change in Developing Countries: A Review Article," *Journal of Economic Literature* 19, no. 1 (1981): 74–82.

Rati Ram and Theodore W. Schultz, "Life Span, Savings, and Productivity," *Economic Development and Cultural Change* 27, no. 3 (April 1979): 394–421.

Julian Simon, "World Population Growth," *Atlantic Monthly* (August 1981): 70–76.

Population Policy

Nick Eberstadt, "Recent Declines in Fertility in Less Developed Countries and What 'Population Planners' May Learn from Them," *World Development* 11, no. 1 (March 1985): 113–38.

"Fertility and Family Planning Surveys: An Update," *Population Reports* Series M, no. 8 (September-October 1985), Johns Hopkins University Press.

W. Parker Mauldin and Bernard Berelson, "Conditions of Fertility Decline in Developing Countries, 1965–75," *Studies in Family Planning* 9, no. 5 (1978).

National Academy of Sciences, *Population Growth and Economic Development: Policy Questions* (Washington, D.C.: National Academy Press, 1986).

Ronald G. Ridker, ed., *Population and Development: The Search for Selective Interventions* (Baltimore and London: Johns Hopkins University Press for Resources for the Future, 1976).

World Bank, *World Development Report 1984* (New York: Oxford University Press, 1984), pp. 51–206.

CHAPTER 8. LABOR'S ROLE

Analyzing Employment Issues

Albert Berry and R. H. Sabot, "Unemployment and Economic Development," *Economic Development and Cultural Change* 33, no. 1 (October 1984): 99–116.

Henry J. Bruton, "Economic Development and Labor Use: A Review," *World Development* (December 1973): 1–22.

J. Keith Hart, "Informal Income Opportunities and the Structure of Urban Employment in Ghana," *Modern African Studies* 2, no. 1 (March 1973): 61–89.

Philip M. Hauser, "The Measurement of Labour Utilisation," *Malayan Economic Review* 19, no. 1 (April 1974): 16–34.

———, "The Measurement of Labour Utilisation—More Empirical Results," *Malayan Economic Review* 22, no. 1 (April 1977): 10–25.

International Labour Office, *Towards Full Employment* (Geneva: ILO, 1970).

S. Mehra, "Surplus Labour in Indian Agriculture," *Indian Economic Review* (April 1966).

David Turnham, assisted by Ingelies Jaeger, *The Employment Problem in Less Developed Countries: A Review of Evidence* (Paris: Organisation for Economic Cooperation and Development, 1971).

Labor Reallocation

Jagdish Bhagwati and Martin Partington, *Taxing the Brain Drain: A Proposal* (Amsterdam: North-Holland, 1976).

Peter Gregory, "An Assessment of Changes in Employment Conditions in Less Developed Countries," *Economic Development and Cultural Change* 28, no. 4 (July 1980): 673–700.

John R. Harris and Michael P. Todaro, "Migration, Unemployment and Development: A Two-Sector Analysis," *American Economic Review* 60 (March 1970): 126–42.

Ragnar Nurkse, *Problems of Capital Formation in Underdeveloped Countries* (Oxford: Basil Blackwell, 1957; first published in 1953).

Michael P. Todaro, "Income Expectations, Rural-Urban Migration and Employment in Africa," *International Labour Review* (1971): 387–414.

Employment Policy

S. J. Burki et al., "Public Works Programs in Developing Countries: A Comparative Analysis" (World Bank Staff Working Paper No. 224, February 1976).

Edgar O. Edwards, ed., *Employment in Developing Nations* (New York and London: Columbia University Press, 1974).

Richard Jolly et al., *Third-World Employment: Problems and Strategy* (Harmondsworth, England: Penguin Books, 1973).

Lyn Squire, *Employment Policy in Developing Countries: A Survey of Issues and Evidence* (New York: Oxford University Press for the World Bank, 1981).

Frances Stewart, "Technology and Employment in LDCs," in *Employment in Developing Nations,* pp. 83–132.

Susumu Watanabe, "Exports and Employment: The Case of the Republic of Korea," *International Labour Review* 106, no. 6 (December, 1972): 495–526.

Louis T. Wells, "Economic Man and Engineering Man: Choice of Technology in a Low-wage Country," in *The Choice of Technology in Developing Countries: Some Cautionary Tales,* C. Peter Timmer, ed. (Cambridge, Mass.: Harvard University Center for International Affairs, 1975), pp. 69–93.

Lawrence White, *Industrial Concentration and Economic Power in Pakistan* (Princeton, N.J.: Princeton University Press, 1974).

CHAPTER 9. EDUCATION

Importance of Education

Mark Blaug, *Economics of Education,* vols. 1 and 2 (London: Penguin Books, 1968, 1969).

———, *Introduction to the Economics of Education* (London: Penguin Books, 1970).

———, *Education and the Employment Problem in Developing Countries* (Geneva: International Labor Office, 1973).

M. Blaug, R. Layard, and M. Woodhall, *Causes of Graduate Unemployment in India* (Harmondsworth, Middlesex, England: Allen Lane, Penguin Press, 1969).

George Psacharopoulos and Maureen Woodhall, *Education for Development: An Analysis of Investment Choices* (New York: Oxford University Press, 1985).

Theodore W. Schultz, " Investment in Human Capital," *American Economic Review* 51 (January 1961): 1–17.

World Bank, *World Development Report 1980* (New York: Oxford University Press, 1980).

Trends and Patterns

Russell Davis, "Planning Education for Employment" (Harvard Institute for International Development, Development Discussion Paper No. 60, June 1979).

Ronald Dore, *The Diploma Disease. Education, Qualification and Development* (Berkeley and Los Angeles: University of California Press, 1976).

John Simmons, "How Effective is Schooling in Promoting Learning? A Review of Research" (World Bank Staff Working Paper No. 200, March 1975).

M. Boissiere, J. B. Knight, and R. H. Sabot, "Earnings, Schooling, Ability, and Cognitive Skills," *American Economic Review* 75, no. 5 (December 1985): 1016–30.

Martin Carnoy, "Rates of Return to Schooling in Latin America," *Journal of Human Resources* (Summer 1967): 359–74.

Philip H. Coombs with Manzoor Ahmed, *Attacking Rural Poverty: How Nonformal Education Can Help* (Baltimore and London: Johns Hopkins University Press, 1974).

Philip J. Foster, "The Vocational School Fallacy in Development Planning," in *Education and Economic Development,* C. A. Anderson and M. J. Bowman, eds. (Chicago: Aldine Publishing Company, 1966), pp. 142–63.

Paolo Freire, *Pedagogy of the Oppressed,* translated from the Portuguese by Myra Bergman Ramos (New York: Seabury Press, 1970).

Ivan Illich, *Deschooling Society* (New York: Harper and Row, 1970).

Herbert S. Parnes, *Forecasting Educational Needs for Economic Development,* Mediterranean Regional Project (Paris: Organisation for Economic Co-operation and Development, 1962).

George Psacharopoulos, "Returns to Education: An Updated International Comparison," *Comparative Education* 17, no. 3 (1981): 321–42.

―――, "Returns to Education: A Further International Update and Implications," *Journal of Human Resources* 20, no. 4 (1985): 583–604.

Jan Tinbergen and H. C. Bos, "A Planning Model for the Educational Requirements of Economic Development," in *Econometric Models for Education* (Paris: Organisation for Economic Co-operation and Development, 1965).

CHAPTER 10. HEALTH AND NUTRITION

Health in the Third World

Samuel H. Preston, "The Changing Relationship between Mortality and Level of Development," *Population Studies* 29, no. 2 (July 1975): 231–48.

―――, *Mortality Patterns in National Populations, with Special Reference to Recorded Causes of Death* (New York: Academic Press, 1976).

World Bank, *Health Sector Policy Paper,* 2nd ed. (Washington, D.C.: World Bank, 1980).

―――, *World Development Report 1980* (New York: Oxford University Press, 1980), pp. 32–104.

Effects of Health on Development

Mohiuddin Alamgir, "The Dimension of Undernutrition and Malnutrition in Developing Countries: Conceptual, Empirical and Policy Issues" (Harvard Institute for International Development, Development Discussion Paper No. 82, February 1980).

S. Basta and A. Churchill, "Iron Deficiency Anemia and the Productivity of Adult Males in Indonesia" (World Bank Staff Working Paper No. 175, April 1974).

Richard Feuchem et al., *Water, Health and Development: An Interdisciplinary Evaluation* (London: Tri-Med Books, 1974), Chapter 9.

Selma Mushkin, "Health as an Investment," *Journal of Political Economy* 70, no. 5, part 2 (Supplement, October 1962): 129–57.

Barry M. Popkin, "Nutrition and Labor Productivity," *Social Science and Medicine* 12C (1978): 117–25.

Nicholas M. Prescott, "Schistosomiasis and Development," *World Development* 7, no. 1 (1979):1–14.

C. Peter Timmer, "Food Policy, Food Consumption, and Nutrition" (Harvard Institute for International Development, Development Discussion Paper No. 124, October 1981).

Burton Weisbrod and Robert E. Baldwin, "Disease and Labor Productivity," *Economic Development and Cultural Change* 22, no. 3 (1974): 414–35.

Malnutrition

Alan Berg, *The Nutrition Factor: Its Role in National Development* (Washington, D.C.: Brookings Institution, 1973).

Shlomo Reutlinger, "Malnutrition: A Poverty Problem or a Food Problem?" *World Development* 5, no. 8 (1977): 715–24

Shlomo Reutlinger and Marcelo Selowsky, *Malnutrition and Poverty: Magnitude and Policy Options,* World Bank Occasional Papers No. 23 (Baltimore: Johns Hopkins University Press, 1976).

Amartya Sen, "Ingredients of Famine Analysis: Availability and Entitlements," *Quarterly Journal of Economics* 96, no. 3 (August 1981): 433–64.

C. Peter Timmer, Walter P. Falcon, and Scott R. Pearson, *Food Policy Analysis* (Baltimore: Johns Hopkins University Press, 1983).

World Bank, *Poverty and Hunger. Issues and Options for Food Security in Developing Countries* (Washington, 1986).

Medical Services

Frederick Golladay and Bernhard Liese, "Health Problems and Policies in Developing Countries" (World Bank Staff Working Paper No. 412, August 1980).

James Kocher and Richard A. Cash, "Achieving Health and Nutritional Objectives within a Basic Needs Framework" (Harvard Institute for International Development, Development Discussion Paper No. 55, March 1979).

Michael Lipton, *Why Poor People Stay Poor: Urban Bias in World Development* (Cambridge, Mass.: Harvard University Press, 1977).

CHAPTER 11. CAPITAL AND SAVINGS

Investment Requirements for Growth

Edward F. Denison, *The Sources of Economic Growth in the United States* (New York: Committee for Economic Development, 1962).

———, *Why Growth Rates Differ* (Washington, D.C.: Brookings Institution, 1967).

International Monetary Fund. *International Financial Statistics Yearbook, 1985* (Washington, D.C. 1985).

Kwang Suk Kim and Michael Roemer, *Growth and Structural Transformation, Studies in the Modernization of the Republic of Korea: 1945–1975* (Cambridge, Mass.: Harvard University Press, 1979).

Paul Streeten, 'The Uses and Abuses of Models in Development Planning, " in *The Teaching of Development Economics,* K. Martin and J. Krall, eds., (London: Cass, 1967), pp. 63–75.

World Bank, *World Development Report 1984* (New York: Oxford University Press, 1984).

———, *World Development Report 1985* (New York: Oxford University Press, 1985).

International Monetary Fund. *Government Financial Statistics Yearbook 1985* (Washington D.C.: International Monetary Fund, 1986).

Raymond F. Mikesell and James E. Zinser, "The Nature of the Savings Function in Developing Countries: A Survey of the Theoretical and Empirical Literature," *Journal of Economic Literature* 11, no. 1 (March 1973): 1–26.

Stanley Please, "Savings Through Taxation: Reality or Mirage?" *Finance and Development* 4, no. 1 (March 1967): pp. 24–32.

Alan Tait, Wilfred Gratz, and Barry Eichengreen, "International Comparisons of Taxation for Selected Developing Countries," *International Monetary Fund Staff Papers* 26, no. 1, (March 1979): 123–56.

Vito Tanzi, "Quantitative Characteristics of Tax Systems in Developing Countries," in *Modern Tax Theory for Developing Countries,* David Newbery and Nicholas Stern, eds. (In press.)

Determinants of Private Savings

Ranadev Banerji, "Small-Scale Production Units in Manufacturing: An International Cross-Section Overview," *Weltwirtschaftliches Archiv* 114, no. 1 (1978).

Donald F. Huddle, "An Analysis of the Savings Behavior of a Group of Colombian Artisan Entrepreneurs," *World Development* 4, no. 4 (October 1978).

Nicholas Kaldor, "Problemas Economicas De Chile," *El Trimestre Economico* 26, no. 102 (April–June 1959): 193, 211–12.

A. E. Kelley and J. Williamson, "Household Savings Behavior in the Developing Economies," *Economic Development and Cultural Change* 16, no. 3 (April 1968).

Constantino Lluch, Alan Powell, and Ross Williams, *Patterns in Household Demand and Savings* (Washington, D.C.: Oxford University Press, 1977).

F. Modigliani, R. Brumberg, and A. Ando, "Life Cycle Hypothesis of Savings: Aggregate Implication and Tests," *American Economic Review* 52, no. 3 (1963).

United Nations, Department of Economic and Social Affairs, *Yearbook of National accounts Statistics 1979* (New York, 1979).

J. G. Williamson, "Personal Savings in Developing Nations: An Intertemporal Cross Section for Asia," *Economic Record* 29, no. 2 (June 1968).

World Bank, *World Development Report 1983* (New York: Oxford University Press, 1983).

International Mobility of Capital and Domestic Savings Mobilization

Jeremy Greenwood and Kent Kimbrough, "Capital Controls and the World Economy," *Canadian Journal of Economics* (1986).

Arnold Harberger, "Vignettes on the World Capital Market," *American Economic Review* 70, no. 2 (May 1980): 331–37.

CHAPTER 12. FISCAL POLICY

Taxation and Public Savings

Roy W. Bahl, "A Regression Approach to Tax Effort and Tax-Ratio Analysis," *International Monetary Fund Staff Papers* 14, no. 4 (1971): 570–608.

Richard M. Bird, "Assessing Tax Performance in Developing Countries," *Finanzachiv,* Band 34, Heft 2 (1975).

Richard Bird, and Oliver Oldman, eds., *Readings on Taxation in Developing Countries,* 3rd Ed. (Baltimore: Johns Hopkins University Press, 1975).

John F. Due, *Indirect Taxation in Developing Economies* (Baltimore: Johns Hopkins University Press, 1970).

Malcolm Gillis, "Federal Sales Taxation: Six Decades of Experience," *Canadian Tax Journal* (January–February 1985).

Malcolm Gillis and Charles E. McLure, Jr., "Taxation and Income Distribution: The Colombian Tax Reform of 1974," *Journal of Development Economics 5,* no. 3 (September 1978): 237, 249.

Peter Heller, "The Under-Financing of Recurrent Development Costs," *Finance and Development* 16, no. 1 (March 1979): 38–41.

International Monetary Fund, *Government Finance Statistics Yearbook 1984* (Washington, D.C.: International Monetary Fund, 1984). Country tables.

——, *Government Finance Statistics Yearbook 1985* (Washington, D.C.: International Monetary Fund, 1985), p. 80.

Richard A. Musgrave, et al., *Fiscal Reform in Bolivia: Final Report and Staff Papers of the Bolivian Mission on Tax Reform* (Cambridge, Mass.: Harvard Law School, International Tax Program, 1981).

Oliver Oldman, and Daniel M. Holland, "Measuring Tax Evasion." (Paper presented at the Fifth Annual General Assembly of the Inter-American Center of Tax Administration, Rio de Janiero, Brazil, May 17, 1971.)

Robert Repetto, "Optimal Export Taxes, " *The Quarterly Journal of Economics* 86, no. 3 (Cambridge, Mass.: Harvard University Press, August, 1972), pp. 396–406.

Harvey Rosen, *Public Finance.* (Homewood, Ill.: Richard D. Irwin, 1985)

Income Distribution

Richard M. Bird and Luc Henry DeWulf, "Taxation and Income Distribution in Latin America: A Critical View of Empirical Studies" (*International Monetary Fund Staff Papers* 20, November 1975): 639–82.

Alejandro Foxley, Eduardo Aninat, and J. P. Arellano, *Redistributive Effects of Government Programs.* (Oxford: Pergamon Press, 1980), Chapter 6.

Charles E. McLure, "Taxation and the Urban Poor in Developing Countries," *World Development* 5, no. 3 (1977): 169–88.

Donald R. Snodgrass, "The Fiscal System as an Income Redistributor in West Malaysia," *Public Finance* 29, no. 1 (January 1974): 56–76.

Economic Stability

Rudiger W. Dornbusch, *Open Economy Macroeconomics* (New York: Basic Books, 1980).

Economic Efficiency

Malcolm Gillis, "Micro- and Macroeconomics of Tax Reform: Indonesia," *Journal of Development Economics* (1986).

Arnold C. Harberger, "The Incidence of Taxes on Income from Capital in an Open Economy: A Review of Current Thinking" (Harvard Institute for International Development Discussion Paper No. 139, August 1982).

Vito Tanzi, "Quantitative Characteristics of Tax Systems in Developing Countries," in *Modern Tax Theory for Developing Countries,* eds. David Newbery and Nicholas Stern, (In press).

Introduction

Anand G. Chandavarkar, "Monetization of Developing Economies," *International Monetary Fund Staff Papers* 24, no. 3 (November 1977): 678–79.

P. J. Drake, *Money, Finance, and Economic Development* (New York: John Wiley and Sons, 1980).

Subrata Ghatak, *Monetary Economics in Developing Countries* (London: MacMillan Press, 1981).

International Monetary Fund, *International Financial Statistics,* various issues, 1970–86.

Ronald I. McKinnon, *Money and Capital in Economic Development* (Washington, D.C.: The Brookings Institution, 1973).

Edward Shaw, *Financial Deepening and Economic Development* (New York: Oxford University Press, 1973).

Inflation and Savings Mobilization

Dale W. Adams, "Mobilizing Household Savings through Rural Financial Markets," *Economic Development and Cultural Change* 26, no. 3 (April 1978): 547–60.

William R. Cline et al., *World Inflation and the Developing Countries.* (Washington, D.C.: Brookings Institution, 1981).

Arnold C. Harberger, "A Primer on Inflation," *Journal of Money, Credit and Banking* 10, no. 4 (November 1978): 505–21.

Albert O. Hirschman, *Journeys Toward Progress: Studies of Economic Policy-making in Latin America* (New York: Twentieth Century Fund, 1963), pp. 208–9.

Michael Roemer, "Ghana, 1950–80: Missed Opportunities," and Yaw Ansu, "Comments," in *World Economic Growth,* Arnold C. Harberger, ed. (San Francisco: Institute of Contemporary Studies, 1984), pp. 201–30.

George M. von Furstenberg, "Inflation, Taxes, and Welfare in LDCs," *Public Finance* 35, no. 2 (1980): 700–710.

Interest Rates and Savings

Charles Beach, Robin Boadway, and Neil Bruce, "Taxation and Savings: Some Life-Cycle Estimates for Canada" (Ontario: Queens University Discussion Paper, 1985).

Michael J. Boskin, "Taxation, Savings and the Rate of Interest," *Journal of Political Economy* 8b, no. 2, part 2 (April 1978): 3–27.

Alberto Giovanni, "The Interest Elasticity of Savings in Developing Countries," *World Development,* Vol. 11 (July 1983): 601–8.

Arnold C. Harberger, "Dynamics of Inflation in Chile," in *Measurement in Economics: Studies in Mathematical Economics in Honor of Yehuda Grunfeld,* Carl Christ, ed. (Palo Alto, Calif.: Stanford University Press, 1963).

Larry Summers, "Capital Taxation and Capital Accumulation in a Life-Cycle Growth Model," *American Economic Review* 71 (September 1981): 533–44.

Colin Wright, "Savings and the Rate of Interest," in *The Taxation of Income from Capital,* Arnold C. Harberger and Martin Bailey, eds. (Washington, D.C.: Brookings Institution Press, 1969).

Financial Development

David Cole and Yung Chul Park, *Financial Development in Korea, 1945–78* (Cambridge, Mass.: Harvard University Press, 1983).

Sebastian Edwards, "Stabilization with Liberalization: An Evaluation of Chile's Experiment with Free-Market Policies 1973–1983," *Economic Development and Cultural Change* 27 (September 1985): 224–53.

Vicente Gablis, "Inflation and Interest-Rate Policies in Latin America," *International Monetary Fund Staff Papers* 26, no. 2 (June 1977): Tables 1, 4, and 6: 334–65.

Sergio Pereira Leite, "Interest-Rate Policies in West Africa," *International Monetary Fund Staff Papers* 29, no. 1 (March 1982): 48–76.

Steven C. Leuthold, "Interest Rates, Inflation and Deflation," *Financial Analysis Journal* (January–February 1981): 28–51.

U.S. Department of Commerce, *Foreign Exchange Trends and Their Implications for the United States* (Washington, D.C., various issues)

World Bank, *Thailand: Industrial Development Strategy* (New York: Oxford University Press, 1980), p. 57.

Monetary Policy and Price Stability

Rudiger Dornbusch, *Open Economy Macroeconomics* (New York: Basic Books, 1980).

Vicente Gablis, "Inflation and Interest Rate Policies in Latin America," *International Monetary Fund Staff Papers* 26, no. 2 (June 1977): Tables 1, 4, and 6: 334–65.

Arnold C. Harberger, "A Primer on Inflation," *Journal of Money, Credit and Banking* 10, no. 4 (November 1978): 505–21.

———, "The Inflation Syndrome," paper presented in "The Political Economy Lecture Series," Harvard University, March 19, 1981.

John Williamson, *The Open Economy and the World Economy* (New York: Basic Books, 1983), pp. 238–41.

CHAPTER 14. FOREIGN SAVINGS: AID AND INVESTMENT

Concepts and Magnitudes

Willy Brandt, chairman, *North-South: A Program for Survival* (Cambridge, Mass.: MIT Press, 1980).

Organization for Economic Cooperation and Development, *Development Cooperation: 1984 Review* (Paris, 1984).

———, *The Flow of Financial Resources to Developing Countries in 1961* (Paris, undated), Table 1.

Lester B. Pearson, chairman, *Partners in Development* (New York: Praeger, 1969).

United States Agency for International Development, *Congressional Presentation* (Washington, D.C.: annually).

World Bank, *World Development Report 1981* (New York: Oxford University Press, 1981), Table 16.

———, *World Development Report 1982* (New York: Oxford University Press, 1982), pp. 118–19.

Foreign Aid

Robert L. Ayres, *Banking on the Poor* (Cambridge, Mass: MIT Press, 1984)

Jagdish Bhagwati and Richard S. Eckaus, eds., *Foreign Aid* (Harmondsworth, England: Penguin Books, 1970).

Joint Ministerial Committee of the Boards of Governors of the World Bank and the

International Monetary Fund on the Transfer of Real Resources to the Developing Countries, *Aid for Development: The Key Issues* (Washington D.C., 1986).

Paul Mosely, "Aid, Savings and Growth Revisited," *Oxford Bulletin of Economics and Statistics* 42 (May 1980): 79–91.

Organization for Economic Cooperation and Development, *Development Cooperation: 1984 Review* (Paris, 1984).

Foreign Investment and the Multinationals

Jack N. Behrman and William A. Fischer, *Overseas R & D Activities of Transnational Corporations* (Cambridge, Mass.: Oelgeschlager, Gunn and Hair, 1980), pp. 107–9.

Fred C. Bergsten, Thomas P. Horst, and Theodore H. Moran, *American Multinationals and American Interests* (Washington, D.C.: Brookings Institution, 1978).

K. Billerbeck, and Y. Yasugi, "Private Direct Foreign Investment," World Bank Staffing Report Paper No. 348 (1979): 4–5.

Byung Soo Chung and Chung H. Lee, "The Choice of Production Techniques by Foreign Firms in Korea," *Economic Development and Cultural Change* 29 (1980): 135–40.

Malcolm Gillis, "Episodes in Indonesian Economic Growth," in *World Economic Growth,* A. C. Harberger, ed. (San Francisco: Institute for Contemporary Studies, 1984), pp. 251–55.

David Goldsborough, "Foreign Direct Investment in Developing Countries," *Finance and Development* (March 1985).

Helen Hughes, and You Pon Seng, *Foreign Investment and Industrialization in Singapore* (Madison: University of Wisconsin Press, 1969) p. 193.

Stephen J. Kobrin, "Foreign Enterprise and Forced Divestment in LDCs," *International Organization* 34 (Winter 1980).

Sanjaya Lall and Paul Streeten, *Foreign Investment, Transnationals and Developing Countries* (Boulder, Colo.: Westview Press, 1977), pp. 104–6.

———, *The Flow of Financial Resources: Private Foreign Investment, Main Findings of a Study on Selected Developing Countries* (United Nations: Document TD/B/C-3 III, May 1973).

Steven Langdon, *Multinationals in the Political Economy in Kenya* (New York: St. Martins Press, 1981), Ch. 4.

Robert E. Lipsey, Irving B. Kraus, and Romualdo A. Roldan, "Do Multinational Firms Adapt Factor Proportions to Relative Factor Prices?" (Cambridge, Mass: National Bureau of Economic Research, Working Paper No. 293 October 1978).

Theodore Moran, ed., *Multinational Corporations* (Lexington, Mass.: Lexington Books, 1985).

Howard Pack, "The Substitution of Labor for Capital in Manufacturing," *Economic Journal* 86 (March 1976): 45–58.

Lewis D. Solomon, *Multinational Corporations and the Emerging World Order* (London: Kennika & Press, 1978), pp. 79–83.

John Stopford, *The World Directory of Multinational Enterprises 1982–1983* (Detroit: Gale Research Company, 1982), pp. 2, 12.

Osvaldo Sunkel, "Big Business and Dependency," *Foreign Affairs* 50 (1972): 518–19.

Raymond Vernon, *Storm over the Multinationals: The Real Issues* (Cambridge, Mass.: Harvard University Press, 1977), pp. 159–61.

L. T. Wells, "The Internationalization of Firms from LDCs," in *Multinationals from Small Countries,* Tamir Agmon and C. P. Kindleberger, eds. (Cambridge, Mass.: MIT Press, 1977).

Lawrence J. White, "The Evidence on Appropriate Factor Proportions," *Economic Development and Cultural Change* 27 (October 1978): 27–59.

Commercial Borrowing

Helen Hughes, "Debt and Development," *World Development* F, no. 1 (1979).

The LDC Debt Crisis

Carol Lancaster and John Williamson, eds., *African Debt and Financing* (Washington, D.C.: Institute for International Economics, 1986).

Jeffrey Sachs, "The LDC Debt Crisis," *NBER Reporter* (Winter 1986): 15–16.

CHAPTER 15. PRIMARY-EXPORT-LED GROWTH

The Structure of Foreign Payments

International Monetary Fund, *Balance of Payments Statistics* (Washington, D.C.: annual).

———, *International Financial Statistics* (Washington, D.C.: monthly).

———, *International Financial Statistics Yearbook* (Washington, D.C.: annual).

Comparative Advantage

Richard E. Caves and Ronald W. Jones, *World Trade and Payments: An Introduction* (Boston: Little, Brown, 1985).

Gerald K. Helleiner, *International Trade and Economic Development* (Baltimore: Penguin Books, 1972).

Charles P. Kindleberger, *Foreign Trade and the National Economy* (New Haven: Yale University Press, 1962).

Peter H. Lindert and Charles P. Kindleberger, *International Economics,* 7th edition (Homewood, Ill: Richard D. Irwin, 1982).

Gerald M. Meier, *International Trade and Development* (Westport, Conn.: Greenwood Press, 1975).

United Nations, *Yearbook of International Trade Statistics* (New York: annual).

John Williamson, *The Open Economy and The World Economy* (New York: Basic Books, 1983).

Primary Exports as an Engine of Growth

Robert E. Baldwin, *Economic Development and Export Growth: A Study of Northern Rhodesia, 1920–1960* (Los Angeles: University of California Press, 1966).

Edward J. Chambers and Donald F. Gordon, "Primary Products and Economic Growth," *Journal of Political Economy* 74 (1966): 315–32.

Albert Fishlow, *American Railroads and the Transformation of the Antebellum Economy* (Cambridge, Mass.: Harvard University Press, 1965).

Robert W. Fogel, "Railroads as an Analogy to The Space Effort: Some Economic Aspects," in *Space Programs: An Exploration in Historical Analogy* (Cambridge, Mass.: MIT Press, 1966).

Albert O. Hirschman, "A Generalized Linkage Approach to Economic Development, with Special Reference to Staples," in *Essays on Economic Development and Cultural Change,* Manning Nash, ed. (Chicago: University of Chicago Press, 1977).

Hla Myint, "The 'Classical Theory' of International Trade and the Underdeveloped Countries," *Economic Journal* 68 (1959): 317–37.

Douglas C. North, "Location Theory and Regional Economic Growth," *Journal of Political Economy* 63 (1955): 243–85.

Scott R. Pearson and J. Cownie, *Commodity Exports and African Development* (Lexington, Mass.: D. C. Heath, 1974).

Michael Roemer, *Fishing for Growth: Export-Led Development in Peru, 1950–67*
(Cambridge, Mass.: Harvard University Press, 1970).

Melville Watkins, "A Staple Theory of Economic Growth," *Journal of Economics
and Political Science* 29 (1963): 141–58.

Barriers to Primary-Export-Led Growth

F. G. Adams and J. R. Behrman, *Commodity Exports and Economic Development*
(Lexington, Mass.: D. C. Heath, 1982).

Jere R. Behrman, *Development, The International Economic Order and Commodity
Agreements* (Reading, Mass.: Addison-Wesley, 1978).

Elliot J. Berg, "Structural Transformation Versus Gradualism: Recent Economic
Development in Ghana and the Ivory Coast," in *Ghana and the Ivory Coast:
Perspectives on Modernization* (Chicago: University of Chicago Press, 1971).

Jagdish N. Bhagwati, ed., *The North-South Debate* (Cambridge, Mass.: MIT Press,
1977).

Jagdish N. Bhagwati, "Immiserizing Growth: A Geometrical Note," *Review of
Economic Studies* 25 (1958): 201–5.

Tony Killick, *Development Economics in Action: A Study of Economic Policies in
Ghana* (London: Heinemann, 1978).

Charles P. Kindleberger, *The Terms of Trade: A European Case Study* (New Haven:
Yale University Press, 1962).

Odin Knudsen and Andrew Parnes, *Trade Instability and Economic Development*
(Lexington, Mass.: Heath Lexington Books, 1975).

Alisdair I. MacBean, *Export Instability and Economic Development* (London:
George Allen and Unwin, 1966).

Gobind Nankani, "Development Problems of Non-fuel Mineral Exporting Countries," *Finance and Development* 17, no. 1 (March 1980): 6–10.

Ragnar Nurkse, *Equilibrium Growth in the World Economy* (Cambridge, Mass.:
Harvard University Press, 1961).

Michael Roemer, "Resource-based Industrialization: A Survey," *Journal of Development Economics* 6 (June 1979): 163–202.

Hans W. Singer, "The Distribution of Trade Between Investing and Borrowing
Countries," *American Economic Review* 40 (May 1950): 470–85.

United Nations (Raul Prebisch), *The Economic Development of Latin America and
its Principal Problems* (Lake Success, N.Y.: 1950).

World Bank, *Commodity Trade and Price Trends* (Washington, D.C.: annual).

CHAPTER 16. IMPORT SUBSTITUTION

The Strategy of Protection

Bela Balassa et al., *The Structure of Protection in the Developing Countries* (Baltimore: Johns Hopkins University Press, 1971).

Bela Balassa and Daniel M. Schydlowsky, "Domestic Resource Cost and Effective
Protection Once Again," *Journal of Political Economy* 80 (1972): 63–69.

Robert E. Baldwin, "The Case Against Infant Industry Protection," *Journal of Political Economy* 77 (1969): 295–305.

Jagdish N. Bhagwati and T. N. Srinivasan, *Foreign Trade Regimes and Economic
Development: India* (New York: Columbia University Press, 1975).

Michael Bruno, "Domestic Resource Costs and Effective Protection: Clarification
and Synthesis," *Journal of Political Economy* 80 (1972): 16–33.

* W. M. Corden, *The Theory of Protection* (London: Oxford University Press, 1971).

* Thomas L. Hutcheson and Joseph J. Stern, "The Methodology of Assistance Policy Analysis," (Harvard Institute for International Development: Development Discussion Paper No. 226, April 1986).

Harry G. Johnson, "Optimal Trade Interventions in the Presence of Distortions," in *Trade Growth and the Balance of Payments,* R. E. Caves et al. (Amsterdam: North Holland, 1965).

Anne O. Krueger, "Trade Policies of Developing Countries," in *Handbook of International Economics* vol. 1, R. W. Jones and P. B. Kenan, eds. (Amsterdam: North Holland, 1984).

Outcomes and Problems

Joel Bergsman, *Brazil: Industrialization and Trade Policies* (London: Oxford University Press, 1970).

Jagdish Bhagwati, *Foreign Exchange Regimes and Economic Development: Anatomy and Consequences of Exchange Control Regimes* (Cambridge, Mass.: Ballinger Press, 1978).

Henry J. Bruton, "The Import Substitution Strategy of Economic Development," *The Pakistan Development Review* 10 (1970): 123–46.

Albert O. Hirschman, "The Political Economy of Import Substitution," *Quarterly Journal of Economics* 82 (1968): 1–32.

Charles P. Kindleberger, "The Disequilibrium System of Foreign Trade and Developing Countries," in *Economics of Trade and Development* James E. Theberge, ed. (New York: John Wiley, 1968).

Anne O. Krueger, *Foreign Trade Regimes and Economic Development: Turkey* (New York: Columbia University Press, 1974).

————, *Foreign Trade Regimes and Economic Development: Liberalization Attempts and Consequences* (Cambridge, Mass.: Ballinger Press, 1978).

J. Clark Leith, *Foreign Trade Regimes and Economic Development: Ghana* (New York: Columbia University Press, 1974).

Stephen Lewis, *Economic Development and Industrial Growth in Pakistan* (London: George Allen and Unwin, 1969).

I. M. D. Little, Tibor Scitovsky, and Maurice Scott, *Industry and Trade in Some Developing Countries* (London: Oxford University Press, 1970).

John H. Power, "Import Substitution as an Industrialization Strategy," *The Philippine Economic Journal* 5 (1966): 167–204.

CHAPTER 17. OUTWARD-LOOKING DEVELOPMENT

The Strategy of Export Substitution

Charles R. Frank, Kwang Suk Kim, and Larry E. Westphal, *Foreign Trade Regimes and Economic Development: South Korea* (New York: Columbia University Press, 1975).

Tony Killick, ed., *The Quest for Economic Stabilization: The I.M.F. and the Third World* (London: Heinemann Educational Books, 1984).

Kwang Suk Kim and Michael Roemer, *Studies in the Modernization of the Republic of Korea, 1945–1975: Growth and Structural Transformation* (Cambridge, Mass.: Harvard University, Press, 1979).

* Asterisks denote more advanced readings.

Anne O. Krueger, *Studies in the Modernization of the Republic of Korea, 1945–1975: The Developmental Role of the Foreign Sector and Aid* (Cambridge, Mass.: Harvard University Press, 1979).

Gustav Ranis, "Industrial Sector Labor Absorption," *Economic Development and Cultural Change* 21 (1973): 347–408.

William G. Tyler, *Manufactured Export Expansion and Industrialization in Brazil* (Tubingen, W. Germany: J.C.B. Mohr, 1976).

John Williamson, ed., *I.M.F. Conditionality* (Washington, D.C.: Institute of International Economics 1983).

Outcomes and Limitations

Vittorio Corbo and Jaime de Melo, eds., "Liberalization with Stabilization in the Southern Cone of Latin America," *World Development* 13 (August 1985): Special Issue.

Joan Nelson, "The Political Economy of Stabilization," *World Development* 12 (October 1984): 983–1006.

John Sheahan, "Market-oriented Economic Policies and Political Repression in Latin America," *Economic Development and Cultural Change* 28 (January 1980): 267–92.

Richard Weisskoff, "The Growth and Decline of Import Substitution in Brazil— Revisited," *World Development* 8 (September 1980): 647–76.

Protection in the North

Jaleel Ahmad, "Prospects of Trade Liberalization Between Developed and Developing Countries," *World Development* 13 (September 1985): 1077–86.

Robert E. Baldwin and J. David Richardson, eds., *International Trade and Finance* (Boston: Little, Brown, 1974), pp. 246–62.

Diane P. Berliner, Kimberly Ann Elliot, and Gary Hufbauer, *Trade Protection in the United States; 31 Case Studies* (Washington: Institute for International Economics, 1986).

Gary Hufbauer and Howard F. Rosen, "Trade Policy for Troubled Industries," *Policy Analyses in International Economics* (Washington: Institute for International Economics, March 1986).

Integration in the South

* Martin Carnoy, "A Welfare Analysis of Latin American Economic Union: Six Industrial Studies," *Journal of Political Economy* 78 (1970): 626–54.

Joseph Grunwald, M. S. Wionczek, and Martin Carnoy, *Latin American Integration and U.S. Policy* Washington: Brookings Institution, 1972).

* Melvyn B. Krauss, "Recent Developments in Customs Union Theory: an Interpretive Survey," *Journal of Economic Literature* 10 (1972): 413–36.

* R. G. Lipsey, "The Theory of Customs Unions: A General Survey," *The Economic Journal* 70 (1960): 493–513.

W. T. Newlyn, "Gains and Losses in the East African Common Market," *Yorkshire Bulletin of Economic and Social Research* 17 (1965): 132–38.

Jacob Viner, *The Customs Union Issue* (New York: Carnegie Endowment for International Peace, 1950).

* Asterisks denote more advanced readings.

Agriculture's Role in Economic Development

Bruce F. Johnston and Peter Kilby, *Agriculture and Structural Transformation* (London: Oxford University Press, 1975).

John Mellor, *The Economics of Agricultural Development* (Ithaca, N.Y.: Cornell University Press, 1966).

_____, *The New Economic Growth* (Ithaca, N.Y.: Cornell University Press, 1976).

Lloyd Reynolds, *Agriculture in Development Theory* (New Haven: Yale University Press, 1976).

T. W. Schultz, *Transforming Traditional Agriculture* (New Haven: Yale University Press, 1964).

Erik Thorbecke, ed., *The Role of Agriculture in Economic Development* (New York: Columbia University Press, 1969).

Self-Sufficiency in Food

R. Barker, E. Bennagen, and Y. Hayami, "New Rice Technology and Policy Alternatives for Food Self-Sufficiency," in International Rice Research Institute, *Economic Consequences of the New Rice Technology* (Los Banos, Philippines: 1978) pp. 337–61.

Lester Brown, *By Bread Alone* (New York: Praeger, 1974).

Richard Goldman, "Staple Food Self-Sufficiency and the Distributive Impact of Malaysian Rice Policy," *Food Research Institute Studies* 14, no. 3, (1975) pp. 251–93.

Land Reform

Ronald P. Dore, *Land Reform in Japan* (London: Oxford University Press, 1959).

William Hinton, *Fanshen* (New York: Vintage Books, 1966).

Elias H. Tuma, *Twenty-six Centuries of Agrarian Reform: A Comparative Analysis* (Berkeley: University of California, 1965).

Louis J. Walinsky, ed., *Agrarian Reform as Unfinished Business: The Selected Papers of Wolf Ladejinsky* (London: Oxford University Press, 1977).

John Wong, *Land Reform in the People's Republic of China* (New York: Praeger, 1973).

Traditional Agriculture

Ester Boserup, *The Conditions of Agricultural Growth* (Chicago: Aldine, 1965).

Dwight H. Perkins, *Agricultural Development in China, 1368–1968* (Chicago: Aldine, 1969).

Sol Tax, *Penny Capitalism* (Chicago: University of Chicago Press, 1963).

Technology of Agricultural Production

Hans B. Binswanger and Vernon W. Ruttan, *Induced Innovation: Technology, Institutions and Development* (Baltimore: Johns Hopkins University Press, 1978).

Dana G. Dalrymple, *Development and Spread of High Yielding Wheat Varieties in Developing Countries* (Washington D.C.: Agency for International Development, 1986).

_____, *Development and Spread of High-Yielding Rice Varieties in Developing Countries* (Washington D.C.: Agency for International Development, 1986).

Yujiro Hayami and Vernon W. Ruttan, *Agricultural Development: An International Perspective* (Baltimore: Johns Hopkins University Press, 1971).

Mobilization of Agricultural Inputs

S. J. Burki, D. G. Davies, R. H. Hook, and J. W. Thomas, *Public Works Programs in Developing Countries: A Comparative Analysis* (World Bank Staff Working Paper No. 224, February 1976).

Uma Lele, *The Design of Rural Development: Lessons from Africa* (Baltimore: Johns Hopkins University Press, 1975).

Dwight H. Perkins and Shahid Yusuf, *Rural Development in China* (Baltimore: Johns Hopkins University Press, 1984).

Agricultural Price Policy

Hussein Askari and John Cummings, *Agricultural Supply Response: A Survey of the Econometric Evidence* (New York: Praeger, 1976).

Elliot Berg et al., *Accelerated Development in Sub-Saharan Africa* (Washington, D.C.: The World Bank, 1981).

Walter P. Falcon and C. Peter Timmer, "The Political Economy of Rice Production and Trade in Asia," in *Agriculture in Development Theory*, L. Reynolds, ed. (New Haven: Yale University Press, 1975).

Raj Krishna, "Agricultural Price Policy and Economic Development," in *Agricultural Development and Economic Growth*, H. M. Southworth and B. F. Johnston, eds., (Ithaca, N.Y.: Cornell University Press, 1967).

C. Peter Timmer, Walter P. Falcon, and Scott R. Pearson, *Food Policy Analysis* (Baltimore: Johns Hopkins University Press, 1983).

CHAPTER 19. NATURAL RESOURCES

Mineral Resources and Growth

Organization of Petroleum Exporting Countries, *Facts and Figures: A Comparative Statistical Analysis* (Vienna: 1981), p. 17.

Minerals: Endowments and Utilization

British Petroleum, *Statistical Review of World Petroleum* (London: June 1984).

Malcolm Gillis, "Malaysia: Public Policies Resource Management and The Tropical Forest in Sabah, Peninsular Malaysia and Sarawak," (unpublished: Duke University, December 1986).

L. Gomez-Pompa, R. Guevara, and G. Yanes, "The Tropical Rain Forest: A Non-Renewable Resource," *Science* 177 (1972): 762–65.

Gobind T. Nankani, "Development Problems of Non-Fuel Mineral Exporting Countries," *Finance and Development* 17, no. 1 (March 1980): 6–10.

United Nations Food and Agricultural Organization, *Forest Resources of Tropical Asia, Africa, Latin America* (Rome: United Nations, 1981).

U.S. House of Representatives, *Energy Factbook* (Washington, D.C.: U.S. Government Printing Office, November 1980).

World Bank, *Energy in the Developing Countries* (Washington, D.C., August 1980).

———, *World Development Report 1985* (New York: Oxford University Press, 1985).

Rents and Returns in Natural Resource Projects

Bela Balassa, "Policy Responses to External Shocks in Selected Latin American Countries," in *Export Diversification and the New Protectionism*, W. Baer and M. Gillis, eds. (Urbana: University of Illinois Press, and National Bureau of Economic Research, 1981).

H. J. Barnett and C. Morse, *Scarcity and Growth: The Economics of Natural Resource Scarcity* (Baltimore: Johns Hopkins University Press, 1963).

D. B. Brooks, ed., *Resource Economics: Selected Works of Orris C. Herfindahl* (Baltimore: Johns Hopkins University Press, 1974).

Hollis P. Chenery, "Restructuring the World Economy, Round II," *Foreign Affairs* (Summer 1981): 1102–20.

W. Max Corden, "Booming Sector and Dutch Disease Economics: A Survey" (Australian National University School of Social Sciences, Working Paper No. 079, 1982).

Malcolm Gillis, "Evolution of Natural Resource Taxes in Developing Countries," *Natural Resources Journal* 22, no. 3 (July 1982): 619–49.

Charles E. Howe, *Natural Resources Economics: Issues Analysis and Policy* (New York: John Wiley and Sons, 1979).

Charles E. McLure, "Market Dominance and the Exporting of State Taxes," *Natural Tax Journal* 34, no. 4 (December 1981).

Robert Repetto, "Optimal Export Taxes in the Short and Long Run: Pakistan Jute Export Policy," *Quarterly Journal of Economics* 86, no. 3 (August 1972): 396–406.

Michael Roemer, "Dutch Disease in Developing Countries: Swallowing Bitter Medicine," in *The Primary Sector in Economic Development,* Matz Lundahl, ed. (Beckenham, England: Croom, Helm, 1985).

V. Kerry Smith, ed., *Scarcity and Growth Reconsidered* (Baltimore: Johns Hopkins Press, 1979).

CHAPTER 20. INDUSTRY

Industry as a Leading Sector

John Friedman and William Alonso, *Regional Development and Planning: A Reader* (Cambridge, Mass.: MIT Press, 1964).

E. J. Hobsbawm, *The Pelican History of Britain,* vol. 3: *Industry and Empire* (Baltimore: Penguin Books, 1969).

David S. Landes, *The Unbound Prometheus: Technological Change and Industrial Development in Western Europe from 1750 to the Present* (London: Cambridge University Press, 1969).

Harry W. Richardson, *City Size and National Spatial Strategies in Developing Countries* (World Bank Staff Working Paper No. 252, April 1977).

Pan A. Yotopoulos and Jeffrey B. Nugent, "A Balanced-Growth Version of the Linkage Hypotheses: A Test," *Quarterly Journal of Economics* 87 (1973): 157–71.

Investment Choices in Industry

American Rural Small-scale Industry Delegation, Dwight H. Perkins, Chairman *Rural Small-scale Industry in the People's Republic of China* (Berkeley: University of California Press, 1977).

Ranadev Banerji, "Small-scale Production Units in Manufacturing: An International Cross-sectional Overview," *Weltwirtschafliches Archive* 114 (1978): 62–68.

Romeo Bautista et al., *Capital Utilization in Manufacturing* (London: Oxford University Press, 1981).

P. N. Dhar and H. F. Lydall, *The Role of Small Enterprises in Indian Economic Development* (New York: Asia Publishing House, 1961).

John Haldi and David Whitcomb, "Economics of Scale in Industrial Plants," *Journal of Political Economy* 75 (1967): 373–85.

Hal Hill, "Choice of Technique in the Indonesian Weaving Industry," *Economic Development and Cultural Change* 31, no. 2 (January 1983): 337–54.

International Labour Office, *Employment, Income and Equality: A Strategy for Increasing Productive Employment in Kenya* (Geneva: 1972).

Alan S. Manne, ed., *Investments for Capacity Expansion: Size, Location and Time Phasing* (Cambridge, Mass.: MIT Press, 1967).

Howard Pack, "Aggregate Implications of Factor Substitution in Industry Processes," *Journal of Development Economics* 11, no. 1 (August 1982): 1–38.

_____, "The Choice of Technique and Employment in the Textile Industry," in *Technology and Employment in Industry*, A. S. Bhalla, ed. (Geneva: International Labour Office, 1975), 153–74.

C. F. Pratten, *Economies of Scale in Manufacturing Industry* (Cambridge: Cambridge University Press, 1971).

F. M. Scherer et al., *The Economics of Multi-Plant Operation: An International Comparisons Study* (Cambridge, Mass.: Harvard University Press, 1975).

Eugene Staley and Richard Morse, *Modern Small Industry for Developing Countries* (New York: McGraw-Hill, 1965).

William F. Steel, *Small-scale Employment and Production in Developing Countries: Evidence from Ghana* (New York: Praeger, 1977).

Frances Stewart, "Manufacture of Cement Blocks in Kenya," in *Technology and Employment in Industry*, A. S. Bhalla, ed. (Geneva: International Labour Office, 1975).

Industry and Development Goals

Robert J. Alexander, *A New Development Strategy* (Maryknoll, N.Y.: Orbis Books, 1976).

John Cody, Helen Hughes, and David Wall, eds., *Policies for Industrial Progress in Developing Countries* (London: Oxford University Press, 1980).

Michael Roemer, Gene M. Tidrick, and David Williams, "The Range of Strategic Choice in Tanzanian Industry," *Journal of Development Economics* 3 (1976): 257–76.

Paul Streeten, "Industrialization in the Unified Development Strategy," *World Development* 3 (1975): 1–9.

CHAPTER 21. PUBLIC ENTERPRISES

The Growth of State Enterprises

Raymond Vernon, "The State-Owned Enterprise in Latin American Export," in *Trade Prospects Among the Americas,* Werner Baer and Malcolm Gillis, eds. (Urbana, Ill.: National Bureau of Economic Research and University of Illinois Press, 1981), pp. 98–114.

World Bank, Financial Studies Division, *Borrowing in International Capital Markets* (Washington, D.C.: World Bank, 1979).

Rationales for Establishing SOEs

Armeane M. Choksi, *State Intervention in the Industrialization of Developing Countries: Selected Issues* (Washington, D.C.: World Bank, 1979).

Berti Walstedt, "State Manufacturing Enterprises in a Mixed Economy" (unpublished manuscript, Washington, D.C.: August 1978).

William Baumol, ed., *Public and Private Enterprises in a Mixed Economy* (New York: St. Martin's, 1980).

Leroy P. Jones, *Public Enterprise and Economic Development* (Seoul: Korea Development Institute, 1976), p. 83.

———, *Public Enterprise and Economic Development: The Korean Case* (Seoul: KDI Press, 1975).

Leroy P. Jones, Edward Mason, and Raymond Vernon, eds., *Public Enterprises in Developing Countries* (New York: Oxford University Press, 1983).

Tony Killick, *Development Economics in Action* (New York: St. Martins Press, 1978), pp. 220–22.

Donald J. LeCraw, "Choice of Technology in Low-Wage Countries: A Non-Neoclassical Approach," *Quarterly Journal of Economics* 93 (November 1979): 631–54.

Harvey Leibenstein, *Beyond Economic Man* (Cambridge, Mass.: Harvard University Press, 1976).

———, "X-Efficiency, Intrafirm Behavior, and Growth," in *Lagging Productivity Growth: Causes and Remedies,* Schlomo Maital and Sidney Meltz, eds. (Cambridge, Mass.: Ballinger Press, 1980).

R. A. McCain, "Competition, Information and Redundancy: X-Efficiency and the Cybernetics of the Firm," *Kyklos* 28 (1975): 286–308.

W. J. Primeaux, "An Assessment of X-Efficiency Gained through Competition," *Review of Economics and Statistics* 59, no. 2 (June 1977): 516–17.

John B. Sheahan, "Public Enterprise in Developing Countries," in *Public Enterprise: Economic Analysis of Theory and Practice,* W. G. Shepherd, ed. (Lexington: Lexington Books, 1976), p. 211.

R. P. Short, "The Role of Public Enterprises: An International Statistical Comparison," (International Monetary Fund, Fiscal Affairs Dept. Paper, May 17, 1983, Table 4).

C. Peter Timmer, "Public Policy for Improving Technology Choice" (manuscript prepared for Alternative Technology, Inc., September 1979): 16–24.

———, "The Choice of Technique in Indonesia," in *The Choice of Technology in Developing Countries,* C. Peter Timmer et al. (Cambridge, Mass.: Harvard University Center for International Affairs, 1975), pp. 1–30.

Louis T. Wells, "Economic Man and Engineering Man," in *The Choice of Technology in Developing Countries,* pp. 71–90.

World Bank, *Economic Memorandum on Uruguay* (Washington, D.C.: 1977), p. 15.

Index

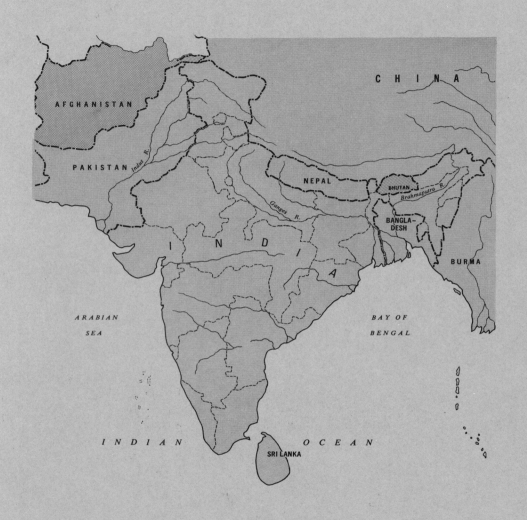

C H I N A

AFGHANISTAN

PAKISTAN

Indus R.

NEPAL

BHUTAN

Brahmaputra R.

BANGLA-
DESH

BURMA

Ganges R.

I N D I A

ARABIAN
SEA

BAY OF
BENGAL

INDIAN OCEAN

SRI LANKA

0   500 **miles**

Gross national product per capita, 1983

☐ $400 and less   ☐ $401 to $1,635   ▓ $1,636 to $5,500   ▨ More than $5,500   ☐ No data

Source: The World Bank Atlas, 1986

SOUTH ASIA